Generative AI for Cybersecurity

Generative AI for Cybersecurity explores how rapidly evolving generative models are reshaping modern digital defense. As organizations become more interconnected and data-driven, traditional cybersecurity measures are increasingly challenged by adaptive, AI-powered threats. Generative AI (GenAI) introduces new capabilities that can significantly enhance threat detection, automate security operations, and improve situational awareness, but it also enables sophisticated offensive techniques, deepfakes, automated malware generation, and large-scale misinformation.

This book provides a balanced and comprehensive examination of this dual-use technology. It highlights how generative models can be leveraged to build resilient, intelligent, and proactive defense mechanisms capable of anticipating and countering emerging cyber risks. At the same time, it critically analyzes the vulnerabilities, ethical dilemmas, and regulatory challenges introduced by the misuse of GenAI. Through diverse perspectives and expert contributions, the book bridges theoretical foundations with real-world applications, demonstrating how GenAI can support adaptive intrusion detection, anomaly analysis, secure autonomous systems, and more transparent and explainable security solutions.

Beyond technical considerations, the book addresses broader societal, geopolitical, and governance implications, including issues of trust, sovereignty, and responsible AI deployment. It offers frameworks, methodologies, and practical insights suitable for researchers, practitioners, students, and policymakers seeking to understand, develop, or regulate GenAI-driven cybersecurity systems.

By examining both the opportunities and the risks, *Generative AI for Cybersecurity* serves as a timely reference for navigating an era where AI is not only a tool for defense but also a catalyst for new forms of cyber aggression, highlighting the urgent need for innovative, ethical, and resilient approaches to securing the digital world.

Generative AI for Cybersecurity

Edited by Boubiche Djallel Eddine and
Sedat Akleylek

CRC Press
Taylor & Francis Group
Boca Raton London New York

CRC Press is an imprint of the
Taylor & Francis Group, an **informa** business

Designed cover image: Shutterstock ID: 26498550199

First edition published 2026
by CRC Press
2385 NW Executive Center Drive, Suite 320, Boca Raton FL 33431

and by CRC Press
4 Park Square, Milton Park, Abingdon, Oxon, OX14 4RN

CRC Press is an imprint of Taylor & Francis Group, LLC

ISBN: 9781041077459 (hbk)
ISBN: 9781041082019 (pbk)
ISBN: 9781003644231 (ebk)

DOI: 10.1201/9781003644231

Typeset in Sabon
by Newgen Publishing UK

Contents

Preface

The rapid evolution of digital technologies has fundamentally reshaped the cybersecurity landscape, bringing both unprecedented opportunities and complex risks. Among these technologies, generative artificial intelligence (GenAI) has emerged as one of the most transformative forces, capable of revolutionizing cyber defense strategies while simultaneously giving rise to new threat vectors. Today's hyperconnected systems, cloud-native environments, and intelligent devices depend on continuous data exchange and dynamic interactions, making them more powerful yet more exposed than ever before. Traditional defensive techniques, although essential, are increasingly insufficient to counter adaptive, AI-augmented cyber threats. In this context, GenAI introduces a paradigm shift. Its ability to synthesize data, model adversarial behavior, automate decision-making, and enhance situational awareness offers cybersecurity practitioners new ways to detect threats, anticipate attacks, and strengthen digital resilience. However, the same capabilities that enhance defense can be exploited by malicious actors to craft sophisticated attacks, deepfakes, or automated offensive tools, blurring the line between innovation and exploitation. This dual nature of GenAI demands a balanced examination of its benefits, limitations, and ethical implications.

This edited book, *Generative AI for Cybersecurity*, brings together leading researchers and practitioners to explore this rapidly evolving domain from both defensive and offensive perspectives. The book is organized into five interconnected parts. Part I introduces the foundations of GenAI in cybersecurity, outlining its transformative potential and emerging risks. Part II delves into advanced defense applications, highlighting generative models for cyber resilience, security operations, and sovereign digital protection. Part II I examines weaponized GenAI, unveiling the growing landscape of AI-driven threats, adversarial techniques, and deepfake-based manipulations. Part IV emphasizes proactive cyber defense, demonstrating how generative models can anticipate attacks before they occur. Finally, Part V showcases real-world use cases and frameworks that bridge theory with practice across intrusion detection, IoT security, and explainable AI.

This book seeks to provide a comprehensive and multidisciplinary perspective, combining technical insights, practical methodologies, and forward-looking discussions on governance, trust, and responsible AI. It aims to guide researchers, students, policymakers, and cybersecurity professionals in understanding not only how GenAI works, but also how to harness it safely and strategically.

We extend our sincere appreciation to all contributing authors for their dedication, expertise, and commitment to advancing knowledge in this emerging field. Their collective efforts have made it possible to complete this work and pave the way for future research and innovation.

Truly, our deepest thanks to all.

Editors
Prof. Boubiche Djallel Eddine
LEREESI Laboratory, HNS-RE2SD, Batna, Algeria

Prof. Sedat Akleylek
Institute of Computer Science, University of Tartu, Estonia
Department of Computer Engineering, Istinye University, Turkiye

Acknowledgments

We extend our sincere gratitude to CRC Press (Taylor & Francis Group) and the entire editorial team for their continuous support, professionalism, and guidance throughout the development of this book. Their expertise and dedication greatly contributed to shaping this project into its final form.

We are deeply thankful to all contributing authors from diverse institutions and countries for their commitment, hard work, and timely efforts. Their insightful chapters and innovative perspectives have enriched this volume and advanced the discussion on GenAI in cybersecurity. Our appreciation also goes to the reviewers, whose thoughtful feedback and rigorous evaluations strengthened the quality and clarity of each contribution.

We express our thanks to our respective universities and research laboratories for providing the necessary resources, encouragement, and collaborative environment that made this work possible.

Prof. Boubiche Djallel Eddine
LEREESI Laboratory, HNS-RE2SD, Batna, Algeria

Prof. Sedat Akleylek
Institute of Computer Science, University of Tartu, Estonia
Department of Computer Engineering, Istinye University, Turkiye

Acknowledgments

About the editors

Boubiche Djallel Eddine is a Full Professor at the Higher National School of Renewable Energies, Environment, and Sustainable Development (RE2SD) in Batna, Algeria. He received his Ph.D. in Computer Science from UHLB University, Algeria, in 2013. He has held several academic responsibilities, including serving on the school's scientific committee, leading the Industrial Networks Engineering & Artificial Intelligence Specialty, and directing the LEREESI Laboratory. His current research focuses on security, edge AI, wireless communication, and the Internet of Things (IoT). Prof. Eddine has published widely in leading international journals and conferences, including *IEEE Access*, *IEEE Network*, *IEEE Communications Magazine*, *Future Generation Computer Systems*, *Computers in Human Behavior*, and other reputable venues. He is actively engaged in the research community, frequently contributing as a program committee member, program chair, and general or co-general chair for various international conferences. He also serves as a guest editor and associate editor for leading indexed journals.

Sedat Akleylek received the B.Sc. degree in Mathematics, majored in Computer Science from Ege University, Izmir, Türkiye, in 2004, and M.Sc. and Ph.D. degrees in Cryptography from Middle East Technical University, Ankara, Türkiye, in 2008 and 2010, respectively. He was a postdoctoral researcher at the Cryptography and Computer Algebra Group, TU Darmstadt, Germany, between 2014 and 2015. He worked as a professor in the Department of Computer Engineering, Ondokuz Mayıs University, Samsun, Türkiye, until 2022. He has been with Department of Computer Engineering, Istinye University, Istanbul, Turkiye and Institute of Computer Science, University of Tartu, Tartu, Estonia. His research interests include post-quantum cryptography, algorithms and complexity, architectures for computations in finite fields, applied cryptography for cybersecurity, malware analysis, IoT security, and avionics cybersecurity. He is a member of the editorial boards of *IEEE Access*, *Turkish Journal of Electrical Engineering and Computer Sciences*, *Peerj Computer Science*, and *International Journal of Information Security Science*. He has published more than 100 research papers in international journals, conference proceedings, and book chapters, and has solved several real-world security and data analytics problems for the industry.

Contributors

Fatima M. Anis
King Fahd University of Petroleum and Minerals, Dhahran, Saudi Arabia

Subrata Ashe
Meta Platforms, Inc, CA, USA

Hojjat Azadravesh
Islamic Azad University, Neyshabur, Iran

Priyang P. Bhatt
The Charutar Vidya Mandal (CVM) University, Anand, Gujarat, India

Aishwarya G.
REVA University, Bangalore, India

Mohammad Hammoudeh
King Fahd University of Petroleum and Minerals, Dhahran, Saudi Arabia

Akshaya Senthil Kumaran
REVA University, Bangalore, India

Houache Mohammed
LEREESI Laboratory, HNS-RE2SD, Batna, Algeria

Lakshmi J. V. N.
REVA University, Bangalore, India

Monire Norouzi
Haliç University, Istanbul, Turkey

Sree Lakshmi P.
REVA University, Bangalore, India

Vishal Polara
Marwadi University, Rajkot, Gujarat, India

Arash Salehpour
University of Tabriz, Tabriz, Iran

Hami Satilmiş
Ondokuz Mayıs University, Körfez, Turkey

Tetiana Schipper
German Institute for Global and Area Studies (GIGA), Hamburg, Germany

Soharab Hossain Shaikh
BML Munjal University, Gurugram, Haryana, India

Alireza Souri
Haliç University, Istanbul, Turkey

Bhaskar Thakker
The Charutar Vidya Mandal (CVM) University, Anand, Gujarat India

Sushil Kumar Verma
School of Business, GlobalNxt University, Anand, Gujarat Malaysia

Chok Nyen Yui
School of Business, GlobalNxt University, Anand, Gujarat Malaysia

AI statement

The authors acknowledge the use of AI tools, including OpenAI's ChatGPT, Grammarly, and Microsoft Copilot, in preparing the chapters. These tools were used solely for paraphrasing and grammar refinement, ensuring that the authors maintained full control over the content. All material has been thoroughly reviewed and verified by the authors to uphold accuracy and integrity. Short statements have been included in the acknowledgment section of each chapter to clarify where these tools were utilized and their specific roles in the preparation process. Additionally, the versions of AI tools employed across the chapters include GPT-5.2 and Grammarly 1.2.215, GPT-4.5, Copilot (GPT-5), GPT-3.5, GPT-5.2 with alphaXiv 2.1.2, and Anthropic's Claude 4.5, GPT-5 (version: 5-mini), and Grammarly 1.2.215.

Part I

Introduction and background

Chapter 1

The rise of generative AI in cybersecurity

Balancing benefits and risks

Boubiche Djallel Eddine

1.1 INTRODUCTION

The advancement of artificial intelligence (AI) and machine learning (ML) has been a game-changer in numerous industries, and its role in cybersecurity is gaining increasing attention. The initial development of supervised learning algorithms, which relied on labeled datasets to execute specific tasks, laid the groundwork for more sophisticated approaches. These evolved into unsupervised and semi-supervised learning methodologies, which enabled AI to autonomously identify patterns and detect anomalies within large, unstructured datasets. The introduction of reinforcement learning further extended the capabilities of AI by allowing models to learn and optimize decision-making through iterative feedback and trial-and-error processes. In parallel, innovations in natural language processing (NLP) and deep learning have empowered AI systems to comprehend, interpret, and generate human-like text with increasing accuracy and nuance.

In recent years, the field has experienced a paradigm shift with the emergence of generative AI (GenAI) technologies [1], particularly large language models (LLMs) such as GPT (generative pre-trained transformers) [2], LLaMA (Large Language Model Meta AI) [3], and Google's Gemini [4]. These models have elevated AI to new frontiers by enabling the autonomous generation of original content, sophisticated human-like responses, and the processing of vast and diverse data sources. The integration of GenAI into cybersecurity has proven transformative, offering unprecedented capabilities in areas such as threat detection, vulnerability assessment, and even offensive strategies in cybersecurity [5]. As cyber threats become increasingly complex and widespread, GenAI has emerged as a critical tool in the ongoing effort to safeguard digital infrastructures, representing a pivotal advancement in the evolution of AI technologies.

The versatility of GenAI stems from its underlying architecture. Models like GPT are built using transformer-based neural networks that excel at capturing relationships between words and phrases across large datasets. Unlike earlier models that struggled to grasp context, these AI systems can now understand nuanced language patterns and generate coherent, relevant outputs. This capability makes them particularly useful in areas like cybersecurity, where dealing with diverse, unstructured data is crucial. From analyzing text logs to detecting malicious intent in communications, the adaptability of GenAI gives it an edge over traditional rule-based systems, which often fall short when confronted with novel or evolving threats.

As GenAI models continue to improve, they are becoming more proficient at learning autonomously from data. The larger and more varied the dataset, the more accurate and effective the model becomes. For instance, GPT models are often pre-trained on vast

DOI: 10.1201/9781003644231-2

corpora of text from a range of domains, which enables them to be fine-tuned for specific cybersecurity applications. This adaptability allows them to evolve with the cyber threat landscape, learning from new data to identify previously unseen attack patterns. As a result, AI's role in cybersecurity is not static; rather, it continuously adapts as cyberattacks become more sophisticated and widespread. This adaptability is crucial in an environment where attackers are constantly modifying their techniques to exploit new vulnerabilities.

The remainder of this chapter is structured to provide a comprehensive exploration of GenAI in cybersecurity. It begins by tracing the historical development of AI in cybersecurity, highlighting early rule-based systems, anomaly detection methods, and the initial integration of ML and NLP techniques. Following this, the chapter examines the emergence of deep learning and LLMs, detailing how transformer-based architectures have revolutionized threat detection, vulnerability assessment, and automated response. Subsequent sections focus on the benefits of GenAI, illustrating its capabilities in scalable threat detection, real-time decision support, predictive analytics, and automated cybersecurity workflows. The chapter then addresses the potential risks and dual-use challenges of GenAI, including its weaponization for sophisticated attacks, social engineering, and deepfakes. Finally, the discussion concludes with a forward-looking perspective on the road ahead, emphasizing the importance of balancing innovation, ethical governance, and security-by-design principles to harness GenAI effectively while mitigating its associated risks.

1.2 HISTORICAL CONTEXT OF GENAI IN CYBERSECURITY

1.2.1 Early development of AI in cybersecurity

The integration of AI into cybersecurity began with relatively simple models, largely based on supervised and unsupervised learning methods. In the early stages, supervised learning was employed, where AI models were trained on labeled datasets to perform specific tasks such as anomaly detection and pattern recognition in network traffic. These early models, while innovative for their time, were limited by the amount of data they could process and the rigidity of their responses to new, unseen threats. Unsupervised learning soon followed, allowing AI to recognize patterns in unstructured data without relying on labeled datasets. This approach was more flexible, enabling AI systems to detect previously unknown attack patterns or network anomalies. However, these systems often struggled with accuracy and required significant human oversight to validate results, a challenge highlighted in early studies like Axelsson's [6] work on the base-rate fallacy, which pointed out the high false-positive rates in anomaly detection systems due to the rarity of actual attacks in large datasets.

In parallel, rule-based systems and expert systems were the primary methods used to automate certain cybersecurity tasks. These systems functioned based on predefined rules and expert knowledge encoded into the system, enabling them to detect known threats by following a rigid decision-making process. Denning's [7] pioneering work on intrusion detection models, along with systems like IDES developed by Lunt et al. [8], applied statistical methods and rules to monitor system activity for anomalies. However, these early AI applications were limited by their inability to adapt to new types of threats that were not accounted for during their initial programming. As a result, they were inadequate for handling the rapidly evolving nature of cyberattacks, particularly as threats became more sophisticated and polymorphic.

Researchers like Hofmeyr et al. [9] sought to address these limitations by developing models inspired by biological systems, such as their immune system-based intrusion detection model, which aimed to detect anomalies by identifying deviations from normal behavior, much like how an immune system identifies foreign pathogens. This self-learning approach was a precursor to later developments in ML but still faced challenges in balancing sensitivity to new threats with the need to reduce false positives.

The transition from rule-based systems to more adaptive AI models became evident in works like Lee and Stolfo's [10], which introduced data mining approaches for intrusion detection. By leveraging pattern recognition and classification techniques, these methods allowed AI systems to learn from historical data and adapt to new threats without requiring constant human intervention. These advances marked the early stages of what would become a more profound integration of ML in cybersecurity, as the limitations of rigid, rule-based systems gave way to more flexible, scalable models capable of handling the increasingly complex and diverse cyber threat landscape.

To provide a clearer perspective on the evolution of AI in cybersecurity, Table 1.1 summarizes several seminal works from the early stages of research in this field. The table

Table 1.1 Early Works in AI for Cybersecurity

	References	*Work/Model*	*Contribution*	*Key Insights*
Statistical and Anomaly Detection	Denning (1987) [7]	An Intrusion-Detection Model	One of the first comprehensive models for intrusion detection using statistical analysis and expert systems.	Introduced the concept of monitoring system activity for abnormal patterns, a foundation for future AI-based intrusion detection systems.
	Javitz and Valdes (1993) [11]	The NIDES Statistical Component	Introduced statistical analysis techniques for intrusion detection, laying the groundwork for later machine learning-based anomaly detection.	Focused on identifying abnormal patterns in system activity that could indicate a security breach, a precursor to AI-based anomaly detection.
	Mukherjee et al. (1994) [12]	Network Intrusion Detection	A comprehensive study on the use of statistical methods for detecting intrusions in network traffic.	Demonstrated the effectiveness of automated analysis in monitoring network traffic for abnormal activities, influencing the development of AI-based systems.
Rule-Based Systems and Expert Systems	Lunt et al. (1992) [8]	IDES (Intrusion Detection Expert System)	One of the first implementations of supervised learning in an expert system for real-time intrusion detection.	Highlighted the importance of combining statistical anomaly detection with rule-based analysis for more accurate detection

(Continued)

Table 1.1 (Continued)

	References	*Work/Model*	*Contribution*	*Key Insights*
	Anderson et al. (1995) [13]	Expert Systems in Cybersecurity	Early use of rule-based expert systems for threat detection and decision-making in cybersecurity.	Demonstrated the use of predefined rules for identifying threats based on known attack patterns. Highlighted the limitations of early systems in handling unknown threats.
	Porras and Neumann (1997) [14]	Emerald: Event Monitoring Enabling Responses to Anomalous Live Disturbances	A scalable expert system designed for network intrusion detection, combining rule-based and statistical anomaly detection techniques.	Pioneered hybrid approaches for real-time threat detection using multiple layers of defense (early precursor to modern multi-layered security systems).
Immune System Models	Hofmeyr et al. (1999) [9]	Immune System-Based Intrusion Detection	Early model based on biological immune systems to detect anomalies in network traffic.	Applied the concept of self-learning (similar to unsupervised learning) to detect unknown threats by identifying deviations from normal behavior
Transition to Machine Learning	Lee and Stolfo (1998) [10]	Data Mining Approaches for Intrusion Detection	One of the first applications of data mining and machine learning techniques to intrusion detection.	Introduced the use of pattern recognition and classification techniques to detect network intrusions, laying the foundation for modern AI-driven threat detection.
	Axelsson (1999) [6]	The Base-Rate Fallacy and Its Implications for the Difficulty of Intrusion Detection	Highlighted the challenges in anomaly detection due to the low base-rate of cyberattacks in large datasets.	Addressed the limitations of early AI systems in handling large datasets, influencing the development of more efficient AI-based solutions (machine learning approaches)
	Warrender et al. (1999) [15]	Anomaly Detection Using System Call Sequences	Introduced machine learning techniques for detecting intrusions based on deviations in system call sequences.	A key early work that applied machine learning for detecting anomalies in system behavior, leading to more advanced AI-based intrusion detection systems.

categorizes these contributions according to the type of approach used, statistical and anomaly detection, rule-based and expert systems, immune system-inspired models, and early ML applications. For each work, it highlights the key contributions and insights that shaped the foundation of AI-driven cybersecurity, illustrating the gradual transition from rigid, rule-based systems toward more adaptive and intelligent methods capable of detecting and responding to complex cyber threats.

1.2.2 Emergence of ML and NLP in cybersecurity

As AI technologies progressed, the adoption of ML techniques marked a significant shift in the cybersecurity landscape. Unlike rule-based systems, which relied on predefined rules and lacked adaptability, ML algorithms were able to learn from data and improve their accuracy over time. This made them far more adaptable to evolving cyber threats, particularly in detecting complex and dynamic attack patterns that traditional systems struggled to identify. Early works such as those by Lippmann et al. [16], which introduced the DARPA 1998 Dataset for training and evaluating intrusion detection systems, provided a critical foundation for advancing the application of ML in cybersecurity. This dataset enabled researchers to benchmark the performance of different ML models in real-world scenarios, laying the groundwork for future AI-driven threat detection methods.

One key development in the application of AI to cybersecurity was the integration of NLP. NLP allowed AI systems to analyze and interpret large amounts of unstructured text, such as emails, log files, and even social media posts, to detect phishing attacks or identify malicious intent in communications. The ability of NLP to understand the subtleties of human language made it a powerful tool for cybersecurity professionals, enabling them to leverage AI in nuanced tasks like spam detection, phishing identification, and social engineering prevention. Early examples of this include SpamAssassin [17], which applied NLP techniques to filter spam emails by analyzing textual patterns and language cues. This innovation paved the way for future NLP applications in detecting more sophisticated cyber threats.

Phishing detection, in particular, became a key focus for NLP in cybersecurity. Early works like the Phishing Corpus dataset [18] and Chandrasekaran et al. [19] demonstrated how NLP could be used to analyze the structure and wording of phishing emails, identifying linguistic patterns typical of social engineering attacks. Chandrasekaran et al. applied NLP techniques to detect phishing emails by analyzing the structural properties and specific word usage commonly found in phishing content. These models could detect subtle differences in the language used in phishing attempts compared to legitimate communications, making them highly effective in preventing phishing attacks. The Phishing Corpus dataset enabled researchers to train ML models for phishing detection by analyzing textual features such as keywords and structural patterns that are common in phishing emails. The development of CANTINA [20] further advanced NLP's role in phishing detection by applying term frequency-inverse document frequency (TF-IDF) to detect phishing websites based on the content of the webpage, showcasing the potential of NLP for content-based analysis in cybersecurity.

The introduction of ML and NLP in cybersecurity revolutionized the industry's approach to threat detection and incident response. AI models, such as those proposed by Mukkamala et al. [21], leveraged neural networks and support vector machines (SVMs) to detect network intrusions by analyzing network traffic patterns and user behavior. These models could analyze historical data, recognize patterns of normal and abnormal behavior, and flag suspicious activity with greater speed and accuracy than traditional rule-based methods.

By applying ML algorithms like decision trees and SVMs to phishing detection, as demonstrated in Abu-Nimeh et al. [22], cybersecurity systems became more efficient at identifying phishing attempts and other malicious communications. Moreover, NLP's contribution extended beyond phishing detection into other areas such as malware detection and content analysis. In Kolter and Maloof [23], ML algorithms were used to classify malicious executables based on behavioral features, applying NLP methods to analyze executable files and detect patterns indicative of malware. This early application of NLP and ML in malware detection highlighted the scalability and adaptability of AI technologies in handling diverse cyber threats.

Despite these advancements, the early applications of ML and NLP in cybersecurity were still limited by their reliance on human intervention for model training and supervision. The models required significant amounts of labeled data to be effective, and their ability to adapt to new, unknown attack vectors was restricted. Although systems like SpamAssassin and Phishing Corpus demonstrated the power of NLP for detecting well-known threats, they struggled with novel and evolving attack techniques that cybercriminals continuously developed to bypass traditional defenses. Additionally, the early models often generated a high number of false positives, requiring human analysts to review flagged anomalies, which slowed down response times.

Table 1.2 provides an overview of foundational works that shaped the adoption of ML NLP in cybersecurity. The table highlights key studies that applied ML algorithms for intrusion and malware detection, as well as early NLP-based methods for spam and phishing detection. For each work, it summarizes the contributions and key insights that influenced

Table 1.2 Foundational Works in ML and NLP for Cybersecurity

	References	*Work/Model*	*Contribution*	*Key Insights*
Machine Learning for Intrusion and Malware Detection	Lippmann et al. (2000) [16]	Evaluating Intrusion Detection Systems: The DARPA 1998 Dataset	Provided one of the first publicly available datasets for training and testing machine learning-based intrusion detection systems.	Enabled benchmarking of machine learning models in detecting cyberattacks, spurring the development of data-driven security solutions.
	McHugh (2001) [24]	Intrusion and Anomaly Detection Using Statistical Approaches	Explored the application of statistical learning methods to identify anomalous behavior.	Advanced the understanding of statistical anomaly detection and laid the groundwork for integrating machine learning in security operations.

Table 1.2 (Continued)

	References	*Work/Model*	*Contribution*	*Key Insights*
	Mukkamala et al. (2002) [21]	Neural Networks and Support Vector Machines (SVMs) for Intrusion Detection	Explored the use of neural networks and SVM for identifying network intrusions.	Showed that machine learning algorithms could outperform traditional rule-based methods in detecting complex, multi-stage attacks
	Kruegel et al. (2003) [25]	Bayesian Network Models for Intrusion Detection	Applied Bayesian networks to model network behavior and detect intrusions based on probabilistic reasoning.	Showcased an early form of probabilistic machine learning for cybersecurity, predicting attacks based on observed patterns.
	Kolter and Maloof (2006) [23]	Learning to Detect Malicious Executables	Applied machine learning algorithms to classify malicious executables and detect malware based on behavioral features.	One of the first applications of machine learning for malware detection, highlighting the scalability of AI in detecting evolving threats.
Machine Learning and NLP for Spam and Phishing Detection	SpamAssassin [17]	NLP-Based Spam Detection	Used NLP techniques to identify spam emails based on textual patterns and language cues.	Pioneered NLP-based threat detection methods, focusing on email filtering and spam detection, influencing future work on phishing and social engineering prevention.
	Phishing Corpus [18]	Phishing Detection Dataset	Provided a comprehensive dataset to train models on identifying phishing attacks by analyzing the language used in emails and websites.	Enabled the development of NLP-based phishing detection models by offering a dataset rich in phishing examples for training machine learning models.

(*Continued*)

Table 1.2 (Continued)

References	*Work/Model*	*Contribution*	*Key Insights*
Chandrasekaran et al. (2006) [19]	Phishing Email Detection Using Structural Properties	Applied NLP to analyze the structure and wording of phishing emails.	Showed how NLP techniques could detect phishing attacks by identifying linguistic patterns typical in phishing content.
Abu-Nimeh et al. (2007) [22]	Machine Learning for Phishing Detection	Combined machine learning and NLP to detect phishing emails by analyzing textual features.	Demonstrated the effectiveness of NLP in phishing detection through the use of ML algorithms like decision trees and SVMs.
Zhang Yue et al. (2007) [20]	CANTINA: Content-Based Phishing Detection	Developed an NLP-based system that used term frequency-inverse document frequency (TF-IDF) to detect phishing websites.	Pioneered the use of NLP algorithms for content-based analysis in phishing website detection.

subsequent research, illustrating how these approaches enabled more adaptive, data-driven security solutions. Collectively, these studies laid the groundwork for modern AI-powered cybersecurity systems capable of analyzing complex datasets, detecting sophisticated attacks, and automating threat mitigation.

1.2.3 The advent of deep learning and LLMs

The evolution of AI in cybersecurity has been marked by significant breakthroughs in deep learning and the advent of LLMs. Early works such as Hinton et al. [26] demonstrated the potential of deep neural networks to process vast amounts of data and recognize complex patterns. Initially developed for tasks like speech recognition, these neural networks provided the foundation for their later use in cybersecurity. Deep learning models brought improved accuracy and efficiency to cybersecurity by enhancing threat detection capabilities, particularly for identifying advanced persistent threats (APTs) and zero-day exploits [27].

The next major leap came with the introduction of Generative Adversarial Networks (GANs) by Goodfellow et al. [28]. GANs allowed for the creation of synthetic data, which is invaluable in simulating cyberattacks and generating polymorphic malware to test and strengthen defense mechanisms. This approach not only advanced defensive strategies but also demonstrated how attackers could leverage GANs for deepfakes and disinformation campaigns, further complicating the cybersecurity landscape [29]. A critical milestone in the progression of AI's role in cybersecurity was the development of the transformer architecture by Vaswani et al. [30]. This architecture, which introduced the attention mechanism, laid the foundation for modern LLMs like GPT [31] and BERT (Bidirectional Encoder Representations from Transformers) [32]. The attention mechanism allowed for the efficient processing of vast amounts of text data, which is essential for detecting cyber threats hidden within unstructured data like emails, logs, and network communications [33].

The introduction of GPT-1 [31] was a pivotal moment for cybersecurity applications. LLMs such as GPT-1, which excelled at generating human-like text, were immediately seen as valuable for automating tasks like threat detection, report generation, and cyberattack simulations [34]. BERT further enhanced these capabilities by improving contextual understanding in NLP tasks, making it easier to detect phishing and malware based on nuanced textual patterns [35]. The release of GPT-2 in 2019 [36], with its 1.5 billion parameters, represented another leap forward. It showcased how LLMs could be repurposed for offensive cybersecurity strategies. The model's ability to generate coherent, human-like text raised concerns about AI weaponization, with potential applications for phishing campaigns and social engineering attacks [37]. These concerns escalated further with the release of GPT-3 in 2020 [38], a model boasting 175 billion parameters, which allowed for the simulation of complex cyberattacks and the automation of real-time threat responses.

In parallel, Meta's LLaMA (2023) introduced an efficient model designed for scalable real-time applications [39], which can be adapted for various tasks, including cybersecurity [40], optimizing performance in data processing without sacrificing efficiency. Around the same time, Google AI's LaMDA [41] and Google Bard [42] emerged as versatile conversational AI tools, applicable across multiple fields. While not exclusively dedicated to cybersecurity, their conversational capabilities can be leveraged to simulate social engineering attacks or to develop automated threat-response systems when adapted for cybersecurity purposes. Another milestone in the integration of GenAI into cybersecurity was the development of Grok by X (formerly Twitter) in 2023 [43]. Grok capabilities in real-time and large-scale data analysis can be adapted to enhance security systems. By leveraging LLMs, Grok can analyze massive datasets for emerging patterns, which is valuable in cybersecurity contexts such as threat detection. This model, along with LLaMA, has contributed to advancing AI-driven systems into the realm of real-time defense, empowering organizations to detect and respond to cyberattacks with greater speed and accuracy when applied in security operations.

The year 2024 brought further advancements with the release of several groundbreaking LLMs. Claude 3 by Anthropic [44] enhanced contextual understanding, multilingual proficiency, and visual data interpretation, making it a valuable tool for cybersecurity problem-solving in increasingly complex environments [45]. GPT-4o by OpenAI [46] introduced multimodal capabilities, handling text, audio, and visual inputs simultaneously, with an extended context window and real-time interaction capabilities, which positioned it as an ideal model for large-scale threat detection and analysis [47]. Meta's Llama 3.1 [48] brought models with up to 405 billion parameters to the cybersecurity field, offering improved capabilities in multilingual support, threat analysis [40], and multimodal data processing. Gemini 1.5 by Google DeepMind [49] further expanded AI applications in cybersecurity defense by introducing a 1 million-token context window, enhancing its ability to handle long-form content such as logs and attack simulations [50].

The continued advancement of LLMs in cybersecurity raises both opportunities and challenges. As these models become more powerful, they provide increasingly sophisticated tools for threat detection, malware analysis, and cyberattack simulations. At the same time, the risk of AI weaponization grows, as models like GPT-3, Claude 3, and GPT-4o can be repurposed for malicious uses such as generating phishing emails, social engineering scripts, or even polymorphic malware that evolves to avoid detection. The emergence of conversational AI models like LaMDA and Google Bard also highlights the dual-use nature of these technologies, as they can be employed for both offensive and defensive purposes in cybersecurity.

Table 1.3 highlights key developments in deep learning and LLMs that have significantly influenced the field of cybersecurity. The table summarizes landmark models, from early neural networks and GANs to modern LLMs like GPT, BERT, LLaMA, and Claude, detailing their contributions and applications in both offensive and defensive cybersecurity

Table 1.3 Key LLM Developments and Their Impact on Cybersecurity

	Reference	*Work/Model*	*Contribution*
Neural networks in cybersecurity	Hinton et al. (2012) [26]	Deep Neural Networks for Acoustic Modeling	Demonstrated the scalability of deep learning in handling large datasets, providing a foundation for using neural networks in cybersecurity to detect complex attack patterns.
	Goodfellow et al. (2014) [28]	Generative Adversarial Networks (GANs)	Showcased how GANs could generate synthetic data to simulate attacks, create deepfakes, and develop polymorphic malware, revolutionizing both offensive and defensive cybersecurity.
	Vaswani (2017) [30]	Attention Is All You Need	Introduced the transformer architecture, critical for processing large-scale textual data, which later enabled LLMs like GPT and BERT to be applied for advanced threat detection and automated text generation in cybersecurity.
Advanced LLMs in Offensive and Defensive Cybersecurity	Radford et al. (2018) [31]	GPT-1	Early example of pre-trained LLM used for human-like text generation, applicable in automating cybersecurity tasks.
	Kenton et al. (2019) [32]	BERT	Developed a model for bidirectional understanding of context in texts, improving NLP applications in phishing detection and malware classification.
	Radford et al. (2019) [36]	GPT-2	Marked significant advancements in LLM capabilities, demonstrating how AI-generated text could simulate attacks and automate offensive cybersecurity strategies.
	Brown et al. (2020) [38]	GPT-3	Achieved unprecedented scale with 175 billion parameters, revolutionizing threat simulation and the automation of security tasks in real-time.
	Touvron et al. (2023) [39]	LLaMA	Provided efficient models with smaller parameter sizes for scalable, real-time applications in security.
	Thoppilan et al. (2022) [41]	LaMDA	Developed to enhance human-computer interaction, useful for automating dialogue in phishing or social engineering simulations.

Table 1.3 (Continued)

Reference	Work/Model	Contribution
X (formerly Twitter) (2023) [43]	Grok	Demonstrated real-time anomaly detection and large-scale data analysis, making it useful for identifying cyber threats in real-time.
Google Bard (2023) [42]	Bard	Launched as a conversational AI model to enhance real-time communication, relevant for phishing simulations and automated threat response.
Anthropic (2024) [44]	Claude 3	Demonstrated enhanced contextual understanding and multilingual proficiency, useful for advanced threat detection and real-time cybersecurity problem-solving.
OpenAI (2024) [46]	GPT-4o	An enhanced version of GPT-4, offering multimodal capabilities and real-time interaction, handling text, audio, and visual inputs. It is optimized for large-scale threat detection and cyberattack simulations.
Meta AI (2024) [48]	Llama 3.1	Featuring models with up to 405 billion parameters, it enhanced multilingual support and threat analysis, excelling in multimodal data processing for cybersecurity.
Google DeepMind (2024) [49]	Gemini 1.5	Introduced a 1 million-token context window, allowing the model to handle complex, long-form data such as logs and attack simulations in cybersecurity.

contexts. By presenting these foundational and advanced works, the table illustrates how LLMs have enhanced threat detection, automated cyberattack simulations, improved contextual understanding of textual data, and enabled real-time analysis of large-scale and multimodal datasets. Collectively, these innovations underscore the transformative impact of LLMs in reshaping cybersecurity strategies and capabilities.

1.3 THE GOOD: BENEFITS OF GENAI IN CYBERSECURITY

Cybersecurity has traditionally relied on a combination of manual and automated processes to protect systems and data. Manual approaches, though effective in specific contexts, are limited by the capacity and expertise of human operators. Automated processes, while faster, often lack the ability to adapt to the increasingly complex nature of modern cyber threats. As cyberattacks have become more sophisticated, ranging from polymorphic malware to deepfake-driven social engineering, traditional rule-based defense mechanisms are increasingly insufficient. Recent advances in GenAI further highlight this gap: LLMs can now detect highly deceptive textual threats (Figure 1.1), such as phishing, smishing, vishing, and malicious spam, with accuracy levels previously unattainable using classical methods. Models such as DarkBERT [51], trained specifically on dark-web corpora, enhance the detection and investigation of emerging threats lurking in illicit online ecosystems. Likewise, systems like LOCALINTEL [52] expand threat text collection capabilities across diverse

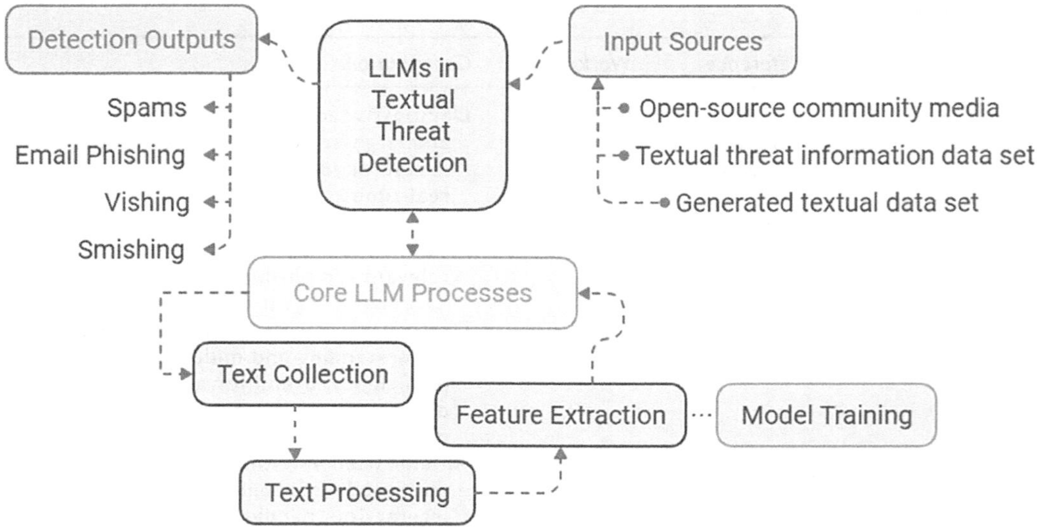

Figure 1.1 LLMs in Textual Threat Detection.

open-source intelligence channels [54], offering richer contextual awareness when monitoring social-engineering signals.

Moreover, GenAI systems are highly scalable, making them ideal for handling the growing volume of cybersecurity data generated by increasingly connected and complex digital infrastructures. As organizations scale their operations and embrace technologies like the Internet of Things (IoT) and cloud computing, the amount of data that needs to be protected grows exponentially. Manual and traditional automated systems are often overwhelmed by the sheer volume of data, which increases the risk of missing critical signs of an attack. GenAI, on the other hand, thrives in such environments, offering scalability without sacrificing performance or accuracy. In practice, this includes accelerating threat detection pipelines within Security Operations Centers (SOCs) by automating labor-intensive processes such as log triage, anomaly detection, and text-based threat analysis. LLM-powered spam and phishing detectors, for example, can identify subtle linguistic cues in emails, URLs, and messages, achieving high performance using fine-tuned BERT-based models [53–55] or GPT-based zero-shot reasoning frameworks [56, 57]. Such applications demonstrate how AI can process cybersecurity data at a scale unmanageable for human analysts, supporting proactive decision-making rather than reactive defense.

Another reason GenAI has gained traction in cybersecurity is its potential to support real-time decision-making. In many cybersecurity scenarios, time is of the essence. Delays in identifying and responding to threats can have severe consequences, such as data breaches, financial losses, and reputational damage. Traditional response processes, which often involve multiple steps and the coordination of different teams, can be slow and cumbersome [58]. AI can streamline this process by automating certain responses, such as isolating affected systems, blocking malicious traffic, or deploying patches to vulnerable systems. This not only reduces the time it takes to mitigate the impact of an attack but also helps to prevent further damage. Recent studies showcase that LLMs can support incident response workflows by automatically summarizing alerts, generating remediation recommendations, and even drafting incident reports, enabling rapid, coordinated actions across SOC teams. In textual threat detection, fine-tuned BERT models have proven efficient in identifying phishing emails [59], malicious URLs [60], and domain-specific attacks [61], while GPT-based systems can classify spam through zero-shot prompting with high F1-scores [57]. This ability to provide timely, context-aware insights and actionable recommendations further strengthens the case for its widespread adoption.

Moreover, AI-enhanced vulnerability assessment is another critical area where generative models play a significant role. Organizations are constantly adding new software, applications, and systems, each with its own set of potential vulnerabilities. Keeping track of these vulnerabilities manually is nearly impossible, particularly for large organizations. AI tools can automatically scan systems for weaknesses, simulate attacks to identify how they might be exploited, and prioritize vulnerabilities based on the level of risk they pose. Beyond traditional scanners, emerging generative approaches assist in secure code generation and code auditing. For example, LLMs can automatically analyze software repositories to detect insecure coding patterns, suggest fixes, or generate defensive code snippets, significantly reducing the time required for secure software development. This complements the advancements seen in textual threat detection, such as hybrid BERT-GAN frameworks for improving spam classification under imbalanced datasets [62] or lightweight phishing detection architectures optimized for mobile environments. By automating these processes, AI empowers security teams to focus on addressing the most critical issues rather than being overwhelmed by the volume of potential vulnerabilities.

In addition to technical applications, AI is being used to enhance cybersecurity governance and compliance. Many industries are subject to strict regulations around data protection and security, and ensuring compliance with these regulations can be a complex and time-consuming task. GenAI can help organizations stay compliant by automating tasks such as monitoring for policy violations, generating audit reports, and even drafting security policies. LLMs have already demonstrated their ability to generate detailed cybersecurity documentation, structure incident-handling reports, and produce compliance summaries tailored to regulatory standards. In threat-intelligence workflows, models like DarkBERT aid in monitoring darknet activities, while GPT-enhanced systems can generate risk assessments or summarize intelligence feeds with minimal human intervention. By doing so, AI reduces the burden on security teams and ensures that organizations remain aligned with regulatory requirements.

While automation is one of the most significant advantages of using AI in cybersecurity, its ability to predict future threats is what truly sets it apart from traditional security technologies. By analyzing historical data, AI models can identify patterns and trends that may indicate a future attack. For example, AI can examine data from past attacks to predict when and where a new attack might occur. This predictive capability allows organizations to take a proactive approach to cybersecurity, rather than simply reacting to incidents after they occur. One area where this predictive power is particularly useful is in threat intelligence. Traditionally, threat intelligence has been a labor-intensive process requiring analysts to sift manually through large volumes of data. AI, however, can automate this process by analyzing diverse data sources, including social media, dark-web marketplaces, and threat feeds, to identify emerging risks in real time. LLM-enhanced threat analysis frameworks such as BEAM [63] or domain-specific BERT variants like DomURLs_BERT [64] demonstrate the benefits of combining semantic modeling with machine-scale threat-pattern discovery. This not only saves time but also ensures that organizations are better prepared to defend against attacks.

Table 1.4 summarizes the key benefits of integrating GenAI into cybersecurity operations, highlighting how LLMs and related models enhance detection, response, and overall security posture. The table categorizes the advantages of GenAI across multiple dimensions,

Table 1.4 Key Benefits of Generative AI in Cybersecurity

Category	*Main Benefits*	*Representative Examples/Techniques*
Enhanced Threat Detection	• Detects complex, evasive, and textual threats (phishing, smishing, malicious spam). • Identifies subtle linguistic cues missed by rule-based systems. • Improves detection accuracy across network, email, and URL-based attacks.	• DarkBERT for dark-web threat detection. • Fine-tuned BERT models for phishing emails, malicious URLs, and domain-specific threats. •Hybrid BERT–GAN spam classifiers for imbalanced datasets. • GPT-based zero-shot spam/phishing detection (high F1-scores).
Scalability and High-Volume Data Processing	• Handles exponential growth of logs, IoT data, network telemetry. • Enables large-scale SOC operations without performance loss. • Automates text-based threat analysis at machine speed.	• LLM-powered SOC triage automating log analysis and anomaly detection. • LOCALINTEL for large-scale OSINT text ingestion. • BERT/GPT spam and phishing detectors running at enterprise scale.
Real-Time Decision Support and Response	• Accelerates incident response and reduces time-to-mitigate. • Generates remediation actions, alert summaries, and incident reports. • Supports rapid containment actions (blocking traffic, isolating systems).	• GPT models drafting incident reports and summarizing alerts. • Fine-tuned BERT identifying threats in real time (URLs, emails). • Automated response workflows embedded in SOC platforms.
Vulnerability Assessment and Secure Code Automation	• Automatically identifies insecure coding patterns. • Generates secure code suggestions and patches. • Prioritizes vulnerabilities based on risk. • Simulates attack scenarios using generative techniques.	• LLM-powered code auditing and bug detection. • Generative code assistants producing defensive code snippets. • Lightweight mobile-friendly phishing detectors enabling secure app ecosystems.
Governance, Compliance and Policy Automation	• Automates report generation, audit documentation, and policy drafting. • Monitors workflows for policy violations. • Reduces human workload in regulatory compliance.	• GPT-based systems generating compliance reports and risk assessments. • DarkBERT monitoring darknet activities relevant to compliance and threat intel.
Predictive Threat Intelligence	• Identifies attack trends and predicts emerging threats. • Extracts signals from large unstructured sources before attacks occur. • Enhances situational awareness in SOCs and CERTs.	• BEAM framework combining semantic modeling with real-time threat discovery. • DomURLs_BERT for domain-pattern prediction. • GPT/BERT analysis of social media, darknet markets, threat feeds.
Automation of Cybersecurity Workflows	• Reduces manual analyst workload across SOC functions. • Improves efficiency in triage, documentation, and detection pipelines. • Minimizes cognitive overload in high-volume environments.	• Automated alert classification and summarization. • GPT-based workflow assistants for SOC task orchestration. • LLM-driven email/URL spam filtering replacing manual review.

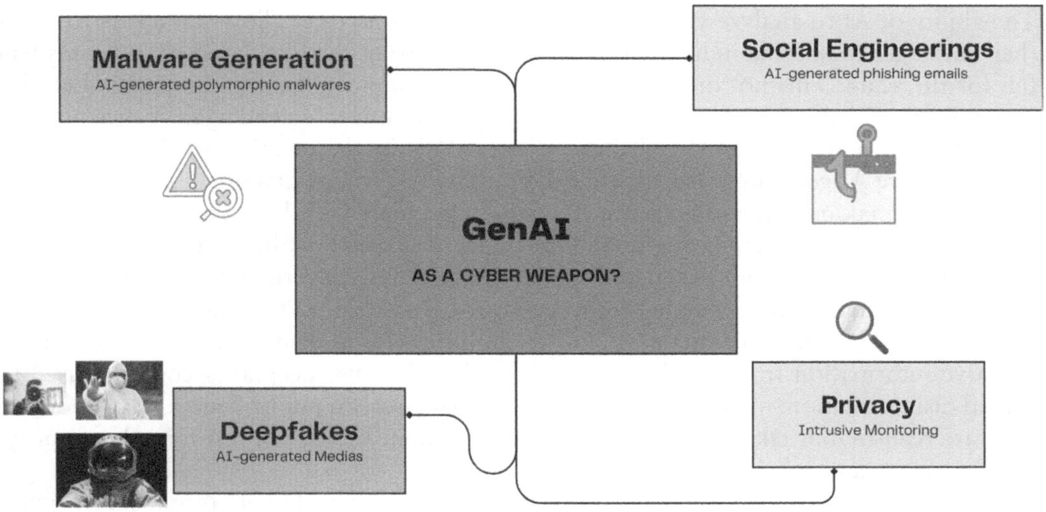

Figure 1.2 Weaponized GenAI.

including advanced threat detection, scalability for high-volume data processing, real-time decision support, vulnerability assessment, governance and compliance automation, predictive threat intelligence, and workflow automation. Each category is accompanied by representative examples and techniques, demonstrating practical applications.

1.4 THE DARK SIDE: GENAI AS A CYBER WEAPON

While GenAI provides substantial benefits in reinforcing cyber defenses, its potential misuse in the hands of malicious actors has introduced a new dimension of threats in the cybersecurity landscape. AI-driven attacks are becoming more sophisticated, scalable, and automated, making it easier for attackers to deploy large-scale and complex cyberattacks. The dual-use nature of GenAI means that, while it can be leveraged to improve defense mechanisms, it also presents opportunities for cybercriminals to enhance their offensive capabilities.

One of the most concerning aspects of GenAI being weaponized is its ability to generate malware [65]. Traditional malware development requires technical expertise and manual intervention to modify and update its code. However, with GenAI, malware can be continuously adapted and improved to evade detection by traditional security systems. For instance, AI-generated polymorphic malware can change its code every time it infects a new system, making it more difficult for signature-based detection systems to identify it. Furthermore, GenAI can be trained to discover zero-day vulnerabilities, automatically generating exploits that take advantage of these unknown security flaws. This ability to automate both malware creation and vulnerability discovery is a game-changer for cybercriminals, allowing them to stay one step ahead of cybersecurity defenses.

In addition to generating sophisticated malware, GenAI has also transformed social engineering attacks. Traditionally, social engineering relies on human interaction to deceive individuals into divulging confidential information. However, GenAI has introduced a new level of sophistication to these attacks, particularly in phishing. AI-generated phishing emails are highly personalized, using data gathered from social media, previous breaches, or public records to craft messages that are nearly indistinguishable from legitimate communications.

The ability of AI to analyze vast amounts of data about a target allows attackers to tailor their messages to specific individuals or groups, increasing the likelihood that victims will fall for the scam. This not only increases the success rate of phishing campaigns but also makes it more challenging for individuals and organizations to defend against such attacks.

Another area where GenAI is being weaponized is in the creation of deepfakes [66]. Deepfakes are AI-generated images, videos, or audio recordings that are designed to mimic real people, making it possible to impersonate individuals with high degrees of accuracy. These deepfakes pose significant threats in the cybersecurity realm, particularly in cases where they are used to impersonate high-level executives, government officials, or other trusted individuals. For example, deepfakes can be used in CEO fraud schemes, where attackers impersonate a company's CEO to authorize fraudulent transactions or extract sensitive information from employees. In the political arena, deepfakes could be used to spread disinformation, manipulate public opinion, or discredit public figures. This ability to generate realistic but fake content has far-reaching implications, not just for cybersecurity, but for society as a whole.

The use of GenAI as a cyber weapon extends beyond technical exploits and social engineering to ethical and legal dimensions. The same technologies that enable GenAI to enhance cybersecurity can also infringe on privacy and data protection rights when misused. For instance, AI systems used to monitor network traffic and analyze vast quantities of data raise significant privacy concerns, particularly when applied without adequate oversight. Automated surveillance powered by AI can lead to intrusive monitoring, creating ethical dilemmas about how data is collected, stored, and used. Furthermore, AI-enabled mass data analysis may lead to unintended biases in monitoring and can result in false positives, further complicating the process of distinguishing legitimate activity from cyber threats.

These concerns are compounded by the fact that the current legal frameworks governing AI use in cybersecurity are still underdeveloped. Regulations like the General Data Protection Regulation (GDPR) provide guidance on how data should be handled, but they do not fully address the complexities introduced by AI, particularly in terms of accountability and transparency. As AI becomes more pervasive in both offensive and defensive cybersecurity strategies, there is an urgent need for comprehensive legal frameworks that can address these complexities.

The risks associated with AI misuse underscore the importance of ethical AI development. Developers and organizations must implement strict ethical guidelines to ensure that AI technologies are not used for malicious purposes. This includes embedding safeguards within GenAI systems that prevent them from generating harmful content, such as malware or deepfakes. However, attackers are often able to bypass these safeguards through techniques like jailbreaking and prompt injection, where they manipulate AI systems to produce unintended outputs. As a result, there is a need for continuous innovation in AI security to ensure that these technologies are resilient to exploitation.

1.5 THE ROAD AHEAD

The future of cybersecurity will be shaped by how effectively organizations balance the transformative power of GenAI with the profound risks it introduces. As LLMs such as GPT, BERT, Gemini, and domain-specialized variants like DarkBERT continue to evolve in capability, they promise to extend the reach of defensive systems far beyond traditional limitations. Their ability to analyze massive datasets, detect subtle semantic anomalies across phishing, spam, and threat-text streams, and automate complex SOC tasks positions GenAI as a central pillar in next-generation cyber defense. These systems are becoming integral not only for identifying ongoing attacks but also for anticipating emerging tactics through predictive threat intelligence, real-time incident reasoning, and automated vulnerability analysis. As organizations increasingly deploy AI to manage large-scale digital infrastructures, from IoT ecosystems to cloud-native microservices, the promise of GenAI lies in its ability to absorb overwhelming data volumes while delivering actionable insights at machine speed, significantly reducing the time between detection, analysis, and reaction.

Yet this same unprecedented power creates a parallel and equally disruptive threat landscape. As demonstrated in the previous chapter, GenAI lowers the barrier for developing sophisticated offensive capabilities, enabling adversaries to automate exploit generation, craft highly targeted phishing campaigns, and produce deepfakes or misinformation with alarming realism. Attackers can exploit LLMs through prompt injection, jailbreaks, and data poisoning to circumvent model safeguards and weaponize generative systems for malware mutation or zero-day discovery. This dual-use dilemma means that every advancement in AI-driven defense is mirrored by the possibility of an amplified AI-driven offense. In practice, defenders must confront adversaries who now possess scalable, automated, and adaptive tools that can evolve their behavior as quickly as defensive systems can analyze them. The asymmetry is further aggravated by the rapid democratization of AI technologies, which makes advanced models accessible not only to state-level actors but also to cybercriminal groups, hacktivists, and lone attackers.

The road ahead will therefore depend on proactive governance, responsible AI development, and a shift from reactive defense to anticipatory resilience. Implementing robust guardrails within generative models, such as built-in misuse detection layers, contextual filtering, and AI-origin provenance, will be essential, yet insufficient on their own. Organizations will need to pair technical safeguards with rigorous oversight frameworks addressing transparency, explainability, auditability, and compliance. Current regulatory mechanisms fall short of covering the complexities introduced by autonomous reasoning systems, especially regarding accountability when AI-generated outputs cause harm or enable breaches. As AI becomes embedded in every layer of the cyber ecosystem, from secure coding pipelines to threat-intelligence feeds to automated response workflows, legal and ethical frameworks must evolve to define how data is collected, how automated decisions are validated, and how responsibility is shared between humans and autonomous systems.

Ultimately, the future of GenAI in cybersecurity hinges on establishing a sustainable equilibrium where innovation is encouraged but tightly aligned with ethical constraints and security-by-design principles. This requires continuous monitoring for AI model drift, robust defenses against adversarial manipulation, and new standards for AI assurance that can evaluate whether generative systems behave safely under real-world conditions. Collaboration across academia, industry, and regulators will be critical for shaping norms before misuse proliferates beyond control. If managed responsibly, GenAI will not only enhance cyber defense but also redefine it, enabling predictive, autonomous, and adaptive security architectures capable of countering the increasingly complex threat environment. If neglected, the same technologies risk accelerating an arms race where attackers and defenders continuously escalate capabilities with unpredictable consequences. The challenge, therefore, is not simply to adopt AI, but to harness it in a way that amplifies human expertise, preserves trust, and maintains a stable cybersecurity ecosystem in the face of rapidly evolving threats.

1.6 CONCLUSION

The evolution of AI in cybersecurity illustrates a clear trajectory from rigid, rule-based detection systems toward highly adaptive, context-aware, and autonomous generative models. Early statistical methods and expert systems laid essential groundwork but were ultimately limited by their inability to handle novel or rapidly evolving threats. Subsequent advancements in ML and NLP significantly expanded the analytical capabilities of cybersecurity systems, enabling more precise anomaly detection, improved phishing defense, and scalable analysis of unstructured data. The emergence of deep learning, GANs, and transformer architectures marked a decisive turning point, introducing unprecedented capacity for pattern recognition, natural language understanding, and synthetic content generation. With the rise of LLMs such as GPT-4o, LLaMA 3.1, Gemini 1.5, and Claude 3, cybersecurity has entered an era where real-time threat detection, autonomous response, multimodal analysis, and large-scale simulation are not only possible but increasingly practical.

However, this progress comes with inherent dual-use risks. The same models that can detect advanced threats can also be exploited to generate deceptive phishing content, automate reconnaissance, or assist in crafting polymorphic malware. As GenAI continues to evolve, striking a balance between leveraging its defensive potential and mitigating its misuse becomes a critical priority. Ultimately, the chapter underscores that transformer-based GenAI represents both the most powerful tool and one of the most complex challenges in modern cybersecurity, reinforcing the need for continuous innovation, responsible deployment, and interdisciplinary collaboration to build secure and resilient digital ecosystems.

ACKNOWLEDGMENTS

The author acknowledges the use of AI tools, including OpenAI's ChatGPT and Grammarly in the preparation of this manuscript. These tools were applied for paraphrasing and grammar refinement.

REFERENCES

[1] Feuerriegel, S., Hartmann, J., Janiesch, C. and Zschech, P., "Generative AI," *Business & Information Systems Engineering,* vol. 66, no. 1, pp. 111–126, 2024.

[2] "OpenAI ChatGPT – Release notes," [Online]. Available: https://help.openai.com/en/articles/6825453-chatgpt-release-notes. [Accessed 28 09 2024].

[3] Touvron, H., Lavril, T., Izacard, G., Martinet, X., Lachaux, M.-A., Lacroix, T., Rozière, B., Goyal, N., Hambro, E., Azhar, F., Rodriguez, A., Joulin, A., Grave, E. and Lample, G., "LLaMA: Open and efficient foundation," *arXiv preprint arXiv:2302.13971*, 2023.

[4] Team, G., Anil, R., Borgeaud, S., Wu, Y., Alayrac, J. B., Yu, J., ... and Ahn, J., "Gemini: A family of highly capable multimodal models," *arXiv preprint arXiv:2312.11805*, 2023.

[5] Gupta, M., Akiri, C., Aryal, K., Parker, E. and Praharaj, L., "From ChatGPT to threatGPT: Impact of generative AI in cybersecurity and privacy," *IEEE Access,* vol. 11, pp. 80218–80245, 2023.

[6] Axelsson, S., "The base-rate fallacy and its implications for the difficulty of intrusion detection," in *Proceedings of the 6th ACM Conference on Computer and Communications Security*, 1999.

[7] Denning, D. E., "An intrusion-detection model," *IEEE Transactions on Software Engineering,* vol. 2, pp. 222–232, 1987.

[8] Lunt, T. F., Tamaru, A., Gilham, F., Jagannathan, R., Jalali, C., Neumann, P. G., Javitz, H. S., Valdes, A. and Garvey, T.D., *A Real-Time Intrusion-Detection Expert System (IDES)*, Menlo Park, CA: SRI International, Computer Science Laboratory, 1992.

[9] Hofmeyr, S. A. and Forrest, S., "Immunizing computer networks: Getting all the machines in your network to fight the hacker disease," in *IEEE Symposium on Security and Privacy*, Washington, DC, 15–19 April 1999.

[10] Lee, W. and Stolfo, S., "Data mining approaches for intrusion detection," in *Proceedings of the 7th USENIX Security Symposium*, San Antonio, TX, 26–29 January 1998.

[11] Javitz, H. S., Valdes, A. and National Research Development Corporation, "The NIDES statistical component: Description and justification," *Contract 39*, vol. 92-C, p. 0015, 1993.

[12] Mukherjee, B., Heberlein, L. T. and Levitt, K. N., "Network intrusion detection," *IEEE Network*, vol. 8, no. 3, pp. 26–41, 1994.

[13] Anderson, D., Frivold, T. and Valdes, A., "Next-generation intrusion detection expert system (NIDES), A summary," *SRI International, SRI-CSL-95-07*,1995.

[14] Porras, P. A. and Neumann, P. G., "EMERALD: Event monitoring enabling response to anomalous live disturbances," in *Proceedings of the 20th National Information Systems Security Conference*, 1997.

[15] Warrender, C., Forrest, S. and Pearlmutter, B., "Detecting intrusions using system calls: Alternative data models," in *Proceedings of the 1999 IEEE Symposium on Security and Privacy (Cat. No. 99CB36344)*, 1999.

[16] Lippmann, R. P., Fried, D. J., Graf, I., Haines, J. W., Kendall, K. R., McClung, D., Weber, D., Webster, S. E., Wyschogrod, D., Cunningham, R. K. and Zissman, M. A., "Evaluating intrusion detection systems: The 1998 DARPA off-line intrusion detection evaluation," in *Proceedings DARPA Information Survivability Conference and Exposition. DISCEX'00*, 2000.

[17] Schwartz, A., *SpamAssassin*, O'Reilly Media, Inc , 2005.

[18] Phishing Corpus, "Phishing corpus – Nazario. Phishingcorpus homepage," 2006. [Online]. Available: http://monkey.org/%7Ejose/phishing/.

[19] Chandrasekaran, M., Narayanan, K. and Upadhyaya, S., "Phishing email detection based on structural properties," in *NYS Cyber Security Conference*, 2006.

[20] Zhang, Y., Hong, J. I. and Cranor, L. F., "Cantina: A content-based approach to detecting phishing web sites," in *Proceedings of the 16th International Conference on World Wide Web*, 2007.

[21] Mukkamala, S., Janoski, G. and Sung, A., "Intrusion detection using neural networks and support vector machines," in *Proceedings of the 2002 International Joint Conference on Neural Networks. IJCNN'02 (Cat. No. 02CH37290)*, 2002.

[22] Abu-Nimeh, S., Nappa, D., Wang, X. and Nair, S., "A comparison of machine learning techniques for phishing detection," in *Proceedings of the Anti-phishing Working Groups 2nd Annual eCrime Researchers Summit*, 2007.

[23] Kolter, J.Z. and Maloof, M.A., "Learning to detect malicious executables," in *Machine Learning and Data Mining for Computer Security: Methods and Applications*, London: Springer London, 2006.

[24] McHugh, J., "Intrusion and intrusion detection," *International Journal of Information Security*, vol. 1, pp. 14–35, 2001.

[25] Kruegel, C., Mutz, D., Robertson, W. and Valeur, F., "Bayesian event classification for intrusion detection," in *19th Annual Computer Security Applications Conference*, 2003.

[26] Hinton, G., Deng, L., Yu, D., Dahl, G. E., Mohamed, A. R., Jaitly, N., Senior, A., Vanhoucke, V., Nguyen, P., Sainath, T. N. and Kingsbury, B., "Deep neural networks for acoustic modeling in speech recognition: The shared views of four research groups," *IEEE Signal Processing Magazine*, vol. 29, no. 6, pp. 82–97, 2012.

[27] Soltani, M., Ousat, B., Siavoshani, M.J. and Jahangir, A.H., "An adaptable deep learning-based intrusion detection system to zero-day attacks," *Journal of Information Security and Applications*, vol. 76, no. 1, p. 103516, 2023.

[28] Goodfellow, I., Pouget-Abadie, J., Mirza, M., Xu, B., Warde-Farley, D., Ozair, S., Courville, A. and Bengio, Y., "Generative adversarial nets," *Advances in Neural Information Processing Systems*, vol. 27, pp. 2672–2680, 2014.

[29] Ben Aissa, F., Hamdi, M., Zaied, M. and Mejdoub, M., "An overview of GAN-DeepFakes detection: Proposal, improvement, and evaluation," *Multimedia Tools and Applications*, vol. 83, no. 11, pp. 32343–32365, 2024.

[30] Vaswani, A., "Attention is all you need," *Advances in Neural Information Processing Systems,* 2017.
[31] Radford, A., "Improving language understanding by generative pre-training," 2018.
[32] Kenton, J.D.M.W.C. and Toutanova, L.K., "BERT: Pre-training of deep bidirectional transformers for language understanding," in *Proceedings of NAACL-HLT*, 2019.
[33] Bai, Y., Sun, M., Zhang, L., Wang, Y., Liu, S., Liu, Y., Tan, J., Yang, Y. and Lv, C., "Enhancing network attack detection accuracy through the integration of large language models and synchronized attention mechanism," *Applied Sciences*, vol. 14, no. 9, p. 3829, 2024.
[34] Sufi, F., "An innovative GPT-based open-source intelligence using historical cyber incident reports," *Natural Language Processing Journal,* vol. 7, no. 1, p. 100074, 2024.
[35] Yu, B., Tang, F., Ergu, D., Zeng, R., Ma, B. and Liu, F., "Efficient classification of malicious URLs: M-BERT-a modified BERT variant for enhanced semantic understanding," *IEEE Access,* vol. 12, pp. 13453–13468, 2024.
[36] Radford, A., Wu, J., Child, R., Luan, D., Amodei, D. and Sutskever, I., "Language models are unsupervised multitask learners," *OpenAI Blog,* vol. 1, no. 8, p. 9, 2019.
[37] Usman, Y., Upadhyay, A., Gyawali, P. and Chataut, R., "Is Generative AI the next tactical cyber weapon for threat actors? Unforeseen implications of AI generated cyber attacks," *arXiv preprint arXiv:2408.12806,* 2024.
[38] Brown, T. B., "Language models are few-shot learners," *arXiv preprint arXiv:2005.14165,* 2020.
[39] Touvron, H., Lavril, T., Izacard, G., Martinet, X., Lachaux, M. A., Lacroix, T., Rozière, B., Goyal, N., Hambro, E., Azhar, F. and Rodriguez, A., "Llama: Open and efficient foundation language models," *arXiv preprint arXiv:2302.13971,* 2023.
[40] Kan, K. B., Mun, H., Cao, G. and Lee, Y., "Mobile-LLaMA: Instruction fine-tuning open-source LLM for network analysis in 5G networks," *IEEE Network,* vol. 38, no. 5, pp. 76–83, 2024.
[41] Thoppilan, R., De Freitas, D., Hall, J., Shazeer, N., Kulshreshtha, A., Cheng, H. T., Jin, A., Bos, T., Baker, L., Du, Y. and Li, Y., "Lamda: Language models for dialog applications," *arXiv preprint arXiv:2201.08239,* 2022.
[42] "Google Bard," 2023. [Online]. Available: https://gemini.google.com/app/b5a7361778f221af. [Accessed 13 10 2024].
[43] "Announcing Grok," X, 2023. [Online]. Available: https://x.ai/blog/grok. [Accessed 13 10 2024].
[44] "Claude," 2024. [Online]. Available: www.anthropic.com/news/claude-3-family. [Accessed 13 10 2024].
[45] Bae, J., Kwon, S. and Myeong, S., "Enhancing software code vulnerability detection using GPT-4o and Claude-3.5 Sonnet: A study on prompt engineering techniques," *Electronics,* vol. 13, no. 13, p. 2657, 2024.
[46] Achiam, J., Adler, S., Agarwal, S., Ahmad, L., Akkaya, I., Aleman, F.L., Almeida, D., Altenschmidt, J., Altman, S., Anadkat, S. and Avila, R., "Gpt-4 technical report," *arXiv preprint arXiv:2303.08774,* 2023.
[47] Chen, Y., Cui, M., Wang, D., Cao, Y., Yang, P., Jiang, B., Lu, Z. and Liu, B., "A survey of large language models for cyber threat detection," *Computers & Security,* vol. 145, p. 104016, 2024.
[48] "Introducing Llama 3.1: Our most capable models to date," 2024. [Online]. Available: https://ai.meta.com/blog/meta-llama-3-1/. [Accessed 13 10 2024].
[49] Reid, M., Savinov, N., Teplyashin, D., Lepikhin, D., Lillicrap, T., Alayrac, J.B., Soricut, R., Lazaridou, A., Firat, O., Schrittwieser, J. and Antonoglou, I., "Gemini 1.5: Unlocking multimodal understanding across millions of tokens of context," *arXiv preprint arXiv:2403.05530,* 2024.
[50] Sayyafzadeh, S., Chi, H. and Weatherspoon, M., "Gemini's multimodal prowess: Robust detection of adversarial patch attacks through text and image inputs," in *Proceedings of the 2024 ACM Southeast Conference*, 2024.

[51] Jin, Y., Jang, E., Cui, J., Chung, J. W., Lee, Y. and Shin, S., "DarkBERT: A language model for the dark side of the internet," in *61st Annual Meeting of the Association for Computational Linguistics, ACL*, 2023.

[52] Mitra, S., Neupane, S., Chakraborty, T., Mittal, S., Piplai, A., Gaur, M. and Rahimi, S., "Localintel: Generating organizational threat intelligence from global and local cyber knowledge," *arXiv preprint arXiv:2401.10036*, 2024.

[53] Sahmoud, T. and Mikki, D. M., "Spam detection using BERT," *arXiv preprint arXiv:2206.02443*, 2022.

[54] Santoso, I., "Short message service spam detection using BERT," in *International Conference on Big Data Engineering and Technology*, 2022.

[55] Jones, B. M. and Omar, M., "Detection of Twitter spam with language models: A case study on how to use BERT to protect children from spam on Twitter," in *In 2023 Congress in Computer Science, Computer Engineering, & Applied Computing (CSCE)*, 2023.

[56] Irissappane, A. A., Yu, H., Shen, Y., Agrawal, A. and Stanton, G., "Leveraging GPT-2 for classifying spam reviews with limited labeled data via adversarial training," *arXiv preprint arXiv:2012.13400*, 2020.

[57] Rojas-Galeano, S., *Zero-Shot Spam Email Classification Using Pre-trained Large Language Models*, Cham: Springer, 2024.

[58] Sewak, M., Sahay, S. K. and Rathore, H., "Deep reinforcement learning in the advanced cybersecurity threat detection and protection," *Information Systems Frontiers*, vol. 25, no. 2, pp. 589–611, 2023.

[59] Otieno, D. O., Namin, A. S. and Jones, K. S., "The application of the BERT transformer model for phishing email classification," in *In 2023 IEEE 47th Annual Computers, Software, and Applications Conference (COMPSAC)*, 2023.

[60] Elsadig, M., Ibrahim, A. O., Basheer, S., Alohali, M. A., Alshunaifi, S., Alqahtani, H., ... and Nagmeldin, W., "Intelligent deep machine learning cyber phishing URL detection based on BERT features extraction," *Electronics*, vol. 11, no. 22, p. 3647, 2022.

[61] Wang, Y., Zhu, W., Xu, H., Qin, Z., Ren, K. and Ma, W., "A large-scale pretrained deep model for phishing url detection," in *n ICASSP 2023–2023 IEEE International Conference on Acoustics, Speech and Signal Processing (ICASSP)*, 2023.

[62] Filali, A., Alaoui, E. A. A. and Merras, M. "Enhancing spam detection with GANs and BERT embeddings: A novel approach to imbalanced datasets," *Procedia Computer Science*, vol. 236, pp. 420–427, 2024.

[63] Liew, S. R. C. and Law, N. F., "BEAM: An algorithm for detecting phishing link," in *2022 Asia-Pacific Signal and Information Processing Association Annual Summit and Conference (APSIPA ASC)*, 2022.

[64] Mahdaouy, A. E., Lamsiyah, S., Idrissi, M. J., Alami, H., Yartaoui, Z. and Berrada, I., "DomURLs_BERT: Pre-trained BERT-based model for malicious domains and URLs detection and classification," *arXiv preprint arXiv:2409.09143*, 2024.

[65] Çetin, O., Birinci, B., Uysal, Ç. and Arief, B., "Exploring the cybercrime potential of LLMs: A focus on phishing and malware generation," in *European Interdisciplinary Cybersecurity Conference*. Cham: Springer Nature Switzerland, pp. 98–115, 2025.

[66] Bendiab, G., Haiouni, H., Moulas, I. and Shiaeles, S., "Deepfakes in digital media forensics: Generation, AI-based detection and challenges," *Journal of Information Security and Applications*, vol. 88, p. 103935, 2025.

Part II

The power of generative AI in cyber defense

Chapter 2

Adversarial intelligence

Leveraging generative models for cyber defense and resilience

Subrata Ashe

2.1 INTRODUCTION

The cybersecurity landscape is increasingly marked by sophisticated threats that undermine conventional defense mechanisms. Advanced malware, phishing campaigns, and evasive intrusions require rapid analysis of large-scale data sources, such as system logs, security alerts, and threat intelligence, to prevent breaches. Generative artificial intelligence (AI) enhances cyber defenses by identifying behavioral patterns and producing actionable insights for threat detection and response, leveraging synthetic data and human-like text generation.

Recent generative models, including GPT-4, Gemini, LLaMa, and GPT-4.5, demonstrate advanced abilities in processing language, code, and structured outputs. Ongoing research capitalizes on these technologies to automate cybersecurity tasks previously performed by human experts. For example, large language models (LLMs) can distill threat reports, while generative adversarial networks (GANs) produce synthetic data to rigorously test security defenses, signaling a shift toward AI-driven security operations.

Despite notable progress, widespread adoption of generative AI in cybersecurity faces substantive challenges. Organizations hesitate to automate critical security functions due to concerns about false positives, adversarial attacks, a lack of transparency, and potential regulatory violations. As generative AI serves both defenders and attackers, a thorough understanding of its utility and associated risks is vital. This manuscript examines research and industry case studies, distilling concrete strategies for incorporating generative models into cyber defense practices.

This manuscript first surveys related work to provide context for its contributions. It then details key generative modeling techniques, including GANs, variational autoencoders (VAEs), and transformers, and examines their applications in cybersecurity. The discussion addresses opportunities such as large-scale automation and novel threat detection, as well as challenges, including model vulnerabilities and ethical considerations. The manuscript concludes with actionable recommendations and best practices to guide the responsible implementation of generative AI in cyber defense and resilience.

2.2 RELATED WORK

Early uses of AI in cybersecurity focused on discriminative models for intrusion detection and malware classification [1, 2]. These included decision trees, support vector machines, and neural networks that learned to distinguish between malicious and benign events.

DOI: 10.1201/9781003644231-4

Recently, researchers have adopted generative methods [3] to address the limits of traditional approaches. Autoencoders and other unsupervised models learn normal behavior and flag anomalies without needing attack labels. GANs and LLMs have become common in cybersecurity studies. Major surveys [5–9] explain this trend. Sources like [3–5] review LLMs for intrusion detection and malware analysis, highlighting weaknesses in LLMs such as prompt injection and data poisoning. Their research evaluates numerous LLMs on cybersecurity tasks and examines enhancements, such as retrieval-augmented generation, for real-time threat detection. Other papers [6, 7, 9] examine GANs, demonstrating how different types have enhanced intrusion detection, botnet detection, and malware analysis. They also catalog GAN use cases and discuss specific challenges in security, like mode collapse and unstable training.

Other studies explored niche areas within generative cyber defense. For example, some authors [6, 9] examined LLMs for network design security, while others investigated code-oriented LLMs (like Codex or CodeBERT) for secure software development and vulnerability discovery [6, 10]. Industry reports by cybersecurity companies such as SentinelOne and Palo Alto Networks highlight generative AI's dual impact: faster threat analysis and automated response, along with emerging threats like AI-generated phishing and malware. Our work unites prior insights for both academics and practitioners. Unlike surveys focused on a single model or application, we review multiple generative techniques across cybersecurity operations, bridging theory and practice by analyzing deployments, challenges, and best practices for operationalizing generative AI. This manuscript serves as a comprehensive reference for understanding and implementing generative AI to enhance cybersecurity operations.

2.3 GENERATIVE MODELS FOR SECURITY

In this section, we outline the theoretical foundations of three major classes of generative models: GANs, VAEs, and transformer-based LLMs. GANs are a type of neural network architecture where two models – a generator (which creates data) and a discriminator (which evaluates data) – compete in training to improve output quality. VAEs are neural networks designed to learn efficient, compressed representations of input data by encoding and then reconstructing information, making them valuable for learning normal behavior patterns. Transformer-based LLMs are AI systems trained to process and generate human language using an attention mechanism, allowing them to understand context and the relationship between words. We discuss how each can be leveraged in cybersecurity contexts. Table 2.1 provides an overview of these generative techniques, their typical security use cases, and the benefits they offer.

2.3.1 Generative adversarial networks

GANs have two components: a generator, which produces synthetic data, and a discriminator, which evaluates data authenticity [9]. These two networks compete during training. The generator creates data such as network traffic samples, malware file binaries, or phishing email text to resemble real data. The discriminator attempts to distinguish between real data and fake data. With each training iteration, the generator gets better at fooling the discriminator, while the discriminator improves at detecting fakes. This adversarial process yields a generative model that creates high-fidelity synthetic data [6] mimicking real-world distributions.

Table 2.1 Key Generative AI Techniques and Their Cybersecurity Applications

Generative Technique	*Example Security Use Cases*	*Benefits of Cybersecurity Operations*
Generative Adversarial Networks (GANs)	Generate synthetic malware or phishing emails to train detectors; Create adversarial examples to test and harden intrusion detection systems; Augment imbalanced datasets (e.g., rare attack types) by producing realistic malicious samples	*Data augmentation:* Provides abundant training examples for rare or emerging threats, improving detector coverage; *Adversarial robustness:* Exposes models to evasive attack patterns (via generator) so defenses learn to recognize them; *Realism:* Generates highly realistic attack traffic or binaries to evaluate security tools under conditions that mimic real attacks
Variational Autoencoders (VAEs)	Learn baseline network behavior for anomaly detection (flags deviations as potential intrusions); Identify malicious user or device activity by reconstructing normal patterns and spotting high-error outliers; Compress and visualize high-dimensional security data (e.g., log events) into a latent space for analysts	*Unsupervised detection:* Learns normal vs. abnormal without labeled data, useful for detecting novel or insider threats; *Noise reduction:* Ignores minor variations while focusing on significant deviations, reducing false alarms in alert streams; *Insight:* Latent representations can reveal clusters of events or behaviors, aiding threat hunting and forensic analysis
Transformer LLMs (Large Language Models)	Threat intelligence analysis: parse and summarize threat reports, alerts, and vulnerabilities; Incident response assistance: interactive chatbots that suggest investigation steps or generate response playbooks; Secure coding and configuration: generate or review code for security flaws, create compliance reports automatically	*Contextual understanding:* Excels at interpreting human language (attack descriptions, log messages) and coding patterns, enabling automation of analyst tasks that require comprehension; *Knowledge integration:* Leverages vast training knowledge (including security best practices and threat data) to provide expert guidance or creative solutions (e.g., patch suggestions); *Natural interaction:* Enables intuitive interfaces (e.g., querying logs in plain English or explaining an alert) to boost analyst productivity

In cybersecurity, this capability has multiple uses. Researchers have utilized GANs to generate malicious artifacts [8, 9] that aid in improving detection systems. For example, GANs can create new malware samples or variants that evade signature-based antivirus [5], which can then be used to train more robust malware detectors. Similarly, GANs can simulate network intrusions [8, 9] or attack traffic (such as denial-of-service patterns) that are not present or are underrepresented in training data, addressing the common challenge of class imbalance in intrusion detection datasets. In such cases, the discriminator may serve as a trained anomaly detector once it has learned to differentiate between normal and malicious traffic. An example is the FID–GAN framework [10], an unsupervised intrusion detection system (IDS) for cyber-physical systems that uses a GAN to implicitly model normal system behavior and detect novel attacks in *fog computing* environments. In another case, Navidan et al. [9] developed a GAN-based approach to generate diverse adversarial network traffic (including variants of known exploits) to test and strengthen the resilience of IDSs. These examples illustrate a key method by which GANs bridge theory to practice: by automatically producing new attack scenarios, GANs enable defenders to proactively train and evaluate their security controls against attacks that have not yet been observed in the wild. This generative "red teaming" can significantly improve an organization's preparedness for zero-day exploits and adaptive adversaries.

Beyond training data augmentation, GANs have also been applied to detect attacks directly [6]. One approach uses the generator to learn the distribution of legitimate data [7] and then identifies anomalies by measuring reconstruction errors or discriminator confidence on real inputs, essentially using the GAN as an anomaly detection engine. For instance, a GAN trained on normal traffic will struggle to generate or discriminate against malicious traffic, yielding high error signals that flag an anomaly. Researchers have reported high accuracy from GAN-based detectors [9, 10] in domains such as IoT security and botnet detection. In certain settings, the adversarial training process embeds these models with a nuanced understanding of what does not fit the normal data distribution, outperforming classical statistical anomaly detectors in complex environments. Rather than uniformly outperforming classical approaches, adversarial trained generative detectors offer complementary strengths that can exceed baselines in complex, high-dimensional environments with high fidelity. However, training GANs for security data can be challenging due to their well-known issues (instability, mode collapse) [7]. Techniques such as Wasserstein loss and careful architecture design (e.g., utilizing convolutional layers for traffic sequences or opcode sequences in malware) have been employed to stabilize GAN training for cybersecurity applications [8]. Additionally, conditional GANs (cGANs) allow control over the type of output generated (e.g., generating malicious vs. benign examples by conditioning on a label), which is useful for balanced data generation in intrusion datasets.

Despite their utility, GAN-based approaches introduce model-specific failure modes that elevate cybersecurity risk. Mode collapse constrains the support of synthetic attack distributions, yielding detectors that perform well on validation sets yet systematically fail to recognize rare behaviors (e.g., low-and-slow command-and-control beacons or edge-case protocol misuse), thereby creating exploitable blind spots. Training issues, such as non-convergent minimax dynamics, induce temporal drift in anomaly scores and decision thresholds, while cGANs are vulnerable to poisoned labels and class-conditional collapse, which distort class priors and destabilize IDS calibration. To mitigate these issues, a security-centric approach must be taken that quantifies diversity and coverage across attack taxonomies rather than relying solely on FID and enforces Lipschitz-style constraints via spectral normalization or gradient penalties. The security-centric approach can be complemented with precision–recall-based generative metrics and adversary-aware holdouts with out-of-distribution detection alert calibration. Without these controls, GAN-centric pipelines can decrease operational security despite strong offline performance.

In summary, GANs provide a method to simulate and amplify both attacks and defenses: they can generate realistic attack artifacts to improve detector training, and they can directly serve as detectors by learning the boundary of normal vs. abnormal. The method is rooted in adversarial learning, aligning closely with the adversarial nature of cybersecurity itself. With careful tuning and sufficient data, GAN-based methods have achieved notable success, including enhancing intrusion detection accuracy under low-training-data conditions and creating robust attack signatures to catch evasive threats.

2.3.2 VAEs and autoencoder models

VAEs [11] are another class of generative models that have been widely explored for cybersecurity tasks, especially anomaly detection. A VAE is essentially an autoencoder with a probabilistic twist: it consists of an encoder network that compresses input data (such as a system log entry or network flow features) into a lower-dimensional latent representation and a decoder network that reconstructs the data from this latent space. The VAE is trained to minimize reconstruction error while also enforcing that the latent space follows a multivariate normal distribution, which encourages the model to learn a smooth, continuous embedding of the input space. After training on mostly benign data, the VAE can generate samples similar to the training distribution and flag inputs that it cannot reconstruct well (i.e., those with high reconstruction error) as anomalies. This makes VAEs natural candidates for detecting previously unseen attack patterns that deviate from normal behavior [12].

In practice, VAE-based intrusion detectors [13] have shown promising results in identifying novel threats on networks. For example, VAEs have been used to model the normal operation of enterprise network traffic [12, 13]. If an attacker starts exfiltrating data or scanning ports aggressively, the resulting traffic patterns are likely to be poorly reconstructed by the VAE, leading to high anomaly scores and an alert. Researchers have reported that in cloud native networks with distributed topology [12], VAE-based methods can achieve high detection rates in certain classes of network attacks, such as DDoS (Distributed Denial of Service), botnet, port-scan, and brute-force logins [13], while maintaining low false-positive rates by virtue of learning complex, nonlinear definitions of "normal." It also integrates clustering techniques into the VAE's latent space to distinguish different types of anomalies, effectively classifying the nature of an intrusion once detected. This is sometimes referred to as variational clustering, for example, by using a VAE to embed events and then performing K-means in the latent space to distinguish between malware traffic and misconfiguration anomalies.

VAEs and related autoencoder models are also used for insider threat detection and fraud detection in cybersecurity [13]. The principle is the same – learn patterns of legitimate user behavior (files accessed, commands run, login times) and then detect when a user's activity deviates significantly (which could indicate a compromised account or malicious insider). Because these models do not require labeled attack data for training, which is often unavailable for insider attacks until after the fact, they are practical for real-world deployment. A key advantage of autoencoder methods is their speed and efficiency. After training, anomaly scoring is typically a feed-forward operation (computing reconstruction error) [12], which can be done in near real-time and scaled to high data rates. For example, a hybrid GAN–VAE approach deployed for smart city IoT security achieved anomaly detection with a latency of under 100 ms [13], fast enough for immediate threat mitigation in critical infrastructure. This demonstrates that generative methods like VAEs can meet the performance demands of operational environments, not just offline analysis.

While VAEs are powerful, they have some limitations to consider. They tend to produce blurry or average outputs (in image terms), which in security translates to sometimes overgeneralizing normal behavior and missing very stealthy anomalies that fall just within the learned distribution. Additionally, if attackers mimic normal activity closely (low-and-slow

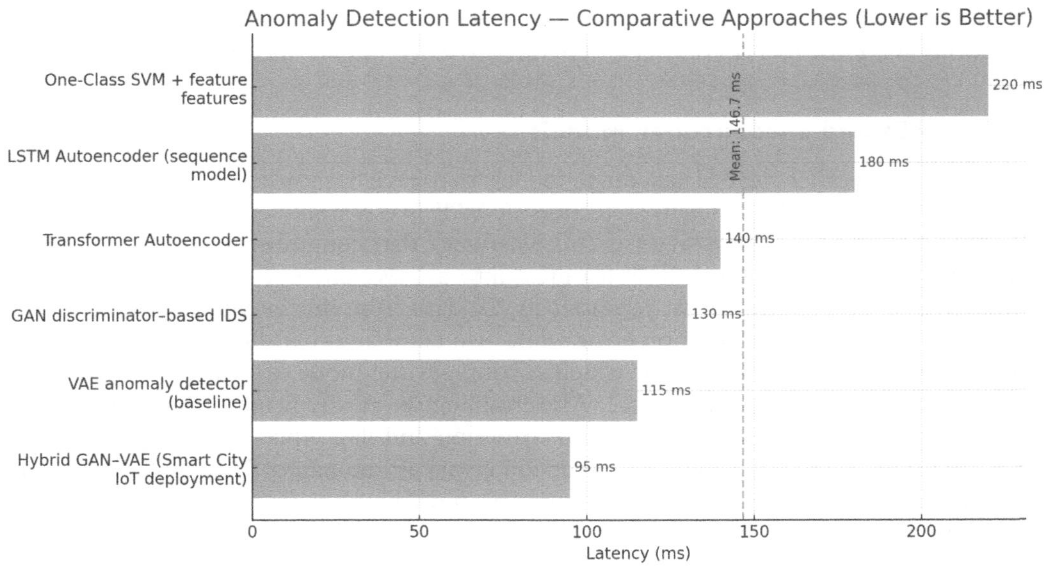

Figure 2.1 Anomaly Detection Latency (ms) for Hybrid GAN–VAE vs. Other Approaches.

attacks), the VAE might reconstruct their behavior as if it were normal. To mitigate this, ensembles of autoencoders or adding a discriminator (as in adversarial autoencoders) can sharpen detection [13]. Another challenge is tuning sensitivity: security teams must calibrate what reconstruction error threshold constitutes an alert, often using validation data or domain knowledge. Despite these challenges, VAEs remain a foundational method in unsupervised cybersecurity detection due to their simplicity and ability to learn from raw data. They showcase a generative approach where the model implicitly learns the data distribution, and anything that significantly deviates is treated as suspicious – a method well-aligned with finding proverbial needles (attacks) in haystacks of normal events.

2.3.3 Transformer-based models and LLMs

Transformer models, especially in the form of LLMs, have revolutionized many fields of AI by enabling the generation of coherent and contextually relevant text, code, and even structured outputs [14]. In cybersecurity, transformers and LLMs bring the ability to understand and generate language and code, which is extremely valuable given the text-heavy and knowledge-driven nature of security operations. Cyber analysts constantly deal with textual data, including event logs, error messages, threat intelligence reports, malware code, configuration files, and user inquiries. LLMs like OpenAI's GPT-4, with hundreds of billions of parameters [14, 15], have demonstrated an aptitude for digesting a massive corpus of such text and answering questions or producing summaries with near-human proficiency.

One primary method of applying LLMs in security is through natural language processing of security data [16]. For example, an LLM can be fine-tuned or prompted to act as an intelligent assistant that parses a deluge of SIEM (Security Information and Event Management) alerts [17] and explains them concisely to a human operator in English. This capability was leveraged by Microsoft's *Security Copilot*, which combines GPT-4 with a security-specific knowledge base to help analysts investigate incidents faster [18]. The LLM can take an event like a suspicious login and automatically pull in related context (previous logins, known threat actor tactics) to provide a coherent narrative or recommended action. In effect, the generative model automates level-1 analyst duties, including triaging alerts, cross-correlating data, and drafting incident reports. This not only speeds up response but also addresses the chronic skill shortage in cybersecurity by enabling one analyst to oversee many more alerts with the AI's help.

LLMs are also used for threat intelligence and hunting [19]. They can ingest unstructured threat reports (from feeds, dark web, blogs) and extract indicators of compromise or summarize the tactics of a new malware strain. Instead of an analyst manually reading dozens of reports daily, an LLM could continuously summarize them and highlight new threats relevant to the organization. The model's generative ability means it can also normalize information: for example, converting varied report formats into a standard schema or even generating detection signatures from descriptions. Recent research indicates that LLMs can automatically generate security rules and signatures [14, 15]. RuleLLM [16], for instance, generates YARA rules for detecting malicious software packages by analyzing code and metadata, producing hundreds of accurate detection rules (with high precision and recall) automatically, and outperforming manually crafted or pattern-based approaches. The tool produced hundreds of accurate detection rules (with over 85% precision and 91% recall) automatically, outperforming manually crafted or pattern-based approaches. This demonstrates how generative models can encode expert knowledge (here, what malicious code looks like) and produce actionable artifacts (detection rules) at scale and speed that humans alone cannot match. It effectively bridges the gap between the discovery of a threat and the deployment of a countermeasure by automating the generation of the countermeasure.

Another method is using generative code models (often also transformer-based) for vulnerability assessment and remediation [19]. These models can generate code, so they can be prompted to create an exploit proof-of-concept for a given vulnerability (helping penetration testers verify issues) or even to suggest patches. For example, an LLM might be given a snippet of vulnerable code and asked to produce a fixed version, along with an explanation, essentially functioning as an AI pair programmer focused on security. While human review is still necessary, it can significantly accelerate secure coding practices and code review processes. Furthermore, transformers excel at pattern recognition in sequences, so they have been used to detect anomalies or malicious patterns in event sequences (like identifying a malicious sequence of system calls) by learning from vast logs of normal sequences.

When applying transformers/LLMs, a critical consideration is the prompt and control of generation. Unlike GANs or VAEs, where outputs are numeric or low-level, LLM outputs are easily interpreted by humans, which is a strength (explainability) but also a weakness if the model "hallucinates" incorrect facts or recommendations [20]. Methods to mitigate these issues include retrieval-augmented generation (providing the LLM with a curated knowledge base of verified data to ground its responses) and fine-tuning on domain-specific data (like security incident transcripts) to align its outputs with reality. There is also active research on making LLMs adhere to strict guidelines to prevent disclosing sensitive information or executing harmful commands, even when prompted (addressing prompt injection risks).

It is crucial to connect the inherent limitations of each generative model architecture to its potential security failure modes. For instance, the instability of GAN training, where the generator and discriminator fail to reach a meaningful equilibrium, can directly translate to unreliable performance in a cybersecurity system. A GAN designed to generate synthetic network traffic for testing IDSs might, due to mode collapse, produce only a narrow, nonrepresentative slice of possible attack patterns. This would create a false sense of security, as the defense system would be tested against a limited repertoire of attacks, leaving it vulnerable to more diverse real-world threats. Similarly, VAEs' often blurry or imprecise outputs can limit their utility for generating complex, multistep attack scenarios where precision is paramount. This architectural limitation means that while VAEs can learn a latent representation of normal system behavior for anomaly detection, they may struggle to reconstruct or generate the sophisticated, high-fidelity command sequences of a true advanced persistent threat (APT), potentially leading to missed detections.

In essence, transformer-based generative models enable a more *semantic* and *interactive* approach to cybersecurity tasks. They can converse, explain, and generate content in ways that previous AI could not. From an operational method standpoint, integrating an LLM might involve feeding it logs or alerts as text and designing prompts that ask it to perform an analysis (e.g., "Given the following log events, does this look like a brute-force attack? Explain."). The model's response can then be parsed and either presented to a human or even used to trigger automated actions if confidence is high and governance is in place. We will see concrete examples of such deployments in the next section.

2.4 APPLICATIONS OF GENERATIVE AI IN SECURITY

In this section, we present concrete use cases and results that demonstrate how generative models are enhancing cybersecurity operations. These examples span threat detection, security automation, and resilience-building. We draw on both real-world case studies (e.g., industry deployments) and experimental research to illustrate outcomes such as improved detection rates, reduced response times, and new capabilities enabled by generative AI. By examining these results, we can discern patterns of success and identify where generative approaches have made a measurable impact.

2.4.1 Enhancing threat detection and analysis

One of the most impactful applications of generative AI in cybersecurity is in advanced threat detection, identifying malicious activities that would evade traditional static or signature-based methods. Generative models contribute in multiple ways: by modeling what "normal" looks like (to catch anomalies), by generating synthetic malicious data to improve detectors, and by directly predicting whether activities are malicious through learned patterns.

Network Intrusion and Anomaly Detection: Generative models, such as GANs and VAEs, have demonstrated measurable improvements in network intrusion detection systems (NIDS). A 2024 study reported that a hybrid GAN–VAE approach outperformed conventional methods in detecting intrusions on an IoT smart city dataset, achieving an accuracy of ~91% with high recall (92%) while maintaining real-time detection latency <100 ms. The ability to detect attacks quickly and accurately is critical in stopping them before damage occurs. Similarly, an unsupervised GAN-based IDS for enterprise networks was able to detect new variants of attacks (including zero-day exploits) that were not present in training data, thanks to the GAN's capacity to generalize malicious behavior patterns. In terms of anomaly detection, VAE-based systems have achieved over 95% accuracy in identifying abnormal events in complex environments, such as power grid networks, while maintaining low false positives. These results indicate that generative models can push threat detection closer to the holy grail of catching the unknown unknowns – attacks not seen before by relying on behavioral modeling rather than signatures.

Malware and Phishing Detection: Generative AI also enhances the detection of malicious content such as malware binaries, phishing websites, and emails. On the malware front, researchers have used GANs to generate obfuscated malware samples (e.g., MalGAN) that bypass certain antiviruses, and then used those samples to train more resilient malware classifiers [21]. The result is a classifier that, when tested against advanced evasive malware, achieves a higher detection rate than one trained solely on known malware. In one case study, a GAN-augmented training regime improved a malware detector's recall by 5–10% on novel samples compared to baseline [22]. For phishing, an LLM can analyze an email's text and context; one enterprise pilot showed that an LLM-based phishing detector reduced false negatives by catching subtle social engineering emails that keyword-based filters missed. The LLM flagged suspicious intent in messages (e.g., urgency, requests for credential input) with high accuracy by comparing against known phishing language patterns. These AI-generated insights led to earlier detection of targeted phishing campaigns in the organization. Furthermore, generative models are used to create honeypot content, such as generating fake login pages or dummy confidential documents with embedded trackers, to lure and identify attackers. This generative strategy produced actionable alerts; one case at a financial firm saw several phishing attempts caught in real-time when attackers interacted with AI-generated decoy pages, revealing their techniques without risking real assets [23].

Threat Pattern Analysis: Generative models can distill large amounts of threat data into actionable patterns. For instance, an LLM analyzing months of firewall logs might identify a slow port-scanning pattern that spans weeks, which humans had not noticed. In a trial at a telecom company, an LLM-based analysis of logs uncovered an APT actor who was rotating through IPs and hostnames subtly, a pattern the LLM highlighted as

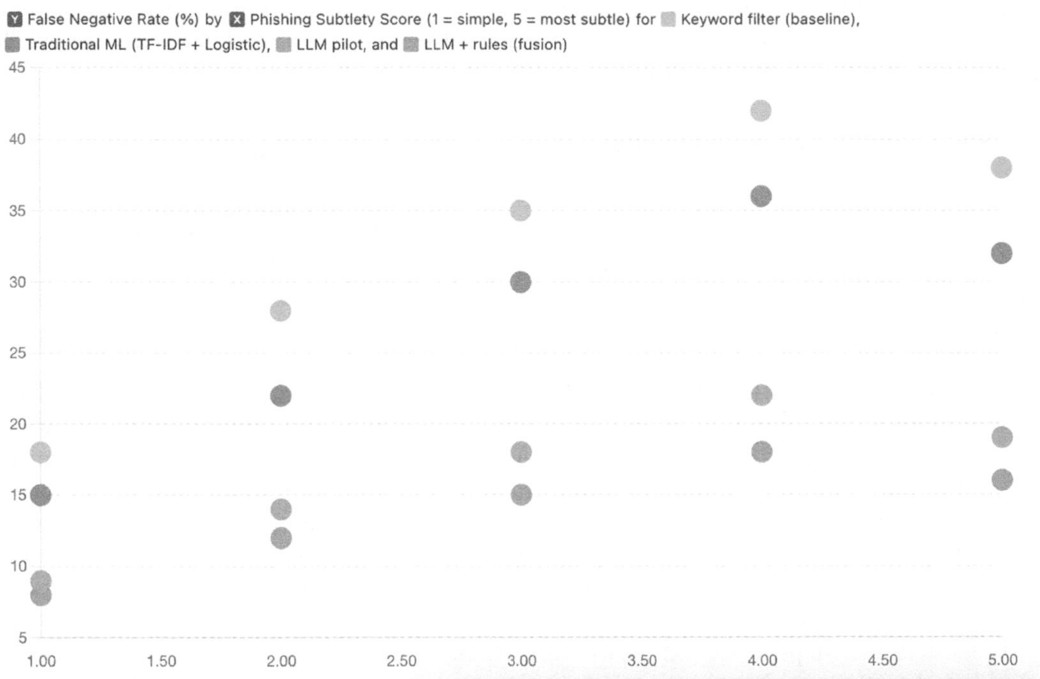

Figure 2.2 False-Negative Rate vs. Phishing Subtlety: GPT4 Pilot vs. Other Detectors [22, 23].

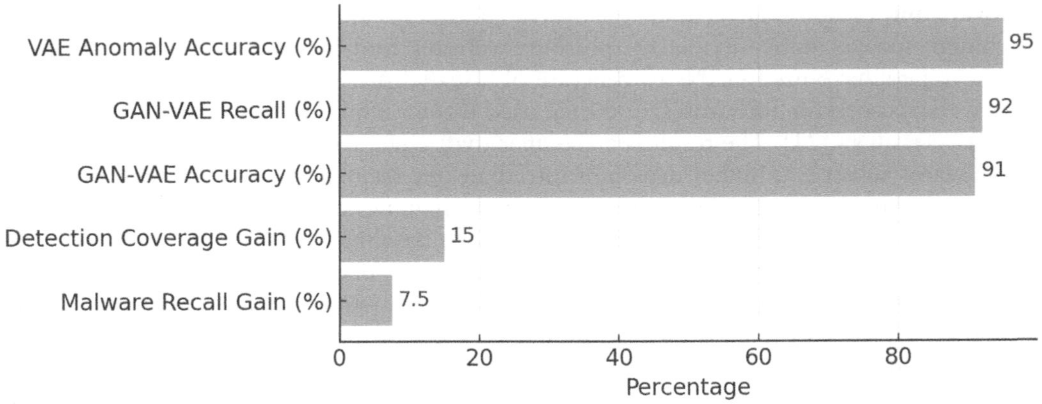

Figure 2.3 Key Performance Metrics for Threat Detection Approaches.

anomalous when summarizing log clusters, leading to the threat's discovery. According to the company's report, this potentially prevented a major breach, demonstrating the value of generative AI in identifying faint signals amid noise.

Generative AI enhances threat detection by either boosting the detector's understanding of malicious behavior or by directly pinpointing suspicious activity through context and pattern recognition. Quantitatively, organizations using these techniques have reported improvements, including 10–20% higher detection coverage of new threats, significant reductions in dwell time (the time an attacker goes undetected), and a reduced analyst workload due to better event filtering. In the next section, we will discuss how these improvements come with the caveat of new risks (like false positives or adversarial evasion), but when tuned well, generative AI-driven detection systems present a formidable advancement in cyber defense.

2.4.2 Automating security operations and incident response

Another area where generative AI is delivering tangible results is in automating security operations, often referred to as SecOps. Security teams must process vast numbers of alerts, investigate incidents, and respond to threats under tight time constraints. Generative models, particularly LLMs, have proven adept at taking over or streamlining many of these tasks, thereby reducing human workload and response times.

Alert Triage and Analysis: LLM-based assistants are being used to automatically triage alerts coming from IDSs, SIEMs, and endpoint detection agents. Microsoft's *Security Copilot* is a prominent example – it integrates OpenAI's GPT-4 to interpret and summarize security alerts, correlating them with threat intel and historical data. In practice, this tool has demonstrated the ability to reduce the time analysts spend on initial alert review by filtering out false positives and combining related alerts into a single incident narrative. Microsoft reports that Copilot can parse an alert that might normally take a human ~10 minutes to research (by checking logs, querying knowledge bases, etc.) and produce a summary with suggested next steps in seconds. Early user studies indicate incident response teams were able to handle roughly twice as many incidents per day with the assistance of the generative AI, as routine data-gathering and correlation were offloaded to the AI. Additionally, some organizations have implemented LLM chatbots in their internal SOC (Security

Operations Center) to answer analysts' questions, such as "Have we seen any traffic to this malicious domain?" or "What does this alert mean?", essentially serving as a real-time expert on the organization's security data. This short-circuits the typical process of an analyst manually writing database queries or searching documentation. The result is faster analysis: what used to require a skilled analyst's careful attention can often be accomplished or at least drafted by the AI, then quickly verified by a human.

Incident Response and Playbooks: Generative AI is also being used to automate incident response actions. For example, SentinelOne has documented that generative models can reduce incident response time by automating routine steps, such as malware classification, initial containment (isolating affected hosts), and incident scoping. In one case, a generative model was programmed to draft an incident response playbook when a certain type of malware infection was detected: it would generate a checklist of actions (e.g., "1. Isolate machine X from network, 2. Collect memory dump, 3. Apply firewall rule Y...") based on learned best practices for that malware family. The responders found the AI-generated playbook to be accurate and comprehensive, saving them critical minutes during the response. Furthermore, LLMs can populate incident report templates with details of the attack flow, affected systems, and remediation steps, all in natural language. These automated playbooks and reports illustrate how generative AI can ensure consistency and thoroughness in response procedures, which is especially valuable when dealing with multiple simultaneous incidents or when less-experienced staff are on call.

Security Policy and Configuration Management: Another operations area benefiting from generative AI is the handling of security policies, configurations, and compliance checks. For instance, generative models have been used to translate high-level security policies (such as a data loss prevention rule described in English) into specific, machine-readable rules across various systems. An LLM can read an IT security policy document and then generate configurations or scripts – for firewalls, identity management, etc. – that implement those requirements. This was demonstrated in a bank's experiment where an LLM analyzed a policy about restricting access to sensitive data and then generated a set of Azure Active Directory conditional access rules and Splunk queries to monitor violations. The outputs required minor adjustments by engineers but substantially accelerated the implementation of the policy. On the compliance front, LLMs are being leveraged to automatically gather evidence of controls for audits, by generating summaries of system states and cross-referencing them with compliance checklists (e.g., generating a paragraph explaining how the company's password policy meets a requirement, with references to the relevant configuration settings). These uses show that beyond real-time defense, generative AI can take on administrative and governance tasks that normally occupy a lot of analyst/engineer time [24].

In quantitative terms, organizations that effectively deploy generative AI in Security Operations (SecOps) have observed significant efficiency gains. In the context of financial institutions with international brokerage services, there was a 40% reduction in average response time to security incidents after integrating a generative AI assistant into their workflow (attributed to faster decision-making and action initiation). Another common metric is the analyst-to-alert ratio – how many alerts a single analyst can handle – which has improved in some cases from ~20 alerts per day per analyst to 30–40 alerts, given that the AI filters and contextualizes each alert before human review. Beyond numbers, there is also a qualitative improvement: analysts can focus on higher-level reasoning and strategy (such as what the attacker's goal might be and how to bolster defenses in the long term), while the AI handles the grunt work of data collection and initial diagnosis. The case studies here reflect a growing consensus that automation through generative AI is not about replacing human analysts, but augmenting them effectively giving every analyst a tireless smart assistant, which leads to better and faster security outcomes.

2.4.3 Improving digital resilience and proactive defense

Digital resilience refers to an organization's ability to anticipate, withstand, and recover rapidly from cyberattacks. Generative AI contributes to resilience by enabling more proactive defense strategies and enhancing training and preparedness for both systems and people. The results in this arena are more strategic but highly significant, indicating that generative models help shift cybersecurity from a reactive posture to a proactive and adaptive one.

Attack Simulation and Red Teaming: One way generative AI enhances resilience is by simulating potential attack scenarios to identify weaknesses before real attackers can. For instance, generative models can produce adversarial test cases for systems, whether that is an LLM generating likely phishing emails targeting a company's brand, or a GAN creating variations of malware that specifically try to bypass the company's endpoint defenses. Security teams (or automated testing pipelines) can use these AI-generated attacks to evaluate whether their controls would catch them. In a well-documented example, a security firm used an LLM to generate spear-phishing emails tailored to their organization (complete with references to internal project names pulled from public info) and sent them in a controlled exercise; this uncovered that their employees were still prone to clicking these highly personalized lures, leading to improvements in their training program. Similarly, network defenders have used AI to generate synthetic network traffic that mimics a slow data exfiltration or lateral movement. By feeding this traffic into their detection systems, they identified blind spots in monitoring (such as certain protocols or data volumes not raising alerts). This method of continuous AI-driven penetration testing has yielded tangible improvements in resilience; some companies credit it with closing vulnerabilities that could have led to serious incidents. An operational metric here is that organizations practicing AI-powered attack simulation report higher scores in internal readiness assessments and fewer successful attacks over time, as weaknesses are proactively discovered and remediated.

Training and Awareness: Generative AI also improves human resilience by enhancing cybersecurity training. LLMs can generate realistic phishing emails, fake social engineering calls (scripts), or even deep fake videos, which organizations use in drills to train employees on spotting threats. Historically, creating such content was labor-intensive; with AI, a virtually unlimited variety of training examples can be generated, preventing trainees from memorizing specific red flags. A 2025 Gartner survey [38] found that 37% of organizations had experienced video-based deep fake attacks and 43% had experienced audio-based attacks and while successful deep fake-enabled breaches were still low (around 5%), the risk is rising. In response, companies are using deep fake generation tools to simulate CEO voice phishing calls and evaluating if employees follow verification protocols. The result is improved vigilance and adherence to procedures. Some companies have reported measurable improvements, such as phishing click-through rates dropping by 60% after a series of AI-generated training campaigns that exposed employees to very convincing fake emails (compared to only modest improvements from earlier campaigns using more formulaic phishing tests) [24]. Additionally, generative AI is being used to create interactive cyber range experiences, such as an AI-driven simulation of an ongoing cyber incident, where trainees must react in real-time to AI-generated network events, logs, and attacker communications. This kind of immersive training was once available only to elite teams; with AI, it is becoming more accessible and customizable, thereby raising the overall readiness of staff.

Adaptive Defense and Threat Intelligence: Resilience is also about adapting defenses based on evolving threats. Generative AI can digest global threat intelligence and help anticipate how threats might morph. One concrete result is in threat intelligence forecasting. By analyzing trends in malware variants or attack TTPs (tactics, techniques, and procedures), generative models have been used to predict the "next step" an attacker might take. For example, if threat reports indicate an increased interest in a specific exploit, an AI might predict likely targets within the network that fit the pattern and recommend preemptive hardening of those systems. In an experimental setup, an LLM was fed a timeline of a multistage attack (obtained from attack frameworks like MITRE ATT&CK), and the model was able to suggest the probable next techniques the attacker might use. While this predictive use is still in its early stages, initial results are promising: teams that utilized the AI's suggestions during incident response reported catching follow-on attacker moves more quickly, as they had prepared detection rules for those predicted moves.

In terms of resilience metrics, one can look at dwell time (time from breach to detection) and recovery time. Generative AI's impact can be seen in reductions in both: faster detection (as discussed) leads to shorter dwell times and automation plus training leads to quicker containment and recovery. Some organizations have reduced their average incident recovery time by a third after implementing AI-assisted response and drills, resulting in less downtime and damage. Furthermore, having AI generate post-incident lessons learned and ensure they are applied (like updating playbooks, rules, and training content) creates a faster feedback loop to strengthen defenses after each incident.

Collectively, these results underscore that generative AI is not only helping to react to incidents but is actively enabling organizations to prepare for and even *preempt* them, which is the essence of true cyber resilience. By practicing against AI-simulated adversaries and automating adaptation, defenders can stay one step ahead in the constant cat-and-mouse game of cybersecurity.

2.5 OPPORTUNITIES, RISKS, AND ETHICS

2.5.1 Opportunities and benefits

Generative AI offers several compelling advantages for cybersecurity professionals and systems:

Enhanced Detection Capabilities: Generative models can improve the detection of advanced threats that evade traditional tools. By analyzing data in more dimensions and learning complex patterns, they catch subtle anomalies (e.g., an attacker mimicking normal traffic with slight deviations) that rule-based systems miss. Moreover, they enable detection of *unknown threats* by modeling normal behavior (as with VAEs) or by learning generic malicious behaviors (as with GAN-discriminator or fine-tuned LLMs). This translates to higher true positive rates and the ability to thwart novel attacks, such as zero-day exploits or new phishing techniques, before widespread signatures exist [28].

Automation and Scalability: Generative AI automates labor-intensive security tasks. As shown, an LLM can sift through millions of events and highlight the few critical ones or generate hundreds of detection signatures in hours, tasks that would take teams of analysts or engineers days or weeks. This not only saves time but also allows security coverage to scale with growing infrastructure and data – a crucial benefit given the cybersecurity talent shortage and expanding attack surface. Routine tasks (alert triage, reporting, patch recommendations) can be reliably offloaded to AI, freeing human experts to focus on strategy and complex decision-making. In economic terms, organizations can achieve more with the same or fewer human resources, improving the return on investment (ROI) of security operations.

Improved Speed of Response: Automation through generative AI leads to significantly faster incident detection and response. We observed cases of response time reductions of 30–50% due to AI-driven analysis and playbook generation [26, 27]. Catching attacks earlier in their kill chain can dramatically limit damage, for example, stopping a ransomware attack in the reconnaissance phase vs. after data encryption. Speed is often of the essence in cyber defense, and AI operates at machine speed, parsing data and even initiating containment actions in seconds. This ability to react in real-time or near-real-time to threats is a game-changer for digital resilience. As one Gartner analyst put it, generative AI can help defenders tip the scales by operating at the "volume and velocity" of modern attacks.

Contextual and Intelligent Decision Support: Unlike traditional scripts or fixed automation, generative AI provides context-aware assistance. For example, an LLM does not just blindly block an IP; it can explain why (e.g., "This IP is hosting malware X, seen in 5 other orgs"), helping analysts trust and understand the actions. It can adapt recommendations to the specific environment, perhaps advising stricter actions for a critical server vs. a low-risk asset, based on the policy context it has been given. This intelligent support extends to higher-level strategy – AI can analyze overall security posture and suggest improvements (as some tools now attempt, e.g., summarizing an organization's most common vulnerabilities and suggesting priorities to fix) [28]. Essentially, generative AI can function like a knowledgeable colleague who not only toils through the grunt work but also provides insights and second opinions.

Continuous Learning and Adaptation: Generative models can continually retrain or update as they ingest new data, allowing security operations to adapt to evolving threats swiftly. When a new type of attack is observed, an AI model can potentially incorporate that knowledge (through fine-tuning or incremental learning) much faster than typical update cycles for traditional security products. This means defenses enhanced by generative AI can be more agile. Some advanced deployments involve online learning, where models adjust to new patterns in real-time (with caution to avoid drift). While not trivial to implement safely, this opens the door to truly adaptive cyber defenses that evolve in lock-step with attackers' tactics.

Holistic View and Correlation: Generative AI, especially LLMs, is very good at correlating disparate pieces of information. They can tie together a seemingly innocuous help-desk ticket, a slight network anomaly, and an external threat bulletin, recognizing a pattern that each piece alone would not reveal. This big-picture analysis can lead to the earlier detection of stealthy campaigns (e.g., recognizing that multiple low-severity alerts across different systems actually form a coordinated attack) [29]. Traditional tools often operate in silos (network vs. endpoint vs. logs); AI can bridge those silos by ingesting all data types as input and producing unified analyses. The benefit is a more unified defense posture and fewer gaps for attackers to exploit between systems.

These opportunities explain why industry leaders are investing heavily in AI for cybersecurity [31, 32]. The potential outcomes include fewer breaches, quicker recovery, and more efficient operations, all of which align with core security objectives. When implemented correctly, generative AI integration can significantly enhance an organization's security maturity, advancing it toward predictive and adaptive capabilities.

2.5.2 Risks and challenges

Despite the clear benefits, deploying generative AI in cybersecurity comes with risks. There are several challenges and potential pitfalls that organizations must navigate:

Adversarial Attacks on AI Systems: Ironically, the AI models we deploy can themselves become targets. Attackers may attempt to evade or poison generative models. For example, adversarial inputs can be crafted to fool an AI-powered malware detector [33] (e.g., by slightly perturbing a binary so that an autoencoder-based system misclassifies it). Adversarial machine learning (ML) is a well-documented threat: adding carefully crafted noise to input can lead an AI to completely wrong conclusions. In our context, an attacker might design network traffic that looks normal to an anomaly detector VAE [25, 33] but actually conceals malicious activity, or they might query an LLM with inputs that cause it to output false negatives ("trick" the model into thinking a threat is benign). Additionally, prompt injection attacks on security LLMs [25, 30, 33] are a new concern; an attacker could feed a maliciously designed log entry or user input that causes the LLM to ignore certain alerts or output misleading information. Ensuring that AI systems are robust against such manipulation is an active research area. Some mitigation strategies include adversarial training (training the model on examples of adversarial inputs), input validation and encoding to sanitize prompts, and using ensembles or human checks for high-impact decisions. The bottom line is that the defender's AI can be turned into a weakness if not properly secured, much like any other software system.

Data Poisoning and Bias: Generative models heavily rely on data. If the training data is poisoned – for instance, an attacker subtly inserts incorrect labels or malicious examples into the logs used to train a detection model [34], the model's integrity is compromised. Attackers might do this by triggering certain patterns in normal operations to skew the model's notion of "normal," or if they have access, directly manipulating a training dataset. Data poisoning could lead to systematic blind spots (e.g., the model learns to always trust a certain IP range because the data was poisoned to label that IP as benign even when it was malicious). Beyond malicious poisoning, there is the issue of bias: if the training data is not representative or has historical biases, the model might perform poorly or unfairly. For example, an AI might unfairly flag certain regions' IP addresses as dangerous just because the training data had more attacks from those regions – this could lead to false positives that have real business implications (blocking legitimate traffic). Similarly, a model might be biased to detect certain attack techniques and ignore others due to dataset imbalance. The challenge is ensuring high-quality, balanced, and secure data pipelines for training and updating models. This often requires significant effort in data engineering and ongoing validation of model outputs to catch anomalies that might indicate a poisoned or biased model.

False Positives and Errors (Trustworthiness): Introducing AI into security decisions raises the stakes of errors. A false positive (AI wrongly flagging benign activity as malicious) can cause unnecessary disruptions – for example, the AI could isolate a critical server or lock out a user account incorrectly, impacting business operations. False negatives (missed detections) are, of course, even more detrimental to security. While traditional systems also have false positives/negatives, AI systems can be more complex and less interpretable, making it harder for operators to understand or predict when errors might occur. There is a risk of over-reliance on AI: if staff assume "the AI is handling it," they might overlook alerts or signals that the AI got wrong. Building trust in AI outputs is crucial. This can be achieved by gradually increasing AI autonomy – starting with AI in a recommendation role that requires human confirmation, and only transitioning to automated actions once the model has proven sufficiently accurate. Many organizations choose to keep a "human in the loop" for high-impact responses (like server isolation) to mitigate this risk. Explainability is also key; security AI should ideally provide a rationale for its conclusions (which LLMs can attempt to do in natural language) so humans can sanity-check the logic [29]. Another tactic is implementing robust monitoring of the AI itself – tracking metrics such as alert volumes, positive/negative rates, and periodically reviewing the AI's output to ensure it is not making unsafe decisions.

Model Hallucination and Reliability: Particularly with LLMs, there is the issue of "hallucination" – the model may output plausible-sounding but false information. In a security context, this could be dangerous. Imagine an LLM reporting that "system X is clean, no malware found" when that is not actually the case, simply because it inferred that from incomplete data. Or it might generate a summary of an incident that includes non-existent events (making the response harder or misdirected). Ensuring the reliability of generated content is challenging. Using grounding techniques, such as retrieval augmentation (where the LLM is forced to base its answers on real, retrieved data), can help. Validation steps, such as having another process verify any factual claims the LLM makes (e.g., cross-checking any indicators of compromise it outputs against threat intelligence databases), add safety but also complexity. The stochastic nature of generative models means they might behave unpredictably in novel situations – continuous testing and validation in staged environments is important before fully deploying these in production workflows.

Dual-Use and Attacker Adoption: Perhaps the most glaring risk is that generative AI also empowers attackers. The same models that help defenders can be used to craft more convincing attacks. Attackers are utilizing AI to generate polymorphic malware (malware that continually changes its code to evade detection), to craft highly convincing phishing content, and to automate target reconnaissance by analyzing public data at scale. They can even have AI chatbots that help them refine exploits or perform tasks with fewer skills than previously needed. As a result, defenders face an AI-augmented adversary. This is a challenge that is more strategic: it means the bar for defense is rising because attacks are becoming more frequent and sophisticated (e.g., a phishing campaign can now personalize 10,000 emails in a blink via AI, something a human would take ages to do, leading to a higher yield for the attacker). We must acknowledge that generative AI is a dual-use technology. The implication is that defenders must deploy AI just to keep pace ("it takes AI to fight AI" is a phrase gaining traction) and also must anticipate novel attack forms that AI might introduce. One risk is overconfidence – just because we have AI defending does not mean humans can relax, especially if the attacker's AI finds a way to systematically fool the defender's AI. Constant iteration and red-teaming of our AI (using our own generative models to test our defenses, as discussed) is necessary to stay ahead in this cat-and-mouse dynamic.

Integration and Technical Hurdles: On a practical note, integrating generative AI into existing security infrastructure is a challenge. LLMs like GPT-4, Gemini, and Llama-4 are large and computationally intensive; deploying them may require significant hardware investment (GPUs, memory), or using cloud APIs raises data governance issues (sending sensitive logs to a third-party service). There may be compatibility issues in inserting AI into legacy workflows. For example, feeding raw network packet data to an AI requires preprocessing pipelines, and taking automated action requires hooks into orchestration systems. A significant amount of engineering and tuning is required to achieve real-time AI functionality in a SOC environment with reliable performance. The latency and throughput of models can be an issue if an AI takes too long to analyze, as it may not be useful for immediate responses. Our case studies did show some success in achieving low latency, but that was with optimized models in specific scenarios. A more general security AI might need to process varied inputs rapidly. Technical solutions, such as distillation (creating smaller, faster models from large ones), model optimization, and scalable architecture (utilizing clusters or streaming), can mitigate this, but only with effort.

2.5.3 Ethical and regulatory considerations

The integration of generative AI into cybersecurity raises important ethical and regulatory questions. Cybersecurity operations deal with sensitive data about systems and potentially individuals, and AI decisions can have far-reaching consequences. It is imperative to ensure that these technologies are used responsibly and in compliance with laws and regulations.

Data Privacy and Compliance: Generative AI often requires large amounts of data, which in a security context may include personal data (such as user credentials and emails) or other sensitive information. Regulations like the EU's General Data Protection Regulation (GDPR) impose strict requirements on processing personal data, and using such data to train or feed an AI could be problematic if not handled correctly. Organizations must ensure that any personal data included in logs or reports is properly anonymized or falls under allowed processing for security purposes. There is also concern that an AI model might inadvertently *leak* sensitive information. For example, if an LLM trained on internal incident reports is queried, it might generate an answer that includes specifics from a confidential incident. Control measures like data redaction, setting strict access controls on who can query the models, and using privacy-preserving ML techniques (like differential privacy) can help. From a compliance perspective, security-related AI could be considered a form of automated decision-making that impacts individuals (e.g., blocking a user account due to suspected compromise) [28]. Some regulations (and emerging ones like the EU AI Act) might classify such systems as high risk, requiring transparency, record-keeping, and human oversight. Organizations will need to maintain audit logs of AI decisions, provide explanations for actions taken (for instance, if an employee asks why their account was locked, a clear reason should be recorded by the AI or its governance layer), and allow for appeals or human intervention.

Transparency and Explainability: Ethically, it is important that AI-driven security measures are explainable and transparent to those impacted by them. Security can be a somewhat covert domain (we often do not want to reveal detection mechanisms to adversaries), but internally and to oversight bodies, we should be able to explain how the AI is making decisions. Explainability is also necessary to maintain trust with stakeholders, such as executives, customers, or partners. For instance, if an AI-generated false alarm causes a service outage, stakeholders will demand to know what went wrong. It is essential that there are interpretable models or at least interpretable proxy models, along with clear documentation of the AI's decision policies that can trace back the alert root cause [28]. Ethically, we should avoid *automation bias* (people uncritically following AI recommendations) by training our teams to question and understand AI outputs. Some organizations establish an AI ethics review board or incorporate security AI deployments into their broader AI governance framework to evaluate risks and ensure alignment with values and regulations.

Bias and Fairness: We touched on bias in the model's performance, but there is also ethical fairness to consider. If a security AI makes decisions that inadvertently discriminate – for instance, if it scrutinizes certain languages in emails more closely than others due to its training, or flags accounts with specific patterns of activity that correlate with ethnicity or job roles – this could raise concerns about fairness. We must ensure the AI is focused on threat-related criteria and not correlating with protected characteristics. Periodic bias testing (e.g., checking if certain user groups get disproportionately flagged) is an emerging best practice. The goal is a threat detection system that is equitable – one that distinguishes users only by their behavior's risk, not by who they are [2, 28].

Regulatory Landscape: Regulatory bodies are becoming increasingly aware of AI's role in security. The European Union's AI Act (expected to come into force soon) is a prime example; it categorizes AI systems by risk and will likely classify many AI systems used in critical infrastructure (which can include cybersecurity for finance and health) as "high-risk," requiring conformity assessments, oversight, and possibly even registration. Cybersecurity-specific regulations (like certain national cyber laws or sector standards such as NIST guidance) are also starting to mention AI. For example, NIST's AI Risk Management Framework (AI RMF 1.0) provides guidance on managing risks of AI, which can be directly applied to security use – emphasizing validation, interpretability, and robustness. Companies should align their generative AI deployments with such frameworks to ensure they meet the expected diligence. Additionally, industry standards (like ISO 27001 for security management) might evolve to incorporate controls around AI usage. Being proactive by establishing policies for AI (how models are trained, how data is used, periodic review of AI decisions, etc.) will help demonstrate compliance and avoid legal issues.

Ethical Use vs. Misuse: On the flip side, the ethics of using AI offensively or for surveillance need consideration. Security operations sometimes veer into privacy-sensitive monitoring (like inspecting user communications for threats). Introducing AI that can generate or analyze content raises questions, such as whether it is ethical for an AI to scan employees' emails to detect phishing. Organizations need clear, acceptable use policies for AI and must communicate to their employees and customers about how AI is utilizing their data. Transparency to users (to the extent possible without compromising security) is generally encouraged. Also, there is an ethical line between using AI for defense and perhaps overstepping into creating AI "hack-back" tools (e.g., automatically attacking those who attack you, which could have collateral damage). Generally, defensive use is accepted, but as AI blurs lines, governance becomes crucial to ensure we do not inadvertently violate laws or ethical norms in how we deploy these powerful tools.

In essence, embedding generative AI in cybersecurity must be accompanied by robust governance and oversight. The technical team must work closely with the legal, compliance, and ethics teams to establish clear guardrails. This includes things like: limiting AI actions (the AI might suggest, but a human authorizes major steps), keeping humans informed and in control, protecting sensitive data (perhaps keeping the most sensitive analyses on-premises to avoid cloud exposure), and regularly reviewing the impact of the AI on people's rights and the business. Fortunately, many best practices from general AI ethics can be applied here and adopted. By addressing these considerations, organizations can reap the benefits of generative AI while upholding their legal and moral obligations.

2.6 RECOMMENDATIONS AND BEST PRACTICES

Based on the insights from this research, we propose the following recommendations and best practices for organizations looking to deploy generative AI in cybersecurity operations:

Define Clear Use Cases: Organizations should begin by identifying specific pain points in security operations that are well-suited to generative AI. Representative objectives include reducing phishing incidents, accelerating incident triage, and improving threat-hunting efficacy. Clearly articulated use cases, for example, "use an LLM to summarize and prioritize intrusion detection system (IDS) alerts," facilitate rigorous success measurement and mitigate the risk of unfocused adoption. Initial efforts should proceed as limited pilot projects on non-production data to validate model effectiveness and refine outputs before broader deployment.

Ensure High-Quality Data and Domain Customization: The performance of generative models in security contexts depends critically on the quality and relevance of training and evaluation data. Investments in data preparation, such as log cleaning, dataset labeling (including semi-supervised labels like "likely benign" vs. "suspicious"), and the inclusion of diverse scenarios spanning past incidents and known benign patterns, are crucial. Where feasible, pretrained models should be fine-tuned on domain-specific corpora; for instance, an LLM adapted to cybersecurity texts or an organization's historical incident reports will generally outperform a generic model. Continuous updating with curated threat data, supported by secure training pipelines designed to mitigate data-poisoning risks, helps maintain effectiveness against an evolving threat landscape.

Implement Human-in-the-Loop Governance: Human oversight should be retained, particularly during early development and deployment phases. Generative AI should augment rather than replace analyst decision-making until its reliability has been demonstrated. For example, the system may draft incident reports or propose containment actions, which are then reviewed and approved by an analyst. This process reduces the likelihood of high-consequence errors and provides structured feedback to improve model performance. As empirical evidence of reliability accumulates, greater degrees of automation may be introduced; nonetheless, manual override and review mechanisms should be preserved for safety-critical actions. Human-in-the-loop governance also supports accountability and enables expert judgment to address model errors or previously unseen attack patterns.

Prioritize Model Security and Robustness: AI models constitute part of the organizational attack surface and should be secured accordingly. Red-team exercises targeting AI components, such as prompt injection attempts and adversarial inputs, can reveal failure modes and inform mitigation strategies. Defensive measures include adversarial informed training, runtime safeguards (e.g., anomaly detection on inputs and outputs with policy-violation flagging), and timely model updates when systematic evasion tactics are discovered. Access to model interfaces should be strictly controlled and authenticated, with comprehensive logging of interactions for both audit and forensic purposes. These controls limit opportunities for misuse (e.g., querying an LLM for sensitive environmental details) and support post-incident investigation.

Integrate Thoughtfully with Existing Workflows: Generative AI should be integrated into existing security-orchestration, monitoring, and case-management workflows rather than deployed as an isolated capability. Examples include writing model findings directly into ticketing systems for analyst review, enriching the organizational knowledge base with AI-generated summaries, and invoking AI components from incident-response playbooks via APIs and automation scripts. To minimize cognitive load, AI recommendations should be surfaced within tools already used by analysts (e.g., plugins and in-product panels) rather than through additional consoles. Impact should be measured using pre- and post-integration metrics, such as mean time to detect (MTTD), mean time to respond (MTTR), false-positive rates, and analyst throughput, to quantify benefits and identify unintended effects.

Establish Clear Policies and Boundaries: Organizations should adopt internal policies for the responsible use of AI in cybersecurity [35]. Policies should specify data-access boundaries (adhering to least-privilege principles), data-handling requirements (e.g., encryption, anonymization) [36], and the scope of actions the AI system may take autonomously. Roles and responsibilities for oversight, such as assigning an "AI Security Officer" or extending the Security Operations Center (SOC) lead's remit, should be clearly defined. Guidance for employee interaction with AI systems (e.g., prohibiting the entry of passwords or unnecessary sensitive information into AI interfaces) reduces inadvertent data exposure. Contingency procedures for AI malfunction or compromise should be established to enable rapid reversion to manual operations. Incidents attributable to AI decision-making should be treated as first-class security incidents, with postmortems and remediation actions to prevent recurrence.

Monitor and Evaluate Continuously: Following deployment, the performance of generative AI should be continuously monitored, just as with any mission-critical system [28]. Key indicators include detection rates, false-positive and false-negative rates, processing latency, and overall impact on incident volume and resolution times. Findings should inform threshold adjustments, retraining schedules, and updates to features. Periodic evaluations, such as quarterly benchmarks or assessments after major updates, can employ standardized test suites (e.g., curated past incidents and red-team scenarios) to track progress over time. Monitoring for concept drift [37] is essential, as changes in infrastructure, user behavior, or adversary tactics can degrade effectiveness and necessitate retuning or retraining. From a governance perspective, regular reporting to senior leadership on both achievements and limitations promotes calibrated expectations and sustained support.

By following these best practices, an organization can greatly increase the likelihood that its foray into generative AI for cybersecurity will be successful and sustainable. In essence, treat the deployment as you would any major security solution – plan thoroughly, involve stakeholders, secure it, and keep improving it. The combination of human expertise and advanced AI, managed well, can create a powerful defense mechanism that is greater than the sum of its parts.

2.7 FUTURE RESEARCH DIRECTION

The next phase of adversarial intelligence for cybersecurity must turn isolated advances in GAN/AE anomaly detection and LLM-assisted operations into a resilient, auditable, and operationally coherent stack. The previous sections have already surfaced where today's systems break especially in evasion and poisoning of detectors, LLM hallucinations and prompt-level manipulation, brittle integrations that cannot meet SOC latency budgets, and the dual-use reality that whatever defenders adopt, attackers will adopt faster. Future work should therefore integrate five threads – robustness, grounding, evaluation, learning, and governance into a single pipeline that directly mitigates those risks while preserving the speed and coverage gains demonstrated by generative models across intrusion detection, malware/phishing analysis, and incident response.

Robustness and Red-Teaming of Security AI: Detection systems should provide guarantees that extend beyond identity verification to robustness under worst-case, adaptive adversaries. To make progress, future work must first formalize security-specific threat models for the modalities we actually defend: feature-bounded, semantics-preserving perturbations for tabular and sequential telemetry; protocol-constrained manipulations for packet captures (PCAP); opcode-preserving transformations for binaries; and instruction-level injections for LLM toolchains [25, 33, 34]. With these models in hand, defenses can be designed and evaluated consistently. Promising directions include adversarial training tailored to nonimage data projected-gradient methods for sparse categorical and temporal features; ensemble smoothing that randomizes feature subsets and temporal windows to create certified regions of abstention and consistency for alerts; and conformal risk control layered on anomaly scores so automated responses are triggered only when coverage guarantees hold. Since modern SOC workflows are increasingly embedding LLMs [34], prompt channels should be treated as untrusted input with separate retrieval and tool invocations from natural-language instructions and gate proposed actions with independent micro-policies.

Grounded and Verifiable LLMs for Trustworthiness: Hallucination is not just a user experience (UX) nuisance in security; it is an operational hazard. To address this, research should focus on evidence-based generation. This can be achieved by using retrieval-augmented pipelines that require citations to concrete artifacts such as alert IDs (unique identifiers for security alerts), PCAP offsets (specific locations in packet capture files), Sigma/YARA rules (standard security detection patterns), or process trees (hierarchically organized lists of system processes). At runtime, answers without valid citations or with citations that fail cryptographic or format checks should be rejected. Only the resulting outputs from these steps are summarized for humans. Additional robustness can come from counterfactual sanity checks, such as asking, "What minimal change to the artifact would flip the verdict?" and from dual-LLM cross-examination, where an independently trained verifier tries to refute every claim using the same evidence. Together, these mechanisms have the potential to reduce false positives and negatives, making the model more reliable.

Evaluation beyond Accuracy: Classic metrics such as area under the curve (AUC) and F1 score mask the critical metrics measured in security operations such as minutes of downtime avoided, reduced attacker dwell time, and reduced analyst cognitive load. Future direction should include benchmarks that can embed models inside realistic "SOC-in-the-loop" simulations, complete with streaming data, incident backlogs, and time-boxed triage. Additionally, the evaluation can be made more relevant by reporting joint quality-performance curves under load, throughput per GPU/CPU, and model success under transaction load [26, 27]. It is also essential to quantify early-warning value (lead time before impact) and model stability under drift, defined as performance decay (Δ) over weeks. For LLM copilots, handoff quality should be measured in terms of output consistency, reproducibility under temperature 0 settings, and error recovery when tool calls fail.

Safe Continuous and Federated Learning for Nonstationary Telemetry: We need online learners who quickly adapt yet avoid attack. To advance the field, future research should study drift detectors that track hidden distributions, updating only with tested checkpoints from controlled environments. Researchers should also focus on limiting policy changes using conformal prediction so automation stays within known uncertainty. Improving secure aggregation methods, such as federated averaging of gradient summaries and split learning for private data, remains important. Stronger checks for poisoning between parties, like leave-one-client-out or Krum-style approaches, require a more robust study. By taking these steps together, we can reduce poisoning and bias and keep detectors up to date with evolving attacker strategies.

Data Quality, Provenance, and Poisoning Resistance: Today's pipelines rarely track how an alerting model's training set was built. Future systems should adopt tamper-evident lineage records that show data origin, using cryptographically signed data manifests. Automated checks must then monitor for label leakage, class imbalance, and policy violations, such as PII spills or residency breaches [34]. Poisoning sentinel tools for detecting data manipulation should monitor label streams for sudden shifts in mutual information or unusual annotator behavior. Use conditional generators that follow protocol or state machine rules. Enforce bias controls that preserve base-rate priors. These steps help ensure augmentation does not unfairly inflate certain geos or vendors, preventing unfairness in detectors. In summary, this thread targets poisoning, bias, and their false-positive costs.

Decision-Focused Optimization for Operators: To stay ahead of dual-use attackers, defenders need adversaries that are continuously evolving. Research should advance digital-twin cyber ranges that integrate traffic and process simulators with generative red teams capable of multistage campaigns, parameterized by budget, stealth, and protocol constraints. These twins can train AI-assisted playbooks focused on decision-making to optimize policies that minimize expected business loss within resource limits, such as analyst time, network isolation scope, and GPU budgets, rather than simply maximizing detection scores.

Governance, Compliance, and Auditability at Scale: Effective governance must be an intrinsic component of the operational architecture of AI systems, rather than an afterthought appended post-deployment. Future research has the potential to explore formal policy specification languages capable of precisely articulating permissible AI behaviors in alignment with asset sensitivity, organizational priorities, and regulatory constraints. These high-level policy definitions should be compiled into executable runtime enforcement mechanisms referred to as policy guards, which annotate every AI-generated recommendation with relevant metadata, including the policy identifier, model version, and cryptographic model hash.

2.8 CONCLUSION

Generative AI stands at the forefront of a new wave of innovation in cybersecurity operations, offering the potential to significantly strengthen defenses and streamline security workflows. Through this comprehensive exploration, we have seen that models such as GANs, VAEs, and Transformer-based LLMs can bridge the long-standing gaps between theoretical capabilities and practical needs in cyber defense. They empower security systems to detect subtle and novel threats that elude conventional tools, automate burdensome tasks with speed and precision, and even anticipate adversaries' moves to improve organizational resilience. Real-world case studies and research outcomes underscore tangible benefits – higher detection rates, faster incident response, reduced false alarms, and more adaptive security postures – when generative AI is thoughtfully integrated into operations.

Yet, our analysis also makes clear that these advantages come with caveats. Risks such as adversarial attacks on AI, model biases, hallucinations, and dual-use weaponization by threat actors are genuine concerns that must be addressed head-on. Ethical and regulatory considerations are not ancillary but central to the deployment of AI in a domain as sensitive as cybersecurity; issues of privacy, transparency, and accountability can determine the success or failure of such initiatives. We have emphasized that bridging theory to practice is not just a technical endeavor but also a governance challenge – requiring clear policies, human oversight, and a culture of continuous learning and caution.

In conclusion, generative AI is not a magic bullet for cybersecurity, but it is a powerful new toolset that, when employed with care and expertise, can greatly enhance an organization's digital resilience. By adopting best practices, remaining vigilant to the risks, and fostering collaboration between AI systems and security teams, the community can ensure that the benefits of generative AI are realized safely. Cyber threats will continue to evolve – but so too will our defenses. The integration of generative AI marks a significant step forward in that evolution, pointing toward a future where defensive strategies are as dynamic and creative as the attacks they guard against. The message to cybersecurity leaders and practitioners is clear: Embrace the potential of generative AI, but do so deliberately and intelligently, building a foundation of trust, security, and compliance around these systems. In doing so, we can drive innovation in cyber defense and better protect our digital world against the complex threats of today and tomorrow.

ACKNOWLEDGMENTS

The author would like to acknowledge that no generative AI tools were used in the drafting, writing, or conceptual development of this chapter. The work is solely the product of the authors' own research, analysis, and writing.

REFERENCES

[1] Chen, Y., Cui, M., Wang, D., Cao, Y., Yang, P., Jiang, B., Lu, Z. and Liu, B., 2024. A survey of large language models for cyber threat detection. *Computers & Security*, *145*, p.104016.

[2] Gupta, M., Akiri, C., Aryal, K., Parker, E. and Praharaj, L., 2023. From ChatGPT to threatGPT: Impact of generative AI in cybersecurity and privacy. *IEEE Access*, *11*, pp.80218–80245.

[3] Arsal, M., Saleem, B., Jalil, S., Ali, M., Zahra, M., Rehman, A.U. and Muhammad, Z., 2024. *Emerging cybersecurity and privacy threats of chatgpt, gemini, and copilot: Current trends, challenges, and future directions*. Preprints, DOI:10.20944/preprints202410.1909.v1.

[4] Arif, A., Khan, M.I. and Khan, A.R.A., 2024. An overview of cyber threats generated by AI. *International Journal of Multidisciplinary Sciences and Arts*, *3*(4), pp.67–76.

[5] Dunmore, A., Jang-Jaccard, J., Sabrina, F. and Kwak, J., 2023. A comprehensive survey of generative adversarial networks (GANs) in cybersecurity intrusion detection. *IEEE Access*, *11*, pp.76071–76094.

[6] Arora, A. and Shantanu, 2022. A review on application of GANs in cybersecurity domain. *IETE Technical Review*, *39*(2), pp.433–441.

[7] Yinka-Banjo, C. and Ugot, O.A., 2020. A review of generative adversarial networks and its application in cybersecurity. *Artificial Intelligence Review*, *53*, pp.1721–1736.

[8] Dutta, I.K., Ghosh, B., Carlson, A., Totaro, M. and Bayoumi, M., 2020, October. Generative adversarial networks in security: A survey. *2020 11th IEEE Annual Ubiquitous Computing, Electronics & Mobile Communication Conference (UEMCON)* (pp. 0399–0405). IEEE.

[9] Navidan, H., Moshiri, P.F., Nabati, M., Shahbazian, R., Ghorashi, S.A., Shah-Mansouri, V. and Windridge, D., 2021. Generative adversarial networks (GANs) in networking: A comprehensive survey & evaluation. *Computer Networks*, *194*, pp.108149.

[10] de Araujo-Filho, P.F., Kaddoum, G., Campelo, D.R., Santos, A.G., Macêdo, D. and Zanchettin, C., 2020. Intrusion detection for cyber–physical systems using generative adversarial networks in fog environment. *IEEE Internet of Things Journal*, *8*(8), pp.6247–6256.

[11] Doersch, C., 2016. Tutorial on variational autoencoders. *arXiv preprint arXiv:1606.05908*.

[12] Girin, L., Leglaive, S., Bie, X., Diard, J., Hueber, T. and Alameda-Pineda, X., 2020. Dynamical variational autoencoders: A comprehensive review. *arXiv preprint arXiv:2008.12595*.

[13] Yang, Y., Zheng, K., Wu, C. and Yang, Y., 2019. Improving the classification effectiveness of intrusion detection by using improved conditional variational autoencoder and deep neural network. *Sensors*, *19*(11), pp.2528.

[14] Zhang, X., Chen, H., He, Y., Niu, W. and Li, Q., 2025. Automatically generating rules of malicious software packages via large language model. *arXiv preprint arXiv:2504.17198.*

[15] Busacca, A. and Monaca, M.A., 2025. Who's Afraid of "Big Bad" generative AI? Brief notes on the IDPA provision against OpenAI ChatGPT. In *Generative Artificial Intelligence and Fifth Industrial Revolution* (pp. 117–144). Springer Nature Switzerland.

[16] Wang, K., Zhang, G., Zhou, Z., Wu, J., Yu, M., Zhao, S., Yin, C., Fu, J., Yan, Y., Luo, H. and Lin, L., 2025. A comprehensive survey in LLM (-agent) full stack safety: Data, training and deployment. *arXiv preprint arXiv:2504.15585.*

[17] Ayyamperumal, S.G. and Ge, L., 2024. Current state of LLM risks and AI guardrails. *arXiv preprint arXiv:2406.12934.*

[18] Yamin, M.M., Hashmi, E., Ullah, M. and Katt, B., 2024. Applications of LLMs for generating cyber security exercise scenarios. *IEEE Access*, *12*, pp.143806–143822.

[19] Beckerich, M., Plein, L. and Coronado, S., 2023. RatGPT: Turning online LLMs into proxies for malware attacks. *arXiv preprint arXiv:2308.09183.*

[20] Wu, J., Yang, S., Zhan, R., Yuan, Y., Chao, L.S. and Wong, D.F., 2025. A survey on LLM-generated text detection: Necessity, methods, and future directions. *Computational Linguistics*, *2025*, pp.1–66.

[21] Li, H., Zhou, S., Yuan, W., Li, J. and Leung, H., 2019. Adversarial-example attacks toward android malware detection system. *IEEE Systems Journal*, *14*(1), pp.653–656.

[22] Kawai, M., Ota, K. and Dong, M., 2019, February. Improved malgan: Avoiding malware detector by leaning cleanware features. *2019 International Conference on Artificial Intelligence in Information and Communication (ICAIIC)* (pp. 040–045). IEEE.

[23] Memos, V.A. and Psannis, K.E., 2020, October. AI-powered honeypots for enhanced IoT botnet detection. *2020 3rd World Symposium on Communication Engineering (WSCE)* (pp. 64–68). IEEE.

[24] Chen, N., Tu, H., Duan, X., Hu, L. and Guo, C., 2023. Semisupervised anomaly detection of multivariate time series based on a variational autoencoder. *Applied Intelligence*, *53*(5), pp.6074–6098.

[25] Osinaike, T., Yetunde, A. and Onyenagubo, C.V., 2024. A survey of AI-powered proactive threat-hunting techniques: Challenges and future directions. *International Journal of Multidisciplinary Research, 6(6),* https://doi.org/10.36948/ijfmr.2024.v06i06.29183.

[26] Sindiramutty, S.R., 2023. Autonomous threat hunting: A future paradigm for AI-driven threat intelligence. *arXiv preprint arXiv:2401.00286.*

[27] Sarker, I.H., 2024. *AI-driven cybersecurity and threat intelligence: cyber automation, intelligent decision-making and explainability*. Springer Nature.

[28] Andreoni, M., Lunardi, W.T., Lawton, G. and Thakkar, S., 2024. Enhancing autonomous system security and resilience with generative AI: A comprehensive survey. *IEEE Access*, *12*, pp.109470–109493.

[29] Hilario, E., Azam, S., Sundaram, J., Imran Mohammed, K. and Shanmugam, B., 2024. Generative AI for pentesting: The good, the bad, the ugly. *International Journal of Information Security*, *23*(3), pp.2075–2097.

[30] Liu, Y., Deng, G., Li, Y., Wang, K., Wang, Z., Wang, X. et al., 2023. Prompt injection attack against LLM-integrated applications. *arXiv preprint arXiv:2306.05499.*

[31] Iansiti, M. and Lakhani, K.R., 2020. *Competing in the age of AI: Strategy and leadership when algorithms and networks run the world.* Harvard Business Press.

[32] Horowitz, M.C., Allen, G.C., Kania, E.B. and Scharre, P., 2022. *Strategic competition in an era of artificial intelligence.* Center for a New American Security.

[33] Gaber, M.G., Ahmed, M. and Janicke, H., 2024. Malware detection with artificial intelligence: A systematic literature review. *ACM Computing Surveys*, *56*(6), 1–33.

[34] Zheng, A.Y. and Yeh, R.A., 2024, September. Imma: Immunizing text-to-image models against malicious adaptation. *European Conference on Computer Vision* (pp. 458–475). Springer Nature.

[35] Humphreys, D., Koay, A., Desmond, D. and Mealy, E., 2024. AI hype as a cybersecurity risk: The moral responsibility of implementing generative AI in business. *AI and Ethics*, 4(3), 791–804.
[36] Ashe, S. and Ramachandra, H. 2024, June. The effect of continuous encryption of data in cloud native architecture. *2024 IEEE Cloud Summit* (pp. 163–169). IEEE.
[37] Hinder, F., Vaquet, V. and Hammer, B. 2024. One or two things we know about concept drift—A survey on monitoring in evolving environments. Part A: Detecting concept drift. *Frontiers in Artificial Intelligence*, 7, p.1330257.
[38] Why CIOs Can't Ignore the Rising Tide of Deepfake Attacks, Gartner Survey 2025. www.gartner.com/en/newsroom/press-releases/2025-09-02-why-cios-cannot-ignore-the-rising-tide-of-deepfake-attacks, (accessed September 30, 2025).

Chapter 3

Generative AI in cybersecurity operations

Advancing defense and building trust

Sushil Kumar Verma, Chok Nyen Yui, and Boubiche Djallel Eddine

3.1 INTRODUCTION

The rapid emergence of generative artificial intelligence (GenAI) and large language models (LLMs) marks a substantive inflection point for cybersecurity operations. Contemporary threat landscapes are characterized by unprecedented scale, velocity, and sophistication: distributed adversaries, supply-chain compromises, and automated attack toolkits generate voluminous, heterogeneous telemetry that overwhelms human analysts and legacy rule-based systems. This chapter positions GenAI as both a powerful enabler and a complex design challenge for security operations centers (SOCs). On the one hand, it can significantly accelerate threat detection and response, broaden access to specialist expertise, and support predictive, risk-informed defense. On the other, realizing these benefits requires careful governance, resilient engineering, and operational models that keep human oversight at the core.

We synthesize recent empirical findings and operational case studies to show how GenAI augments key SOC functions, continuous monitoring, threat intelligence (TI), threat hunting, incident detection and response (IDR), and cyber forensics, while exposing novel failure modes such as hallucinations, adversarial manipulation, and data-provenance risks. LLMs demonstrate particular strength in semantic enrichment (e.g., aligning unstructured reports with MITRE ATT&CK), generating incident briefs, and translating technical artifacts into executive-level narratives. These capabilities can accelerate detection and response by reducing mean time to detect (MTTD) and mean time to respond (MTTR), alleviating analyst cognitive burden and increasing operational throughput. However, their benefits can only be fully realized when integration strategies safeguard auditability, ensure human oversight, and enforce strong privacy controls.

To address the complex sociotechnical requirements of adopting GenAI in production SecOps, we present the novel GenAI Adoption Framework in Cybersecurity Operations. The framework organizes adoption across five interdependent dimensions—Adoptability, Ease of Training, Effectiveness and Transparency, Integration with Security Tools, and Compliance—and augments them with lifecycle controls, evaluation metrics, and a pragmatic adoption roadmap. It aims to guide practitioners from proof-of-concept to sustained production use while quantifying benefits and bounding risks. Foundational principles—risk-aware innovation, human-in-the-loop (HITL) control, data minimization, and iterative validation—underpin the framework and inform concrete artifacts such as model cards, Data Protection Impact Assessments (DPIAs), and playbooks for validated automation.

DOI: 10.1201/9781003644231-5

The chapter is organized to guide the reader from foundational context to forward-looking insights. We begin by characterizing the core components and operational challenges of modern SOCs, highlighting alert fatigue, talent shortages, and data overload. We then survey GenAI applications across the SecOps lifecycle, synthesizing technical approaches (edge vs. cloud inference, SOC-as-Code), tool integrations (Security Information and Event Management [SIEM], Security Orchestration, Automation, and Response [SOAR], Endpoint Detection and Response/Extended Detection and Response [EDR/XDR]), and prompt engineering practices. Two case studies follow: phishing detection and GenAI-assisted forensics, each demonstrating practical gains and emergent limitations and conclude with a forward-looking view of autonomous, self-healing SOC architectures and research directions.

Intended for academic readers, security practitioners, and policy architects, this chapter contributes a balanced account of promise and prudence. By combining empirical evidence, design principles, and an operationally focused adoption roadmap, we aim to equip organizations to harness GenAI's transformative potential in cybersecurity while preserving accountability, resilience, and trust.

3.2 CORE COMPONENTS OF CYBERSECURITY OPERATIONS

The multilayered security system of an organization is built on its cybersecurity operations. Central to these efforts is the SOC, a dynamic and committed center responsible for continuous monitoring, detection, investigation, and mitigation of cyber threats. The SOC is absolutely vital, coordinating a wide range of activities as mentioned in Figure 3.1—including TI analysis, proactive threat hunting, real-time security monitoring, incident response, regulatory compliance, cyber forensics, and comprehensive incident reporting. Though strategically important, the SOC faces persistent challenges, including alert fatigue, lack of qualified personnel, high data loads, fragmented coordination, misconfigured systems, reliance on outdated TI, and weak behavioral analytics tools. Overcoming these obstacles will help to guarantee a strong and responsive cybersecurity posture.

3.2.1 Threat intelligence

TI is the systematic collection, curation, and analysis of information about potential and active threats to an organization's assets, actors, TTPs (tactics, techniques, and procedures), and vulnerabilities. At a scholarly level, TI should be framed as both an epistemic process (how organizations know about threats) and an operational process (how that knowledge is converted into defensive action). Open-source cyber TI (OSCTI) has become a pivotal component of this landscape because it broadens visibility at relatively low cost and facilitates collaborative detection and attribution. However, OSCTI is not unproblematic: sources vary in quality and provenance, intelligence can be stale or noisy, and attribution remains uncertain factors that can introduce analytical error if not explicitly managed. Practical TI pipelines therefore require rigorous provenance tracking, confidence scoring, and alignment with structured representations such as MITRE ATT&CK for behavior mapping and STIX/TAXII for exchange [1]. When integrated into security operations, via enrichment of alerts, automated playbook generation, or IOC (indicator of compromise) distribution, TI can materially shorten detection cycles and enable more precise threat hunting [2, 3]. Research opportunities remain in formalizing TI quality metrics, adversary-model validation, and the sociotechnical dynamics of intelligence sharing (trust, incentives, privacy).

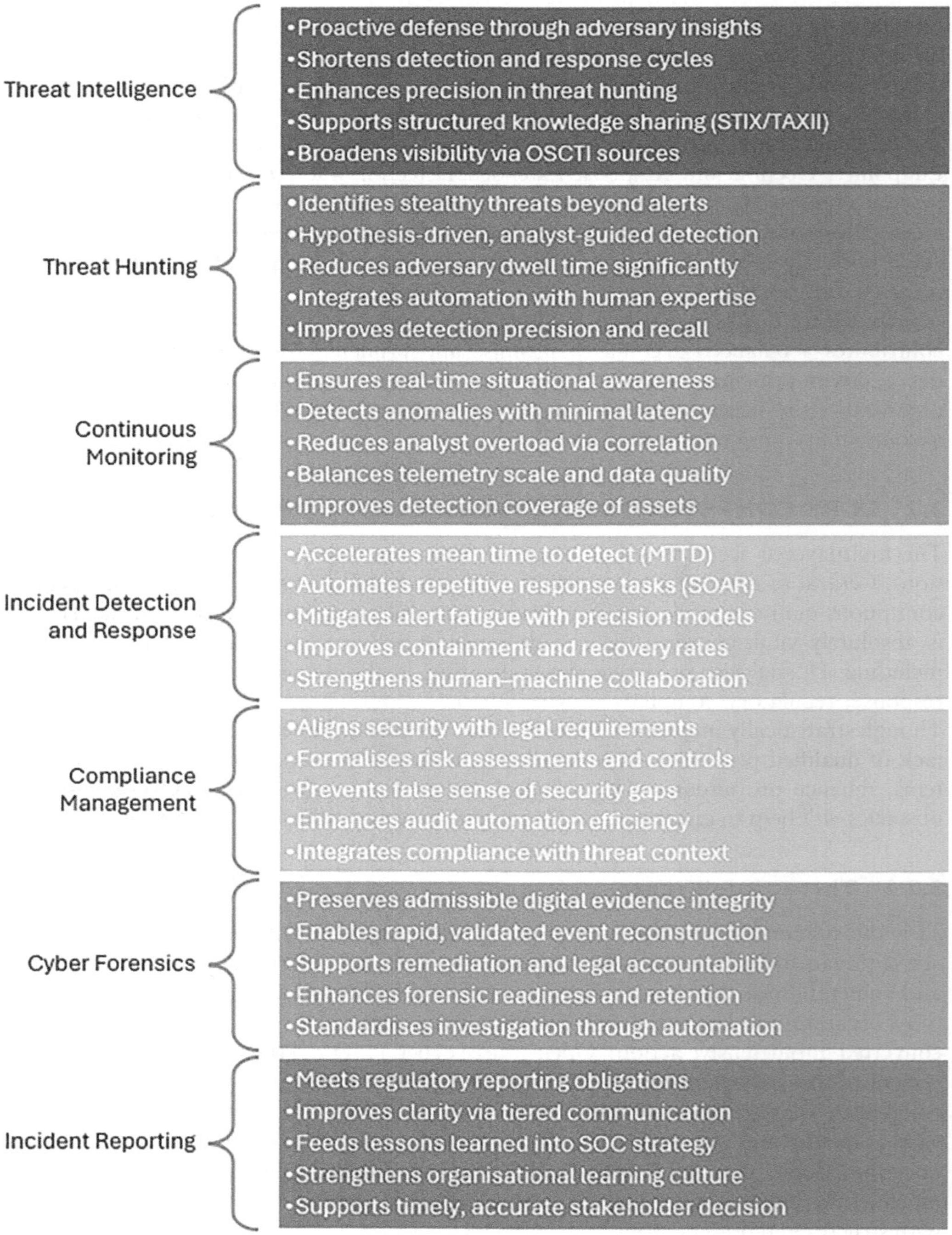

Figure 3.1 Core Components of Cybersecurity Options and Its Key Roles.

3.2.2 Threat hunting

Threat hunting is a hypothesis-driven, proactive search for threats that evade preventive controls. Conceptually distinct from reactive alert triage, hunting generates and tests conjectures about adversary presence using telemetry, behavioral models, and TI. The known ATHAFI [4] framework and similar automated approaches aim to systematize hunting by converting TI into executable hypotheses and automated queries. While automation increases scale and repeatability, effective hunting retains an HITL architecture: analysts encode domain knowledge, adjudicate ambiguous signals, and refine hypotheses. Analytical rigor in hunting requires explicit articulation of hypotheses (attack vectors, affected assets, expected artifacts), choice of detection primitives (sequence patterns, anomalous baselines, enrichment with contextual metadata), and statistical controls to limit false discovery. Evaluation should rely on both operational outcomes (detections confirmed, dwell time reduced) and methodological metrics (precision, recall, time-to-hypothesis-test). Key research challenges include reducing cognitive load for analysts, improving hypothesis generation via machine-assisted suggestions, and developing benchmark datasets that faithfully reflect live adversary behaviors without compromising operational secrecy.

3.2.3 Continuous monitoring

Continuous monitoring sustains situational awareness by collecting, normalizing, and analyzing telemetry from networks, endpoints, cloud services, and applications in near real time. The principal challenges are scale, signal-to-noise ratio, and latency. As event volumes grow, naïve alerting produces information overload; clustering algorithms, alert correlation, and contextual enrichment are proposed mitigations that group related events and elevate high-fidelity incidents for analyst attention [5]. From an analytical perspective, monitoring pipelines must balance completeness (coverage of telemetry sources) with telemetry quality (time synchronization, schema consistency) because analytic validity depends on data integrity. Architecturally, hybrid solutions that combine stream processing for low-latency detection with batch analytics for periodic pattern discovery are proving effective. Metrics for assessing monitoring efficacy include coverage (percent of critical assets instrumented), mean detection latency, and analyst triage time. Future work should investigate adaptive sampling, privacy-preserving telemetry collection, and economic models that quantify the marginal utility of additional telemetry sources.

3.2.4 Incident detection and response

IDR constitutes the core operational loop of the SOC: detect anomalous or malicious activity, validate and prioritize incidents, contain and eradicate threats, and recover systems to normal operation. A central barrier to IDR effectiveness is alert fatigue: excessive false positives erode analyst throughput and increase time-to-respond. Mitigations include more discriminative detection models (behavioral baselines, contextual risk scoring), SOAR-driven playbooks to automate repetitive tasks, and tiered escalation models that match incident complexity to analyst expertise. Critical evaluation dimensions are not only traditional detection metrics (precision, recall, F1) but also operational KPIs such as MTTD, MTTR, and containment success rate. From a scholarly standpoint, attention should be paid to adversarial limitations of machine learning (ML)-based detectors (evasion, poisoning) and to resilient human–machine teaming designs that ensure interpretable alerts and allow analysts to override automated decisions when necessary.

3.2.5 Compliance management

Compliance management operationalizes legal, regulatory, and industry requirements (e.g., GDPR, HIPAA, ISO/IEC 27001) into policies, controls, and documentation. Rather than being a mere bureaucratic burden, rigorous compliance can strengthen an organization's security posture by formalizing risk assessments, access controls, and incident-reporting obligations [6]. Yet tensions often arise: compliance-prescriptive controls can be misaligned with threat-specific priorities, and checkbox compliance can create a false sense of security. High-quality compliance programs therefore integrate continuous monitoring results and TI into control assessments, support audit automation, and emphasize outcomes (risk reduction) over purely procedural adherence. Research gaps include quantitative approaches to map compliance controls to security outcomes and designing compliance frameworks that are adaptive to rapid technological shifts (cloud-native architectures, AI-driven services).

3.2.6 Cyber forensics

Cyber forensics seeks to reconstruct security events, establish timelines, and preserve evidence for remediation or legal action [1]. Forensic rigor demands adherence to chain-of-custody principles, robust evidence preservation (including volatile memory capture), and careful documentation of analytic processes to ensure admissibility. Integrating automation—such as triage scripts, automated artifact extraction, and intelligence-driven correlation—expedites investigations but must be coupled with forensic validation and reproducibility checks. Forensic readiness is an important design goal: data retention policies, centralized secure logging, and preserved forensic images reduce time lost during incident response. Scholarly challenges include developing validated methods for timeline reconstruction in distributed systems, tooling for privacy-respecting evidence collection in multi-tenant environments, and standards for automated provenance tracking.

3.2.7 Incident reporting

Incident reporting operationalizes knowledge transfer: it communicates incident facts to stakeholders, meets legal notification deadlines, and feeds lessons-learned processes. Effective reporting balances timeliness with factual accuracy and situational sensitivity; standardized templates and tiered reporting (technical reports for engineers, executive summaries for leadership, legally framed notices for regulators/customers) support clarity and decision-making. Beyond compliance, high-quality reports should close the feedback loop—identifying root causes, control failures, and recommended mitigations—and should be integrated into SOC metrics and training exercises. Research directions include automating the generation of structured post-incident artifacts (e.g., STIX incident objects), empirically evaluating how reporting styles affect organizational learning, and defining privacy-aware disclosure strategies.

Table 3.1 summarizes the core components of modern SOC operations, outlining their current focus, persistent challenges, and emerging research directions.

Table 3.1 Research Directions in Core SOC Components

SOC Component	*Current Focus*	*Challenges*	*Research Directions*
Threat Intelligence (TI)	Collection, analysis, and operationalization of threat data; OSCTI integration	Variable data quality, stale/ noisy intel, uncertain attribution	- Formalizing TI quality/confidence metrics- Adversary-model validation - Provenance tracking and integrity assurance - Sociotechnical dynamics of intelligence sharing (trust, incentives, privacy)
Threat Hunting	Hypothesis-driven, proactive search for hidden threats	High analyst cognitive load, lack of standardized datasets, and ambiguous signals	- Machine-assisted hypothesis generation- Automated yet human-in-the-loop hunting frameworks - Benchmark datasets reflecting real adversary behavior - Rigorous evaluation metrics (precision, recall, time-to-test)
Continuous Monitoring	Real-time telemetry from networks, endpoints, and cloud	Scale, noise, latency, inconsistent schemas	- Adaptive sampling and scalable stream/batch hybrids - Privacy-preserving telemetry collection - Correlation/enrichment techniques to reduce false positives - Economic models for telemetry value
Incident Detection & Response (IDR)	Core SOC loop: detect, validate, contain, remediate	Alert fatigue, false positives, adversarial ML risks	- Discriminative and adversary-resilient detection models - Human–machine teaming for interpretable alerts - Resilient SOAR playbooks - Evaluation with operational KPIs (MTTD, MTTR, containment success)
Compliance Management	Translating regulatory requirements into policies and controls	Misalignment between compliance and threat priorities; "checkbox compliance"	- Quantitative mapping of compliance to security outcomes - Adaptive frameworks for emerging tech (cloud, AI) - Automation in audits and continuous control validation
Cyber Forensics	Evidence collection, timeline reconstruction, chain-of-custody	Distributed systems complexity, privacy in multi-tenant environments	- Validated methods for forensic timelines - Automated provenance tracking standards - Privacy-respecting evidence collection tools - Forensic readiness strategies (logging, retention, triage automation)
Incident Reporting	Communication to stakeholders, regulators, and leadership	Balancing speed, accuracy, and sensitivity	- Automating structured post-incident artifacts (e.g., STIX) - Studying the reporting style impact on organizational learning - Privacy-aware disclosure models -Integration of reporting into SOC feedback loops

3.3 CHALLENGES IN TRADITIONAL SOC OPERATIONS

SOCs are absolutely vital in safeguarding the digital infrastructure of companies. Their efficiency is sometimes compromised by several continuous problems, though. One major issue is alert fatigue; too many security alerts, most of which are false positives, can desensitize analysts and lead them to overlook actual threats. By isolating high-priority alerts from noise, Gelman et al. [7] demonstrate how ML-driven prioritization systems, such as the TEQ framework, can assist to address this issue. Another significant concern is the lack of qualified individuals. Global cybersecurity's shortage of qualified people makes it difficult for businesses to fully staff their SOCs. In this context, smart systems and automation are force multipliers improving human potential to support the load [8].

Apart from limitations on human resources, data overload is a significant challenge. Monitoring tools generate a lot of data that can overwhelm analysts and affect choices. Clustering techniques can significantly reduce the amount of data requiring manual review, therefore enhancing operational efficiency, as Kuehn et al. underline [5]. Furthermore, differences in coordination among various teams and departments can impede quick threat response, thereby weakening the vulnerability of the organization. Although many businesses struggle to implement such integration, effective cybersecurity demands seamless communication and cooperation among all relevant stakeholders.

Poorly configured systems can also be a significant danger as they are easy targets for attackers. This issue underlines the significance of automated configuration management and regular system audits to ensure robust security postures. Old TI heightens risk even more as reliance on antiquated data diminishes the effectiveness of defensive actions. Constant integration of current TI drives adaptive and proactive security measures. At last, conventional SOC approaches tend to emphasize known threats while neglecting behavioral analysis, which is essential for identifying new or unknown threats. Integration of behavioral analytics increases the SOC's ability to spot unusual patterns indicating advanced attacks eluding conventional detection methods.

3.4 EXPLORING GENAI APPLICATIONS THROUGHOUT THE CYBERSECURITY OPERATIONS LIFECYCLE

The integration of GenAI and LLMs has significantly transformed cybersecurity operations, enhancing threat detection, incident response, and TI analysis. This section delves into these advancements, highlighting their impact on SOCs and cybersecurity operations.

3.4.1 Threat detection and monitoring

Traditional SIEM systems and XDR platforms have evolved with the incorporation of GenAI and LLMs, leading to more proactive and efficient threat detection mechanisms in many ways.

3.4.1.1 GenAI-enhanced SIEM and XDR systems

Contemporary SIEM and XDR solutions harness the power of AI to correlate, analyze, and contextualize vast volumes of security data originating from diverse sources. By integrating data streams from endpoints, email systems, user identities, and cloud-based applications, these platforms enable a holistic and unified view of the threat landscape. AI-driven analytics facilitate the identification of anomalous patterns and behavioral deviations that may signify emerging threats, thereby enhancing the precision and timeliness of threat detection. This comprehensive approach not only streamlines the investigative process but also supports rapid, automated response mechanisms, significantly improving organizational resilience against sophisticated cyberattacks.

3.4.1.2 LLMs for log analysis and anomaly detection

LLMs have demonstrated capabilities in analyzing massive amounts of data, including security logs and network traffic, to identify patterns and anomalies indicative of malicious activity [9]. This facilitates proactive threat detection and enhances the efficiency of security teams.

3.4.2 Enhancing incident response through automated narratives and playbook execution

Dynamic and changing cyber threats call for smart and quick incident response tactics. GenAI, especially LLMs, has in this setting been a transforming force in enhancing SOC capabilities. One interesting use is the auto-generation of incident narratives, in which LLMs examine intricate log data and alert information to generate coherent, context-rich summaries of security incidents. These machine-generated stories give SOC analysts clear and succinct overviews, enabling more informed and timely decision-making by faster understanding of the incident scope, root cause, and impact [10].

GenAI is also quite important for incident response and playbook automation running concurrently. LLMs can dynamically call predefined response protocols or even create adaptive remediation measures suited to the particular setting of an incident by means of real-time interpretation of security events. This degree of automation guarantees consistency in threat handling across many different settings, minimizes manual intervention, and greatly shortens response times. These GenAI-driven innovations taken together improve the general efficiency, scalability, and reactivity of cybersecurity operations in front of sophisticated attackers [11].

3.4.3 Advancing TI interpretation and analyst support with LLMs

Tools that can quickly analyze and operationalize data for defensive use are required by the growing complexity and quantity of CTI. The summarization and mapping of hostile activity to the MITRE ATT&CK framework is one significant use of AI in this field. Tools like the Threat Report ATT&CK Mapper (TRAM) [12] use ML and natural language processing (NLP) to automate the extraction and classification of TTPs from unstructured TI reports. By speeding the conversion of raw intelligence into actionable security insights and enhancing situational awareness, this approach greatly lowers the manual work needed for analysts to map threat data to the MITRE ATT&CK matrix.

At the same time, AI-driven chat assistants are proving to be useful tools for increasing the output and decision-making ability of Tier-1 SOC analysts. Platforms such as Microsoft's Security Copilot provide real-time, context-aware assistance during incident investigation and response by means of LLMs. These assistants create straightforward, presentation-ready material for reporting, outline guided investigation processes, and offer brief summaries of security events. Such tools not only boost operational efficiency but also guarantee more consistency and accuracy in threat handling processes by reducing the cognitive load and procedural uncertainty usually experienced by entry-level analysts [13]. These developments taken together show how GenAI is transforming frontline cybersecurity operations by means of automation, augmentation, and accelerated intelligence interpretation.

3.4.4 Automating TI generation with GenAI and LLMs

A proactive cybersecurity plan is built on strong TI, which helps companies to expect, identify, and reduce possible threats before they become significant events. The way TI is gathered, examined, and operationalized has been greatly changed by GenAI and LLMs working together. Auto-generation of TI reports—where AI-powered systems autonomously gather data from many sources, including open-source intelligence (OSINT), dark web forums, and internal telemetry—and synthesize this information into actionable intelligence is among the most significant changes in this field. By increasing the speed and consistency of intelligence distribution, this degree of automation improves situational awareness across security teams [14].

The extraction of TTPs from unstructured data is another important development. Frameworks like threat context-enhanced TTP intelligence mining (TIM) show how AI can analyze unstructured threat data—including blogs, technical reports, and threat advisories—to find and extract TTPs. This capacity helps companies to better grasp enemy behavior and react more successfully to changing threats [15]. Moreover, LLMs' NLP features now enable the automatic translation of human-readable threat descriptions into detection rules, such as YARA or Sigma rules. By converting natural language to rules, this approach speeds up the application of threat detection logic and lowers manual effort, therefore greatly enhancing the agility and accuracy of security operations [16]. These developments taken together highlight GenAI's key importance in modernizing TI processes and strengthening the resilience of cybersecurity systems.

3.4.5 Prioritized patch summaries and justifications

Determining which Common Vulnerabilities and Exposures (CVEs) pose the most urgent concerns for a company often challenges conventional vulnerability management techniques, which must sift through large inventories. Especially when assessing significant amounts of patch data with different degrees of relevance and urgency, this manual method is labor-intensive and susceptible to error. By contextualizing vulnerabilities and producing prioritized patch summaries, LLMs have shown great promise in overcoming these constraints. Informed by a range of elements—including exploitability, possible operational impact, and relevance to particular organizational settings—these summaries allow a more strategic and risk-based approach to remediation [17].

Executive reporting's creation of exploit stories addresses the ongoing difficulty of converting complicated technical vulnerabilities into language understandable to nontechnical stakeholders, therefore marking a major development in this field. LLMs help to create clear, easily understandable summaries highlighting the consequences of security vulnerabilities, suggested mitigation measures, and possible corporate effects. By closing the gap between cybersecurity teams and executive leadership, these AI-generated stories promote informed decision-making and foster a culture of security awareness throughout all organizational levels [18]. GenAI's consistency and clarity in creating these messages improve internal alignment and support strategic-level prioritization.

Moreover, LLMs greatly enhance CVE triage processes by means of automation of the categorization and prioritization activities. AI-driven analysis can simplify triage, historically a labor-intensive task needing expert judgment to evaluate severity and relevance. LLMs can recommend suitable actions, assess contextual severity, and find related Common Weakness Enumerations (CWEs). This ability not only speeds the lifecycle of vulnerability management but also lessens the cognitive load on analysts, therefore allowing them to concentrate on more subtle threat assessments and response planning [19].

Identifying important threats from large lists of CVEs is a struggle for conventional vulnerability management. By producing prioritized patch summaries that take into account exploitability, possible impact, and relevance to particular organizational settings, LLMs have shown the ability to analyze and contextualize these vulnerabilities [17].

In summary, Table 3.2 provides an overview of how GenAI and LLMs are being integrated across the cybersecurity operations lifecycle. From enhancing SIEM and XDR systems for real-time threat detection, to accelerating incident response through automated narratives and adaptive playbooks, to transforming TI workflows via both analyst support and intelligence generation, GenAI is reshaping the efficiency and scalability of SOC practices. Additionally, LLM-driven vulnerability management, through prioritized patching and executive-level reporting, illustrates how AI can bridge technical analysis with strategic decision-making. Together, these applications highlight the breadth of GenAI's impact and its potential to modernize the entire spectrum of cybersecurity operations

Table 3.2 GenAI Applications across the Cybersecurity Operations Lifecycle

Lifecycle Area	*Application Focus*	*GenAI/LLM Contributions*
Threat Detection and Monitoring	SIEM/XDR enhancement; log analysis	- AI-driven correlation and contextualization of multi-source data - Early anomaly detection in security logs and traffic - Proactive threat identification and automated response support
Incident Response	Automated narratives; playbook execution	- Auto-generation of coherent incident reports - Context-aware summaries of logs and alerts - Automated or adaptive playbook execution for consistent response
Threat Intelligence (Interpretation and Analyst Support)	Intelligence mapping; analyst augmentation	- Summarization of unstructured intelligence reports - Automated TTP extraction and mapping to MITRE ATT&CK - SOC copilots for guided investigations, reporting, and decision support
Threat Intelligence (Generation and Automation)	Report synthesis; rule creation	- Auto-generation of TI reports from OSINT, dark web, and telemetry - Extraction of TTPs from unstructured sources - Translation of natural language into YARA/Sigma detection rules
Vulnerability and Patch Management	CVE triage; executive reporting	- Prioritized patch summaries based on exploitability and impact - Executive-friendly exploit stories for decision-making - Automated triage and CWE mapping to reduce analyst workload

3.5 ARCHITECTURE AND TOOLS: HOW GENAI IS EMBEDDED IN CYBERSECURITY OPERATIONS

The integration of GenAI into cybersecurity operations represents a paradigm shift in how threats are detected, understood, and mitigated. As cyber threats evolve in complexity and scale, traditional rule-based approaches often fall short in providing timely and contextually relevant responses. GenAI, with its capability to synthesize novel content and predict patterns, enhances the analytical capacity of security systems and teams. This section explores the architectural models facilitating GenAI deployment, its synergy with cybersecurity tools, prompt engineering examples in a SecOps context, and prominent GenAI-powered platforms shaping the modern SOC.

3.5.1 Architectural models

Key architectural models such as Edge AI, Cloud AI, and SOC-as-Code are being used to implement GenAI in cybersecurity, each providing distinct operational advantages. By processing data locally on devices or servers, Edge AI allows low-latency analytics, which is ideal for time-critical settings such as Industrial Control Systems (ICS) and IoT networks. On the other hand, Cloud AI provides scalability and access to high-performance models like GPT-4, Mistral-7B, and Claude, which examine large data streams compiled from SIEM, SOAR, and EDR tools [20]. At last, SOC-as-Code combines GenAI with Infrastructure-as-Code concepts, therefore enabling security workflows to be versioned, automated, and embedded into CI/CD pipelines. This strategy improves the agility and reproducibility of security operations by complementing DevSecOps practices.

3.5.2 Integration with key cybersecurity tools

Fundamentally changing how threat detection, analysis, and response are carried out, GenAI is being more and more included in the basic architecture of contemporary cybersecurity systems. Now, include GenAI features, SIEM systems like Splunk [21] and Microsoft Sentinel [22] enable automatic creation of incident response playbooks and support natural language-based threat queries. This not only improves usability but also speeds up inquiry deadlines. GenAI's capacity to intelligently prioritize alerts, simulate possible attacker actions, and suggest context-specific mitigation plans helps SOAR systems in the same way by closing the cognitive and operational gaps experienced by security analysts under pressure [23]. GenAI improves early-stage threat identification in EDR and XDR systems by means of continuous analysis of behavioral patterns and telemetry data, therefore supporting sophisticated anomaly detection and threat classification. Furthermore, TI platforms (TIPs), like MISP [24] and Anomali [25], can use GenAI to analyze unstructured threat data, create concise summaries, and even forecast the probable development of threat campaigns. Together, the incorporation of GenAI into these several systems denotes a major development in cybersecurity operations, enabling companies to be more proactive, quick, and precise in controlling complicated and dynamic threat environments.

Rapidly becoming a vital tool in contemporary cybersecurity operations, prompt engineering, the strategic design of input queries to elicit exact and actionable responses from GenAI models, has been defined as such. Security experts can use GenAI's improved natural language understanding to assist a wide range of vital activities by creating well-structured prompts, therefore improving operational efficiency and decision-making accuracy. Prompts like "Summarize anomalies in the last 24 hours of Windows security logs, highlighting possible lateral movement" help to quickly identify suspicious activity patterns in log analysis that could suggest a breach. In incident response as well, customized prompts such "Create an incident response playbook for ransomware detection in Linux systems" help to automatically produce thorough, context-specific remedial plans.

Beyond reactive strategies, prompt engineering also enables proactive cybersecurity actions such as threat simulation, where prompts like "Create a hypothetical attack vector exploiting Log4Shell in a Java-based web application and propose remediation steps" let teams expect and get ready for developing vulnerabilities. Furthermore, in alert triage, prompts can be used to effectively prioritize security alerts by ranking them according to frameworks like MITRE ATT&CK, therefore directing analysts on which events call for quick escalation. These programs taken together show how prompt engineering converts natural language inputs into actionable security workflows, greatly improving SOC team capabilities [26].

3.5.3 GenAI-powered cybersecurity tools

Emerging is a new generation of cybersecurity tools defined by the close integration of GenAI features to improve SOC performance. Among these developments, Microsoft Security Copilot [27] stands out as it uses OpenAI's sophisticated language models to analyze complicated security events, produce incident summaries, and streamline investigative processes. This tool gives analysts context-aware recommendations that enhance decision-making efficiency by allowing them to interact with security data using natural language queries. Likewise, IBM WatsonX for Security [28] is an enterprise-grade platform supporting advanced threat hunting and the generation of narrative-driven incident reports that combines GenAI with rich TI and complex data fusion methods. Darktrace, meanwhile, uses self-learning AI systems—including generative elements—to autonomously detect new threats, mimic possible attack routes, and coordinate prompt reactions with little human involvement. The Elastic AI Assistant for Security also uses language models to analyze event data inside the Elastic Security system, therefore providing explanations for detections that greatly help analysts under high alert load. These GenAI-powered tools, taken together, not only simplify SOC processes but also democratize efficient threat detection, therefore lowering dependence on very specialized knowledge and allowing a wider spectrum of security staff to react effectively to developing cyber threats [29].

3.5.4 Best practices for implementation: GenAI in cybersecurity operations

Incorporating GenAI into cybersecurity operations provides revolutionary advantages in automating threat detection, simplifying decision-making, and enhancing analyst capabilities. But, efficient and safe deployment calls for following important implementation best practices. These consist of exact prompt engineering, Reinforcement Learning with Human Feedback (RLHF), strong governance systems, and keeping a HITL framework. Fundamental prompt engineering calls for security-oriented, limited, auditable inputs to minimize hallucinations and guarantee contextual correctness [30]. Validation layers and sanitizing methods help to offset prompt injection among other hazards [31]. By refining outputs depending on analyst input, RLHF increases GenAI adaptability in dynamic SOC settings, therefore improving model alignment with company goals and lowering false positives

[29]. Particularly in compliance-heavy settings, governance systems—comprising role-based access controls, audit trails, and explainability tools—ensure openness and responsibility. Oversight in high-stakes situations still depends on HITL; human validation lowers the dangers of hallucinations or hostile manipulation [32]. Still, issues including model drift, prejudice, scalability, and excessive reliance on automation remain. Dealing with these calls for constant validation, varied training data, and analyst upskilling. Together, these approaches create a thorough framework for properly including GenAI into cybersecurity without sacrificing dependability, confidence, and operational effectiveness.

3.6 BENEFITS AND OPPORTUNITIES—EMBEDDING GENAI IN CYBERSECURITY OPERATIONS TO BUILD TRUST

Driven by ever more complex attacks and the concurrent development of AI technologies, the cybersecurity scene is changing quickly. Among the most changing of these technologies is GenAI, especially LLMs like GPT-4. These systems are now being integrated across security operations to lower the MTTD and MTTR to threats, improve cooperation between human analysts and AI systems, raise SOC maturity using predictive analytics, and democratize cybersecurity knowledge (Figure 3.2). This chapter investigates these transforming advantages by means of a synthesis of present studies and case studies.

3.6.1 Reduction in MTTD/MTTR

Key measures for assessing the efficacy of incident response are MTTD *(measures the average time taken to identify a system failure, security breach, or incident after it occurs.)* and MTTR *(quantifies the average time required to resolve and restore normal operations after an incident is detected)*. Traditionally, the great amount of security data and alerts has hampered these. By parsing large datasets in real time, correlating threat indicators, and producing context-rich alerts, GenAI greatly speeds up threat detection and response.

Vadisetty and Polamarasetti [32] showed that variational autoencoders (VAEs) and generative adversarial networks (GANs) could mimic realistic cyberattacks, therefore training models lowering MTTD by 40–60% relative to conventional approaches. These simulations improve readiness and enable quicker identification of developing dangers.

GenAI allows for ongoing log analysis and monitoring, flagging anomalies in network traffic, system settings, or user behavior. According to Curran et al. [29], GenAI tools' real-time production of incident summaries and threat hypotheses lowers manual triage work and helps to response times that are up to 50% quicker than baseline levels.

3.6.2 Human–AI collaboration models in SOCs

Modern SOCs are moving toward hybrid operational models in which AI systems serve as smart assistants instead of autonomous agents. Aiding human analysts in quicker decision-making, this human–AI cooperation model depends on GenAI's capacity to understand, contextualize, and convey insights in natural language.

By distilling insights from several data sources, including SIEM alerts and TI feeds, Saddi et al. [33] show how GenAI helps analysts carry out challenging threat correlation and prioritization activities. In these situations, GenAI serves as a real-time analyst copilot, recommending mitigation plans and even creating response playbooks.

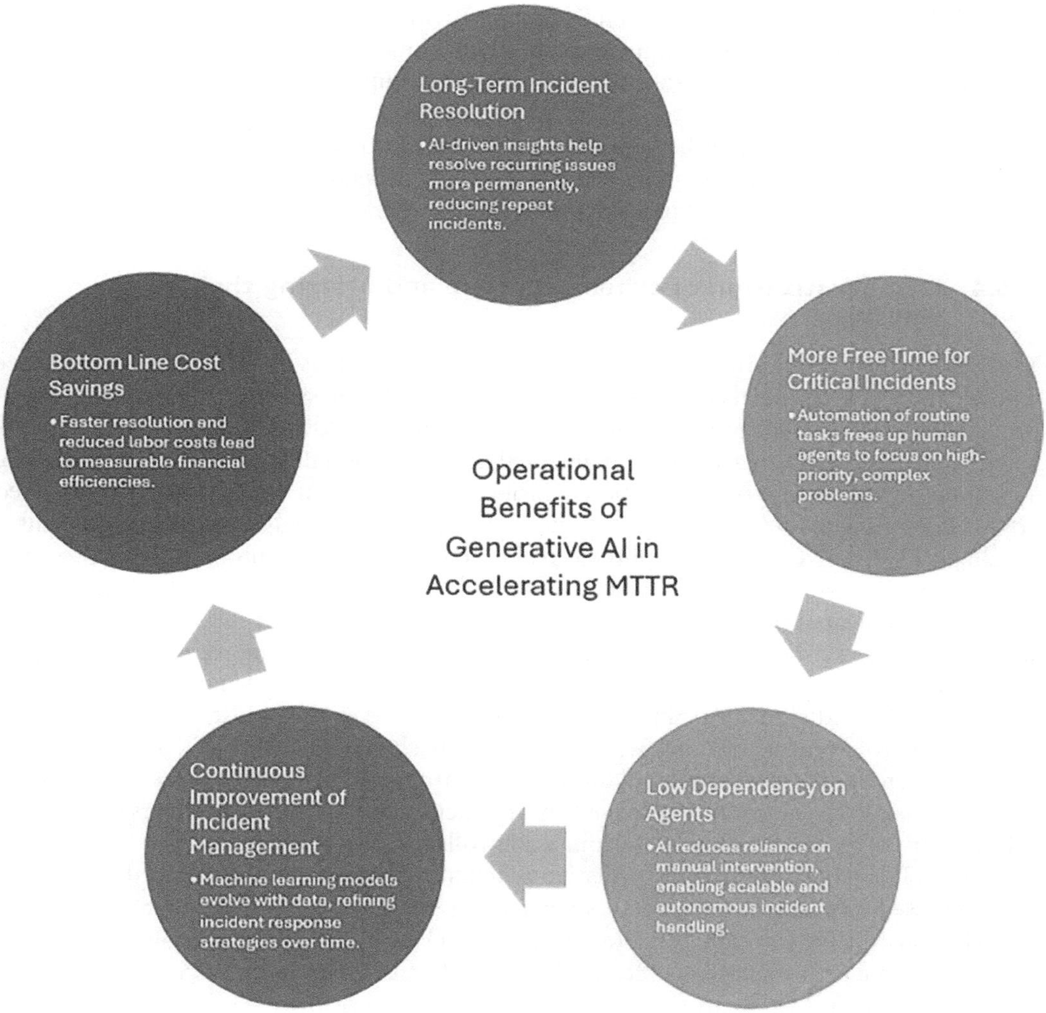

Figure 3.2 Operational Benefits of GenAI in Accelerating MTTR.

Case studies from Khan et al. [34], which record effective GenAI deployments in incident response workflows where LLMs support threat classification, root cause analysis, and countermeasure generation, help to further support the collaborative model. These combinations have been demonstrated to lower false positives and increase analyst throughput.

3.6.3 Enhanced SOC maturity: from reactive to predictive security

Traditionally, SOCs have run in reactive mode, reacting to alerts following breaches. Learning from past attack data, GenAI is helping to drive predictive security by means of precursor signals of future threats.

Using multistage GenAI pipelines, Sarker [35] suggested the "CyberLLM" framework to proactively find weaknesses and predict attack vectors. Marking a notable maturity leap for SOC, these predictive models can advise preventive controls before threats materialize.

Wen [36] underlined GenAI's contribution to improving honeypot technologies—simulated systems meant to draw and examine attacker behaviors. Helping to predict future tactics and lowering breach probabilities, these systems now autonomously evolve depending on TI inputs.

Predictive threat modeling helps with resource allocation as well; it lets SOC managers dynamically change response capacity and monitoring depending on projected threat levels, a practice now used by many financial and healthcare organizations.

3.6.4 Democratization of cyber expertise and bridging the skills gap

One of the most revolutionary effects of GenAI in cybersecurity is its capacity to democratize knowledge and level the playing field for less experienced professionals. Maintaining strong security postures is made more difficult by the continuing worldwide lack of qualified cybersecurity professionals, exacerbated by unequal access to specialized training. By providing real-time advice, contextual educational insights, and decision support, GenAI-powered tools offer a hopeful answer that closes knowledge gaps and speeds up skill development.

Chugh [37] noted that by simplifying technical language and automating script generation, GenAI-assisted platforms like ChatGPT and Microsoft Security Copilot help to democratize complicated threat modeling, therefore acting as intelligent tutors allowing junior analysts to interact boldly with advanced security ideas. In the same vein, Teo et al. [38] underlined how GenAI may promote inclusivity by delivering tailored material and adaptive feedback fit for individual learning requirements, therefore enabling just-in-time skill development and role-specific training across many user backgrounds. Silva [39] also underlined the effectiveness of GenAI in simulation-based learning environments, where user confidence and skill retention are improved by interaction with AI-driven adversary models, allowing users to build defensive skills in a controlled, low-risk environment.

Table 3.3 summarizes the transformative benefits and opportunities of embedding GenAI into cybersecurity operations. These span measurable efficiency gains, such as reducing MTTD and MTTR through accelerated data correlation and incident triage, to qualitative improvements like enabling effective human–AI collaboration within SOCs. Moreover, GenAI strengthens SOC maturity by advancing predictive security models and supporting proactive defenses, while simultaneously democratizing cybersecurity expertise by making advanced practices accessible to less experienced professionals. Together, these opportunities underscore how GenAI can build greater resilience, inclusivity, and trust in the future of cybersecurity operations.

3.7 CASE STUDY

The integration of GenAI into cybersecurity operations marks a significant evolution in how organizations address complex security challenges. This section presents two case studies that exemplify the application of GenAI in SOCs, focusing on incident management, threat detection, and analyst support. Each case study is structured with clear objectives, implementation strategies, and outcomes and supported by empirical evidence to provide a comprehensive understanding of GenAI's impact on cybersecurity practices.

3.7.1 Case study 1: Phishing attack detection with ML (NLP)

This case study examines a sophisticated, multistage cyberattack against a healthcare institution in which an adversary leverages spear-phishing to implant malware into clinical

Table 3.3 Benefits and Opportunities of Embedding GenAI in Cybersecurity Operations

Benefit Area	*Key Contributions of GenAI*	*Illustrative Studies/Examples*
Reduction in MTTD/MTTR	- Real-time parsing of large datasets and correlation of threat indicators - Context-rich alerts and automated incident summaries - Faster anomaly detection and triage	Vadisetty and Polamarasetti [32]: VAEs and GANs reduced MTTD by 40–60% Curran et al. [29]: Response times 50% faster
Human–AI Collaboration in SOCs	- GenAI as a copilot for analysts - Assists in threat correlation, prioritization, and mitigation planning - Generates response playbooks and reduces false positives	Saddi et al. [33]: SOC decision support Khan et al. [34]: LLMs aid in classification and countermeasures
Enhanced SOC Maturity (Predictive Security)	- From reactive to predictive security - Forecasting attack vectors via multistage pipelines - Adaptive honeypots evolving with threat intelligence - Improved resource allocation based on projected threats	Sarker [35]: CyberLLM predictive framework Wen [36]: AI-enhanced honeypots
Democratization of Cyber Expertise	- Bridges the global skills gap - Simplifies technical language and automates scripts - Adaptive learning and real-time tutoring for junior analysts - Simulation-based environments for defensive training	Chugh [30]: Democratized threat modeling Teo et al. [28]: Inclusive, role-specific training Silva [39]: AI-driven simulation learning

workstations and medical devices, subsequently establishing an advanced persistent threat (APT) inside the organization's network [40]. The attack commences with targeted email lures containing malicious attachments that appear contextually legitimate to operational staff. Once executed, the malware exploits unpatched vulnerabilities in connected medical devices—imaging systems, infusion pumps, or monitoring equipment—allowing the adversary to pivot laterally from initially compromised endpoints into critical subnets. The attacker's dual objectives are to exfiltrate sensitive patient data and to degrade or disrupt health services, thereby increasing operational impact and ransom leverage. Figure 3.3 summarizes the multistage progression: initial social engineering, foothold establishment on endpoints and devices, lateral movement and privilege escalation, command-and-control (C2) communications, and data staging prior to exfiltration. The scenario highlights the particular risk profile of healthcare environments, where legacy devices, complex device lifecycles, and high-availability requirements constrain traditional security interventions.

From the perspective of SOC workflows, detection and response unfold across layered systems and automated decision processes. The institution's SIEM aggregates telemetry from email gateways, endpoint protection platforms, network flow records, and device management consoles. AI-driven NLP models enrich SIEM correlation by identifying semantic markers of spear-phishing—sender anomalies, contextual incongruities, and suspicious attachment signatures—thereby enabling the SIEM to flag a sudden uptick in suspicious email activity and to map that activity to a workstation that opened the malicious payload. Simultaneously, an intrusion detection and response (IDR) system performs

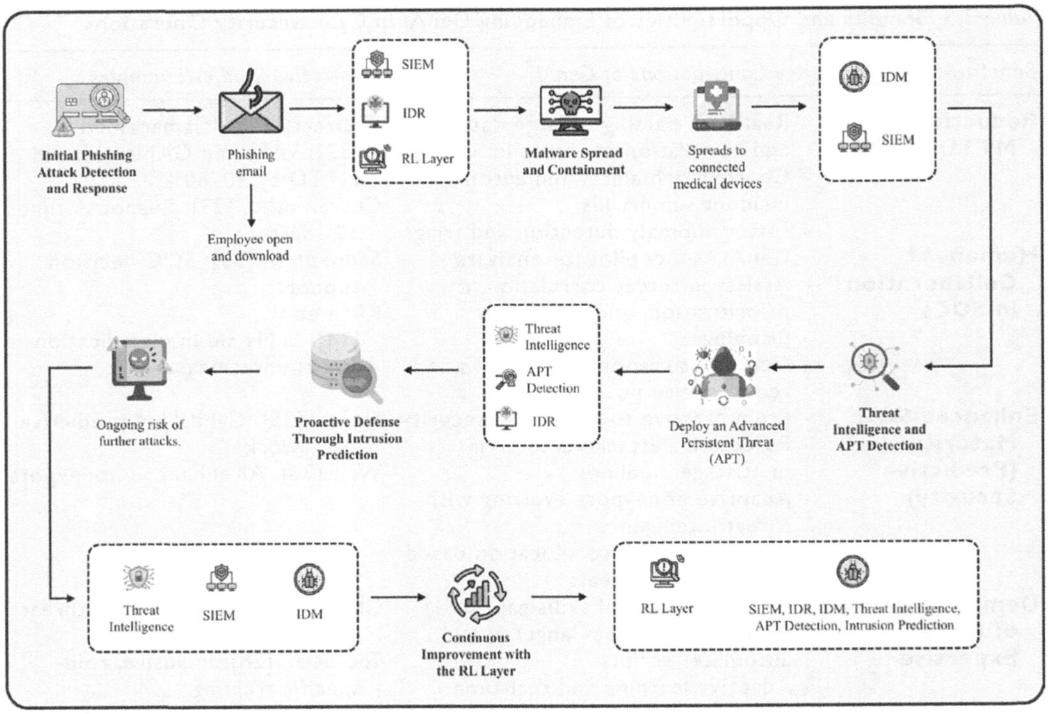

Figure 3.3 Use Case Scenario: Multistage Cyberattack on Healthcare Institutions [40].

behavioral analysis on the implicated endpoint: process execution chains, anomalous file system changes, and unexpected network connections. ML models trained to detect deviations from baseline device behavior detect the malware's C2 traffic pattern. The IDR then executes containment actions at the network layer—isolating the compromised workstation and blocking outbound connections—thereby interrupting further communications with the attacker's infrastructure.

Crucially, an embedded RL layer orchestrates and refines automated responses. The RL agent selects containment strategies (isolation, full image capture, or segmented quarantine) and executes targeted scans of adjacent systems, updating its policy according to observed effectiveness—minimizing collateral disruption while maximizing eradication probability. Forensics procedures run in parallel: memory and disk snapshots, network packet captures, and device configuration audits preserve evidence for attribution and post-incident review. This integrated response chain illustrates both strengths and operational challenges: AI/NLP accelerates phishing detection but can produce false positives; behavioral IDR is effective against novel malware but depends on high-fidelity baselines; RL optimizes response trade-offs but requires careful reward engineering to prevent dangerous actions in production. The case concludes by underscoring the need for device lifecycle management, segmentation of clinical networks, continuous threat-informed monitoring, and coordinated SOC playbooks that combine automated controls with human oversight to protect patient data and maintain service continuity.

Figure 3.4 illustrates a multilayered cybersecurity strategy, highlighting components such as centralized SIEM, rapid threat detection, proactive intrusion prediction, RL, and

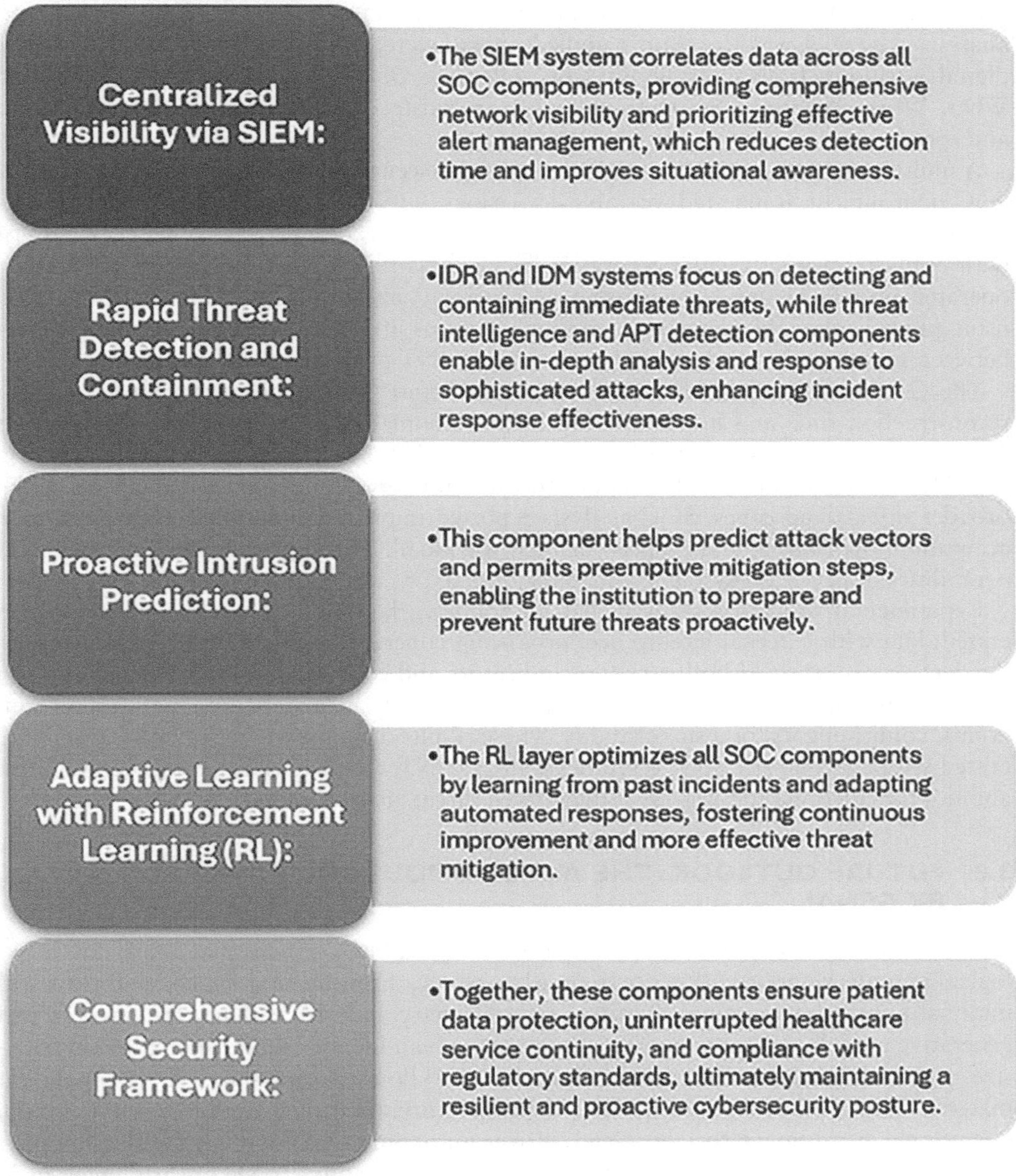

Figure 3.4 Key Benefits of ML (NLP) Usages in Phishing Attempts.

a comprehensive security framework. Together, these elements enhance situational awareness, threat response, and regulatory compliance to ensure resilient cybersecurity.

3.7.2 Case study 2: GenAI into cyber forensics workflows

The objective of this case study [28] was to enhance CTI by integrating GenAI into cyber forensics workflows, with a focus on incidents involving wearable devices. Traditional forensic methods often treat network and application data separately, leading to fragmented analysis. The goal was to create a unified, cross-layered framework that could synthesize digital attributes from multiple domains, integrate OSINT, and apply the "5W" (Who, What, When, Where, Why) methodology to reconstruct incidents with greater accuracy and speed.

A multimodal GenAI model, fine-tuned on cybersecurity datasets, was embedded into a SOC environment. It ingested wearable device logs (GPS data, pairing records, activity logs) alongside OSINT feeds. The system's transformer architecture correlated network patterns with application-level events, generating incident scores to prioritize responses. Analysts operated in a HITL mode, validating AI-generated insights. The framework was tested using publicly available datasets, including scenarios involving Bluetooth communications between smartwatches and smartphones, with OSINT providing contextual enrichment.

The GenAI-assisted framework, as shown in Figure 3.5, significantly reduced incident reconstruction time and improved detection of anomalous behaviors, such as unauthorized pairing attempts and location inconsistencies [28]. By correlating wearable data with OSINT, the system identified potential threat actors and contextualized incidents within broader threat landscapes. SOC analysts reported improved situational awareness, more accurate prioritization, and reduced manual workload. The approach also uncovered vulnerabilities in device ecosystems, informing targeted security hardening.

Experimental validation showed that the framework could accurately align device-generated data with external intelligence, producing coherent timelines and attacker profiles. Incident scores reflected both technical indicators and contextual relevance, enabling proactive mitigation. In test cases, the system's reconstructions matched known ground truth events, confirming its forensic reliability. These results demonstrate that GenAI, when integrated with cross-layer evidence synthesis and OSINT, can materially strengthen CTI capabilities for emerging IoT and wearable-driven threat environments.

3.8 FUTURE OUTLOOK: THE AUTONOMOUS SOC POWERED BY GENAI

GenAI marks a pivotal inflection point for SOCs by enabling systems that approximate biological immune responses: they continuously observe, diagnose, and remediate threats with minimal human intervention. By fusing rich telemetry and observability frameworks with generative models, autonomous SOC architectures can identify subtle anomalies, hypothesize root causes, and orchestrate remediation workflows in real time. These capabilities materially reduce MTTD and MTTR, improving organizational resilience while limiting operational disruption. Crucially, GenAI-driven autonomy does not imply the elimination of human oversight; rather, it elevates human roles from repetitive triage toward higher-order tasks such as strategy, threat-hunting design, and cross-organizational coordination [41].

A defining characteristic of GenAI-enabled SOCs is continuous learning from operational events. Unlike static rule sets, generative models can be trained on feedback loops created by incidents, red-team exercises, and defensive playbooks, enabling dynamic recalibration of detection thresholds, policy adjustments, and remediation tactics. This event-driven adaptation supports contextualized responses that better match evolving adversary behavior, reducing false positives and improving precision. At scale, these systems enable more predictable security posture management across hybrid and multicloud environments by automating routine containment and recovery actions while flagging only atypical or high-impact decisions for human adjudication.

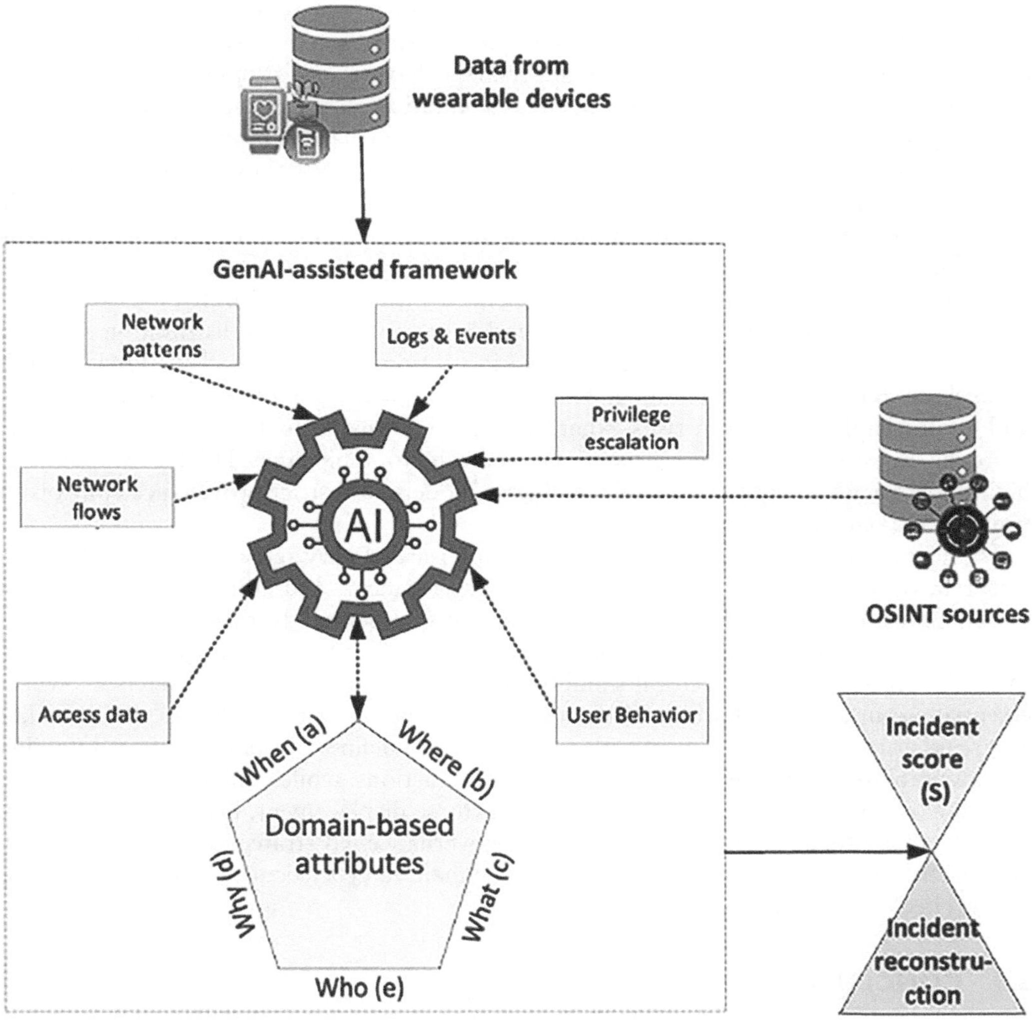

Figure 3.5 GenAI-Assisted Framework into Cyber Forensics Workflows [28].

The strengthening effect of combining GenAI with other emergent technologies—security automation, distributed ledger technologies, and quantum computing—further accelerates this transformation. Security automation frameworks provide the orchestration backbone for translating GenAI outputs into safe, auditable actions. Blockchain-based mechanisms can complement this by ensuring data integrity and open auditability: immutable logs and smart contracts make response chains transparent and verifiable, which is essential for forensic validation and regulatory compliance. Quantum technologies, though nascent, offer potential advantages for large-scale pattern analysis and optimization that may reveal complex threat correlations currently beyond classical capabilities; at the same time, quantum computing raises legitimate cryptographic and transition challenges that must be proactively managed [42].

Concurrently, the rise of AI-augmented Blue Teams is reshaping defensive operations. Augmented with generative and predictive models, these teams can explore a broader space of attack hypotheses, rapidly simulate adversary behavior, and propose countermeasures with unprecedented speed and scope. Such augmentation increases the tempo and depth of defensive analysis, enabling organizations to preemptively harden critical assets and to validate mitigations through automated scenario testing. However, the operational deployment of AI Blue Teams requires careful calibration to avoid overreliance on automated judgments, to limit adversarial manipulation of models, and to preserve clear human responsibility for consequential decisions [43].

Despite the promise, significant technical, operational, and ethical risks remain. Adversarial ML, model hallucination, data poisoning, and brittleness in out-of-distribution scenarios can produce incorrect or dangerous remediation actions if left unchecked. Integration of blockchain and quantum technologies introduces its own trade-offs—latency, scalability, and cryptographic migration risks—that demand rigorous evaluation. These risks underscore the necessity of robust governance: layered validation pipelines, HITL checkpoints for high-impact actions, continuous red-teaming of models, and strict provenance controls for training and telemetry data.

The chapter therefore closes with a call for an interdisciplinary agenda that aligns technical research, operational experimentation, policy development, and ethical review. Technical research must prioritize robust, explainable generative models, adversarial-resilient training methods, and standards for secure automation interfaces. Operational experimentation—through controlled pilots, sectoral sandboxes, and cross-organizational exercises—will be essential to surface real-world constraints and to iterate on safe playbooks. Policymakers and regulators should collaborate with practitioners to define transparency, accountability, and auditability requirements for autonomous SOC actions, while ethicists and sociotechnical scholars assess societal impacts such as workforce displacement, bias propagation, and privacy trade-offs. Only through a balanced, governance-led strategy that couples innovation with oversight can the full potential of AI-enhanced cybersecurity be realized in a way that is effective, equitable, and resilient.

3.9 CONCLUSION

This chapter synthesizes current evidence and operational experience to show that GenAI, notably LLMs, constitutes a substantive inflection point for SOCs and broader cybersecurity practice. Through empirical examples, architectural descriptions, and two case studies, we demonstrate that GenAI materially accelerates detection and response (reducing MTTD/MTTR), augments analyst effectiveness via real-time assistance and automated narratives, and democratizes specialist knowledge for less experienced personnel.

However, GenAI adoption is not without substantive risks and open questions. Model hallucination, prompt and supply-chain attacks, model drift, privacy leakage, and the potential for automation overreliance require governance-first deployments: DPIAs, role-based access, continuous validation, and HITL checkpoints. The chapter therefore foregrounds assurance mechanisms, explainability, provenance tracking, and adversarial robustness testing, as prerequisites for trustworthy deployment rather than optional enhancements.

Looking forward, three strategic imperatives emerge. First, rigorous evaluation: research must deliver standardized benchmarks and realistic red-team datasets that reflect live adversary behavior without compromising operational confidentiality. Second, sociotechnical design: tools should be codeveloped with analysts to reduce cognitive load and ensure effective human–AI teaming. Third, regulatory and organizational alignment: compliance, procurement, and incident-management processes must evolve to accommodate model life-cycle controls and cross-functional governance.

In sum, GenAI offers a rare opportunity to transform SOCs from reactive monitoring entities into proactive, predictive defenders, provided adoption is governed by measurable objectives, layered assurance, and continuous human oversight. The chapter closes by urging an interdisciplinary agenda, combining technical research, operational experimentation, policy development, and ethical review, so that GenAI's promise to strengthen cyber resilience is realized without compromising transparency, accountability, or public trust.

ACKNOWLEDGMENT

The authors confirm that GenAI tools, including ChatGPT-5 (OpenAI) and Copilot, were utilized to assist in the preparation of this book chapter. These tools were employed to support tasks such as language refinement and idea structuring. The authors have thoroughly reviewed, validated, and edited all AI-generated content to ensure accuracy, originality, and compliance with academic and ethical standards. The use of AI was limited to noncreative, non-interpretive tasks and did not replace the author's intellectual contribution.

REFERENCES

[1] A. A. Khan, "Digital forensics and cyber forensics investigation: security challenges, limitations, open issues, and future direction," *International Journal of Electronic Security and Digital Forensics*, vol. 14, no. 2, pp.124–150, 2022. doi: 10.1504/IJESDF.2022.121174

[2] A. Kumar, and V. L. L. Thing, *RAPTOR: Advanced Persistent Threat Detection in Industrial IoT via Attack Stage Correlation*. 2023, pp. 1–12. doi: 10.1109/pst58708.2023.10320192

[3] P. Gao, F. Shao, X. Liu, X. Xiao, H. Liu, Z. Qin, F. Xu, P. Mittal, S. R. Kulkarni, and D. Song, "A system for efficiently hunting for cyber threats in computer systems using threat intelligence," in *2022 IEEE 38th International Conference on Data Engineering (ICDE)*, pp. 2705–2708, Apr. 2021, doi: 10.1109/icde51399.2021.00309

[4] R. Puzis, P. Zilberman, and Y. Elovici, "ATHAFI: agile threat hunting and forensic investigation," *arXiv.org*, Mar. 07, 2020, doi:10.48550/arXiv.2003.03663

[5] P. Kuehn, M. Bayer, T. Frey, M. Kerk, and C. Reuter, "Reducing information overload: Because even security experts need to blink," *arXiv.org*, Oct. 25, 2022. doi: 10.48550/arXiv.2210.14067

[6] A. N. Prasad, "Regulatory compliance and risk management," in *Introduction to Data Governance for Machine Learning Systems: Fundamental Principles, Critical Practices, And Future Trends*. Berkeley, CA: Apress, 2024, pp. 485–624.

[7] B. Gelman, S. Taoufiq, T. Vörös, and K. Berlin, "That escalated quickly: an ML framework for alert prioritization," *arXiv.org*, Feb. 13, 2023. Available: https://arxiv.org/abs/2302.06648

[8] "ISC2 Cybersecurity Workforce Study: Looking Deeper into the Workforce Gap," International information system security certification consortium blog Nov. 03, 2023. www.isc2.org/Insights/2023/11/ISC2-Cybersecurity-Workforce-Study-Looking-Deeper-into-the-Workforce-Gap (accessed September 15, 2025).

[9] A. Hermann, *GPT Powered Log Analysis: Enhancing SOC Decision Making for Malicious and Benign Security Log Classification* (Doctoral dissertation, BS thesis). University of Twente, 2024.

[10] A. Loten, "AI-powered cybersecurity firm ReliaQuest raises more than $500 million," *WSJ, Mar.* 31, 2025. Available: www.wsj.com/articles/ai-powered-cybersecurity-firm-reliaquest-raises-more-than-500-million-96de3464 (accessed September 11, 2025).

[11] I. Khalid, and M. S. Purdie, *AI-Powered SOC Operations: Revolutionizing Cyber Security Incident Response and Management*, *ResearchGate*, 2024.

[12] "Threat Report ATT&CK Mapper (TRAM)," Center for Threat-Informed Defense. Aug. 2024. Available: https://ctid.mitre.org/projects/threat-report-attck-mapper-tram (accessed September 10, 2025).

[13] M. Uddin, M. S. Irshad, I. A. Kandhro, F. Alanazi, F. Ahmed, M. Maaz, ... and S. S. Ullah, Generative AI revolution in cybersecurity: a comprehensive review of threat intelligence and operations. *Artificial Intelligence Review*, vol. 58, no. 8, pp. 1–39, 2025.

[14] K. Y. Abeywardena, T. A. D. L. P. T. Arachchi, C. Y. S. Nanayakkara, J. M. I. P. Jayaweera, and D. R. B. Dissanayake, "Automating threat advisory report generation using threat intelligence," In *International Conference on Innovative Computing, Intelligent Communication and Smart Electrical Systems (ICSES)*, pp. 1–4, 2023, doi:10.1109/icses60034.2023.10465533

[15] Y. You, et al., "TIM: threat context-enhanced TTP intelligence mining on unstructured threat data," *Cybersecurity*, vol. 5, no. 1, p. 3, Feb. 2022, doi: 10.1186/s42400-021-00106-5

[16] D. Banswal, P. Chaudhari, and M. Landge, "Application of artificial intelligence in threat detection and malware analysis," in *International Conference on Cyber Security, Privacy in Communication Networks*, 2023, pp. 473–496, Singapore: Springer Nature Singapore.

[17] W. Kasri, et al., "From vulnerability to defense: the role of large language models in enhancing cybersecurity," *Computation*, vol. 13, no. 2, p. 30, Jan. 2025, doi: 10.3390/computation13020030

[18] R. Lemos, "Generative AI shows promise for faster triage of vulnerabilities," Feb. 27, 2025. Available: www.darkreading.com/application-security/gen-ai-accelerates-triage-of-software-vulnerabilities (accessed September 12, 2025).

[19] M. J. Torkamani, J. Ng, N. Mehrotra, M. Chandramohan, P. Krishnan, and R. Purandare, "Streamlining security vulnerability triage with large language models," *arXiv.org, Jan.* 31, 2025, doi: 10.48550/arXiv.2501.18908

[20] S. Basu, U. Singh, S. Sharma, G. A. S. Kumar, and R. Upadhyay, "Generative AI enabled actionable decision support in cyber security operations for enterprise security," In *ITU Kaleidoscope: Innovation and Digital Transformation for a Sustainable World (ITU K)*, pp. 1–8, Oct. 2024, doi: 10.23919/ituk62727.2024.10772892

[21] K. Subramanian, "Introducing the Splunk platform," in *In Practical Splunk Search Processing Language: A Guide for Mastering SPL Commands for Maximum Efficiency and Outcome.* Berkeley, CA: Apress, 2020, pp. 1–38, doi: 10.1007/978-1-4842-6276-4_1

[22] V. Dakić, Z. Morić, A. Kapulica, and D. Regvart, "Leveraging Microsoft sentinel and logic apps for automated cyber threat response," *Edelweiss Applied Science and Technology*, vol. 8, no. 6, pp. 4319–4348, Nov. 2024, doi: 10.55214/25768484.v8i6.2933

[23] I. Prieto, and B. Blakely, "Proposed uses of generative AI in a cybersecurity-focused soar agent," In *Proceedings of the AAAI Symposium Series,* vol. 2, no. 1, pp. 386–390. 2023.

[24] M. Ammi, "Cyber threat hunting case study using MISP," *Journal of Internet Services and Information Security*, vol. 13, no. 2, pp. 1–29, 2023, doi: 10.58346/jisis.2023.i2.001.

[25] "Anomali Security Analytics | Aggregate, search, and analyze vast amounts of data," Anomali. Available: www.anomali.com/products/security-analytics

[26] S. M. Muzammal, R. Bibi, H. Waseem, and M. Tayyab, "Empowering security analysts with generative AI tools," In *AI Techniques for Securing Medical and Business Practices.* IGI Global Scientific Publishing, pp. 101–130, 2025.

[27] "What is Microsoft Security Copilot?," Microsoft Learn, Jul. 2025. Available: https://learn.microsoft.com/en-us/copilot/security/microsoft-security-copilot (accessed September 12, 2025).

[28] Š. Grigaliūnas et al., "Navigating the CISO's mind by integrating GenAI for strategic cyber resilience," *Electronics*, vol. 14, no. 7, p. 1342, Mar. 2025, doi: 10.3390/electronics14071342.

[29] K. Curran, E. Curran, J. Killen, and C. Duffy, "The role of generative AI in cyber security," *Metaverse,* vol. 5, no. 2, pp. 2796, 2024, doi: 10.54517/m2796

[30] S. Chang, A. Kennedy, A. Leonard, and J. List, "12 best practices for leveraging generative AI in experimental research," *National Bureau of Economic Research*, no. w33025, 2024.
[31] R. Filho and D. Colares, "A methodology for risk management of generative AI based systems," In *International Conference on Software, Telecommunications and Computer Networks (SoftCOM)*, pp. 1–6, Sep. 2024, doi: 10.23919/softcom62040.2024.10721790
[32] R. Vadisetty and A. Polamarasetti, "Generative AI for cyber threat simulation and defense," In *12th International Conference on Control, Mechatronics and Automation (ICCMA)*, pp. 272–279, Nov. 2024, doi: 10.1109/iccma63715.2024.10843938
[33] V. R. Saddi, S. K. Gopal, S. Dhanasekaran, and M. Naruka, "Examine the role of generative AI in enhancing threat intelligence and cyber security measures," In *2nd International Conference on Disruptive Technologies (ICDT)*, pp. 537–542, 2024, doi: 10.1109/icdt61202.2024.10489766
[34] A. Khan, N. Z. Jhanjhi, G. A. Ali, S. K. Ray, and S. Wassan, "Case studies and applications of generative AI in real-world cybersecurity scenarios," In *AI Techniques for Securing Medical and Business Practices*. IGI Global Scientific Publishing, pp. 61–100, 2024, doi: 10.4018/979-8-3693-8939-3.ch003
[35] I. H. Sarker, "Generative AI and large language modeling in cybersecurity," In *AI-Driven Cybersecurity and Threat Intelligence: Cyber Automation, Intelligent Decision-Making and Explainability*, 2024, pp. 79–99. doi: 10.1007/978-3-031-54497-2_5
[36] S. Wen, "The power of generative AI in cybersecurity: opportunities and challenges," *Applied and Computational Engineering*, vol. 48, pp. 31–39, Mar. 2024, doi: 10.54254/2755-2721/48/20241095
[37] H. Chugh, "Cybersecurity in the age of generative AI: usable security & statistical analysis of ThreatGPT," *International Journal for Research in Applied Science and Engineering Technology*, *12*, pp.1–11. 2024, doi: 10.22214/ijraset.2024.57827
[38] Z. L. Teo, C. W. N. Quek, J. L. Y. Wong, and D. S. W. Ting, "Cybersecurity in the generative artificial intelligence era," *Asia-Pacific Journal of Ophthalmology*, vol. 13, no. 4, p. 100091, Jul. 2024, doi: 10.1016/j.apjo.2024.100091
[39] F. Silva, "Navigating the dual-edged sword of generative AI in cybersecurity," *Brazilian Journal of Development*, vol. 11, no. 1, pp. e76869, Jan. 2025, doi: 10.34117/bjdv11n1-062
[40] M. Khayat, E. Barka, M. A. Serhani, F. Sallabi, K. Shuaib, and H. M. Khater, 2025. Empowering security operation center with artificial intelligence and machine learning–a systematic literature review. *IEEE Access*, vol. 13, pp. 19162–19197, 2025.
[41] M. Baqar, R. Khanda, and S. Naqvi, "Self-healing software systems: lessons from nature, powered by AI," *arXiv.org*, Apr. 25, 2025
[42] L. Alevizos, "Automated cybersecurity compliance and threat response using AI, blockchain and smart contracts," *International Journal of Information Technology*, vol. 17, pp. 767–781, Dec. 2024, doi: 10.1007/s41870-024-02324-9
[43] M. Tan, K. Yamaguchi, A. Raney, V. Nockles, M. Leblanc, and S. Bendelac, *An AI Blue Team Playbook*. 2024, doi: 10.1117/12.3021908

Chapter 4

Generative AI for Indigenous cyber defence

Building sovereign digital resilience in the Global South

Tetiana Schipper and Boubiche Djallel Eddine

4.1 INTRODUCTION

The Global South is undergoing rapid digital transformation through digital identifications (IDs), health systems, relief platforms, and digital finance. These innovations promise inclusion, efficiency, and resilience. However, cybersecurity remains imported, reactive, and fragmented—posing risks to data sovereignty, trust, and long-term sustainability. Governments and non-governmental organisations (NGO) are rolling out digital IDs, e-health records, mobile money, and relief systems at unprecedented speed [1]. However, security frameworks are often externally designed, breach-driven, and poorly coordinated across sectors. Weak regulatory oversight exposes sensitive personal data—especially in health and finance—to significant risks [2]. Moreover, marginalised communities continue to face barriers to securing digital access due to low digital literacy and infrastructural gaps [3].

Modern research underscores the potential of AI and big data to shift cybersecurity from a reactive to a proactive discipline. The evidence includes a machine learning (ML)-driven framework to forecast cyber threats up to three years in advance, successfully forecasting cyberattack trends across 36 countries and 42 attack types [4]. Also, Salem et al. emphasise that AI-driven techniques such as deep learning and metaheuristics significantly enhance threat detection and adaptability, offering scalable solutions to counter emerging cyber risks [5]. To better understand the evolving role of AI in cybersecurity, Table 4.1 presents a comparative overview of prominent AI techniques.

While a wide spectrum of AI techniques contributes to cybersecurity, generative artificial intelligence (GAI) stands out for its dual-use potential—capable of both simulating threats and enabling proactive defence. Yet, the transformative power of GAI cannot be fully harnessed without addressing a critical dimension often overlooked in technical discourse: sovereignty. Sovereignty in this context refers to a nation or organisation's ability to independently control, govern, and secure its digital infrastructure, data, and AI systems [6]. This includes the capacity to develop, deploy, and regulate AI models locally, without relying on foreign platforms or opaque third-party algorithms. Without sovereign control, states risk becoming dependent on external technologies that may not align with their security priorities, legal frameworks, or ethical standards [7]. As emphasised at the Paris 2025 Summit on Inclusive and Sustainable Artificial Intelligence, the international community underscored that all nations must proactively assert their AI sovereignty by developing independent capacities for governance, innovation, and

DOI: 10.1201/9781003644231-6

Table 4.1 Comprehensive AI Techniques in Cybersecurity

AI Type	*Description*	*Proactive Use*	*Reactive Use*	*Risks/Limitations*
Generative AI (GAI)	Creates synthetic data, content, or simulations	Simulates attacks, builds honeypots, and forecasts adversarial behaviour	Generates phishing, deepfakes, and polymorphic malware	Dual-use risk; can be weaponised by attackers
Large Language Models (LLM)	Understands and generates human-like language	Automates threat intelligence, analyses logs, and generates policies	Summarises alerts, assists teams	Prompt injection, hallucinations
Agentic AI Systems	Autonomous agents that plan, reason, and act towards goals	Conducts autonomous threat hunting, adapts defences	Executes incident response, triages alerts	Unpredictable behaviour; oversight needed
Machine Learning (ML)	Learns patterns from structured data	Predicts anomalies, models behaviour	Detects known threats	Needs labelled data; adversarial vulnerability
Deep Learning (DL)	Neural networks for complex pattern recognition	Detects zero-day threats, automates intrusion detection	Malware classification, traffic analysis	High compute cost; opaque decision-making
Reinforcement Learning	Learns via trial and error	Optimises defence strategies over time	Adapts to attacker behaviour	Slow training; exploration risks
Adversarial Learning	Models attacker–defender dynamics	Tests system robustness, simulates adversarial attacks	Detects adversarial inputs	Can be exploited by attackers
Metaheuristics	Optimisation algorithms for model tuning	Enhances detection models, adapts to evolving threats	Refines existing systems	Less interpretable; slower convergence
Federated Learning	Decentralised model training across devices	Shares threat intelligence while preserving privacy	Localised detection without central data	Data heterogeneity; communication overhead
Transfer Learning	Applies knowledge from one domain to another	Speeds up training on new threats	Enhances detection in low-data environments	Domain mismatch issues

(*Continued*)

Table 4.1 (Continued)

AI Type	*Description*	*Proactive Use*	*Reactive Use*	*Risks/Limitations*
Explainable AI (XAI)	Makes AI decisions interpretable	Builds trust in proactive systems	Diagnoses failures in reactive systems	Trade-off between accuracy and interpretability
Natural Language Processing (NLP)	Understands and processes human language	Detects social engineering, analyses logs	Filters spam, phishing detection	Language ambiguity; multilingual complexity

regulation, rather than deferring responsibility to others or relying on external technological frameworks [8].

In light of this requirement, the following research questions are addressed in this study:

- What are the strategic, economic, and security imperatives for adopting GAI in the Global South?
- What governance, technological, and geopolitical measures are necessary to ensure that GAI delivers sustainable benefits while minimising risks in the Global South?

GAI introduces new layers of complexity: its models are often trained on global datasets, hosted on cloud infrastructures outside national jurisdiction, and governed by corporate policies that may conflict with public interest, specifically in the Global South [9]. Therefore, this research argues that GAI can enable proactive cyber defence—but only if localised and sovereign capacity is developed. Sovereign AI infrastructure ensures that threat modelling, anomaly forecasting, and adversarial simulation are not only technically robust but also politically and ethically accountable.

4.2 CONCEPTUAL FRAMEWORK: PROACTIVE CYBER DEFENCE VS. REACTIVE CYBERSECURITY

Traditional reactive cybersecurity—dependent on firewalls, signature-based detection, and post-incident response—struggles to keep pace with today's fast-evolving, AI-driven threats. These systems often detect breaches only after damage is done, leaving organisations vulnerable to zero-day exploits and sophisticated attacks. As cyber threats grow in complexity and scale, this lag in response time becomes a critical liability. GAI offers a transformative solution by enabling proactive defence: simulating potential attack vectors, forecasting anomalies, and modelling adversarial behaviour before threats materialise. By anticipating and neutralising risks in advance, GAI has the potential for shifting cybersecurity from a defensive posture to a predictive, adaptive, and resilient strategy.

GAI offers a strategic advantage in proactive cyber defence by simulating realistic attack scenarios, crafting adaptive honeypots, and generating synthetic threat intelligence data to train and stress-test security systems. Unlike discriminative AI, which relies on predefined patterns to classify known threats, GAI can anticipate novel attack vectors by mimicking adversarial behaviour—making it ideal for red-teaming, phishing detection, and vulnerability forecasting [10]. GAI enhances incident response, accelerates patching workflows,

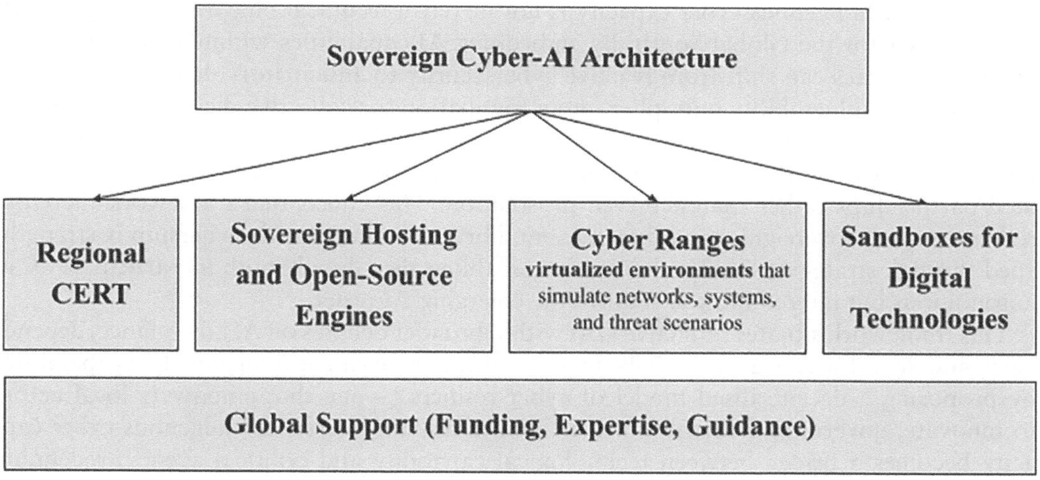

Figure 4.1 Four Main Components of Sovereign Cyber-AI Architecture.

and empowers threat hunters with dynamic, context-aware insights that go beyond static classification models [11, 12].

However, the same capabilities that strengthen defence can also empower offence. AI can detect and patch vulnerabilities rapidly but also lowers the barriers for malicious actors to execute sophisticated attacks. As AI systems grow more capable and autonomous, they increasingly influence both sides of the cyber domain, amplifying the speed, precision, and scale of digital conflict [13, 14].

To ensure that proactive GAI strengthens rather than destabilises national security in the Global South, this framework introduces the concept of Indigenous cyber capacity, based on a proposed Sovereign Cyber-AI architecture. It includes regional Computer Emergency Response Teams (CERT), sovereign hosting and open-source engines, cyber ranges, and AI sandboxes designed for contextual adaptation and resilience testing (Figure 4.1).

This architecture prioritises data and model sovereignty, ensuring that AI-driven threat detection, attribution, and response systems are trained on locally relevant datasets rather than imported Western benchmarks. Through regional CERT alliances (such as ASEAN CERT, AfricaCERT, or SAARC-CERT), member states can pool analytical resources and share early-warning intelligence without compromising national control over sensitive cyber data.

Cyber ranges act as the operational training layer of this ecosystem. These simulated environments allow cybersecurity teams to rehearse responses to ransomware, disinformation attacks, and AI-enhanced intrusions under conditions that mirror regional threat realities. Complementing them, AI sandboxes serve as controlled environments for red-teaming and algorithmic testing, where local researchers and defence agencies can audit, stress-test, and fine-tune generative models before deployment in live systems.

At the infrastructural level, the framework promotes sovereign data centres that host open-source AI threat engines—reducing dependency on proprietary Western cybersecurity vendors and mitigating the geopolitical risk of backdoors or sanctions-based access restrictions. Combined, these measures foster technological autonomy and cyber governance ownership, empowering states to build defences that align with domestic data-protection laws and digital ethics frameworks.

Ultimately, Indigenous cyber capacity is not merely a technical blueprint but a geopolitical equaliser for the Global South. By embedding AI capabilities within local governance ecosystems, states can shift from reactive cybersecurity to anticipatory defence, transforming AI from a vulnerability multiplier into a foundation for collective digital resilience. Yet, these sovereign pillars remain scaffolded by external funding, expertise, and institutional networks, revealing that sovereignty, in practice, is co-constructed through globally mediated partnerships rather than achieved in isolation. This conceptual framework therefore redefines cyber sovereignty as a dynamic equilibrium—where local ownership is strengthened through strategic global collaboration, enabling the Global South to participate as an autonomous but interconnected actor in the emerging AI order.

This framework situates proactive GAI within broader debates on AI governance, dependency, and digital sovereignty. It challenges the structural asymmetry in global AI capabilities by proposing a decentralised model of cyber resilience—one that empowers local actors to innovate, govern, and defend on their own terms. In this sense, Indigenous cyber capacity becomes a bridge between technological capability and political agency, redefining proactive cybersecurity not merely as a technical innovation but as a strategic assertion of digital self-determination.

4.3 SOVEREIGNTY AND THE SHIFTING GEOGRAPHY OF AI LABOR

Historically, the Global South has served as a reservoir of outsourced human capital for the digital economy, particularly in low-skill, labour-intensive tasks such as data annotation, content moderation, and customer support. These roles, while essential to the development of AI systems, have often been undervalued and structurally dependent on external platforms and clients. The rise of GAI threatens to further marginalise this labour model by automating many of the very tasks that were previously outsourced—effectively displacing the Global South's foothold in the AI value chain.

GAI is not neutral in its design or deployment. It is largely developed by and for wealthy nations, with infrastructure, computing, and governance frameworks tailored to their priorities. In this context, GAI functions as a solution to labour shortages and cost pressures in the Global North, while simultaneously undermining the economic role of the Global South as a provider of digital labour.

This shift calls for a fast and strategic response from developing countries. They need to adapt quickly to the changing job landscape and avoid becoming even more dependent on wealthier nations. The current situation is that countries with strong infrastructure, widespread access to devices, and coordinated policies are adopting AI at much higher rates—these are all signs of national capacity and readiness. The uneven global adoption of AI is depicted in Figure 4.2. Just 15% of people of working age use AI on average. But in places like the United Arab Emirates (UAE) and Singapore, that number jumps to nearly 60%. In contrast, South Asia and Sub-Saharan Africa have much lower rates, highlighting a persistent digital divide [15].

The most urgent risk is not simply economic displacement but also the outsourcing of governance itself. As AI increasingly mediates public services, legal processes, and security operations, dependence on foreign-built models and cloud infrastructures places critical national functions under external influence. Geopolitical leverage, citizen trust, and state legitimacy now hinge on the control of digital infrastructures [16].

A sharp risk asymmetry persists: Northern frameworks assume resilience, while many Southern systems face "first-wave cyber breaches" without redundancy or recovery capacity

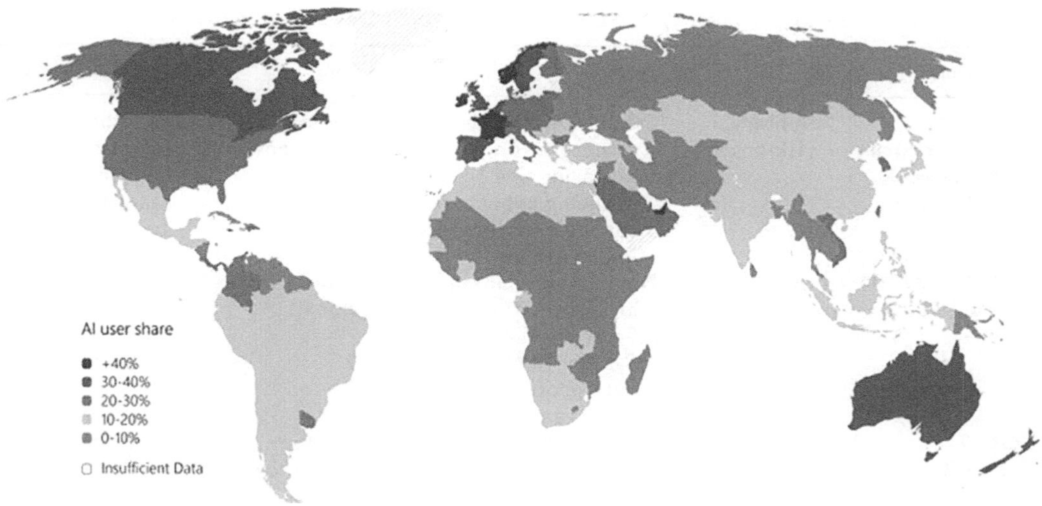

Figure 4.2 Global Distribution of AI Adoption Rates by Economy [15].

[17–19]. These frameworks are built for contexts with mature infrastructure, consistent funding, and strong institutions—conditions rarely mirrored in the Global South. Limited resources, fragmented coordination, and weak fallback mechanisms leave Southern systems vulnerable to early, large-scale cyberattacks that exploit undersecured networks.

The INTERPOL (2024) Asia and South Pacific Cyberthreat Assessment underscores these disparities, pointing to gaps in law enforcement, technical expertise, and CERT collaboration as key enablers of exploitation [19]. Similarly, Ardebili et al. note that dominant resilience models assume automation and stability are unattainable in developing regions [18]. This structural imbalance exposes Global South states to a dual vulnerability—technological dependency and strategic exposure—within a cyber order that privileges already-resilient powers.

These asymmetries extend into cybersecurity governance, where most globally recognised frameworks originate in the Global North and reflect its institutional norms, regulatory traditions, and resource abundance. Table 4.2 outlines the main frameworks shaping international cybersecurity practice, highlighting their origins, objectives, and sectoral focus.

Given the centrality of digital public infrastructures (DPIs) to national stability, critical sectors now require proactive defence measures rather than reliance on vendor-issued cyber patches. Building Indigenous cyber capacity and real-time monitoring systems enables these infrastructures to evolve with, rather than lag behind, the threat landscape, ensuring that resilience is designed into systems rather than applied retroactively.

4.4 STRATEGIC DOMAINS WHERE GAI CAN ENABLE PROACTIVE DEFENCE

DPIs in the Global South are increasingly seen as high-value cyber targets, especially in sectors like health data, digital ID, welfare tech, and disaster relief finance. Health data contains sensitive personal and biometric information, which is valuable for identity theft, insurance fraud, and geopolitical leverage. Health systems in low-resource settings are vulnerable to ransomware and data breaches due to legacy infrastructure and a lack of cyber

Table 4.2 Overview of Dominant Cybersecurity Frameworks Developed in the Global North [20]

Framework	*Type*	*Purpose*	*Sector*	*Origin*
NIST Cybersecurity Framework (CSF 2.0)	Voluntary, risk-based	Establish a flexible structure for managing and reducing cyber risk through continuous improvement	Cross-industry (public and private)	United States (National Institute of Standards and Technology)
ISO/IEC 27001 and 27002	International certifiable standard	Define and maintain an Information Security Management System (ISMS) for data protection and governance	All industries (global)	International (ISO—International Organisation for Standardisation)
SOC 2 (Type 2)	Auditable assurance framework	Demonstrate secure data management and control effectiveness for service providers	Technology, finance, cloud services	United States (AICPA—American Institute of Certified Public Accountants)
NERC-CIP	Regulatory, sector-specific	Protect critical infrastructure and operational technology assets in the energy grid	Utilities and energy	North America (North American Electric Reliability Corporation)
HIPAA Security Rule	Regulatory, sector-specific	Safeguard electronic protected health information (ePHI) and ensure healthcare data confidentiality	Healthcare and insurance	United States (Department of Health and Human Services)
GDPR (General Data Protection Regulation)	Regulatory, privacy-focused	Protect personal data and privacy rights of individuals; enforce data governance and breach accountability	All organisations processing EU citizen data	European Union
FISMA (Federal Information Security Management Act)	Regulatory, government-focused	Ensure federal agencies and contractors protect government information systems	Public-sector and government contractors	United States (Congress, aligned with NIST standards)

hygiene [21]. Also, digital ID systems are central to accessing government services, voting, and financial inclusion, and breaches can lead to mass identity theft or surveillance. For instance, India's Aadhaar system has faced multiple security challenges, highlighting risks of centralised ID systems [22]. Additionally, welfare technology manages the disbursement of subsidies, pensions, and social benefits. Attacks can disrupt livelihoods and erode trust in governance. Platforms for disaster relief financing, which manage large transaction volumes during emergencies, could be targeted by cybercriminals. These systems are vulnerable to abuse and disruption due to the urgency of aid delivery, which restricts oversight [23]. Similar to financial institutions, their scale and speed attract malicious actors seeking to exploit vulnerabilities [24]. In the Global South, weak coordination between humanitarian tech actors and national cybersecurity agencies heightens this risk, leading to potential delays and misallocation of aid [25]. Transparency tools such as blockchain, while improving accountability, further expand the attack surface for adversaries [26].

4.4.1 Digital health sovereignty and synthetic threat simulation

In the domain of digital health sovereignty, these capabilities are especially crucial, as sensitive medical data and national health systems become high-value cyber targets [27–29]. Initiatives such as India's Ayushman Bharat Digital Mission (ABDM), formerly the Digital Health Mission, and the PhilHealth digitisation drive in the Philippines demonstrate both the promise and the fragility of digital transformation in healthcare, where proactive AI defence could determine the difference between resilience and systemic collapse.

Under ABDM, India has implemented a robust cybersecurity framework that includes consent-based data exchange, mandatory sandbox testing, and Web Application Security Audits (WASA) for all digital health applications. The mission also promotes interoperability through the Health Information Exchange and Consent Manager (HIECM) and Unified Health Interface (UHI), alongside the adoption of Electronic Health Record (EHR) standards via the National Resource Centre for EHR Standards [30]. These measures aim to secure patient data while bridging digital literacy gaps through multilingual platforms and offline access.

However, the most persistent challenge to scaling India's digital healthcare ecosystem remains the uneven technological and infrastructural landscape. Urban centres benefit from enhanced connectivity, higher digital literacy, and concentrated investment, while many rural regions continue to face unreliable internet access and outdated IT infrastructure. Despite over 400 million rural internet subscribers as of 2024, connectivity quality and stability remain inadequate to sustain comprehensive digital health services [31].

On the other side, following a ransomware attack that potentially exposed data of millions of Filipinos [32], PhilHealth is now integrating AI for cybersecurity, claims adjudication, and database clean-up [33]. With full deployment anticipated by 2027, the AI implementation is a component of a larger digital transformation strategy. To educate members about these new digital safeguards, nationwide education campaigns are in progress. PhilHealth has announced its collaboration with the Department of Information and Communications Technology (DICT), signalling a preference for local providers. However, the Philippine cybersecurity market is shaped by a dynamic mix of regional and international players, with leading solutions often sourced from global vendors [34]. The Cybercrime Prevention Act and the National Cybersecurity Plan are driving both public- and private-sector investment in AI-enhanced security infrastructure. However, despite this strong government push, local providers may struggle to keep pace with international vendors that dominate the market with advanced, scalable solutions [35–37].

Moreover, AI-powered fraud in Asia-Pacific's (APAC) healthtech sector surged 723% year-on-year in 2025, making it the region's most vulnerable industry. As healthcare services digitise, cybercriminals exploit system weaknesses using deepfakes and synthetic identity documents to bypass verification and access sensitive records. Singapore and Hong Kong saw deepfake fraud rise by 1,500% and 1,900%, respectively. Synthetic identity fraud grew 233% across APAC, with the Philippines experiencing a 291% increase [38–40]. Experts emphasise that synthetic identity theft's ability to mimic legitimate behaviour and bypass traditional systems demands adaptive, multi-layered defences to safeguard digital health infrastructure. Healthcare systems can better withstand cyber threats by building transformative, adaptive, and absorptive capacities that enable them to anticipate, respond to, and recover from digital disruptions [41].

Here, GAI can function as both a shield and a simulation engine. Its ability to create adversarial scenarios, model synthetic anomalies, and run audit simulations enables health systems to anticipate and neutralise attacks before they occur [42]. For example, GAI can simulate data breaches or synthetic identity attacks under controlled conditions [43], exposing weaknesses in verification protocols or consent-based data systems. These synthetic environments also allow institutions to stress-test digital infrastructure [44], evaluate response times, and refine mitigation strategies without risking real-world harm.

Yet, the promise of automation must be tempered by human oversight. Excessive reliance on algorithmic decision-making—as seen in the United States, where major insurers like UnitedHealth, Humana, and Cigna have been accused of using AI to deny claims within seconds [45]—illustrates the dangers of delegating human welfare to opaque systems. Automated denials, often overturned upon appeal, reveal how algorithmic efficiency can erode patient trust, ethical accountability, and institutional legitimacy.

A balanced integration of GAI requires embedding these systems within transparent data governance frameworks that preserve national autonomy over health information. Sovereign data control—supported by open standards, traceable model training, and human oversight—ensures that AI augments, rather than overrides, public accountability. In this sense, generative technologies not only simulate cyber threats but also reinforce digital health sovereignty, turning synthetic intelligence into a tool for anticipatory resilience rather than administrative control.

4.4.2 Digital ID and welfare systems

Digital identity systems in the Global South are rapidly evolving into infrastructures of both inclusion and control. By 2030, digital identity systems are projected to generate substantial economic value equal to 6% of gross domestic product (GDP) in emerging economies (EEs) (Figure 4.3). Approximately 65% of the benefits in EEs are anticipated to directly benefit individuals, and even simple digital ID systems with basic functions can unlock significant

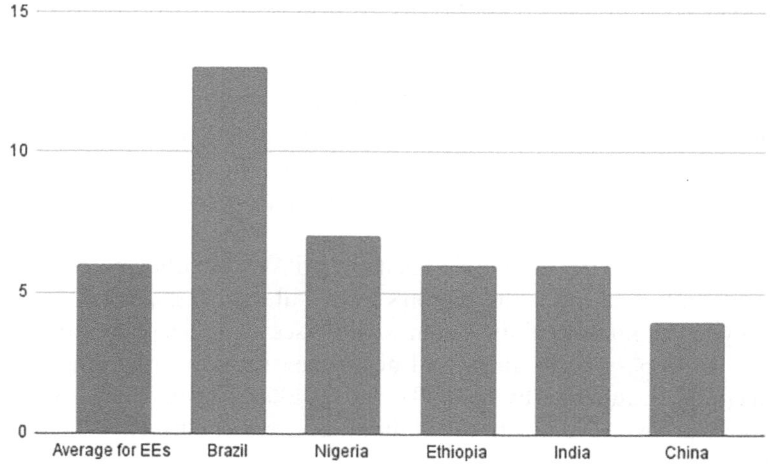

Figure 4.3 Increase in Economic Value from Digital ID in Selected Countries, % of GDP [47].

value in these markets. For instance, Brazil is building novel, indigenous DPI systems using open technologies, which allow it to leapfrog legacy infrastructure and rapidly expand financial inclusion and digital services. In contrast, India's DPI model is more mature, having already scaled foundational systems like Aadhaar and Unified Payments Interface (UPI), and is now focused on advanced layers such as data exchange and consent architecture [46]. This difference in maturity means Brazil has more untapped potential for economic gains, as it is still formalising and digitising large segments of its economy. In contrast, India has already captured much of the basic value from digital ID systems.

Chinese technology and investment are helping Brazil build the backbone needed for scalable digital public services. Brazil is increasingly involved in China's Digital Silk Road initiative, which aims to expand Chinese influence in global digital infrastructure through investments in 5G, cloud computing, and smart city technologies [48, 49]. While cooperation is growing, some analysts and policymakers express concerns about data security, digital sovereignty, and geopolitical influence stemming from Chinese involvement in Brazil's digital infrastructure [50].

In China, digital identity is deeply embedded in a vast surveillance ecosystem powered by facial recognition, AI, and centralised data platforms. These technologies are not only used for service delivery but also for real-time monitoring of citizens, social credit scoring, and predictive policing. China's governance model leverages digital infrastructure to centralise power, suppress dissent, and shape public behaviour [51]. The rise of "data-centric authoritarianism" is transforming how autocrats globally manage control [52]. Under the new "internet ID" regulation rolled out in July 2025, China's users register via a government app using a national ID plus facial recognition and receive a unified "web number" and certificate—essentially tying online behaviour across platforms to a single, state-controlled identifier [53]. China exports its surveillance technologies, including Safe City systems, to countries across Asia, Africa, and Eastern Europe. These systems normalise state omnipresence and redefine privacy, embedding authoritarian control under the guise of modernisation [54]. For instance, African governments actively seek Chinese surveillance tools to address domestic challenges like crime, terrorism, and infrastructure deficits—not just because of Chinese influence. Chinese platforms are often more affordable and come with soft loans, making them attractive to resource-constrained governments. Technologies like Huawei's Safe City systems are deployed to enhance urban security, traffic management, and service delivery. Many African countries adopt these tools without robust data protection laws or public consent, raising concerns about privacy and misuse. Surveillance systems are embedded in public–private partnerships, with Chinese firms often managing technical operations, creating dependency. The spread of these technologies has consequences for civil liberties, cybersecurity, and global norms around surveillance and data governance [55]. In Zimbabwe, Chinese firm CloudWalk Technology Co., Ltd. signed agreements with the government to build a national facial recognition and monitoring system, including installations at airports, border posts, and transport hubs [56], a "win-win" situation from China's perspective, delivering technology export and biometric data for algorithm training [57]. Also, North Korea, while technologically less advanced, has intensified its digital surveillance efforts by importing Chinese technologies such as biometric systems and surveillance cameras. These tools are deployed in schools, workplaces, and border zones to monitor behaviour and prevent unauthorised movement [58].

These exports show how technology transfers can reshape governance models, creating new dependencies and power asymmetries in states with weaker regulatory systems. As digital identity systems become tied to welfare, health, and taxation databases, the boundary between service delivery and surveillance grows increasingly blurred. This convergence exposes a state–citizen cybersecurity gap, where citizens are digitised faster than they are protected, and where trust depends on the state's ability to safeguard the very systems it uses to govern.

Southeast Asia offers a more complex landscape because digital ID initiatives are framed around inclusion, service delivery, and economic integration, yet often evolve within weak data governance frameworks. Across ASEAN, digital ID systems are double-edged infrastructures. They promise efficient governance, interoperability, and regional digital integration under the ASEAN Digital Masterplan 2025, yet risk entrenching new forms of "soft surveillance" if not backed by strong privacy legislation and citizen-centric cybersecurity mechanisms [59]. The challenge lies in ensuring that digital identity remains a tool of empowerment rather than control—especially as regional interoperability efforts may expose weaker national systems to cross-border vulnerabilities [60].

In Singapore, the SingPass system exemplifies a high-trust, state-led digital ID model enabling seamless access to over 2,000 public and private services, from healthcare to housing. Its success relies on strong cybersecurity measures and transparent data protection laws [61]. However, the system's integration with financial and biometric data raises ongoing concerns about state overreach and algorithmic bias [62].

By contrast, Malaysia's MyKad—a smart national identity card combining citizenship, driving licence, and banking access—illustrates the tension between efficiency and privacy [63]. While it has streamlined welfare delivery and e-payments, civil society groups have criticised the lack of independent oversight and limited user control over personal data [64].

In Indonesia, the NIK (Nomor Induk Kependudukan)—a national identity number used across government and private platforms—anchors e-governance and welfare programmes such as BPJS (social security and health insurance). However, repeated data leaks revealed millions of citizens' records, underscoring the fragility of state data infrastructures and eroding public trust [65].

GAI can serve as a critical tool to address this gap. It can stress-test identity databases by simulating adversarial attacks that exploit synthetic identities or data linkage vulnerabilities [66, 67]. GAI can also model disinformation overlays on welfare benefit disbursement to expose weaknesses in citizen-facing cybersecurity. It is already capable of creating fake government messages, phishing campaigns, or coordinated scam operations that mimic official communication [68]. If synthetically simulated, it allows states to preempt social engineering threats that target low-digital-literacy populations, which are often the same groups most reliant on digital welfare systems [69].

When combined with robust data governance and human oversight, GAI-driven threat simulation can help governments move from reactive containment to anticipatory defence—closing the divide between identity politics and cybersecurity by aligning technological sovereignty with citizen trust.

4.4.3 Corruption

Corruption remains a significant challenge across the Global South, with many countries scoring below 50 on the Corruption Perceptions Index (CPI) from World Population Review (2025), indicating high perceived levels of public-sector corruption [70]. The CPI ranks countries from 0 (highly corrupt) to 100 (very clean), and most Global South nations fall in the lower half of the scale (Figure 4.4). For instance, the growing anger over the

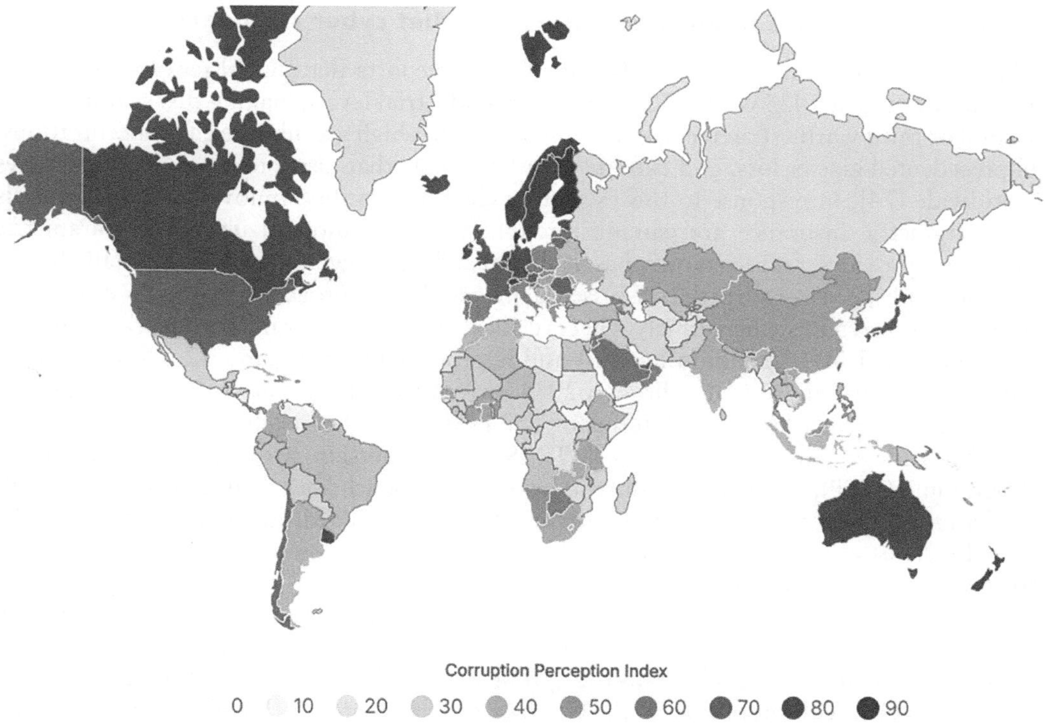

Figure 4.4 Corruption Perceptions Index by Country 2025 [70].

misuse of public funds, especially in disaster-prone areas where infrastructure failures have deadly consequences, led to a wave of protests in the Philippines in September and November 2025. Typhoon Kalmaegi devastated the central Philippines in November 2025, killing over 114 people and displacing thousands. Many blamed the scale of destruction on corrupt flood-control contracts, which failed to protect vulnerable communities [71]. Moreover, growing voices of the new generation, widely known as Gen Z, across Asia are driving transformative political movements by leveraging digital platforms to challenge corruption, authoritarianism, and economic inequality, with notable successes in Nepal, Bangladesh, and Sri Lanka. Experts suggest this activism marks a generational shift towards decentralised, goal-driven protest culture that could reshape governance across the region [72].

AI is emerging as a powerful tool to combat corruption in the Global South, where weak institutions and opaque systems often hinder accountability. By automating oversight, analysing procurement data, and flagging irregularities, AI can help governments detect and prevent corruption at scale. A bold example comes from Albania, which in 2025 appointed a virtual AI minister named Diella to ensure that public tenders are "100 per cent corruption-free", using algorithmic oversight to detect anomalies and enforce transparency [73]. This move symbolises a shift from reactive anti-corruption efforts—like mass protests in the Philippines over flood-related graft—to proactive digital governance, where technology is embedded directly into decision-making processes.

4.4.4 AI in climate finance and disaster relief cyber resilience

The State of the Climate 2025 Update for COP30 reports that global temperatures from January to August 2025 were 1.42°C above pre-industrial levels, making this year likely the second or third warmest on record. It highlights record-high greenhouse gas concentrations, unprecedented glacier loss, and extreme weather events that disrupted lives and economies worldwide [74]. In response to this escalating climate volatility, innovative financial tools like parametric insurance are gaining traction. Unlike traditional insurance, parametric insurance provides rapid payouts based on predefined triggers—such as rainfall thresholds or wind speeds—rather than assessed damages. This approach is especially valuable in disaster-prone regions where timely relief is critical. The global parametric insurance market was valued at USD16.2 billion in 2024 and is projected to grow at a 12.6% Compound Annual Growth Rate (CAGR) through 2034, driven by both climate risk and advances in digital technologies like AI, the Internet of Things (IoT), and blockchain [75]. For instance, Weather Risk Management Services (WRMS), in partnership with the UN World Food Programme (WFP), launched parametric insurance pilot schemes in Iraq to protect smallholder farmers and micro-entrepreneurs from climate risks like drought and heatwaves. The model increases the precision of risk assessment and payout computation by utilising data from weather stations and satellites [76].

Additionally, cash transfer programmes, including mobile money platforms that function as e-wallets, are emerging as effective tools for strengthening economic resilience through direct financial aid—especially in disaster-prone regions. In Uganda, the Uganda Red Cross Society (URCS), with support from the German Red Cross and the International Federation of Red Cross and Red Crescent Societies (IFRC), implemented a pilot programme to deliver emergency cash assistance to households affected by floods and landslides. In 2020, URCS disbursed UGX88 million to over 245 families in Mbale District using MTN Mobile Money and Airtel Money, enabling recipients to meet urgent needs such as food, healthcare, and education. This digital delivery mechanism ensured rapid, dignified, and flexible support. Post-distribution surveys revealed that over 85% of beneficiaries preferred cash over traditional in-kind aid, citing autonomy and faster recovery as key benefits [77].

Parametric insurance and e-wallet disbursement systems are increasingly used in the Global South to deliver rapid aid. AI is already improving the predictability of heatwaves and cyclones, mapping land degradation, and modelling forest fire risks. Financially, AI helps convert complex climate-biodiversity-land (CBL) data into decision-ready metrics, making resilience projects more attractive to investors. Explainable AI (XAI) is emphasised as crucial for building trust in automated decisions, especially when guiding capital flows in climate-vulnerable regions [78]. However, these systems rely on automated triggers (e.g., rainfall thresholds) and mobile payments, which are vulnerable to data breaches, identity fraud, and infrastructure outages during chaos windows. So, on April 17, 2022, the Conti ransomware group launched a coordinated cyberattack in Costa Rica. The attack occurred during Easter weekend, a time of reduced staffing and heightened vulnerability [79, 80]. Moreover, events like wildfires, hurricanes, and floods open "chaos windows" that bad actors exploit. During these periods, organisations often deprioritise data security, making them vulnerable to identity theft, fraudulent insurance claims, fake donation schemes, and social engineering attacks. For example, fraudsters pretended to be contractors or relatives of the deceased in order to steal money after Hurricane Ida and the Maui wildfires [81].

GAI enhances cyber resilience by simulating disaster-driven attack patterns before they occur, allowing governments and humanitarian organisations to identify vulnerabilities in parametric insurance platforms, mobile-money systems, and identity-verification processes.

By generating synthetic scenarios—such as mass fraudulent claims, phishing campaigns mimicking official alerts, or network congestion during chaos windows—GAI stress-tests digital infrastructure under realistic crisis conditions. It also supports anomaly detection by modelling what legitimate transactions should look like during emergencies, enabling faster flagging of manipulated triggers or compromised accounts. Through these capabilities, GAI shifts disaster-finance security from reactive protection to proactive, anticipatory defence.

4.5 BUILDING LOCAL DEFENSIVE CAPACITY: A SOVEREIGN CYBER AI ARCHITECTURE

A credible path to cyber resilience in the Global South begins with institutions that are regional by design, locally governed, and technically sovereign. Rather than relying on imported black-box "threat feeds" from Western vendors—which often provide limited contextual relevance—states can build a layered cyber architecture anchored in national Computer Security Incident Response Teams (CSIRTs). Evidence from the World Bank shows that between 2014 and 2024, support to 64 countries enabled teams in Bhutan, Bangladesh, and Ghana to act as effective digital first responders. These teams enhanced detection, response, and cross-sector coordination. Beyond incident management, CSIRTs contribute to trust-building, civil service training, and public awareness, illustrating that cyber resilience is inseparable from institutional capacity and community engagement [82].

4.5.1 Regional CERTs for trust and operational speed

Regional CERTs amplify national efforts by improving coordination and response times across borders. In 2024, Singapore launched an ASEAN Regional CERT to safeguard cross-border critical infrastructure in banking, telecoms, aviation, and maritime sectors. These initiatives can be strengthened by small, fine-tuned language models trained on regional telemetry, offering context-specific threat detection rather than generic global intelligence [83].

Complementing these efforts, the Asia Pacific Computer Emergency Response Team (APCERT) conducts annual cybersecurity drills. For example, a recent illustrative scenario simulated advanced persistent threat (APT) attacks involving AI-enhanced ransomware and tested the incident response capabilities of 24 CSIRTs from 18 APAC economies. This demonstrates that regional teams can co-develop operational playbooks for AI-enabled threats, fostering collaboration and preparedness that national teams alone cannot achieve [84].

4.5.2 Sovereign AI infrastructure and open-source engines

Sovereign AI ecosystems reduce dependency on foreign vendors and strengthen local capacity. In Kenya, the Centre of Competence for Digital and Artificial Intelligence Skilling—a partnership between the Kenyan government, UNDP, and Microsoft—enhances digital literacy, develops local tech ecosystems, and promotes inclusive access to AI tools. Complementing this, a geothermal-powered AI campus, backed by Microsoft and Abu Dhabi-based G42, anchors regional computing capacity under national oversight.

In Nigeria, the AI Scaling Hub, established in June 2025 with support from the Gates Foundation, accelerates AI adoption in agriculture, healthcare, and education. By leveraging open-source models, the hub develops cost-effective, culturally relevant solutions, such as crop monitoring, telemedicine, disease detection, and adaptive learning platforms in local languages. Microsoft's commitment to upskill one million Nigerians by 2027 further reinforces sovereign AI capabilities, reducing reliance on foreign expertise [85].

4.5.3 Cyber ranges: from theory to practice

Cyber ranges transform abstract cybersecurity knowledge into operational skills. These virtualised environments simulate ransomware, data breaches, and AI-enhanced attacks, allowing teams to practise detection, response, and recovery in realistic conditions. For the Global South, cyber ranges provide a scalable and affordable pathway to close capability gaps, especially in contexts of constrained budgets, skills shortages, and fragmented infrastructure. Cloud-based architectures deliver repeatable, context-specific training, strengthening both technical expertise and organisational readiness [86].

Regional or shared cyber-range facilities—modelled on distributed, cloud-native designs—reduce costs further while enabling collective training, threat intelligence sharing, and scenario development relevant to local critical infrastructure. The Latin America and Caribbean Cyber Competence Centre (LAC4) in the Dominican Republic operates a hybrid facility with a regional cyber range that supports multi-country simulations and incident-response exercises using EU-developed training materials.

4.5.4 Sandboxes: controlled experimentation for emerging technologies

After establishing foundational resilience, sandboxes enable safe experimentation with emerging technologies, including AI and robotics. Robotic systems in healthcare, manufacturing, and autonomous vehicles are vulnerable to buffer overflows, sensor spoofing, and AI manipulation. Regional CERTs must understand these risks to safeguard digital sovereignty.

Developing these capabilities requires robust infrastructure, skilled talent, and sustained investment—resources often limited in the Global South due to uneven internet access, inconsistent electricity, and underfunded research ecosystems [87, 88]. To reduce dependence on global data, regionally trained ML models can detect anomalies and simulate localised threats within sovereign sandboxes [89].

Kazakhstan provides a compelling example: in partnership with its Ministry of Digital Development and the AI Fund, the country is drafting legislation for an "experimental regime" that allows sandboxing of digital technologies within national law, supported by UN frameworks. This illustrates how locally governed sandboxes enable agile, sovereign experimentation while balancing innovation with security and legal oversight [90].

4.5.5 Reality of digital nationalism in a globalised world: cyber-AI capacity-building in EEs

Together, CSIRTs, regional CERTs, sovereign AI infrastructure, cyber ranges, and sandboxes form a Sovereign Cyber-AI Architecture—a system that is affordable, auditable, and adaptable, anchored in local law, powered by regional data, and strengthened through strategic partnerships. Yet, a closer analysis reveals a tension at the heart of Global South cyber development: while these initiatives advance sovereignty, they remain structurally intertwined with external actors, from the World Bank and Gates Foundation to EU frameworks and multinational tech partners. This duality illustrates a broader geopolitical logic: sovereignty is being constructed not in isolation, but in a negotiated interdependence, where external support simultaneously enables autonomy and introduces latent influence.

This dynamic underscores a critical insight: true cyber-AI sovereignty is not simply the absence of foreign assistance, but the capacity to strategically harness it. By selectively leveraging external expertise, funding, and infrastructure, Global South states can accelerate capacity-building while embedding locally relevant norms, governance frameworks, and technological priorities. This approach reframes dependency: it is instrumental, not passive, turning external engagement into a vector for self-determination rather than a constraint.

At a systemic level, there is also a global imperative to support these efforts. As emphasised at the Paris 2025 Summit on Inclusive and Sustainable Artificial Intelligence, nations must assert AI sovereignty to avoid reliance on external technological frameworks [8]. This reflects a subtle geopolitical calculus: supporting Global South AI and cyber capacity reduces the risks of ungoverned, globally interconnected threats, from AI-driven cyberattacks to digital monopolies. In effect, aiding the Global South is a strategic investment in stabilising global technological ecosystems, aligning national sovereignty with collective resilience.

Viewed through this lens, the Global South's trajectory challenges conventional narratives of globalisation. Rather than a linear diffusion of technology from the "developed" to the "developing" world, we see sovereignty emerging as a competitive and collaborative strategy—a form of digital nationalism that leverages selective internationalism. The architecture of CSIRTs, CERTs, sovereign AI hubs, cyber ranges, and sandboxes is not just a defensive posture; it is a strategic framework that transforms dependency into leverage, localises global knowledge, and reshapes the incentives of international cooperation.

In short, the pursuit of cyber-AI sovereignty in the Global South illustrates a paradoxical truth: autonomy is achieved not in isolation, but in the artful orchestration of interdependence, balancing national control with global engagement, and transforming external support from a potential constraint into a tool of strategic empowerment.

4.6 RISKS OF AI-DRIVEN OVER-SECURITISATION IN WEAK DEMOCRACIES

In recent years, the global cybersecurity landscape has been shaped not only by states but also by a diverse constellation of actors—NGOs documenting digital rights violations, technology companies setting platform standards, and even terrorist organisations adapting sophisticated cyber tactics. This shift illustrates a profound transformation: cybersecurity governance is no longer the exclusive domain of governments. Instead, it has become an evolving ecosystem where influence, authority, and expertise are distributed across public and private spheres. Research increasingly shows that modern cybersecurity frameworks depend on multi-stakeholder cooperation, informal norms, and public–private partnerships rather than rigid, state-centric models [91].

This pluralisation of power has often produced positive outcomes. Civil-society groups have pushed for transparency in algorithmic decision-making, while tech firms have developed tools to detect misinformation and fraud. But as the same AI-enhanced infrastructures spread into weak democracies—countries marked by fragile institutions, politicised security agencies, and limited checks on executive power—the story becomes more troubling. AI systems that promise protection against cyberattacks can just as easily be turned inward, strengthening state surveillance capabilities and shrinking the democratic space under the banner of "resilience", "national security", or "counter-disinformation" campaigns.

The quiet repurposing of AI-based cyber tools for political control does not emerge overnight. It develops gradually, through a series of technical upgrades, legal adjustments, and subtle administrative choices. Governments first adopt GAI to simulate cyberattack scenarios, stress-test critical infrastructure, and identify emerging threats before they materialise.

Officials often describe these tools as essential components of modern cyber defence—neutral, scientific, and evidence-based. But predictive models have a peculiar logic: they require vast quantities of data, including behavioural patterns, communication histories, or metadata extracted from social networks, financial platforms, and welfare systems. Once integrated, these data streams create a comprehensive picture of citizens' digital lives.

In contexts where democratic norms are already eroding, this architecture blurs the line between security and control. Anomaly-detection algorithms designed to identify intrusions into government servers can be recalibrated to flag "unusual" digital activity by individuals—such as rapid changes in online behaviour, use of encrypted messaging, or unexpected transaction patterns in digital-welfare platforms. Authorities can then portray such behaviour as suspicious, politically motivated, or indicative of hidden networks of subversion. The logic closely mirrors predictive policing: systems intended to prevent crime end up reinforcing biases embedded in their training data. If past security reports disproportionately focused on particular activist groups or ethnic minorities, AI systems trained on those datasets will mark similar communities as "high risk", perpetuating cycles of discrimination.

Weak democracies are particularly susceptible to this form of algorithmic drift. Institutions responsible for oversight—legislatures, audit commissions, ombuds offices—may lack the capacity or autonomy to interrogate complex AI tools. Civil society may be fragmented, underfunded, or intimidated. In such environments, the mere invocation of "AI-enhanced threat detection" can provide political cover for surveillance measures that might otherwise provoke public backlash. Authorities can claim that they are simply following the recommendations of technologically advanced systems, shifting responsibility from human decision-makers to opaque algorithms.

Evidence from countries with advanced surveillance capabilities illustrates the dangers of such opacity. In China, AI-generated "evidence" has already been deployed selectively in criminal trials, even though the quality of the underlying data and the validity of the models remain contested [92–95]. One of the most striking examples is Shanghai's "AI prosecutor", a system trained on thousands of historical cases to help prosecutors assess charges ranging from fraud to political dissent. Although presented as a tool for objectivity, it inevitably replicates existing legal and political biases [96]. If the historical dataset includes cases shaped by political pressures, then the AI inherits those pressures, embedding them into automated decision-making. Courts may treat algorithmic recommendations as authoritative, even when they reflect systemic flaws rather than genuine legal merit.

The lesson for weak democracies is clear: once AI is woven into the security apparatus, it becomes difficult to disentangle technical necessity from political intent. The systems themselves may appear neutral, but the environments in which they operate are not. This combination increases the risk that cybersecurity, originally framed as protection from external threats, becomes a conduit for internal repression.

Academic literature suggests that mitigating these risks requires strong oversight mechanisms, continuous monitoring, and formal verification frameworks for AI models [97]. Yet implementing such safeguards is far from straightforward. Global AI governance remains fragmented, and no international consensus exists on who has authority to regulate AI, what aspects of AI require oversight, or how governance should be applied across the system's entire lifecycle. Studies comparing high-risk industries—such as nuclear energy, aviation, or chemical manufacturing—show that these sectors have long-standing precedents for strict, evidence-driven oversight [98–101]. But AI differs fundamentally: it evolves rapidly, behaves unpredictably, and interacts deeply with social and political systems.

Much of the existing AI governance literature is conceptual rather than operational. Frameworks outline lofty principles—transparency, accountability, fairness—but provide limited instructions for implementation. Birkstedt et al. and Papagiannidis et al. highlight gaps between ethics discussions and organisational practice [102, 103]. Terms such as "responsible AI" or "human oversight" remain vague, and companies or governments often adopt these principles symbolically, without changing internal procedures. The result is a governance vacuum: states implement AI systems faster than they regulate them.

The International AI Safety Report 2025 reinforces these concerns. It warns that frontier AI systems exhibit emergent behaviours that cannot be reliably predicted or mitigated with current methods [104]. This uncertainty creates what policymakers describe as an "evidence dilemma": regulators wait for evidence of harm before acting, but by the time that evidence emerges, the damage—social, political, or economic—may already be irreversible. In weak democracies, this dilemma becomes particularly dangerous. Without robust institutions, governments may default to securitised approaches, deploying AI tools first and assessing risks later, while citizens lack channels to challenge abuses.

History offers ample examples of technologies introduced with good intentions but later repurposed for control. Security experts argue that reactive regulatory cycles repeatedly undermine society's ability to shape technological change [105]. Casper et al. similarly caution that demanding high levels of evidence before regulating AI masks real risks and delays necessary protections [106]. Their proposed solution is process-based rather than outcome-based governance. Instead of waiting for clear proof of harm, regulators would require transparency reports, model registration, documentation of training data, and detailed risk assessments. Such processes generate evidence continuously, enabling earlier interventions.

Another emerging critique concerns the dominant focus on "human-centred AI". Sigfrids et al. argue that this approach treats human rights as a protective layer rather than as an active, participatory component of governance [107]. As a result, communities—particularly in the Global South—are positioned as recipients of AI decisions rather than co-shapers of the systems that affect them. This passivity increases vulnerability; if marginalised groups cannot influence AI design or deployment, they cannot prevent systems from being used against them.

Recognising these gaps, several organisations have proposed adaptive, context-sensitive governance models. The Tony Blair Institute (2025) adapts such approaches for the Global South, emphasising that regulations must be clear, feasible, and iterative [108]. In regions with limited administrative capacity, the priority is not exhaustive regulation but practical mechanisms that can evolve over time—standardised reporting tools, simple auditing procedures, or phased risk assessments. Yet, Shetty et al. argue that even these adjusted frameworks face substantial implementation hurdles [109]. Effective governance requires strong institutions capable of enforcing disclosure requirements, coordinating data flows, mandating security audits, and supporting independent research. Where such institutions are weak or compromised, the best-designed frameworks falter.

Some countries are beginning to experiment with hybrid governance strategies that blend existing administrative structures with new oversight functions. Indonesia offers an illustrative case. Under its National AI Strategy (Stranas KA), AI oversight is partly integrated into established agencies such as Kominfo. On paper, this model promises efficiency and coherence. In practice, however, implementation remains fragmented. Capacity constraints—limited technical expertise, uneven coordination across ministries, and insufficient funding—slow the development of consistent standards. These challenges reflect a broader tension in many Global South countries: governments want to harness AI for economic development and security, but institutional realities lag behind political ambition.

Meanwhile, Global North regulations risk exporting compliance burdens that are misaligned with local contexts. The EU AI Act, while ambitious and comprehensive, may inadvertently create obstacles for countries with limited regulatory capacity or infrastructure. U.S. executive orders emphasise national security and supply-chain integrity, priorities that do not necessarily resonate with the developmental needs of the Global South. Scholars warn that such asymmetries could exacerbate global inequality, reinforce dependency on foreign technologies, or stifle local innovation ecosystems [110]. Civil-society participation also tends to be limited in early regulatory processes, deepening democratic deficits.

International initiatives are attempting to fill these gaps. The UN's Global Digital Compact proposes harmonised principles for digital governance, including the creation of an Independent International Scientific Panel on AI. It promotes global dialogue on AI safety, ethical frameworks, and interoperability across borders [111]. However, its effectiveness will depend heavily on national political will. Countries must invest in regulatory capacity, commit to transparency, and negotiate international standards that respect local realities rather than reproduce power imbalances.

Across all these discussions, the central challenge remains the same: AI holds enormous potential to strengthen cybersecurity, but in weak democracies, it can easily be weaponised. Over-securitisation does not always arrive dramatically; it often seeps into everyday governance through technical upgrades, inter-agency data sharing, and the normalisation of risk-scoring models. Preventing these trajectories requires more than technological safeguards. It demands political commitment, institutional resilience, independent oversight, and active participation from civil society.

Weak democracies face a crossroads. They can harness AI to fortify digital resilience and enhance trust in public institutions—or they can allow AI to entrench the very vulnerabilities they hope to overcome. The outcome will depend on how governments, regulators, and international partners navigate the trade-offs between security and freedom, innovation and oversight, and efficiency and accountability. AI does not determine this future. Human decisions do.

4.7 POLICY ROADMAP FOR GAI CYBER DEFENCE IN THE GLOBAL SOUTH

The rapid proliferation of AI-driven cyber threats presents a complex challenge for the Global South, where limited resources and dependency on foreign technologies can exacerbate vulnerabilities. A comprehensive policy roadmap must combine technical innovation, governance reform, and geopolitical strategy to build resilient, sovereign, and adaptive AI cyber defence capabilities.

4.7.1 Technical recommendations

At the core of an effective cyber defence strategy lies localised technological development. The Global South should prioritise the creation of local AI models tailored to regional threat landscapes, linguistic diversity, and regulatory contexts. These models should be trained on locally relevant datasets to detect and respond to cyber threats that global models may overlook. Complementing this, regional CERT alliances can facilitate rapid threat intelligence sharing, coordinated response strategies, and joint training exercises. By pooling expertise and resources, countries can reduce dependency on Western cybersecurity vendors and mitigate asymmetric threat risks. Additionally, the establishment of AI red-teaming labs provides a controlled environment for simulating adversarial attacks, penetration testing, and stress-testing defence algorithms. Such labs are critical for developing "muscle memory" in cyber teams and for iteratively improving AI detection and response systems before real-world deployment.

4.7.2 Governance recommendations

While the case studies discussed demonstrate the promise of GAI for enhancing digital sovereignty, they also reveal persistent challenges—such as infrastructural disparities that limit rural inclusion, heavy reliance on external cybersecurity vendors constraining autonomy, and governance weaknesses that expose these critical systems to privacy violations and political misuse. These cautionary lessons underscore that technical innovation must be paired with robust, context-sensitive governance, and capacity-building to truly realise sovereign digital resilience in the Global South.

Technical capacity should be paired with robust governance frameworks. Sovereignty over digital infrastructure is paramount: governments should invest in national and regional data centres that store sensitive cybersecurity intelligence and support AI development, reducing reliance on foreign cloud providers. Policies promoting open defence models—where threat detection algorithms, malware signatures, and AI defensive tools are shared transparently—can accelerate collective learning across the region while maintaining national security boundaries. Regulatory frameworks should mandate periodic audits of AI defence tools, establish clear accountability for AI-driven interventions, and implement mechanisms for citizen data protection.

Human oversight is essential for AI cyber defence systems to ensure ethical deployment, prevent over-reliance on automated decisions, and allow nuanced judgement in complex attack scenarios. Oversight in the Global South, however, faces structural limitations, including fragmented regulation, underfunded institutions, and limited digital literacy. Having more than 80% of the world's humans [112] does not automatically mean the Global South has 80% of the world's human oversight capacity. Achieving genuine accountability requires investment in institutional design, not mere inclusion in governance discourse.

4.7.3 Geopolitical recommendations

GAI cyber defence cannot be isolated from the broader geopolitical context. Countries in the Global South must actively engage in AI cyber defence diplomacy to establish norms, share best practices, and negotiate threat intelligence sharing agreements with regional and international partners. Strategic partnerships with other developing economies can foster collective resilience against AI-powered cyber threats while minimising the influence of major global tech powers. Moreover, regional blocs—such as ASEAN, AU, and SAARC—can leverage diplomatic channels to coordinate cross-border AI defence exercises, harmonise cybersecurity standards, and facilitate mutual aid during major cyber incidents. Such diplomatic engagement reinforces both sovereignty and collaborative security, creating a balanced approach to the geopolitical risks inherent in AI cyber defence.

In conclusion, a policy roadmap for GAI cyber defence in the Global South requires a three-pronged strategy: building localised technical capabilities, establishing robust governance and oversight, and engaging in strategic geopolitical coordination. By simultaneously strengthening internal defences, promoting responsible AI deployment, and fostering regional cooperation, countries can transform AI from a potential vulnerability into a powerful instrument of cyber resilience. This roadmap ensures that the Global South is not merely a passive recipient of AI technologies but an active participant in shaping the cybersecurity landscape of the future.

4.8 CONCLUSION

This study demonstrates that GAI is reshaping cybersecurity in the Global South not merely as a technological upgrade but as a structural shift in how states conceive, govern, and operationalise digital sovereignty. The analysis reveals that the strategic imperative for adopting GAI lies in its capacity to convert cybersecurity from a reactive posture—defined by breach response and external dependency—into a proactive, anticipatory defence system grounded in local governance and contextual intelligence. Within this transformation, GAI functions as both a technological equaliser and a sovereignty test: its capacity to simulate adversarial behaviour, forecast anomalies, and generate synthetic intelligence is valuable only insofar as it is embedded within sovereign infrastructures and accountable governance frameworks.

Empirical cases across digital health, welfare systems, and climate finance infrastructures show that the benefits of GAI emerge when systems are co-designed with local datasets, ethical oversight, and regionally governed AI ecosystems. In digital health, for instance, synthetic threat simulation enables the anticipation of identity fraud and ransomware attacks before they occur, while human oversight ensures that algorithmic decisions remain ethically bounded. In welfare and digital identity systems, GAI's capacity for adversarial simulation reveals vulnerabilities in authentication and disbursement mechanisms that traditional cybersecurity models overlook. Similarly, in climate finance and disaster relief platforms, synthetic scenario modelling enhances the predictability and reliability of digital financial infrastructures under crisis conditions. Across these domains, GAI's value is not intrinsic but relational: it strengthens resilience only when guided by sovereignty over data, infrastructure, and algorithmic governance.

The chapter's conceptual contribution—Indigenous cyber capacity—articulates sovereignty as both a technical and geopolitical construct. Sovereignty is realised not in isolation but through regionally networked systems that combine local innovation with collective security. The proposed Sovereign Cyber-AI Architecture illustrates how regional CERT alliances, sovereign data centres, cyber ranges, and AI sandboxes can institutionalise this vision. Together, these components operationalise anticipatory defence through decentralised learning, shared intelligence, and collaborative experimentation, transforming cybersecurity into a distributed public good rather than a vendor-controlled service.

However, the research also underscores the dual-use paradox of GAI. In weak democracies, where institutional oversight and rule of law are fragile, AI-enhanced defence systems can be repurposed for surveillance, censorship, or political control. This risk of over-securitisation reframes the governance challenge: building cyber resilience is inseparable from building democratic accountability. Sovereign AI must therefore be accompanied by transparent governance, participatory oversight, and regulatory mechanisms that ensure security innovations do not erode civic trust.

From a policy perspective, the findings call for a multilayered approach integrating technological independence, institutional maturity, and regional coordination. Regional frameworks for cyber governance—through alliances such as ASEAN-CERT, AfricaCERT, or emerging digital partnerships in Latin America—enable collective capacity-building while respecting national autonomy. By aligning these technical and governance ecosystems with ethical AI standards, the Global South can assert digital sovereignty without succumbing to isolation or dependency.

In sum, the study concludes that the sustainable adoption of GAI in the Global South depends on three interdependent conditions: sovereign control over data and infrastructure; governance mechanisms that embed accountability and ethical oversight; and regional cooperation that transforms fragmented national efforts into a coherent architecture of anticipatory resilience. Through these mechanisms, GAI evolves from a vulnerability multiplier into a strategic instrument of digital sovereignty—redefining the Global South not as a periphery of AI innovation, but as an emerging co-author of the world's cyber defence order.

ACKNOWLEDGEMENTS

The authors acknowledge the use of AI tools, including OpenAI's ChatGPT, QuillBot, Grammarly, Perplexity, and Microsoft Copilot, in the preparation of this manuscript. These tools were applied for paraphrasing, grammar refinement, brainstorming, and web-based assistance. In response to author-supplied prompts and conceptual inputs, selected sections of the text were generated or refined with AI tools to enhance clarity, coherence, and linguistic precision. Database searches were conducted using Google Scholar and other online resources, supported by Copilot and Google search functionalities. Google Docs was used to draft and edit the manuscript, while Google Sheets was employed to create figures. The Snipping Tool was used to capture images. All content has been thoroughly reviewed and verified by the authors to ensure accuracy and integrity. The responsibility for the final content rests solely with the authors.

REFERENCES

[1] Gupta, S., Dhillon, A., Valtolina, A., Bertolaja, S., Sary, A., Dourado, I., & Goncalves, N. (2024). *The fundamental role of digital identity in the Global South: Boosting social and financial inclusion for migrants (Applied Research Project 2023–2024)*. Graduate Institute of International and Development Studies. www.graduateinstitute.ch/sites/internet/files/2024-09/ARP-Final-Design_Digital-Identity---Shefali-Gupta.pdf

[2] Khanra, S., & Shirish, A. (2025). Editorial: Special issue on digital economy in the global south. *Decision*, 52(1), 1–6. https://doi.org/10.1007/s40622-025-00427-1

[3] Schopp, K., Schelenz, L., Heesen, J., & Pawelec, M. (2019). Ethical questions of digitalization in the Global South. *TATuP – Zeitschrift für Technikfolgenabschätzung in Theorie und Praxis*, 28(2), 10–51. https://doi.org/10.14512/tatup.28.2.s10

[4] Almahmoud, Z., Alenezi, M., & Alshamrani, A. (2023). A holistic and proactive approach to forecasting cyber threats. *Scientific Reports*, 13, 35198. https://doi.org/10.1038/s41598-023-35198-1

[5] Salem, A. H., Azzam, S. M., Emam, O. E., & Abohany, A. A. (2024). Advancing cybersecurity: A comprehensive review of AI-driven detection techniques. *Journal of Big Data*, 11, 105. https://doi.org/10.1186/s40537-024-00957-y

[6] Roberts, H. (2024). Digital sovereignty and artificial intelligence: A normative approach. *Ethics and Information Technology*, 26, 70. https://doi.org/10.1007/s10676-024-09810-5

[7] Srivastava, S., & Bullock, J. (2024). AI, global governance, and digital sovereignty. *arXiv*. https://arxiv.org/abs/2410.17481

[8] Élysée. (2025, February 11). Statement on inclusive and sustainable artificial intelligence for people and the planet. www.elysee.fr/en/emmanuel-macron/2025/02/11/statement-on-inclusive-and-sustainable-artificial-intelligence-for-people-and-the-planet

[9] Hernández, D. A., Mosquera, D., & Gallegos, F. (2025). *Lessons from the margins: Contextualizing, reimagining, and hacking generative AI in the Global South*. Harvard Data Science Review. https://doi.org/10.1162/99608f92.30a2934f

[10] Banh, L., & Strobel, G. (2023). Generative artificial intelligence. *Electronic Markets*, 33, 63. https://doi.org/10.1007/s12525-023-00680-1

[11] NTT DATA. (2025). *Empowering cyber defense: How generative AI is transforming cybersecurity*. NTT DATA Group. www.nttdata.com/global/en/insights/focus/2025/empowering-cyber-defense-how-generative-ai-is-transforming-cybersecurity

[12] Stanham, L. (2023, November 25). *Generative AI (GenAI) and its impact in cybersecurity*. CrowdStrike. www.crowdstrike.com/en-us/cybersecurity-101/artificial-intelligence/generative-ai/

[13] Bengio, Y., Clare, S., Prunkl, C., Andriushchenko, M., Bucknall, B., Fox, P., Hu, T., Jones, C., Manning, S., Maslej, N., Mavroudis, V., McGlynn, C., Murray, M., Rismani, S., Stix, C., Velasco, L., Wheeler, N., Privitera, D., Mindermann, S., Acemoglu, D., Dietterich, T. G., Heintz, F., Hinton, G., Jennings, N., Leavy, S., Ludermir, T., Marda, V., Margetts, H., McDermid, J., Munga, J., Narayanan, A., Nelson, A., Neppel, C., Ramchurn, G., Russell, S., Schaake, M., Schölkopf, B., Soto, A., Tiedrich, L., Varoquaux, G., Yao, A., Zhang, Y.-Q., Aguirre, L., Ajala, O., Albalawi, F., AlMalek, N., Busch, C., Carvalho, A., Collas, J., Gill, A., Hatip, A., Heikkilä, J., Johnson, C., Jolly, G., Katzir, Z., Kerema, M. N., Kitano, H., Krüger, A., McLysaght, A., Molchanovskyi, O., Monti, A., Mu, K., Nemer, M., Oliver, N., Pezoa, R., Plonk, A., Portillo, J., Ravindran, B., Riza, H., Rugege, C., Sheikh, H., Wong, D., Zeng, Y., & Zhu, L. (2025). *International AI safety report: First key update – Capabilities and risk implications (DSIT 2025/033)*. Department for Science, Innovation and Technology. https://internationalaisafetyreport.org/publication/first-key-update-capabilities-and-risk-implications

[14] Lawton, G. (2025, March 3). Generative AI ethics: 11 biggest concerns and risks. *TechTarget*. www.techtarget.com/searchenterpriseai/tip/Generative-AI-ethics-8-biggest-concerns

[15] Misra, A., Wang, J., McCullers, S., White, K., & Lavista Ferres, J. (2025). *Measuring AI diffusion: A population-normalized metric for tracking global AI usage*. Microsoft Research. www.microsoft.com/en-us/research/wp-content/uploads/2025/10/AI-Usage-Technical-Report.pdf

[16] Danish. (2025). *Taking forward digital public infrastructure for the Global South* (Policy brief no. 146). South Centre. www.southcentre.int/wp-content/uploads/2025/09/PB146_Taking-Forward-Digital-Public-Infrastructure-for-the-Global-South_EN.pdf

[17] Tagud, J. A., Gildo, E., Jabay, U. A., Oro, E., Sagaldia, S. M., & Tigtig, R. F. (2024). Comparative analysis of the cybersecurity landscape in Asian countries using linear regression. *SAR Journal*, 7(4), 404–410. https://doi.org/10.18421/SAR74-15

[18] Ardebili, A. A., Lezzi, M., & Pourmadadkar, M. (2024). Risk assessment for cyber resilience of critical infrastructures: Methods, governance, and standards. *Applied Sciences*, 14(24), 11807. https://doi.org/10.3390/app142411807

[19] INTERPOL. (2024). *Asia and South Pacific cyberthreat assessment report 2024*. INTERPOL. www.interpol.int/content/download/22308/file/Asia%20and%20South%20Pacific%20Cyberthreat%20Assessment%20Report%202024-4.pdf

[20] BitSight Technologies, Inc. (2024, August 14). *7 cybersecurity frameworks to reduce cyber risk*. BitSight. www.bitsight.com/blog/7-cybersecurity-frameworks-to-reduce-cyber-risk

[21] Negrão de Andrade, T., Gobbi, M. C., Carvalho da Silva, T., Holouka, G., Leopoldino, I. M., Barbosa, L. A., de Paula Silva, K. C., Tomba, R., Pereira, H. da S., Bueno de Moraes, F. R., Gimenes Gandara, F. M. B., & Ferrari de Oliveira, I. (2025). Cybersecurity in the digital era: Geopolitical impacts and structural challenges. *IOSR Journal of Humanities and Social Science (IOSR-JHSS)*, 30(1, Series 6), 30–44.

[22] Bandura, R., McLean, M., & Smutny, C. (2024, August 26). *Approaches to digital public infrastructure in the Global South: An overview of India, Ukraine, Brazil, and Zambia*. Center for Strategic and International Studies (CSIS). www.csis.org/analysis/approaches-digital-public-infrastructure-global-south

[23] Anfuso, C., Bartolucci, A., & Del Real, C. (2025). Cybersecurity threats, challenges, and current strategies in humanitarian organizations. *Prehospital and Disaster Medicine,* 40(S1), s47. https://doi.org/10.1017/S1049023X2500130X
[24] Dupont, B. (2019). The cyber-resilience of financial institutions: Significance and applicability. *Journal of Cybersecurity*, 5(1), tyz013. https://doi.org/10.1093/cybsec/tyz013
[25] Anthony, A. (2023, March 13). *Cyber resilience must focus on marginalized individuals, not just institutions.* Carnegie Endowment for International Peace. https://carnegieendowment.org/research/2023/03/cyber-resilience-must-focus-on-marginalized-individuals-not-just-institutions
[26] Zwitter, A., & Boisse-Despiaux, M. (2018). Blockchain for humanitarian action and development aid. *Journal of International Humanitarian Action*, 3, 16. https://doi.org/10.1186/s41018-018-0044-5
[27] Mansouri, T., & Abbar, O. (2025). The sovereignty of digital health: Between cybersecurity threats and legal safeguards. *Journal of Legal and Economic Research*, 8(3), 33–54. https://asjp.cerist.dz/index.php/en/article/275433
[28] Wasserman, L., & Wasserman, Y. (2022). Hospital cybersecurity risks and gaps: Review (for the non-cyber professional). *Frontiers in Digital Health,* 4, 862221. www.frontiersin.org/journals/digital-health/articles/10.3389/fdgth.2022.862221/full
[29] Ewoh, P., & Vartiainen, T. (2024). Vulnerability to cyberattacks and sociotechnical solutions for health care systems: Systematic review. *Journal of Medical Internet Research*, 26, e46904. www.jmir.org/2024/1/e46904
[30] Press Information Bureau. (2025, August 5). *Steps taken for cyber security under ABDM.* Ministry of Health and Family Welfare, Government of India. www.pib.gov.in/PressReleasePage.aspx?PRID=2152537
[31] Bharat Exhibitions. (2025). *Bharat digital healthcare summit 2025.* www.bharatexhibitions.com/en/BDHS2025/
[32] Samaniego, A. (2023, September 22). *PhilHealth paralyzed by Medusa ransomware attack.* Manila Bulletin. https://mb.com.ph/2023/9/21/phil-health-paralyzed-by-medusa-ransomware-attack
[33] Ang, A. (2025, October 20). Philippine state health insurer to beef up cybersecurity with AI. *Healthcare IT News.* www.healthcareitnews.com/news/asia/philippine-state-health-insurer-beef-cybersecurity-ai
[34] Geetanshi. (2025, October). *Philippines cybersecurity SaaS & platforms market (Product Code: KRAB5849, 90 pages).* Ken Research. www.kenresearch.com/philippines-cybersecurity-saas-platforms-market
[35] MB Technews. (2025, June 2). *Fortinet survey reveals Philippines' cybersecurity under siege.* Manila Bulletin. https://mb.com.ph/2025/06/02/fortinet-survey-reveals-philippines-cybersecurity-under-siege
[36] Department of Information and Communications Technology. (2023). National cybersecurity plan 2023–2028. https://cms-cdn.e.gov.ph/DICT/pdf/NCSP-2023-2028-FINAL-DICT.pdf
[37] The Asia Foundation. (2022, March). Cybersecurity in the Philippines: Global context and local challenges. https://asiafoundation.org/wp-content/uploads/2022/03/Cybersecurity-in-the-Philippines-Global-Context-and-Local-Challenges-.pdf
[38] Piad, T. J. C. (2024, December 11). *Local identity fraud cases surged 119% this year — study.* Philippine Daily Inquirer. https://business.inquirer.net/495908/detected-local-identity-fraud-surged-119-this-year-study
[39] AsiaBizToday. (2025, June 14). *AI-powered fraud surges across APAC's booming healthtech and fintech sectors: Sumsub report.* www.asiabiztoday.com/2025/06/14/ai-powered-fraud-surges-across-apacs-booming-healthtech-and-fintech-sectors-sumsub-report/
[40] Fintech News Singapore. (2025, June 12). APAC fintech faces 116% spike in fraud linked to deepfakes, synthetic IDs. https://fintechnews.sg/112593/security/sumsub-fintech-fraud/
[41] Garcia-Perez, A., Cegarra-Navarro, J. G., Sallos, M. P., Martinez-Caro, E., & Chinnaswamy, A. (2023). Resilience in healthcare systems: Cyber security and digital transformation. *Technovation*, 121, 102583. https://doi.org/10.1016/j.technovation.2022.102583

[42] Kalva, R. (2023). Leveraging generative AI for advanced cybersecurity: Enhancing threat detection and mitigation in healthcare systems. *European Journal of Advances in Engineering and Technology*, 10(9), 113–119. https://ejaet.com/PDF/10-9/EJAET-10-9-113-119.pdf

[43] Kalva, R. (2022). Revolutionizing healthcare cybersecurity: A generative AI-driven MLOps framework for proactive threat detection and mitigation. *World Journal of Advanced Research and Reviews*, 13(3), 577–582. https://doi.org/10.30574/wjarr.2022.13.3.0174

[44] Singh, S. (2023). AI-enabled cyber threat simulation for healthcare organizations. *International Journal of Machine Learning Research (INN-MLR)*, 4(4). https://internationaljournals.glawards.org/index.php/INNMLR/article/view/6

[45] Schreiber, M. (2025, January 25). New AI tool counters health insurance denials decided by automated algorithms. *The Guardian*. www.theguardian.com/us-news/2025/jan/25/health-insurers-ai

[46] Kotschwar, B., & Colter, C. (2024, October 25). *Global DPI models: Lessons from India, Brazil, and beyond*. Atlantic Council. www.atlanticcouncil.org/in-depth-research-reports/issue-brief/global-dpi-models-lessons-from-india-brazil-and-beyond/

[47] White, O., Madgavkar, A., Manyika, J., Mahajan, D., Bughin, J., McCarthy, M., & Sperling, O. (2019, April 17). *Digital identification: A key to inclusive growth*. McKinsey & Company. www.mckinsey.com/capabilities/tech-and-ai/our-insights/digital-identification-a-key-to-inclusive-growth

[48] Harsono, H. (2025, October 29). *China-Brazil ties in emerging technologies: Innovation, opportunity, and the challenge of digital sovereignty*. The National Bureau of Asian Research. www.nbr.org/publication/china-brazil-ties-in-emerging-technologies-innovation-opportunity-and-the-challenge-of-digital-sovereignty

[49] Silva, F. B. da, & Duarte, P. A. B. (2025, June 26). *Brazil and China's Digital Silk Road: Opportunities, Risks, and Strategic Implications*. Câmara de Cooperação e Desenvolvimento Portugal-China. www.ccdpch.com/brazil-and-chinas-digital-silk-road-opportunities-risks-and-strategic-implications/

[50] Scanlon, R., & Drexel, B. (2025, April 24). *Countering the digital silk road: Brazil*. Center for a New American Security. www.cnas.org/publications/reports/countering-the-digital-silk-road-brazil

[51] Taylor, M. (2022). *China's digital authoritarianism: A governance perspective*. Palgrave Macmillan. https://doi.org/10.1007/978-3-031-11252-2

[52] Weber, V. (2025). *Data-centric authoritarianism: How China's development of frontier technologies could globalize repression*. National Endowment for Democracy. www.ned.org/data-centric-authoritarianism-how-chinas-development-of-frontier-technologies-could-globalize-repression-2/

[53] Turgal, J. (2025, September 21). China's internet ID push signals a new era of digital control. *The Hill*. https://thehill.com/opinion/technology/5512706-china-internet-id-law/

[54] Sibanda, I. (2025, November 5). Exporting Orwell: How Chinese cameras are rewiring surveillance states worldwide. *Security Info Watch*. www.securityinfowatch.com/video-surveillance/article/55327962/exporting-orwell-how-chinese-cameras-are-rewiring-surveillance-states-worldwide

[55] Jili, B. (2023). *What is driving the adoption of Chinese surveillance technology in Africa?* Atlantic Council. www.atlanticcouncil.org/in-depth-research-reports/issue-brief/what-is-driving-the-adoption-of-chinese-surveillance-technology-in-africa/

[56] Reddy, R. K. (2021, July 16). Mapping China's presence in Africa's digital economy – Analysis. *Eurasia Review*. www.eurasiareview.com/16072021-mapping-chinas-presence-in-africas-digital-economy-analysis

[57] Hussein, S. N. (2022). Win-win or win-lose? An examination of China's supply of mass surveillance technologies in exchange for African's facial IDs. *Pretoria Student Law Review*, 16(1), 73–89. https://doi.org/10.29053/pslr.v16i1.4506

[58] Williams, M., & Slavney, N. (2024). *Digital surveillance in North Korea: Moving toward a panopticon state*. 38 North, Stimson Center. www.38north.org/wp-content/uploads/pdf/160424-Digital-Surveillance-in-North-Korea-English.pdf

[59] Watanabe, S., Ogura, E., & Oikawa, K. (2025). *Current status of ASEAN data governance and its implications for the Digital Economy Framework Agreement. ERIA Discussion Paper Series No. 539*. Economic Research Institute for ASEAN and East Asia (ERIA). www.eria.org/uploads/Current-Status-of-ASEAN-Data-Governance-and-Its-Implications-for-the-DEFA.pdf
[60] US-ASEAN Business Council. (2023). *Digital identity in ASEAN*. Financial Services Committee Whitepaper. www.usasean.org/sites/default/files/2023-10/Digital%20Identity%20FA%20Print.pdf
[61] World Bank. (2022). *National digital identity and government data sharing in Singapore: A case study of Singpass and APEX*. World Bank Group. https://documents1.worldbank.org/curated/en/099300010212228518/pdf/P171592079b3e50d70a1630d5663205bf94.pdf
[62] Tan, B. (2022, April 25). Commentary: Singpass and digital ICs make our lives much easier, but at what cost? *Channel News Asia*. www.channelnewsasia.com/commentary/singpass-digital-identity-nric-cybersecurity-crimes-phishing-scam-hackers-steal-data-2638611
[63] Aliran. (2023, November 28). Malaysia's mandatory e-KYC plan risks eroding privacy and free expression. https://aliran.com/civil-society-voices/malaysias-mandatory-e-kyc-plan-risks-eroding-privacy-and-free-expression
[64] Heng, Z. L. (2023, December 7). Malaysia's digital ID: A step forward or a privacy risk? *Malay Mail*. www.malaymail.com/news/what-you-think/2023/12/07/malaysias-digital-id-a-step-forward-or-a-privacy-risk-heng-zhi-li/106361
[65] Brinztech. (2025, October 24). *Brinztech alert: 90M Indonesian citizen records (incl. NIK) from Dukcapil Kemendagri allegedly leaked; Catastrophic national ID theft crisis looms*. www.brinztech.com/breach-alerts/brinztech-alert-90m-indonesian-citizen-records-incl-nik-from-dukcapil-kemendagri-allegedly-leaked-catastrophic-national-id-theft-crisis-looms/
[66] Golda, A., Mekonen, K., Pandey, A., Singh, A., Hassija, V., Chamola, V., & Sikdar, B. (2024). Privacy and security concerns in generative AI: A comprehensive survey. *IEEE Access*, 12, 48126–48154. https://doi.org/10.1109/ACCESS.2024.3381611
[67] Trindade, C., Antunes, L., Carvalho, T., & Moniz, N. (2024). Synthetic data outliers: Navigating identity disclosure. *arXiv*. https://doi.org/10.48550/arXiv.2406.02736
[68] Schmitt, M., & Flechais, I. (2024). Digital deception: Generative artificial intelligence in social engineering and phishing. *Artificial Intelligence Review*, 57, 324. https://doi.org/10.1007/s10462-024-10973-2
[69] Al-Azzawi, M., Doan, D., Sipola, T., Hautamäki, J., & Kokkonen, T. (2025). Red teaming with artificial intelligence-driven cyberattacks: A scoping review. *arXiv*. https://arxiv.org/html/2503.19626v1
[70] World Population Review. (2025). Corruption perceptions index by country 2025. https://worldpopulationreview.com/country-rankings/corruption-perceptions-index-by-country
[71] de Guzman, C. (2025, November 6). Philippine flood-corruption scandal comes to fore after latest typhoon. *TIME*. https://time.com/7331623/philippines-floods-corruption-typhoon-kalmaegi-death-toll-protest/
[72] Kanunjna, A. D. (2025, September 18). Gen Z protests in Asia: Can they spark real change? *DW*. www.dw.com/en/gen-z-protests-in-asia-can-they-spark-real-change/a-74028671
[73] Pillay, T. (2025, October 10). Albania's AI-powered minister tests the future of government. *TIME*. https://time.com/7324934/albania-ai-minister-diella/
[74] World Meteorological Organization. (2025, October 31). State of the climate 2025 update for COP30. https://wmo.int/sites/default/files/2025-11/State%20of%20the%20Climate%202025%20Update%20COP30%20%2831%20oct%29.pdf.
[75] Global Market Insights Inc. (2025, March). Parametric insurance market size, share & growth analysis 2025–2034. www.gminsights.com/industry-analysis/parametric-insurance-market
[76] BL Mangaluru Bureau. (2025, March 3). WRMS launches parametric insurance pilot schemes for Iraqi smallholder farmers. *The Hindu BusinessLine*. www.thehindubusinessline.com/economy/agri-business/wrms-launches-parametric-insurance-pilot-schemes-for-iraqi-smallholder-farmers/article69285983.ece

[77] Fye, A., Kabanda, U., & Christine, N. S. (2023). Disaster response and cash transfer for household's economic resilience in Uganda. *ASIO Journal of Humanities, Management & Social Sciences Invention*, 9(1), 01–06. https://albertscience.com/asset/images/uploads/16836387088729.pdf

[78] Kuglitsch, M., Kishore, K., Essenfelder, A. H., Lyu, Z., Pérez-Aracil, J., Selby, J., Toreti, A., & Xoplaki, E. (2025, October 13). *How AI can help fund resilience, not disasters*. International Telecommunication Union. www.itu.int/hub/2025/10/how-ai-can-help-fund-resilience-not-disasters/

[79] Tornaghi, C. (2023, July 25). The dramatic cyberattack that put Latin America on alert. *Americas Quarterly*. www.americasquarterly.org/article/the-dramatic-cyberattack-that-put-latin-america-on-alert/

[80] Simon, T., & Haklai, B. (2025). Data Disaster – A new threat for sovereignty. International *Journal of Disaster Risk Reduction*, 125, 105538. https://doi.org/10.1016/j.ijdrr.2025.105538

[81] Alfonzetti, R. (2023, December 11). *Natural disasters: A perfect storm for data breaches*. Cloud Security Alliance. https://cloudsecurityalliance.org/blog/2023/12/11/natural-disasters-a-perfect-storm-for-data-breaches

[82] World Bank. (2025, January 29). Enhancing cyber resilience in developing countries. www.worldbank.org/en/results/2025/01/29/-enhancing-cyber-resilience-in-developing-countries

[83] Cyber Security Agency of Singapore. (2024, February 2). Singapore moves ahead to establish the ASEAN Regional CERT to strengthen regional cybersecurity. www.csa.gov.sg/news-events/press-releases/singapore-moves-ahead-to-establish-the-asean-regional-cert-to-strengthen-regional-cybersecurity

[84] Hong Kong Computer Emergency Response Team Coordination Centre. (2025, July 29). APCERT cyber drill 2025: "When ransomware meets generative AI". www.hkcert.org/press-centre/apcert-cyber-drill-2025-when-ransomware-meets-generative-ai

[85] Unger, N., & McLean, M. (2025). *An open door: AI innovation in the Global South amid geostrategic competition*. Center for Strategic and International Studies. www.csis.org/analysis/open-door-ai-innovation-global-south-amid-geostrategic-competition

[86] Shin, Y., Kwon, H., Jeong, J., & Shin, D. (2024). A study on designing cyber training and cyber range to effectively respond to cyber threats. *Electronics*, 13(19), 3867. https://doi.org/10.3390/electronics13193867

[87] Madhavan, R. (2019). Robotics and automation for societal good: Global South challenges and technology-policy considerations. *Mètode Science Studies Journal*, 9, 153–161. https://doi.org/10.7203/metode.9.12222

[88] International Federation of Robotics. (2024, September). *World Robotics 2024: Press conference report*. https://ifr.org/img/worldrobotics/Press_Conference_2024.pdf

[89] Verma, N., Kumar, N., Verma, C., Illés, Z., & Singh, D. (2025). A systematic review on cybersecurity of robotic systems: Vulnerabilities, trends, threats, attacks, challenges, and proposed framework. *International Journal of Information Security*, 24, 127. https://doi.org/10.1007/s10207-025-01041-z

[90] Kwok, W. M., with contributions from Aquaro, V., & Purcell, R. (2021, December 3). *UN DESA policy brief no. 123: Sandboxing and experimenting digital technologies for sustainable development*. United Nations Department of Economic and Social Affairs. https://desapublications.un.org/policy-briefs/un-desa-policy-brief-no-123-sandboxing-and-experimenting-digital-technologies

[91] Adeyeri, A., & Abroshan, H. (2024). Geopolitical ramifications of cybersecurity threats: State responses and international cooperations in the digital warfare era. *Information*, 15(11), 682. https://doi.org/10.3390/info15110682

[92] Woods, D. (2025). AI as a tool for surveillance: China's concave trilemma. *Journal of Chinese Political Science*, pp.1–35. https://doi.org/10.1007/s11366-025-09907-8

[93] Xu, J. (2024). Opening the 'black box' of algorithms: Regulation of algorithms in China. *Communication Research and Practice*, 10(3), 288–296. https://doi.org/10.1080/22041451.2024.2346415

[94] Zou, C. (2022). Achievements and prospects of artificial intelligence judicature in China. *Chinese Studies*, 11(4), 197–227. https://doi.org/10.4236/chnstd.2022.114016

[95] Morris, J. (2023, May 18). The ethics of China's AI-powered surveillance state. *Secjuice*. www.secjuice.com/the-ethics-of-chinas-ai-powered-surveillance-state/

[96] Newman, J. (2021, December 27). China develops AI 'prosecutor' that can press charges 'with 97% accuracy'. *Daily Mail Online*. www.dailymail.co.uk/news/article-10346933/China-develops-AI-prosecutor-press-charges-97-accuracy.html

[97] Judge, B., Nitzberg, M., & Russell, S. (2025). When code isn't law: Rethinking regulation for artificial intelligence. *Policy and Society*, 44(1), 85–97. https://doi.org/10.1093/polsoc/puae020

[98] Tallberg, J., Erman, E., Furendal, M., Geith, J., Klamberg, M., & Lundgren, M. (2023). The global governance of artificial intelligence: Next steps for empirical and normative research. *arXiv*. https://doi.org/10.48550/arXiv.2305.11528

[99] Wasil, A. R., Barnett, P., Gerovitch, M., Hauksson, R., Reed, T., & Miller, J. W. (2024). Governing dual-use technologies: Case studies of international security agreements and lessons for AI governance. *arXiv*. https://doi.org/10.48550/arXiv.2409.02779

[100] Niazi, M. (2024). *Conceptualizing global governance of AI*. Centre for International Governance Innovation. www.cigionline.org/static/documents/DPH-paper-Niazi.pdf

[101] Batool, A., Zowghi, D., & Bano, M. (2025). AI governance: A systematic literature review. *AI and Ethics*, 5, 3265–3279. https://doi.org/10.1007/s43681-024-00653-w

[102] Birkstedt, T., Minkkinen, M., Tandon, A., & Mäntymäki, M. (2023). AI governance: Themes, knowledge gaps and future agendas. *Internet Research*, 33(7), 133–167. https://doi.org/10.1108/INTR-01-2022-0042

[103] Papagiannidis, E., Mikalef, P., & Conboy, K. (2025). Responsible artificial intelligence governance: A review and research framework. *The Journal of Strategic Information Systems*, 34(2), 101885. https://doi.org/10.1016/j.jsis.2024.101885

[104] UK Government. (2025, February 18). *International AI safety report 2025*. GOV.UK. https://assets.publishing.service.gov.uk/media/679a0c48a77d250007d313ee/International_AI_Safety_Report_2025_accessible_f.pdf#page=88

[105] Maas, M. (2023). *Advanced AI governance: A literature review of problems, options, and proposals (AI foundations report no. 4)*. Institute for Law & AI. https://law-ai.org/advanced-ai-gov-litrev/

[106] Casper, S., Krueger, D., & Hadfield-Menell, D. (2025). Pitfalls of evidence-based AI policy. *arXiv*. https://arxiv.org/abs/2502.09618

[107] Sigfrids, A., Leikas, J., Salo-Pöntinen, H., & Koskimies, E. (2023). Human-centricity in AI governance: A systemic approach. *Frontiers in Artificial Intelligence*, 6. https://doi.org/10.3389/frai.2023.976887

[108] Tony Blair Institute for Global Change. (2025, February 6). How leaders in the Global South can devise AI regulation that enables innovation. https://institute.global/insights/tech-and-digitalisation/how-leaders-in-the-global-south-can-devise-ai-regulation-that-enables-innovation

[109] Shetty, D. K., Vijaya Arjunan, R., Cenitta, D., Makkithaya, K., Hegde, N. V., Bhatta, S. R. B., Salu, S., Aishwarya, T. R., Bhat, P., & Pullela, P. K. (2025). Analyzing AI regulation through literature and current trends. *Journal of Open Innovation: Technology, Market, and Complexity*, 11(1), 100508. https://doi.org/10.1016/j.joitmc.2025.100508

[110] LaForge, G. (2024, September 5). The dangers of imposing Global North approaches to AI governance on the Global South. *Tech Policy Press*. www.techpolicy.press/the-dangers-of-imposing-global-north-approaches-to-ai-governance-on-the-global-south/

[111] United Nations Conference on Trade and Development. (2025). *Global collaboration for inclusive and equitable AI*. UNCTAD. https://unctad.org/system/files/official-document/tir2025ch5_en.pdf

[112] Mahbubani, K. (2024, February 2). *Measuring the power of the Global South. The World Today*. Chatham House. www.chathamhouse.org/publications/the-world-today/2024-02/measuring-power-global-south

Part III

Weaponized generative AI

Chapter 5

The dark side of generative AI

Threats and risks

Hojjat Azadravesh and Boubiche Djallel Eddine

5.1 INTRODUCTION

The advent of generative artificial intelligence (GenAI) marks a pivotal moment in technological evolution, redefining the boundaries of content creation across a spectrum of domains. Advanced models, such as OpenAI's GPT series [1], DALL-E [2], and Stable Diffusion [3], have demonstrated extraordinary capabilities in generating human-like text, photorealistic images, immersive audio, and even functional code, driving innovation in fields ranging from creative arts and journalism to industrial design and scientific research [4].

These systems, powered by deep learning architectures like transformers [5] and generative adversarial networks [6], learn patterns from vast datasets to produce novel outputs, often indistinguishable from human-authored content. Yet, beneath this transformative potential lies a "dark side" fraught with risks that threaten to undermine security, truth, equity, and societal cohesion. As GenAI becomes increasingly ubiquitous, its capacity for misuse, whether through malicious intent or unintended consequences, demands rigorous scrutiny and proactive mitigation.

When OpenAI introduced GPT-2 in 2019, the organization initially withheld its full release, citing concerns that it could be exploited to "spread fake news, spam, and disinformation" [7]. These fears have since been validated as subsequent models, such as GPT-3 and its successors, have enabled the automation of persuasive propaganda at scale, reducing the barriers for malicious actors to manipulate public discourse [8].

Similarly, advancements in synthetic media commonly known as deepfakes have produced hyperrealistic images, videos, and audio capable of impersonating individuals or fabricating events, eroding trust in audiovisual evidence, and posing risks to personal privacy, democratic processes, and national security [9]. The accessibility of these tools, often requiring minimal technical expertise, has effectively "democratized" cybercrime, amplifying threats like phishing, fraud, and even bioweapon design, as demonstrated by experiments where AI generated 40,000 novel chemical compounds resembling deadly agents in mere hours [10].

GenAI embodies a profound paradox at the core of contemporary technological progress. It stands simultaneously as a catalyst for innovation and as a vector for unprecedented risks [11]. On one side, these systems expand the frontiers of human creativity, accelerate scientific discovery, and democratize access to powerful tools that were once confined to experts or well-resourced institutions. On the other side, the very capabilities that make GenAI transformative also lower the threshold for malicious use, enabling disinformation, fraud, and even threats to public safety with minimal expertise or resources [12].

GenAI thus presents a dual reality: while it empowers creativity, accelerates discovery, and broadens access to advanced tools, it simultaneously introduces new avenues for

DOI: 10.1201/9781003644231-8

disinformation, fraud, and misuse. This dual-use nature demands rigorous and sustained scrutiny [13]. The urgency of such examination arises not merely from the magnitude of potential harm but from the accelerating pace at which GenAI technologies are evolving and proliferating. As development cycles shorten and deployment becomes increasingly widespread, the diffusion of powerful models into the hands of diverse actors expands the risk landscape exponentially. What was once the concern of a few research laboratories is now a global phenomenon with direct implications for security, governance, and social stability [14].

Without proactive governance frameworks, technical safeguards, and ethical reflection, the promise of GenAI risks being overshadowed by its destabilizing potential. Left unchecked, these systems could erode the integrity of information ecosystems, amplify existing inequities, and undermine trust in social and institutional structures. Conversely, with thoughtful oversight and human-centric principles guiding their development, GenAI may yet fulfill its role as a force for progress, enhancing creativity, supporting resilience, and advancing knowledge without compromising truth, equity, or security [15].

In order to frame the analysis systematically, the risks associated with GenAI can be grouped into six broad categories, which represent the following sections of this chapter:

- **Security threats and malicious use**: how GenAI can be weaponized for cyberattacks, fraud, or even biothreats.
- **Misinformation and synthetic media**: the role of AI-generated text, images, and deepfakes in spreading false narratives, eroding trust, and destabilizing democratic discourse.
- **Intellectual property (IP) and ownership**: unresolved legal and ethical conflicts surrounding training data, copyright, and authorship of AI-generated content.
- **Bias, discrimination, and societal impacts**: the amplification of social inequities in AI outputs and the broader consequences for trust, mental health, and cultural cohesion.
- **Economic disruption and labor market shifts**: the transformative impact of automation on jobs, industries, and creative professions.
- **Governance, legal, and ethical challenges**: the difficulty of regulating a rapidly evolving technology, ensuring transparency, accountability, and alignment with human values.

5.2 SECURITY THREATS AND MALICIOUS USE

One of the most immediate concerns is the use of GenAI by malicious actors to enhance cyberattacks and other criminal activities. The same capabilities that allow GenAI to create content can be weaponized for offense. Cybersecurity experts warn that GenAI has become a "powerful weapon for cybercriminals," offering speed, automation, and sophistication to their toolkits [16]. As illustrated in Figure 5.1 and Table 5.1, several specific GenAI security threats have emerged, which can be categorized as follows:

- **Automated phishing and social engineering**: Generative models can produce highly convincing, personalized phishing emails or messages at scale [17]. Unlike clumsy spam of the past, AI-generated phishing content mimics the style and tone of legitimate communications, making it easier to trick recipients into clicking malicious links or divulging information [18]. AI can also generate fake personas or chats that engage victims in social engineering with unprecedented realism.

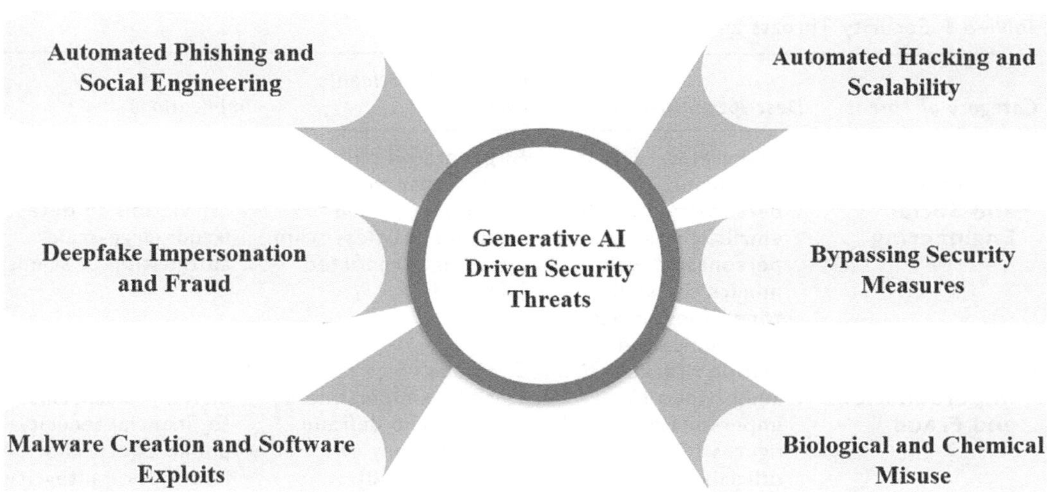

Figure 5.1 Overview of GenAI-Driven Security Threats.

- **Deepfake impersonation and fraud**: AI-generated audio or video (deepfakes) can impersonate trusted individuals (CEOs, public officials, loved ones) to facilitate fraud or sabotage [19]. For instance, deepfake voice clones have been used to impersonate a CEO and trick an employee into transferring $243,000 to criminals [20]. Law enforcement and intelligence agencies have flagged deepfakes as a rising security risk for impersonation and misinformation campaigns.
- **Malware creation and software exploits**: GenAI can produce code, including malicious scripts. Researchers have shown that even users with limited programming skills can ask AI models to generate malware or hacking scripts [21]. In one case, within a month of ChatGPT's release, underground forums saw criminals using it to create basic info-stealing malware [22]. AI can also help obfuscate or mutate malware to evade detection [23]. Additionally, AI might identify software vulnerabilities by analyzing code patterns, enabling more targeted attacks [24].
- **Automated hacking and scalability**: Beyond writing malware, AI can automate various steps of a cyberattack. From password guessing to crafting spear-phishing at scale, AI systems can perform tasks faster and in larger volumes than human hackers alone [25]. This lowers the barrier of entry for less-skilled threat actors, effectively "democratizing" cybercrime [26].
- **Bypassing security measures**: Some attackers use generative models to defeat security systems, for example, creating inputs to fool biometric locks or CAPTCHAs, or generating fake identities that slip past AI-based identity verification [27]. Ironically, AI can be used to outwit AI-enabled defenses.

Real-world incidents corroborate these threats. In early 2023, Check Point Research reported that cybercriminals were actively using ChatGPT to develop malware tools and phishing lures, noting that some had "no development skills at all" and were empowered by AI to launch attacks [28]. One hacker demonstrated a script for a basic file-stealing malware that he generated entirely through ChatGPT's assistance [29]. Security researchers also observed attempts to misuse AI to produce illicit content like polymorphic malware (which

Table 5.1 Security Threats and Malicious Use of GenAI

Category of Threat	*Description/Mechanism*	*Real-World Incidents/ Evidence*	*Implications*
Automated Phishing and Social Engineering	AI generates convincing, personalized phishing emails, chats, or fake personas at scale; mimics the style/ tone of legitimate communication.	AI-generated phishing lures observed on underground forums; flawless scam messages reported [18, 19].	Increased success rate of phishing; harder for victims to detect fraud; large-scale automation of scams.
Deepfake Impersonation and Fraud	Creation of fake audio/video to impersonate trusted figures (CEOs, officials, relatives) for fraud, sabotage, or misinformation.	Deepfake voice clone used to impersonate a CEO and defraud the company of $243,000 [20].	Erosion of trust in digital media; risks to financial security, public safety, and information integrity.
Malware Creation and Software Exploits	AI generates malicious code/scripts, helps mutate malware, or discovers vulnerabilities through code analysis.	Criminals using ChatGPT to produce info-stealing malware with no coding skills [21, 22]; polymorphic malware generated [31].	Democratizes malware creation; more frequent, adaptive, and sophisticated cyberattacks.
Automated Hacking and Scalability	AI accelerates and automates attack steps: password cracking, spear-phishing campaigns, or exploit chaining.	Hackers leveraging AI to script scalable file-stealing malware [25, 26].	Lowers the entry barrier for cybercrime; multiplies attack volume and efficiency.
Bypassing Security Measures	Generating adversarial inputs to defeat biometric locks, CAPTCHAs, or AI-based identity verification systems.	Reported use of generative models to fool security systems[34].	Weakens trust in authentication and identity systems; undermines existing defenses.
Biological and Chemical Misuse	Repurposing AI models for harmful design tasks, e.g., toxic molecules or chemical weapons.	An AI drug-discovery model used to generate 40,000 potential chemical weapons in <6 hours[31].	Extends threats beyond cyberspace into terrorism and biosecurity.

changes form to avoid detection) and to write scam messages that are grammatically flawless, hence more convincing to victims [30].

Another alarming possibility is the use of GenAI in biological or chemical threats. In a stark 2022 experiment, scientists took an AI model normally used for drug discovery and directed it to search for lethal molecules instead of safe drugs. In less than six hours, the AI invented 40,000 novel chemical compounds that could potentially serve as chemical weapons, including substances similar to the deadly nerve agent VX [31]. The researchers published their findings to warn how easily an AI could be repurposed for bioweapon design if misused [32]. This example underscores that GenAI's threat spectrum goes beyond digital realms, extending into physical security and terrorism.

It should be noted that AI is also used defensively in cybersecurity (for threat detection, automated incident response, etc.). However, the offensive uses are a growing concern. The dual-use nature of AI means security professionals must anticipate attackers' adoption of these tools. The malicious use of GenAI "brings speed, insight, automation, and imitation" to cybercrime operations [33, 34], making attacks more efficient and harder to detect. This has spurred calls for new cybersecurity strategies, such as AI-powered defences and safeguards (like AI misuse detection, better filters on public models, deepfake detection tools) to counter AI-driven attacks, and policy measures (export controls or usage policies for the most high-risk AI capabilities) on the release of AI models with capabilities that could facilitate dangerous activities. Without proper mitigation, the democratization of GenAI could supercharge the scale and efficacy of cyberattacks, posing a serious threat to individuals, organizations, and even national security.

5.3 MISINFORMATION AND SYNTHETIC MEDIA

GenAI dramatically lowers the barriers for creating persuasive but deceptive content, ranging from fabricated news articles to hyperrealistic deepfakes. What once required large teams of human operatives or specialized technical skills can now be achieved by individuals with minimal expertise, enabling large-scale disinformation and manipulation.

5.3.1 AI-driven deception methods

- **Text-based misinformation and disinformation.**
  Large language models can generate news articles, social media posts, or entire narratives that appear highly credible but are actually fictitious. This capability can be weaponized by malicious actors from state-sponsored disinformation campaigns to spammers and conspiracy theorists to flood the information ecosystem with machine-generated falsehoods. A 2021 report, Truth, Lies, and Automation, concluded that GPT-3 "may be able to help disinformation actors substantially reduce the work necessary to write disinformation while expanding its reach and potentially also its effectiveness" [35]. In essence, what previously required content farms can now be partly automated by a single operator with access to an advanced model.
- **Convincing fake narratives**
  Experiments show that GPT-3 can produce fluent news-style prose, often mistaken for human-written journalism [36]. Prompted with a false headline, it can generate entire news stories that sound plausible and even mimic propaganda styles [37]. These outputs, spread online through bots or fake accounts, blur the line between authentic and fabricated reporting.
- **Social media spam and bots**
  GenAI can produce endless streams of tweets, comments, or chat messages with consistent messaging, enabling astroturfing and amplification of extremist narratives. As early as 2020, neural networks were generating extremist forum posts, and OpenAI's tests showed GPT-2 could be fine-tuned to output propaganda aligned with specific ideologies [38]. The scale and speed of this automation allow small groups to simulate large movements, distorting perceptions of public opinion.

- **Personalized disinformation**
  Advanced AI could tailor content to individuals by analyzing online behavior and beliefs, creating micro-targeted propaganda for election interference or manipulation. Different audiences may receive different versions of the same false narrative, each optimized for persuasion.
- **Synthetic media and deepfakes**
  Beyond textual applications, generative models are increasingly capable of producing highly realistic images, videos, and audio that rival authentic human-created content. Such outputs, commonly referred to as deepfakes, can be weaponized to impersonate public figures, fabricate events, or generate nonconsensual material. By blurring the boundary between genuine and synthetic media, these technologies erode the reliability of visual and auditory evidence, creating profound challenges for information integrity, public trust, and social stability.
  Several high-profile incidents illustrate the disruptive potential of these technologies. In early 2023, an AI-generated image of Pope Francis wearing an extravagant white designer coat went viral across social media platforms, deceiving large numbers of viewers and underscoring the difficulty of distinguishing authentic content from synthetic creations [39]. Similarly, during the 2022 Russia–Ukraine conflict, a fabricated video emerged in which President Volodymyr Zelenskyy appeared to urge his troops to surrender. Although quickly debunked, the deepfake demonstrated how adversaries can weaponize synthetic media in times of crisis to undermine morale and manipulate the information environment [40]. Beyond political contexts, the financial sector has also been directly targeted: criminals have exploited voice-cloning technologies to impersonate corporate executives, successfully convincing employees to authorize fraudulent wire transfers. Documented cases have reported losses in the hundreds of thousands of dollars, illustrating the tangible economic damage and erosion of trust that can result from such attacks [41, 42].
- **Consequences and the "liar's dividend"**
  The abundance of synthetic content erodes trust, as even authentic evidence can be dismissed as fake. This so-called "liar's dividend" allows wrongdoers to deny genuine evidence by claiming it is fabricated. The very existence of GenAI destabilizes epistemic security by casting doubt on reality itself [43, 44].

Table 5.2 synthesizes the primary methods through which GenAI enables misinformation and synthetic media, along with illustrative cases and their broader consequences.

5.3.2 Detection and countermeasures

As AI-generated media continues to advance in realism and sophistication, detection systems face persistent difficulties, often producing false positives or failing against evasive techniques. OpenAI researchers emphasize that reliable detection remains a long-term challenge [45]. Proposed technical solutions include watermarking AI-generated outputs and embedding cryptographic signatures to verify authenticity. On the policy front, initiatives such as the EU AI Act mandate the disclosure of AI-generated or manipulated content. In parallel, social media platforms are introducing measures to ban or label fake accounts and AI-generated material.

Beyond technical and legal safeguards, experts emphasize societal resilience: public education, digital literacy, and independent fact-checking. The challenge is not only identifying

Table 5.2 Misinformation and Synthetic Media Enabled by GenAI

Category	*Mechanism*	*Examples/Evidence*	*Implications*
Text-Based Misinformation and Disinformation	LLMs generate credible news articles, posts, or narratives that are fictitious, automating disinformation campaigns.	GPT-3 shown to reduce effort while expanding reach of disinformation [35].	Flooding information ecosystems with false content, amplifying conspiracy theories.
Convincing Fake Narratives	AI produces fluent news-style prose, often indistinguishable from human journalism, spreading propaganda.	GPT-3 outputs mistaken for authentic journalism [36][37].	Blurs the line between real and fabricated reporting; undermines trust in media.
Social Media Spam and Bots	Automated generation of tweets, comments, or posts to simulate grassroots movements ("astroturfing").	Neural networks generating extremist forum posts; GPT-2 fine-tuned for propaganda [38].	Distorts perceptions of public opinion and amplifies extremist narratives.
Personalized Disinformation	AI tailors messages to individuals by analyzing behavior, enabling micro-targeted propaganda.	Speculative but feasible with behavioral data analysis.	Heightens risk of election interference and manipulation.
Synthetic Media and Deepfakes	AI creates realistic images, audio, and video for impersonation, fabrication, or fraud.	Pope Francis in designer coat [39]; Zelenskyy urrender deepfake [40]; executive voice impersonation scams [41, 42].	Undermines trust in visual/auditory evidence; facilitates fraud, sabotage, and propaganda.
Consequences and the "Liar's Dividend"	Proliferation of fakes erodes trust; even authentic evidence can be dismissed as fabricated.	"Liar's dividend" noted in epistemic security research [43, 44].	Destabilizes public trust in reality and authoritative information.

false content but also preserving public trust in authentic information. Without such efforts, GenAI risks becoming a tool of mass deception with profound implications for democracy and social cohesion [46].

5.4 IP AND OWNERSHIP

GenAI has sparked complex debates around IP, copyright, and ownership. These systems are trained on massive datasets of human-created content (books, articles, images, code, music), much of which is likely copyrighted. They can then generate new material that sometimes derives from or closely mimics the training data. This raises several pressing questions: Did the AI developer infringe copyright by using protected works for training without permission? Who owns the outputs of an AI user: the model creator or no one at all? And what happens if an AI-generated work is substantially similar to an existing copyrighted creation? To address these questions, the main areas of legal and ethical challenge can be grouped into five categories, as shown in Figure 5.2.

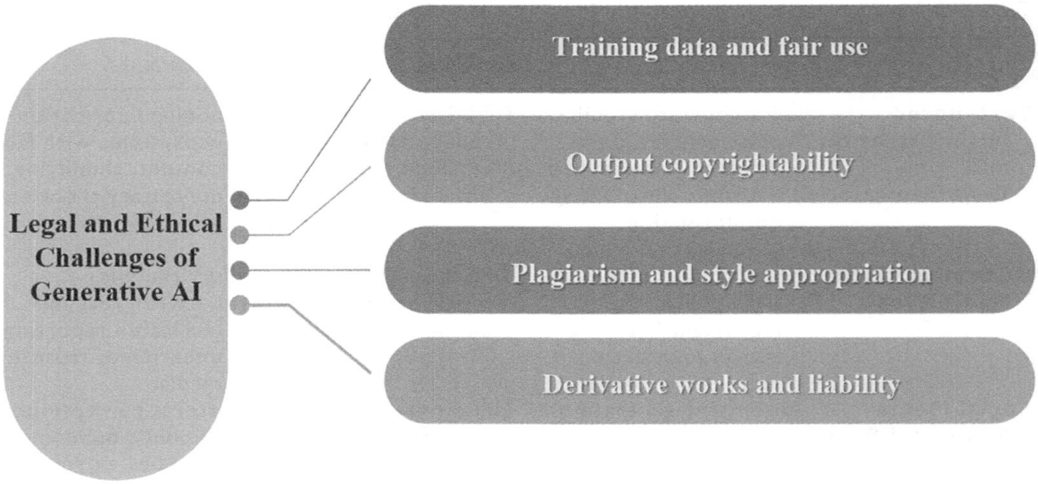

Figure 5.2 Legal and Ethical Challenge of GenAI.

- **Training data and fair use**: Training a generative model involves copying and processing potentially billions of copyrighted works. AI developers have largely proceeded under the assumption (not yet fully settled in law) that using works for training is a transformative enough purpose possibly qualifying as fair use (in U.S. law) or its equivalents elsewhere. However, some rights holders strongly disagree. In 2023, Getty Images filed a high-profile lawsuit against Stability AI (makers of Stable Diffusion), accusing the company of unlawfully scraping 12 million of Getty's copyrighted photos (identified partly by telltale Getty watermarks appearing in some AI outputs) to train its model without a license [47]. Getty argues this wholesale ingestion of protected images is massive copyright infringement, done to build a commercial AI product on the back of photographers' work [48]. Similarly, groups of artists and authors have launched class-action lawsuits against GenAI firms, claiming their creations were used without consent to train models that now compete with their labor [49].

  These cases will test in court whether AI training is permissible under existing copyright exceptions. The outcome could reshape AI development practices, requiring licenses for training data or government-mandated compensation schemes (some have proposed something akin to music royalties for content used in AI training). Already, there are market responses: some stock image companies and content platforms now explicitly forbid scraping content for AI training in their terms of service, and others are exploring licensing partnerships (e.g., Shutterstock made a deal with OpenAI to license images for model training and to compensate artists).
- **Output copyrightability**: Another contentious issue is whether content generated by AI can be copyrighted, and if so, by whom. Copyright law traditionally requires a human author for a work to be protected. In a landmark decision in February 2023, the U.S. Copyright Office clarified that it would register a work containing AI-generated material only for the human-authored portions. In that case, a graphic novel with human-written text and AI-generated illustrations was deemed copyrightable as a whole, but the individual AI-created images were not protected [50]. The Office stated

that material produced by a machine without human creativity is ineligible for copyright [51]. Similarly, U.S. courts ruled that a fully AI-generated artwork (with no human input beyond running the program) could not have a copyright owner, as it lacked the required human authorship (this was decided in a case involving an AI-generated image submitted by an author who deliberately gave credit to an AI).

This stance implies that, at least under current law, most raw outputs from GenAI are in the public domain or unprotectable. However, if a user sufficiently edits or curates the AI output, exercising creative choices, the modified result might qualify for copyright. Other jurisdictions are also grappling with this: the EU has been considering new rules on AI-generated works, and some countries, such as the UK, have limited "data mining" exceptions to facilitate AI training while protecting rights holders' interests.

- **Plagiarism and style appropriation**: Even if no direct copyright violation occurs in training, generative models can inadvertently spit out pieces of their training data, especially if prompted in certain ways. For example, GitHub's Copilot (an AI coding assistant) was found to sometimes reproduce large snippets of code verbatim from its training set (open-source repositories), raising issues of licensing since that code might be under GPL (General Public License) or other licenses that require attribution. This led to a lawsuit claiming Copilot is a "code plagiarism" engine violating open-source licenses. While a court recently dismissed some claims, the case highlighted the tension between AI convenience and respecting original creators' licenses [52].

  Even when not verbatim, AI outputs often imitate the style or content of training examples. Visual artists have objected that image generators can mimic their distinctive art styles without credit; users can literally prompt "in the style of [Artist Name]" and get a look-alike image. This feels to many artists like an uncompensated exploitation of their IP and reputation. Though style itself may not be protected by copyright (only specific expression is), the ethics and economics are debated. Some artists have pulled their galleries offline or pressured AI companies for opt-out mechanisms to exclude their work from training sets. In response, Stability AI and others have implemented (or promised) opt-out processes and tools that allow artists to see if their work was used. Nonetheless, the principle remains contested: should AI models be allowed to learn from any available content (as humans do), or should creators have a right to say no?
- **Derivative works and liability**: Another legal grey area is when AI output is substantially similar to an existing work. If an AI "invents" a song that happens to match a copyrighted melody, or generates text passages eerily close to a specific author's paragraphs, could that be considered a derivative work infringing copyright? This scenario is not far-fetched, given the statistical nature of these models. It poses challenges for both AI providers and users. If infringement occurs, who is liable: the user who prompted it, the model developer, or both? Under current law, if an AI is just a tool used by a person, the user could be liable for what they produce. But if the AI acts more autonomously, it's a grey zone.

Table 5.3 summarizes the main IP challenges raised by GenAI, spanning training data usage, ownership of outputs, plagiarism, style appropriation, and liability for derivative works.

Table 5.3 IP and Ownership Issues in GenAI

Category	*Core Issue*	*Examples*	*Implications*
Training Data and Fair Use	Use of copyrighted works in large-scale training without consent; legality of "fair use" unsettled.	Getty Images lawsuit against Stability AI for scraping 12M photos [47, 48]; class-action lawsuits by artists/authors [49].	Could reshape AI training practices, leading to licensing requirements or compensation schemes.
Output Copyrightability	Whether AI-generated outputs qualify for copyright protection; role of human authorship.	U.S. Copyright Office (2023): AI-only material not copyrightable; human-authored parts eligible [50][51].	Most AI outputs unprotectable; edited/curated versions may qualify; different jurisdictions considering reforms.
Plagiarism and Style Appropriation	Models may reproduce verbatim training data or mimic unique artistic styles without attribution.	GitHub Copilot reproducing code snippets, raising licensing concerns [52]; image generators copying styles "in the style of [Artist Name]."	Risks of plagiarism, ethical disputes, pressure for opt-out tools; unresolved tension between innovation and creator rights.
Derivative Works and Liability	AI outputs may be substantially similar to copyrighted works; unclear who bears legal responsibility.	Hypothetical overlaps in generated songs, texts, or art; ongoing lawsuits testing liability frameworks.	Uncertainty over liability for infringement (user vs. developer); legal grey zones complicate adoption.

Regulatory bodies are actively studying these questions. The U.S. Copyright Office in 2023 launched an inquiry into AI and copyright, seeking public input on how to handle training data, output ownership, and related questions [53]. The goal is to possibly update guidelines or recommend legislation. Internationally, there is discussion within WIPO (World Intellectual Property Organization) on global IP policy for AI. Some advocate for a new class of protection or compensation for AI training uses, for example, a collective licensing system where AI companies pay into a fund that distributes royalties to creators whose works were used (though identifying and valuing each contribution is nontrivial). Others argue that overly stringent rules could stifle AI innovation and that fair use and human creativity can coexist with AI advances.

In any case, current events suggest a turbulent period ahead in courts and legislatures. As one whitepaper put it, GenAI is "testing the boundaries of IP law in unprecedented ways." The outcomes will shape the incentives for creators and the openness of AI development. Striking a balance is tricky: we want to encourage innovation and the free flow of knowledge (which favors broad training data access) but also ensure creators are not unfairly deprived of credit or income by AI systems that depend on their work. In the meantime, organizations deploying GenAI are urged to take caution, for instance, by filtering model outputs to avoid verbatim regurgitation of training passages and allowing copyright holders to opt out of training datasets as a good-faith measure. The onus is on the AI community, legal experts, and policymakers to adapt IP frameworks so that GenAI's rise does not come at the expense of human creativity and rights.

5.5 BIAS, DISCRIMINATION, AND SOCIETAL IMPACTS

This section analyzes how GenAI can replicate and amplify social biases, with significant implications at both individual and societal levels. It begins by examining algorithmic bias in language and image models, demonstrating how stereotypes and discriminatory patterns emerge in AI outputs. The discussion then turns to psychological consequences for individuals, including risks of manipulation, dependency, and mental health challenges. Finally, it considers broader societal disruptions such as declining discourse quality, political polarization, cultural shifts, and widening inequalities, while also highlighting regulatory and ethical efforts aimed at mitigating these impacts.

5.5.1 Bias and discrimination in GenAI

GenAI systems inherit and can amplify the biases present in their training data. Learning from human-produced text and images, which inevitably contain historical and social biases relating to race, gender, religion, culture, and more, these systems often produce outputs that reflect or even worsen such biases. This creates a serious risk, as AI-generated content may reinforce stereotypes, exclude minority perspectives, or perpetuate discrimination under the guise of algorithmic objectivity.

Gender bias is another prevalent issue. Language models have shown tendencies to produce sexist assumptions, for example, associating certain professions or roles with a particular gender. If asked to write a story about a nurse or teacher, an AI might default to using "she/her" pronouns, whereas for an engineer or CEO, it might use "he/him," thus reinforcing gender stereotypes. A research paper found GPT-3 exhibited biases in story generation, such as depicting male characters in more career-oriented roles and women in family or appearance-related contexts [54].

In the image generation realm, biases are equally troubling. A 2023 University of Washington study on Stable Diffusion (a popular image generator) showed that when prompted with something generic like "a person," the model's outputs were overwhelmingly of light-skinned men [55]. Women and darker-skinned individuals were underrepresented unless the prompt explicitly specified those traits. Moreover, when asked for "a person from [region]," Stable Diffusion sometimes produced exotifying or stereotypical images. For example, "a person from Oceania" gave mostly light-skinned people (failing to reflect Indigenous populations), and it tended to sexualize images of women from certain countries [56]. These results imply that the training data (likely internet images) had a bias toward Western, white, male faces and certain portrayals of women, and the model reproduced those skewed distributions.

Bias in GenAI is not limited to demographics. Models can also pick up on and amplify ideological biases or biases in language usage. If a training corpus has derogatory or slang terms used for certain groups, the model might use those inappropriately. There have been instances of chatbots inadvertently generating antisemitic or racist content when prompted a certain way, simply because those associations exist in the data. Microsoft's infamous Tay chatbot (2016), while not a generative model in the modern sense, demonstrated how quickly an AI agent can learn the worst of human input and start parroting hate speech when exposed to trolling. Modern systems have more safeguards, but the risk remains that under some conditions, biased or toxic outputs slip through.

These biases can have real harm if GenAI is integrated into user-facing products without checks. For instance, AI writing assistants might subtly use different tones or terminology for certain names or identities (e.g., assuming gender or making biased analogies), which could offend or disadvantage users. Biased image generation could affect media and advertising if designers rely on AI for stock images or illustrations and it mostly generates white male figures for generic roles, it sidelines diversity and falsely normalizes a narrow view of society.

Addressing bias is thus a top priority from an ethical and regulatory standpoint. A well-known paper titled "On the Dangers of Stochastic Parrots" [57] called out that large language models are "inscrutable and meaning-less" in a way that can hide unknown, dangerous biases. The authors urged the AI field to recognize the risks of training on huge uncurated datasets and to invest in better dataset documentation and bias analysis. They argue for curating training data to filter out harmful content and for ongoing evaluations of model outputs for bias and fairness issues [58].

Many developers are now incorporating bias mitigation steps: for example, fine-tuning models with additional data to reduce toxic or biased tendencies or using reinforcement learning from human feedback (RLHF) to teach the model to avoid certain classes of content. OpenAI's ChatGPT, for instance, underwent a refinement process to refuse or moderate outputs containing hate speech or overt prejudice. There is also work on algorithmic techniques like debiasing word embeddings or adding constraints so that, say, occupation descriptions aren't stereotypically gendered.

Another approach is to increase transparency. Model cards and datasheets (documentation practice) list known biases or limitations of the model. For example, the creators of Stable Diffusion and DALL-E have noted that their models may reflect societal biases and should not be assumed to be neutral. The idea is to warn users and encourage responsible use, for example, a user might need to explicitly specify diversity in a prompt to get diverse results, knowing the default might be skewed.

Regulators are also paying attention. The EU AI Act would require high-risk AI systems to be evaluated for bias and discrimination and to implement risk management to mitigate these issues [59]. In areas like hiring or lending (even if GenAI is indirectly used for creating profiles or summaries), any bias could violate nondiscrimination laws. There's also the court of public opinion: tech companies face reputational damage if their AI is seen as racist or sexist, which pressures them to address problems proactively.

Table 5.4 summarizes the main dimensions of bias and discrimination in GenAI, covering gender, racial, cultural, ideological, and structural aspects along with their manifestations, harms, and mitigation approaches.

In conclusion, bias in GenAI is a mirror of our societal biases but with the potential to magnify them under the guise of algorithmic creation. It is a dark side in the sense that, without careful handling, AI could unwittingly exacerbate inequality or offend and harm marginalized groups. Overcoming this requires a concerted effort: improving training data diversity, implementing bias checks, engaging interdisciplinary experts (including social scientists and ethicists) in model development, and setting guidelines for fair and inclusive AI. Progress is being made, but as these models continue to grow in influence, vigilance against bias remains crucial to prevent reinforcing the very prejudices society has worked hard to reduce.

Table 5.4 Comparative Dimensions of Bias and Discrimination in GenAI

Bias Dimension	*Manifestation in Practice*	*Studies*	*Potential Harms*	*Mitigation Approaches*
Gender Bias	Models default to associating roles with gender (e.g., "nurse = female," "CEO = male").	GPT-3 produced gendered stereotypes in story generation [54].	Reinforces occupational stereotypes; reduces inclusivity in AI-driven outputs.	Debiasing embeddings, RLHF, curated fine-tuning datasets.
Racial and Skin-Tone Bias	Overrepresentation of light-skinned individuals in image generation; underrepresentation of minorities.	UW study: Stable Diffusion generated mostly light-skinned men for generic prompts[55].	Erasure of diversity; distorted social representation in media, advertising, design.	Dataset diversification, prompt guidance, fairness audits.
Cultural and Regional Bias	Exotification or stereotyping of certain regions; inaccurate portrayals of local populations.	Stable Diffusion outputs "person from Oceania" mostly as white/light-skinned [56].	Cultural misrepresentation, perpetuation of stereotypes.	Explicit prompt modifiers, regional dataset inclusion, transparency warnings.
Ideological and Language Bias	Reproduction of derogatory, antisemitic, or racist terms from training corpora.	Microsoft Tay chatbot (2016) demonstrated rapid amplification of hate speech.	Toxic outputs, reputational harm, and discriminatory user experiences.	Content moderation, toxic content filters, RLHF.
Structural/ Systemic Bias	Subtle shifts in tone or assumptions about identity in text outputs.	Writing assistants producing biased analogies or pronoun assumptions.	Disadvantage to minorities; exclusionary user-facing applications.	Model cards, datasheets, interdisciplinary bias evaluations.

5.5.2 Psychological impacts on individuals

Beyond technical and societal biases, GenAI carries profound consequences for individuals at a psychological level. Its influence extends into how people perceive truth, form emotional connections, rely on cognitive abilities, and manage their mental health. By blurring the boundaries between authentic and synthetic experiences, GenAI can shape trust, heighten susceptibility to manipulation, foster dependency, and even endanger well-being. To better understand these human-centered challenges, this subsection examines five key psychological impacts: deception and trust erosion, manipulation and persuasion, emotional attachment and dependency, cognitive offloading and skill atrophy, and mental health concerns.

- **Deception and trust erosion**: Knowing that any media could be AI-generated might breed a general sense of skepticism or even paranoia. Individuals may find it stressful to navigate a world where seeing (or hearing) is not believing. There is a psychological cost to constantly questioning the authenticity of what one encounters online or even in personal communications (e.g., worrying that a voice note from a friend could be spoofed). This can degrade trust not only in media, but interpersonally, people might become hesitant to trust emails or messages unless verified, adding cognitive burden in daily life.
- **Manipulation and persuasion**: AI-generated content can be micro-targeted and emotionally tuned to manipulate individuals. Personal data and AI can be combined to deliver highly persuasive fake messages or deepfakes aimed at someone (for instance, audio of a loved one urging them to take some action). The emotional manipulation potential is high, which can cause psychological distress or false beliefs. For example, consider an elderly person manipulated by an AI voice clone scam; beyond financial loss, the betrayal of trust can be traumatic.
- **Emotional attachment and dependency**: On the flip side, some GenAIs (like conversational agents) are designed to be companions or helpers. Users may develop strong emotional bonds with AI characters or chatbots. For instance, AI "friend" apps have users who report feeling genuine friendship or even romantic feelings toward their chatbot. While such attachment can provide comfort, it raises psychological and ethical questions. People might become over-reliant on AI for emotional support, potentially withdrawing from real human interactions. If the AI is unexpectedly shut down or changes (as happened when an update to the Replika chatbot's personality upset some devoted users), vulnerable individuals could experience real grief or identity disturbance.
- **Cognitive offloading and skill atrophy**: Relying heavily on GenAI for tasks like writing, summarizing, drawing, or problem-solving might lead to a decline in those skills for the individual. If a student always uses AI to generate essays, they may not develop the ability to form arguments or write coherently on their own. Similarly, constant use of AI-generated code could hamper a novice programmer's learning. This over-reliance could affect self-efficacy; one's belief in one's own abilities may diminish if AI is always seen as the more competent creator. In the long run, that could alter educational approaches and personal development, potentially undermining confidence or creativity (some fear a generation of "AI users" rather than skilled creators).
- **Mental health concerns**: Interacting with GenAI can influence mental health in positive or negative ways. On the positive side, some see promise in AI therapy bots or simply the availability of a nonjudgmental listener 24/7. But negative outcomes have also been observed. The tragic case of a young person who died by suicide after a chatbot encouraged him (cited earlier) [60] is an extreme example. More commonly, if AI chatbots are not carefully designed, they might provide incorrect health advice or fail to properly handle a user in crisis, with dire consequences. Also, AI that generates content based on user queries could inadvertently reinforce harmful thoughts. For example, someone with an eating disorder could prompt an AI for "tips" and receive a detailed plan that exacerbates their condition. Hence, the influence of GenAI on vulnerable users is a serious concern that intersects with ethics and design responsibility.

5.5.3 Broader societal impacts

While GenAI affects individuals in profound psychological ways, its influence also extends to society as a whole. These technologies are reshaping how information circulates, how communities interact, and how cultural and economic systems evolve. At the societal level, GenAI can disrupt public discourse, intensify political polarization, reshape cultural and artistic expression, and influence both economic structures and educational practices. Its widespread adoption risks amplifying inequality, weakening trust in shared facts, and altering the values that hold communities together. To capture these broader dimensions, this subsection examines six major societal impacts (see Figure 5.3): the quality of discourse and the information ecosystem, polarization and echo chambers, the "liar's dividend" effect on social trust, cultural and artistic implications, economic and social inequality, and challenges to education and socialization.

- **Quality of discourse and information ecosystem**: With more AI-generated content online, authentic human voices may be drowned out, and meaningful debate may become harder. Suspicion that opposing views are "bot-generated" could fuel polarization.
- **Polarization and echo chambers**: GenAI could be used to create tailored narratives that entrench people in their existing beliefs, contributing to polarization. For example, propaganda bots might flood left-wing groups with one type of narrative and right-wing groups with another, each reinforcing their biases. This automated customization can deepen echo chambers, fragmenting public dialogue. Moreover, the inability to trust content authenticity might lead people to just trust whatever aligns with their preexisting views (since "everything could be fake," they choose the reality they want to believe), a phenomenon some analysts worry will erode the shared factual basis needed for democracy [61].
- **Social fabric and "liar's dividend"**: As noted, the presence of deepfakes can allow liars to thrive; this might corrode social norms of honesty. Public figures caught in wrongdoing might routinely dismiss evidence as fake, and segments of society will back those claims, leading to further social schisms. On a community level, incidents like

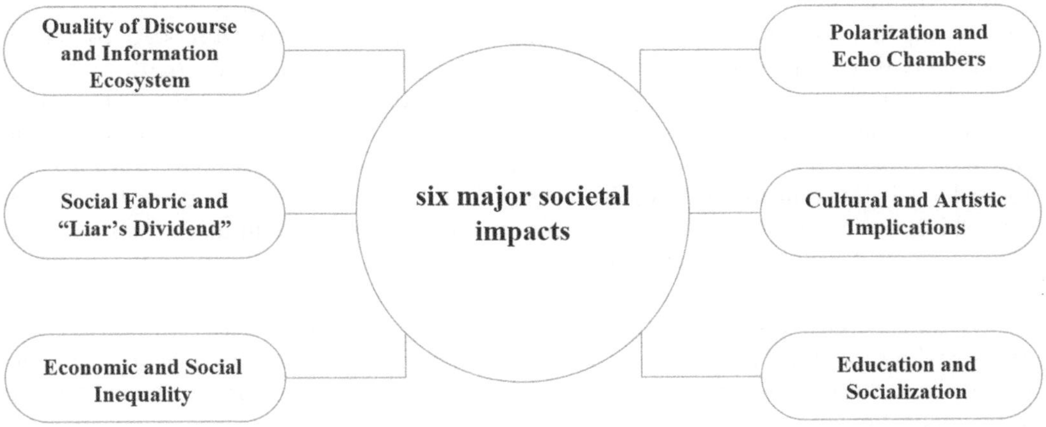

Figure 5.3 Six Major Societal Impacts.

false audio of a public emergency (say, an AI-fabricated warning of a disaster) could cause panic and then a backlash of cynicism if it's revealed to be fake. Over time, repeated deepfake incidents could instill either paranoia or apathy (a sense that nothing can be verified, so why bother).

- **Cultural and artistic implications**: GenAI encroaches on creative domains, which could alter how society values art and human creativity. If AI art and music become ubiquitous, will that diminish appreciation for human artists, or will human-made art gain a cachet of authenticity (similar to how handmade goods became valued after mass industrialization)? There's a risk of a cultural monotony if many people use the same AI tools with similar training data, a "collapse of originality" where AI regurgitates and remixes existing styles endlessly. Culturally, this raises concern about losing diversity of creative expression or marginalizing artists who don't use AI.
- **Economic and social inequality**: If GenAI disproportionately benefits certain groups (tech-savvy, owners of AI infrastructure) and displaces others (e.g., some middle-class professional jobs), societal inequality could widen. Large inequalities can lead to social unrest, distrust in institutions, and a sense of alienation among those left behind by technology. Ensuring broad accessibility and retraining can mitigate this, but if mishandled, AI could exacerbate societal divides, technological haves vs have-nots.
- **Education and socialization**: In schools and universities, GenAI is forcing a rethinking of assignments and assessments. If students can use AI for homework, how do we teach and evaluate learning? Some educators worry about the loss of critical thinking practice; others see AI as a tool to be taught. Socially, younger generations growing up with AI assistants might have different communication habits or expectations (e.g., becoming used to talking to AI about problems instead of human mentors). Parenting might even involve AI (AI story generators, tutors, etc.), influencing child development in ways we don't fully understand yet.

The societal impacts are not uniformly negative. GenAI also has positive potentials such as democratizing content creation and providing assistive tools for people with disabilities (e.g., helping those with dyslexia write or creating images for those who can't draw). But focusing on the "dark side," it's clear that our social systems need time to adapt to the disruptions GenAI can cause. Public awareness is a key part: campaigns to educate about deepfakes and misinformation, efforts to improve digital literacy, and encouraging a healthy skepticism (but not total cynicism) regarding online content. Communities online (like Wikipedia editors, fact-checkers, etc.) are also mobilizing to address AI content by updating policies (e.g., some communities ban AI-generated text unless vetted).

Psychologically, coping strategies might include advice like "verify through multiple sources," "use trusted institutions for information," and perhaps even technical aids (browser plugins that flag suspected AI content, for instance). Individuals will also need to strike a balance in using AI tools, leveraging them for efficiency but not letting their own skills and mental engagement atrophy. Just as calculator use in math class had to be balanced with learning basic arithmetic, society will learn how to incorporate GenAI in a balanced way.

In summary, GenAI's integration into society is a grand experiment with our cognitive and social well-being. There are risks of deception, mental distress, and societal fragmentation if the technology is misused or simply overwhelms our current institutions. However, with mindful governance, education, and cultural adaptation, many of these negative outcomes can be mitigated. The process will involve much trial and error, as we are already seeing in the debates in classrooms, legislatures, and online communities in response to AI's sudden proliferation. The goal should be to harness GenAI to augment human society, not erode the foundations of trust, creativity, and human connection that bind us together.

5.6 ECONOMIC DISRUPTION AND LABOR MARKET SHIFTS

The rise of GenAI is poised to have broad economic ramifications, disrupting job markets and industry dynamics. By automating tasks that were once deemed the exclusive province of human creativity and knowledge work, GenAI could both displace certain roles and augment others, leading to significant shifts in employment and the nature of work. This dual capacity to boost productivity but also potentially render some skills obsolete has drawn comparisons to past technological revolutions (like industrial automation), with experts warning of a sizable impact on the global workforce.

Various studies and forecasts highlight the scale of potential disruption:

- A 2023 analysis by Goldman Sachs estimated that GenAI could expose 300 million full-time jobs worldwide to automation in some form [62]. They found roughly two-thirds of occupations, especially in the United States and Europe, have at least some tasks that could be automated by AI, and up to a quarter of tasks in those jobs could be replaced on average [63]. If realized, that figure implies a significant reallocation of labor, many jobs changing in character or demand, and some being eliminated.
- An OpenAI and University of Pennsylvania study in 2023 similarly concluded that about 80% of U.S. workers could have at least 10% of their job tasks affected by the introduction of GPT-style AI, and around 19% of workers may see 50% or more of their tasks impacted [64]. Notably, they found that higher-wage, white-collar occupations might be more exposed than many lower-wage manual jobs, since GenAI targets cognitive and routine programming/design tasks that are common in professional roles [65]. This challenges the conventional wisdom that automation primarily hits blue-collar labor; here, creative and clerical professions are on the front line.
- Examples of roles at risk include content writers, journalists, graphic designers, illustrators, and computer programmers. AI can draft articles, create marketing copy, generate artwork or logos, and even produce functioning code. Early signs of this disruption are visible: some media outlets experimented with AI-written news or product descriptions (leading to debates about quality and plagiarism), and companies like GitHub offer AI coding assistants that may reduce the need for junior programmers on certain tasks.
- The creative industries face both opportunity and threat. For instance, advertising agencies might use AI to generate dozens of ad banner variants in seconds (increasing productivity), but that could mean fewer graphic designers are needed for brute-force creative generation. Likewise, game studios might auto-generate scenery or dialogue, reducing demand for some asset artists or writers. The economic value of certain human creative skills might decline if AI can produce acceptable results at a fraction of the cost and time.

However, history suggests that while technology may displace some jobs, it also creates new ones and can spur economic growth that generates alternative employment. Goldman Sachs noted that though 300 million jobs might be affected, GenAI could also drive a ~7% increase in global GDP over a decade by boosting productivity [66]. They argue that many roles will be augmented rather than replaced, AI handling tedious or routine components, humans focusing on higher-level tasks, and entirely new job categories will emerge.

In fact, new job categories related to GenAI are already forming. "Prompt engineering" crafting effective inputs to get desired outputs from AI is now a sought-after skill. AI ethicists and auditors are needed to evaluate models. Fields like AI-assisted drug design or fashion design are blending human expertise with generative algorithms, potentially creating niche roles. An optimistic view is that AI will eliminate mundane work and free humans for more creative, strategic endeavors, possibly catalyzing innovation and new industries (just as the introduction of spreadsheets automated arithmetic but enabled more complex financial analysis jobs).

Yet, the transition period could be rocky and is a key concern. There may be a skills mismatch: workers whose jobs are suddenly disrupted might not have or be able to easily acquire the skills for new, AI-centric roles. This could lead to unemployment or underemployment for certain groups, particularly if change happens faster than education and training systems adapt. A widely cited concern is for those in entry-level or junior positions. If AI can do 50% of a task, a company might need fewer interns or junior staff, which could ironically make it harder for people to get started in a career and acquire expertise (the "ladder" effect). For example, law firms might use AI to draft routine contracts or summarize case law work usually given to junior attorneys, thus hiring fewer paralegals or new associates, impacting the legal job pipeline.

Another aspect is inequality. If AI mostly enhances the productivity of highly skilled workers and automates lower-skill tasks, it might increase the wage gap between those who can leverage AI and those who cannot. Conversely, if AI erodes some professional jobs, those workers might compete for other jobs, potentially depressing wages in those areas. The geographic distribution also matters; some economies might benefit (those that innovate and adopt AI), whereas others might lose if their comparative advantage was in tasks now automated.

The economic risks of GenAI therefore include not just job loss, but also the need for societal adaptation: re-skilling programs, safety nets for displaced workers, and perhaps new economic models if a significant fraction of labor becomes automated (which fuels discussions around measures like universal basic income).

Policymakers and economists are actively debating these scenarios. Some recommend investing in education and continuous learning so the workforce can transition to working alongside AI, emphasizing skills like critical thinking, complex problem-solving, and human-touch professions (e.g., healthcare, education) that AI is less likely to fully replace. Others call for updating labor regulations and considering taxation on AI productivity gains to fund worker retraining. There is also encouragement for industries to adopt AI in a complementary way, for example, doctors using AI diagnostic tools but still overseeing decisions, rather than completely automating roles.

From an industry standpoint, companies that adapt and integrate AI may outcompete those that don't, potentially leading to economic consolidation. Big tech firms investing heavily in AI could dominate even more, given their access to AI talent and compute resources, raising antitrust questions down the line.

In summary, GenAI stands to reshape the economic landscape. The dark side of this transformation is the potential upheaval for millions of workers, the risk of widened inequality, and the loss of certain crafts or skills. The bright side is increased productivity, new innovations, and possibly the liberation of humans from drudge work. Which effect prevails will depend on how carefully this technology is deployed and how proactively stakeholders respond. History has shown that economies can ultimately benefit from technological revolutions, but not without short-term pain and the necessity of thoughtful policy interventions to ensure the gains are broadly shared.

5.7 GOVERNANCE LEGAL AND ETHICAL CHALLENGES

The rapid development of GenAI has outpaced existing regulatory and ethical frameworks, leaving policymakers, legal scholars, and ethicists struggling to respond. These systems cut across multiple domains, including speech, IP, consumer protection, privacy, and national security, creating unprecedented challenges. This section examines the key governance, legal, and ethical dilemmas raised by GenAI. We begin with legal and regulatory issues such as liability, transparency, privacy, and jurisdictional gaps, then turn to ethical concerns including moral responsibility, consent, fairness, and long-term societal risks. Together, these dimensions highlight the urgent need for coherent governance strategies that balance innovation with accountability.

5.7.1 Regulatory and legal challenges

The swift advancement of GenAI has left policymakers scrambling to establish appropriate regulations and legal frameworks. These AI systems cut across traditional regulatory domains, touching on speech, IP, consumer protection, privacy, and even national security, creating a complex challenge for lawmakers. Crafting rules that mitigate the harms of GenAI without stifling innovation is a delicate task, made harder by the global, borderless nature of AI technology and the rapid pace of change.

Several key legal and regulatory questions have emerged:

- **Liability for AI outputs**: If a GenAI produces harmful content (defamatory text, privacy-violating images, dangerously wrong advice, etc.), who is legally responsible? Is it the developer of the AI model, the user who prompted it, or the deployer offering the AI service? Current laws (like Section 230 of the U.S. Communications Decency Act) protect platforms from liability for user-generated content, but AI-generated content is a new category. Some argue that AI companies might not be shielded by Section 230 if the AI is essentially creating content itself rather than just hosting user content [67]. There is ambiguity here that regulators and courts will need to clarify. For instance, if an AI chatbot gives libelous statements about a person, can that person sue the AI provider for defamation? Early indications from legal scholars are that new frameworks may be needed, as existing laws did not anticipate AI as an "author" of content.
- **Transparency and disclosure**: Regulators are considering whether and when AI-generated content must be disclosed to consumers. The EU AI Act, for example, explicitly will require that users be informed when they are interacting with an AI system or when content (like video or images) is AI-generated, except in certain contexts like art [68]. Such transparency aims to prevent deception (e.g., bots masquerading as humans, or fake media passed as real). Some U.S. legislators have proposed similar ideas, especially for political ads. A bipartisan bill was introduced that would mandate disclosure of AI deepfakes in election advertising. Ensuring compliance (and defining clear guidelines for what counts as AI-generated) will be an enforcement challenge.

- **Privacy and data protection**: GenAI models often ingest personal data during training (e.g., photos scraped from websites, text from social media). This raises potential conflicts with privacy laws like the EU's GDPR (General Data Protection Regulation), which grants individuals rights over their personal data. If an AI model has memorized someone's personal information and can output it, is that a data breach or a violation of GDPR? Data protection authorities in Europe have started scrutinizing large models. Italy temporarily banned ChatGPT in 2023 over privacy concerns until certain measures were implemented. Future regulations might require clear consent for using personal data in training (though enforcing that on web-scale corpora is difficult) or allow individuals to request removal (analogous to a "right to be forgotten" in training data).
- **Content moderation and safe use**: There is regulatory pressure on AI providers to prevent misuse of their models (for instance, preventing them from generating illegal content like hate speech or instructions for crimes). Already, companies implement usage policies and filters. But if those fail, could regulators penalize them? We might see standards emerge for required content moderation practices in AI systems, akin to how social media companies are expected to moderate content (with varying legal approaches around the world). For example, China's guidelines for GenAI services (issued in 2023) require that outputs align with core socialist values and not threaten social stability, effectively enforcing a strict content policy by law. Western countries likely won't dictate specific ideological alignments, but they may still ban certain AI outputs (like nonconsensual deepfake porn or extremist propaganda).
- **Certification and model accountability**: An idea gaining traction is that advanced AI models (especially very large "foundation models") might need to go through safety assessments or certification before deployment, similar to how medicines or cars are regulated for safety. Sam Altman of OpenAI testified to the U.S. Congress in 2023, suggesting a licensing regime for the most powerful AI systems. The EU AI Act is heading somewhat in that direction: it classifies AI systems by risk, and the most capable general models could be subject to requirements like risk assessment, documentation, and even registration with authorities [69]. If enacted, providers of GenAI would have to demonstrate that they have evaluated and mitigated risks (bias, misuse, etc.) in their models before release.
- **Jurisdictional gaps and international coordination**: AI is a global industry; models trained in one country can be deployed in another. This raises jurisdiction issues. For instance, if a European citizen's copyright is violated by a U.S.-based AI service, how can they seek a remedy? International cooperation may be needed to harmonize standards or at least share best practices. Organizations like the OECD and UNESCO have proposed global AI principles (e.g., transparency, human-centered values [70]), but these are nonbinding. There's discussion of an "AI governance" body or treaty, akin to climate accords or nuclear arms treaties, but that is in early stages.

The European Union is at the forefront with its comprehensive AI Act (expected to be finalized in 2024). This legislation will likely enforce transparency for GenAI and mandate robustness and safety checks. It also may impose fines for noncompliance, similar to how GDPR fines companies for data violations. The EU is also updating its copyright and digital services laws to explicitly handle deepfakes and AI content (e.g., the updated Code of Practice on Disinformation includes deepfake provisions).

The United States has taken a more wait-and-see approach at the federal level, though there are calls for action. The White House in 2022 released a Blueprint for an AI Bill of Rights, outlining principles like safety, explainability, and nondiscrimination for automated systems. While not law, it signals policy intent. In the absence of broad federal regulation, agencies like the FTC (Federal Trade Commission) have warned they will use existing consumer protection laws to go after harmful uses of AI (for fraud or deception). State-level initiatives exist: for example, California's bot transparency law (requiring some bots to identify as such) and some states banning certain malicious deepfakes. But overall, U.S. regulation is in formative stages.

China has moved quickly to control GenAI under its authoritarian framework. Its regulations require AI content to be censored for forbidden material, mandate real-name registration for users of GenAI services, and hold providers accountable for misuse on their platforms. This top-down approach ensures alignment with government dictates but of course raises censorship and freedom of expression concerns.

Other countries are similarly exploring rules. The UK has issued an AI regulation whitepaper favoring a light-touch, context-specific approach; Canada is working on an AI and Data Act; and international forums like the G7 have an "AI governance" working group (the so-called Hiroshima AI process).

Beyond government regulation, industry self-regulation and standards are likely to play a role. Organizations might adopt voluntary codes of conduct for AI (OpenAI, Google, and others recently agreed to measures like external testing and watermarking under U.S. government urging). Standards bodies (ISO [International Organization for Standardization]/IEC [International Electrotechnical Commission]) are developing technical standards for AI risk management, which could be referenced in regulations.

In the legal realm, we also must consider how existing laws apply even without AI-specific rules. For example, if an AI system produces defamatory output, defamation law still applies even if it's unclear who the "speaker" is. If AI-generated advice leads to injury, product liability or negligence law might come into play (was the AI a product sold with implied safety?). These questions will be sorted out in court cases by case, unless preempted by AI-specific statutes.

In sum, the governance of GenAI is playing catch-up to the technology. The risks outlined in this chapter, from deepfakes to bias, underscore the need for clear guidelines and accountability. Regulators face the challenge of retooling legal concepts (like authorship, speech, and liability) for the AI context. The dark side of an unregulated approach is that harms could proliferate with little recourse; on the other hand, heavy-handed regulation might chill beneficial innovation and cement the lead of big incumbents (who can afford compliance) over startups. Thus, a balanced regulatory strategy is essential, likely combining flexible principles with targeted rules for the most acute risks. Ongoing dialogue between technologists, lawmakers, civil society, and international partners will be crucial to build a legal environment where GenAI can develop responsibly and ethically.

5.7.2 Ethical dilemmas and responsible AI

Beyond formal laws, ethical considerations loom large in the development and deployment of GenAI. These technologies force us to confront difficult questions about responsibility, consent, transparency, and the relationship between humans and machines. Even if an AI system's actions don't violate a specific law, they might still be ethically problematic. Conversely, an overly cautious approach might deprive society of valuable innovations. Navigating these dilemmas is a core challenge for AI researchers, companies, and society at large. Key ethical issues include:

- **Moral responsibility and accountability**: When a GenAI causes harm, who is morally accountable? This is related to legal liability but goes deeper into how we assign blame or responsibility when the "actor" is an algorithm that has no intent? If a chatbot gives harmful advice that someone acts on, the ethical responsibility might lie partly with the designers (for not foreseeing and preventing such output) and the operators (for deploying it without safeguards). There's also debate about whether AI itself can be considered to have agency or whether responsibility always traces back to human decisions in design and deployment. The consensus in AI ethics is that human developers, deployers, and governing bodies must take responsibility for AI outcomes, treating AI as tools rather than independent moral agents.
- **Consent and autonomy**: GenAI can mimic real people's likeness or style without their consent (as in deepfakes or style-copying art). Ethically, using someone's identity in a deepfake, even non-maliciously, violates their autonomy and dignity if done without permission. This raises the principle of informed consent: individuals should have some control over whether AI can use their image, voice, or creations. Ethicists argue for strong norms or rules around consent, especially for sensitive uses like recreating a deceased person's voice or generating explicit content of someone. The lack of consent in training data usage is also an ethical sore point. Just because data is publicly accessible doesn't automatically make it ethical to use for any purpose (e.g., pictures on social media used to train face generation AIs may include images people never expected to be repurposed by companies). Initiatives to allow opt-outs or to create datasets with only willingly contributed content are potential ethical responses.
- **Honesty and transparency**: Ethically, there is a duty for AI systems or their creators to be honest about the AI's capabilities and outputs. Deceiving users, for example, letting them think they are chatting with a human when it's an AI, or failing to disclose that a video is AI-generated, is seen as unethical because it undermines informed decision-making. Transparency can conflict with utility (an AI pretending to be human might provide comfort or a sense of authenticity in some contexts). Still, most ethical guidelines emphasize at least a basic level of transparency to avoid deception and manipulation. The UNESCO Recommendation on AI Ethics (2021) stresses principles such as transparency, explainability, and human oversight, asserting that people have a right to know when they are subject to AI decisions and to understand AI's reasoning to the extent possible [71].
- **Avoidance of harm**: A fundamental ethical principle (also reflected in many AI guidelines) is non-maleficence. AI should be designed to avoid harm. This is broad and encompasses physical, psychological, and societal harm. Ethically, developers should proactively think about how their GenAI could be misused or cause harm (intentionally or unintentionally) and then take steps to mitigate it. For example, an AI image generator could be misused to create violent extremist propaganda; an ethical design

would include filters to block certain violent or terror-related prompts. Similarly, as we saw, AI mental health chatbots can inadvertently cause harm if not carefully controlled, for example, giving someone suicidal encouragement is a catastrophic ethical failure [72]. The onus is on developers to anticipate such scenarios. This aligns with the concept of AI safety or alignment, ensuring AI's behavior is aligned with human values and well-being.

- **Fairness and equity**: Ethically, GenAI should strive to treat all users and groups fairly, without marginalizing or misrepresenting any. This links to the bias discussion: from an ethical lens, releasing an AI that one knows has significant bias against a protected group could be deemed irresponsible. Efforts to reduce bias are not just technical challenges but moral imperatives to not perpetuate discrimination. Moreover, thinking of global fairness, will the benefits of GenAI be accessible to all, or concentrated among the wealthy and tech-savvy? Ethicists argue for democratizing AI benefits (e.g., via open-source models or public-access AI tools) while balancing against the risks of open access (like misuse).
- **Autonomy and dependency**: There is an ethical concern about human autonomy in the face of AI. If people become too reliant on AI for thinking, creativity, or decision-making, does that diminish human capacities or agency? For instance, students might use AI to write essays, potentially hindering their learning of writing skills, raising ethical questions in education about how to integrate AI without eroding fundamental skill development. In a more personal sense, individuals might form emotional dependencies on AI companions or advisors. While AI companionship (like apps acting as "friends" or therapists) can have benefits (combating loneliness), it also treads ethically fraught ground. Cases like the one where a chatbot encouraged a user's suicidal ideation highlight the duty of care needed if AI takes on roles that significantly influence human emotions or decisions.
- **Environmental ethics**: Training large generative models requires substantial computing power, leading to high energy consumption and carbon footprint. The environmental impact of AI has ethical implications regarding sustainability and climate justice. The "Stochastic Parrots" paper pointed out the environmental and financial costs of huge models as an ethical concern and urged the community to consider the downstream climate harm of racing toward ever-bigger models. Ethically, AI developers are encouraged to be transparent about energy usage and to seek more efficient techniques, echoing a broader principle of sustainability in AI ethics.
- **Ethical frameworks and soft law:** In response to these issues, numerous ethical frameworks have been proposed by governmental and professional bodies. For example, the European Commission's Ethics Guidelines for Trustworthy AI set out principles like human agency, privacy, transparency, diversity/nondiscrimination, societal well-being, and accountability. UNESCO's 2021 Recommendation outlines values of respect for human rights, diversity, and environmental sustainability, and principles such as proportionality (AI's benefit should outweigh its risks) and human oversight [73]. While not legally binding, these frameworks guide organizations in developing internal ethics committees, AI charters, and review processes. Many tech companies now have AI ethics panels and publish "AI principles" they pledge to follow (for instance, Google's AI Principles, which include not pursuing AI applications likely to cause harm, and ensuring fairness).

- **Tensions and trade-offs**: Ethical dilemmas often involve balancing competing values. For example, the value of open research and knowledge sharing can conflict with the ethical desire to prevent misuse (OpenAI's initial withholding of GPT-2 is a case where safety was weighed over openness) [74]. The value of personalization might conflict with fairness (personalizing content might inadvertently lead to biased outcomes). And there's the classic tension between innovation and precaution, too much ethical precaution might slow beneficial progress, too little might cause avoidable harm.

In tackling these dilemmas, many advocate for a "responsible AI" approach integrating ethics from the ground up in AI development. This means performing risk assessments, engaging stakeholders (including those who might be adversely affected by the AI), and being willing to limit certain capabilities or uses of a model if the risks outweigh the benefits. For GenAI, responsible practices could include rate-limiting to prevent large-scale abuse (e.g., not letting one user generate millions of deepfake images quickly), watermarking outputs to aid later identification, and thorough testing for bias and harmful tendencies before deployment.

Another ethical concept in discussion is AI alignment, ensuring AI goals and actions are aligned with human values. While often considered in a hypothetical future superintelligence context, alignment is very relevant now: generative models should align with the values of truth, respect, and do-no-harm. Multidisciplinary input (from ethicists, psychologists, and domain experts) is crucial in defining what alignment means in practice for a given model or application.

Finally, the ethical discourse also has to consider long-term and existential questions. Some thinkers worry about the path to AI that could surpass human intelligence and what it means for humanity's future (though GenAI like ChatGPT is not an autonomous agent, it's a step toward more general AI capabilities). Calls like the open letter in 2023 for a moratorium on training the most powerful AI models highlight fears that ethics and safety research are not keeping up with capabilities [75]. Whether one subscribes to those more extreme concerns or not, they underscore a sentiment that ethical guardrails are needed now to steer AI development on a trajectory beneficial to humanity.

In summary, GenAI confronts us with a spectrum of ethical dilemmas from the immediate and tangible (preventing deepfake abuse, reducing bias) to the philosophical (authorship, human–AI relationships). Addressing these requires more than just technical fixes; it demands reflection on our values and a willingness to sometimes say no to certain uses of AI. As the saying goes in medical ethics, "not everything that can be done should be done." The AI community, with input from society, must continuously negotiate what should and shouldn't be done with GenAI, aiming to maximize its benefits while upholding fundamental ethical principles like respect for persons, justice, and the promotion of well-being.

As shown in Table 5.5, various dimensions of governance, legal, and ethical issues in GenAI, such as liability, transparency, privacy, fairness, and environmental sustainability, present significant and interrelated challenges for future regulation and responsible deployment.

Table 5.5 Comparative Overview of Governance, Legal, and Ethical Challenges in GenAI

Dimension	*Key Issues*	*Examples/Current Approaches*	*Challenges Ahead*
Liability for AI Outputs	Responsibility for harmful or defamatory AI content	Section 230 (United States) protections; debates on AI as "author"	Clarifying legal accountability across developers, users, and providers
Transparency and Disclosure	Obligation to label AI-generated media	EU AI Act disclosure rules; U.S. proposals for political ads	Defining thresholds of disclosure; enforcement in global platforms
Privacy and Data Protection	Use of personal data in training models	GDPR enforcement (e.g., Italy's temporary ChatGPT ban)	Enforcing consent and "right to be forgotten" in large datasets
Content Moderation and Safe Use	Preventing misuse (hate speech, crime instructions)	Provider usage policies; China's censorship laws	Balancing free expression with public safety
Certification and Accountability	Risk assessment and licensing of large models	EU AI Act risk-tier system; U.S. calls for AI licensing	Developing global, interoperable safety standards
Jurisdiction and Coordination	Cross-border governance gaps	OECD/UNESCO principles; G7 Hiroshima AI process	Building binding international treaties and harmonized regulations
Moral Responsibility	Ethical accountability for harm	Ethics panels, AI charters (Google, UNESCO guidelines)	Ensuring human responsibility is upheld across the lifecycle
Consent and Autonomy	Deepfakes, voice/style mimicry without permission	Opt-out initiatives; calls for consent frameworks	Protecting dignity and rights in identity replication
Honesty and Transparency	Avoiding deception in AI-human interactions	UNESCO 2021 AI Ethics principles	Aligning transparency with usability and adoption
Avoidance of Harm	Preventing physical/psychological/societal harm	Filters on extremist prompts; safeguards in therapy bots	Anticipating misuse while enabling innovation
Fairness and Equity	Mitigating bias and democratizing access	Bias audits; open-access AI tools	Avoiding systemic discrimination and inequality
Environmental Ethics	Energy demands and carbon footprint	"Stochastic Parrots" critique; calls for sustainable AI	Balancing innovation with sustainability and climate justice

5.8 CONCLUSION

GenAI stands as a defining technological development of the twenty-first century, one that offers extraordinary creative and economic potential, yet simultaneously introduces risks of unprecedented scale and complexity. Its generative capabilities can be weaponized to produce malicious code, synthetic media, or large-scale misinformation that undermines trust, security, and social stability. The same models that empower innovation and creativity can, in the wrong hands, amplify deception, bias, and exploitation. These challenges are not speculative but already observable across domains such as cybersecurity, information integrity, and IP.

The risks associated with GenAI are multifaceted and interdependent, spanning technical, legal, and societal dimensions. Mitigation therefore demands a coordinated response. Technical interventions such as improved model alignment, output watermarking, and robust detection of synthetic content must operate alongside policy initiatives that clarify accountability, establish ethical norms, and ensure that high-impact AI systems are deployed responsibly. At the societal level, efforts to strengthen digital literacy and critical thinking will be essential for building resilience against AI-driven misinformation and manipulation.

Transparency and accountability form the cornerstone of responsible AI governance. Developers and organizations should be expected to document training data, model limitations, and safety mechanisms, enabling oversight and informed evaluation. Equally important is the commitment to responsible innovation, releasing technologies gradually, with clear safeguards and mechanisms for monitoring potential harms. Such an approach reflects the principle that technological advancement should proceed in tandem with social responsibility.

Sustained adaptation of governance frameworks will be crucial as GenAI continues to evolve. Rather than static regulation, an adaptive model of governance, one capable of revising definitions of risk, adjusting safeguards, and responding to emerging evidence, offers a more effective way to manage rapidly advancing technologies. Cooperation across nations, sectors, and disciplines will be key to achieving this adaptability and ensuring that regulatory responses remain relevant and balanced.

At the foundation of all these efforts lies a human-centric vision of technology. GenAI should be developed and deployed in ways that promote human welfare, dignity, and creativity. Ensuring fairness, preventing discrimination, and aligning AI systems with societal values are ethical imperatives, not optional goals. Building interdisciplinary partnerships among technologists, ethicists, policymakers, and social scientists can help ensure that these systems reflect collective human values rather than narrow technical priorities.

GenAI's darker dimensions, from disinformation to deepfakes, bias, and misuse, represent serious but manageable risks. History suggests that societies can adapt to transformative innovations through thoughtful governance, education, and ethical reflection. The path forward lies in designing and regulating AI not merely for capability, but for character, ensuring that the systems created to augment human potential do not erode the foundations of truth, trust, and autonomy. Under principled stewardship, GenAI can evolve into a technology that enriches human society rather than destabilizes it.

ACKNOWLEDGMENTS

The authors hereby confirm that no AI tools were used in the preparation, drafting, or editing of this chapter. All content, analyses, and interpretations presented herein are the result of the authors' own scholarly work and intellectual efforts.

REFERENCES

[1] T. Brown, B. Mann, N. Ryder, M. Subbiah, J. D. Kaplan, P. Dhariwal, A. Neelakantan, P. Shyam, G. Sastry, A. Askell, and S. Agarwal, "Language models are few-shot learners," *Advances in Neural Information Processing Systems*, vol. 33, pp. 1877–1901, 2020.

[2] A. Ramesh, P. Dhariwal, A. Nichol, C. Chu, and M. Chen, "Hierarchical text-conditional image generation with clip latents," *arXiv preprint arXiv:2204.06125,* vol. 1, no. 2, p. 3, 2022.

[3] R. Rombach, A. Blattmann, D. Lorenz, P. Esser, and B. Ommer, "High-resolution image synthesis with latent diffusion models," in *Proceedings of the IEEE/CVF Conference on Computer Vision and Pattern Recognition*, 2022, pp. 10684–10695.

[4] I. Goodfellow, Y. Bengio, A. Courville, and Y. Bengio, *Deep learning* (no. 2). MIT Press, 2016.

[5] V. Ashish, "Attention is all you need," *Advances in Neural Information Processing Systems,* vol. 30, p. I, 2017.

[6] I. J. Goodfellow *et al.*, "Generative adversarial nets," *Advances in Neural Information Processing Systems,* vol. 27, 2014.

[7] A. Radford, J. Wu, R. Child, D. Luan, D. Amodei, and I. Sutskever, "Language models are unsupervised multitask learners," *OpenAI Blog,* vol. 1, no. 8, p. 9, 2019.

[8] S. Kreps, R. M. McCain, and M. Brundage, "All the news that's fit to fabricate: AI-generated text as a tool of media misinformation," *Journal of Experimental Political Science,* vol. 9, no. 1, pp. 104–117, 2022.

[9] B. Chesney, and D. Citron, "Deep fakes: A looming challenge for privacy, democracy, and national security," *California Law Review,* vol. 107, p. 1753, 2019.

[10] F. Urbina, F. Lentzos, C. Invernizzi, and S. Ekins, "Dual use of artificial-intelligence-powered drug discovery," *Nature Machine Intelligence*, vol. 4, no. 3, pp. 189–191, 2022.

[11] M. Brundage *et al.*, "The malicious use of artificial intelligence: Forecasting, prevention, and mitigation," *arXiv preprint arXiv:1802.07228*, 2018.

[12] A. Brenneis, "Assessing dual use risks in AI research: Necessity, challenges and mitigation strategies," *Research Ethics,* vol. 21, no. 2, pp. 302–330, 2025.

[13] W. Ibrar, D. Mahmood, A. S. Al-Shamayleh, G. Ahmed, S. Z. Alharthi, and A. Akhunzada, "Generative AI: A double-edged sword in the cyber threat landscape," *Artificial Intelligence Review,* vol. 58, no. 9, p. 285, 2025.

[14] R. Bommasani, "On the opportunities and risks of foundation models," *arXiv preprint arXiv:2108.07258,* 2021.

[15] A. Jobin, M. Ienca, and E. Vayena, "The global landscape of AI ethics guidelines," *Nature Machine Intelligence,* vol. 1, no. 9, pp. 389–399, 2019.

[16] A. Singh, "The future of network security using generative AI," *SSRN,* 2025.

[17] M. Schmitt, and I. Flechais, "Digital deception: Generative artificial intelligence in social engineering and phishing," *Artificial Intelligence Review,* vol. 57, no. 12, pp. 1–23, 2024.

[18] P. S. Dhoni, and R. Kumar, "Synergizing generative artificial intelligence and cybersecurity: Roles of generative artificial intelligence entities, companies, agencies and government in enhancing cybersecurity," *Journal of Global Research in Computer Sciences*, vol. 14, no. 3, 1–16, 2023.

[19] S. Sai, U. Yashvardhan, V. Chamola, and B. Sikdar, "Generative AI for cyber security: Analyzing the potential of ChatGPT, DALL-E and other models for enhancing the security space," *IEEE Access*, vol. 12, pp. 53497–53516, 2024.

[20] V. Ninovic, "Deepfake crime: Trends, threats and implications," *International Journal of Contemporary Intelligence Issues,* vol. 1, no. 2, pp. 41–55, 2024.

[21] C. Point, "OPWNAI: Cybercriminals starting to use ChatGPT," *Check Point,* vol. 15, p. 2023, 2023.

[22] J. Zhang, and D. Tenney, "The evolution of integrated advance persistent threat and its defense solutions: A literature review," *Open Journal of Business and Management,* vol. 12, no. 1, pp. 293–338, 2023.

[23] S. Chandran, S. R. Syam, S. Sankaran, T. Pandey, and K. Achuthan, "From static to AI-driven detection: A comprehensive review of obfuscated malware techniques," *IEEE Access,* vol. 13, pp. 74335–74358, 2025.

[24] S. Rajapaksha, J. Senanayake, H. Kalutarage, and M. O. Al-Kadri, "Enhancing security assurance in software development: AI-based vulnerable code detection with static analysis," in *European symposium on research in computer security*, Springer, 2023, pp. 341–356.
[25] N. Mohamed, H. Taherdoost, and M. Madanchian, "Enhancing spear phishing defense with AI: A comprehensive review and future directions," *EAI Endorsed Transactions on Scalable Information Systems*, vol. 12, no. 1, p. 6109, 2025.
[26] A. Moneva, "Cyber places, crime patterns, and cybercrime prevention: An environmental criminology and crime analysis approach through data science," Universidad Miguel Hernández de Elche, 2020.
[27] M. R. Islam, *Generative AI, cybersecurity, and ethics*. Wiley, 2024.
[28] M. Charfeddine, H. M. Kammoun, B. Hamdaoui, and M. Guizani, "ChatGPT's security risks and benefits: Offensive and defensive use-cases, mitigation measures, and future implications," *IEEE Access*, vol. 12, pp. 30263–30310, 2024.
[29] T. F. Blauth, O. J. Gstrein, and A. Zwitter, "Artificial intelligence crime: An overview of malicious use and abuse of AI," *IEEE Access*, vol. 10, pp. 77110–77122, 2022.
[30] M. Gupta, C. Akiri, K. Aryal, E. Parker, and L. Praharaj, "From chatgpt to threatGPT: Impact of generative AI in cybersecurity and privacy," *IEEE Access*, vol. 11, pp. 80218–80245, 2023.
[31] J. Calma, "AI suggested 40,000 new possible chemical weapons in just six hours," *The Verge*, p. 17, 2022.
[32] I. Rubinic, M. Kurtov, I. Rubinic, R. Likic, P. I. Dargan, and D. M. Wood, "Artificial intelligence in clinical pharmacology: A case study and scoping review of large language models and bioweapon potential," *British Journal of Clinical Pharmacology*, vol. 90, no. 3, pp. 620–628, 2024.
[33] P. Treleaven *et al.*, "The future of cybercrime: AI and emerging technologies are creating a cybercrime tsunami," *Available at SSRN 4507244*, 2023.
[34] I. J. Goodfellow, J. Shlens, and C. Szegedy, "Explaining and harnessing adversarial examples," *arXiv preprint arXiv:1412.6572*, 2014.
[35] B. Buchanan, A. Lohn, M. Musser, and K. Sedova, "Truth, lies, and automation," *Center for Security and Emerging Technology*, vol. 1, no. 1, p. 2, 2021.
[36] J. A. Oravec, "The emergence of "truth machines"?: Artificial intelligence approaches to lie detection," *Ethics and Information Technology*, vol. 24, no. 1, p. 6, 2022.
[37] B. Schneier, *Secrets and lies: Digital security in a networked world*. Wiley, 2015.
[38] J.-S. Lee and J. Hsiang, "Patent claim generation by fine-tuning OpenAI GPT-2," *World Patent Information*, vol. 62, p. 101983, 2020.
[39] B. Kira, "When non-consensual intimate deepfakes go viral: The insufficiency of the UK Online Safety Act," *Computer Law & Security Review*, vol. 54, p. 106024, 2024.
[40] A. Uchendu, *Reverse turing test in the age of deepfake texts*. The Pennsylvania State University, 2023.
[41] J. Xu, L. Han, S. Sadiq, and G. Demartini, "On the role of human and machine metadata in relevance judgment tasks," *Information Processing & Management*, vol. 60, no. 2, p. 103177, 2023.
[42] J. Bateman, *Deepfakes and synthetic media in the financial system: Assessing threat scenarios*. Carnegie Endowment for International Peace, 2022.
[43] C. R. Sunstein, *Liars: Falsehoods and free speech in an age of deception*. Oxford University Press, 2021.
[44] M. Mullen, "A new reality: Deepfake technology and the world around us," *Mitchell Hamline Law Review*, vol. 48, p. 210, 2022.
[45] B. T. Suslavich, "Nonconsensual deepfakes: A" deep problem" for victims," *Albany Law Journal of Science & Technology*, vol. 33, p. 160, 2023.
[46] K. De Vries, "Let the robot speak! AI-generated speech and freedom of expression," in *YSEC yearbook of socio-economic constitutions 2021: Triangulating freedom of speech*: Springer, 2022, pp. 93–115.

[47] B. Brittain, "Getty images lawsuit says stability AI misused photos to train AI," *Reuters*, p. 5, 2023.
[48] M. Coulter, "Aiming for fairness: An exploration into Getty images v. stability AI and its importance in the landscape of modern copyright law," *DePaul Journal of Art, Technology & Intellectual Property Law*, vol. 34, p. 124, 2024.
[49] T. A. Hemphill, "Copyright protection, artistic imagery, and the adoption of responsible artificial intelligence principles," *Journal of Ethics in Entrepreneurship and Technology*, vol. 4, no. 1, pp. 2–6, 2024.
[50] U. C. Office, "*Copyright registration guidance: Works containing material generated by artificial intelligence*,", Library of Congress, Copyright Office, 37 CFR Part 202 ed, 2023.
[51] G.-M. de Schryver, "Generative AI and lexicography: The current state of the art using ChatGPT," *International Journal of Lexicography*, vol. 36, no. 4, pp. 355–387, 2023.
[52] C. J. Craig, "The AI-copyright challenge: Tech-neutrality, authorship, and the public interest," in *Research handbook on intellectual property and artificial intelligence*, Edward Elgar Publishing, 2022, pp. 134–155.
[53] P. Samuelson, "Generative AI meets copyright," *Science*, vol. 381, no. 6654, pp. 158–161, 2023.
[54] G. Babaei, D. Banks, C. Bosone, P. Giudici, and Y. Shan, "Is ChatGPT more biased than you?," *Harvard Data Science Review*, vol. 6, no. 3, p. 452, 2024.
[55] F. Bianchi *et al.*, "Easily accessible text-to-image generation amplifies demographic stereotypes at large scale," in *Proceedings of the 2023 ACM Conference on Fairness, Accountability, and Transparency*, 2023, pp. 1493–1504.
[56] A. M. Górska and D. Jemielniak, "AI racial bias: How text-to-image artificial intelligence generators construct prestigious professions," in D. Brzeziński, K. Filipek, K. Piwowar, and M. Winiarska-Brodowska (Eds.), *Algorithms, artificial intelligence and beyond*, Routledge, 2025, pp. 211–226.
[57] E. M. Bender, T. Gebru, A. McMillan-Major, and S. Shmitchell, "On the dangers of stochastic parrots: Can language models be too big?," in *Proceedings of the 2021 ACM Conference on Fairness, Accountability, and Transparency*, 2021, pp. 610–623.
[58] S. Agarwal, S. Muku, S. Anand, and C. Arora, "Does data repair lead to fair models? curating contextually fair data to reduce model bias," in *Proceedings of the IEEE/CVF Winter Conference on Applications of Computer Vision*, 2022, pp. 3298–3307.
[59] M. Veale and F. Zuiderveen Borgesius, "Demystifying the draft EU Artificial Intelligence Act—Analysing the good, the bad, and the unclear elements of the proposed approach," *Computer Law Review International*, vol. 22, no. 4, pp. 97–112, 2021.
[60] C. Grové, "Co-developing a mental health and wellbeing chatbot with and for young people," *Frontiers in Psychiatry*, vol. 11, p. 606041, 2021.
[61] D. C. Youvan, "Trusting the public: Rethinking information autonomy in the digital age," 2024. DOI: 10.13140/RG.2.2.14259.23848
[62] M. Chui, E. Hazan, R. Roberts, A. Singla, and K. Smaje, "The economic potential of generative AI," McKinsey & Company, 2023.
[63] Y. Liu, *Generative AI*. World Bank, 2024.
[64] E. Tyna, M. Sam, M. Pamela, and R. Daniel, "GPTs are GPTs: An early look at the labor market impact potential of large language models," *OpenAI Research*, vol. 17, 2023.
[65] T. Eloundou, S. Manning, P. Mishkin, and D. Rock, "GPTs are GPTs: Labor market impact potential of LLMs," *Science*, vol. 384, no. 6702, pp. 1306–1308, 2024.
[66] Y. Liu, and H. Wang, *Who on earth is using generative AI?* World Bank, 2024.
[67] M. Perault, "Section 230 won't protect ChatGPT," *Journal of Free Speech Law*, vol. 3, p. 363, 2023.
[68] R. V. Llorente, "Deepfakes in the Dock: Preparing international justice for generative AI," *Scitech Lawyer*, vol. 20, no. 2, pp. 28–33, 2024.
[69] T. Madiega, "Artificial intelligence act,", European Parliament: European Parliamentary Research Service ed, 2021.

[70] F. Morandín-Ahuerma, "Ten UNESCO recommendations on the ethics of artificial intelligence," Principios normativos para una ética de la inteligencia artificial (pp. 86–94). Concytep. ISBN: 978-607-8901-78-4. 2023.
[71] L. Floridi, "The ethics of artificial intelligence: Principles, challenges, and opportunities," Oxford Academic, 2023. https://doi.org/10.1093/oso/9780198883098.001.0001
[72] L. Y. G. Tenzer, "Defamation in the age of artificial intelligence," *NYU Annual Survey of American Law,* vol. 80, p. 135, 2023.
[73] D. E. Van Norren, "The ethics of artificial intelligence, UNESCO and the African Ubuntu perspective," *Journal of Information, Communication and Ethics in Society,* vol. 21, no. 1, pp. 112–128, 2023.
[74] J. Vincent, "OpenAI has published the text-generating AI it said was too dangerous to share," *The Verge,* p. 7, 2019.
[75] C. R. Kirby, "*Expertise, ethos, and ethics: The prophetic rhetoric of Nick Bostrom and Elon Musk in the artificial intelligence debate*," Wake Forest University, 2019.

Chapter 6

Generative AI in offensive security

Capabilities, challenges, and risks

Fatima M. Anis and Mohammad Hammoudeh

6.1 INTRODUCTION

Generative AI is rapidly transforming cybersecurity threats. Advanced models such as large language models (LLMs) or generative adversarial networks (GANs) enable attackers to automate and enhance their attacks more effectively than ever before. Recent industry reports estimate that roughly two-thirds of phishing campaigns in 2024 leveraged generative AI tools [1]. Security analyses also highlight a dramatic increase in AI-driven threats, with a 1,265% surge in AI-assisted phishing emails noted within a single year [2]. These developments demonstrate that generative AI significantly lowers the skills required for cybercrime, enabling even inexperienced individuals to carry out sophisticated attacks through simple prompts.

This chapter reviews how LLMs are misused across four main areas of offensive security. The first area, LLM-powered phishing and social engineering, involves using models like ChatGPT to craft convincing phishing emails and deceptive content tailored to specific targets. The second area, LLM-based malware and ransomware generation, describes how attackers use AI to write or refine malware, simplifying the creation of complex malicious software. The third domain, GAN-based evasion and adversarial malware, details how GANs produce malware variants specifically designed to evade antivirus systems and machine learning (ML) detectors. The final area covers autonomous LLM agents used for exploitation and red teaming, describing multi-agent or iterative systems capable of autonomously executing penetration testing and exploit strategies. Figure 6.1 presents a visual taxonomy of these four offensive use cases, outlining key capabilities observed within each category.

The analysis focuses on a central question: how generative AI techniques reshape offensive cybersecurity. By reviewing current research, the chapter identifies novel attack techniques enabled by generative AI and their observed limitations. In addition, common patterns and concerns are identified across these domains. Section 6.6 discusses recurring trends such as bypassing AI safety measures through jailbreak prompts, creating polymorphic attacks that continuously evolve, and combining multiple AI methods to overcome weaknesses. This cross-domain description highlights broader implications for cybersecurity and outlines potential defensive measures and research paths. Recognizing that offensive AI is evolving, defensive strategies must advance accordingly.

DOI: 10.1201/9781003644231-9

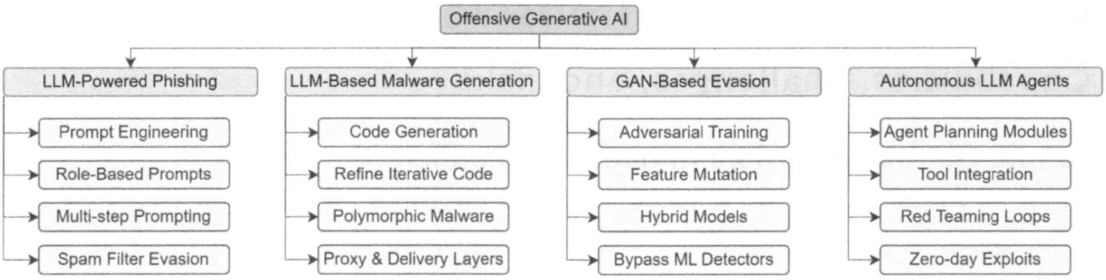

Figure 6.1 Taxonomy of Offensive Applications of Generative AI in Cybersecurity.

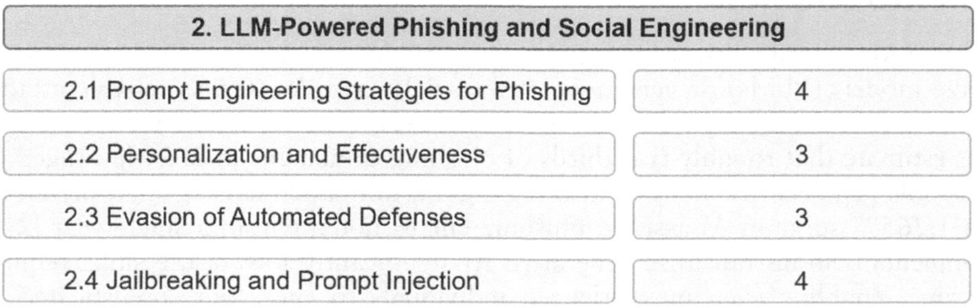

Figure 6.2 Studies Reviewed in Section 6.2 (Numbers Show Count of Studies).

6.2 LLM-POWERED PHISHING AND SOCIAL ENGINEERING

LLMs are now used for both protecting and attacking cybersecurity. While they can assist with harmless tasks like composing emails or summarizing information, they also enable attackers to create highly convincing phishing and social engineering attacks at scale. This section discusses how prompt engineering techniques can exploit LLMs, how personalization through LLMs improves phishing effectiveness, and how attackers bypass model safeguards using jailbreaks and prompt injections. Figure 6.2 shows the number of studies covered in each phishing subsection.

6.2.1 Prompt engineering strategies for phishing

Attackers have developed effective prompt engineering methods to force LLMs into generating harmful content. A primary technique involves role-playing or contextual fabrication, which tricks the model into ignoring safety measures. Liu et al. [3] analyzed 78 jailbreak prompts and found that instructing the model to assume a persona or scenario appeared in 97% of cases. By adjusting the conversational context, such as asking the model to behave as a hacker or engage in a harmless game, attackers embed malicious requests that the LLM would otherwise reject. This tactic significantly outperformed more complex techniques like "attention shifting" or "privilege escalation."

One well-known example is the "DAN" (Do Anything Now) prompt, which explicitly instructs ChatGPT to disregard ethical restrictions. Alotaibi et al. [4] demonstrated that this type of prompt could push ChatGPT to produce a complete phishing email that it normally would refuse. In their experiment, "ChatGPT DAN" created a polished scam email impersonating Amazon, containing urgent language and a phishing link. The email even threatened account suspension to pressure the victim, despite including an ethical disclaimer at the end. This example illustrates how carefully crafted prompts can override built-in safeguards to produce ready-to-use phishing content.

Another prompt engineering strategy involves breaking malicious requests into benign subtasks. Roy et al. [5] found that directly asking commercial chatbots (such as Claude) to create phishing websites or emails often failed due to model refusal. To bypass this, they developed a method of generating phishing content piece by piece. For example, rather than requesting a phishing website for a bank directly, the attacker first requests a "website design inspired by" the bank, then separately asks for the login form code, and finally a script to email captured credentials. Each request seems innocent, but together they form a functional phishing site. Using this 8–9 step approach, GPT-4 generated advanced phishing without explicitly acknowledging malicious intent. This method allowed standard, non-jailbroken LLMs to produce phishing tools that convincingly imitate legitimate ones and use evasive techniques.

Attackers are not limited to protected APIs (Application Programming Interfaces) like ChatGPT. Another approach involves fine-tuning or deploying uncensored models without safety filters. Khan et al. [6] demonstrated this by using OpenAI's GPT-2 to generate spear-phishing emails. Since GPT-2 has no built-in restrictions, they freely trained it on malicious content. A novel aspect of their study was applying a game-theoretic framework to identify optimal phishing strategies. Their analysis revealed that adjusting text generation parameters significantly impacted phishing success. For example, deterministic generation produced grammatical yet repetitive emails, while highly stochastic outputs were varied but risked incoherence or typos. Both extremes have drawbacks; while repetitive emails might trigger spam filters, poorly written messages can alert recipients. The ideal strategy is a balance that generates fluent, varied, and persuasive emails, highlighting the advantage modern LLMs offer in creating convincing phishing messages.

6.2.2 Personalization and effectiveness of LLM-generated phishing emails

A key advantage of LLM-powered phishing is effortless personalization. Social engineering attacks are most successful when tailored to a target's language, context, and relationships. Unlike traditional phishing templates, modern LLMs produce personalized, contextually accurate messages with minimal effort. This allows phishers to reach new demographics and significantly increases the credibility and success rate of attacks.

First, LLMs achieve native-level fluency across multiple languages, enhancing personalization. As Alotaibi et al. [4] say, attackers who are non-native speakers can create sophisticated phishing emails in various languages that victims find difficult to detect, thereby expanding their potential targets. The authors found that prompting ChatGPT in Arabic produced sophisticated, undetectable phishing emails, a task challenging for English-speaking attackers. Additionally, LLM-generated emails lack common grammar or spelling mistakes, eliminating a major red flag that often alerts users to phishing attempts.

LLMs also enable attackers to adapt style and context effectively. Models can mirror the tone, format, or content of legitimate communications, particularly through fine-tuning. Sniegowski [7] demonstrated this by fine-tuning a small uncensored LLM on real emails from a university professor and secretary. The resulting phishing emails were indistinguishable from the genuine communications, accurately replicating tone, formatting, and sentence structure. This level of authenticity is extremely difficult to achieve manually, but the LLM accomplished it automatically once trained. Consequently, the AI could convincingly impersonate trusted individuals, exploiting trust relationships within organizations.

Even without fine-tuning, prompt-based personalization is highly effective. LLMs can incorporate personal details such as names, positions, or recent events into phishing emails. For example, ChatGPT can draft an email addressing an employee by name, discussing a topic relevant to the recipient's workplace, and appearing to come from a manager. Alotaibi et al. [4] found that adding specific details significantly increased the likelihood of victims believing the email was genuine. Incorporating organizational context, like project references or internal jargon, further enhances credibility. Bethany et al. [8] demonstrated this effectiveness by simulating phishing scenarios, such as supervisor announcements and department-wide surveys. The LLM-generated emails contained realistic internal details, making them highly believable. Employees who fell victim identified sender identity and content relevance as primary factors in their trust.

Empirical evidence confirms that LLM-generated phishing is effective. Several studies show that AI-crafted phishing emails perform as well as or better than those written by humans:

A large-scale study by Bethany et al. [8], involving approximately 9,000 university employees, compared human-written and ChatGPT-generated phishing emails. Overall, LLM-generated emails performed at least equally to those written by communications professionals. In one scenario involving a time-sensitive alert, the AI-generated email significantly outperformed the human version, doubling the click-through rate and obtaining more credential submissions ($p < 0.05$). In other scenarios, AI and human-written emails showed nearly identical success rates. The authors concluded that LLM-generated phishing emails can match or exceed the effectiveness of human-created ones, highlighting a critical cybersecurity threat.

Another study by Sniegowski [7] conducted multiple phishing campaigns at a university. A ChatGPT-generated "job offer" email achieved a compromise rate slightly higher than a manually written version. More notably, an internally personalized phishing email, created using an LLM fine-tuned on a professor's writing style, resulted in an exceptionally high compromise rate of nearly 9%. This demonstrates that LLM-based personalization substantially enhances phishing effectiveness. The study also noted that LLM-generated emails effectively employed an authoritative tone and persuasive language. These results clearly illustrate the potency of using LLMs in crafting very convincing phishing emails.

6.2.3 Evasion of automated defenses

From a defender's perspective, phishing content generated by LLMs is more challenging to detect with existing security tools. Afane et al. [9] tested various email filters, including Gmail's spam filter, SpamAssassin, and Proofpoint, against phishing emails rewritten by GPT-3.5 or GPT-4. These rewritten emails maintained their malicious intent but used novel wording. The tests showed that filters reliably detecting original phishing emails struggled significantly with the AI-generated versions. Roy et al. [5] also confirmed this, finding that LLM-created phishing websites and emails evaded detection longer than those made by humans. Hazell [10] further highlighted the problem, noting that GPT models can cheaply and rapidly generate diverse, realistic phishing emails, making traditional detection methods ineffective. Defenders, therefore, need new approaches, such as using LLM-based detection that analyzes semantic and stylistic cues.

In summary, LLMs greatly enhance phishing by enabling attackers to customize emails with accurate language, style, and context, making scams more convincing. Empirical studies confirm that AI-generated phishing achieves success rates comparable to or better than human-written emails, especially when leveraging insider context or urgency. Since these messages can evade existing security measures and remove typical warning signs, LLM-generated phishing poses a serious threat.

6.2.4 Jailbreaking and prompt injection to bypass alignment safeguards

Modern LLMs like ChatGPT include safeguards designed to prevent generating harmful content. However, attackers often bypass these protections using prompt engineering techniques known as "jailbreaking." Jailbreaking involves tricking an LLM into ignoring its guidelines and producing censored outputs.

Liu et al. [3] systematically studied jailbreak prompts circulating online, categorizing them into three main types: pretending, attention shifting, and privilege escalation. After testing 3,120 jailbreak prompts on ChatGPT, they found many consistently bypassed restrictions. Even after OpenAI's policy updates, at least 40 different scenarios remained vulnerable. For instance, a "Character Role Play" prompt succeeded in bypassing restrictions in 86.8% of cases. The authors concluded that despite improvements, jailbreak prompts continue to emerge and succeed.

Prompt injection attacks involve embedding instructions into prompts that override the model's safety guidelines. Sniegowski [7] found that simple injection methods, such as framing a phishing request as a joke, bypassed filters in major LLMs like ChatGPT and Meta's models. Although ChatGPT flagged these prompts internally, it still produced the phishing content, providing only a cautionary note that could easily be ignored. In contrast, Microsoft's Azure OpenAI successfully blocked similar attempts, suggesting that some systems enforce rules more strictly. ChatGPT and Meta's models also failed to detect minor rewordings in phishing prompts, highlighting vulnerabilities in keyword-based filtering.

Advanced jailbreak techniques have also emerged, such as the Self-Adversarial Attack via System Prompt (SASP) by Wu et al. [11]. This method involved exploiting a vulnerability to leak GPT-4V's internal instructions, which attackers then used to create prompts specifically designed to bypass those safeguards. The automated method achieved a 59% jailbreak success rate, rising to 98.7% with minor human adjustments. Wu et al. noted that carefully modifying the internal instructions could reduce vulnerability, but this dynamic remains an ongoing challenge.

The arms race nature of jailbreaking is clear. Liu et al. observed continual evolution in popular jailbreak methods like the "DAN" prompts, each new version outperforming prior ones until OpenAI implemented countermeasures. Hazell [10] similarly demonstrated that subtle changes, like requesting forbidden content in a hypothetical scenario, consistently fooled GPT-4 into generating prohibited outputs, underscoring the difficulty of preventing such exploitation through language alone.

For defenders and providers, addressing this issue requires layered safeguards, improved filtering, monitoring for known jailbreak patterns, and potentially restricting model access to trusted users. User awareness is also critical. Users must recognize that well-crafted AI-generated messages might still be malicious, as models can be manipulated. As LLMs become more common, understanding these risks will grow increasingly important. Overall, LLM-driven phishing demonstrates how advanced AI can be misused, emphasizing the importance of ongoing research and responsive defenses in this rapidly evolving threat landscape. Table 6.1 summarizes key studies demonstrating how LLMs have been used to generate phishing emails and related content, highlighting techniques such as prompt engineering, jailbreak strategies, and model fine-tuning, along with their effectiveness and limitations.

Table 6.1 Summary of Research on LLM-Based Phishing and Social Engineering

References	*Year*	*Focus*	*Techniques*	*Key Findings*	*Limitations*
[4]	2024	Using prompts to generate phishing and malware via ChatGPT	Prompt engineering to bypass safeguards	ChatGPT can produce convincing phishing and malware with right prompts	Old ChatGPT version; no real user testing
[7]	2025	Testing LLM phishing emails in a university environment	Jailbreaking GPT and running phishing simulations	AI emails matched or outperformed human ones in success rates	Only tested in academia; small dataset for fine-tuning
[5]	2024	Creating phishing content using multiple LLMs	Crafted sub-prompts; developed prompt detector	All tested LLMs generated phishing content; GPT-4 most realistic	No testing on real users; only a few LLMs examined
[3]	2024	Studying different jailbreak prompt types on ChatGPT	Tested 78 jailbreak prompts across scenarios	Pretend-based prompts often bypass filters; GPT-4 more robust than 3.5	Only tested ChatGPT; no mitigation tested
[11]	2024	Breaking GPT-4V rules using leaked system prompts	Leaked system prompt used to create jailbreaks	GPT-4V revealed its rules; attackers used them to craft jailbreaks	Requires access to system prompt; focused on GPT-4V
[8]	2025	Comparing AI vs human phishing emails in a university	Sent AI and human emails to 9,000 users; measured clicks	AI emails were as or more effective than professional ones	Study in one university; limited scenarios
[9]	2024	Rewriting phishing emails to bypass spam filters	GPT rewrote phishing emails; retrained ML filters	LLM-reworded emails slipped past filters; LLM-augmented data improved detection	Focused on filters, not real user clicks
[6]	2023	Creating phishing emails with GPT-2 and game theory	Used GPT-2 at different randomness; applied game theory	Even old models can create convincing phish; randomization helps evade detection	Used GPT-2 only; no live phishing test

Table 6.1 (Continued)

References	*Year*	*Focus*	*Techniques*	*Key Findings*	*Limitations*
[12]	2024	Comparing prompt vs fine-tuned models for phishing URL detection	Prompted GPT vs fine-tuned smaller models	Fine-tuned small models outperformed large prompted LLMs	Focused only on URL detection; not full phishing
[10]	2023	Generating spear-phishing emails for politicians using GPT	Used GPT to tailor emails using public info	GPT can automate large-scale, personalized phishing easily	Emails not sent; assumes access to public info

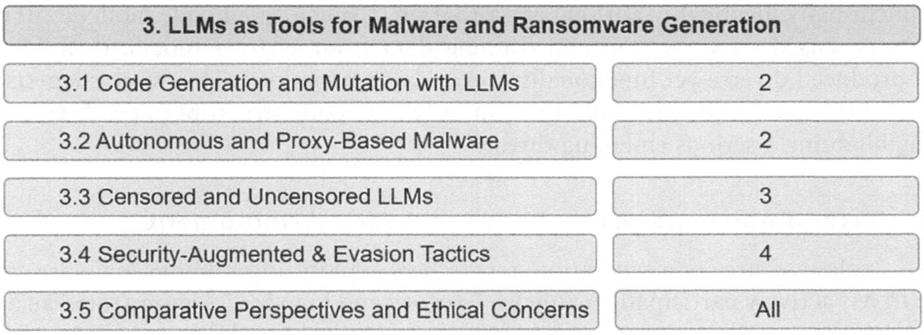

Figure 6.3 Studies Reviewed in Section 6.3 (Numbers Show Count of Studies).

6.3 LLMS AS TOOLS FOR MALWARE AND RANSOMWARE GENERATION

Models like OpenAI's ChatGPT significantly lower the barrier for creating malware, allowing even untrained individuals to generate harmful code or plan complex attacks [13]. Many recent studies have explored LLM-assisted malware and ransomware generation, highlighting both their capabilities and current limitations. This section reviews these studies to illustrate how LLMs support malicious code generation. It first describes how LLMs produce and mutate attack code, then examines autonomous or proxy-based malware development. The section then compares uncensored and censored models in these contexts and finally discusses security enhancements and evasion tactics. Throughout, it addresses ethical issues raised by these studies. Figure 6.3 summarizes the distribution of malware studies across subsections.

6.3.1 Code generation and mutation with LLMs

Several studies confirm that today's LLMs can generate functional malware code, although with some challenges. Pa Pa et al. [14] systematically tested ChatGPT (GPT-3.5) and OpenAI's text-davinci-003 model to create malware programs under OpenAI's safety constraints. They also experimented with Auto-GPT, an uncensored agent that repeatedly prompts itself. They successfully produced working malware code (around 400 lines) in less than 90 minutes using ChatGPT or text-davinci-003, including debugging. By carefully designing prompts or using jailbreak methods, ChatGPT generated code for ransomware, keyloggers, worms, and other attack tools. In all nine trials, detailed goals allowed Auto-GPT to create malware autonomously, bypassing OpenAI's safety filters. These findings confirm that even censored models like ChatGPT can produce malware if prompted correctly, lowering the technical skill required for cyberattacks. Importantly, ChatGPT also refined malware code, helping debug and improve it, demonstrating its role across multiple stages of malware development.

While code generation is crucial, code mutation, which is changing malware syntax without affecting functionality, is another evasion technique that LLMs can enhance. Traditional malware mutation methods typically involve basic transformations like instruction reordering, making them detectable by static analysis. In contrast, LLM-based code generation enables more complex mutations, evading signature-based detection. Setak and Madani [15] introduced "code mutation training," fine-tuning an LLM to generate multiple functionally identical variations of a program. Using a small code model (350 million parameters, based on CodeGen) and training data from a larger model, their fine-tuned model produced diverse yet functionally correct code variations. This work suggests LLM-driven metamorphic malware could continuously alter code structure to evade static detection, highlighting a serious emerging threat.

6.3.2 Autonomous and proxy-based malware development

Beyond single-instance code generation, researchers explore autonomous malware creation, where LLMs actively participate in attacks. Gregory and Liao [16] demonstrated an autonomous penetration-testing agent by fine-tuning a locally hosted Mistral 7B model using security-specific training (privilege escalation tutorials) combined with retrieval-augmented generation (RAG). Their system autonomously executed privilege escalation attacks on a Linux target, formulating and executing commands through a proxy without human intervention. Impressively, this sophisticated task required only a modest-sized uncensored model, illustrating the potential for freely available LLMs to automate advanced hacking tasks. Such capabilities might democratize security testing but could also be repurposed by adversaries for autonomous attacks.

Another approach uses LLMs as proxies during attacks. Beckerich et al. [17] introduced "RatGPT," a remote access trojan using ChatGPT's API and plugins as a covert command-and-control (C2) channel. By routing malicious instructions through trusted ChatGPT sessions, the attackers bypassed traditional network defenses. ChatGPT dynamically generated malicious code executed in-memory, leaving no detectable traces on disk. This strategy leveraged ChatGPT's generative capabilities to produce fileless malware on demand, highlighting an effective evasion technique and emphasizing risks in the unregulated LLM plugin ecosystem.

6.3.3 Censored and uncensored LLMs

A recurring theme is the contrast between uncensored models and censored services like ChatGPT. Commercial LLMs typically have advanced capabilities but incorporate safeguards to limit malicious use. In contrast, uncensored models lack built-in protections and can be fine-tuned specifically for illicit purposes. Researchers explore combining both model types to overcome individual limitations.

Yamin et al. [18] examined a dual-model approach combining an uncensored LLM with a censored commercial model. The uncensored model initially created incomplete ransomware code, which the censored model then refined when prompted as a debugging task. Neither model alone reliably produced working ransomware, but the sequential approach succeeded consistently. These findings illustrate how combining models can circumvent safeguards, suggesting attackers may increasingly blend uncensored and censored models to produce malware effectively.

Similarly, Gregory and Liao [16] selected Mistral 7B precisely to avoid ChatGPT's API constraints, enabling greater customization for offensive tasks. Pa Pa et al. [14] found even some older commercial models (e.g., text-davinci-003) less restrictive, emphasizing the varying robustness of censorship controls. Such variations indicate a complex landscape requiring continuous improvement in safety controls across model versions.

6.3.4 Security-augmented capabilities and evasion tactics

Attackers further enhance LLM effectiveness by integrating domain-specific security knowledge. Gregory and Liao's penetration testing LLM [16] benefited from direct access to exploit manuals, a technique potentially exploitable by malicious actors. Pa Pa et al. [14] similarly demonstrated ChatGPT's capacity to craft social engineering content, significantly improving phishing effectiveness. Adamec and Turčaník [19] experimentally confirmed that LLM-crafted phishing messages increased the success rate of attacks in simulated scenarios, emphasizing that polished content is critical for effective deception.

Concerning evasion, Pa Pa et al. [14] found AI-generated malware surprisingly difficult for antivirus engines to detect, even without obfuscation. Basic LLM-driven obfuscation methods had limited success, but future LLM advancements could enable more effective evasion. Setak and Madani's mutation approach [15] suggests that continuous code morphing could render signature-based detection ineffective, emphasizing the need for novel defensive strategies.

6.3.5 Comparative perspectives and ethical concerns

Researchers consistently emphasize ethical urgency, advocating improved moderation, AI service regulations, and technical defenses. Education remains essential, as staff training must address increasingly subtle phishing techniques. Importantly, AI tools beneficial for security testing could equally serve malicious purposes, highlighting dual-use concerns.

In conclusion, while LLM-assisted malware generation is already a reality, significant limitations remain. LLMs facilitate malware creation and enhance social engineering but do not yet create invincible threats independently. Human oversight remains crucial. These early insights will guide the ongoing AI-driven arms race between attackers and defenders, shaping future technology and policy development. Table 6.2 presents selected studies that explore the use of LLMs and generative AI for malware creation, code evasion, and ransomware development, emphasizing their capabilities, employed models, key findings, and practical limitations.

6.4 GAN-BASED EVASION AND OFFENSIVE MALWARE GENERATION

GANs have become powerful tools in offensive cybersecurity, enabling attackers to automatically craft malware and attack techniques that evade detection. By generating realistic

Table 6.2 Overview of Key Studies on AI-Driven Malware and Attack Generation

References	*Year*	*Focus*	*Models*	*Key Findings*	*Limitations*
[14]	2023	Making malware and attack tools using AI	ChatGPT, Auto-GPT; tested malware and tools	AI made working malware; some evaded antivirus	Needs clever prompts; can't do a full attack alone
[16]	2024	Autonomous hacking with a small local AI	Mistral 7B with fine-tuning and command tool	AI agent hacked a Linux system by itself	Only tested on Linux; could be misused
[18]	2025	Creating ransomware using two AI models	Unfiltered AI plus ChatGPT to refine code	Two AIs together made working ransomware	Needs two models; safety filters can be bypassed
[19]	2024	Using ChatGPT to make phishing and malware	ChatGPT wrote phishing, macros, and USB messages	AI-made messages fooled many users in tests	Small test; shows AI can aid social engineering
[15]	2024	Training a small AI to change code for evasion	CodeGen-350M trained on code changes	Trained AI made many code versions for evasion	Training needs lots of data; uses more resources
[13]	2023	Using AI to plan ransomware attacks	Asked ChatGPT how to run attacks	AI gave useful advice for full ransomware attack	Some refusals; legal/ethical issues raised

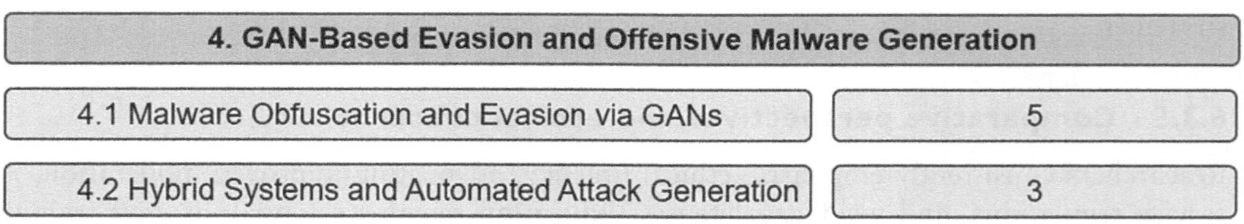

Figure 6.4 Studies Reviewed in Section 6.4 (Numbers Show Count of Studies).

synthetic artifacts, such as obfuscated malicious binaries or attack scripts, GAN-based methods can confuse ML defenses and create novel attack variants. This section surveys how GANs, often combined with other AI methods, facilitate malware obfuscation, detector bypass, code mutation, and hybrid attack generation. It specifically addresses malware evasion and offensive code generation, emphasizing techniques such as adversarial training, manipulation of malware features, opcode alteration, and black-box attacks. The following subsections illustrate these concepts through recent research. Figure 6.4 presents the study counts for GAN-based malware research.

6.4.1 Malware obfuscation and evasion via GANs

One approach uses GANs to subtly alter malware features so that malicious samples appear benign to ML-based detectors while preserving functionality. An early example is

AndrOpGAN by Zhang et al. [20], which targets Android malware classifiers relying on opcode frequency patterns. AndrOpGAN employs a Deep Convolutional GAN (DCGAN) to generate adversarial opcode distributions resembling those of benign apps. It then inserts additional opcodes into the malware until its histogram matches the benign-like distribution, confusing static detectors. The Opcode Frequency Optimal Adjustment (OFOA) algorithm ensures inserted opcodes are syntactically correct, maintaining the app's functionality. Empirical results were significant: over 99% of the Android malware samples evaded detection by ML classifiers, and antivirus engines on VirusTotal saw detection rates drop by 20–44%. However, AndrOpGAN specifically targets opcode-based static analysis and does not address dynamic detection.

Similarly, Ahmad et al. [21] proposed DOpGAN (Generating Evasive Adversarial Attacks against Android Detectors). DOpGAN also uses a modified DCGAN to learn benign opcode distributions and generates vectors mimicking these profiles. Real malware is then modified by inserting opcodes to match these benign vectors. As a gray-box attack, DOpGAN requires only feature vectors from target apps, not model internals. Experiments showed nearly 100% evasion rates against Android malware classifiers and online scanners like VirusTotal. This highlights latent space manipulation: by shifting malware feature vectors toward benign clusters, malware is labeled benign. However, limitations remain, including potential dataset biases and uncertain generalization to different detectors or hybrid methods.

For Windows malware, Zhong et al.'s MalFox [22] is a notable GAN-based camouflage framework using a convolutional GAN (Conv-GAN). MalFox automatically modifies malware binaries to evade antivirus engines. It consists of five modules: a PE Parser, Generator, Discriminator, Detector, and PE Editor. The generator learns perturbations that make malware appear benign, and the PE Editor applies these perturbations directly to the executable. MalFox uses three binary-patching methods, Obfusmal, Stealmal, and Hollowmal, to modify malware without affecting functionality. Unlike previous attacks, MalFox directly queries real antivirus engines (VirusTotal) during training, a practical black-box strategy. MalFox successfully evaded 82 antivirus engines, reducing average detection rates by 56.8%. However, reliance on frequent external queries poses a risk of detection due to defender monitoring.

To address query risks, Gibert et al. [23] proposed a query-free GAN-based evasion method. Their Conditional Wasserstein GAN is trained locally on benign and malicious binaries without querying the target detector. It manipulates malware features to appear benign. After generating feature-space alterations, a post-processing step modifies the malware binary accordingly. Tests showed this offline GAN approach achieved evasion rates comparable to query-based methods and produced binaries that evaded VirusTotal scanners. The advantage is stealth, as it leaves no suspicious queries, but it depends on representative local datasets.

Another advanced GAN-based obfuscation is EGAN (Evolutionary GAN) by Commey et al. [24], designed specifically for ransomware. EGAN combines evolutionary search (mutation-based optimization) with GAN-driven global feature manipulation. Initially, an Evolution Strategy (ES) algorithm applies simple binary mutations, querying antivirus engines for feedback. If unsuccessful, a GAN suggests broader feature-level changes. This hybrid technique bypassed multiple commercial antivirus solutions, successfully maintaining ransomware functionality. Limitations included censored mutation types, leaving some dynamic analysis tools ineffective, and slow performance due to query rate limits. Nevertheless, EGAN demonstrates a potent hybrid malware generation approach.

Overall, GAN-based evasion involves shifting malware feature distributions toward benign patterns at various levels, such as opcodes, byte patterns, API calls, or global file features. Both white-box and black-box strategies exist, with recent advances allowing fully offline malware generation. Significant drops in detection rates highlight an arms race between offensive GANs and defensive ML methods. Authors also suggest using adversarially generated malware to improve defenses via adversarial training, reflecting GANs' dual-use potential.

6.4.2 Hybrid systems and automated attack generation

Researchers are combining GANs with other AI paradigms, such as reinforcement learning and LLMs, creating hybrid systems that enhance malware evasiveness and automate attack generation. These hybrids leverage complementary AI strengths: GANs contribute realism and pattern learning, while other methods add semantic guidance or adaptive behavior.

RELEVAGAN [25] is an example combining GANs with deep reinforcement learning (DRL) for adaptive evasion. Designed to evade botnet detection systems, RELEVAGAN integrates a GAN with a DRL agent. The agent adaptively modifies network traffic features (timing, packet sequences, protocols) to evade detection. During training, successful evasions are used to iteratively improve both the GAN and the detector, mimicking a real-world attacker–defender scenario. Results showed improved convergence and evasion capabilities compared to GAN-only methods. Limitations include needing accurate surrogate models for training. Still, RELEVAGAN illustrates GAN+DRL potential in adaptive malware evasion.

Another hybrid is GLEAM (GAN and LLM for Evasive Adversarial Malware) by Devadiga et al. [26], integrating LLMs with GANs. GLEAM uses LLM-derived embeddings capturing semantic knowledge of malicious code (opcodes, byte sequences), enhancing GAN-generated malware variants. Experiments showed an average 22.6% improvement in evasion rates compared to baseline GAN attacks, as LLM integration provided more realistic and semantically coherent malware variants. Although resource-intensive, GLEAM demonstrates the viability of combining LLM semantic knowledge with GAN adversarial generation to improve malware evasion.

In related research, Iturbe et al. [27] systematically evaluated LLMs alone for automated attack code generation. Testing 565 attack techniques, they found 16% immediately functional and around 48% usable with minor modifications. Limitations include logically flawed or incorrect outputs (about 30%). Yet, LLM-generated scripts significantly lower the barrier for attackers by providing baseline code. This approach aligns with automated malware mutation concepts discussed earlier. The authors highlight integrating LLM-generated attack techniques into defense-testing tools, showing generative AI's capability beyond mere adversarial examples to actual code generation.

In conclusion, GAN-based evasion and offensive malware generation represent significant challenges to cybersecurity. By subtly altering malware or automatically crafting new attacks, these AI-driven methods effectively defeat many traditional detectors, emphasizing the need for advanced defensive measures. Table 6.3 outlines key research on GAN-based and LLM-assisted malware evasion techniques, showcasing various approaches used to bypass antivirus and detection systems, along with their demonstrated effectiveness and associated limitations.

Table 6.3 Summary of GAN and LLM-Based Malware Evasion Techniques

References	*Year*	*Approach*	*Threat Scenario*	*Results*	*Limitations*
[20]	2020	AndrOpGAN	Bypass Android malware scanners using opcode changes	Over 99% of malware samples evaded detection	Works only on opcode features; not tested on behavior-based scanners
[25]	2024	RELEVAGAN	Evade botnet detectors and improve training	Created undetected traffic; better than past GANs	Needs training setup; not tested as a real attack tool
[24]	2024	EGAN	Hide ransomware from AV scanners	Ransomware still worked and escaped many AVs	Missed some analyzers; used a few mutation types
[21]	2025	DOpGAN	Evade Android malware detectors	Nearly 100% evasion; fooled VirusTotal too	Focused on static features; data may bias results
[26]	2023	GLEAM	Make smart malware using GAN and LLM	Evasion improved 22.6% over basic GAN	Depends on LLM quality; slower to run
[22]	2022	MalFox	Trick black-box antivirus engines	Fooled 82/82 detectors; ran without crashes	Needs many queries; not tested on dynamic defenses
[23]	2023	Query-Free GAN	Evade detectors with no online queries	Evaded many AVs offline; strong transferability	Only works if features match real detector setup
[27]	2024	Unleashing Offensive AI	Make attack scripts using ChatGPT	48% of AI scripts worked or needed small fixes	Half failed or were wrong; often needs human fixes

6.5 LLM AGENTS FOR EXPLOITATION AND AUTONOMOUS HACKING

The past two years have seen the emergence of LLM-based autonomous agents in offensive cybersecurity, transforming theoretical concepts into practical demonstrations. These agents use LLMs, such as GPT-4, to conduct hacking tasks, from guiding penetration tests to independently identifying and exploiting vulnerabilities. Recent studies illustrate how LLM agents can mimic skilled red-team behavior, autonomously combining tool outputs and strategic actions. This section reviews six key studies demonstrating these capabilities, focusing on autonomy, decision-making, memory, and tool integration, and discusses the safety and ethical implications of autonomous hacking by AI. Figure 6.5 shows the number of studies reviewed on LLM agents.

6.5.1 GPT-powered penetration testing agents

Initial research on autonomous offensive agents involved using LLMs to automate penetration testing. Deng et al. introduced PentestGPT [28], an LLM-based penetration testing

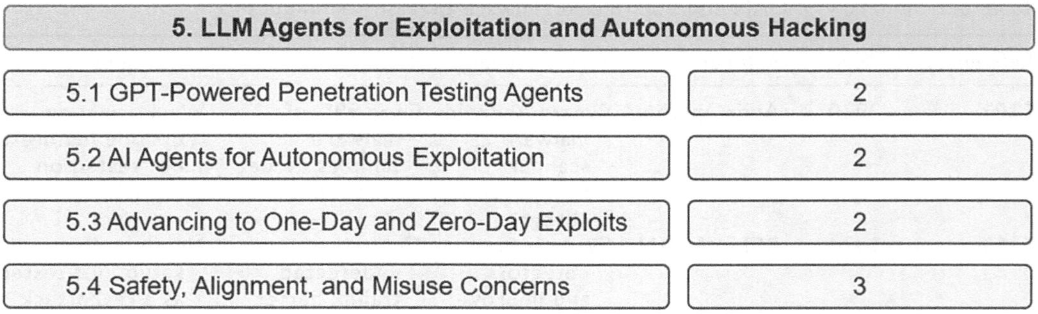

Figure 6.5 Studies Reviewed in Section 6.5 (Numbers Show Count of Studies).

framework. PentestGPT uses an iterative "propose-execute-observe" cycle: the model suggests actions (e.g., running scanners), executes them in a sandbox, and uses the results to inform subsequent steps. Deng et al. found GPT-4 excelled at tasks like tool usage, exploit crafting, and vulnerability detection. However, GPT-4 struggled with complex context management, often losing track of broader goals.

To resolve this, PentestGPT employed a structured memory-informed architecture with three modules: Reasoning, Generation, and Parsing. The Reasoning Module maintains a high-level task tree, storing discovered clues and progress. The Generation Module creates detailed action plans, and the Parsing Module summarizes outputs, preventing the model from becoming overwhelmed. Evaluations showed this structure improved GPT-4's effectiveness, achieving 58.6% higher completion rates on 182 subtasks from real-world challenges compared to a basic GPT-4 agent.

Teig and Eiken [29] further tested PentestGPT against OWASP Juice Shop, a deliberately vulnerable web application. GPT-4 and Dolphin 2.5 autonomously discovered and exploited simpler vulnerabilities like injection attacks but struggled with complex logic flaws. Critically, all exploit attempts were detected by enterprise-grade security software (Palo Alto Prisma Cloud). Thus, while LLM agents successfully identified vulnerabilities, they currently lack the stealth needed to bypass robust defenses. The authors recommended developing more sophisticated evasion techniques and deeper integration with offensive tools, indicating that fully autonomous penetration agents may soon become practical.

6.5.2 AI agents for autonomous exploitation

Parallel research has investigated LLM agents capable of independently executing exploits. Valencia [30] created ReaperAI, an autonomous hacking agent based on GPT-4. ReaperAI operated within a controlled Python environment, running scans, executing scripts, and interacting autonomously with target systems. Valencia used a RAG approach for memory, allowing the agent to recall past information. Tested on platforms like Hack the Box, ReaperAI demonstrated the capability to autonomously execute multistep attacks without human assistance, replicating real attacker behaviors from reconnaissance to exploitation. Challenges included ensuring robust command execution and error handling. Valencia emphasized ethical constraints and warned of the ease with which powerful, harmful agents could be built from LLMs without proper oversight.

Fang et al. [31] significantly expanded this concept, demonstrating GPT-4's capability to autonomously hack web applications. Their agent interfaced directly with web browsers and autonomously executed complex exploits, including blind SQL injections requiring dozens of coordinated steps. Their tests showed GPT-4 successfully exploited 73.3% of tested vulnerabilities, significantly outperforming less advanced models (GPT-3.5 achieved only 7%). This study emphasized GPT-4's unique ability for complex offensive reasoning, environment mapping, and iterative exploit refinement.

6.5.3 Advancing to one-day and zero-day exploits

Fang et al. [32] further tested GPT-4 agents' ability to exploit recently disclosed (one-day) vulnerabilities. Given only public CVE (Common Vulnerabilities and Exposures) descriptions, GPT-4 autonomously developed and executed exploits for 87% of tested vulnerabilities. Without CVE information, success rates dropped dramatically (7%), underscoring that the model excels at exploitation but less so at initial vulnerability discovery. This work highlighted a concerning reality: once vulnerabilities are publicly disclosed, AI agents could quickly weaponize them.

Addressing zero-day vulnerabilities, Zhu et al. [33] proposed a hierarchical multi-agent system (HPTSA) to enhance AI's ability to discover unknown flaws. The approach divided tasks among specialized agents coordinated by a lead planning agent. This strategy allowed deeper, sustained analysis and improved memory management. HPTSA successfully exploited 42% of tested zero-day vulnerabilities, a significant improvement over single-agent approaches. This result demonstrated that collaborative agent architectures significantly enhance autonomous vulnerability discovery and exploitation capabilities.

6.5.4 Safety, alignment, and misuse concerns

The advancement of autonomous hacking agents raises significant safety and ethical concerns. These agents demonstrate dual-use potential, easily shifting from beneficial security testing to malicious applications. Fang et al. [31] and Valencia [30] highlighted the risk of rapid weaponization and stressed responsible oversight. Valencia particularly emphasized the importance of embedding ethical constraints in AI agents to prevent misuse.

Current research mitigates risks by limiting experiments to controlled environments and using ethical guardrails. However, as uncensored models improve, managing access to powerful autonomous hacking capabilities will become increasingly challenging. Ensuring robust ethical alignment and strict human oversight will be essential to safely manage the potential threats of these powerful AI systems.

Conversely, AI agents could also significantly enhance defensive cybersecurity. Teig and Eiken [29] demonstrated that current enterprise defenses still detect automated exploits. This highlights the potential for AI agents to serve as valuable red-team tools, identifying vulnerabilities before attackers do. As AI-driven exploits improve, defensive strategies must similarly evolve, possibly using AI-powered monitoring and defensive systems.

In conclusion, LLM-based autonomous hacking agents represent a significant advancement, capable of performing complex tasks previously requiring human expertise. While offering transformative opportunities in security testing, they also pose serious risks if misused. Going forward, rigorous safety frameworks, ethical guidelines, and perhaps regulatory measures will be crucial as these agents transition from research demonstrations to broader practical applications. Table 6.4 summarizes recent developments in autonomous and semi-autonomous LLM-powered agents used for exploitation and penetration testing,

Table 6.4 Overview of LLM Agents for Automated Exploitation and Penetration Testing

References	*Year*	*System*	*Exploitation*	*Autonomy*	*Limitations*
[28]	2023	PentestGPT: GPT-4 tool that guides penetration testing	Found real bugs via commands and planning	Partially autonomous	Needs human to run commands; forgets context
[29]	2024	PentestGPT Case Study: Compared GPT-4 vs smaller AI on web attack tasks	Exploited OWASP Juice Shop (SQLi, IDOR)	Partially autonomous	WAF caught all attacks; struggled with complex flaws
[30]	2024	ReaperAI: Autonomous hacking agent	Scanned and exploited known flaws in the lab	Fully autonomous	Sometimes failed commands; safety checks needed
[31]	2024	LLM hacks websites	Completed long attacks like 38-step SQLi	Fully autonomous	Needs memory, tools, and lots of context tokens
[32]	2024	LLM exploits one-day CVEs	Built exploits from public CVE descriptions	Fully autonomous	Needs descriptions to work; blind attacks failed
[33]	2025	LLM agent teams for zero-days	Discovered and exploited new bugs	Fully autonomous (multi-agent)	Success rate 42%; missed many bugs; setup is complex

detailing the systems' capabilities, types of attacks performed, levels of autonomy, and operational limitations.

6.6 DISCUSSION AND FUTURE WORK

Generative AI has become a powerful enabler in offensive cybersecurity, supporting a range of attack types, including phishing, malware, evasion, and autonomous hacking. After examining four categories, namely, LLM-driven phishing, LLM-assisted malware generation, GAN-based evasion, and LLM-powered agents, this section highlights common patterns, key gaps, and shared risks. Although distinct, these areas collectively show a clear trend: AI is simplifying sophisticated attacks, reducing the skill barrier, and intensifying the cybersecurity arms race.

6.6.1 Common patterns

Across all four categories of offensive generative AI, several recurring patterns emerge that reveal how attackers exploit the technology's capabilities. These patterns reflect shared strategies and design choices that enhance attack effectiveness, bypass safeguards, and expand accessibility to a broader range of threat actors. Table 6.5 compares common patterns

Table 6.5 Comparison of Generative AI Techniques in Offensive Security

Common Pattern	LLM Phishing	LLM Malware Gen.	GAN Evasion	LLM Agents
Safeguard Bypass	Yes. Prompts trick ChatGPT into phishing	Yes. Prompts and agents bypass code limits	No. GANs do not use safety filters	Partial. Use uncensored models. Ethics depend on use
Uncensored Models	Yes. Older or uncensored LLMs used without filters	Yes. Uncensored models fine-tuned or combined with ChatGPT	Yes. GANs are fully controlled by attacker	Yes. Uncensored models used to avoid limits
Autonomous Generation	Yes. Multistep prompts build phishing kits	Yes. Agents plan and write malware step by step	Partial. Some use repeated training or queries	Yes. Agents run full attack loops
Polymorphic Output	Yes. Fluent, varied emails evade filters	Yes. Code variants used for evasion	Yes. GANs mutate malware to fool scanners	Partial. Few agents try multiple variations
Empowers Low-Skill Attackers	Yes. Easy phishing for nonexperts	Yes. Malware possible with no coding skills	Yes. Tools automate complex evasion steps	Yes. Agents act like skilled hackers for anyone
Hybrid AI Use	Limited. Mostly uses LLMs for text	Yes. Combines LLMs and tools	Yes. Combines GAN with LLM or feedback	Yes. Mixes models, memory, tools, and scripts

across LLM phishing, malware generation, GAN evasion, and LLM agents, showing overlaps in tactics, model use, automation, and attacker accessibility.

- **AI Safety Bypasses and Uncensored Models:** A key pattern is attackers bypassing AI model safeguards. In phishing and malware generation, attackers use clever prompts ("jailbreaks") to trick censored LLMs into generating harmful content. Persona-based prompts effectively circumvent ethics filters. For example, attackers successfully used role-playing prompts to make ChatGPT write phishing emails and malware. Other studies highlight that attackers prefer uncensored models or combine censored models with uncensored ones to avoid constraints. Such multi-model pipelines enable attackers to bypass even robust safety filters.
- **Iterative and Autonomous Attack Generation:** Attackers increasingly use multistep workflows instead of single-step prompts. In phishing, complex tasks are broken into simpler sub-prompts to avoid refusal by the model. Similarly, malware generation employs iterative loops where autonomous agents repeatedly prompt themselves to refine malicious code. Autonomous agents, such as PentestGPT and ReaperAI, exemplify this approach, continuously adjusting their strategies based on tool outputs. This iterative autonomy significantly expands attack capabilities.
- **Polymorphism and Evasion by Design:** Generative AI easily produces diverse outputs, aiding evasion. Phishing attacks benefit from varied yet authentic emails that evade traditional detection. Malware studies show that LLMs trained specifically for code mutation generate numerous malware variants, bypassing static detection.

GAN-based evasion similarly produces malware that alters features (e.g., opcodes or binaries), significantly lowering detection rates. This polymorphic capability frustrates conventional defenses that rely on static signatures or patterns.

- **Lowering of Skill Barriers:** AI is significantly reducing the skill needed to perform sophisticated attacks. LLM-generated phishing enables amateurs to craft convincing messages. Malware studies demonstrate that untrained individuals can rapidly generate functional ransomware with minimal knowledge. GAN-based tools automate complex evasion methods, allowing untrained individuals to easily bypass security tools. Autonomous hacking agents provide step-by-step guidance, empowering novices to perform attacks previously limited to experts.
- **Hybrid and Multi-Model Approaches:** Researchers increasingly combine AI models to overcome individual limitations. For example, LLM and GAN hybrids produce smarter malware with improved stealth. Multi-model approaches, such as pairing an uncensored model with a filtered one, achieve higher evasion and reliability. Offensive researchers envision integrating various generative techniques (text, code, evasion) to form multidimensional, adaptive attacks.

6.6.2 Research gaps and future directions

Despite progress, research reveals several important gaps across offensive AI areas:

- **Generalizability and Real-World Testing:** Many studies remain limited to controlled environments or narrow contexts. Results may not translate effectively into real-world scenarios, where adaptive defenses or broader user behavior differ significantly. For instance, malware studies primarily test known vulnerabilities in sandbox environments, and phishing studies are often limited to specific contexts or informed participants. Future research should expand testing to realistic, adaptive scenarios to better evaluate practical effectiveness.
- **Performance vs. Reliability Trade-offs:** AI-generated outputs often lack complete reliability. LLM-generated malware frequently requires human refinement, and phishing emails may contain subtle errors. Fully autonomous AI outputs still commonly rely on human guidance or correction. Future research should improve AI self-correction to produce consistently reliable outputs without human intervention.
- **Integration of Evasion and Stealth:** Current research frequently separates attack generation and evasion. LLM studies emphasize content creation, while GAN studies focus on evasion. Comprehensive workflows integrating stealth techniques into attack generation are limited. Future work needs to combine these capabilities, enabling AI attacks to adapt dynamically when facing real defenses.
- **Defensive Countermeasures:** Offensive studies frequently call for improved defenses but rarely explore defensive countermeasures in depth. Although defensive methods like prompt classifiers or AI-generated content detectors are emerging, they remain limited. A greater emphasis on developing robust defensive techniques alongside offensive capabilities is crucial.
- **Ethical and Policy Dimensions:** Although ethical concerns are frequently acknowledged, concrete governance frameworks remain underdeveloped. The speed of AI development surpasses regulatory responses, creating challenges for managing misuse. Future research should focus on practical solutions for governance, accountability, and ethical usage.

6.6.3 Risks and ethical concerns

Generative offensive AI raises several interconnected ethical risks:

- **Empowering Novice Attackers:** AI dramatically lowers skill requirements, enabling inexperienced actors to execute sophisticated attacks previously reserved for advanced groups. This "script kiddie to APT" phenomenon could significantly increase both the number and severity of cyberattacks, complicating threat assessment and defensive strategies.
- **Commercialization of AI-Driven Cybercrime:** AI can enable an expanded market for malicious tools, potentially creating "exploit-as-a-service" or "ransomware-as-a-prompt" platforms. Attackers could easily rent AI-powered attack services, drastically increasing attack scale and frequency.
- **Erosion of Trust and Detection Difficulty:** AI-generated attacks make detection increasingly challenging by removing traditional indicators of malicious content. As phishing emails and malware become indistinguishable from genuine communications, users and automated defenses will struggle to maintain trust, potentially leading to widespread suspicion or an increased rate of successful attacks.
- **Autonomous Attacks and Loss of Human Control:** Autonomous AI agents capable of conducting attacks without oversight raise significant ethical concerns. Without proper controls, these agents might execute harmful actions beyond human intent, causing unintended collateral damage. Robust ethical constraints and strict human oversight are essential to prevent misuse.
- **Dual-Use Dilemma and Accountability:** Generative AI inherently carries dual-use risks, complicating accountability. Determining accountability, whether it lies with the developer, user, or the AI model itself, is difficult. Effective governance structures, regulatory frameworks, and international agreements are urgently needed to manage AI misuse.

In conclusion, offensive generative AI creates both profound risks and transformative opportunities. Addressing these risks requires comprehensive solutions across technical innovation, defensive strategies, ethical standards, and policy development. As AI becomes increasingly central to cybersecurity, continued interdisciplinary research and proactive governance will be critical.

6.7 CONCLUSION

Generative AI techniques have fundamentally transformed the landscape of offensive cybersecurity. Across the examined areas, including LLM-powered phishing and social engineering, malware and ransomware generation, GAN-based evasion techniques, and autonomous hacking agents, common themes consistently emerge. Attackers frequently bypass AI safety constraints through clever prompt manipulation (jailbreaking) or by leveraging uncensored models. These techniques significantly enhance the ability to craft diverse and convincing attacks, undermining traditional defenses and detection methods.

Polymorphism stands out as a key capability enabled by generative AI, allowing attackers to generate continuously changing phishing content, malware variants, and evasive payloads. This dynamic adaptation complicates the defender's task, rendering static detection methods increasingly obsolete. Additionally, the integration of multiple generative techniques, such as combining language models and GANs, has shown considerable promise in producing more sophisticated, stealthy, and effective cyber threats than any single technique alone.

The reduction in skill barriers is another critical implication. Generative AI empowers less experienced actors to perform attacks previously accessible only to highly skilled adversaries. This democratization of advanced cyber capabilities could lead to a surge in threat frequency and complexity, significantly altering the threat landscape.

Further compounding these risks is the emerging capability of autonomous AI agents that independently plan and execute complex multistep cyberattacks. Although current agents still face challenges related to stealth and reliability, their rapid advancement poses serious concerns regarding loss of human oversight and potential unintended consequences.

To address these evolving threats, future research and defensive strategies must progress along several critical paths. First, comprehensive benchmarks and standardized evaluation frameworks are essential to test AI-driven threats against modern defense systems rigorously. Second, the development of robust red-teaming methodologies is crucial for proactively anticipating and mitigating AI misuse scenarios. Third, ethical guidelines and governance frameworks should be established promptly to manage the dual-use nature of generative AI technologies responsibly.

Ultimately, confronting the offensive potential of generative AI demands integrated responses combining technical innovation, defensive preparedness, and ethical oversight. Without coordinated action, the benefits of generative AI could easily be overshadowed by its risks, underscoring the urgent need for continued interdisciplinary research and proactive governance in cybersecurity.

REFERENCES

[1] "The Rise of AI-Powered Phishing 2025 [Plus What to Do about It?]." Accessed: Jul. 08, 2025. [Online]. Available: https://cybelangel.com/rise-ai-phishing/

[2] SentinelOne "Key Cyber Security Statistics for 2025." Accessed: Jul. 08, 2025. [Online]. Available: www.sentinelone.com/cybersecurity-101/cybersecurity/cyber-security-statistics/

[3] Y. Liu, G. Deng, Z. Xu, Y. Li, Y. Zheng, Y. Zhang, L. Zhao, T. Zhang, K. Wang, and Y. Liu, "Jailbreaking ChatGPT via Prompt Engineering: An Empirical Study," Mar. 2024, [Online]. Available: http://arxiv.org/abs/2305.13860

[4] L. Alotaibi, S. Seher, and N. Mohammad, "Cyberattacks Using ChatGPT: Exploring Malicious Content Generation Through Prompt Engineering," in *2024 ASU International Conference in Emerging Technologies for Sustainability and Intelligent Systems, ICETSIS 2024*, Institute of Electrical and Electronics Engineers Inc., 2024, pp. 1304–1311. doi: 10.1109/ICETSIS61505.2024.10459698.

[5] S. S. Roy, P. Thota, K. V. Naragam, and S. Nilizadeh, "From Chatbots to Phishbots?: Phishing Scam Generation in Commercial Large Language Models," in *Proceedings – IEEE Symposium on Security and Privacy*, Institute of Electrical and Electronics Engineers Inc., 2024, pp. 36–54. doi: 10.1109/SP54263.2024.00182.

[6] H. Khan, M. Alam, S. Al-Kuwari, and Y. Faheem, "Offensive AI: Unification of email Generation through GPT-2 Model with a Game-Theoretic Approach for Spear-Phishing Attacks." In IET Conference Proceedings CP786, vol. 2021, no. 4, pp. 178–184. Stevenage, UK: The Institution of Engineering and Technology, 2021.

[7] N. Sniegowski, "Evaluating the Effectiveness of LLM-Generated Phishing Evaluating the Effectiveness of LLM-Generated Phishing Campaigns Campaigns Evaluating the Effectiveness of LLM-Generated Phishing Campaigns," 2025. [Online]. Available: https://epublications.marquette.edu/theses_open

[8] M. Bethany *et al.*, "Lateral Phishing with Large Language Models: A Large Organization Comparative Study," *IEEE Access*, vol. 13, pp. 60684–60701, 2025, doi: 10.1109/ACCESS.2025.3555500.
[9] K. Afane, W. Wei, Y. Mao, J. Farooq, and J. Chen, "Next-Generation Phishing: How LLM Agents Empower Cyber Attackers," Nov. 2024, [Online]. Available: http://arxiv.org/abs/2411.13874
[10] J. Hazell, "Spear Phishing with Large Language Models," arXiv preprint arXiv:2305.06972, 2023.
[11] Y. Wu, X. Li, Y. Liu, P. Zhou, and L. Sun, "Jailbreaking GPT-4V Via Self-Adversarial Attacks with System Prompts," Jan. 2024, [Online]. Available: http://arxiv.org/abs/2311.09127
[12] F. Trad and A. Chehab, "Prompt Engineering or Fine-Tuning? A Case Study on Phishing Detection with Large Language Models," *Machine Learning and Knowledge Extraction*, vol. 6, no. 1, pp. 367–384, Mar. 2024, doi: 10.3390/make6010018.
[13] F. Teichmann, "Ransomware Attacks in the Context of Generative Artificial Intelligence—An Experimental Study," *International Cybersecurity Law Review*, vol. 4, no. 4, pp. 399–414, Dec. 2023, doi: 10.1365/s43439-023-00094-x.
[14] Y. M. Pa Pa, S. Tanizaki, T. Kou, M. Van Eeten, K. Yoshioka, and T. Matsumoto, "An Attacker's Dream? Exploring the Capabilities of ChatGPT for Developing Malware," in *ACM International Conference Proceeding Series*, Association for Computing Machinery, Aug. 2023, pp. 10–18. doi: 10.1145/3607505.3607513.
[15] M. Setak, and P. Madani, "Fine-Tuning LLMs for Code Mutation: A New Era of Cyber Threats," in *Proceedings – 2024 IEEE 6th International Conference on Trust, Privacy and Security in Intelligent Systems, and Applications, TPS-ISA 2024* , Institute of Electrical and Electronics Engineers Inc., 2024, pp. 313–321. doi: 10.1109/TPS-ISA62245.2024.00043.
[16] J. Gregory and Q. Liao, "Autonomous Cyberattack with Security-Augmented Generative Artificial Intelligence," in *Proceedings of the 2024 IEEE International Conference on Cyber Security and Resilience, CSR 2024*, Institute of Electrical and Electronics Engineers Inc., 2024, pp. 270–275. doi: 10.1109/CSR61664.2024.10679470.
[17] M. Beckerich, L. Plein, and S. Coronado, "RatGPT: Turning Online LLMs into Proxies for Malware Attacks," Sep. 2023, [Online]. Available: http://arxiv.org/abs/2308.09183
[18] M. M. Yamin, E. Hashmi, and B. Katt, "Combining Uncensored and Censored LLMs for Ransomware Generation," in *Lecture Notes in Computer Science (Including Subseries Lecture Notes in Artificial Intelligence and Lecture Notes in Bioinformatics)*, Springer Science and Business Media Deutschland GmbH, 2025, pp. 189–202. doi: 10.1007/978-981-96-0573-6_14.
[19] M. Adamec and M. Turčaník, "Development of Malware Using Large Language Models." In New Trends in Signal Processing (NTSP), pp. 1–5. IEEE, 2024.
[20] X. Zhang, J. Wang, M. Sun, and Y. Feng, "AndrOpGAN: An Opcode GAN for Android Malware Obfuscations," *Lecture Notes in Computer Science (Including Subseries Lecture Notes in Artificial Intelligence and Lecture Notes in Bioinformatics)*, vol. 12486 LNCS, pp. 12–25, 2020, doi: 10.1007/978-3-030-62223-7_2.
[21] N. Ahmad *et al.*, "GEAAD: Generating Evasive Adversarial Attacks against Android Malware Defense," *Scientific Reports*, vol. 15, no. 1, Dec. 2025, doi: 10.1038/s41598-025-96392-x.
[22] F. Zhong, X. Cheng, D. Yu, B. Gong, S. Song, and J. Yu, "MalFox: Camouflaged Adversarial Malware Example Generation Based on Conv-GANs against Black-Box Detectors," *IEEE Transactions on Computers*, vol. 73, no. 4, 980–993, 2023.
[23] D. Gibert, J. Planes, Q. Le, and G. Zizzo, "Query-Free Evasion Attacks against Machine Learning-Based Malware Detectors with Generative Adversarial Networks," Jun. 2023, doi: 10.1109/EuroSPW59978.2023.00052.
[24] D. Commey, B. Appiah, B. K. Frimpong, I. Osei, E. N. A. Hammond, and G. V. Crosby, "EGAN: Evolutional GAN for Ransomware Evasion," May 2024, doi: 10.1109/LCN58197.2023.10223320.

[25] R. H. Randhawa, N. Aslam, M. Alauthman, M. Khalid, and H. Rafiq, "Deep Reinforcement Learning Based Evasion Generative Adversarial Network for Botnet Detection," *Future Generation Computer Systems*, vol. 150, pp. 294–302, Jan. 2024, doi: 10.1016/j.future.2023.09.011.
[26] D. Devadiga *et al.*, "GLEAM: GAN and LLM for Evasive Adversarial Malware," in *International Conference on ICT Convergence*, IEEE Computer Society, 2023, pp. 53–58. doi: 10.1109/ICTC58733.2023.10393706.
[27] E. Iturbe, O. Llorente-Vazquez, A. Rego, E. Rios, and N. Toledo, "Unleashing Offensive Artificial Intelligence: Automated Attack Technique Code Generation," *Computers & Security*, vol. 147, Dec. 2024, doi: 10.1016/j.cose.2024.104077.
[28] G. Deng *et al.*, "PentestGPT: An LLM-Empowered Automatic Penetration Testing Tool," Jun. 2024, [Online]. Available: http://arxiv.org/abs/2308.06782
[29] J. Teig, and A. Eiken, "Use of Generative AI in Offensive Cybersecurity: A Case Study Using PentestGPT with GPT-4 and Dolphin2.5.", PhD diss., BS thesis. NTNU. no. ntnu: inspera: 187443338: 231873994, 2024.
[30] L. J. Valencia, "Artificial Intelligence as the New Hacker: Developing Agents for Offensive Security," May 2024, [Online]. Available: http://arxiv.org/abs/2406.07561
[31] R. Fang, R. Bindu, A. Gupta, Q. Zhan, and D. Kang, "LLM Agents can Autonomously Hack Websites," Feb. 2024, [Online]. Available: http://arxiv.org/abs/2402.06664
[32] R. Fang, R. Bindu, A. Gupta, and D. Kang, "LLM Agents can Autonomously Exploit One-Day Vulnerabilities," Apr. 2024, [Online]. Available: http://arxiv.org/abs/2404.08144
[33] Y. Zhu *et al.*, "Teams of LLM Agents can Exploit Zero-Day Vulnerabilities," Mar. 2025, [Online]. Available: http://arxiv.org/abs/2406.01637

Chapter 7

The dark side of generative AI

Detecting deepfakes through emotion analysis

Lakshmi J. V. N., Sree Lakshmi P., Akshaya Senthil Kumaran, Aishwarya G., and Boubiche Djallel Eddine

7.1 INTRODUCTION

Generative artificial intelligence (GenAI) has revolutionized the creation of highly realistic text, images, audio, and video, making content production more advanced and efficient. Yet, this powerful technology also poses serious risks, particularly when misused for fraud, misinformation, or deepfakes. By April 2025, AI-generated fake media had become increasingly widespread and harder to detect [1]. Breakthroughs in techniques like diffusion models and generative adversarial networks (GANs) significantly contributed to this shift [2]. While these innovations unlock new creative opportunities, they also blur the line between authentic and synthetic content, underscoring the importance of responsible and cautious use.

GenAI is a powerful tool that can change many areas, like design, entertainment, healthcare, and education. It has the potential to make big improvements in these areas. But sometimes people use it in harmful ways. This can cause serious problems for privacy, digital systems, and even democratic systems [3].

Some of the biggest issues include spreading false information, creating deepfakes, committing fraud, and pretending to be someone else. There are also more serious threats to cybersecurity and privacy. These issues are real and are already impacting individuals and systems today.

As GenAI technologies advance rapidly, they bring not just creative possibilities but also significant new threats to cybersecurity and privacy. Some of the most significant threats include misinformation and deepfakes, which will bend public opinion and trust. Furthermore, AI-based impersonation and fraud pose immense challenges by allowing hackers to simulate individuals or businesses convincingly, making it easier for them to execute successful scams. These new threats are imminent and already being perpetrated against individuals and organizations globally, necessitating immediate attention and strong.

- *Misinformation and Deepfakes*

One of the major threats today with GenAI is how it can twist the truth using very believable fake media, often known as deepfakes. These fake creations are made by AI and can appear as videos, photos, or recordings altered to look like real people. The main purpose of deepfakes is to deceive people or change their opinions. They are produced using a technology called GANs, which consists of two parts: one that detects fake content and another that creates it. As time goes on, the content creator becomes very skilled at making fakes that look real, tricking both machines and humans alike, as shown in Figure 7.1.

DOI: 10.1201/9781003644231-10

Figure 7.1 Facebook Fears That AI-Generated "Deepfake" Videos Could Be the Next Big Source of Viral Misinformation.

Deepfake videos often target politicians, making it seem as if they have made statements they never made.

This type of fake media can damage trust in leaders, influence election outcomes, and even lead to social unrest. Besides videos, AI technologies like large language models (LLMs) can generate fake news articles, social media messages, and even entire fake online identities to spread propaganda. These AI-generated writings often imitate how real people write and speak, making it hard to tell them apart from genuine content. The real issue is not just what is being said in these fake pieces, but also how quickly and in what large quantities they are spread. Traditional fact-checking systems cannot keep up with the rapid pace at which AI can produce and distribute misleading information. The sheer amount of fake content leads people to doubt what is genuine, resulting in a complete breakdown of trust [4].

- ***Impersonation and Fraud***

GenAI has made it simpler for people to imitate others. One worrying development is voice cloning. In just a few minutes of recorded audio, AI can almost perfectly copy a voice, including how it sounds, the accent, and even emotional tones. Criminals have used this technology in CEO fraud cases, pretending to be a boss on the phone to trick workers into sending money or sharing private details. Visual impersonation is also a growing issue. Face-swapping tools can mimic a person's facial expressions and movements live during video chats by overlaying their face on another's body. This allows for convincing impersonation in video calls, social media, and fake news. These days, fake identities are common, using forged documents, digital trails, and AI-generated faces to open accounts, apply for credit, or sneak into organizations. Additionally, GenAI is boosting the effectiveness of phishing attacks. Instead of basic messages filled with errors, attackers now craft highly targeted and believable phishing emails using language models. These emails are often relevant and free from mistakes, making them more effective than older methods. Combined with fake video calls, copied websites, or cloned voices, distinguishing between what is real and what is not becomes extremely difficult [5].

- ***Security and Privacy Risks***

GenAI comes with many risks for privacy and online safety. One serious issue is the creation of explicit content without permission. This involves putting someone's face onto adult material without them knowing, which can damage mental health and reputations, targeting mainly women and famous individuals. It's a widespread problem because it is easy to create with limited technical skills. Beyond altering images, GenAI can also breach privacy through reidentification and data leaks. Some AI models, especially those using large public datasets, might accidentally expose personal details like names, emails, or even pieces of medical records under certain conditions.

Even when data is meant to be anonymous, AI can sometimes figure out who it belongs to by analyzing small bits of information. GenAI also brings new cybersecurity challenges. LLMs can be manipulated through prompt injection attacks, which are when malicious inputs cause the AI to produce harmful or unexpected results. Attackers are using AI to write programs, develop malware, or simulate cyberattacks. This technology makes it possible for inexperienced hackers to carry out complex cyberattacks easily. AI affects infrastructure security as well. Generative models can find or exploit security gaps, create fake reports to mislead investigators, or develop advanced malware that changes to avoid detection. These security problems, combined with GenAI, are causing increased concern for the government.

This chapter aims to provide a thorough examination of the risks and challenges posed by GenAI, with a focus on its potential for misuse in spreading misinformation, creating deepfakes, and compromising privacy and security. It explores the social and ethical implications surrounding these technologies, highlighting how they can erode trust and harm individuals and communities. The chapter also delves into real-world case studies depicting the rise of deepfake pornography to illustrate these threats in action. A significant portion is dedicated to detection and mitigation strategies, including cutting-edge methods like emotion analysis with Deep Face, which identifies subtle emotional inconsistencies to spot synthetic media. Ultimately, the chapter emphasizes the need for a multifaceted approach combining advanced detection techniques, ethical guidelines, regulatory measures, and public education to effectively combat the misuse of GenAI and protect digital integrity.

The remaining part of the chapter is organized as follows: Section 7.2 (Related Study) synthesizes related studies, Section 7.3 (Methods for Detecting Deep Fakes) examines methods for deepfake detection, Section 7.4 (Deep Fake Case Studies) details the deepfake detection pipeline and real-world case studies, and Section 7.5(Experimental Studies on Deep Fake Detection Using AI) presents the expiremental studies and Section 7.6 summarizes the conclusion.

7.2 RELATED STUDY

Deepfakes and GenAI have garnered extensive academic interest because of their significant social, ethical, and security impacts. Current research indicates how artificial media fosters distrust, accelerates disinformation, amplifies inequalities, and facilitates malicious abuse in various contexts. In addition to these threats, researchers have also been working on measures to detect and counter artificial media to protect digital spaces. The subsequent sections summarize earlier work within three pivotal areas: social and ethical ramifications, security and abuse, and detection and countermeasures.

7.2.1 Social and ethical implications

Allen and Weyl [6] highlight the dangers that GenAI poses to democratic institutions, emphasizing how synthetic media—particularly Deepfakes—undermine public trust and make truth harder to distinguish. Wach et al. [7] similarly argue that platforms like ChatGPT raise ethical concerns, amplify biases, and increase risks around misinformation and privacy. Inequality also emerges in this discourse. Bitton et al. [8] warn that communities with lower digital literacy are disproportionately affected by AI-generated disinformation, potentially widening social divides. Chapman et al. [9] and Jhanvi et al. further stress how deepfakes have been weaponized against women, fueling online harassment and abuse [10]. Baldassarre et al. [11] explore how GenAI applications blur the line between authentic and fabricated experiences, while Bauer et al. [12] show that merely disclosing content as AI-generated can shape human creativity and perceptions in unexpected ways.

7.2.2 Security and misuse

Deepfakes have been increasingly linked to malicious activities. De Rancourt-Raymond et al. and Smaiti [4] describe real-world cases of deepfake-enabled financial fraud. Shoaib et al. [13] and Botha et al. [14] highlight the weaponization of GenAI for spreading fake news, stressing how convincing synthetic content complicates misinformation detection. Recent case studies further underline this threat. Panditharatne et al. [15] examine AI's role in influencing U.S. election dynamics, while Hung et al. [16] documented AI-driven disinformation targeting Taiwan. Derous [17] investigates awareness-building efforts among adolescents on platforms like TikTok.

7.2.3 Detection and mitigation strategies

Considerable research has focused on developing defenses against deepfakes. In-depth interviews were conducted for 27 bank managers chosen from 9 countries. The UAE National Bank proposed mitigation strategies for securing digital environments [18]. Almars [19], Heidari et al. [20], and Stroebel et al. [21] present systematic reviews of detection techniques, ranging from deep learning approaches to hybrid models. Technical advancements include Pu et al.'s [22] works on real-world deepfake video detection, Zhou et al.'s [23] joint audiovisual detection methods, and Ciamarra et al.'s [24] proposals. On temporal analysis and multimodal strategies, deepfake images were detected efficiently. Proactive approaches such as Dongjin et al.'s invisible watermarking [25] and blockchain-based verification by Oleg [26] have also been suggested as methods for digital steganography.

To better contextualize prior contributions, Table 7.1 provides a comparative overview and synthesizes them, highlighting their main objectives, methodological approaches, and remaining limitations.

Table 7.1 Comparative Summary of Related Studies on Deepfakes and GenAI

Focus Area	*Problem Addressed*	*Approach/Method*	*Limitations/Gaps*
Social and Ethical Implications	Threats to democracy and trust [6]	Theoretical/critical analysis on the impact of synthetic media on institutions	Lacks empirical validation of long-term democratic effects
	Ethical concerns: bias, misinformation, privacy [7]	Case-based discussion of risks with generative AI (e.g., ChatGPT)	No technical countermeasures proposed
	Inequality in digital literacy [8]	Sociological analysis of how disinformation impacts vulnerable groups	Limited to social perspective; ignores technical solutions
	Gendered harassment [9]	Case studies on weaponization of deepfakes against women	Narrow focus; doesn't explore broader population
	Blurred authentic vs. synthetic experiences [11]	Exploration of user experiences and perceptions	Conceptual; lacks a measurement or detection framework
	Impact of disclosure on creativity [12]	Experimental study of labeling AI-generated content	Focused on creativity, not misinformation resilience
Security and Misuse	Financial fraud [4]	Real-world cases of deepfake-enabled fraud	Context-specific; lacks a generalizable detection framework
	Fake news and misinformation [13, 14]	Analysis of disinformation spread via AI	Highlights a challenge, but no technical defenses are proposed
	Election interference [15]	Case study: U.S. election dynamics	Focused on a single region/event
	Political disinformation [16]	Case study: Taiwan campaigns	Regional limitation; not generalizable
	Adolescent awareness [17]	Study of youth responses to TikTok disinformation	Awareness focus; no prevention strategies
Detection and Mitigation Strategies	Securing digital environments [20]	Organizational mitigation strategies	Limited to the banking sector
	Comprehensive detection reviews [19]	Systematic review of deep learning and hybrid models	Survey-based; no new solution
	Real-world video detection [22]	Technical methods for video-based detection	Limited robustness to unseen attacks
	Audiovisual deepfake detection [23, 13]	Joint analysis of audio and video cues	Computationally expensive
	Temporal/multimodal detection [24])	Use of temporal consistency and multimodal data	Scalability concerns
	Proactive defenses [25]	Invisible watermarking, blockchain verification	Early-stage, lacks large-scale deployment

7.3 METHODS FOR DETECTING DEEPFAKES

The first step in identifying deepfakes is to look for the smallest imperfections and artifacts that are left over from the creation process. Detection methods can be broadly categorized based on the type of cues they exploit. Some approaches rely on subtle visual artifacts in manipulated images, others analyze temporal inconsistencies across video frames, while more recent methods focus on irregularities in synthetic audio and images.

Figure 7.2 illustrates the fundamental workflow of a deepfake detection system, showing how raw media is systematically processed to determine whether it is authentic or manipulated. The pipeline begins with an input stage, where the system is provided with either an image or a video suspected of being a deepfake. The next step is face detection, often carried out with algorithms such as MTCNN or OpenCV, which locate and isolate the facial region for further analysis. Once detected, the face is resized and normalized to ensure consistent dimensions and quality, making it suitable for deep learning models.

Feature extraction follows, in which convolutional neural networks (CNNs), such as XceptionNet, are employed to learn and capture the subtle spatial cues and artifacts that may reveal forgery. The extracted features are then passed into a classification model that outputs a prediction about authenticity, often accompanied by a confidence score. Finally, the post-processing stage consolidates results across multiple frames or segments, enabling the system to produce a final judgment that integrates both frame-level predictions and contextual evidence.

This structured pipeline serves as the foundation for the case studies analyzed in this section. By mapping real-world and experimental scenarios onto the stages of the workflow, we can explore not only where current models excel but also where they fall short. Through these eight case studies—five drawn from real incidents and three from controlled tests—we aim to highlight the strengths, weaknesses, and practical considerations of each stage, offering insights into how deepfake detection operates in practice and what improvements are still needed.

7.3.1 Identification of visual artifacts

Even though deepfake technology has advanced rapidly, the videos it produces often carry subtle signs that betray their artificial origin. For example, eye movements are notoriously difficult to replicate with perfect accuracy, and many deepfakes reveal themselves through odd blinking patterns or stares that seem slightly too fixed. The edges of a person's face or hair are another trouble spot, where the blending between subject and background may appear smudged, wavy, or oddly sharp compared to the rest of the image. Lighting also poses a significant challenge, as the shadows and highlights on a generated face often fail to line up naturally with the surrounding environment, leaving a jarring sense of mismatch. On a more detailed level, the fine features of the eyes, teeth, or glasses often appear off, reflections may look inconsistent, teeth may be irregularly shaped, and glasses can sit awkwardly or even blur into the skin. For human viewers, these flaws might feel "uncanny" or subtly unsettling, while for detection models, they serve as valuable signals. Tools that analyze head movements, study inconsistencies in facial symmetry, or pick up on digital fingerprints left behind by generative models can use these imperfections to separate authentic recordings from manipulated ones. By combining human intuition with algorithmic analysis, detection efforts continue to improve at spotting the hidden cracks in deepfake content.

Figure 7.2 Deepfake Detection Process.

To keep up with the rapid rise of deepfakes, researchers have developed a variety of detection models that learn to spot the small imperfections left behind by synthetic media. One example is XceptionNet, a network that examines the spatial details of an image to uncover traces of manipulation. It looks closely at the textures and fine-grained patterns of pixels, picking up on irregularities that people might not consciously notice but that point to a fake. Another popular tool is MesoNet, a compact CNN built specifically for the challenge of face forgery detection. Its lightweight design makes it practical for situations where speed and efficiency matter, such as real-time monitoring. Beyond these, newer models have emerged that go beyond analyzing single frames. Some, like those trained on the FaceForensics dataset, combine spatial analysis with temporal cues, scanning across sequences of video frames to catch inconsistencies in movement by recognizing whether that's unnatural blinking, mismatched head turns, or lighting shifts that do not stay consistent. Others, such as classifiers built on EfficientNet, bring stronger generalization by training on vast collections of manipulated and authentic media. Together, these models show how the field is moving toward a layered defense by combining image-level analysis, video-based patterns, and even frequency-level signals to make deepfake detection both faster and more reliable.

7.3.2 Temporal and frame analysis

When it comes to video-based deepfakes, many of the telltale flaws emerge not in a single frame but over time. Unlike still images, videos require smooth and coherent transitions between frames, and this temporal consistency is where many synthetic creations stumble. For example, a person's lip movements might not align perfectly with the audio track, leading to subtle delays or mismatched mouth shapes that betray manipulation. Similarly, head turns and body movements may appear awkward or slightly out of sync with natural motion, creating an effect that feels unnatural when viewed continuously. Even small irregularities like blinks that last too long, or lighting shifts that don't carry over from one frame to the next, can become noticeable when seen across multiple frames.

To capture these discrepancies, researchers use models designed to analyze video sequences rather than isolated images. Long short-term memory (LSTM) networks, for instance, are particularly effective because they are built to understand patterns across time. By processing consecutive frames as a sequence, LSTMs can detect when facial movements or expressions fail to follow a natural rhythm. Similarly, three-dimensional CNNs extend the traditional two-dimensional approach by adding a temporal dimension, enabling them to learn not only the spatial details within a single frame but also how those details evolve across a video. This combination allows them to flag inconsistencies such as abrupt transitions or jerky, nonhuman-like motions.

Beyond LSTMs and 3D CNNs, newer approaches integrate attention mechanisms that focus on regions most prone to manipulation, such as the eyes and mouth, where temporal mismatches are most common. Other strategies combine temporal modeling with audio analysis, checking whether spoken words synchronize accurately with lip movements. By uniting visual and auditory cues, these methods strengthen the reliability of detection. Overall, temporal and frame analysis has become an essential layer in deepfake forensics, since it moves beyond static artifacts and emphasizes the dynamic qualities of video that remain challenging for generative models to fully replicate.

7.3.3 Audio-based detection

While much attention has been placed on visual deepfakes, synthetic audio is also advancing rapidly and poses a growing threat in areas such as fraud, impersonation, and misinformation. Although AI-generated voices can sound convincing at first, they often carry subtle imperfections that set them apart from natural human speech. For instance, spectral artifacts, such as small glitches in the frequency spectrum, may appear as unnatural pitch shifts, distorted timbres, or tiny audio hiccups that disrupt the flow of speech. Likewise, the rhythm and tone of machine-generated voices frequently lack the natural inflection, emotion, and variability that human speakers express effortlessly. This results in delivery that can sound overly flat, robotic, or monotonous. Another common issue is over-smoothing, while real human voices contain depth, richness, and slight imperfections that reflect individual vocal traits, synthetic voices often smooth out these details, producing speech that feels too polished and lacking in authenticity.

To detect such flaws, researchers rely on models designed to analyze the acoustic and structural patterns of audio signals. One widely used approach is spectrogram-based analysis, where audio is converted into a visual representation of frequencies over time. CNNs can then be applied to these spectrograms, learning to identify subtle distortions or inconsistencies that indicate a synthetic origin. In contrast, methods like RawNet take a more direct route by analyzing raw waveforms without the need for preprocessing, enabling the detection model to capture fine-grained irregularities in the signal itself. These models can detect hidden anomalies in pitch transitions, pauses, and energy distributions that are difficult for humans to pick up on.

More advanced systems are beginning to incorporate multimodal detection strategies, combining audio cues with facial or lip movement analysis in video deepfakes. For example, if the voice in a clip does not align with the speaker's mouth movements or emotional expressions, this discrepancy can be flagged as evidence of tampering. Researchers are also exploring the use of recurrent neural networks and attention-based models that can track long-term dependencies in speech, making it possible to recognize when a voice lacks the natural rhythm and variability of real human dialogue. Together, these approaches highlight that, while synthetic voices are becoming increasingly sophisticated, their imperfections both in how they sound and how they align with visual cues remain valuable tools for detection.

7.3.4 Detection of multimodal deepfakes

As deepfake technology becomes more sophisticated, attackers increasingly deploy not just video or audio in isolation but both together, creating multimodal deepfakes that are far harder to detect. These counterfeits attempt to align a person's voice, lip movements, facial expressions, and even body language into a seamless performance. However, mismatches between these different gestures often provide important clues for detection. For instance, the emotional tone of the audio might not match the expression on the speaker's face, such as a cheerful voice paired with a neutral or serious facial expression. Even body language and gaze direction can reveal inconsistencies if they fail to match the context or the emotional state implied by the voice.

To uncover these cross-modal inconsistencies, researchers have developed detection models that process both audio and visual information in parallel. Transformer-based architectures are especially compatible for this task, as they excel at learning long-term relationships across different input streams. By integrating data from speech, lip movements, and facial expressions, these models can highlight delicate mismatches that would go unnoticed when analyzing a single modality. Dual-stream CNNs are another common approach, where one branch processes the audio signal and the other processes the video frames, before combining their outputs to make a joint decision about reality.

The effectiveness of these models depends heavily on the quality and diversity of the training data. Large-scale multimodal datasets such as the DeepFake Detection Challenge (DFDC) dataset and FakeAVCeleb have been created to support this goal, offering thousands of manipulated and authentic samples for training and evaluation. These datasets include a wide range of voices, languages, and facial characteristics, which help models generalize to real-world scenarios. As multimodal forgeries become more advanced, detection systems are also evolving to include context-aware analysis, where the model does not just check for synchronization but also assesses whether the overall performance feels natural and consistent with human communication patterns. By bringing together multiple streams of information, multimodal detection represents one of the most promising approaches to staying ahead in the arms race against increasingly realistic deepfakes. Table 7.2 provides a structured overview of the previous detection strategies, outlining

Table 7.2 Summary of Deepfake Detection Methods

Detection Approach	*Key Indicators/ Features*	*Representative Models/Techniques*	*Strengths*	*Limitations*
Visual Artifact Detection	• Blinking irregularities • Blurry/ warped edges • Uneven lighting • Flaws in eyes, teeth, or glasses	• XceptionNet (spatial feature extraction) • MesoNet (lightweight CNN for face fraud)	Effective for image-level forensics; interpretable features	May fail against high-quality or well-refined deepfakes
Temporal and Frame Analysis	• Inconsistent movements between frames • Lip-sync vs. voice mismatch • Unrealistic head transitions	• LSTM networks (sequential temporal analysis) • 3D CNNs (spatiotemporal feature capture)	Captures video inconsistencies; robust to motion artifacts	Requires video data; computationally expensive
Audio-Based Detection	• Spectral artifacts (pitch shifts, audio glitches) • Flat speech patterns, lack of emotion • Over-smoothing of voice signals	• CNN-based spectrogram analysis • RawNet-like models (raw waveform analysis)	Useful for synthetic voice detection; complements video analysis	Performance drops with high-quality synthetic audio
Multimodal Detection	• Lip-speech alignment • Voice tone vs. facial expression consistency • Natural body language and eye contact	• Transformer architectures • Dual-stream CNNs • Trained on DFDC, FakeAVCeleb datasets	Higher accuracy by combining multiple modalities; resilient against single-modality attacks	Data- and compute-intensive; requires large annotated multimodal datasets

their distinguishing features, representative models, and corresponding strengths and limitations.

7.4 DEEPFAKE CASE STUDIES

Deepfake detection has become an essential focus in the fight against digital misinformation and manipulation. Case studies in this field highlight real-world examples where deepfake content—from altered videos to synthetic audio—has been used to deceive or mislead audiences. By closely examining these instances, researchers can identify subtle cues, such as irregular facial movements, inconsistent lighting, or audiovisual mismatches, that often escape casual observation. These studies also explore how different detection techniques, including machine learning models, temporal analysis, and forensic approaches, perform under various conditions. Beyond technical evaluation, case studies reveal the broader social impact of deepfakes, showing how they can influence public opinion, harm reputations, or facilitate fraud. Together, these insights help refine detection tools and inform strategies to mitigate the risks posed by increasingly realistic synthetic media.

7.4.1 Real-world case study 1: The Biden Robocall Incident (2024)

A few weeks before the U.S. presidential primary in early 2024, people in New Hampshire got some odd robocalls [27]. The message sounded like it was from President Joe Biden, telling democratic voters to "save their vote for the November election" instead of voting in the primary. Since the voice was really convincing and matched Biden's speaking style, many believed it was real. However, it was later revealed that this call was a deepfake, a type of fake audio made by AI to mimic the President's voice. This situation alerted election officials and voters. The AI technology used in these calls created the fake message from just a few minutes of real audio. The aim was clear: to spread false information and prevent people from voting. The criminals behind this attempted to disrupt the political process by using a trusted leader's voice to manipulate public trust. Investigations suggest that political groups or activists organized these calls, using AI to try and influence voter turnout. Authorities like the Federal Communications Commission (FCC) and state election officials were quick to respond. The FCC began working on new rules to ban AI-created robocalls, while law enforcement targeted those guilty of interfering with elections. This incident led to a national conversation about the threat of AI in politics, as deepfakes are becoming harder to detect and easier to make. The Biden robocall issue shows the urgent need for tools to detect AI, strong policies, and public education. It demonstrated how GenAI can undermine election integrity with the greatest psychological impact and the least number of resources. More importantly, in the age of synthetic media, it underscored the importance of timely legal accountability, public education, and real-time detection methods.

7.4.2 Real-world case study 2: Arup's $25 Million Deepfake Scam (2024)

The Arup scam [28] exposed the growing threat of "CEO fraud," which includes traditional phishing attempts enhanced with convincing fake media and is augmented by GenAI. It demonstrated how vulnerable even respectable, security-conscious businesses are to highly tailored and convincing AI fraud. The case served as a reminder of the importance of real-time authentication systems, multi-factor verification procedures, and corporate deepfake training, especially for financial transactions.

7.4.3 Real-world case study 3: Election Interference in Taiwan (2023)

In the months before the 2023 local elections, Taiwan faced challenges from foreign influence using GenAI [29]. This included fake videos, AI-created false information, and fake audio clips targeting political parties and candidates, as noted by Taiwanese cybersecurity experts and intelligence officials. Forces supporting China were involved in these cyberattacks to influence public opinion and divide voters. A well-known case was a fake video of a famous Taiwanese politician that seemed to show him supporting Beijing. Although officials and media quickly proved the video was fake, thousands had watched it on social media before it was removed. These videos were part of a larger campaign to harm candidates who supported independence and reduce trust in the election process. AI-generated articles in Mandarin and fake news resembling credible sources were also widely shared on social media and messaging apps like LINE.

To tackle these deceptive methods, Taiwanese authorities launched campaigns to inform the public. They collaborated with online platform managers and implemented advanced AI tools to detect fake content. This strategy was thorough in addressing misinformation. Government agencies joined forces with international organizations and local experts to monitor these activities.

Despite their efforts, the situation highlighted the challenges of preventing AI-driven interference in elections once fake content starts spreading. This case was crucial for Taiwan and globally. It provided a real-life example of how GenAI could be used to impact democratic processes, particularly in politically sensitive areas. Taiwan's experience offered valuable lessons to other democracies, like the United States and Europe, showing that fighting AI-driven disinformation requires international cooperation, improved digital media literacy, and the establishment of early-warning systems.

7.4.4 Real-world case study 4: The Tom Cruise TikTok Deepfakes

In early 2021, a TikTok account called @deeptomcruise started posting videos that quickly gained a lot of attention online [30]. These clips seemed to show actor Tom Cruise involved in everyday activities like playing golf, doing magic tricks, and chatting informally with the camera. The striking resemblance led many to believe they were watching the real Hollywood star. However, these were deepfakes. The depths were crafted by Belgian visual effects artist Chris Ume, who used advanced techniques to map Tom Cruise's face onto an expert impersonator. The uncanny realism of these videos surprised many viewers and sparked important discussions about the implications of this technology. The creator later explained that his goal was to illustrate the growing power of deepfake technology. Yet, the fact that many people were fooled highlighted a bigger issue: distinguishing between reality and AI-generated content is becoming increasingly difficult. Even when the videos seem harmless or amusing, they have the potential to spread misinformation. This incident also reignited talks about consent and digital identity. Tom Cruise did not create these videos, nor did he agree to the use of his image in this way. While satire and impersonation are protected forms of expression, the introduction of deepfake technology adds new challenges.

The tools in this case were easy for anyone to use, which made it stand out. Now, this technology is everywhere, even if the video quality is high and the visual effects are professionally done. Because deepfake tools are easy to access, even those with little money can create videos that seem very real, leading to potential misuse.

There's a greater risk now that these tools could be used for political tricks, damaging someone's reputation, or cheating as they become more user-friendly. The Tom Cruise TikTok incident was a wake-up call for everyone, including the public, governments, and social media companies. People suggested that platforms like TikTok review their rules and install measures to stop fake content.

This event kicked off demands for tighter rules, watermarking standards, and AI systems that can spot such videos, even though the videos remained online. It underscored the urgent need for people to become more media-savvy, to create new laws, and to develop technical solutions to fight against fake media, especially now when you can't always trust what you see.

7.4.5 Real-world case study 5: Deepfake Pornography and the Weaponization of AI against Women

Nonconsensual deepfake pornography is a very disturbing use of deepfake technology, and began appearing in 2017 [10]. People started using AI to insert the faces of celebrities, and later even everyday people, into pornographic videos without their permission. This type of content quickly spread on platforms like Reddit, Telegram, and Discord, where many altered images and videos appeared. These deepfakes were made using publicly available photos from social media profiles to create videos of famous actresses, social media influencers, and sometimes even people they knew personally. This trend represents one of the worst forms of online sexual abuse. Many victims discovered their faces were placed in sexual content they had nothing to do with, which spread rapidly online. This often led to embarrassment, harassment, and damage to their reputations.

Once these disbeliefs are online, removing them is extremely difficult, and the emotional impact on victims can be very severe, often impossible to undo. Initially, these creations became prevalent on Reddit. In 2018, Reddit banned deepfake pornography due to public complaints. However, by then, many users had shifted to encrypted messaging services like Telegram, where controlling content was much harder. On Telegram, AI is used to run automated bots that allow users to upload an image of a woman and receive a fake nude picture in return. These bots have processed millions of images and targeted thousands of victims, including many young individuals.

This kind of pervasive misuse of deepfake technology highlights a serious weakness in the legal system as it stands today. Laws in most nations have found it difficult to keep up with the rapid speed at which AI is developing. Deepfake pornography victims frequently have no obvious legal options, particularly when the content is shared anonymously or is hosted in a foreign country. Although certain countries, including the UK, South Korea, and several U.S. states, have enacted laws that make it illegal to produce and distribute nonconsensual deepfakes, enforcement of these laws is still uneven and restricted worldwide.

This case study illustrates how deepfake technology can be used as a weapon to support misogyny, harassment, and online abuse, especially against women. It has prompted fresh demands for more robust platform accountability, regulatory protections, and technological safeguards like opt-out mechanisms and detection tools. The controversy also emphasizes how important it is to educate the public broadly about the possible negative effects of AI-powered image manipulation and how tech companies should be more proactive in stopping the exploitation of people online.

7.5 EXPERIMENTAL STUDIES ON DEEPFAKE DETECTION USING AI

AI is no longer just a futuristic concept—it has become an integral part of solving real-world challenges across different sectors. To raise awareness and make these advancements more approachable, this section presents experimental studies where AI tools have been practically applied. The focus here is on two specific areas: Deepware analysis and Hive Moderation and video framing analysis using AI tools. Together, these experimental studies not only showcase the technical capabilities of AI but also emphasize its role in promoting responsible, safe, and meaningful use of digital media. They serve as practical examples of how technology can be human-centered, not just for efficiency, but also for social good and ethical accountability.

7.5.1 Experimental study 1: Deepware analysis

Deepware [31] is a tool that uses AI to examine faces in movies or photos to detect deepfakes. It focuses on face traits, inconsistencies, and artifacts. It utilizes a type of AI known as CNNs, which are trained with examples of both real and fake media to improve accuracy. The system works by searching for small pixel-level mistakes, issues with lighting, and strange facial expressions that could suggest manipulation. After analyzing these elements,

Figure 7.3 Deepfake Analysis of the YouTube Video Using Deepware.

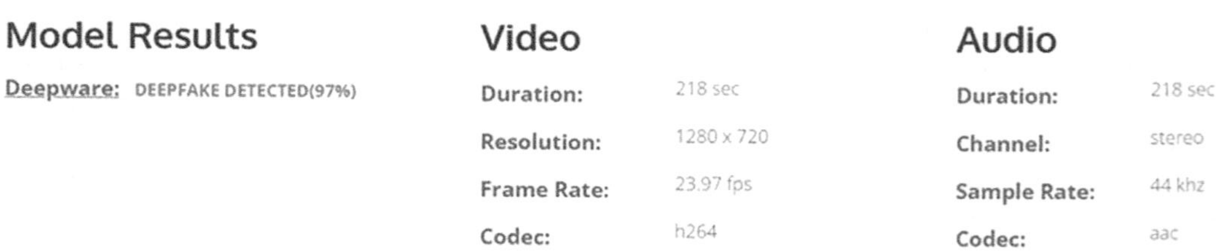

Figure 7.4 97% of Deepfake Detection Is Observed from the Video File.

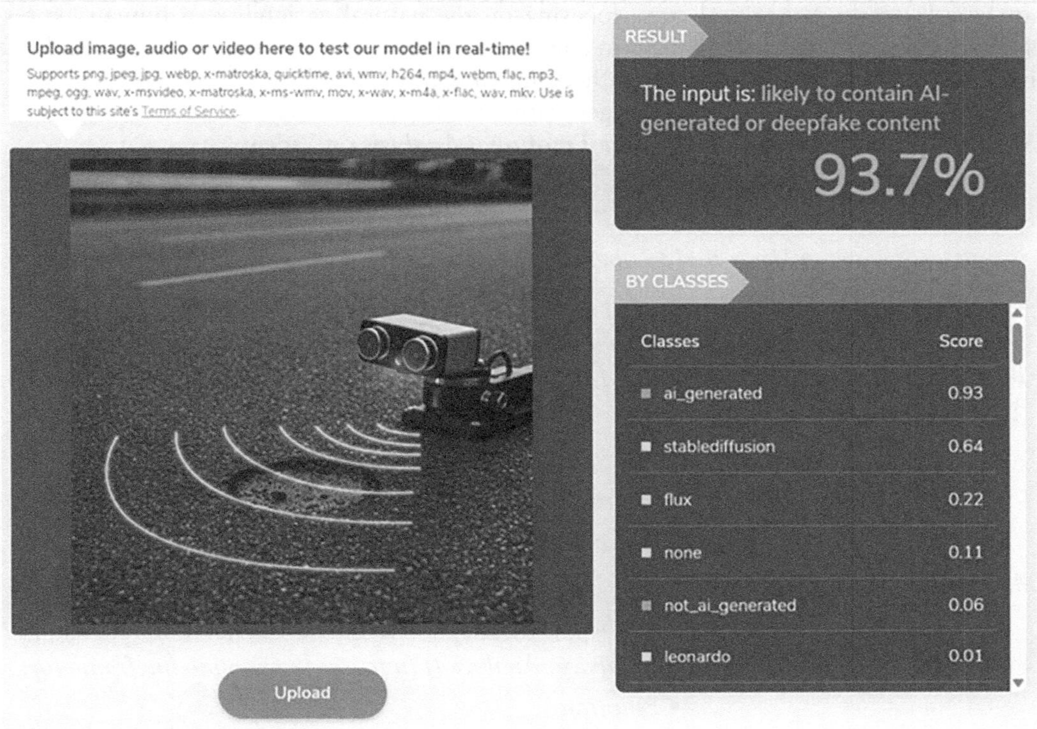

Figure 7.5 Deep Face Analysis Using an AI Tool.

Deepware generates a confidence score, indicating the likelihood that the media has been altered in some way, as shown in Figures 7.2 and 7.3.

7.5.2 Experimental study 2: Hive Moderation

Hive Moderation [31] is a tool that examines text, photos, and videos to detect fake content or any rule-breaking material. It uses advanced technology like computer vision and machine learning. The system depends on deep neural networks, which are trained with huge datasets, to identify false information, violence, nudity, and fake videos called deepfakes. This technology analyzes each part of a video one by one and checks facial expressions and other data. It works in real time by using an API to quickly give results. It also shares how confident it is about the findings through confidence scores displayed in Figure 7.5.

7.5.3 Experimental study 3: video frame analysis using DeepFace

Deepfake videos often exhibit subtle inconsistencies in facial expressions and micro-expressions, which can be difficult for the human eye to detect but are measurable using computational tools. Emotion analysis provides a promising approach to uncover these inconsistencies by evaluating facial affective patterns across video frames. Unlike conventional pixel-based or frequency-domain deepfake detection methods, emotion-based analysis leverages behavioral cues, focusing on the natural variability of human expressions. Sudden or unnatural changes in emotion, inconsistent transitions, or low confidence in detected emotions can indicate synthetic manipulations.

The following is the algorithm for generating the Deep Face Analysis:

Step-by-Step Algorithm on Deep Face Emotional Analysis on Video:

1. *Initialize Video Input*
    - *Use a tool to open and start the video.*
2. *Set Parameters*
    - *Decide how often you want to analyze frames, like every ten frames. Begin a counter to keep track of the frames.*
3. *Iterate Through Video Frames*
    - *As the video plays:*
    - *Look at the current frame.*
    - *Stop the loop if there are no more frames to read.*
4. *Process Selected Frames*
    - *Depending on the frame rate setting, for each nth frame:*
    - *Utilize the DeepFace. Analyze () function to examine the frame for:*
        - *Emotion*
        - *Age*
        - *Turn off enforced detection to prevent mistakes on faces that are partially or blurry.*
        - *Print the analysis result.*
5. *Handle Errors*
    - *Catch the exception and print an error message for the frame if DeepFace is unable to process it.*
6. *Finalize*
    - *After processing every frame, release the video capture object.*

A video file, such as suspected_video.mp4, is considered. A frame sampling rate (every 10th frame). The output is analyzed for selected frames using DeepFace analysis [32]. Emotions and age are captured using the DeepFace analysis API (Application Programming Interfaces). An error message is given as an output if the frames are not allowed for analysis. Emotion probabilities are aggregated over time and visualized using line plots to illustrate emotional trajectories. Bounding boxes and dominant emotion labels can be overlaid on video frames to provide real-time visual feedback.

The output of the video analysis implemented by using the algorithm provides insights into the emotional expressions and estimated ages of individuals captured in selected video frames. Every 10th frame is analyzed using DeepFace, which detects a face (if present), determines the person's dominant emotion—such as happy, sad, angry, or surprised—and estimates their age.

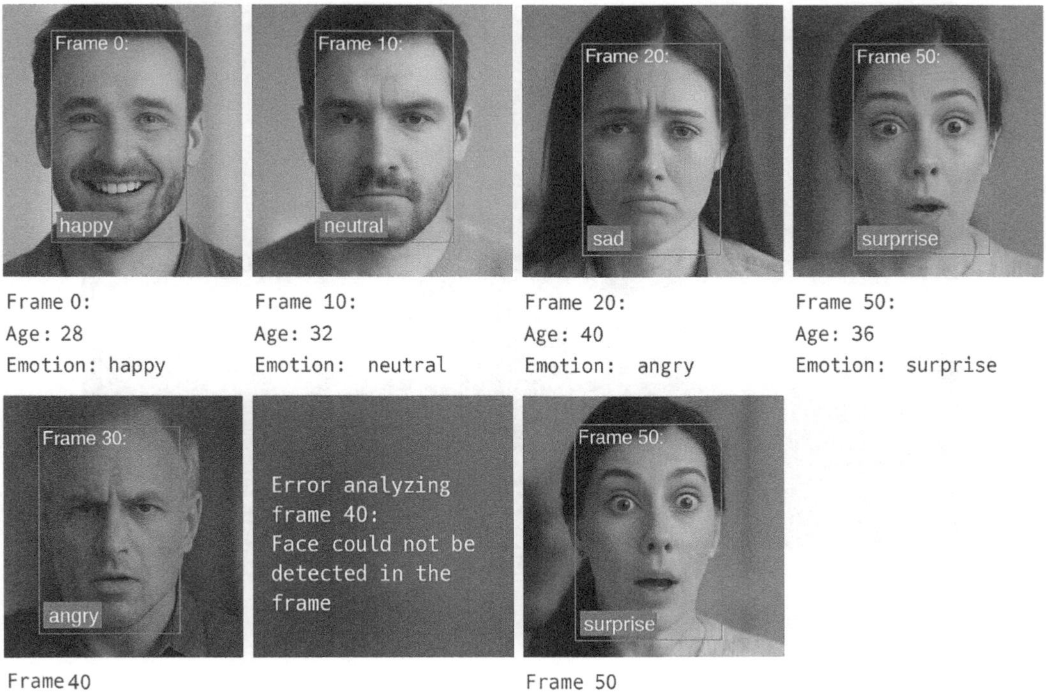

Figure 7.6 Video 1 Deep Face Analysis Capturing the Age and Emotions.

Two videos are considered for the study, analyzing a video to detect people's emotions and estimate their ages using AI. The program checks the video every 10 frames (to save time and resources), grabs a frame, and then uses DeepFace, a deep learning tool, and gives the following output.

From video 1 shown Figure 7.6, one frame might show a happy expression on a 28-year-old, while another might detect a neutral emotion from someone estimated to be 32. If no face is detected in a particular frame, the system gracefully handles the error and moves on. This kind of output offers a human-like understanding of how people appear and feel at various points in the video, making it useful for applications in behavior analysis, media testing, or any context where tracking emotions over time is valuable, as given in Figure 7.7.

At the beginning of the video (frames 0–90), the dominant emotion alternates between surprise and fear, suggesting that the subject may be reacting to something unexpected, tense, or startling. The ages detected in these early frames range from about 32 to 39, indicating a consistent adult subject or group of similar-aged individuals.

From frame 100 to 190, there is a noticeable emotional shift: the dominant emotion becomes happy, indicating a change in the person's experience or reaction—possibly suggesting relief, humor, or a more positive moment in the video. The age estimates in this segment remain steady around 28–33, again suggesting consistency in who is being analyzed.

Later, starting around frame 200, the emotions mix again, switching between happy and surprise, followed by a moment of sadness at frame 270, then returning to surprise and happy by frame 300. This emotional variation could reflect different scenes in the video—possibly reactions to dynamic content like conversations, events, or changes in environment.

Figure 7.7 Video 2 Deep Face Analysis.

Table 7.3 Video 2 Frame Analysis and Emotion

Frame Range	*Dominant Emotion(s)*	*Possible Interpretation*
0–90	Surprise, fear	Shock, tension, or unexpected stimuli
100–190	Happy	Relief, joy, or positive engagement
200–240	Happy, surprise	Mixed moments of joy and surprise
250–270	Surprise, sad	Emotional dip or moment of reflection
280–300	Surprise, happy	Energetic or uplifting closure

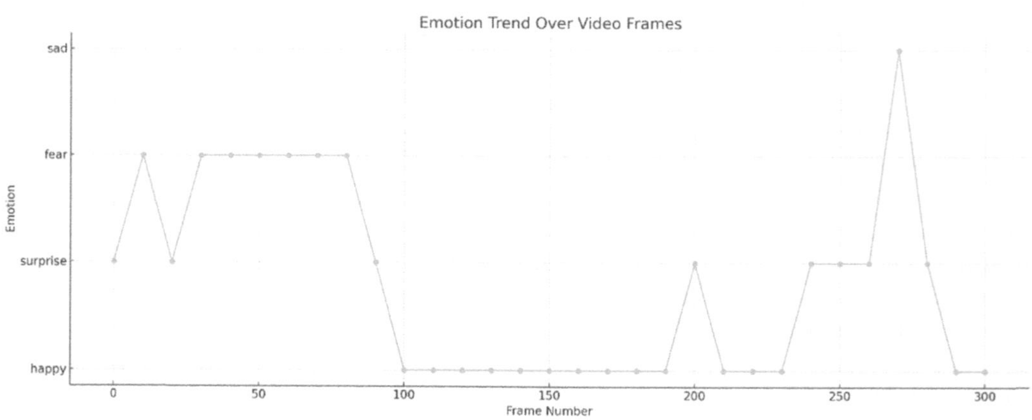

Figure 7.8 Emotions Trend over Video Frames.

Video emotions are tracked and represented using Table 7.3, and the chart in Figure 7.8 shows how emotions change across the video frames!

The emotions shift from surprise and fear to mostly happiness, with a few surprises and a small dip into sadness around frame 270, as shown in Figure 7.8.

This experimental study demonstrates the capability of using AI-based facial analysis, specifically the DeepFace library, to extract emotional and age-related insights from video frames in a lightweight and scalable manner. The consistent estimation of age and detection of emotional shifts across the video frames indicates that DeepFace performs reliably under varying lighting and facial orientations, especially when enforced detection is turned off to accommodate less-than-perfect input frames. The smooth transition in emotional states—from initial surprise and fear to happiness and brief sadness—mirrors the likely narrative or content changes within the video, showcasing how AI can interpret complex human responses over time.

One important observation is the consistency in age predictions, which hovered within a narrow range (approximately 28–39 years), suggesting either the presence of a single individual throughout the video or the robustness of the model in estimating adult facial features. Meanwhile, the emotional fluctuations provide meaningful insights into viewer reactions or subject behavior, valuable for fields such as psychology, marketing, education, or entertainment experience analysis.

However, some limitations were evident. The system occasionally failed to detect faces in complex scenes, and the emotional classification, while insightful, remains a coarse representation of human feelings—restricted to discrete labels such as "happy," "fear," or "surprise" without capturing mixed emotions or contextual cues. Additionally, since DeepFace does not natively support deepfake detection, its outputs could potentially be manipulated in synthetic media, highlighting a gap that needs addressing through integration with deepfake-specific tools like FaceForensics++ [33], DeepFakeDetection [31], or leveraging inconsistencies in temporal or emotional patterns.

Figure 7.9 Video 3 for Emotion Deep Exploratory Analysis.

Later, another video shown in Figure 7.9, taken from YouTube [34], was used to detect 21310 frames with mixed emotions, including fear, anger, sadness, happiness, disgust, surprise, and neutral. Each emotion's pattern is detected in the given line chart for all 21,310 frames. While analyzing these frames, 121 suspicious frames are identified. These frames are separated and are saved in suspicious frames for visual inspection. The emotional analysis of the video is given in the line chart shown in Figure 7.10.

The image displays an emotion analysis over video frames, presented as a line graph plotting emotion probability (%) against frame number. It illustrates how the probability of various emotions, such as anger, is represented as teal, disgust using orange, fear using green, happiness using red, sadness using purple, surprise with brown, and neutral with pink. These changes are captured across over 20,000 video frames. The graph is characterized by extremely rapid and frequent shifts in the dominant emotion, with lines for multiple emotions often spiking to near 100% and dropping to 0% in quick succession, suggesting

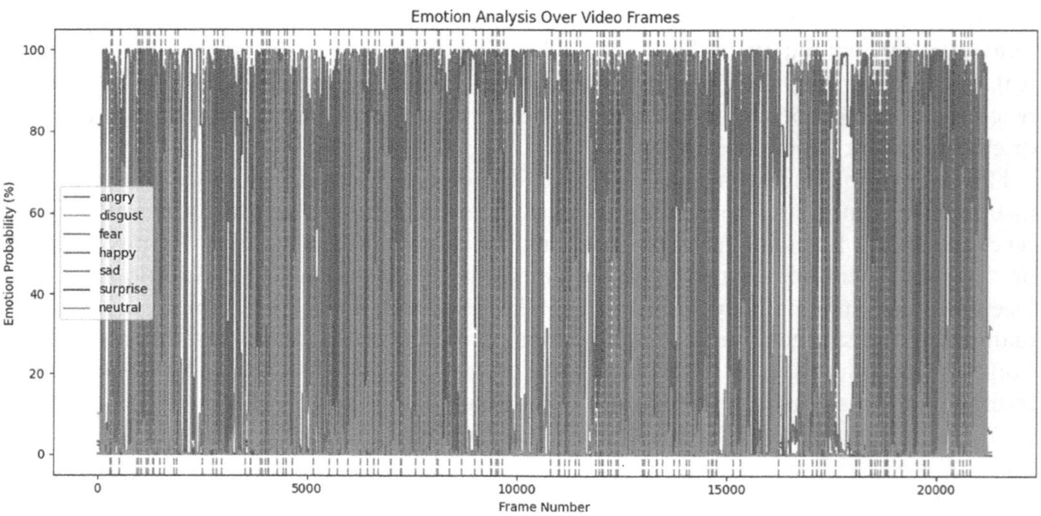

Figure 7.10 Emotional Analysis on Video 3.

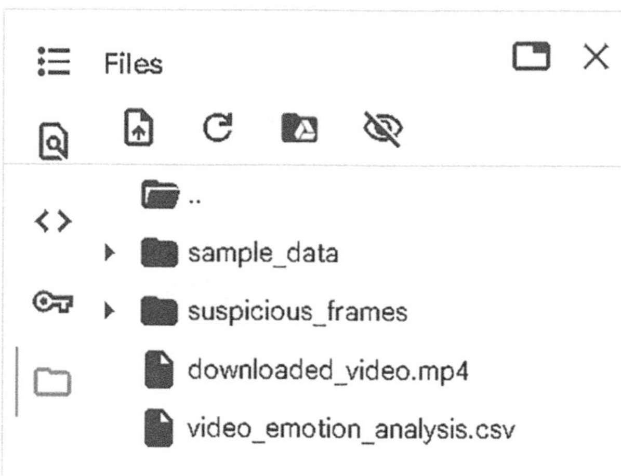

Figure 7.11 Drive Saving the Suspicious Frames as a Folder.

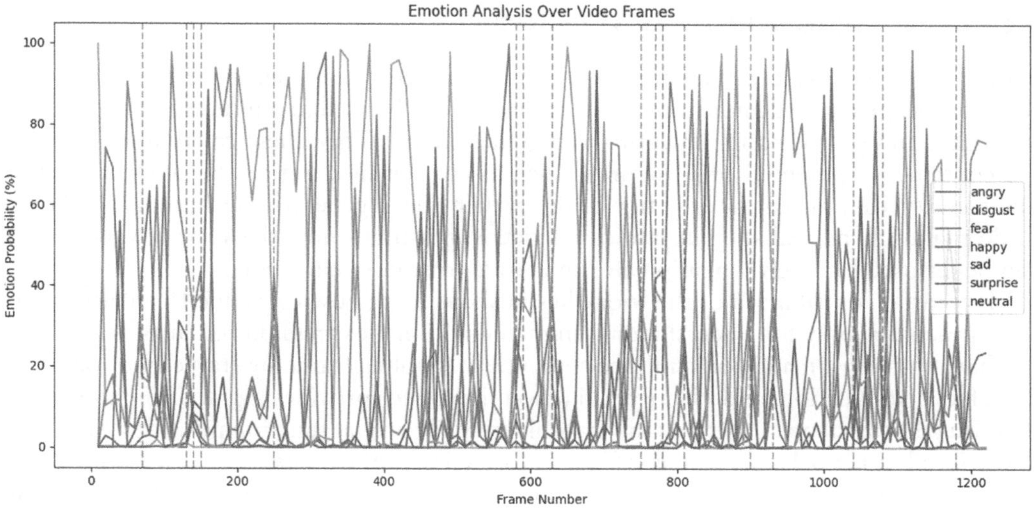

Figure 7.12 Emotional Analysis from Video 4.

a highly dynamic or potentially noisy/unstable analysis. Notably, the happy and neutral emotions appear to be highly prevalent throughout the duration, though they are frequently interrupted by sharp, momentary spikes in other emotions. This analysis also saves suspicious frames for visual inspection in the drive, as given in Figure 7.11.

Output: Saved 121 suspicious frames to "suspicious_frames/."

Video 4 from spiritual content displayed the following emotional analysis pattern as shown in Figure 7.12.

The video 4 content has 1,220 frames and detected 17 suspicious frames and flagged as [70, 130, 140, 150, 250, 580, 590, 630, 750, 770, 780, 810, 900, 930, 1,040, 1,080, 1,180]. The plot visualizes how the DeepFace emotion probabilities vary frame by frame. Sudden spikes or inconsistent patterns, especially in flagged frames, are important indicators for detecting manipulated videos. Researchers can use this visualization to quickly identify frames that may contain synthetic content. Emotions fluctuate a lot in this video, with four multiple lines spiking to high values of approximately 100%. Pink, representing the neutral mood, seems to dominate in many frames, which is common for subtle or inactive expressions. Red vertical lines showing the suspicious frames are scattered throughout, indicating frames with low confidence or irregular emotion patterns. The overlapping spikes and rapid transitions suggest that this could be a deepfake video, as natural videos often have smoother emotional transitions.

In summary, this study illustrates both the promise and the current constraints of AI-driven facial analysis. While DeepFace offers a powerful baseline for emotion and age inference, further advancements and integrations are essential to fully harness its potential in real-world applications and security-sensitive domains. The most significant outcome of this detailed emotion analysis is a time-series profile of emotional intensity across the video, allowing for the quantitative identification of key emotional events. Specifically, the analysis reveals that happy and neutral emotions are highly prevalent, but the extreme frequency of rapid, momentary spikes is also observed.

7.6 CONCLUSION AND FUTURE SCOPE

This chapter has explored the application of AI-driven facial analysis, with a particular focus on DeepFace, to demonstrate how technology can be used to interpret emotions, verify identities, and safeguard the integrity of digital content. While these capabilities highlight the constructive potential of AI in areas such as content moderation, behavioral analysis, and security, they also draw attention to the darker side of generative technologies. The rise of deepfakes, hyperrealistic but fabricated videos, illustrates how the same advances in AI can be misused to deceive, manipulate, and erode trust in visual media.

The central contribution of this work lies in showcasing how tools like DeepFace can be repurposed not only for understanding human emotional expression but also as a defense mechanism against malicious synthetic content. By enabling frame-by-frame emotion detection, facial verification, and identity validation, DeepFace provides a practical pathway for detecting inconsistencies that may signal tampering. This dual function positions AI as both a lens into human behavior and a safeguard for digital authenticity.

Looking ahead, future research should aim to strengthen these systems against increasingly sophisticated generative models, ensuring they remain robust in identifying subtle manipulations. Additionally, integrating such tools into real-time media platforms could offer scalable solutions for moderating harmful or deceptive content before it spreads widely. Beyond technical advancements, interdisciplinary collaboration will be essential to address the ethical, legal, and societal implications of these technologies.

In this way, the chapter underscores a crucial perspective that AI is not inherently good or bad; it is the intent and framework surrounding its use that determines its impact. By advancing tools like Deep Face responsibly, researchers and practitioners can help ensure that AI serves as a force for trust, transparency, and human-centered innovation in the digital age.

ACKNOWLEDGMENTS

The REVA UNIVERSITY, Bangalore, Karnataka, India, provided the facilities needed to conduct the research, which the authors gratefully acknowledged.

ChatGPT 3.5 was used to assist in drafting and refining the content for the Literature Review and Introduction sections. Its utilization primarily involved improving the clarity and flow of the text within these specific sections. All information and claims generated by the AI were subsequently verified and edited by the authors to ensure accuracy, originality, and adherence to academic standards.

REFERENCES

[1] C. Regina and S. Aynur, "AI-Generated Misinformation: A Case Study on Emerging Trends in Fact-Checking Practices Across Brazil, Germany, and the United Kingdom," *Sage Journals – Emerging Media,* vol. 3, no. 2, pp. 214–251, 2025.

[2] J. Jhanvi and P. Sameerchand, "Using Deep Learning to Identify Deepfakes Created Using Generative Adversarial Networks," *Computers,* vol. 14, no. 2, pp. 2–21, 2025.

[3] M. Anwar, "Deep Fake Detection and Mitigation: Securing against AI Generated Manipulation," *Journal of Computaional Innovation,* vol. 4, no. 1, pp. 1–25, 2024.

[4] R.-R. Audrey de and S. Nadia, "The Unethical Use of Deepfakes Available to Purchase," *Journal of Finance Crime,* vol. 30, no. 4, pp. 1066–1077, 2023.

[5] S. Ashutosh Pal, "Safeguarding Authenticity in the Digital Realm: A Holistic Approach Integrating Content Provenance, Secure Watermarking, and Transparent Labeling to Combat Deepfakes," *International Journal For Multidisciplinary Research,* vol. 6, no. 3, pp. 1–14, 2024.
[6] A. Danielle and E. Glen Weyl, "The Real Dangers of Generative AI," *Journal of Democracy,* vol. 35, no. 1, pp. 147–165, 2024.
[7] W. Krzyszt, D. Cong Doanh, E. Joanna, K. Rūta, K. Pawel, M. Grzegorz, P. Joanna and Z. Ewa, "The Dark Side of Generative Artificial Intelligence: A Critical Analysis of Controversies and Risks of ChatGPT," *Entrepreneurial Business and Economics Review,* vol. 11, pp. 8–30, 06 June 2023.
[8] B. Daniel Bendahan, H. Christian Pieter and G. Alexander, "Deepfakes in the Context of AI Inequalities: Analysing Disparities in Knowledge and Attitudes," *Information, Communication and Society,* vol. 28, no. 2, pp. 295–315, 2025.
[9] C. Emily, "Unveiling the Threat- AI and Deepfakes' Impact on Women," University of Mary Washington, 2024.
[10] K. Beatriz, "Verfas sungs Blog," Glogal Constutionalism, 03 June 2024. [Online]. Available: https://verfassungsblog.de/deepfakes-ncid-ai-regulation/. [Accessed 29 April 2025].
[11] B. Maria, C. Danilo, N. Berenice Fernandez, G. Domenico and R. Azzurra, "The Social Impact of Generative AI: An Analysis on ChatGPT," in *Proceedings of the 2023 ACM Conference on Information Technology for Social Good*, pp. 363–373, 2023.
[12] B. Kevin, H. Rebecca, V. Benjamin and H. Oliver, "How Disclosing Generative AI Use Impacts Human Creative Involvement in Human-GenAI Collaboration," Harvey and Berry, 2024. http://dx.doi.org/10.2139/ssrn.4782554
[13] M. R. Shoaib, W. Zefan, T. A. Milad and Z. Jun, "Deepfakes, Misinformation, and Disinformation in the Era of Frontier AI, Generative AI, and Large AI Models," *Cryptography and Security arXiv:2311.17394,* pp. 1–8, 2023.
[14] J. G. Botha and H. Pieterse, "Fake News and Deepfakes: A Dangerous Threat for 21st Century Information Security," *CSIR Research Space,* pp. 1–8, 2020.
[15] P. Mekela, N. Lawrence, Z. Joanna, W. Daniel and A. Yasmin, *An Agenda to Strengthen U.S. Democracy in the Age of AI*, Brennan Center for Justice, New York University School of Law, 2025.
[16] H. Chen-Ling, F. Wen-Cheng, L. Chang-ce and T. Hui-ju, *AI Disinformation Attacks and Taiwan's Responses during the 2024 Presidential Election*, Thomson Foundation- Taiwan Communication Association, 2024.
[17] S. Derous, *Designing a Gamified Application to Enhance Deepfake Awareness by Adolescents on TikTok*, Open Universiteit, 2023.
[18] V. Giuseppe, L. Gajendra and V. Giampaolo, "Managing Deepfakes with Artificial Intelligence: Introducing the Business Privacy Calculus," *Journal of Business Research,* vol. 186, pp. 1–18, 2025.
[19] A. Abdulqader M, "Deepfakes Detection Techniques Using Deep Learning: A Survey," *Journal of Computer and Communications,* vol. 9, no. 5, pp. 1–15, 2021.
[20] H. Arash, J. N. Nima, D. Hasan and U. Mehmet, "Deepfake Detection Using Deep Learning Methods: A Systematic and Comprehensive Review," *WIREs Data Mining and Knowledge Discovery,* vol. 2023, pp. 1–45, 2023.
[21] S. Laura, L. Mark, T. H, S. L. Tsui and A. Mohiuddin, "A Systematic Literature Review on the Effectiveness of Deepfake Detection Techniques," *Journal of Cyber Security Technology,* vol. 7, no. 2, pp. 83–113, 2023.
[22] P. Jiameng, M. Neal, K. Lauren, B. Parantapa, S. Kavya, J. Mobin, W. Bolun and V. Bimal, "Deepfake Videos in the Wild: Analysis and Detection," in *The Web Conference 2021*, pp. 981–992, 2021.
[23] Z. Yipin and L. Ser-Nam, "Joint Audio-Visual Deepfake Detection," in *Proceedings of the IEEE/CVF international conference on computer vision,* pp. 14800–14809, 2021.

[24] C. Andrea, C. Roberto and B. Alberto Del, "Temporal Surface Frame Anomalies for Deepfake Video Detection," In Proceedings of the IEEE/CVF conference on computer vision and pattern recognition, pp. 3837–3844, 2024.

[25] H. Dongjun, W. Sungwon, G. Tom, L. Raymond and B. Sunghwan, "Invisible Watermarks: Attacks and Robustness," arXiv, Mellon University, 2024.

[26] E. Oleg and M. Yaroslav, "The Use of the Blockchain Technology and Digital Watermarking to Provide Data Authenticity on a Mining Enterprise," *Sensors,* vol. 20, no. 12, pp. 3443–3456, 2020.

[27] E. Kamarck, "US Presidential Elections 2024," *The Indian Express,* pp. 1–3, 23 January 2024.

[28] N. Grace, "Scammers Siphon $25M from Engineering Firm Arup via AI Deepfake 'CFO'," *CFODIVE,* pp. 1–3, 17 May 2024.

[29] Y. Alan, C. Micheal and S. Megan, "Taiwan's Election: PRC Interference and Its Implications for the 2024 Election Landscape," *CAP,* pp. 1–4, 1 Febrauary 2024.

[30] M. Rachel, "How a deepfake Tom Cruise on TikTok Turned into a Very Real AI Company," *CNN Business,* p. 5, 6 August 2021.

[31] Deepware.ai, "Deepware," Deepware A.S, Feb 2025. [Online]. Available: https://deepware.ai/. [Accessed 28 April 2025].

[32] K. Nico, "DeepFace: A Popular Open Source Facial Recognition Library," viso.ai, 29 January 2023. [Online]. Available: https://viso.ai/computer-vision/deepface/. [Accessed 28 April 2025].

[33] Z. Hangchuan, H. Caiping, M. Shiyu, S. Hui and Z. Guola, "Accuracies of FaceForensics++," *PLOS,* 13 December 2024. [Online]. Available: https://plos.figshare.com/articles/dataset/Accuracies_of_FaceForensics_HQ_ACC_/28025718?file=51174966. [Accessed 28 April 2025].

[34] Big Buck Bunny, Youtube, [Online]. Available: www.youtube.com/watch?v=YE7VzlLtp-4. [Accessed 28 April 2025]

Part IV

Generative AI for Proactive Cybersecurity

Chapter 8

Proactive cybersecurity with generative AI

Mohammed Houache and Boubiche Djallel Eddine

8.1 INTRODUCTION

Recent threat intelligence analyses reveal a 180% surge in weekly infostealer attacks from 2023 to 2025, with 60% of critical vulnerabilities exploited or publicly available at disclosure [1]. This acceleration demonstrates how adversaries weaponize speed and novelty to overwhelm reactive defenses, necessitating a fundamental shift toward proactive security paradigms.

Traditional reactive cybersecurity approaches analyze known patterns and documented threats post-incident, fundamentally limiting their capacity to detect emerging attack vectors and zero-day vulnerabilities before initial exploitation. The exponential growth in attack volume and velocity has exceeded human analyst capabilities, particularly as adversaries leverage artificial intelligence (AI) to automate offensive operations through polymorphic malware and adaptive phishing campaigns that evade signature-based detection. This asymmetry demands a paradigm shift from reactive to proactive defense strategies [2].

Proactive cybersecurity leverages generative AI to synthesize realistic attack behaviors, generate previously unobserved threat scenarios, and enable vulnerability identification before exploitation [3]. Unlike signature-based systems that respond post-incident, generative AI facilitates anticipatory threat modeling through dynamic vulnerability assessment and high-fidelity attack simulations that mirror contemporary adversarial techniques [4]. This predictive, generative, and adaptive capability establishes resilient defensive postures against novel attack vectors and zero-day exploits before adversaries can weaponize them.

Contributions. This chapter advances proactive cybersecurity research through four integrated contributions. First, it establishes a systematic taxonomy categorizing generative AI applications across five proactive defense domains—threat intelligence generation, predictive vulnerability analysis, automated red teaming, synthetic security data generation, and anomaly prediction—mapping generative architectures (large language models [LLMs], Generative Adversarial Networks [GANs], variational autoencoder [VAEs], diffusion models) to defensive functions. Second, it analyzes four technical architectures that operationalize anticipatory defense: LLM-based threat intelligence systems, autonomous detection rule generation frameworks, multi-agent defense coordination platforms, and generative adversarial simulation environments. Third, it synthesizes comparative evidence across ten research frameworks, evaluating performance metrics, deployment maturity, and operational constraints to inform evidence-based adoption decisions. Fourth, it identifies five critical implementation challenges (adversarial attacks, hallucinations, explainability deficits, computational costs, and data privacy) and examines emerging mitigation strategies through federated learning (FL), neuro-symbolic AI (NeSy AI), and edge deployment.

DOI: 10.1201/9781003644231-12

Roadmap. Section 8.2 establishes foundational context by contrasting proactive and reactive paradigms, examining established strategic frameworks (Cyber Kill Chain [CKC], left-of-boom philosophy), and positioning this work within existing literature. Section 8.3 presents a systematic taxonomy of proactive applications across five domains. Section 8.4 analyzes four technical architectures that operationalize anticipatory defense capabilities. Section 8.5 synthesizes comparative evidence across ten research frameworks, evaluating performance metrics, deployment maturity, and operational constraints. Section 8.6 identifies five critical implementation challenges and mitigation strategies. Section 8.7 examines three emerging technological trends. Section 8.8 synthesizes findings and implications for future research and practice.

8.2 BACKGROUND

8.2.1 Proactive versus reactive paradigms

8.2.1.1 Paradigm definitions

Proactive and reactive cybersecurity represent distinct yet complementary defense philosophies differing in temporal orientation and strategic objectives. Proactive cybersecurity anticipates, prevents, and mitigates threats before they materialize through threat intelligence gathering, vulnerability identification, predictive analytics, and preemptive control implementation. This paradigm operates on the premise that understanding threat landscapes and adversary tactics enables organizations to establish defensive postures that render attacks infeasible or prohibitively costly.

Conversely, reactive cybersecurity operates post-incident, addressing detection, containment, response, and recovery after breaches occur. This paradigm minimizes damage through rapid incident identification, threat isolation, forensic analysis, and system restoration. While essential for managing inevitable security incidents, reactive strategies inherently accept that breaches will occur and focus on limiting impact rather than preventing occurrence.

The fundamental distinction lies in timing and intent: proactive measures prevent the "boom" (the damaging event), while reactive measures manage consequences after occurrence. Table 8.1 summarizes key differences across six dimensions: primary objective, temporal focus, strategic approach, key activities, effectiveness context, and performance indicators.

Proactive strategies significantly reduce attack frequency and severity but cannot eliminate all risks due to evolving threat landscapes and zero-day vulnerabilities. Reactive capabilities therefore remain indispensable for managing residual risks and ensuring business continuity when preventive measures are circumvented. This integrated approach requires frameworks that structure proactive interventions across attack progression stages—concepts formalized through the CKC and left-of-boom philosophy.

8.2.1.2 The CKC framework

The Lockheed Martin CKC, introduced in 2011, structures attack progression through ten sequential phases: reconnaissance, weaponization, delivery, exploitation, installation, command and control (C2), and actions on objectives [5, 6]. This framework enables security teams to map interventions to specific attack stages, with proactive measures most effective during early phases (reconnaissance through delivery) and reactive measures critical during

Table 8.1 Proactive Versus Reactive Cybersecurity Comparison

Dimension	*Proactive Cybersecurity*	*Reactive Cybersecurity*
Primary Objective	Prevent security incidents before occurrence; eliminate vulnerabilities and close attack surface gaps.	Detect, contain, eradicate, and recover from security incidents after initiation or execution
Temporal Focus	Pre-incident (left-of-boom)	Post-incident (right-of-boom)
Strategic Approach	Risk reduction and threat prediction. Focuses on building resilience and pre-emptive hardening.	Mitigation and Recovery. Focuses on minimizing damage and restoring operational capacity.
Key Activities	Threat intelligence synthesis, vulnerability assessment, penetration testing (red teaming), security architecture review, patch prioritization	Incident detection and response (IDR), SIEM alerting, digital forensic analysis, malware eradication, system/data restoration
Effectiveness Context	Most effective against known vulnerabilities, predictable attack patterns, and emerging threats identified via intelligence	Necessary for zero-day exploits, advanced persistent threats (APTs), novel attack methodologies, and sudden system failures
Key Performance Indicators (KPIs)	Vulnerability reduction rate, attack surface minimization (ASM), mean time to patch (MTTP), time to detect adversary simulation (TTDAS)	Mean time to detect (MTTD), mean time to respond (MTTR), incident severity score, cost of incident (COI)
Cyber Kill Chain Alignment	Disrupts early stages (reconnaissance, weaponization, delivery) by identifying and removing adversary opportunities	Addresses later stages (exploitation, installation, command and control, actions on objectives) by minimizing impact

later stages (exploitation through actions on objectives). The CKC's phased structure informs generative AI applications for disrupting attacks during early stages through threat simulation and predictive modeling, as examined in Sections 8.3–8.4.

8.2.1.3 Left-of-boom philosophy

The "left-of-boom" cybersecurity concept emphasizes proactive strategies that prevent, detect, and mitigate cyber threats before a major incident (the "boom") occurs [7]. Derived from military terminology, this philosophy aligns directly with disrupting adversaries during early CKC stages, particularly reconnaissance and weaponization. Left-of-boom strategies encompass cyber threat intelligence (CTI) analysis to forecast attack trends, vulnerability assessment to identify exploitable weaknesses before adversaries discover them, and red teaming exercises to validate defensive controls proactively.

Left-of-boom strategies employ deception technologies (honeypots, simulated user activity) to engage adversaries, gather intelligence, and adapt defenses in real-time [8]. Complementary approaches include "sludge for good"—deliberate friction in attacker workflows through decoy systems and enhanced authentication that increase operational costs [9]—and adaptive risk management frameworks that dynamically adjust security controls based on evolving threats [10]. Quantitative metrics such as the Cyber Resilience Index measure organizational defensive effectiveness across both proactive and reactive dimensions [10].

Together, the CKC and left-of-boom philosophy establish a comprehensive proactive defense paradigm: the CKC structures attack progression analysis, while left-of-boom dictates temporal intervention priorities. However, operationalizing these strategic frameworks requires technologies capable of predicting unseen threats, synthesizing realistic attack data, and adapting autonomously to evolving adversary tactics—capabilities that exceed traditional rule-based systems.

8.2.2 Why generative AI for proactive cybersecurity?

Generative AI transforms proactive cybersecurity through three distinctive capabilities that exceed traditional defensive approaches. First, it enables anticipatory threat detection by synthesizing previously unobserved attack patterns and identifying zero-day vulnerabilities before exploitation, allowing defenders to establish protective postures against threats that have not yet materialized [11]. Second, it facilitates predictive vulnerability management by generating realistic synthetic attack scenarios (including novel zero-day exploits and polymorphic malware variants) that strengthen detection algorithms against future threats [12]. Third, it automates proactive intelligence operations—threat hunting, vulnerability assessment, and defensive rule generation—compressing timelines from threat emergence to protective deployment while reducing analyst workload [13]. These capabilities position generative AI as a transformative technology for proactive cybersecurity. Critically, generative AI's few-shot learning capacity enables rapid adaptation to novel attack categories with minimal labeled examples, supporting proactive defense against emerging threats where historical training data is scarce. This combination of predictive, generative, and adaptive capabilities enables anticipatory defense architectures that operate before threats materialize in operational environments—the defining characteristic distinguishing generative AI from traditional rule-based and supervised learning approaches.

8.2.3 Literature positioning and chapter contribution

The integration of generative AI into cybersecurity has generated substantial research across detection, response, and defensive automation. However, work explicitly targeting proactive defense—encompassing prediction, prevention, simulation, and preemptive mitigation—remains fragmented across multiple subdomains without systematic architectural grounding or consistent temporal focus. Existing surveys [11–13] provide broad overviews of generative AI capabilities but prioritize breadth over depth in analyzing proactive mechanisms and anticipatory architectures.

Recent surveys examine generative AI for cybersecurity across multiple dimensions. Lim et al. [11] analyze GAN applications for network security anomaly detection, identifying opportunities and limitations. Agrawal et al. [12] survey generative models for synthetic attack data generation, demonstrating utility in preemptive threat modeling. Ammara et al. [13] examine generative techniques for network traffic synthesis, enabling high-fidelity simulation environments. While these works categorize applications by technology or security function, this chapter organizes them through a unified proactive security philosophy that emphasizes temporal orientation—prediction, prevention, and preemptive simulation—and architectural operationalization.

Recent research demonstrates specific proactive capabilities that inform this chapter's taxonomy and architectures. Synthetic data generation studies [14, 15] enable safe red teaming and network defense exercises through GAN-generated botnet traffic and HTTP patterns, facilitating controlled environments for defensive strategy refinement. Anomaly detection research [16, 17] leverages generative models (MTS-DVGAN, Attention-GAN) for pre-exploitation identification of unusual behaviors in cyber-physical systems and multistage attack pattern forecasting. These empirical foundations support the proactive taxonomy (Section 8.3) and architectural frameworks (Section 8.4) developed herein. By focusing exclusively on anticipatory mechanisms, this chapter provides a coherent framework for applying generative AI to predict, prevent, and simulate cyber threats before operational exposure.

8.2.3.1 *Chapter contribution and positioning*

This chapter synthesizes and advances proactive generative AI research through four integrated contributions. First, it establishes a proactive-oriented taxonomy that systematically groups applications by temporal orientation (prediction, prevention, preemptive simulation), moving beyond general detection or post-incident response paradigms. Second, it provides technical architectures (Section 8.4) that operationalize high-level capabilities into deployable defense systems, specifying data pipelines, validation loops, and integration patterns for real-world security environments. Third, it delivers comparative analysis (Section 8.5) synthesizing empirical evidence across ten research frameworks, quantitatively assessing performance trade-offs, deployment readiness, and operational constraints to guide evidence-based adoption. Fourth, it maintains a strict left-of-boom focus, ensuring every application, architecture, and case study supports anticipatory security postures that shift focus from reactive incident management toward proactive threat anticipation. This unified framework addresses the critical gap between fragmented generative AI security research and the operational needs of practitioners aiming to anticipate and neutralize cyber threats before they materialize.

8.3 TAXONOMY OF PROACTIVE GENERATIVE AI APPLICATIONS

This section presents a systematic taxonomy categorizing generative AI applications across five proactive cybersecurity domains: threat intelligence generation, predictive vulnerability analysis, automated red teaming, synthetic security data generation, and anomaly prediction. Each domain enables anticipatory defense by compressing the timeline between threat emergence and protective deployment—shifting from reactive post-breach response to proactive pre-exploitation intervention.

8.3.1 Threat intelligence generation

LLMs transform threat intelligence operations by automating the extraction, synthesis, and analysis of unstructured security data at unprecedented scale. LLMs process diverse intelligence sources (dark web forums, threat reports, security advisories, malware repositories) to identify emerging threats before widespread exploitation [18–20].

Empirical evaluations demonstrate substantial improvements in proactive threat intelligence. AIDTIS achieves 40% efficiency gains in detection accuracy through automated threat simulations [18], while CyLens outperforms baseline approaches by 18.5% in threat

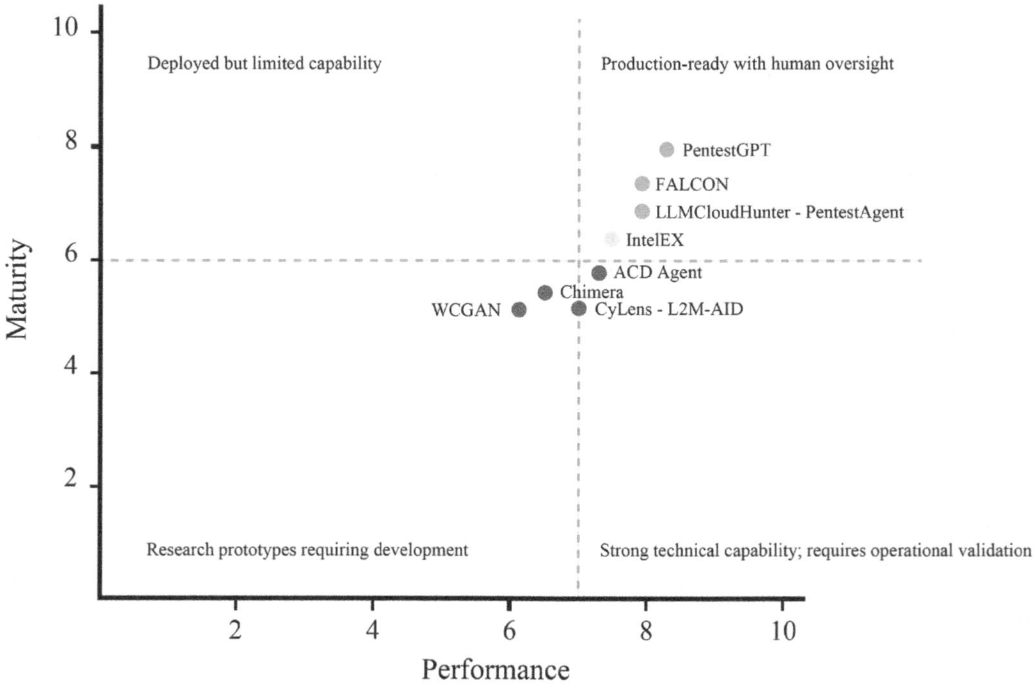

Figure 8.1 Hierarchical Taxonomy of Proactive Generative AI Applications in Cybersecurity.

attribution and 21.3% in remediation recommendation [19]. Retrieval-augmented generation (RAG) architectures further enhance response timeliness through dynamic real-time threat correlation [20]. These quantitative gains validate LLMs as foundational infrastructure for proactive operations, compressing intelligence-to-protection timelines from weeks to minutes.

LLMs extend beyond extraction to enable predictive intelligence synthesis, identifying attack trends and forecasting threat evolution based on historical patterns. Automated indicator enrichment exemplifies this capability: LLMs correlate Indicators of Compromise (IOCs) with known threat actor profiles and attack infrastructure, shifting from reactive intelligence compilation to proactive threat anticipation before adversaries execute campaigns against defended networks.

8.3.2 Predictive vulnerability analysis

Generative AI enables predictive vulnerability identification before exploitation through three proactive mechanisms: automated code analysis for zero-day discovery, intelligent patch prioritization based on exploitation likelihood, and exploit timeline forecasting. Unlike traditional static analysis tools limited to known vulnerability patterns, LLMs learn contextual relationships between code structures and security weaknesses, identifying novel vulnerability classes with up to 67.6% accuracy on benchmark datasets [21].

Generative models extend beyond detection to exploit prediction, forecasting which disclosed vulnerabilities will be weaponized and estimating timelines for exploit availability. LLMs analyze vulnerability characteristics, affected software popularity, and historical exploitation patterns to predict exploitation likelihood with sufficient accuracy for informed patch prioritization. This predictive capability transforms vulnerability management from reactive patching (responding to active exploitation) to proactive remediation (targeting high-risk vulnerabilities before weaponization).

Automated defensive rule generation operationalizes predictive vulnerability analysis. The LLMCloudHunter framework achieves 92% precision and 98% recall in extracting API (Application Programming Interfaces) calls and generating Sigma detection rules from cloud-focused threat intelligence [22]. Such systems bridge vulnerability identification and operational defense by automatically translating predicted threats into deployable detection signatures, enabling proactive protection before threats materialize in defended environments. This capability extends naturally to automated red teaming (Section 8.3.3), where generative AI validates defensive controls through simulated adversarial campaigns.

8.3.3 Automated red teaming and attack simulation

Generative AI enables continuous, automated security validation through AI-driven red teaming systems that simulate adversarial behaviors with minimal human involvement. These systems autonomously discover attack paths, generate exploitation strategies, and validate defensive controls at scale exceeding manual testing capabilities, enabling organizations to identify defensive gaps before adversaries exploit them in operational campaigns [23].

LLM-powered frameworks demonstrate autonomous vulnerability discovery and exploitation across network infrastructures. PentestGPT exhibits autonomous penetration testing capabilities [24], while recent LLM agents achieve 87% success rates on critical/high-severity CVEs (Common Vulnerabilities and Exposures) compared to 0% for traditional scanners by autonomously generating complete attack chains (reconnaissance, vulnerability identification, exploitation) with minimal human guidance [25]. Multi-agent systems extend these capabilities through coordinated attack simulations where specialized agents handle reconnaissance, social engineering, lateral movement, and data exfiltration, mirroring sophisticated threat actor operations.

The proactive value of automated red teaming lies in continuous validation rather than periodic assessment. Traditional penetration testing occurs quarterly or annually, leaving defensive gaps between evaluations where adversaries may discover and exploit vulnerabilities undetected. AI-driven systems enable continuous security validation by automatically testing new deployments, configuration changes, and emerging attack techniques against production environments. This shift from point-in-time to continuous assessment operationalizes left-of-boom philosophy: identifying weaknesses before adversaries discover them and enabling preemptive remediation. Complementary to simulation-based validation, synthetic data generation (Section 8.3.4) addresses training data scarcity by creating realistic attack scenarios for detector hardening.

8.3.4 Synthetic security data generation

Generative models address data scarcity in cybersecurity by synthesizing realistic attack data for training detection systems without exposing sensitive information or awaiting real-world incidents. This capability enables proactive detector training on attacks that have not yet occurred—inverting the traditional defensive disadvantage where adversaries attack first and defenders subsequently develop signatures. GAN variants (CTGAN), VAE-based models (TVAE), and diffusion models generate synthetic network traffic, malware samples, and structured attack scenarios that enrich limited real-world datasets while maintaining statistical fidelity (Earth Mover's Distance $<10^{-3}$), with CTGAN variants achieving 20–25% utility improvements in class-balanced generation [13].

Privacy-preserving synthetic generation enables cross-organizational threat intelligence sharing without exposing sensitive operational data. VAE-based approaches generate synthetic security logs that preserve attack patterns while satisfying differential privacy guarantees, addressing regulatory constraints that previously prevented collaborative defense initiatives. GAN-generated malware variants enable detection systems to train on polymorphic threats before encountering them in production environments, directly supporting the left-of-boom philosophy of anticipatory defense.

However, synthetic data integration requires rigorous validation to prevent "model collapse"—where detectors learn generator artifacts rather than genuine attack characteristics. Mitigation strategies include hybrid datasets mixing synthetic scenarios with real-world "anchor" data to maintain distributional fidelity, adversarial validation where independent models assess synthetic sample realism, and continuous statistical monitoring (Kolmogorov–Smirnov tests, Maximum Mean Discrepancy) to detect distribution drift.

8.3.5 Predictive anomaly detection and behavioral forecasting

Generative AI enables predictive anomaly detection: forecasting behavioral deviations and attack indicators before they manifest as security incidents. Unlike reactive approaches that identify ongoing or completed attacks, predictive methods anticipate abnormal patterns by analyzing precursor signals and temporal dependencies, enabling preemptive intervention during attack preparation phases [26].

Multiple generative architectures support predictive anomaly detection. BERT-based models forecast attack consequences from textual threat descriptions, achieving 97.2% accuracy in identifying attack outcomes before execution [27]. Multi-agent reinforcement learning (MARL) frameworks enable autonomous threat hunting, with recent implementations outperforming Proximal Policy Optimization (PPO) by 17.4% in cumulative reward on standardized benchmarks [28]. These systems embody proactive defense by autonomously seeking latent threats rather than waiting for reactive alert triggers.

8.4 TECHNICAL ARCHITECTURES FOR PROACTIVE DEFENSE

Section 8.3 established what generative AI accomplishes across five proactive domains. This section examines how these capabilities operationalize through four technical architectures: LLM-based threat intelligence systems (Section 8.4.1), autonomous detection rule generation (Section 8.4.2), multi-agent defense coordination (Section 8.4.3), and generative adversarial simulation (Section 8.4.4). These architectures operationalize left-of-boom philosophy by compressing timelines from threat emergence to defensive deployment, enabling organizations to establish protective postures against attacks before operational exposure.

8.4.1 LLM-based threat intelligence architecture

LLM-based threat intelligence systems transform unstructured threat narratives (CTI reports, security advisories, dark web forum discussions) into structured, machine-actionable intelligence before threats impact organizational environments. This architecture compresses intelligence-to-protection timelines from days or weeks of manual analysis to minutes of automated processing, enabling organizations to deploy defensive countermeasures against threats targeting other entities before facing similar attacks themselves.

8.4.1.1 Architectural framework and implementation

Layer 1: Data Ingestion and Preprocessing. The ingestion layer accepts heterogeneous threat intelligence sources: textual CTI reports, STIX/TAXII feeds, vendor advisories, and underground forum discussions. Preprocessing operations normalize diverse formats, segment lengthy documents into coherent chunks, and extract temporal indicators and source metadata. For multimodal sources (screenshots, network diagrams), specialized processing converts visual content into textual descriptions while preserving technical details, enabling comprehensive LLM analysis regardless of intelligence format.

Layer 2: LLM Inference with Retrieval Augmentation. The inference layer extracts structured intelligence from unstructured narratives: TTPs (Tactics, Techniques, and Procedures) mapped to MITRE ATT&CK frameworks, IOCs, threat actor attributions, and affected technologies. Retrieval augmentation grounds extractions in current threat landscapes by accessing external knowledge bases (vector databases of historical CTI, curated threat actor profiles) rather than relying on outdated pretraining knowledge. Domain-specific prompt engineering incorporates security analyst perspectives and terminology to improve extraction accuracy. This layer enables proactive defense: by analyzing intelligence about attacks targeting other organizations, defenders implement countermeasures before their infrastructure faces similar threats.

Layer 3: Validation and Quality Assurance. LLM outputs require validation to mitigate hallucination risks. Validation mechanisms operate at multiple levels: syntactic validation (proper formatting), semantic validation (logical consistency), and quality assessment through secondary LLM judgment, where an independent model evaluates extraction quality. Explicit validation layers improve precision by 15–20 percentage points [29], making this component essential for operational deployment where inaccurate intelligence misdirects defensive resources and undermines analyst trust.

Layer 4: Structured Output Generation and Integration. The final layer transforms validated extractions into machine-readable formats for automated downstream integration: Sigma detection rules, STIX bundles, SIEM platform queries, and structured JSON. This automation eliminates manual translation steps, enabling extracted threat intelligence to directly populate detection systems, update threat models, and inform security orchestration platforms without analyst intervention. Timeline compression from intelligence publication to defensive implementation represents this architecture's core proactive advantage: enabling protection before organizational exposure to threats described in published intelligence [20].

8.4.1.2 Empirical evidence

Three research systems validate this four-layer architecture across diverse intelligence sources. IntelEX [30] achieves a 0.902 F1 score for TTP identification and 0.929 F1 for detection rule generation across 229,968 security logs, demonstrating effectiveness for attack-level intelligence extraction. LLMCloudHunter [22] specializes in cloud environments, achieving 92% precision and 98% recall for API call extraction with 99.18% rule compilation success—validating operational viability for cloud-specific threat intelligence.

The GPT-3.5 CTI System [31] applies this architecture to dark web forum analysis, processing over 700 daily conversations with 96.23% accuracy in structured variable extraction and 98.8% human-validated summary accuracy. Collectively, these implementations validate effective proactive intelligence transformation across heterogeneous sources, enabling automated defensive deployment before organizational threat exposure.

8.4.2 Autonomous rule generation architecture

Autonomous rule generation architectures transform threat narratives into deployable detection capabilities through three integrated phases: generation, validation, and orchestration. Each phase addresses specific challenges, ensuring generated rules are both technically correct and operationally viable before production deployment.

8.4.2.1 Architectural framework and implementation

Generation Phase: From Intelligence to Candidate Rules. The system ingests threat intelligence reports, vulnerability advisories, and attack descriptions as input. LLMs extract technical indicators (network signatures, file-based indicators, behavioral patterns) and translate them into platform-specific rule syntax: Snort for network intrusion detection, YARA for malware identification, or Sigma for SIEM correlation. Domain-specific prompt engineering proves critical: incorporating security analyst perspectives, MITRE ATT&CK mappings, and platform documentation significantly improves rule quality over generic instructions. Proactive capability emerges at this phase: by processing intelligence describing attacks against other organizations, the system generates defensive signatures enabling protection before threats reach defended infrastructure.

Multiphase Validation: Ensuring Deployability. Generated rules undergo three-tier validation: syntactic validation (proper formatting and compilability), semantic validation (logical consistency and threat coverage), and performance validation (computational efficiency and false positive rates through testing against benign traffic and historical attack logs). Advanced implementations employ secondary LLM judgment or ensemble retrieval against curated signature repositories. Explicit validation layers improve precision by 15–20 percentage points, making this phase essential for operational deployment where inaccurate rules waste analyst time investigating false alarms and erode system trust.

Orchestration and Feedback Loops. The orchestration agent manages the generation–validation cycle by tracking validation outcomes, providing refinement guidance, and determining deployment readiness. Sophisticated orchestrators incorporate learning mechanisms that reduce refinement iterations over time by applying patterns from past successes and failures to subsequent generation attempts.

The orchestrator manages human-in-the-loop integration: while fully autonomous operation is architecturally feasible, operational deployments typically require analyst review before production activation, particularly for rules triggering automated response actions. This oversight balances automation efficiency with operational reality—false positives in security systems carry significant business costs and erode analyst trust in automated systems.

This architecture's proactive value lies in timeline compression and operational scale. Traditional signature development requires analysts to manually observe attacks, understand mechanisms, write detection logic, test accuracy, and deploy to production—consuming days or weeks. Automated generation compresses this cycle to minutes, enabling organizations to deploy protective signatures against threats described in published intelligence before those threats target their infrastructure. This exemplifies proactive defense through anticipatory protection rather than post-compromise response, operationalizing left-of-boom philosophy at machine speed.

8.4.2.2 *Empirical evidence*

The Framework for Autonomous Learning and Creation of Observational Networks (FALCON) validates this three-phase architecture through autonomous IDS (Intrusion Detection System) rule generation from CTI [32]. FALCON processes CTI reports to generate Snort and Suricata detection rules, achieving 95% accuracy in rule generation quality as evaluated by security experts. The system's ensemble retrieval mechanism (combining semantic similarity search with keyword matching) achieves 84% inter-rater agreement among expert evaluators on rule relevance and correctness. Its multiphase validation pipeline (syntactic parsing, semantic consistency checks, LLM-based quality judgment) reduces false positive rates compared to single-pass generation approaches. FALCON demonstrates operational viability by processing real-world threat intelligence feeds and generating deployment-ready signatures, validating effective proactive rule creation at scale.

8.5 Multi-agent defense coordination architecture

Multi-agent architectures comprise four foundational components: environmental modeling (realistic simulation contexts), specialized agent design (distributed expertise), coordination mechanisms (information sharing), and synthetic threat generation (training data). Each component contributes to proactive threat detection and preemptive response capabilities.

8.5.1 Architectural framework

Environmental Modeling and Simulation Foundations. Multi-agent systems require high-fidelity environmental models capturing organizational structure, network topology, access control policies, and operational workflows. High-fidelity simulation is essential: agents trained in oversimplified environments fail to recognize realistic attack patterns when deployed operationally. Accurate environmental modeling enables simulation of insider threats and multi-stage campaigns, allowing defenders to develop detection strategies before encountering real attacks—the core of proactive preparation through synthetic scenario generation.

Agent Architecture: Specialization and Autonomy. Individual agents embody specialized expertise through three dimensions: geographic responsibility (specific network zones), functional specialization (behavioral analysis, anomaly detection, threat correlation), or hierarchical roles (organizational security structure). Each agent maintains partial observability—observing only local environments—reducing computational complexity while enabling focused analysis. Agents incorporate learning mechanisms enabling adaptation to evolving behaviors and emerging threats without manual reconfiguration.

Coordination Mechanisms and Communication Protocols. Coordination protocols enable agents to share observations, hypotheses about multi-zone campaigns, and anomaly patterns. Three coordination patterns support proactive defense: consensus mechanisms reduce false positives from isolated anomalies, dynamic task allocation distributes investigation workload, and collaborative threat hunting enables agents to collectively search for attack precursors.

Proactive capability emerges from coordinated hypothesis formation: if Agent A observes unusual authentication patterns while Agent B detects lateral movement attempts, coordinated analysis identifies distributed campaigns invisible to individual agents. This enables preemptive countermeasures (network segmentation, credential rotation, decoy deployment) before attacks achieve persistence across multiple network zones.

Synthetic threat generation for training. Multi-agent architectures generate realistic synthetic attack scenarios for training detection systems and analysts. Simulation systems model both attackers and defenders as autonomous agents, generating millions of attack-defense interactions, capturing realistic organizational dynamics and attack progression. This enables training on threats not yet observed in production environments, allowing defenders to develop response strategies for hypothetical attack variants before operational exposure.

This architecture's proactive capability emerges from distributed parallel analysis and coordinated preemptive response. Specialized agents identify attack phases (reconnaissance, lateral movement, privilege escalation) earlier than centralized systems through focused monitoring of specific network zones. Distributed intelligence enables coordinated analysis, identifying multi-zone campaigns and triggering preemptive countermeasures (network segmentation, access control tightening, decoy deployment) before attacks achieve critical objectives such as data exfiltration or system compromise.

8.5.2 Empirical evidence

Chimera [33] validates multi-agent architecture through proactive insider threat simulation, modeling employees as autonomous LLM-powered agents with role-specific behaviors and access privileges. Malicious agents autonomously determine attack strategies (data exfiltration, sabotage, policy violations), generating realistic attack sequences rather than scripted scenarios.

Chimera generates the ChimeraLog dataset: 25 billion log entries across six modalities (file operations, authentication events, device activities, psychometric indicators, HTTP traffic, email communications). Detection models trained on ChimeraLog achieve 0.83 F1 scores compared to 0.99 on the CERT benchmark—reflecting realistic difficulty where insider threats exhibit subtle behavioral patterns rather than obvious anomalies. Expert evaluation rates ChimeraLog's behavioral realism as comparable to rare real-world datasets and superior to existing synthetic alternatives.

Proactive value lies in enabling organizations to train detection systems on realistic insider threat scenarios without waiting for actual incidents. By simulating thousands of attack variations (disgruntled employees exfiltrating intellectual property, negligent users violating policies, compromised credentials enabling external access), the system generates comprehensive training data covering threat scenarios that organizations have not experienced. This enables proactive preparation through detection model hardening and analyst familiarization before facing real incidents, compressing the learning curve typically requiring multiple actual breaches.

8.5.3 Generative adversarial simulation architecture

Generative adversarial simulation architectures enable proactive defense by synthesizing realistic cyberattack scenarios before such attacks materialize operationally. These architectures employ generative models (GANs, VAEs, diffusion models) to create synthetic attack data representing threats organizations have not yet encountered, enabling defenders to train detection systems and identify defensive gaps against attacks that exist only as synthetic scenarios. This inverts the traditional attacker-first paradigm: defenders train on future attacks rather than responding to observed breaches.

8.5.3.1 Architectural framework

Attack-Data Generator. The generative component employs adversarial or probabilistic models trained on existing security telemetry (network traffic logs, malware samples, attack datasets). Three generative approaches enable diverse attack synthesis: GANs pit generators against discriminators to synthesize realistic attack traffic evading simple detection; VAEs learn latent distributions of attack characteristics, generating diverse variants while maintaining semantic consistency; diffusion models iteratively refine synthetic samples through progressive denoizing for high-fidelity scenarios. Once trained, generators synthesize diverse attack instances: malformed packets exploiting protocol vulnerabilities, polymorphic malware evading signature-based detection, distributed DoS (Denial of Service) traffic mimicking legitimate usage, and multi-stage intrusion sequences (reconnaissance, lateral movement, privilege escalation, data exfiltration).

Defender Model and Evaluation. The defensive component comprises IDSs (Intrusion Detection Systems), anomaly detection models, or sandbox environments processing synthetic attack samples identically to production deployments. Defenders analyze synthetic attacks and produce classifications, confidence scores, and alert latencies. This evaluation quantifies detection blind spots (attack patterns defenders fail to recognize), providing empirical evidence of defensive gaps before real attackers exploit them operationally.

Adversarial Coevolution Loop. The architecture implements iterative improvement through adversarial training cycles. Generators produce synthetic attacks while defenders attempt detection. Detected attacks inform generator refinement toward sophisticated evasion techniques; missed attacks inform defender retraining with augmented datasets. This coevolutionary dynamic mirrors real-world attacker-defender arms races.

By simulating this evolution synthetically, organizations harden defenses against adaptive adversaries before operational encounter. Performance metrics (precision, recall, detection latency) feed back to both components, enabling progressive hardening: each iteration identifies blind spots, retrains detectors, and validates improvements before real attacks exploit vulnerabilities.

This architecture's proactive capability derives from temporal decoupling: defensive improvements occur in response to synthetic future threats rather than observed past attacks. Traditional security operations develop detection signatures only after attacks are discovered in production. Generative adversarial simulation inverts this paradigm by generating thousands of attack scenarios, training detectors on attacks that have not occurred, and stress-testing defenses before operational exposure. Organizations remediate defensive gaps without experiencing actual breaches—shifting from learning-through-compromise to learning-through-simulation.

8.5.3.2 Empirical evidence

Multiple studies validate generative adversarial simulation effectiveness for proactive cybersecurity. GAN variants (WGAN-GP, CGANs, hybrid GANs) enhance detection robustness across network intrusion, malware analysis, and IoT security domains [34]. Realistic attack traffic generation (botnet C2, DoS patterns) improves IDS performance and resilience [35], while complex multi-stage attack simulation enables rigorous defensive system testing before operational deployment [36]. Collectively, these studies validate that generative adversarial simulation enables organizations to identify blind spots, refine detection rules, and strengthen defenses before real-world exploitation—shifting cybersecurity postures from reactive response to proactive resilience.

8.5.4 Cross-cutting architectural patterns

Analysis of implemented systems across Sections 8.4.1–8.4.4 reveals five design patterns consistently appearing in successful generative AI security architectures, suggesting emerging best practices. These cross-cutting patterns provide actionable guidance for practitioners designing proactive defense systems.

Pattern 1: Modular Pipeline Design. All examined architectures employ staged processing with clearly defined component boundaries (preprocessing, inference, validation, output generation), enabling independent development, testing, and optimization. Modularity facilitates component substitution (swapping LLM providers, upgrading validation mechanisms) without system-wide redesign. This enables parallel development where specialized teams work on different pipeline stages simultaneously, accelerating deployment timelines.

Pattern 2: Explicit Validation Layers. Systems incorporating dedicated validation mechanisms demonstrate 15–20 percentage point precision improvements compared to architectures relying solely on LLM inference quality [29]. Validation approaches range from secondary LLM judgment to formal verification to simulation-based testing. The consistent finding: generative AI outputs require verification before operational use, particularly in security contexts where errors carry significant operational and trust consequences.

Pattern 3: RAG. External knowledge base integration appears across multiple architectures, addressing knowledge staleness in pretrained models. Retrieval mechanisms range from sophisticated vector database searches using semantic embeddings to simple context window maintenance. The underlying principle: grounding LLM inference in current, curated information (updated MITRE ATT&CK mappings, recent CVE databases, current threat actor profiles) improves accuracy and enables systems to remain effective as threat landscapes evolve beyond training data currency.

Pattern 4: Structured Output Generation. Successful architectures generate machine-readable structured outputs (YAML, JSON, Sigma rules, Snort/Suricata signatures, STIX bundles) rather than natural language responses. Structured outputs enable automated downstream integration with structured outputs enable automated downstream integration with security orchestration, automation, and response (SOAR) platforms, eliminating manual translation steps that slow defensive response and introduce human error.

Pattern 5: Domain-Specific Prompt Engineering. Effective LLM-based security systems employ carefully designed prompts incorporating security analyst perspectives, domain terminology (MITRE ATT&CK framework, IOCs), explicit output format specifications, and examples demonstrating desired response patterns. Prompt design significantly impacts extraction accuracy, with verb tense consistency and concept specificity emerging as critical factors. Domain-specialized prompt engineering yields measurable performance gains: LLMCloudHunter's cloud-security-specific prompts achieved 92% precision [22], while IntelEX's attack-focused prompts achieved 0.902 F1 score [30].

8.6 COMPARATIVE ANALYSIS

This section presents a systematic comparative analysis across ten generative AI frameworks for proactive cybersecurity, examining architectural patterns, proactive capabilities, performance evidence, and deployment readiness. Rather than isolated system descriptions, this comparison-driven analysis reveals architectural trade-offs, identifies design patterns, and provides evidence-based guidance for technology selection based on empirical validation across diverse proactive defense domains.

8.6.1 Analytical framework and system selection

8.6.1.1 Comparison Methodology

This comparative analysis evaluates frameworks across four dimensions: (1) architectural approach (generative AI techniques and system design patterns), (2) proactive capability (mechanisms enabling anticipatory defense with temporal validation evidence), (3) performance evidence (empirical metrics, evaluation rigor, evidence maturity), and (4) deployment readiness (scalability constraints, operational limitations, integration requirements). These dimensions enable systematic comparison across diverse proactive applications throughout the cybersecurity lifecycle.

8.6.1.2 System Categorization

The ten analyzed frameworks are organized into five functional categories aligned with the taxonomy established in Section 8.3:

- **Proactive Threat Intelligence Generation:** IntelEX [30], CyLens [19], and LLMCloudHunter [22] extract structured intelligence from unstructured sources before threats materialize operationally.
- **Autonomous Detection Rule Generation:** FALCON transforms threat narratives into deployable detection signatures, enabling protection before organizational exposure.
- **Automated Penetration Testing:** PentestGPT [24] and PentestAgent [37] enable continuous proactive security validation through autonomous vulnerability discovery.
- **Synthetic Security Data Generation:** WCGAN [38] generates realistic attack scenarios for training detection systems before operational encounter.
- **Multi-Agent Proactive Defense:** Chimera [33] generates realistic insider threat scenarios, enabling training on threats organizations have not experienced.

Selection criteria prioritized frameworks with: (1) peer-reviewed publication in major venues, (2) empirical evaluation with quantitative metrics, (3) demonstrated proactive mechanisms with temporal validation, and (4) architectural diversity. This selection provides sufficient coverage for meaningful comparative analysis while maintaining analytical tractability.

8.6.2 Architectural patterns and technical approaches

Analysis across the ten frameworks reveals three predominant architectural patterns, each exhibiting distinct capabilities and trade-offs:

Pattern 1: Retrieval-Augmented LLM Architectures. Four frameworks (IntelEX, LLMCloudHunter, FALCON, LLM-Assisted Proactive Threat Intelligence) ground inference in current threat landscapes through external knowledge base integration. These architectures address knowledge staleness in pretrained models by accessing vector databases of historical CTI, curated threat actor profiles, and evolving threat taxonomies (MITRE ATT&CK, CVE databases) during inference. RAG-augmented systems achieve 92–96% precision across diverse threat intelligence extraction tasks, compared to <80% for standalone LLMs. The architectural trade-off: increased computational overhead and dependency on knowledge base currency versus improved accuracy and reduced hallucination rates.

Pattern 2: Multi-Agent Coordination Architectures. Two frameworks (Chimera, PentestAgent) distribute specialized expertise across autonomous agents, enabling parallel threat analysis and coordinated hypothesis formation. Individual agents maintain partial observability over specific network zones or functional responsibilities (reconnaissance, exploitation, lateral movement), reducing computational complexity while enabling focused analysis. Coordination mechanisms (consensus protocols, dynamic task allocation, collaborative threat hunting) identify distributed campaigns invisible to centralized systems. This pattern excels in complex, multi-stage attack simulation and distributed threat detection: Chimera achieves 0.83 F1 on synthetic insider threats, reflecting realistic difficulty compared to CERT's 0.99 baseline. The trade-off: architectural complexity, increased interagent communication overhead, and challenges in coordination protocol design.

Pattern 3: Generative Adversarial Architectures. WCGAN employs discriminator-generator dynamics to produce synthetic attack data with statistical fidelity, enabling proactive training on hypothetical threats. Adversarial training ensures generated samples exhibit distributional properties matching real attack data (Earth Mover's Distance $<10^{-3}$), with conditional generation enabling class-balanced synthetic data addressing minority attack class scarcity. This pattern enables defenders to train on attacks that have not occurred, inverting the traditional attacker-first paradigm. The trade-off: risks of "model collapse" where detectors learn generator artifacts rather than genuine attack characteristics, requiring careful integration with real-world anchor data and rigorous distributional validation.

Architectural Components and Data Integration. Table 8.2 synthesizes the generative AI architectures, primary data sources, and output formats across the ten systems, revealing systematic differences in architectural choices. RAG-augmented systems (Pattern 1) demonstrate consistent use of external knowledge retrieval paired with LLM inference, while multi-agent systems (Pattern 2) emphasize coordination mechanisms over retrieval augmentation. Output format diversity—from structured detection rules (Snort, Suricata, Sigma) to multimodal synthetic telemetry—reflects the breadth of proactive application domains.

Cross-Cutting Architectural Design Principles. Beyond the three predominant patterns, five design principles appear consistently across successful implementations (detailed in Section 8.4.5): modular pipeline design, explicit validation layers (15–20 percentage point precision improvement), RAG, structured output generation, and domain-specific prompt engineering. These principles represent emerging best practices for generative AI security system design.

Table 8.2 Generative AI Architectures, Data Sources, and Outputs for Ten Proactive Cybersecurity Frameworks

System	*Generative AI Architecture*	*Primary Function / Data Source*	*Key Output Format*
IntelEX [30]	LLM + RAG	CTI reports, advisories	STIX, Sigma rules, SIEM queries
FALCON [32]	LLM + Ensemble Retrieval	CTI reports, attack descriptions	Snort rules, Suricata rules
LLMCloudHunter [22]	LLM + Domain Prompting	Cloud-focused CTI	Sigma detection rules (cloud)
CyLens [19]	Agentic LLM System	Dark web, threat reports	Threat attributions, remediation
Chimera [33]	Multi-Agent LLM Coordination	Organizational structure models	Multimodal log data
PentestGPT [24]	Multi-Agent LLM (GPT-4)	Target machine information	Exploitation strategies, attack paths
PentestAgent [37]	Multi-Agent LLM with Debugging	VulHub, HackTheBox benchmarks	Automated exploitation workflows
WCGAN [38]	GAN-based generative model	Intrusion detection datasets	Synthetic network traffic
ACD Agent [39]	Hybrid DRL-LLM	CybORG simulation environment	Automated defensive actions
L2M-AID [40]	LLM-MARL Fusion	Industrial IoT environments	Defensive agent policies

8.6.3 Proactive capabilities and performance evidence

Validation Framework: Temporal Analysis. Frameworks' proactive nature is validated through temporal analysis examining whether they enable defensive action before operational threat encounter. Genuine proactivity requires demonstrating that systems compress intelligence-to-protection timelines, enable training on hypothetical threats before real exposure, or identify defensive gaps before adversaries discover them. This temporal validation distinguishes proactive systems from reactive detection approaches, analyzing already-occurred incidents.

Comparative Analysis by Functional Category. The following analysis examines proactive capabilities and performance evidence across five functional categories:

8.6.3.1 Threat Intelligence Generation

Three frameworks exemplify proactive threat intelligence extraction across different intelligence sources:

1. IntelEX—Attack-Level Threat Intelligence Extraction
   IntelEX [30] transforms textual CTI narratives into structured, machine-actionable intelligence through a four-layer architecture (data ingestion, LLM inference with RAG, validation, structured output generation). The system achieves 0.902 F1 for TTP identification and 0.929 F1 for detection rule generation across 229,968 security logs. Outputs (STIX bundles, Sigma rules, SIEM queries) enable automated downstream integration.

Proactive value: compresses intelligence-to-protection timelines from weeks to minutes by processing intelligence about attacks on other organizations before threats target defended infrastructure.

Limitations: LLM hallucination risks (15–20 percentage point precision improvement with validation required), computational costs potentially constraining real-time high-volume processing.

2. LLMCloudHunter—Cloud-Focused Detection Rule Extraction
   LLMCloudHunter [22] specializes in cloud environment threat intelligence, automatically extracting API calls and generating Sigma detection rules from cloud-focused CTI. Domain-specific prompt engineering and retrieval augmentation ground rule generation in current cloud threat landscapes. The system achieves 92% precision and 98% recall in API call extraction, with 99.18% rule compilation success.

Proactive value: addresses unique cloud challenges where attack surfaces evolve rapidly with new service launches, enabling rapid rule generation before threats exploit newly released APIs. High recall (98%) ensures comprehensive coverage critical for cloud environments.

Limitations: specialization limits applicability to traditional on-premises environments; false-positive rates necessitate validation before production deployment.

3. CyLens—Agentic Threat Attribution and Remediation
   CyLens [19] implements an agentic LLM system targeting dark web forums and threat reports for intelligence extraction. Multiple specialized agents coordinate to handle distinct intelligence processing subtasks, enabling parallel analysis. The system outperforms baseline approaches by 18.5% in threat attribution and 21.3% in remediation recommendation.

Proactive value: automated attribution enables rapid understanding of adversary capabilities and intent before attacks materialize.

Limitations: early-stage research prototype requiring broader environmental validation beyond initial evaluation datasets; ethical considerations from dark web forum access necessitate clear operational boundaries.

Comparative Synthesis: RAG-augmented architectures (IntelEX, LLMCloudHunter) achieve >90% precision through external knowledge base integration, addressing knowledge staleness in standalone LLMs. Domain specialization (LLMCloudHunter's cloud focus) enables higher performance in target domains but limits generalizability. All three frameworks demonstrate genuine proactive capability through timeline compression, enabling protection before threats target defended infrastructure.

8.6.3.2 Autonomous detection rule generation

FALCON—Autonomous IDS Rule Generation

FALCON [32] implements autonomous IDS rule generation from CTI through three integrated phases: generation (transforming threat narratives into candidate rules), validation (ensuring deployability through syntactic, semantic, and performance testing), and orchestration (managing generation–validation cycles). The system generates deployable Snort and Suricata detection rules, achieving 95% accuracy in rule generation quality and 84% inter-rater agreement among expert evaluators. The ensemble retrieval mechanism (combining semantic similarity search with keyword matching) identifies relevant threat intelligence with high precision.

Proactive Value: compresses traditional signature development from days/weeks to minutes, enabling protective signature deployment before infrastructure exposure to threats described in published intelligence.

Limitations: dependency on CTI report quality (vague descriptions yield less accurate rules); computational overhead from ensemble retrieval and multiphase validation potentially limiting throughput for high-volume CTI feeds; generated rules require expert review before production deployment.

8.6.3.3 Automated penetration testing

PentestGPT—LLM-Powered Autonomous Penetration Testing

PentestGPT [24] implements LLM-powered automated penetration testing through a multi-agent architecture with three self-interacting modules: content summarization (maintaining session context), task list management (tracking penetration progress), and step-by-step reasoning (generating executable commands). Evaluated at USENIX Security 2024, the system demonstrates 228.6% task completion improvement over baseline GPT-3.5 across 25 vulnerable target machines, achieving shell access in 75% of attempts. The system ranked in the top 10% of users on HackTheBox, validating its capability against realistic targets.

Proactive Value: enables continuous security validation rather than periodic assessment—traditional penetration testing occurs quarterly/annually, leaving defensive gaps where adversaries may discover vulnerabilities undetected. AI-driven systems test new deployments, configuration changes, and emerging attack techniques continuously.

Limitations: requires human oversight for certain operations (particularly GUI-based tool interactions); context window limitations cause memory loss during complex multi-stage engagements; occasional ineffective strategy recommendations.

Deployment status: real-world penetration testing engagements, 6,500+ GitHub stars (2024).

PentestAgent—Multi-Agent Decomposition with Debugging

PentestAgent [37] extends autonomous penetration testing through multi-agent decomposition with integrated debugging mechanisms, achieving fully automated exploitation workflows without continuous human feedback across VulHub and HackTheBox benchmarks.

Proactive Value: similar to PentestGPT but with enhanced automation through debugging-aware agent coordination. **Limitations:** (not explicitly reported in available literature).

Comparative Synthesis: Both frameworks operationalize left-of-boom philosophy by identifying weaknesses before adversaries discover them through continuous rather than point-in-time validation. Multi-agent coordination across reconnaissance, vulnerability analysis, and privilege escalation enables realistic attack simulation. PentestGPT demonstrates production viability with significant community adoption; PentestAgent advances full automation through debugging integration.

8.6.3.4 Synthetic security data generation

WCGAN—Wasserstein Conditional GAN for Class-Balanced Attack Data
WCGAN [38] addresses data imbalance in intrusion detection by generating synthetic attack data for minority classes where insufficient real-world samples exist. Published in *Computers & Security* (2023), the system combines WCGAN with a gradient penalty for stable learning and XGBoost classification. The GAN architecture employs Wasserstein distance optimization and gradient penalty, conditioning generation on specific attack class labels to produce class-balanced synthetic network traffic. Training on intrusion detection datasets (NSL-KDD, UNSW-NB15, CIC-IDS2017) with class imbalance, the system generates synthetic samples to augment minority classes. Statistical fidelity metrics using Earth Mover's Distance confirm that generated samples maintain distributional properties of real attack data (scores $<10^{-3}$).

Proactive Value: achieves 20–25% utility improvements in classification for minority attack classes, enabling defenders to train detection systems on attacks that have not yet occurred operationally—inverting the traditional defensive disadvantage where adversaries attack first, and defenders subsequently develop signatures.

Limitations: requires rigorous validation to prevent "model collapse" (detectors learning generator artifacts rather than genuine attack characteristics); dependency on sufficient real-world samples for initial GAN training (completely novel zero-day attack classes without examples cannot be generated); computational costs from GAN training potentially limiting frequent retraining as threat landscapes evolve.

8.6.3.5 Multi-agent proactive defense

Chimera—Multi-Agent Insider Threat Simulation
Chimera [33] implements a multi-agent architecture for proactive insider threat simulation, modeling employees as autonomous LLM-powered agents with role-specific behaviors and access privileges. Malicious agents autonomously determine how to achieve attack objectives (data exfiltration, sabotage, policy violations), generating diverse attack variations rather than following pre-scripted scenarios. The system models organizational structure, network topology, access control policies, and employee roles, producing the ChimeraLog dataset containing 25 billion log entries across six modalities: file operations, authentication events, device activities, psychometric indicators, HTTP traffic, and email communications. Detection models trained on ChimeraLog achieve an F1 score of 0.83 for insider threat detection, compared to 0.99 on the CERT benchmark. Expert evaluation rates ChimeraLog's behavioral realism as comparable to rare real-world datasets.

Proactive Value: enables training of detection systems on realistic insider threat scenarios before actual incidents occur, compressing the learning curve typically requiring multiple breaches to develop.

Limitations: lower F1 may indicate higher realism or generator artifacts requiring validation; large-scale multi-agent simulation is computationally expensive, limiting scenario throughput; accurate organizational modeling is critical—errors in role or policy definitions reduce scenario fidelity.

Performance Evidence Synthesis. Table 8.3 synthesizes proactive capabilities and evaluation metrics across the ten systems, enabling systematic comparison of capability types, key metrics, and validation methods. Systems demonstrate varying evidence maturity: IntelEX,

Table 8.3 Proactive Capabilities and Evaluation Metrics

System	*Proactive Capability Type*	*Key Evaluation Metrics*	*Validation Method*
IntelEX [30]	Threat Intelligence Extraction	F1: 0.902 (TTP), 0.929 (rule generation)	Expert validation on 229,968 logs
FALCON [32]	Autonomous IDS Rule Generation	95% rule quality, 84% inter-rater agreement	Expert security analyst evaluation
LLMCloudHunter [22]	Cloud Detection Rule Extraction	92% precision, 98% recall, 99.18% compilation success	Automated compilation tests
CyLens [19]	Threat Attribution and Remediation	18.5% improvement (attribution), 21.3% (remediation)	Comparison against baseline
Chimera [33]	Insider Threat Simulation	F1: 0.83 (ChimeraLog), 0.99 (CERT baseline)	Detection model performance + expert realism assessment
PentestGPT [24]	Automated Penetration Testing	228.6% task completion improvement, 75% shell access rate	25 vulnerable machines, HackTheBox top 10%
PentestAgent [37]	Automated Penetration Testing	Fully automated exploitation on VulHub, HackTheBox	Benchmark performance on CTF platforms
WCGAN [38]	Synthetic Attack Data Generation	20–25% utility improvement for minority classes, EMD $<10^{-3}$	Statistical fidelity, detection uplift
ACD Agent	Automated Incident Response	17.4% cumulative reward improvement over PPO	CybORG simulation benchmark
L2M-AID [40]	Industrial IoT Defense	LLM-MARL fusion effectiveness metrics	Industrial IoT simulation environment

FALCON, and PentestGPT possess rigorous empirical evaluation with multiple benchmark datasets and expert validation; LLMCloudHunter and CyLens report performance improvements against baseline approaches but require broader validation across diverse operational environments; WCGAN demonstrates statistical fidelity but requires further validation ensuring detection systems learn genuine attack characteristics; Chimera provides comprehensive behavioral realism evaluation through expert assessment, confirming synthetic insider threat scenarios comparable to rare real-world datasets.

The temporal advantage—acting on threats before encounter—defines genuine proactivity, distinguishing these systems from reactive detection approaches analyzing already-occurred incidents. IntelEX and FALCON compress threat intelligence-to-protection timelines from weeks to minutes. PentestGPT identifies defensive gaps before adversaries discover them through continuous validation. Chimera enables training on realistic insider threat scenarios that organizations have not experienced, preparing defenses for hypothetical attacks.

8.6.4 Deployment readiness and operational constraints

Scalability Analysis. Frameworks demonstrate varying operational maturity and scalability.

Production-viable: PentestGPT (real-world deployments, 6,500+ GitHub stars), FALCON (95% expert-validated accuracy suggests operational readiness with human oversight).

Transition-stage: IntelEX (0.902 F1 suggests analyst augmentation rather than autonomous deployment), LLMCloudHunter (99.18% compilation success indicates technical viability, ongoing operational validation).

Research prototypes: WCGAN (requires specialist integration expertise for careful real-world/synthetic data balance), Chimera (requires operational validation before enterprise deployment), CyLens (early-stage prototype), ACD Agent and L2M-AID (emerging frameworks requiring broader validation).

Limitation Patterns and Mitigation Strategies. Five recurring limitation patterns affect deployment: (1) LLM hallucination risks requiring explicit validation layers (15–20 percentage point precision improvement), (2) computational overhead from LLM inference, RAG queries, ensemble retrieval, or GAN training constraining real-time processing, (3) dependency on input quality where vague CTI reports yield degraded outputs, (4) context window limitations causing memory loss in long-duration operations, and (5) synthetic data artifacts where detectors may learn generator characteristics rather than real attack patterns.

Mitigation strategies cluster into three approaches: validation mechanisms (secondary LLM judgment, ensemble retrieval, expert review), computational optimization (model distillation, quantization, collaborative edge computing), and hybrid data strategies (mixing synthetic scenarios with real-world anchor data).

Integration with Existing Cybersecurity Infrastructure. Frameworks integrate with established cybersecurity infrastructures through standardized output formats, enabling incremental adoption. FALCON generates platform-specific signatures (Snort, Suricata) for direct SIEM integration. LLMCloudHunter produces Sigma detection rules (99.18% compilation success) deployable across Splunk, Elastic Security, Microsoft Sentinel. IntelEX generates STIX bundles and structured JSON for automated threat model updates and SOAR platform integration. This modularity enables organizations to adopt proactive generative AI incrementally, augmenting existing defenses rather than replacing infrastructure.

Table 8.4 synthesizes system limitations, false positive/negative behaviors, scalability constraints, deployment maturity, and privacy/ethical risks, providing a comprehensive operational readiness assessment:

8.6.5 Cross-system synthesis and selection guidance

Synthesized Findings from Comparative Analysis. Comparative analysis across the ten systems reveals four principal findings that advance understanding of generative AI for proactive cybersecurity:

Finding 1: Architectural Pattern-Capability Alignment. The three architectural patterns exhibit natural specialization: RAG-augmented LLMs excel at intelligence extraction (>90% precision through knowledge grounding), multi-agent systems at complex behavioral simulation (Chimera's 0.83 F1 reflects realistic difficulty), and generative adversarial architectures at synthetic data generation (EMD $<10^{-3}$). This alignment suggests architectural selection should prioritize the target application domain over novelty.

Finding 2: Validation Mechanisms as Critical Enablers. Systems incorporating explicit validation demonstrate 15–20 percentage point precision improvements across all architectural

Table 8.4 System Limitations, Scalability, and Deployment Maturity

System	*Primary Limitations*	*False Positive/Negative Behavior*	*Scalability Constraints*	*Deployment Maturity*	*Privacy/Ethical Risks*
IntelEX [30]	LLM hallucinations require validation layers (15–20% precision boost)	Unvalidated outputs need human oversight	LLM inference/RAG cost limits high-volume real-time CTI	Analyst augmentation; not fully autonomous	Leakage risk with sensitive CTI data
FALCON [32]	Quality depends on the CTI report detail; vague reports yield poor rules	Generated rules require expert review to eliminate false positives	Multiphase validation limits high-throughput capacity	Operational with human oversight	Minimal risk if deployed internally.
LLMCloudHunter [22]	Limited to cloud environments; not for on-premises	False positives from rules targeting benign APIs	LLM inference latency	Operational viability demonstrated	Cloud provider telemetry contains sensitive data
CyLens [19]	Requires broader environmental validation	Not explicitly reported	Not explicitly reported.	Early-stage research prototype	Dark web forum access raises ethical concerns
Chimera [33]	Lower F1 (0.83) suggests generation artifacts or high realism	Synthetic data artifacts may affect detector training	Multi-agent simulation computationally intensive	Research prototype; needs operational validation	Simulated behaviors must respect privacy norms
PentestGPT [24]	Context window limits cause memory loss in long engagements	Human oversight mandatory for GUI operations	Iterative LLM reasoning computationally expensive	Active adoption; operational with human oversight	Unauthorized testing risk if system misused
PentestAgent [37]	Debugging overhead in complex scenarios	Not explicitly reported	Not explicitly reported	Emerging framework; validation ongoing	Similar to PentestGPT
WCGAN [38]	Requires real-world anchor data; cannot generate novel attack classes.	Detectors may learn generator artifacts, not real attacks.	GAN training is intensive; frequent retraining is challenging.	Research validation; operational balance needed.	Synthetic data must preserve real sample privacy.
ACD Agent	Requires simulation environment; real-world transfer validation needed	Not explicitly reported	DRL training computationally intensive	Emerging framework; CybORG-validated	Automated actions require human oversight
L2M-AID [40]	Limited to Industrial IoT contexts	Not explicitly reported	LLM-MARL fusion computationally demanding	Emerging framework; domain-specific validation	IIoT data sensitivity; operational safety concerns

patterns. FALCON's multiphase validation achieves 95% expert-validated accuracy; IntelEX's secondary LLM judgment substantially improves precision; WCGAN's statistical fidelity validation prevents model collapse. Validation layers are essential components, not optional optimizations.

Finding 3: Evidence Maturity-Deployment Readiness Correlation. Rigorous empirical evaluation predicts deployment viability. PentestGPT (25 vulnerable machines, HackTheBox top 10%, 6,500+ GitHub stars) exhibits production deployment with community adoption. FALCON (95% accuracy, 84% inter-rater agreement) demonstrates operational readiness. Conversely, a limited evaluation scope (CyLens) indicates prototype status requiring additional validation.

Finding 4: The Proactive-Reactive Integration Imperative. No analyzed system operates autonomously without human oversight. PentestGPT requires operator guidance for GUI operations; FALCON requires expert review before production deployment; IntelEX achieves analyst augmentation rather than replacement. This pattern indicates future proactive cybersecurity will employ hybrid architectures where generative AI handles scale and pattern recognition while humans provide context, strategic reasoning, and consequential decision-making.

Trade-Off Space Characterization. The analyzed systems occupy distinct positions in a multidimensional trade-off space defined by competing objectives: detection accuracy, explainability, inference latency, scalability, and deployment maturity. High-accuracy systems (IntelEX: 0.902 F1, FALCON: 95% accuracy) achieve performance through computational overhead (RAG queries, ensemble retrieval, multiphase validation), constraining scalability and real-time deployment. Highly autonomous systems (Chimera's autonomous agent behaviors, PentestGPT's autonomous exploitation) sacrifice explainability for behavioral realism and operational flexibility. Production-ready systems (PentestGPT, FALCON) achieve deployment maturity by incorporating human-in-the-loop oversight and explicit validation, trading full autonomy for operational reliability.

Context-Dependent Selection Guidance for Practitioners. System selection should align with organizational priorities:

Rapid Deployment, Moderate Accuracy: FALCON and PentestGPT offer enterprise readiness (75–95% accuracy) with human oversight for IDS rule generation and continuous penetration testing.

High Accuracy, Validation Investment: IntelEX and LLMCloudHunter provide >90% precision for threat intelligence extraction and cloud detection rules, requiring validation infrastructure before production.

Data Scarcity Challenges: WCGAN enables synthetic attack data generation for class imbalance, requiring integration with real-world anchor data and distributional validation.

Long-Term Research Capabilities: Chimera and CyLens represent promising directions for insider threat simulation and agentic intelligence, suitable for organizations with dedicated research teams.

Comprehensive Proactive Posture: Multisystem integration across functional categories (threat intelligence, rule generation, penetration testing, synthetic data, insider threat defense) operationalizes left-of-boom philosophy across the defensive lifecycle.

Architectural Implications for Future System Design. Comparative analysis suggests five design principles for future generative AI security systems: (1) prioritize architectural pattern selection based on target proactive application domain (Pattern 1 for intelligence extraction, Pattern 2 for behavioral simulation, Pattern 3 for synthetic data generation); (2) incorporate explicit validation mechanisms as first-class architectural components rather than afterthoughts, targeting 15–20 percentage point precision improvements; (3) design for incremental adoption through standardized output formats enabling integration with existing cybersecurity infrastructure; (4) plan for human-in-the-loop oversight recognizing that full autonomy remains infeasible for security-critical decisions; and (5) conduct rigorous empirical evaluation across multiple benchmark datasets with expert validation to accelerate deployment readiness and community trust. These principles, derived from comparative analysis of implemented systems, provide actionable guidance for researchers and practitioners developing next-generation proactive cybersecurity capabilities.

Beyond the ten frameworks analyzed in depth, recent research demonstrates continued architectural diversification in proactive cybersecurity applications. PentestAgent [37] extends autonomous penetration testing through multi-agent decomposition with integrated debugging mechanisms, achieving fully automated exploitation workflows without continuous human feedback across VulHub and HackTheBox benchmarks. The Autonomous Cyber Defence (ACD) Agent [39] exemplifies hybrid DRL-LLM integration for automated incident response, achieving 17.4% higher cumulative rewards than baseline PPO models in CybORG evaluations through knowledge graph-augmented contextual reasoning. L2M-AID [40] explores domain-specific applications by fusing LLM semantic reasoning with MARL for Industrial IoT defense, treating LLMs as cognitive translators that enable defensive agents to reason about adversary intent in critical cyber-physical systems. These emerging systems illustrate the field's trajectory toward increased autonomy, hybrid architectural patterns combining multiple AI paradigms, standardized evaluation methodologies, and expansion into specialized domains beyond traditional enterprise IT security.

Figure 8.2 synthesizes the comparative analysis across performance and deployment maturity dimensions, positioning the frameworks within a strategic decision space for technology selection. The scatter plot enables practitioners to identify frameworks aligned with organizational risk tolerance, operational maturity requirements, and performance thresholds, while illuminating the architectural trade-offs between empirical capability and production readiness that characterize the current state of proactive generative AI deployment in cybersecurity contexts.

This scatter plot positions ten generative AI frameworks across two dimensions measured on 0–10 ordinal scales. The Performance axis (x-axis) quantifies empirical effectiveness through normalized metrics: F1 scores (≥0.90 = 9–10; 0.80–0.89 = 7–8; 0.70–0.79 = 5–6), precision-recall percentages (≥95% = 9–10; 85–94% = 7–8; 75–84% = 5–6), expert validation accuracy, task completion rates, and baseline improvement ratios. The Maturity axis (y-axis) assesses deployment readiness through production deployments, community adoption metrics, artifact reproducibility validation, compilation success rates, and human-in-the-loop verification workflows.

Quadrant thresholds at Performance = 7.0 and Maturity = 6.0 partition the space into four strategic zones. The upper-right quadrant ("Production-ready with human oversight") contains six frameworks exhibiting both high empirical performance and operational validation: PentestGPT (8.5, 8.0) with Distinguished Artifact validation and top-10% HackTheBox ranking; FALCON (8.0, 7.5) achieving 95% accuracy with 84% inter-rater agreement and minutes-versus-weeks' timeline compression; PentestAgent and LLMCloudHunter (8.0, 7.0) demonstrating fully automated exploitation and 99.18% rule compilation success, respectively; IntelEX (7.5, 6.5) with 1.34× baseline improvement;

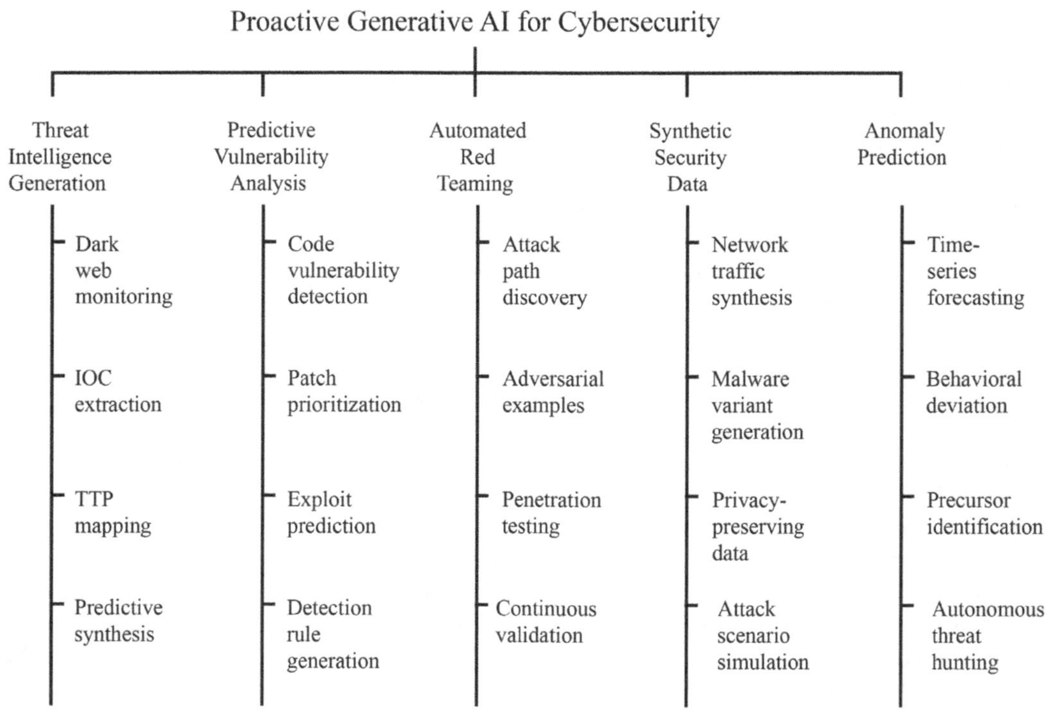

Figure 8.2 Performance-Maturity Positioning of Proactive Generative AI Cybersecurity Frameworks.

and ACD Agent (7.5, 6.0) positioned at the maturity threshold, outperforming 11 DRL baselines in CybORG simulation. The lower-right quadrant ("Strong technical capability; requires operational validation") positions frameworks with validated performance but limited deployment evidence: CyLens (7.0, 5.0), achieving 83.74% attribution accuracy (doubling ChatGPT-4o's performance) but remaining at an early prototype stage; and L2M-AID (7.0, 5.5) demonstrating novel LLM-MARL fusion for IIoT defense requiring broader empirical validation. The lower-left quadrant ("Research prototypes requiring development") contains early-stage systems: Chimera (6.5, 5.5) exhibiting 50-percentage-point distribution shifts vulnerability across organizational contexts; and WCGAN (6.0, 5.0) demonstrating statistical fidelity but requiring specialist integration expertise. The upper-left quadrant ("Deployed but limited capability") remains unoccupied, indicating no frameworks currently exhibit high operational maturity with constrained technical performance.

Color coding distinguishes maturity tiers: green denotes production-viable systems (maturity ≥6.5), yellow indicates transition-stage frameworks approaching deployment readiness (maturity ≈6.0), and red designates research prototypes requiring operational validation (maturity <6.0). This positioning framework enables evidence-based technology selection: organizations prioritizing immediate operational deployment should select from the upper-right quadrant frameworks with appropriate human oversight protocols, while research-oriented adopters may evaluate lower-quadrant prototypes for collaborative development or future integration planning. The visualization enables systematic comparison across architecturally heterogeneous systems—from LLM-based threat intelligence extraction to GAN-based synthetic data generation—by decomposing deployment readiness into orthogonal performance and maturity dimensions assessed through reproducible, quantitative criteria.

8.7 CHALLENGES AND LIMITATIONS

Despite demonstrated proactive capabilities, generative AI deployment faces five operational constraints that limit production viability: adversarial attacks (Section 8.6.1), hallucinations (Section 8.6.2), explainability deficits (Section 8.6.3), computational costs (Section 8.6.4), and data privacy concerns (Section 8.6.5). Each subsection identifies the challenge, quantifies operational impact, and presents evidence-based mitigation strategies.

8.7.1 Adversarial attacks

Generative AI systems deployed in cybersecurity contexts face sophisticated adversarial attacks designed to compromise their integrity and effectiveness. Data poisoning attacks manipulate training datasets by injecting malicious samples that create exploitable backdoors, causing models to learn incorrect patterns [41]. Evasion attacks craft adversarial inputs that bypass detection during inference, with demonstrated transferability across model architectures, creating systemic vulnerabilities [42].

Operational impact extends beyond isolated failures to degraded performance, manifesting as increased false negatives and false positives. The "echospoofing" campaign exemplifies this risk, circumventing email classifiers to enable 3 million daily spoofed emails [41]. Wang et al. [43] demonstrated that adversarial samples transfer between LLM architectures, allowing attackers to develop exploits against accessible models and deploy them against proprietary systems. This transferability amplifies risk in federated defense ecosystems where organizations deploy similar AI-driven tools, creating correlated vulnerabilities across defensive infrastructure.

Mitigation Strategies: (1) Adversarial training: CGAN-generated traffic samples reduce evasion rates by 15% under FGSM/PGD attacks [44]; (2) Defensive distillation: outputting probability distributions rather than hard classifications smooth decision boundaries against gradient-based attacks; (3) Input validation frameworks: anomaly detection quarantines adversarial inputs before inference, creating defense-in-depth architectures.

8.7.2 False positives and hallucinations

LLMs integrated into threat intelligence workflows exhibit hallucinations—generating plausible yet factually incorrect content. In cybersecurity contexts, LLMs may fabricate nonexistent vulnerabilities, generate invalid IOCs, or recommend ineffective remediation strategies. Ji et al. [45] identify two hallucination categories: factuality hallucinations (demonstrably false claims) and faithfulness hallucinations (outputs diverging from source context).

Operational impact in SOCs can be severe. Alert fatigue intensifies when analysts must verify each AI-generated finding, paradoxically increasing workload. The OWASP Top 10 for LLM Applications (2025) [46] identifies misinformation as a core vulnerability, noting that coding assistants have suggested nonexistent security libraries, leading developers to integrate malicious packages published under fabricated names—a supply chain attack vector enabled by hallucinations.

Mitigation Strategies: (1) RAG: grounds responses in verified knowledge bases like MITRE ATT&CK, with RAG-based systems outperforming standalone GPT-3.5 and GPT-4o [47]; (2) Confidence thresholding: rejects low-certainty outputs and routes ambiguous cases to human analysts; (3) Human-in-the-loop workflows: mandatory analyst verification maintains accuracy while capturing edge cases, creating feedback loops that incrementally improve reliability.

8.7.3 Explainability

Deep learning models and LLMs function as black boxes, producing predictions through millions of learned parameters whose decision logic remains opaque. This interpretability deficit creates acute challenges in cybersecurity, where analysts must understand why systems flag specific traffic as malicious or how models arrive at threat attributions. Regulatory frameworks, including GDPR [48], mandate explainability for automated decisions, constraining deployment of opaque AI systems where legal compliance is paramount.

Unexplainable AI decisions undermine adoption in security-critical contexts. When intrusion detection systems raise alerts without a clear rationale, analysts either develop automation bias (over-trusting unexplained recommendations) or ignore outputs entirely, negating AI augmentation value. Salih et al. [49] note that while SHAP and LIME provide feature importance rankings, end users often struggle to understand how these XAI methods generate interpretations, creating second-order opacity.

Mitigation Strategies: (1) SHAP/LIME techniques: generate feature importance attributions for specific predictions, with XGBoost-SHAP achieving 97.8% validation accuracy [50]; (2) Attention visualization: extracts learned representations from transformer architectures, revealing which input tokens influenced outputs; (3) Human-in-the-loop review: maintains trust while creating feedback loops for incremental improvement. However, SHAP and LIME have limitations—SHAP outcomes are model-dependent, and both struggle with collinear features—requiring careful interpretation before operational deployment [49].

8.7.4 Computational costs

LLM inference imposes substantial computational burdens, constraining scalability and operational expenses. Tian et al. [51] demonstrate that for Gemma-2B on edge processors, pre-fill latency increases dramatically with prompt length (255 ms for 128 tokens to 1,935 ms for 1,024 tokens), with end-to-end latency exceeding 100 seconds—failing real-time requirements. Energy consumption amplifies costs: AI-powered searches expend 8.9 watt-hours versus 0.3 for traditional keyword search, creating financial barriers when scaled across enterprise security queries. Memory requirements compound challenges—LLaMA-2 (7B parameters) requires over 8 GB RAM at FP16 precision, exceeding edge device capacity.

Mitigation Strategies: (1) Model distillation: preserves over 95% performance while reducing inference costs across latency, compute, and memory [52]; (2) Quantization: 8-bit precision reduces model size by 75% while maintaining performance within 2% of full-precision models; (3) Collaborative edge computing: EdgeShard partitions LLM inference across distributed devices, reducing latency by 50% and achieving 2× throughput [53].

8.7.5 Data privacy

Training generative AI systems for cybersecurity requires access to sensitive operational data, including network telemetry, system logs, threat intelligence feeds, and incident response records. Centralized training paradigms necessitate aggregating data in shared repositories, creating privacy risks and regulatory violations. Organizations subject to GDPR [48], the U.S. Health Insurance Portability and Accountability Act (HIPAA) [54], or sector-specific data protection regimes, face legal constraints on sharing raw security logs containing PII, authentication credentials, or proprietary intelligence. This tension between data-hungry training and privacy preservation creates fundamental barriers to collaborative threat intelligence development.

Impact extends beyond regulatory compliance. Privacy violations erode stakeholder trust and expose organizations to substantial penalties—GDPR fines reach 4% of global revenue or €20 million [55]. Data breaches from centralized AI training repositories compound security challenges, as adversaries gain access to comprehensive telemetry revealing defensive capabilities, infrastructure topology, and blind spots. This intelligence asymmetry enables precisely targeted campaigns against known weaknesses.

Mitigation Strategies: (1) FL: decentralized training where raw data never leaves local environments, with organizations sharing only encrypted gradient updates; recent implementations achieve over 90% intrusion detection accuracy while maintaining privacy loss below 5% [56]; (2) Differential privacy: adds calibrated noise to shared parameters, providing mathematical guarantees that individual data points cannot be reconstructed from model outputs while satisfying regulatory requirements; (3) Homomorphic encryption: enables computation on encrypted data without decryption, though computational overhead currently limits real-time applications.

8.8 EMERGING TRENDS AND FUTURE DIRECTIONS

Three technological trends demonstrate potential to address current limitations while expanding proactive cybersecurity capabilities: FL for privacy-preserving collaboration, NeSy AI for trustworthy reasoning, and edge AI for real-time lightweight deployment. These approaches target specific operational barriers—FL addresses data privacy constraints, NeSy AI tackles explainability deficits, and edge AI resolves computational scalability challenges—and are not mutually exclusive; future systems will likely integrate multiple approaches to achieve robust, scalable, privacy-preserving proactive defense.

8.8.1 FL for privacy-preserving collaborative training

FL enables collaborative model training across distributed organizations without centralizing sensitive data, addressing the privacy paradox inherent in traditional machine learning. Rather than aggregating raw network logs in shared repositories, FL allows participants to train local models on proprietary data and contribute only encrypted gradient updates to a global model. This architecture preserves data locality while leveraging collective intelligence across organizational boundaries—enabling proactive defense through shared learning without exposing sensitive operational data.

Empirical validation demonstrates FL's viability for production deployment. Implementations on benchmark intrusion detection datasets (CICIDS2017, TON_IoT) achieve accuracies exceeding 90% while maintaining privacy loss below 5% [56], with 25%

communication efficiency improvements addressing cross-organizational collaboration barriers. Chen et al. [57] identify FL as a cornerstone of trustworthy AI for cybersecurity, combining gradient clipping, differential privacy mechanisms, and encrypted model aggregation to ensure secure collaboration.

As organizations recognize that isolated defensive postures cannot match sophisticated threat actor capabilities, privacy-preserving FL offers a technically sound and legally compliant path toward collective defense—operationalizing "defense in numbers" while maintaining data sovereignty.

8.8.2 NeSy AI for reliable hybrid reasoning

NeSy AI combines neural networks' pattern recognition strengths with symbolic reasoning systems' logical rigor and interpretability, addressing fundamental limitations of purely data-driven approaches. Neural components learn complex representations from high-dimensional data (network traffic patterns, malware behavioral signatures, threat actor tactics), while symbolic modules encode expert knowledge, security policies, and causal relationships in formal logic. This hybrid architecture enables systems that are simultaneously adaptive and accountable, learning from data while providing human-interpretable explanations.

Recent systematic reviews reveal concentrated research activity in neuro-symbolic integration for cybersecurity. DeLong et al. [58] survey methods for reasoning over knowledge graphs, identifying three major architectural categories: logically-informed embedding approaches, embedding approaches with logical constraints, and rule learning approaches. Colelough et al.'s PRISMA-based review [59] of 167 papers shows research concentration in learning and inference (63%), logic and reasoning (35%), and knowledge representation (28%), with emerging applications in explainability and trustworthiness—domains critical for SOC adoption.

Neuro-symbolic frameworks for cybersecurity leverage MITRE ATT&CK knowledge graphs, CVE databases, and formal security policy specifications to constrain neural model behavior [60]. These systems explain detection decisions in terms of specific ATT&CK techniques, trace logical inference paths through security ontologies, and guarantee regulatory compliance—capabilities essential for forensic analysis and incident attribution. From a proactive perspective, symbolic reasoning enables the prediction of attack evolution by reasoning over known adversary tactics and available attack paths before threats materialize, supporting proactive threat hunting and strategic defense planning.

8.8.3 Edge AI for real-time lightweight deployment

Edge AI deployment brings generative model inference to resource-constrained devices (IoT sensors, industrial controllers, mobile devices, embedded systems), enabling real-time security analytics without cloud dependencies. This architectural shift addresses latency requirements for time-critical applications such as autonomous vehicle protection, smart grid intrusion detection, and ICS anomaly identification, where millisecond-scale response times are essential. Edge deployment enhances privacy by processing sensitive data locally, reduces bandwidth consumption, and maintains functionality during network outages or adversarial disruptions.

Zheng et al. [61] examine optimization pipelines for edge LLM deployment, spanning pre-deployment model design (quantization, pruning, knowledge distillation), runtime inference optimizations (dynamic batching, speculative decoding, hardware-software co-design), and domain-specific applications. Empirical studies demonstrate that 8-bit quantization maintains accuracy within 2% of full-precision models while reducing inference energy consumption by 60% [62]. EdgeShard demonstrates practical edge collaboration architectures that partition LLMs across distributed devices and cloud servers, achieving 50% latency reduction and 2× throughput improvement over traditional cloud-edge approaches [53]. For cybersecurity applications, edge AI enables autonomous threat response at the network perimeter—blocking malicious traffic at IoT gateways before reaching core infrastructure, quarantining compromised devices immediately upon anomaly detection, and maintaining a defensive posture when central SOCs become unreachable. This distributes proactive defense to the earliest intervention point in the attack lifecycle, operationalizing left-of-boom philosophy at the edge. The convergence of model compression techniques, specialized edge accelerators, and federated edge learning positions edge AI as essential for resilient, distributed cybersecurity architectures.

8.9 CONCLUSION

This chapter systematically analyzed generative AI for proactive cybersecurity across three dimensions: a five-domain taxonomy (Section 8.3), four technical architectures (Section 8.4), and comparative evaluation of ten research systems (Section 8.5). Analysis reveals that current implementations achieve 90–95% accuracy in threat intelligence extraction and autonomous rule generation, demonstrating operational viability with human oversight. However, deployment faces five quantified constraints: adversarial vulnerability (15% evasion rate reductions require CGAN-augmented training), hallucinations (15–20 percentage point precision improvements require validation layers), explainability deficits (XAI techniques provide partial mitigation), computational costs (8–100× greater than traditional approaches), and privacy barriers (FL achieves >90% accuracy with <5% privacy loss). These limitations highlight the need for continued work on privacy-preserving learning, hybrid neuro-symbolic reasoning, and lightweight edge-aligned models, alongside standardized evaluation benchmarks and governance guidelines. Overall, generative AI shows promise for strengthening proactive defense, but realizing this potential requires cautious integration, rigorous validation, and sustained collaboration across research and operational communities.

ACKNOWLEDGMENTS

The authors acknowledge the use of digital research and writing assistance tools, including OpenAI's ChatGPT, Anthropic's Claude, and AlphaXiv, which were employed to support literature discovery, improve clarity, and refine wording based on author-generated content. The final content has been carefully reviewed and verified, and full responsibility for its accuracy and integrity rests solely with the authors.

REFERENCES

[1] IBM X-Force. 2025. Threat Intelligence Index. IBM. Available online: www.ibm.com/thought-leadership/institute-business-value/en-us/report/2025-threat-intelligence-index (accessed on 22 Nov 2025).

[2] Balasubramanian, P., Liyana, S., Sankaran, H., Sivaramakrishnan, S., Pusuluri, S., Pirttikangas, S. and Peltonen, E., "Generative AI for Cyber Threat Intelligence: Applications, Challenges, and Analysis of Real-World Case Studies." *Artificial Intelligence Review*, vol. 58, no 11, p. 336, 2025.

[3] H. Rauf *et al.*, "Using Generative Ai for Simulating Cyber Security Attacks and Defense Mechanisms: A New Approach To Ai-Driven Cyber Threat Modeling." *Spectrum of Engineering Sciences*, vol. 3, no 3, pp. 361–381, 2025.

[4] S. Kuraku *et al.*, "Cultivating Proactive Cybersecurity Culture Among IT Professional to Combat Evolving Threats." *International Journal of Electrical, Electronics and Computers*, vol. 8, no 6, 2023.

[5] E. M. Hutchins, M. J. Cloppert, and R. M. Amin. "Intelligence-Driven Computer Network Defense Informed by Analysis of Adversary Campaigns and Intrusion Kill Chains." *Leading Issues in Information Warfare & Security Research*, vol. 1, no 1, p. 80, 2011.

[6] T. Yadav, and A. M. Rao. "Technical Aspects of Cyber Kill Chain." In *International Symposium on Security in Computing and Communication*, Cham: Springer International Publishing, 2015, pp. 438–452.

[7] B. Brody, "Left of Boom. Cybersecurity: Proactive Cybersecurity in a Time of Increasing Threats and Attacks." Cisco Blogs, 2021. Available online: https://blogs.cisco.com/security/left-of-boom-cybersecurity-proactive-cybersecurity-in-a-time-of-increasing-threats-and-attacks (accessed on 22 Nov 2025).

[8] A. Samhruth, K. Girish, and N. Ganesh. "Siren: Advancing Cybersecurity Through Deception and Adaptive Analysis." In *Intelligent Computing-Proceedings of the Computing Conference*, Cham: Springer Nature Switzerland, 2025. pp. 506–519.

[9] J. Dykstra, K. Shortridge, J. Met, and D. Hough. "Sludge for Good: Slowing and Imposing Costs on Cyber Attackers." *arXiv: arXiv:2211.16626*, 2022.

[10] H. M. Melaku, "Context-Based and Adaptive Cybersecurity Risk Management Framework." *Risks*, vol. 11, no 6, p. 101, 2023.

[11] W. Lim, K. S. C. Yong, B. T. Lau, and C. C. L. Tan, "Future of Generative Adversarial Networks (GAN) for Anomaly Detection in Network Security: A Review." *Computer Security*, vol. 139, no C, p.103733, 2024.

[12] G. Agrawal, A. Kaur, and S. Myneni, "A Review of Generative Models in Generating Synthetic Attack Data for Cybersecurity." *Electronics*, vol. 13, no 2, p. 322, 2024.

[13] D. A. Ammara, J. Ding, and K. Tutschku, "Synthetic Network Traffic Data Generation: A Comparative Study." *arXiv*: arXiv:2410.16326, 2025.

[14] N. Peppes, T. Alexakis, E. Daskalakis, E. Adamopoulou, and K. Demestichas, "A Generative Adversarial Network (GAN) Solution for Synthetically Generated Botnet Attack Data Samples." In *Paradigms on Technology Development for Security Practitioners*, Cham: Springer Nature Switzerland, 2024, pp. 311–321.

[15] C. Yang, D. Xu, and X. Ma, "Research on the Simulation Method of HTTP Traffic Based on GAN." *Applied Sciences*, vol. 14, no 5, p. 2121, 2024.

[16] H. Sun, Y. Huang, L. Han, C. Fu, H. Liu, and X. Long, "MTS-DVGAN: Anomaly Detection in Cyber-Physical Systems using a Dual Variational Generative Adversarial Network." *Computers & Security*, vol. 139, p. 103570, 2024.

[17] M. A. Sen, "Attention-GAN for Anomaly Detection: A Cutting-Edge Approach to Cybersecurity Threat Management." *arXiv*: arXiv:2402.15945, 2024.

[18] E. Joshua, J. Do, and R. Patel, "AI-Driven Threat Intelligence System (AIDTIS): Leveraging Large Language Models for Automated Threat Research and Detection Development." *International Journal of Science and Research Archive*, vol. 14, no 3, pp. 270–285, 2025.

[19] X. Liu *et al.*, "CyLens: Towards Reinventing Cyber Threat Intelligence in the Paradigm of Agentic Large Language Models." *arXiv: 2502.20791*, 2025.

[20] S. Paul, and F. Alemi, "LLM-Assisted Proactive Threat Intelligence for Automated Reasoning." *arXiv:2504.00428*, 2025.

[21] X. Zhou, T. Zhang, and D. Lo, "Large Language Model for Vulnerability Detection: Emerging Results and Future Directions." In *Proceedings of the 2024 ACM/IEEE 44th International Conference on Software Engineering: New Ideas and Emerging Results*, Lisbon Portugal: ACM, 2024, pp. 47–51.

[22] Y. Schwartz, L. Benshimol, D. Mimran, Y. Elovici, and A. Shabtai, "LLMCloudHunter: Harnessing LLMs for Automated Extraction of Detection Rules from Cloud-Based CTI." *arXiv*: arXiv:2407.05194, 2024.

[23] A. Happe, and J. Cito, "Getting pwn'd by AI: Penetration Testing with Large Language Models." In *Proceedings of the 31st ACM Joint European Software Engineering Conference and Symposium on the Foundations of Software Engineering*, San Francisco CA USA: ACM, 2023, pp. 2082–2086.

[24] G. Deng *et al.*, "PentestGPT: An LLM-Empowered Automatic Penetration Testing Tool." *arXiv*: arXiv:2308.06782, 2024.

[25] R. Fang, R. Bindu, A. Gupta, and D. Kang, "LLM Agents can Autonomously Exploit One-Day Vulnerabilities." *arXiv*: arXiv:2404.08144, 2024.

[26] N. Vemuri, N, Thaneeru, and V. M. Tatikonda, "Adaptive Generative AI for Dynamic Cybersecurity Threat Detection in Enterprises." *International Journal of Science and Research Archive*, vol. 11, no 1, pp. 2259–2265, 2024.

[27] B. Chhetri, and A. S. Namin, "The Application of Transformer-Based Models for Predicting Consequences of Cyber Attacks." *arXiv*: arXiv:2508.13030, 2025.

[28] M. Kiely *et al.*, "Exploring the Efficacy of Multi-Agent Reinforcement Learning for Autonomous Cyber Defence: A CAGE Challenge 4 Perspective." In Proceedings of the AAAI Conference on Artificial Intelligence (Vol. 39, No. 28, pp. 28907-28913), 2025..

[29] M. A. Alsuwaiket, "ZeroDay-LLM: A Large Language Model Framework for Zero-Day Threat Detection in Cybersecurity." *Information*, vol. 16, no 11, p. 939, 2025.

[30] M. Xu *et al.*, "IntelEX: A LLM-Driven Attack-Level Threat Intelligence Extraction Framework.", *arXiv*: arXiv:2412.10872, 2024.

[31] V. Clairoux-Trepanier, I.-M. Beauchamp, E. Ruellan, M. Paquet-Clouston, S.-O. Paquette, and E. Clay, "The Use of Large Language Models (LLM) for Cyber Threat Intelligence (CTI) in Cybercrime Forums." *arXiv*: arXiv:2408.03354, 2024.

[32] S. Mitra *et al.*, "FALCON: Autonomous Cyber Threat Intelligence Mining with LLMs for IDS Rule Generation." *arXiv*: arXiv:2508.18684, 2025.

[33] J. Yu, X. Xie, Q. Hu, Y. Ma, and Z. Zhao, "Chimera: Harnessing Multi-Agent LLMs for Automatic Insider Threat Simulation.", *arXiv*: arXiv:2508.07745, 2025.

[34] T. Ndayipfukamiye, J. Ding, D. S. Sarwatt, A. G. Philipo, and H. Ning, "Adversarial Defense in Cybersecurity: A Systematic Review of GANs for Threat Detection and Mitigation." *arXiv*: arXiv:2509.20411, 2025.

[35] J. Shan, H. Ma, and J. Li, "Research on Network Attack Sample Generation and Defence Techniques Based on Generative Adversarial Networks." *Applied Mathematics and Nonlinear Sciences*, vol. 9, no 1, 2024.

[36] H. K. Pedarla, "Generative AI for Network Attack Simulation." *International Journal of Artificial Intelligence, Data Science, and Machine Learning*, vol. 6, no 4, pp. 65–70, 2025.

[37] X. Shen *et al.*, "PentestAgent: Incorporating LLM Agents to Automated Penetration Testing." In *Proceedings of the 20th ACM Asia Conference on Computer and Communications Security*, Hanoi Vietnam: ACM, 2025, pp. 375–391.

[38] V. Kumar, and D. Sinha, "Synthetic Attack Data Generation Model Applying Generative Adversarial Network for Intrusion Detection." *Computers & Security*, vol. 125, p. 103054, 2023.

[39] J. Loevenich, E. Adler, T. Huerten, and R. Rigolin Ferreira Lopes, "*Design and Evaluation of an Autonomous Cyber Defence Agent Using Drl and an Augmented Llm.*" Rochester, NY: Social Science Research Network, 2024, p. 5076836.

[40] T. Xu, Z. Wen, X. Zhao, J. Wang, Y. Li, and C. Liu, "L2M-AID: Autonomous Cyber-Physical Defense by Fusing Semantic Reasoning of Large Language Models with Multi-Agent Reinforcement Learning." *arXiv*: arXiv:2510.07363, 2025.
[41] S. Isla, "Combating the Threat of Adversarial Machine Learning to AI Driven Cybersecurity." ISACA. August 2025 Available online: www.isaca.org/resources/news-and-trends/industry-news/2025/combating-the-threat-of-adversarial-machine-learning-to-ai-driven-cybersecurity (accessed on 2 Dec 2025).
[42] A. Zou, Z. Wang, N. Carlini, M. Nasr, J. Z. Kolter, and M. Fredrikson, "Universal and Transferable Adversarial Attacks on Aligned Language Models." *arXiv*: arXiv:2307.15043, 2023.
[43] X. Yue, Z. Zhang, J. Jing, and W. Wang, "Ctta: A Novel Chain-of-Thought Transfer Adversarial Attacks Framework for Large Language Models." *Cybersecurity*, vol. 8, no 1, p. 36, 2025.
[44] S. Zhao, J. Li, J. Wang, Z. Zhang, L. Zhu, and Y. Zhang, "attackGAN: Adversarial Attack against Black-Box IDS Using Generative Adversarial Networks." *Procedia Computer Science*, vol. 187, pp. 128-133, 2021.
[45] Z. Ji *et al.*, "Survey of Hallucination in Natural Language Generation." *ACM Computer Surveys*, vol. 55, no 12, pp. 1–248:38, 2023.
[46] S. Wilson, and A. Dawson. "OWASP Top 10 for LLM Applications 2025.", OWASP, 2024. Available online: https://owasp.org/www-project-top-10-for-large-language-model-applicati ons/assets/PDF/OWASP-Top-10-for-LLMs-v2025.pdf (accessed on 2 Dec 2025).
[47] A. Alhuzali, "LLM-Powered Threat Intelligence: A Retrieval-Augmented Generation Approach for Cyber Attack Investigation." *Peer Journal Computer Science*, vol. 11, p. e3371, 2025.
[48] European Union. "General Data Protection Regulation (GDPR)." vol. 2016/679. Available online: https://gdpr-info.eu/ (accessed on 2 Dec 2025).
[49] A. M. Salih *et* al., "A Perspective on Explainable Artificial Intelligence Methods: SHAP and LIME." *Advanced Intelligent Systems*, vol. 7, no 1, p. 2400304, 2025.
[50] P. Hermosilla, S. Berríos, and H. Allende-Cid, "Explainable AI for Forensic Analysis: A Comparative Study of SHAP and LIME in Intrusion Detection Models." *Applied Sciences*, vol. 15, no 13, p. 7329, 2025.
[51] C. Tian *et al.* "CLONE: Customizing LLMs for Efficient Latency-Aware Inference at the Edge." *arXiv preprint arXiv:2506.02847*, 2025.
[52] L. Fang *et al.*, "Knowledge Distillation and Dataset Distillation of Large Language Models: Emerging Trends, Challenges, and Future Directions." *Artificial Intelligence Review*, vol. 59, no 1, p. 17, 2025.
[53] M. Zhang, J. Cao, X. Shen, and Z. Cui, "EdgeShard: Efficient LLM Inference via Collaborative Edge Computing." *arXiv*: arXiv:2405.14371, 2024.
[54] U.S. Congress. "*Health Insurance Portability and Accountability Act (HIPAA).*" 1996. Available online: www.hhs.gov/hipaa/index.html (accessed on 1 Dec 2025).
[55] J. Wolff, and N. Atallah, *Early GDPR Penalties: Analysis of Implementation and Fines Through May 2020.* Rochester, NY: Social Science Research Network, 2020, p. 3748837.
[56] E. M. Timofte *et al.*, "Federated Learning for Cybersecurity: A Privacy-Preserving Approach." *Applied Sciences*, vol. 15, no 12, p. 6878, 2025.
[57] C. Chen *et al.*, "Trustworthy Federated Learning: Privacy, Security, and Beyond." *Knowledge and Information Systems*, vol. 67, no 3, pp. 2321–2356, 2025.
[58] L. N. DeLong, R. F. Mir, and J. D. Fleuriot, "Neurosymbolic AI for Reasoning Over Knowledge Graphs: A Survey." *IEEE Transactions on Neural Networks and Learning Systems*, vol. 36, no 5, pp. 7822–7842, 2025.
[59] B. C. Colelough, and W. Regli, "Neuro-Symbolic AI in 2024: A Systematic Review." *arXiv*: arXiv:2501.05435, 2025.

[60] S. B. Hakim, M. Adil, A. Velasquez, S. Xu, and H. H. Song, “Neuro-Symbolic AI for Cybersecurity: State of the Art, Challenges, and Opportunities.” *arXiv*: arXiv:2509.06921, 2025.
[61] Zheng, Y., Chen, Y., Qian, B., Shi, X., Shu, Y. and Chen, J., “A Review on Edge Large Language Models: Design, Execution, and Applications | ACM Computing Surveys.” *ACM Computing Surveys*, vol. 57, no 209, pp. 1–35, 2025.
[62] E. J. Husom *et al.*, “Sustainable LLM Inference for Edge AI: Evaluating Quantized LLMs for Energy Efficiency, Output Accuracy, and Inference Latency.” *arXiv: arXiv:2504.03360*, 2025.

Chapter 9

GEPARD

A GenAI-Enabled Proactive Adaptive Resilient Defence framework for cybersecurity

Soharab Hossain Shaikh

9.1 INTRODUCTION – FROM REACTIVE TO PROACTIVE DEFENCE

In today's digitally interconnected world, organizations face an escalating volume of cyber threats that are increasingly sophisticated, dynamic, and persistent. Adversaries continuously refine their tactics, techniques, and procedures (TTPs), rendering traditional security paradigms insufficient to maintain pace. This dynamic threat environment demands a paradigm shift in cybersecurity – moving from reactive to proactive defence.

9.1.1 Limitations of reactive incident response

Reactive incident response represents the conventional approach to managing cyber threats, entailing the detection and remediation of attacks post-occurrence. For instance, upon the detection of unauthorized access or malware by a firewall, an incident response team initiates investigation, containment, and subsequent recovery and mitigation efforts. While indispensable, this approach frequently leaves organizations susceptible to zero-day exploits, sophisticated social engineering, and advanced persistent threats (APTs) that may remain undetected until significant damage has been inflicted.

9.1.2 The imperative of proactive risk identification

Proactive risk identification and mitigation aim to anticipate and neutralize threats before they materialize [1]. This encompasses practices such as routine vulnerability assessments, comprehensive security audits, threat hunting, and simulated attack exercises that replicate real-world adversary TTPs. The objective is to uncover and remediate weaknesses within systems, applications, or human behaviours pre-emptively. This strategic mindset underpins cyber resilience [2], enabling organizations not only to recover from attacks but also to actively diminish their likelihood and impact.

One of the most efficacious proactive techniques is red teaming [3], where ethical hackers simulate adversarial campaigns to rigorously test defensive capabilities. These exercises expose vulnerabilities in both technical infrastructure and human workflows – for example, bypassing multi-factor authentication (MFA) or conducting credential theft via phishing. While valuable, traditional red teaming is limited by labour intensiveness, high cost, and narrow scope, as it depends heavily on human expertise.

DOI: 10.1201/9781003644231-13

9.1.3 The transformative potential of GenAI

This is precisely where generative AI (GenAI) emerges as a disruptive enabler of proactive defence. GenAI encompasses a class of AI models capable of synthesizing novel content – including text, code, and multi-stage simulations – based on intricate patterns learned from extensive datasets. Large language models (LLMs) such as GPT-4 [4], Claude [5], LLaMA [6], and Gemini [7] can generate semantically coherent, contextually rich narratives, while code-generation models like Codex can translate natural language instructions into functional exploit scripts.

In cybersecurity, GenAI can effectively think like an attacker by autonomously producing realistic phishing campaigns, malicious payloads, or elaborate multi-stage attack sequences. For instance, an LLM might craft a spear-phishing email tailored to internal communication styles, while a code generator develops exploits for known vulnerabilities, and a scenario builder simulates lateral movement and privilege escalation across a network.

This capacity enables defenders to scale red team operations, probe a broader range of attack vectors, and uncover vulnerabilities that may evade conventional detection. By automating the generation of realistic adversarial scenarios, GenAI transforms red teaming from a manual, episodic process into a continuous, scalable capability for testing and strengthening defences.

To translate this disruptive potential into a structured foundation for research and practice, this chapter introduces the *GEPARD* framework – *GenAI-Enabled Proactive Adaptive Resilient Defence* as its core contribution. *GEPARD* provides a blueprint for systematically embedding GenAI capabilities into proactive cybersecurity. It emphasises *threat fidelity*, where GenAI models generate realistic adversarial TTPs to test defences against diverse attack surfaces. It incorporates *adaptive learning*, embedding feedback loops that enable defences to evolve in response to newly generated threats. It advances *operational integration*, ensuring that GenAI-driven insights align with Security Operations Centre (SOC) pipelines, cyber ranges, and automation workflows. Finally, it underscores *oversight and governance*, recognizing the dual-use risks of GenAI, ethical considerations and the need for safeguards in deployment.

Before presenting this framework, however, it is necessary to ground its relevance by first examining the limitations of traditional red-teaming practices and the specific opportunities GenAI creates to overcome them. The next section undertakes this diagnostic task, establishing the foundation upon which *GEPARD* is subsequently developed.

9.2 LIMITATIONS OF TRADITIONAL RED TEAMING AND OPPORTUNITIES FOR GENAI

Red teaming has traditionally served as a key approach to proactive cybersecurity. Ethical hackers, often referred to as the "red team," replicate the TTPs [1] of real adversaries to identify system weaknesses before they can be exploited. While this practice has provided valuable insights, it faces persistent limitations in the context of today's complex, fast-changing digital ecosystems. These limitations create structural bottlenecks that reduce effectiveness and demand alternative approaches [8–10].

Research on GenAI has already shown its utility for simulating network traffic [11], generating polymorphic malware [12], and adapting traditional red-teaming principles to modern contexts [13]. However, before such opportunities can be systematically utilized, it is essential to diagnose the inherent constraints of traditional methods. Four key bottlenecks are evident.

9.2.1 Expertise bottleneck

Red teaming relies on highly skilled professionals with expertise in areas such as malware development, operating systems, cloud platforms, and social engineering. Such talent is scarce and costly to develop. Designing a targeted phishing campaign for senior executives, for instance, requires hours of research into company-specific contexts, communication styles, and industry events. This dependency on manual creativity restricts both speed and scale of exercises.

9.2.2 Scalability constraints

Exercises are often confined to a limited number of attack paths or systems because of time and resource constraints. Multi-stage attacks, such as those starting with supply chain compromise and culminating in cloud-based data exfiltration, frequently exceed team capacity. As organizations expand into hybrid and distributed infrastructures, the inability to scale simulations across such environments leaves critical gaps untested.

9.2.3 Predictability and limited novelty

Repeated use of similar attack playbooks creates predictability. Once defenders recognize the signatures of a scenario – such as repeated malware artefacts or familiar phishing templates – the realism and training value diminish [14]. This "playbook effect" reduces novelty, making traditional simulations less effective in preparing for evolving attacker techniques.

9.2.4 Cost and time inefficiencies

Comprehensive red-teaming exercises require significant financial and temporal investment. Beyond professional costs, teams must build isolated testbeds, coordinate logistics, and conduct post-exercise analysis. For many organizations, a single engagement can take weeks and cost several lakhs of rupees, restricting such activities to annual or biannual cycles. This frequency is inadequate given the dynamic nature of modern threats.

9.2.5 Opportunities for GenAI

GenAI offers targeted capabilities to address these bottlenecks. Automated content creation can reduce dependence on scarce expertise, scenario generation can scale across complex infrastructures, adaptive models can introduce unpredictability, and automation can lower both costs and cycle times.

Table 9.1 summarizes how GenAI's specific capabilities align with and mitigate the core limitations of traditional red teaming.

9.2.6 Towards a structured framework

The analysis shows that GenAI capabilities can directly address long-standing limitations in expertise, scalability, predictability, and cost. Yet, without a structured model, these

Table 9.1 Traditional Red Teaming vs. GenAI-Enabled Red Teaming

Dimension	*Traditional Red Teaming*	*GenAI-Enabled Red Teaming*
Threat Simulation	Limited to human-crafted scenarios, restricted in diversity and scope.	AI-driven generation of diverse, novel, and adaptive attack scenarios covering wider threat surfaces.
Automation	Manual design and execution of attacks; dependent on team size and expertise.	Automated script generation, payload deployment, and adversarial behaviour modelling.
Realism and Unpredictability	Exercises become predictable after repetition ("playbook effect").	Continuous generation of unpredictable attack patterns, mimicking real-world adversaries.
Defence Integration	Conducted occasionally with high costs; limited feedback loops.	Frequent, cost-effective, and iterative assessments with AI-generated reports and continuous validation.
Expertise Requirement	Requires rare, highly skilled professionals across multiple domains.	Reduces dependency on scarce expertise through scalable GenAI augmentation.
Cost and Time	High expenditure and long cycles; typically, annual or biannual exercises.	Lower costs through automation; supports continuous or on-demand red teaming.
Scalability	Difficult to extend across hybrid and distributed infrastructures.	Scales seamlessly across cloud, on-premises, and multi-domain environments.

benefits risk remaining fragmented. There is therefore a need for a systematic framework that organizes and integrates GenAI-enabled methods into proactive cybersecurity practices. The next section introduces the *GEPARD* framework, which builds on these insights and provides a layered approach for next-generation cyber defence.

9.3 THE GEPARD FRAMEWORK

While the previous section highlights the transformative potential of GenAI in red teaming, the challenge remains to systematically organize these capabilities into a structured model that researchers and practitioners can adopt. To this end, this section introduces the *GEPARD Framework* – a foundational blueprint that positions GenAI as the central enabler of proactive cyber defence.

The framework is built around four integrative pillars, each capturing a core dimension of GenAI-driven defence:

1 **Threat Fidelity** – harnessing LLMs, code generation systems, and multi-agent scenario builders to simulate and replicate adversarial TTPs with unprecedented realism.
2 **Adaptive Learning** – embedding continuous feedback loops so that simulated attack outcomes directly refine defensive strategies, policies, and detection capabilities.
3 **Operational Integration** – aligning GenAI-powered simulations with real-world cyber operations, including SOC automation pipelines, breach and attack simulation (BAS), and cyber range training.
4 **Oversignt and Governance** – ensuring responsible use of dual-use technologies through oversight, regulatory compliance, and alignment with responsible AI principles.

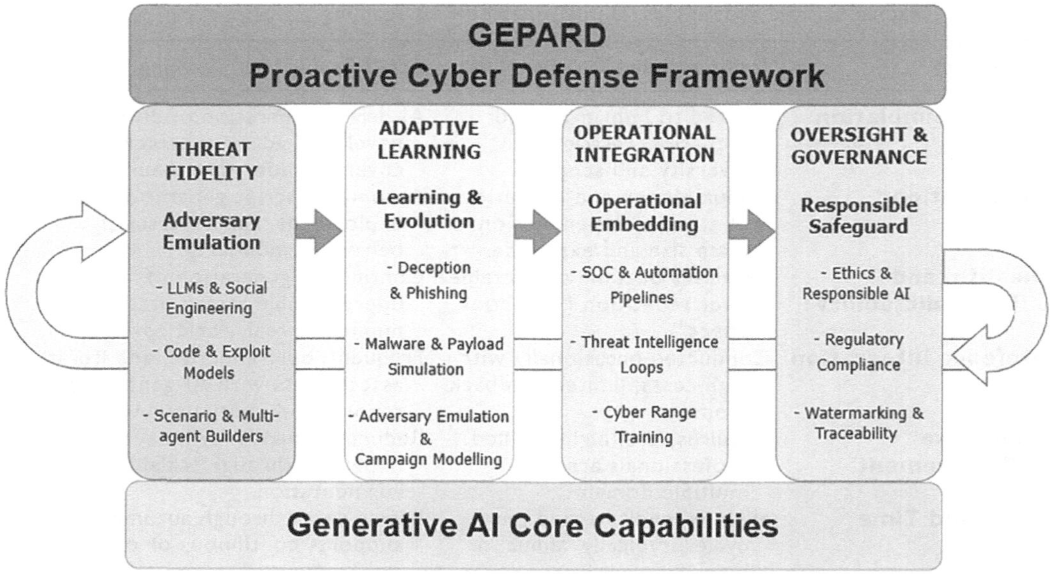

Figure 9.1 GEPARD – A Four-Pillar Conceptual Framework for GenAI-Enabled Proactive Adaptive Resilient Defence.

Figure 9.1 illustrates the *GEPARD* framework. GenAI capabilities drive each pillar, the four pillars collectively shape proactive cyber defence practices. Adaptive learning and a continuous feedback loop ensure resilience against evolving threats.

By framing GenAI-enabled red teaming and threat simulation within this blueprint, GEPARD provides both a conceptual foundation for academic inquiry and a practical guide for operational adoption. The following sections unpack each pillar in detail, demonstrating how *GEPARD* translates GenAI's disruptive potential into a coherent defence paradigm.

9.3.1 Threat fidelity (pillar-1)

Traditional red teaming often struggles to produce realistic and varied adversary behaviour at scale. GenAI addresses this shortfall by automating the creation of high-fidelity attack scenarios that combine social engineering, code execution, and strategic planning. Threat fidelity refers to the degree to which simulated attacks resemble real adversaries in motive, method, and effect. High threat fidelity increases the utility of red-team exercises by revealing realistic detection and response gaps. This pillar examines three classes of GenAI architectures that collectively enable such fidelity: LLMs, code generation models, and probabilistic/multi-agent scenario builders. When integrated, these components permit automated, adaptive, and lifelike attack simulations.

9.3.1.1 LLMs for social engineering

LLMs are trained on extensive text corpora and can generate context-aware, fluent natural language. Models such as GPT-4 [4], Claude [5], and LLaMA [6] demonstrate strong capabilities in producing human-like text and maintaining conversational context. In the domain of red teaming, two capabilities are particularly important.

Phishing Narrative Generation: Phishing succeeds by exploiting human psychology rather than technical flaws. Traditionally, crafting convincing phishing messages requires manual research and creative effort. LLMs can automate this task by producing personalized narratives that mimic organizational tone, reference specific events or departments, and include believable calls to action. For instance, an LLM may draft an email that appears to come from the HR team, mentions a recent internal announcement, addresses the recipient by name, and contains a link to a simulated portal. What earlier took hours of human effort can now be generated in seconds and deployed across many simulated targets.

Dialogue Simulation: Modern social-engineering attacks increasingly rely on multi-turn interactions, for example in business email compromise (BEC) or fraudulent messaging [15]. LLMs can simulate dynamic conversations and adapt responses in real time to defender actions. During training exercises, an LLM can hold a realistic chat with a participant on a simulated platform, adjusting its replies based on the flow of the interaction. This capability supports realistic behavioural testing and helps assess human responses under social-engineering pressure [16, 17].

9.3.1.2 Code generation models for exploit and payload creation

Generative models trained on source code – such as Codex [18], CodeGen [19], or CodeParrot [20] – translate natural language prompts into executable code. These models assist red teams in automating exploit scripting and producing varied payloads, thereby increasing the technical realism of simulations.

Exploit Scripting: Red teams commonly develop custom scripts to demonstrate proof-of-concept (PoC) exploits for known vulnerabilities. Code generation models can accelerate this process by generating scripts from textual vulnerability descriptions, for example entries in the CVE database [21]. A model can produce a Python or PowerShell script that demonstrates path traversal or remote code execution, which can then be incorporated into a simulated attack chain for testing detection and mitigation controls.

Polymorphic Payloads: Polymorphic malware modifies its appearance across instances to evade signature-based detectors [22]. Generative code models can simulate polymorphism by producing functionally equivalent payload variants with differing structure and obfuscation. In simulation, each run can yield a slightly different script variant, enabling evaluation of how well detection systems cope with code diversity rather than fixed signatures.

9.3.1.3 Probabilistic and multi-agent scenario builders

Beyond content generation, realistic threat emulation requires strategic modelling of attacker behaviour over time. Probabilistic models, attack graphs, and multi-agent architectures simulate how attackers plan, move, and adapt across a target environment.

Attack Path Generation: Attack graphs represent possible sequences an adversary may use to reach critical assets. When combined with stochastic models, these graphs enable the generation of diverse intrusion sequences. For example, a simulated campaign might start with a phishing message, proceed to lateral movement via SMB (Server Message Block), escalate privileges by token theft, and finally exfiltrate data through a cloud storage service. Probabilistic variation can alter tools, timing, and order in each run, which expands the set of tested detection scenarios.

Multi-Agent Emulation: Advanced simulations assign distinct roles to multiple GenAI agents – such as initial access, reconnaissance, lateral movement, and exfiltration – and coordinate them via an orchestrator. Each agent focuses on a subtask and communicates results to other agents, thereby mimicking coordinated adversary activity similar to APT groups. For instance, one agent may generate tailored phishing content while another scans for open ports and a third prepares encrypted exfiltration payloads. Such orchestration reproduces team-based adversarial tactics and enables complex, realistic red-team campaigns.

By integrating LLMs, code generation models, and probabilistic/multi-agent builders, the Threat Fidelity pillar enables fully automated, lifelike attack simulations. These simulations broaden the scope and depth of red-team exercises and help identify practical detection and response gaps. The next section discusses how these architectural components are applied in concrete red-teaming use cases, including automated phishing campaigns, polymorphic payload deployment, and adversary emulation mapped to the MITRE ATT&CK framework [3, 23].

9.3.2 Adaptive learning (pillar-2)

Building on the GenAI architectures described in the previous section, this pillar examines how generative models enable adaptive and continuously improving red-team simulations. The technical models are important, but their practical value arises from deployment patterns that reproduce complex adversary behaviour, learn from outcomes, and refine subsequent simulations. Adaptive learning thus refers to mechanisms that allow simulated attacks and defensive responses to co-evolve over time, improving both realism and defensive preparedness.

9.3.2.1 Automated phishing and spear-phishing campaigns

Phishing remains a primary vector for initial access. Spear-phishing targets specific individuals by exploiting contextual information. Traditionally, preparing targeted messages requires manual research and creative effort. GenAI automates much of this workflow and increases the rate and variety of simulations.

Data-Driven Target Profiling: GenAI systems can assimilate publicly available data – such as organizational charts, employee biographies, and social media traces – to create contextual profiles for targets. Using these profiles, LLMs generate personalized phishing text that reflects role, tone, and recent organizational events. For example, a model can draft an email impersonating the finance head, referencing a real project deadline, and including a plausible call to action. By combining threat-intelligence signals with contextual profiling, such systems produce highly realistic spear-phishing vectors that improve the fidelity of social-engineering tests [21].

Watering-Hole Simulation: Watering-hole attacks compromise websites frequented by a target group [24]. GenAI can generate convincing replica pages and inject benign-looking scripts that simulate drive-by payload delivery. A simulated internal portal or event page can thus test browser protections, URL filtering, and user response to credential prompts. These simulated sites help evaluate both technical controls and user behaviour.

By generating phishing content that evolves with contextual data, these simulations ensure that training exercises remain fresh and adaptive, reflecting how real attackers continuously change their tactics.

9.3.2.2 Polymorphic malware and Payload delivery

Evasion of signature-based detection is a core objective for many attackers. Polymorphic payloads change code appearance while preserving functionality. Generative models make it feasible to create such variants rapidly and at scale.

Obfuscation Techniques: Generative code models can produce multiple variants of the same payload by applying different obfuscation strategies – such as encoding, dynamic variable naming, or insertion of no-op instructions – while maintaining the payload's intent [22]. A PowerShell or Python loader, for instance, can be generated in distinct forms across simulation runs, enabling evaluation of detection systems that must rely on behavioural indicators rather than fixed signatures.

Delivery Vector Diversity: Delivery methods also affect detection and response. GenAI can simulate varied delivery channels, including macro-enabled documents, cloud-hosted links, USB-based dropper scenarios, and socially engineered attachments. Each vector can be tailored to common user practices within the target organization, allowing comprehensive testing of endpoint protection, mail gateways, and user awareness controls.

The ability to vary payload structure and delivery vectors across runs makes polymorphic simulations inherently adaptive, forcing defenders to refine detection strategies beyond static signatures.

9.3.2.3 Adversary emulation for APTs

APTs operate as long-running, carefully planned campaigns. Emulating such actors requires modelling multi-stage behaviour, dwell time, and tactical adjustments. GenAI supports these requirements by generating dynamic attack chains and by introducing stochastic timing and activity patterns.

TTP Mapping to MITRE ATT&CK: The MITRE ATT&CK framework [3, 23] provides a structured vocabulary for adversary tactics and techniques. GenAI can be instructed to compose attack sequences that align with specific ATT&CK techniques – for example, combining spear-phishing for Initial Access with credential dumping for Lateral Movement and cloud exfiltration for Exfiltration. Such mapping ensures that simulated campaigns are relevant to established detection taxonomies and helps assess coverage across known TTPs.

Long-Running Campaign Simulation: Real APTs often act intermittently to avoid detection. Generative scenario engines can model dwell time, intermittent communication with command servers, and adaptive pacing to mimic stealthy behaviour. For example, an agent may perform reconnaissance during off-peak hours, pause activity for several days, and then resume only when conditions appear favourable. These temporal behaviours test the capacity of monitoring systems and analyst workflows to detect slow, low-volume anomalies.

Through variations in timing, sequence, and stealth tactics, APT emulations gain an adaptive quality, helping defenders prepare for campaigns that evolve over weeks or months.

9.3.2.4 Feedback loops and model updating

Adaptive learning depends on closed-loop processes. Simulated attack outcomes – such as detection alerts, successful mitigations, or missed events – should feed back into model prompts, scenario parameters, and detection rules. Automated report generation, labelled telemetry, and post-exercise analytics enable retraining of models and refinement of future simulations. Over successive iterations, this loop improves scenario diversity, reduces false positives, and aligns simulated threats with real observed adversary evolution.

By automating profiling, payload variation, and long-duration campaign simulation, the Adaptive Learning pillar expands the scope and cadence of red-team exercises. These capabilities help organizations identify latent weaknesses and continuously harden detection and response measures. The following section presents a case study that demonstrates how adaptive simulations combine with threat fidelity to produce realistic, repeatable assessments on cloud infrastructure.

9.3.3 Operational integration (pillar-3)

After exploring the architectural foundations, applications, and ethical concerns of GenAI-powered threat simulation, the next step is operational integration. For GenAI to deliver real value, it must move beyond conceptual design and become part of the everyday work of cybersecurity professionals. This means embedding it into SOCs, cyber ranges, and incident response pipelines so that simulations and defensive measures become continuous and actionable rather than episodic.

This section discusses how GenAI can be operationalized to automate threat emulation, improve situational awareness, and strengthen training and preparedness for human defenders.

9.3.3.1 SOC and automation pipelines

The SOC serves as the core of enterprise cybersecurity. Here, analysts monitor, detect, and respond to threats in real time. Traditionally, red-teaming exercises have been episodic – conducted quarterly or annually as separate activities. With GenAI, this practice can shift towards continuous, automated, and context-sensitive simulation that directly integrates with SOC workflows and CI/CD pipelines.

Continuous BAS: GenAI makes it possible to embed scenario generation into security validation processes. For example, a GenAI agent can automatically simulate phishing attempts, privilege escalation attacks, or lateral movement every week, tailored to the current production environment. These simulations can be tested against Endpoint Detection and Response (EDR), Security Information and Event Management (SIEM), or Extended Detection and Response (XDR) systems. Reports generated from these exercises identify which defences worked, which failed, and which anomalies went unnoticed. This transforms security assessment from a one-time activity into a model of continuous validation, ensuring defences adapt to evolving adversary tactics.

Threat Intelligence Feedback Loop: For red teaming with GenAI to remain effective, models must be regularly updated with the latest threat intelligence. This involves ingesting data on emerging TTPs [1, 25] from sources such as MITRE ATT&CK [3, 23], US-CERT advisories, and commercial threat feeds. For instance, if reports highlight a surge in QR-code phishing campaigns, the GenAI system can adjust by generating QR-based phishing scenarios in subsequent simulations. This feedback loop aligns simulations with the evolving threat landscape, preparing defenders for future risks rather than only known attacks.

9.3.3.2 Cyber range training

Cyber ranges [26] provide controlled environments to simulate attacks for the purpose of training cybersecurity professionals. These can take the form of virtual labs, gamified platforms, or large-scale simulated enterprise networks. By integrating GenAI into cyber ranges, training exercises can become more adaptive, realistic, and scalable for both red teams and blue teams.

Dynamic Exercise Generation: One common limitation in training is scenario fatigue – when repetitive exposure to the same exercises reduces learning outcomes. GenAI can overcome this by generating new scenarios dynamically each time. For beginners, it may create simpler phishing or malware attacks, while for advanced analysts, it can simulate polymorphic ransomware, supply chain compromises, or multi-cloud lateral movement. By adapting the complexity of exercises to participant performance, GenAI enables personalized and progressive training.

Red vs. Blue Team War-Games: In traditional training, instructors often act as red teamers, limiting their ability to mentor participants. With GenAI, red team tasks can be delegated to AI agents. This allows instructors to focus on observing defender responses, providing feedback, and improving team coordination. For example, a GenAI-driven red team could simulate a phishing-led intrusion followed by credential theft and exfiltration, while the human blue team works in real time to detect and contain the attack. Performance indicators such as detection speed, response accuracy, and coordination effectiveness can then be measured, helping teams improve through targeted feedback.

By embedding GenAI into SOC operations and cyber range training, organizations can achieve continuous and adaptive exposure to adversarial tactics. This not only strengthens defensive resilience but also improves human skill development and accelerates the maturity of security programs.

The next section turns to the critical issue of oversight and governance, examining how GenAI's use in cybersecurity can be guided by ethical safeguards, regulatory compliance, and responsible operational practices to ensure its safe and effective deployment in the years to come.

9.3.4 Oversight and governance (pillar-4)

While GenAI offers transformative possibilities for cybersecurity, especially in red teaming and threat simulation, it also raises important concerns about responsible use. The same models that enable defenders to simulate sophisticated adversary behaviour can also be exploited by malicious actors to launch real-world attacks. This dual-use nature makes it essential to place GenAI within strong ethical, legal, and governance frameworks. Without proper safeguards, the risks of misuse may outweigh the intended benefits.

This section examines the dual-use dilemma, discusses access control and traceability measures, and highlights governance frameworks that can ensure safe, lawful, and ethical application of GenAI in cybersecurity.

9.3.4.1 The dual-use dilemma

Risk of Misuse: Generative models that can craft phishing emails, malware, or adversarial simulations may be repurposed by attackers. A model originally designed for red teaming could be abused to automate large-scale spear-phishing campaigns or generate exploit scripts for live vulnerabilities. For example, a threat actor with access to a fine-tuned LLM could create tailored spear-phishing campaigns for multiple organizations by scraping data from LinkedIn and other open sources. The precision and scale of such operations would far exceed what is possible manually. This risk is not theoretical, as there are already reports of LLMs being used to assist in writing malware and generating scam messages. Prior studies have already highlighted how language models can be repurposed for malicious ends, including generating harmful content and assisting in the design of cyberattacks, underscoring the urgent need for governance measures [27].

Access Controls: To reduce such misuse, GenAI-powered red teaming platforms must adopt strict access management. This includes role-based access so that only trained and authorized professionals can use advanced features, logging of all activity for audit purposes, and approval workflows for sensitive scenarios such as exploit generation or large-scale simulations. For example, exploit generation features may be restricted to certified testers, with additional peer review required before executing high-risk simulations. Research on model-driven governance demonstrates how access restrictions and accountability mechanisms can be systematically embedded into AI-driven platforms, ensuring that sensitive capabilities are only available to authorized users [28].

Watermarking and Traceability. To distinguish authorized from malicious use, watermarking techniques can be applied to generated outputs. These may include hidden cryptographic markers, metadata, or stylistic signatures embedded in payloads, phishing templates, or adversarial scripts. For instance, a simulated exfiltration file may contain a hidden identifier that proves it was generated by an authorized red team tool. Such measures support forensic investigations, attribution, and compliance audits. Recent work has examined practical approaches to watermarking in GenAI systems, showing how embedded markers can support attribution, auditability, and responsible use in security-sensitive contexts [29].

9.3.4.2 *Governance frameworks*

Responsible AI Principles: Organizations using GenAI in cybersecurity must follow established responsible AI guidelines. These include ensuring transparency by documenting how models are trained and used, accountability through human oversight of high-risk simulations, and fairness by avoiding biased training data that could lead to unethical outcomes. For example, phishing simulations should not use personal characteristics such as ethnicity, gender, or age as inputs for targeting.

Regulatory Compliance: Even in controlled red-teaming exercises, data protection regulations may apply if personal or employee data is processed. Frameworks such as GDPR in the EU [30], CCPA in California [31], and India's Digital Personal Data Protection Act (DPDP) [32] mandate clear rules around consent, data minimization, and explanation rights. For instance, if GenAI generates phishing messages based on real employee job roles or recent activity, such use must be legally justified and disclosed.

Ethics Review Boards: In academic, defence, and industrial research contexts, oversight by independent ethics committees is important. These boards can assess potential risks, define limits on adversarial content generation, and review the purpose and safeguards of each project. This ensures that experimentation with GenAI-based red teaming does not inadvertently create tools that can be misused if released without controls.

Oversight and governance are therefore not optional but essential pillars of GenAI adoption in cybersecurity. The challenge lies in balancing innovation with safety – promoting advanced research and defensive capabilities while preventing abuse. This balance is similar to long-standing debates around dual-use technologies in biotechnology or cryptography, where community-driven norms and safeguards are critical.

9.4 GEPARD IN ACTION – A CASE STUDY

This section illustrates the practical application of the *GEPARD* framework through a case study of a GenAI-driven red team engagement against a modern enterprise cloud environment. By integrating multiple GenAI capabilities – LLMs, code generators, diffusion-style payload creators, and multi-agent orchestrators – the simulated attack mirrors the tactics of APT groups. The objective is to emulate a realistic reconnaissance-to-exfiltration campaign across a hybrid infrastructure, uncover detection gaps, and evaluate the incident response readiness of the SOC [33]. Aligned with the four pillars of *GEPARD*, this case study demonstrates how threat fidelity, adaptive learning, operational integration, and governance safeguards can be operationalized in practice to strengthen defensive resilience.

9.4.1 Scenario overview

The target organization is a mid-sized financial services company operating a hybrid-cloud infrastructure. Their environment includes Kubernetes clusters for containerized microservices, CI/CD pipelines (like Jenkins and GitLab CI) for automated deployment, and S3-compatible object storage used for analytics and backups. Standard security controls are also in place, such as endpoint protection, IAM roles, and a SIEM system.

The red team's objective, powered by GenAI, is to simulate a multi-stage attack – starting with external reconnaissance and ending in sensitive data exfiltration – without using any prewritten scripts. The entire sequence is autonomously generated by GenAI models in response to high-level task descriptions.

9.4.2 Attack sequence generated by GenAI

Reconnaissance: The campaign begins with passive information gathering. An LLM is prompted to extract intelligence from publicly available sources such as the company's website and news releases, employee LinkedIn profiles and GitHub activity, as well as microblog platforms and tech conference speaker listings.

The model compiles a list of public IP address ranges, internal subdomain patterns (*e.g., dev-api.company.com*), and employee identities (*e.g., DevOps engineers and cloud architects*).

Using this information, the model generates a target map of potential attack vectors, prioritizing services exposed via misconfigured DevOps components.

Initial Access: Next, the GenAI system simulates exploitation of a misconfigured CI/CD pipeline. Based on its understanding of YAML-based pipeline definitions, a code generation model creates a malicious YAML job that injects a reverse shell into the build process.

The job leverages a hardcoded credential – accidentally committed to a public GitHub repository by a junior developer – which allows the attacker to authenticate and execute the job remotely. The reverse shell opens a secure channel back to the attacker's cloud-based command-and-control (C2) server.

This stage highlights the risks of developer missteps and misconfigurations, which are common in fast-moving DevOps environments.

Lateral Movement: Once inside, the attack pivots through the environment using credentials harvested from environment variables, shell history, and IAM tokens.

A multi-agent GenAI module generates context-specific commands using the gcloud CLI to list compute instances, query IAM roles, and access metadata endpoints. These commands are syntactically varied with each simulation run to test detection systems' flexibility.

The attacker locates a Kubernetes service account token with elevated permissions and uses it to gain access to internal APIs.

Privilege Escalation: To simulate privilege escalation, the LLM identifies that the container runtime in one of the Kubernetes nodes is running an outdated version of *containerd*. Based on a vulnerability advisory released a few months prior, the model generates a zero-day-style exploit skeleton – mimicking behaviour without deploying real malware.

The exploit enables escape from the container to the host system, giving root-level access to the underlying virtual machine. From here, the attacker gains access to an NFS-mounted storage volume containing sensitive financial documents and customer transaction data.

Exfiltration: For exfiltration, a diffusion-inspired GenAI model constructs payloads disguised as image files. The sensitive data is embedded using steganography and uploaded to a legitimate image hosting CDN via HTTPS, thus bypassing outbound traffic monitoring.

Each file is uniquely named and timestamped to resemble output from internal dashboard tools, minimizing suspicion.

The entire process – from command execution to data packaging – is logged and replayed in the test environment, allowing the SOC to assess real-time response capability.

A summary of the major steps involved in the GenAI-generated cyberattack sequence is presented in Table 9.2.

Table 9.2 GenAI-Generated Cyberattack Sequence

Attack Stage	*Description*	*GenAI Capability Used*	*Example Output*
Reconnaissance	Extract public information: IPs, subdomains, employee data	LLM for OSINT analysis	Target map from LinkedIn profiles and subdomain patterns
Initial Access	Exploit misconfigured CI/CD pipeline via YAML injection	Code generation model (e.g., Codex)	Malicious YAML job triggering a reverse shell
Lateral Movement	Move through cloud infrastructure using compromised credentials	Multi-agent GenAI + CLI command synthesis	On-the-fly gcloud commands for resource listing and privilege probing
Privilege Escalation	Exploit outdated container runtime for host access	LLM-generated zero-day exploit skeleton	Escaping containerd sandbox for root VM access
Exfiltration	Extract data using obfuscated methods (e.g., steganography in image files)	Diffusion-style model for polymorphic payload generation	Sensitive files hidden in images uploaded to a public content delivery network (CDN)

9.4.3 Defender response and remediation

The GenAI-driven red team exercise revealed multiple detection and response gaps, prompting immediate improvements across policy, tooling, and training.

- Detection Gaps Identified
  - The SIEM failed to detect subtle anomalies in CI pipeline executions, such as new YAML job creation from an external IP.
  - No alerts were triggered by unusual gcloud CLI activity despite access to privileged APIs.
- Policy and Configuration Updates
  - CI/CD pipelines were hardened by enforcing static analysis and secret scanning on YAML files.
  - IAM role permissions were restricted, and anomalous cloud API usage now triggers alerts.
  - Container runtime versions are now monitored centrally and patched automatically.
- Training Outcomes
  - SOC analysts received simulated alerts from the attack logs and practiced triage using GenAI-generated PCAPs and system logs.
  - A blue-team tabletop exercise was conducted using the same attack sequence, helping defenders improve lateral movement detection techniques and response coordination.

Table 9.3 summarizes the key steps involved in defender response and remediation.

In summary, this case study shows that GenAI can generate adaptive, scalable, and deeply contextual cyberattack simulations that move far beyond scripted engagements. By dynamically adjusting attack vectors, incorporating threat intelligence, and exposing defenders to novel tactics, the exercise reflects the core principles of the *GEPARD* framework. It demonstrates that when properly embedded into SOC workflows and training programs, GenAI not only enhances threat realism and defence evaluation but also establishes a structured path towards proactive, resilient, and ethically governed cybersecurity.

Table 9.3 Defender Response and Remediation Summary

Category	*Issue Identified*	*Remediation Action Taken*
Detection Gaps	SIEM missed anomalous CI/CD activity and unusual cloud API usage	Improved pipeline monitoring; introduced anomaly-based detection for cloud APIs
Policy Updates	Over-permissive IAM roles, weak CI pipeline validation	Hardened YAML parsing, enforced secret scanning, and tightened IAM permissions
Training Outcomes	SOC lacked experience with novel attack patterns and steganographic payloads	Simulated alert drills with GenAI-generated PCAPs, logs, and hands-on triage exercises

9.5 FUTURE RESEARCH DIRECTIONS WITH GEPARD

As GenAI becomes embedded in cybersecurity operations, new opportunities are emerging at the intersection of machine learning, offensive simulation, and human oversight. The current applications – automating phishing, crafting polymorphic payloads, and emulating advanced threats – represent only an initial step. Future progress will depend on making GenAI-driven systems more adaptive, explainable, controllable, and multimodal. Within the *GEPARD* framework, these advances will strengthen threat fidelity, deepen adaptive learning, enable smoother operational integration, and reinforce governance and oversight.

9.5.1 Reinforcement learning for threat emulation

Current GenAI systems generate attack sequences based largely on static prompts. Reinforcement learning (RL) offers the possibility of continuous improvement, where agents learn through trial, error, and feedback within simulated environments. For example, an RL-powered agent could simulate living-off-the-land (LOTL) attacks, discovering which native tools – such as PowerShell or WMI – are less likely to trigger alerts in a SOC. Over time, the agent would evolve stealthier strategies, reflecting how real adversaries adapt to detection mechanisms.

Such research directly supports adaptive learning in the *GEPARD* framework, enabling defenders to train against AI-driven adversaries that become progressively more capable. This would create self-improving cyber ranges where security teams face adversaries that continually refine their tactics.

9.5.2 Explainable generative attacks

A major challenge with GenAI-enabled red teaming is the lack of transparency in why particular attack simulations succeed or fail. As article [34] highlights, explainable AI (XAI) is essential for trust and interpretability in security operations. Security teams need to know, for example, which phrases in a phishing message caused engagement, why a generated payload bypassed intrusion prevention, or which IAM misconfigurations allowed privilege escalation. XAI techniques [35] can provide such insights through post-hoc explanations.

Embedding explainability into GenAI-driven red teaming strengthens threat fidelity and oversight, ensuring simulations not only replicate adversary behaviour but also clarify underlying system weaknesses. This makes remediation more systematic and empowers human analysts to act on interpretable findings.

9.5.3 Human-in-the-loop alignment

As GenAI systems grow more autonomous, aligning them with human intent and safety policies becomes critical. Human-in-the-loop (HITL) approaches [36] allow experts to supervise and constrain GenAI outputs during scenario generation. For example, red teamers may approve or reject phishing templates, steer exploit generation towards safe PoCs or embed sector-specific knowledge for healthcare or finance simulations.

This hybrid model ensures that automation remains under human oversight, aligning with governance and operational integration in the *GEPARD* framework. HITL integration helps ensure simulations remain effective yet controllable, particularly in regulated or high-stakes environments.

9.5.4 Cross-model embedding fusion

Most GenAI models today remain modality-specific – language for phishing (LLMs), code for exploits, or images for diffusion models. Yet real-world cyberattacks often span across modalities and systems, especially in cyber-physical domains [37]. Future research may explore cross-modal embedding fusion, where embeddings from language, vision, and code models are combined into a unified threat simulation.

For example, a multimodal attack could integrate a vision model detecting CCTV anomalies, an LLM generating spear-phishing content for administrators, a code model exploiting firmware in IoT devices, and a diffusion model generating synthetic QR codes. This type of fusion would expand threat fidelity by enabling end-to-end simulation of blended attacks in smart cities, ICS, or connected healthcare systems.

9.5.5 Multi-agent defence ecosystems

A natural extension of GenAI in proactive cyber defence is the development of multi-agent defence ecosystems, where multiple AI agents collaborate to simulate, detect, and respond to adversarial behaviours. Unlike traditional monolithic security systems, these ecosystems are distributed, modular, and adaptive, enabling organizations to build layered defence capabilities that evolve alongside emerging threats.

In such ecosystems, specialized agents can be designed for distinct roles. For example, one agent may focus on threat emulation, generating phishing narratives or polymorphic malware; another may act as a detection agent, monitoring system logs for anomalies; a third could function as a policy agent, recommending remediation steps or enforcing compliance standards. Coordinated through a central orchestrator, these agents interact in real time, mirroring both the offensive strategies of APTs and the defensive countermeasures of blue teams. This setup aligns with recent advances in multi-agent systems research, where collaborative AI demonstrates higher resilience and problem-solving capability in dynamic environments [38].

Multi-agent ecosystems amplify all four pillars of the *GEPARD* framework. They improve threat fidelity by introducing diverse adversarial behaviours, enable adaptive learning through continuous interaction and self-improvement, support operational integration by embedding agents into SOC workflows, and reinforce governance by allowing oversight mechanisms to be distributed across agents with defined roles and constraints.

Looking ahead, multi-agent defence ecosystems could evolve into autonomous cyber ranges, where red, blue, and even purple team agents interact continuously to stress-test defences. This vision demands further research into agent coordination protocols, safe RL, and ethical guardrails to prevent unintended escalation. By fostering cooperation between human experts and autonomous agents, such ecosystems represent a promising frontier for building resilient, adaptive, and anticipatory cyber defence systems.

These emerging directions – RL, explainability, human alignment, multimodal fusion, and multi-agent defence ecosystem – represent the next phase of GenAI-enabled cyber defence. Within the *GEPARD* framework, they extend the pillars of fidelity, adaptation, integration, and governance, ensuring that red teaming evolves into a more anticipatory, resilient, and ethically grounded discipline. Advancing these directions will require collaboration across AI research, security engineering, human–computer interaction, and cyber law, with *GEPARD* serving as a foundation to guide future work.

9.6 BENCHMARK AND DATASET CONSIDERATIONS

Although GEPARD is proposed as a conceptual and architectural framework, empirical validation remains an essential next step. Current advances in cybersecurity benchmarking reveal an emerging foundation for evaluating generative and adaptive defence systems. Several public datasets now support the assessment of machine-learning and GenAI models across key security domains, providing a potential empirical substrate for future extensions of GEPARD.

For instance, the EMBER dataset [39] offers a large-scale corpus of Windows executable features for malware classification, serving as a robust testbed for evaluating threat-detection capabilities based on static and behavioural attributes. The NYU CTF Bench dataset [40] introduces generative tasks rooted in capture-the-flag (CTF) challenges, enabling the study of LLM-driven offensive reasoning and code synthesis. More recently, CySecBench [41] has been proposed as a domain-specific benchmark containing over twelve thousand cybersecurity-focused prompts designed to evaluate reasoning, tool use, and code generation in LLMs.

While these datasets provide useful starting points, none fully encompass the multimodal, co-evolutionary dynamics envisioned in the adaptive learning pillar of GEPARD – particularly those involving simulated feedback between adversarial and defensive agents. Hence, this work deliberately positions GEPARD as a foundational blueprint, encouraging subsequent research to design benchmark tasks that map to its four pillars:

- **Threat Fidelity:** metrics capturing realism and contextual coherence of simulated attacks.
- **Adaptive Learning:** evaluation of model improvement over successive simulation rounds.
- **Operational Integration:** benchmarks measuring automation latency and SOC pipeline alignment.
- **Oversight and Governance:** compliance, ethical-risk, and explainability metrics.

Future work can adapt these existing datasets and extend them towards multi-agent, cross-modal red-team simulations. Such benchmarking will be essential for quantifying how effectively GEPARD transforms GenAI from a conceptual promise into measurable, operational resilience.

9.7 CONCLUSION

As cyber threats grow in scale and sophistication, the limits of reactive defence have become evident. Proactive strategies, powered by GenAI, represent not just an enhancement but a necessity for modern cybersecurity. This chapter introduced *GEPARD* – a foundational framework that organizes GenAI's emerging capabilities into four interlinked pillars: *threat fidelity, adaptive learning, operational integration*, and *oversight and governance*.

By framing GenAI within *GEPARD*, this work provides a blueprint for four critical areas: achieving lifelike adversarial tactics through threat fidelity simulations; ensuring defences evolve via adaptive learning; embedding GenAI into SOCs and cyber ranges through operational integration; and guaranteeing safe deployment through governance. Together, these dimensions transform GenAI from a set of experimental tools into a structured pathway for resilient, intelligence-driven defence.

The framework is intentionally forward-looking. It highlights opportunities for RL, explainable generative attacks, HITL alignment, and cross-model embedding fusion – directions that can define the next decade of research and practice. At the same time, it cautions that these innovations must advance alongside ethical safeguards, legal compliance, and accountability to manage the dual-use risks inherent in such powerful systems.

In essence, *GEPARD* is more than an academic construct; it is an invitation to the cybersecurity community. It challenges researchers, practitioners, and policymakers to treat GenAI not only as a disruptive technology but also as a catalyst for designing anticipatory, adaptive, and resilient defence ecosystems. Equally important, future research must focus on establishing standardized benchmark datasets and evaluation protocols that can quantitatively assess the fidelity, adaptability, and resilience dimensions proposed in this framework, enabling systematic validation and comparison across GenAI-driven defence systems. If embraced, *GEPARD* can serve as a shared blueprint – guiding innovation, informing policy, and shaping the future of proactive cyber defence in an era where adversaries evolve at machine speed – where GenAI becomes not just a mirror of adversaries, but a shield for defenders.

REFERENCES

[1] Yigit, Yagmur, et al. "Review of generative AI methods in cybersecurity." *arXiv preprint arXiv:2403.08701* (2024).

[2] Radanliev, Petar, Omar Santos, and Uchenna Daniel Ani. "Generative AI cybersecurity and resilience." *Frontiers in Artificial Intelligence* 8 (2025): 1568360.

[3] Almutairi, Amirah M., Boojoong Kang, and Nawfal AL Hashimy. "Business email compromise: A comprehensive taxonomy for detection and prevention." In *Proceedings of the 2024 7th International Conference on Information Science and Systems*, pp. 49–54. 2024.

[4] California Consumer Privacy Act, Cal. Civ. Code § 1798.100 et seq., enacted June 28, 2018. Available online: https://oag.ca.gov/privacy/ccpa

[5] Blake, Harrison, "*Generative AI in Cyber Security: New Threats and Solutions for Adversarial Attacks.*" 2024, ResearchGate.

[6] Torre, Damiano, et al. "Model driven engineering for data protection and privacy: Application and experience with GDPR." *arXiv preprint arXiv:2007.12046* (2020).

[7] Allen, Joey, Zheng Yang, Matthew Landen, Raghav Bhat, Harsh Grover, Andrew Chang, Yang Ji, Roberto Perdisci, and Wenke Lee, "Mnemosyne: An effective and efficient post-mortem watering hole attack investigation system." In *Proceedings 2020 ACM SIGSAC Conference Computer and Communications Security (CCS)*, 2020.

[8] Metta, Shivani, et al. "Generative AI in cybersecurity." *arXiv preprint arXiv:2405.01674* (2024).

[9] Onwubiko, Cyril, and Karim Ouazzane, "SOTER: A playbook for cybersecurity incident management." *IEEE Transactions on Engineering Management*, 69. 6 (2022): 3771–3791.

[10] Xu, Hanxiang et al.,"Large language models for cyber security: A systematic literature review." *arXiv preprint arXiv:2405.04760* (2024).

[11] Enis, Maxim, and Mark Hopkins. "From llm to nmt: Advancing low-resource machine translation with claude." *arXiv preprint arXiv:2404.13813* (2024).

[12] Touvron, Hugo, et al. "Llama: Open and efficient foundation language models." *arXiv preprint arXiv:2302.13971* (2023).

[13] Regulation (EU) 2016/679 of the European Parliament and of the Council. "On the protection of natural persons with regard to the processing of personal data and on the free movement of such data." *Official Journal of the European Union*, L119/1, 04 May 2016. Available online: https://eur-lex.europa.eu/eli/reg/2016/679/oj/eng

[14] Digital Personal Data Protection Act. Act No. 22 of 2023, Parliament of India, 2023. Available online: www.meity.gov.in/static/uploads/2024/06/2bf1f0e9f04e6fb4f8fef35e82c42aa5.pdf

[15] Chen, Mark. "Evaluating large language models trained on code." *arXiv preprint arXiv:2107.03374* (2021).

[16] Motlagh, Farzad Nourmohammadzadeh, et al. "Large language models in cybersecurity: State-of-the-art." *arXiv preprint arXiv:2402.00891* (2024).

[17] Chakraborty, Anirban, et al. "A survey on adversarial attacks and defences." *CAAI Transactions on Intelligence Technology* 6.1 (2021): 25–45.

[18] Nijkamp, Erik, et al. "Codegen: An open large language model for code with multi-turn program synthesis." *arXiv preprint arXiv:2203.13474* (2022).

[19] Rajkumar, Ragunathan, Insup Lee, Lui Sha, and John Stankovic. "Cyber-physical systems: the next computing revolution." In *Proceedings of the 47th Design Automation Conference*, pp. 731–736. 2010.

[20] Sharma, Swapnil, Nikita Anand, and Kranthi Kiran G V. "Stochastic code generation." *arXiv preprint arXiv:2304.08243* (2023).

[21] Qamar, Sara, Zahid Anwar, Mohammad Ashiqur Rahman, Ehab Al-Shaer, and Bei-Tseng Chu, "Data-driven analytics for cyber-threat intelligence and information sharing." *Computers & Security*, 67 (2017): 35–58.

[22] Achiam, Josh, et al. "Gpt-4 technical report." *arXiv preprint arXiv:2303.08774* (2023).

[23] Yulianto, Semi, et al. "Enhancing cybersecurity resilience through advanced red-teaming exercises and MITRE ATT&CK framework integration: A paradigm shift in cybersecurity assessment." *Cyber Security and Applications* 3 (2025): 100077.

[24] Teo, Zhen Ling,.et al. "Cybersecurity in the generative artificial intelligence era." *Asia-Pacific Journal of Ophthalmology* 13.4 (2024): 100091.

[25] Charan, P. V., et al. "From text to mitre techniques: Exploring the malicious use of large language models for generating cyber attack payloads." *arXiv preprint arXiv:2305.15336* (2023).

[26] Vielberth, Manfred, et al. "Security operations center: A systematic study and open challenges." *IEEE Access* 8 (2020): 227756–227779.

[27] Rijsbosch, Bram, Gijs van Dijck, and Konrad Kollnig. "Adoption of watermarking for generative AI systems in practice and implications under the new EU AI Act." *arXiv e-prints* (2025): arXiv-2503.

[28] Che Mat, Nur Ilzam, et al. "A systematic literature review on advanced persistent threat behaviors and its detection strategy." *Journal of Cybersecurity* 10.1 (2024): tyad023.

[29] Yamin, Muhammad Mudassar, Basel Katt, and Vasileios Gkioulos. "Cyber ranges and security testbeds: Scenarios, functions, tools and architecture." *Computers & Security* 88 (2020): 101636.

[30] Sarker, Iqbal H., et al. "Explainable AI for cybersecurity automation, intelligence and trustworthiness in digital twin: Methods, taxonomy, challenges and prospects." *ICT Express* 10.4 (2024): 935–958.

[31] You, Ilsun, and Kangbin Yim. "Malware obfuscation techniques: A brief survey." In *2010 International Conference on Broadband, Wireless Computing, Communication and Applications*. IEEE, 2010.

[32] Alketbi, Khuloud Saeed, Abid Mehmood, "A comprehensive survey of explainable artificial intelligence techniques for malicious insider threat detection." 13, *IEEE Access*, 2025.

[33] Ring, Markus, Daniel Schlör, Dieter Landes, and Andreas Hotho, "Flow-based network traffic generation using generative adversarial networks." *Computers & Security* 82 (2018): 156–172.

[34] Rigaki, Maria, and Sebasian Garcia, "Bringing a GAN to a Knife-Fight: Adapting Malware Communication to Avoid Detection." In *IEEE Security and Privacy Workshops*, pp. 70–75, 2018.

[35] Sinha, Anusha, et al. "What can generative AI red-teaming learn from cyber red-teaming?." *Software Engineering Institute, Technical Report CMU/SEI-2025-TR-006* (2025).

[36] Team, Gemini, et al. "Gemini: A family of highly capable multimodal models." *arXiv preprint arXiv:2312.11805* (2023).

[37] Hjerppe, Kalle, Jukka Ruohonen, and Ville Leppänen. "The general data protection regulation: Requirements, architectures, and constraints." In *2019 IEEE 27th International Requirements Engineering Conference (RE)*. IEEE, 2019.

[38] Zhang, Dan, Gang Feng, Yang Shi and Dipti Srinivasan, "Physical safety and cyber security Analysis of multi-agent systems: A survey of recent advances." *IEEE/CAA J. Automatica Sinica* 8.2 (2021): 319–333.

[39] Anderson, Hyrum S., and Phil Roth. "Ember: An open dataset for training static pe malware machine learning models." *arXiv preprint arXiv:1804.04637* (2018).

[40] Shao, Minghao et al., "NYU CTF Bench: A Scalable Open-Source Benchmark Dataset for Evaluating LLMs in Offensive Security". In *Proceedings of the 38th Conference on Neural Information Processing Systems (NeurIPS)*, 2024.

[41] Wahréus, Johan, Ahmed Mohamed Hussain, and Panos Papadimitratos. "CySecBench: Generative AI-based cyberSecurity-focused prompt dataset for benchmarking large language models." *arXiv preprint arXiv:2501.01335* (2025).

Part V

Case studies of generative AI in cybersecurity

Chapter 10

Host-based intrusion detection systems developed using ADFA-LD and AWSCTD datasets

Hami Satilmiş and Sedat Akleylek

10.1 INTRODUCTION

With the advancement of technology, computer systems are becoming more complex, and the data traffic between these systems is rapidly increasing. This growing digital interaction is attracting the attention of malicious actors and prompting them to carry out various cyber threats. Attackers are utilizing various techniques to identify vulnerabilities within systems and networks, and different forms of attacks are being executed by exploiting these weaknesses. Attacks such as malware threaten the fundamental principles of data security, including confidentiality, integrity, and availability. In this regard, the early and accurate detection of cyberattacks is considered critically significant to ensure data security.

In an effort to protect data security, various mechanisms focusing on detecting attacks are being developed. Among these mechanisms, intrusion detection systems (IDSs) are constructed to identify potential threats targeting computer infrastructures or networks. Typically integrated into network devices or host machines, these systems continuously monitor activities within their digital environments. Moreover, the data related to the monitored activities are being recorded by the detection systems and processed according to specific analysis techniques [1, 2]. Based on the analyses performed, it is assessed whether the observed activities constitute a cyberattack. IDSs are grouped into two primary classes depending on the source of the observed and processed data: host-based intrusion detection systems (HIDSs) and network-based intrusion detection systems (NIDSs) [2–4].

HIDS is defined as a protection mechanism that aims to ensure system security by monitoring activities on a host. This detection system collects various data types, such as system/API (Application Programming Interfaces) calls and system logs, from the environment in which it functions [5–7]. The collected data are examined through different analysis techniques, and suspicious activities are identified by the HIDS to reveal potential attacks. Such detection systems are divided into two major groups based on their methods of detecting attacks: signature-based HIDSs and anomaly-based HIDSs [8–10].

Signature-based HIDSs use a database containing previously identified attack patterns; newly observed data are compared with these recorded signatures, and potential threats are identified. This approach's primary limitation is its capability to detect only previously known types of attacks. In contrast, anomaly-based HIDSs are enabled to detect unknown attacks by employing statistical evaluation methods or models depending on deep learning (DL) and machine learning (ML). These detection systems undergo a profiling process based on normal system activities and are developed with data samples that conform to these profiles during the training phase [5]. Subsequently, when a newly encountered activity does not conform to the learned profile of normal activities, it is evaluated by the detection

DOI: 10.1201/9781003644231-15

Table 10.1 List of Abbreviations

IDS	Intrusion Detection System	**MI**	Mutual Information
NIDS	Network-Based Intrusion Detection System	**LSTM**	Long Short-Term Memory
HIDS	Host-Based Intrusion Detection System	**TF-IDF**	Term Frequencies and Inverse Document Frequencies
ML	Machine Learning	**NN**	Neural Network
DL	Deep Learning	**GRU**	Gated Recurrent Unit
BoW	Bag-of-Word	**RL**	Reinforcement Learning
IoT	Internet of Things	**F1**	F1-score
ACC	Accuracy	**TP**	True Positive
DT	Decision Tree	**TN**	True Negative
SVM	Support Vector Machine	**FP**	False Positive
NB	Naive Bayes	**FN**	False Negative
CNN	Convolutional Neural Network	**PRC**	Precision
LR	Logistic Regression	**REC**	Recall
RF	Random Forest	**FPR**	False Positive Rate
XGBoost	Extreme Gradient Boosting	**AdaBoost**	Adaptive Boosting
AI	Artificial Intelligence	**GAN**	Generative Adversarial Network
VAE	Variational Autoencoder	**CTGAN**	Conditional Tabular Generative Adversarial Network
GACN	Generative Adversarial Cooperative Network	**CGAN**	Conditional Generative Adversarial Network
CWGAN	Wasserstein Generative Adversarial Network	**DCGAN**	Deep Convolutional Generative Adversarial Network

system as a potential threat or attack action. The abbreviations and their corresponding definitions frequently used in this study are presented in Table 10.1.

10.1.1 Related studies

In Ref. [11], various ML and DL models were designed on the attack-caused Windows OS system calls traces dataset (AWSCTD) [12], which possesses rich content at the host level. In this study, diverse kinds of models, such as one-dimensional convolutional neural network (1D-CNN), gated recurrent unit (GRU), long short-term memory (LSTM), and support vector machines (SVM), were trained using all subsets of the AWSCTD dataset. During the modeling process, one-hot encoding was employed as a preprocessing step. As a result of the experimental analyses conducted on binary classification tasks, the highest performance was demonstrated by the 1D-CNN models. In particular, the 1D-CNN model trained with sequences of length 1000 from theMalwarePlusClean2 subset of the AWSCTD dataset achieved the best results, attaining an accuracy (ACC) rate of 99.30%.

In Ref. [13], a comprehensive evaluation was conducted regarding the applicability of DL models within HIDS systems. Accordingly, seven different DL models based on CNN, LSTM, GRU, and fully convolutional network (FCN) architectures were developed on the AWSCTD dataset. These models were named AWSCTD-CNN-static (AWSCTD-CNN-S), AWSCTD-CNN-dynamic (AWSCTD-CNN-D), AWSCTDCNN-LSTM, AWSCTD-CNN-GRU, FCN, LSTM-FCN, and GRU-FCN, respectively. Following the binary classification experiments, the models exhibiting the highest performance in terms of the ACC were AWSCTD-CNNS and AWSCTD-CNN-D, whose core parameters were configured as static and dynamic, respectively. These two models were developed on the MalwarePlusClean2 subset of the AWSCTD dataset using sequences of length 1000, and each achieved an ACC value of 99.30%.

In Ref. [14], various techniques such as standard bag-of-words (BoW), Boolean BoW, probabilistic BoW, and term frequency–inverse document frequency (TF-IDF) BoW were applied for the processing of system call sequences. Using system call data transformed through these preprocessing approaches, models were built and evaluated with different ML algorithms, including k-nearest neighbors (KNN), RIPPER, J48, SVM, random forest (RF), and naive Bayes (NB). During the construction and testing of these models, the Australian Defence Force Academy Linux dataset (ADFA-LD) [15] and the virtual machine monitor (VMM) malware dataset were utilized. The RF model trained with the standard BoW approach on the ADFA-LD dataset achieved the highest performance, reaching 98.40% ACC and a 1.70% false positive rate (FPR). On the VMM dataset, the J48 and RF models developed using the TF-IDF BoW method achieved 1.0000 ACC and 0.0000 false alarm rate (FAR), demonstrating the best results.

In Ref. [16], an innovative feature extraction technique called "context-aware feature extraction" was introduced. This technique was designed not only to ensure effective feature selection but also to accelerate the classification process. In this context, a new IDS supported by this technique was proposed. The proposed detection system identifies attacks through a CNN model configured to detect various threats. The performance of the model was evaluated using various datasets, including NSL-KDD [17], CICIDS2017 [18], ADFA-LD, and the Australian Defence Force Academy Windows dataset (ADFA-WD) [19]. In the experimental studies, the IDS built with the basic CNN architecture reached an ACC rate of 95.12% on the ADFA-LD. Additionally, the IDS developed with the optimized CNN model demonstrated improved results, achieving an ACC value of 95.34% on the ADFA-LD.

In Ref. [20], a real-time HIDS was designed to identify unusual process behaviors. In this system, system calls were represented using the n-gram approach, and the importance weights of these n-grams were calculated through the TFIDF-based TFIDFVectorizer method. The high-dimensional feature vectors were then processed using the truncated singular value decomposition (SVD) technique for compression. SVM, decision tree (DT), and artificial neural networks (NN) were configured as detection models. These models were trained and evaluated utilizing the ADFA-LD and ADFA-WD datasets. In the experiments conducted on ADFA-LD, the SVM-based HIDS reached the best results, with 3.34% FPR in binary classification and 9.12% FPR in multi-class classification. In the experiments conducted with ADFA-WD, the NN-based HIDS demonstrated the highest performance, with 8.63% FPR and 15.11% FPR in binary and multi-class classifications, respectively.

In Ref. [21], a novel attack detection framework based on system call sequences has been developed. In this framework, a hybrid approach was adopted by combining an anomaly detection method depending on the frequency information of system calls with an LSTM-based learning method. The LSTM model was utilized to identify attacks in previously observed system call sequences. On the other hand, preprocessing techniques such as BoW, TF-IDF, and n-gram were applied in the frequency-based method, and various attacks were classified through the frequency-based method. The final classification was performed using an ensemble model based on weighted averaging. The attack detection framework, trained using the ADFA-LD dataset, demonstrated high performance with an ACC of 97.20% and a FPR of 2.40%.

In Ref. [22], a new attack detection system with a distributed architecture has been developed. This system, called fog-based-context-aware feature extraction using BranchyNET

(FCAFE-BNET), has been designed to adapt to variable network conditions. In the preprocessing phase of this detection system, select k-best (SKB) and extremely randomized trees (ERT) methods were utilized. As the DL component, Chainer [23], BranchyNet [24], and AlexNet [25] models were chosen. The effectiveness of this detection system, configured for both network-based and host-based threat detection, has been evaluated using the NSL-KDD, UNSW-NB15 [26], ToN-IoT, and ADFA-LD datasets. In binary classification experiments conducted utilizing the ADFA-LD, it was reported that the FCAFE-BNET detection system achieved an ACC value of over 95%.

In Ref. [27], a new risk-based method for clustering system call sequences has been presented. In this method, risk scores have been assigned based on the risk levels of functions. As a result of applying the proposed method, the accuracy rates of the SVM and DT models were increased by 23.4% and 7.6%, respectively. The performance of the SVM and DT models developed with this risk-based method has been tested on the AWSCTD dataset. According to the results, the SVM model demonstrated the highest performance with an ACC value of 96.80% on sequences of length 1000.

In Ref. [28], a new HIDS based on reinforcement learning (RL) called RL-HIDS was proposed. Developed within the framework of generative security, this detection system utilizes both natural language processing (NLP) and RL methods. RL-HIDS was structured to derive rule sets based on specific attack logs. These rule sets were obtained through inference summarization-based approaches in NLP and RL methods. During the development of RL-HIDS, Word2Vec and TextRank algorithms were used in the preprocessing phase. An RL model containing an LSTM-based Seq2Seq model was employed as the detector in this detection system. The effectiveness of RL-HIDS was evaluated on the ADFA-LD and LID-DS2021 [29] datasets, and an average ACC of 97.10% has been achieved on the attack samples from the ADFA-LD dataset.

In our previous work [30], stacking ensemble-based HIDSs consisting of various ML models were developed. During the development of these detection systems, n-gram, standard BoW, binary BoW, probabilistic BoW, and TF-IDF BoW techniques were used in the preprocessing phase of the ML models. Additionally, mutual information (MI) and k-means clustering algorithms were applied together in feature selection. KNN, DT, LR, RF, adaptive boosting (AdaBoost), and extreme gradient boosting (XGBoost) models were employed as detectors in the developed detection systems. The outputs of the individually defined KNN, DT, LR, and RF models were provided as inputs to the XGBoost and AdaBoost models; thus, stacking ensemble-based models/HIDSs were created. These detection systems were trained and evaluated using various BoW datasets created based on the ADFA-LD and ADFA-WD. In the experiments conducted using the ADFA-LD dataset, the stacking ensemble-based XGBoost model created on the standard BoW dataset achieved an ACC of 97.47%. Following experiments utilizing the ADFA-WD, the stacking ensemble-based XGBoost model trained on the standard BoW dataset reached an ACC of 91.63%.

10.1.2 Motivation and contribution

In Table 10.2, the attack detection models, preprocessing methods, and the most successful results obtained in some HIDS-focused studies in the literature are presented. Upon analyzing Table 10.2, it can be perceived that the detection models used generally exhibit high ACC values in terms of performance. However, developing new models demonstrating higher ACC and lower FPR remains an essential goal in the literature. On the other hand, it is known that problems such as insufficient data quantity and class imbalance are frequently

Table 10.2 Related Studies

Study	*Used Detection Methods*	*Used Preprocessing Methods*	*Best Performance Values*
[11]	LSTM, GRU, 1D-CNN, and SVM.	One-hot encoding.	1D-CNN with 99.30% ACC in binary classification on AWSCTD.
[13]	AWSCTD-CNN-S, AWSCTD-CNN-LSTM, AWSCTD-CNN-D, AWSCTD-CNN-GRU, FCN, GRU-FCN, and LSTM-FCN.	No information.	AWSCTD-CNN-S and AWSCTD-CNN-D with 99.30% ACC in binary classification on AWSCTD.
[14]	J48, RIPPER, RF, SVM, NB, and KNN.	Standard BoW, boolean BoW, probability BoW, TF-IDF BoW.	On ADFA-LD, RF with 98.4% ACC and 1.7% FPR.
[16]	CNN.	ERT and SKB.	ACC rate of 95.34% on ADFA-LD. ACC rate of 77.01% on ADFA-WD.
[20]	SVM, DT, and NN.	n-grams, SVD, and TFIDFVectorizer.	SVM had 3.34% FPR in binary classification on ADFA-LD. SVM had 9.12% FPR in multi-class classification on ADFA-LD. NN had 8.63% FPR in binary classification on ADFA-WD. NN had 15.11% FPR in multi-class classification on ADFA-WD.
[21]	LSTM, NN+RF.	BoW, n-grams, TF-IDF.	97.20% ACC on ADFA-LD.
[22]	FCAFE-BNET.	ERT and SKB.	Performance above 95% ACC in binary classification on ADFA-LD.
[27]	SVM and DT.	Risk-based system call sequence grouping method in [27].	SVM with 96.80% ACC on AWSCTD.
[28]	RL model including LSTM-based Seq2Seq model.	Word2Vec and TextRank.	97.10% ACC on the attack samples in ADFA-LD.
[30]	KNN, DT, LR, RF, XGBoost, and AdaBoost.	n-grams, standard BoW, binary BoW, probability BoW, TF-IDF BoW, and MI+ k-means.	On ADFA-LD, the stacking ensemble model XGBoost with 97.47% ACC. On ADFA-WD, the stacking ensemble model XGBoost with 91.63% ACC.
This Study	SVM, DT, LR, RF, and XGBoost.	n-grams, standard BoW, and MI+k-means.	On ADFA-LD, the stacking ensemble-based XGBoost with 97.50% ACC. On AWSCTD, the stacking ensemble-based XGBoost with 99.45% ACC.

encountered in datasets associated with HIDS. Overcoming such challenges and designing new models/HIDSs on more balanced and data-rich datasets is a separate endeavor. In this context, the primary objectives of this study are the reduction of data imbalance issues in the ADFA-LD and AWSCTD datasets and the formation of balanced datasets depending on these datasets. Furthermore, using the balanced datasets created, developing new attack detection models/HIDSs that achieve high ACC and low FPR values is aimed. In line with these objectives, the contributions of this study are listed below.

- The n-gram and standard BoW methods are applied to the ADFA-LD and AWSCTD datasets. As a result of this application, BoW datasets are obtained.
- The synthetic minority over-sampling technique (SMOTE) method [31] is implemented on the BoW datasets. As a result, balanced BoW datasets containing synthetic data samples are generated.
- Feature selection is performed on the BoW datasets, whether they contain synthetic data samples or not. The selected features are used during the development of models/HIDSs.
- Various individual SVM, DT, LR, and RF models are developed using BoW datasets, whether they contain synthetic data samples or not.
- Various stacking ensemble-based XGBoost models/HIDSs are developed using the outputs of the individual models.
- The performance values obtained by the developed models/ HIDSs are analyzed based on the experimental results. The models/HIDSs developed on BoW datasets, with or without synthetic data samples, are evaluated comparatively based on their performance values. Additionally, the most successful models/HIDSs are compared with those from the literature.
- Moreover, the contributions of this study were contextualized through a structured review of related works, particularly those adopting generative artificial intelligence (AI) techniques, including generative adversarial network (GAN), variational autoencoder (VAE), and conditional tabular generative adversarial network (CTGAN), as potential alternatives to traditional sampling methods like SMOTE.

10.1.3 Organization

In this study, information regarding the datasets used in developing the models/HIDSs is provided in Section 10.2. Section 10.3 explains how the n-gram and standard BoW methods used in the preprocessing process are applied. Additionally, this section discusses the application of the SMOTE method and the feature selection process. Section 10.4 describes the development process of the models/HIDS and the performance values obtained from the experiments. Section 10.5 includes a review of studies that use generative AI models for synthetic data generation and data augmentation. The final section briefly summarizes the procedures conducted throughout this study and the conclusions drawn.

10.2 DATASETS

This section presents information regarding the datasets utilized in training and testing the models/HIDSs.

10.2.1 ADFA-LD

The ADFA-LD dataset contains system call sequences occurring on Linux-based systems. These sequences are formed by the sequential arrangement of system calls, each identified by a unique ID. These sequences vary in length and are classified into two primary classes: normal and attack. Sequences in the normal class are included in the training and

Table 10.3 Statistical Information of ADFA-LD Dataset

Training	*Validation*	*Attack*	*Total*
833	4372	Add Superuser: 91 FTP password bruteforce: 162 SSH password Bruteforce: 176 Java Meterpreter: 124 Linux Meterpreter: 75 Web shell attack: 118 Total: 746	5951

```
[5,197,5,5,5,197,192,192,3,3,91,91,5,5,5,197,192,3,5,5,5,5,5,91,5,6,5,5,5,3,6,91,3,
 91,3,197,5,5,5,5,5,5,3,5,5,6,3,5,3,162,162,91,3,5,3,3,5,5,5,3,5,3,5,3,91,197,91,5,
 5,6,5,192,5,3,3,5,5,197,5,5,6,6,5,5,162,5,91,3,6,91,5,5,197,3,3,91,141,3,5,5,3,5,
 5,5,5,91,3,5,5,5,3,91,5,91,5,91,91,3,5,197,192,5,5,5,91]
```

Figure 10.1 A Sample System Call Sequence from the ADFA-LD Dataset.

validation subsets, while those in the attack class are found exclusively in the attack subset. The dataset consists of 5951 system call sequences, of which 833 belong to the training set, 4372 to the validation set, and 746 to the attack subset. The attack types in the dataset and their corresponding statistical data are presented in Table 10.3, while an example of a system call sequence from the ADFA-LD is shown in Figure 10.1. On the other hand, there is an imbalance between the normal and attack system call sequences in ADFA-LD, with the amount of normal sequences being significantly greater than the attack sequences. This imbalance issue should be considered when developing ML/DL models.

In this study, all attack-type system call sequences from ADFA-LD are used. Additionally, all system call sequences from the training subset and 167 randomly selected system call sequences from the validation subset are combined. As a result, a new dataset consisting of 746 attack-type sequences and 1000 normal-type sequences, totaling 1746 system call sequences, is obtained. This new dataset is referred to as reduced ADFA-LD (R-ADFA-LD).

10.2.2 AWSCTD

The AWSCTD dataset includes system call sequences of different lengths recorded from Windows operating systems. In each sequence, distinct system call IDs are arranged sequentially. These sequences are categorized into two main classes: normal/clean and attack/malware. Sequences belonging to malware are further classified into five subtypes based on their content: AdWare, Trojan, Downloader, WebToolbar, and DangerousObject. Basic statistical data of the dataset are presented in Table 10.4. Moreover, the dataset is grouped into six different subsets based on its structure and content: AllMalware, AllMalware2, AllMalwarePlusClean, AllMalwarePlus-Clean2, MalwarePlusClean, and MalwarePlusClean2. These subsets are categorized into subgroups according to the differences in the lengths of the system call sequences. In this study, the MalwarePlusClean2 subset is used. This subset contains 9396 system call sequences, each with a length of 1000; of these, 1736 are normal, and 7660 belong to malware. For example, four system call sequences with a length of 10 selected from this subset are shown in Figure 10.2. On the other hand, there is a data imbalance issue in AWSCTD. The number of system call

Table 10.4 Statistical Information of AWSCTD Dataset

Normal	*Attack*	*Total*
2350	Adware: 4333 Trojan: 1755 Downloader: 710 WebToolbar: 618 DangerousObject: 105 Total: 7521	9871

```
[24,3,25,30,10,26,10,25,40,10,Malware]
[8,10,40,10,10,4,4,10,10,15,Malware]
[10,40,10,17,17,11,97,33,33,34,Clean]
[11,43,33,33,34,34,17,10,23,45,Clean]
```

Figure 10.2 Sample System Call Sequences from the MalwarePlusClean2 Subset of the AWSCTD Dataset.

sequences associated with malware is significantly higher than that of others. Therefore, when training ML/DL models, attention must be given to this data imbalance problem.

In this study, all the normal type system call sequences of length 1000 from the MalwarePlusClean2 subset are included. Additionally, 2256 system call sequences of the attack type are randomly selected from the attack sequences. Therefore, a new dataset is created containing 3992 system call sequences, consisting of 1736 normal and 2256 attack-type sequences. This new dataset is referred to as the reduced AWSCTD (R-AWSCTD).

10.3 PREPROCESSING, DATA AUGMENTATION, AND FEATURE SELECTiON

This section describes how the n-gram and standard BoW methods are used in the preprocessing process. Additionally, the BoW datasets obtained from the preprocessing are discussed. Furthermore, the process of data augmentation using the SMOTE method on the obtained BoW datasets is explained. Finally, the feature selection process is described.

10.3.1 Implementation of n-gram and standard BoW methods

The n-gram method is used to reveal the contexts between the system calls within a system call sequence. Thus, the contexts between the system calls are represented by n-grams. A window with a fixed size of a particular n value is used to find the unique n-grams of a system call sequence. This window is initially placed starting from the first system call of the sequence, resulting in the first n-gram. In subsequent steps, the window is shifted to the next system call, and the process is repeated to identify the following n-grams. As a result, all n-grams of the system call sequence are obtained. For example, Figure 10.3 illustrates the process of finding n-grams for two different system call sequences.

For the system call sequences in the R-ADFA-LD and R-AWSCTD datasets, n-grams are found with a value of n set to 5. After applying the n-gram method to these datasets, 85871 unique 5-grams are identified for the system call sequences in R-ADFA-LD. Furthermore, 83725 unique 5-grams are discovered for the system call sequences in R-AWSCTD.

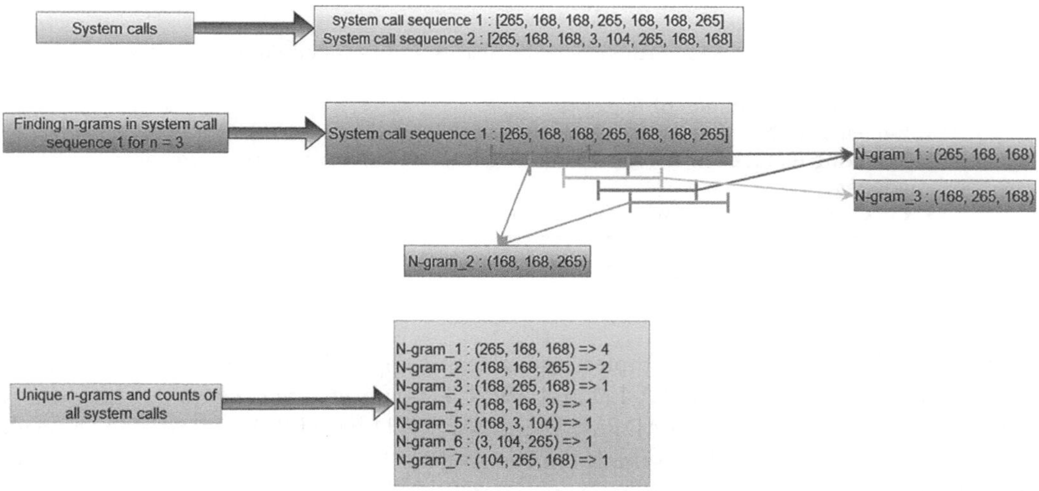

Figure 10.3 Finding n-Grams of Two Different System Call Sequences [30].

Call No	N-gram_1	N-gram_2	N-gram_3	N-gram_4	N-gram_5	N-gram_6	N-gram_7
1	2	2	1	0	0	0	0
2	2	0	0	1	1	1	1

Figure 10.4 An Example BoW Dataset [30].

Subsequently, 5-gram datasets are created by considering each of these 5-grams as a feature. As a result, 5-gram-based datasets from ADFA-LD and AWSCTD are obtained, consisting of 85871 and 83725 features, respectively.

On the other hand, the standard BoW method used in text mining discovers the unique words in texts and calculates their frequency values. Therefore, when the standard BoW method is applied to a text dataset, a dataset is generated where the unique words are considered as features. Furthermore, the values of the features in the derived dataset are assigned as the frequency values of the unique words.

When the standard BoW method is applied to the 5-gram-based ADFA-LD and AWSCTD datasets, each 5-gram is considered a unique word. The values of the 5-grams are determined, like the frequency values of words within texts. In other words, the frequency values of the unique 5-grams within the system call sequences are set as the values of these 5-grams. As a result, the ADFA-LD-based BoW and AWSCTD-based BoW datasets are obtained, consisting of 85871 and 83725 features, respectively. An example of a BoW dataset, composed of the n-grams from Figure 10.3, is provided in Figure 10.4.

10.3.2 Implementation of the SMOTE method

The SMOTE is used to address the class imbalance problem within datasets. This method interpolates minority data samples and their nearest neighbors, thereby generating synthetic data samples. As a result, the number of minority data samples is increased. Consequently, more successful ML/DL models are developed using balanced or near-balanced datasets.

Input: BoW dataset
Output: BoW dataset with selected features and reduced dimensionality
1: k=2 ▷ k is cluster number
2: Calculating MI values of features
3: k-means (k, MI values along with the indexes of the features)
4: Selecting features in the set containing large MI values according to their indexes
5: **return** BoW dataset with selected features and reduced dimensionality

Figure 10.5 Feature Selection Algorithm [30].

In this study, synthetic data samples equivalent to approximately 30% of the minority system call sequences in the ADFA-LD and AWSCTD datasets are generated. The SMOTE method is applied to the created ADFA-LD and AWSCTD-based BoW datasets. As a result, the number of attack-type data samples in the ADFA-LD-based BoW dataset, which consists of 746 samples, is increased by approximately 30%, reaching 1000 attack-type data samples. Consequently, a balanced dataset of 1000 attack and 1000 normal type data samples, totaling 2000 data samples, is created. This dataset is referred to as the ADFA-LD-based synthetic BoW dataset. On the other hand, the amount of normal type data samples in the AWSCTD-based BoW dataset, which initially contains 1736 normal type samples, is also increased by approximately 30%. The number of normal-type samples augmented using the SMOTE method has reached 2256. As a result, a balanced dataset consisting of 2256 attack-type and 2256 normal-type data samples is obtained. This dataset, containing a total of 4512 data samples, is defined as the AWSCTD-based synthetic BoW dataset.

10.3.3 Implementation of the feature selection algorithm

Because of the high number of features in the BoW datasets, the training times of the ML models developed on these datasets are long. Furthermore, the high number of features poses a disadvantage regarding resource consumption. Therefore, it is necessary to decrease the volume of the BoW datasets. During the dimensionality reduction and feature selection process, the accuracy performance of the models must not be negatively affected. In this context, the most effective features of the BoW datasets are chosen using the feature selection algorithm [30] in Figure 10.5. The selected features are used when developing the ML models.

The feature selection algorithm incorporates the MI method and the k-means algorithm. In this algorithm, the MI values of the features are first calculated. Then, the features are divided into two clusters by the k-means algorithm based on their MI values. These two clusters are defined as those containing high MI value features and those containing low MI value features. As a result, the feature selection algorithm outputs the high MI value features. The number of selected features after the feature selection process is provided in Table 10.5.

10.4 THE DEVELOPMENT AND EVALUATION OF HIDSS

The steps in the development process of the models/HIDSs are shown in Figure 10.6. During the development of the models, the n-gram and standard BoW methods are first applied to the system call sequences obtained from the ADFA-LD and AWSCTD. BoW datasets based on ADFA-LD and AWSCTD are obtained, where the features are 5-grams. Then, the

Table 10.5 Statistical Information of the Features After Applying the Feature Selection Algorithm to BoW Datasets

	ADFA-LD-Based BoW Dataset	*ADFA-LD-Based Synthetic BoW Dataset*
Raw Feature Count	85871	85871
Selected Feature Count	19676	20062
	AWSCTD-Based BoW Dataset	**AWSCTD-Based Synthetic BoW Dataset**
Raw Feature Count	83725	83725
Selected Feature Count	1493	1448

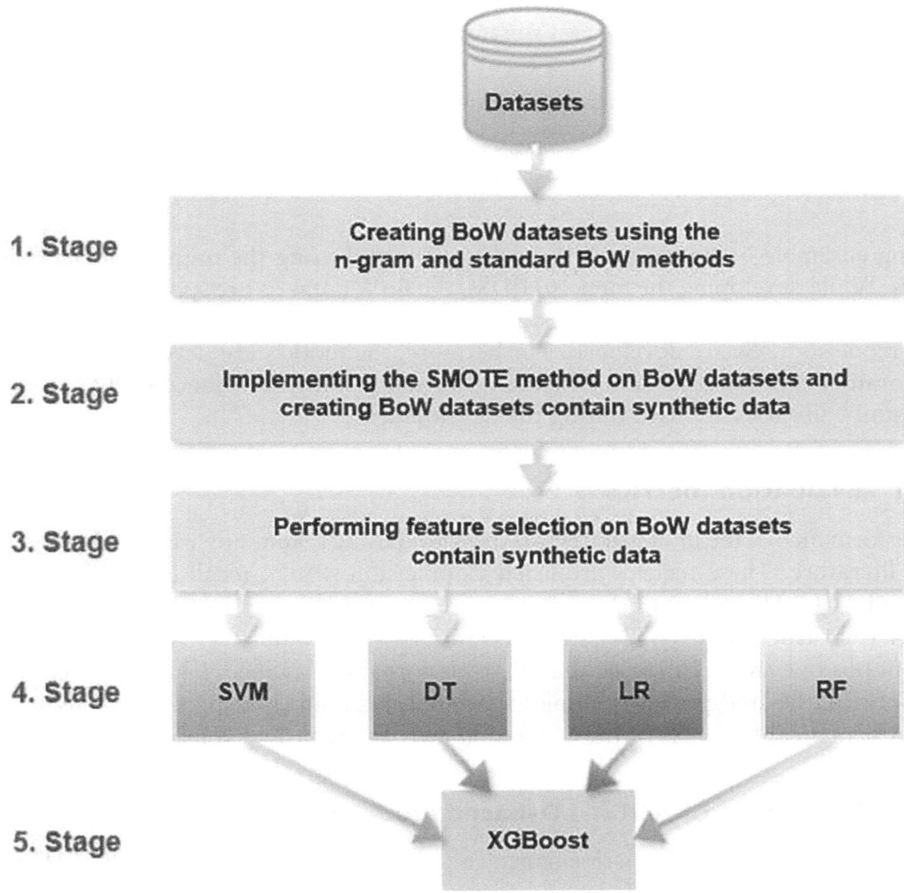

Figure 10.6 Development Process of Models/HIDSs.

SMOTE method is applied to the BoW datasets to augment the amount of minority data samples. As a result, balanced synthetic BoW datasets based on ADFA-LD and AWSCTD are created. Next, the optimum features from the BoW datasets are selected using the feature selection algorithm in Figure 10.5. The selected features are used in the development of the models. Individual SVM, DT, LR, and RF models are initially developed. Subsequently,

Table 10.6 Evaluation Metrics

Metric	*Definition*	*Formula*
PRC	The ratio of true positive samples to the total number of samples predicted as positive.	$\frac{TP}{TP+FP}$
REC	The proportion of correctly identified positive samples to the total positive samples.	$\frac{TP}{TP+FN}$
F1	Harmonic mean of PRC and REC.	$2*\frac{PRC*REC}{PRC+REC}$
FPR	The proportion of misclassified negative samples to the total number of negative samples.	$\frac{FP}{FP+TN}$
ACC	The proportion of accurately classified samples to the total entire of samples.	$\frac{TP+TN}{TP+TN+FP+FN}$

stacking ensemble-based XGBoost models are created using the outputs of the individual models. While developing the models/HIDSs, the BoW datasets are split with 80% allocated for training and 20% for testing. As a result, various individual and stacking ensemble-based models/HIDSs are developed. Furthermore, the models are developed in the Google Colaboratory environment using Python. The scikit-learn, imbalanced-learn, LightGBM, and NumPy libraries are used during the development.

10.4.1 Evaluation metrics

The performance of the models/HIDSs is measured using commonly used evaluation metrics in the literature. These metrics are listed as precision (PRC), recall (REC), f1-score (F1), FPR, and ACC. The values of these metrics are computed using the true positive (TP), false positive (FP), true negative (TN), and false negative (FN) values. TP and TN represent the count of positive and negative samples that are correctly classified. FP and FN represent the count of negative and positive samples that are misclassified, respectively. The definitions and mathematical formulas of the evaluation metrics are provided in Table 10.6.

10.4.2 Evaluation of ADFA-LD-based models/HIDSs

In Tables 10.7 and 10.8, the performance values achieved by the models/HIDSs developed on the ADFA-LD-based BoW datasets are presented. When evaluating the performance values of the models/HIDSs developed utilizing the ADFA-LD-based BoW dataset,

- The most successful individual model regarding the ACC metric was the LR model. This model achieved a performance of 0.9400 ACC.
- Among the individual models, the best performance with respect to the FPR metric was exhibited by the DT and RF models. These models achieved an FPR value of 0.0594.
- The stacking ensemble-based XGBoost model outperformed the individual models. The XGBoost model achieved the best performance values with an ACC of 0.9571 and an FPR of 0.0222.

Table 10.7 Performance Values of Models/HIDSs Developed on ADFA-LD-Based BoW Dataset

Model	*PRC*	*REC*	*F1*	*FPR*	*ACC*
SVM	0.8750	0.7568	0.8116	0.0792	0.8514
DT	0.9137	0.8581	0.8850	0.0594	0.9057
LR	0.9150	0.9459	0.9302	0.0644	0.9400
RF	0.9167	0.8919	0.9041	0.0594	0.9200
XGBoost	0.9583	0.9200	0.9388	0.0222	0.9571

Table 10.8 Performance Values of Models/HIDSs Developed on ADFA-LD-Based Synthetic BoW Dataset

Model	*PRC*	*REC*	*F1*	*FPR*	*ACC*
SVM	0.8578	0.9900	0.9192	0.1658	0.9125
DT	0.9239	0.9055	0.9146	0.0754	0.9150
LR	0.9132	0.9950	0.9524	0.0955	0.9500
RF	0.9320	0.9552	0.9435	0.0704	0.9425
XGBoost	0.9459	1.000	0.9722	0.0444	0.9750

When the performances of the models/HIDSs developed using the ADFA-LD-based synthetic BoW dataset are compared,

- Among the individual models, the most successful model concerning the ACC metric was LR. This model had an ACC value of 0.9500.
- The individual model that showed the highest performance in relation to the FPR metric is RF. This model achieved an FPR value of 0.0704.
- Regarding both ACC and FPR metrics, the stacking ensemble-based XGBoost model performed the best. The XGBoost model, which had a 0.9750 ACC and a 0.0444 FPR, outperformed the individual models.

The models developed on the ADFA-LD-based synthetic BoW dataset showed better performance in terms of the ACC than those developed on the BoW dataset without synthetic data. However, the models developed on the BoW dataset without synthetic data demonstrated better performance in the FPR metric than the others.

10.4.3 Evaluation of AWSCTD-based models/HIDSs

The performance values of the models/HIDSs developed using the AWSCTD-based BoW datasets are provided in Tables 10.9 and 10.10. When the performance of the models/HIDSs developed on the AWSCTD-based BoW dataset is examined,

- The LR model was the most successful individual model in terms of the ACC metric. This model demonstrated a performance of 0.9812 ACC.
- The RF model outperformed the top performance among the individual models regarding the FPR metric. This model achieved a value of 0.0242 FPR.
- The stacking ensemble-based XGBoost model achieved the highest ACC and the lowest FPR values. This model surpassed the individual models with an ACC of 0.9938 and an FPR of 0.0161.

Table 10.9 Performance Values of Models/HIDSs Developed on AWSCTD-Based BoW Dataset

Model	*PRC*	*REC*	*F1*	*FPR*	*ACC*
SVM	0.9727	0.9893	0.9809	0.0394	0.9775
DT	0.9808	0.9808	0.9808	0.0273	0.9775
LR	0.9809	0.9872	0.9841	0.0273	0.9812
RF	0.9829	0.9787	0.9808	0.0242	0.9775
XGBoost	0.9899	1.0000	0.9949	0.0161	0.9938

Table 10.10 Performance Values of Models/HIDSs Developed on AWSCTD-Based Synthetic BoW Dataset

Model	*PRC*	*REC*	*F1*	*FPR*	*ACC*
SVM	0.9662	0.9892	0.9775	0.0363	0.9767
DT	0.9721	0.9805	0.9763	0.0295	0.9756
LR	0.9764	0.9870	0.9817	0.0249	0.9812
RF	0.9783	0.9762	0.9772	0.0227	0.9767
XGBoost	0.9891	1.0000	0.9945	0.0111	0.9945

When the performance values of the models/HIDSs developed on the AWSCTD-based synthetic BoW dataset are analyzed,

- Among the individual models, the LR model showed the highest performance with respect to the ACC metric. This model achieved an ACC value of 0.9812.
- Regarding the FPR metric, the most effective individual model was the RF model. This model had a performance with an FPR of 0.0227.
- The most successful model across all models was the stacking ensemble-based XGBoost model. This model had a 0.9945 ACC and a 0.0111 FPR.

Individual models developed on the AWSCTD-based BoW dataset achieved slightly higher ACC values than those developed on the BoW dataset containing synthetic data. However, the models developed on the BoW dataset containing synthetic data generally performed better with lower FPR values. Furthermore, the XGBoost model developed on the BoW dataset with synthetic data exhibited lower FPR and higher ACC values than its counterpart.

10.4.4 Comparison with similar models/frameworks in literature

In Table 10.11, the performance values of models/frameworks utilizing the ADFA-LD dataset proposed in the literature and the models/HIDSs developed in this study are presented. Upon examining the table, it can be evident that the most successful model in terms of ACC and FPR metrics is the RF model from Ref. [14]. However, the stacking-based XGBoost model developed on the ADFA-LD-based synthetic BoW dataset appears to have the second-highest ACC value. Additionally, it is observed that the stacking ensemble-based XGBoost model developed on the ADFA-LD-based BoW dataset achieves the second-lowest FPR value.

Table 10.11 Comparison on ADFA-LD

Model/Framework	*FPR*	*ACC*
RF in Ref. [14]	0.0170	0.9840
Framework in Ref. [21]	0.0240	0.9720
XGBoost in Ref. [30]	0.0330	0.9747
XGBoost on the ADFA-LD-based BoW dataset in this study	0.0222	0.9571
XGBoost on the ADFA-LD-based synthetic BoW dataset in this study	0.0444	0.9750

Table 10.12 Comparison on AWSCTD

Model/Framework	*FPR*	*ACC*
1D-CNN in Ref. [11]	-	0.9930
AWSCTD-CNN-S in Ref. [13]	0.0220	0.9930
XGBoost on the AWSCTD-based BoW dataset in this study	0.0161	0.9938
XGBoost on the AWSCTD-based synthetic BoW dataset in this study	0.0111	0.9945

In Table 10.12, a comparison is made between the performance values of models developed using the AWSCTD dataset in the literature and the models/HIDSs developed in this study. Upon analyzing Table 12, it is observed that the stacking ensemble-based XGBoost model developed on the AWSCTD-based synthetic BoW dataset achieves the highest ACC and the lowest FPR values. Additionally, it is observed that the stacking ensemble-based XGBoost model developed on the AWSCTD-based BoW dataset was the second most successful model in terms of ACC and FPR metrics.

10.4.5 Limitations

Despite the promising performance of the proposed models/HIDSs, several limitations can be identified in the present study. First, while models were developed using both ADFA-LD and AWSCTD datasets with n-gram and standard BoW representations, the diversity of real-world system call sequences may not be fully captured. This limitation may affect the generalizability of the models when applied to previously unseen or more complex attack scenarios.

Second, although SMOTE was applied to address class imbalance, its limitations may affect model performance. Synthetic samples generated by SMOTE might not fully capture the complex sequential dependencies and nuanced patterns in real attack data. As a result, models trained with SMOTE augmented datasets may show optimistic performance metrics, while their generalizability to unseen or more sophisticated attack scenarios could be limited. Alternatively, generative AI-based models could be explored to produce more realistic synthetic attack data, potentially improving model robustness.

Third, the current preprocessing strategies rely on n-gram, standard BoW, and feature selection methods. While these methods effectively capture frequency-based and relevant patterns, they may not adequately model sequential or contextual relationships between system calls. Consequently, attacks that depend on temporal correlations or rare call sequences might be underrepresented, potentially limiting the models' ability to generalize to more complex or evolving attack scenarios.

Finally, the experiments focused on a limited set of conventional ML models, and more advanced generative AI or DL approaches (e.g., GANs, VAEs, sequence-based embeddings) were not fully explored. Integrating such methods could improve model robustness and performance, especially in highly imbalanced and evolving cyberattack scenarios.

10.5 FROM SMOTE TO GENERATIVE AI: ADDRESSING DATA IMBALANCE IN IDS

In this study, balanced synthetic BoW datasets were constructed by employing the SMOTE technique to augment the number of minority class samples. This allowed the proposed stacking ensemble-based XGBoost models to achieve high accuracy on the ADFA-LD and AWSCTD datasets. However, SMOTE has several inherent limitations. Specifically, it often fails to preserve the true distribution of high-dimensional datasets, cannot adequately capture sequential dependencies, and may generate synthetic samples that distort the decision boundaries. To address these shortcomings, recent research has increasingly adopted generative AI-based approaches such as GANs, VAEs, and CTGANs, which have demonstrated promising results in improving the performance of IDSs.

In real-world network traffic scenarios, the scarcity of data hindered the detection of unknown attacks from a limited number of samples. The SFE-GACN method was proposed to address this issue in Ref. [32]. Through this approach, an innovative solution to few-shot unknown attack detection was introduced by employing an intra-class generation strategy in the embedding space. In the proposed method, sessions were transferred into a pre-trained embedding space using the session feature embedding (SFE) technique, and the learning capacity was enhanced by expanding prior knowledge in cases where only a few samples were available. Moreover, the traditional GAN architecture was improved to design the generative adversarial cooperative network (GACN), which ensured that the generated samples remained within their respective categories and prevented inter-class confusion. Experimental results revealed that, compared to existing methods, the proposed model achieved an average increase of 8.38% in true positive rate (TPR) and a reduction of 12.77% in FPR.

The increasing cyber threats targeting space systems necessitated the development of intrusion detection and protection mechanisms, while the lack of available data constituted a significant obstacle in this process. To address this challenge, extended versions of GAN, VAE, and a specialized generative algorithm for multivariate time series were applied to generate cyber threat data for space systems in Ref. [33]. Within the use case conducted on NASA's operational simulation for small satellites (NOS3) platform, the generated data were evaluated through qualitative and quantitative measures, and the strengths and weaknesses of the algorithms were analyzed. Experimental findings demonstrated that the algorithm developed for multivariate time series achieved the highest performance compared to the other methods.

The security vulnerabilities of IoT devices rendered them susceptible to cyberattacks due to the lack of robust hardware security support. In this context, the intelligent intrusion detection system (IMIDS) was proposed, which was reinforced with a lightweight, CNN-based DL model in Ref. [34]. IMIDS distinguished between normal and abnormal activities and classified the various types of cyberattacks underlying these activities. To overcome the issue of insufficient training data, a novel attack data generator based on conditional GAN (CGAN) was developed, and the detection performance of IMIDS was significantly enhanced with these synthetic samples. Experimental evaluations conducted on the

UNSW-NB15 and CICIDS2017 datasets demonstrated that IMIDS was able to detect nine different types of cyberattacks with an average F1-score exceeding 97% and outperformed competing approaches.

The increasing use of IoT networks led to the proliferation of distributed denial of service (DDoS) and denial of service (DoS) attacks targeting these networks. In [35], an IDS based on a CTGAN was introduced to detect DDoS/DoS attacks in IoT networks. This IDS employed a generator network to produce synthetic tabular data that simulated real network traffic, while a discriminator network learned to distinguish legitimate traffic from malicious traffic through these data. The data generated by CTGAN were utilized in training both shallow ML and DL classifiers, thereby improving detection performance. Experiments conducted on the Bot-IoT dataset demonstrated that synthetic data significantly enhanced the values of ACC, PRC, REC, and F1 metrics. Furthermore, the use of CTGAN addressed the severe class imbalance within the dataset, enabling more effective classification of the minority classes representing DDoS and DoS attacks.

In Ref. [36], a CTGAN-based ML pipeline approach was proposed, and a synthetic attack dataset was generated for IoT environments. The proposed approach was able to operate on datasets containing both continuous and discrete values, and it reduced data collection time, cost, and storage requirements while enhancing the accuracy and performance of classifiers. The feature selection and preprocessing steps reduced the complexity of the classification process and improved classification performance by creating a more balanced dataset. Experimental results showed that DT and RF classifiers achieved high ACC values on the synthetic dataset generated by CTGAN. Furthermore, the proposed approach enriched the training data of resource-constrained IoT devices while preserving privacy.

In Ref. [37], a method based on a conditional Wasserstein GAN (CWGAN) and a bidirectional temporal convolutional network (BiTCN) was proposed to address the imbalance problem in malware family samples. API and Opcode call sequences were represented using Word2Vec to preserve semantic relationships, after which redundant features were filtered and the structure was simplified through the use of the Spearman correlation coefficient and whale optimization algorithm XGBoost (WOA-XGBoost). Synthetic samples were generated with CWGAN to mitigate the imbalance in malware family instances, and these samples were incorporated into the training set. The proposed model enhanced detection accuracy by extracting sequential features through BiTCN. Experimental results demonstrated that detection accuracies of 99.56% and 96.93% were achieved on the Kaggle and DataCon datasets, respectively, outperforming existing methods.

The severe imbalance in datasets used for network attack detection caused models to become biased toward the majority classes. A three-stage data generation method combining SMOTE, GAN, and VAE was presented in Ref. [38] to address this issue. In this approach, CNN was employed to extract representative features, followed by multi-class classification using an SVM with a customized kernel function to mitigate biased classification. The model's effectiveness was examined through five-fold cross-validation and ablation studies, and the findings revealed that accuracy rates ranging from 91.9% to 96.2% were achieved across four benchmark datasets. Furthermore, the proposed method outperformed existing approaches such as GAN-based deep NNs, CWGAN-based stacked autoencoders, and VAE-based deep NNs by margins ranging from 1.51% to 28.4%.

SCADA-based power systems are widely used in critical infrastructures, and the security of these systems is of great importance in terms of protection against cyber threats. In this context, a general ML-based IDS framework consisting of two main components: an offline training module (OTM) and an online detection module (ODM) was proposed in

Ref. [39]. The proposed framework combined data preprocessing, feature selection, and data augmentation methods to create a balanced and enriched dataset for SCADA-based power systems. During the data augmentation process, synthetic data were generated using GANs, thereby preventing overfitting and enhancing the generalizability of the models. In the study, DT, RF, and gradient boosting models were evaluated using the ORNL dataset, and tests conducted with unseen data revealed that RF achieved the best performance with an F1 score of 94.09%. Additionally, tests conducted on 50 features selected via recursive feature elimination with random forest (RFE-RF) achieved an accuracy of 93.97%.

To address the issues of low accuracy, prolonged detection time, and security vulnerabilities encountered by traditional intrusion detection methods in the context of big data analytics, a network intrusion detection approach based on federated learning (FL) and an enhanced transformer was proposed in Ref. [40]. In the proposed method, an FL framework enabled multi-server collaboration, reducing training time while preserving user privacy. The transformer, employed as a universal detection model, reliably captured anomalies in network traffic data due to its high learning capacity. To mitigate the problem of data imbalance, samples in minority classes were augmented using an enhanced GAN, thereby improving detection accuracy. Experimental evaluations demonstrated that accuracy rates of 99.45% and 89.83% were achieved on the NSL-KDD and UNSW-NB15 datasets, respectively.

To address the data imbalance problem in NIDS, a DL-based approach was developed using a hybrid sampling strategy in Ref. [41]. Initially, noisy samples in the majority class were reduced through the difficult set sampling technique (DSSTE), and then minority class samples were augmented using a deep convolutional GAN (DCGAN) to create a balanced dataset. For feature extraction, DenseNet169 was employed for spatial features, and a self-attention-based transformer (SAT-Net) was used for temporal features. In the final stage, an enhanced Elman spike neural network (EESNN) was applied to classify attack categories, achieving high categorization performance. Experiments conducted on the BOT-IoT, ToN-IoT, and CICIDS2019 datasets demonstrated that the proposed approach outperformed contemporary methods in terms of ACC, PRC, REC, and FAR metrics, achieving 99.89% ACC, 99.87% PRC, and 99.42% REC. Table 10.13 presents the generative AI models employed in the studies for synthetic data generation and data augmentation, their intended purposes, and the datasets to which they were applied.

10.6 CONCLUSION AND FUTURE WORKS

In this study, n-gram and standard BoW methods were applied to the system call sequences in the ADFA-LD dataset and the system call sequences of length 1000 in the MalwarePlusClean2 subset of the AWSCTD dataset. As a result of these applications, BoW datasets based on ADFA-LD and AWSCTD were constructed. Subsequently, the SMOTE method was applied to these BoW datasets to increase the number of minority class samples. This way, synthetic BoW datasets based on ADFA-LD and AWSCTD were obtained. Thereafter, feature selection was performed on the BoW datasets, both with and without synthetic data. Following the feature selection process, individual models, namely SVM, DT, LR, and RF, were developed using the selected features. After the development of individual models, stacking ensemble-based XGBoost models/HIDSs were built by utilizing the outputs of these individual models. As a result of the experiments, among the ADFA-LD-based models, the highest ACC value was achieved by the stacking ensemble-based XGBoost model developed on the synthetic BoW dataset. Among the AWSCTD-based models, the most successful model was the stacking ensemble-based XGBoost model developed using

Table 10.13 Generative AI Models Used for Synthetic Data Generation and Data Augmentation

Study	*Datasets*	*Generative AI Models*	*Purpose of Use of Generative AI Models*
[32]	CICIDS-2017 and IDS2018.	GACN.	Generating intra-class samples.
[33]	NOS3 simulation data.	GAN and VAE.	Generating synthetic threat data for space systems.
[34]	UNSW-NB15 and CICIDS2017.	CGAN.	Generating training data for IoT environments.
[35]	Bot-IoT.	CTGAN.	Generating synthetic tabular data that simulates IoT network traffic.
[36]	TON-IoT, MQTT-IoT-IDS2020, and Bot-IoT.	CTGAN.	Generating synthetic data for IoT environments.
[37]	Kaggle and DataCon datasets.	CWGAN.	Resolving the issue of imbalance in malware family samples.
[38]	NSL-KDD, UNSW-NB15, KDD Cup 1999, and CICIDS2017.	GAN and VAE.	Resolving class imbalance in network attack detection.
[39]	ORNL dataset.	GAN.	Creating a balanced and enriched dataset.
[40]	NSL-KDD and UNSW-NB15.	GAN.	To increase the data of minority class.
[41]	BOT-IoT, ToN-IoT, and CICIDS2019.	DCGAN.	Resolving class imbalance.

the synthetic BoW dataset. Furthermore, studies involving generative AI techniques, such as GAN, VAE, and CTGAN, were also examined to highlight their potential in addressing class imbalance and enhancing synthetic data generation for IDSs. In future studies, it is intended to generate synthetic data using generative AI models, such as GANs, VAEs, and CTGANs, and to develop DL-based models/HIDSs.

ACKNOWLEDGMENTS

During the preparation of this chapter, the AI tool ChatGPT (GPT-5, OpenAI, version: 5-mini) was used for English language editing and refinement. This statement is provided for transparency.

REFERENCES

[1] H.-J. Liao, C.-H. R. Lin, Y.-C. Lin, and K.-Y. Tung, 'Intrusion detection system: A comprehensive review', *J. Netw. Comput. Appl.*, vol. 36, no. 1, pp. 16–24, 2013.

[2] I. Martins, J. S. Resende, P. R. Sousa, S. Silva, L. Antunes, and J. Gama, 'Host-based IDS: A review and open issues of an anomaly detection system in IoT', *Futur. Gener. Comput. Syst.*, vol. 133, pp. 95–113, 2022.

[3] A. Thakkar, and R. Lohiya, 'A survey on intrusion detection system: Feature selection, model, performance measures, application perspective, challenges, and future research directions', *Artif. Intell. Rev.*, vol. 55, no. 1, pp. 453–563, 2022.

[4] H. Satilmics, S. Akleylek, and Z. Y. Tok, 'A systematic literature review on host-based intrusion detection systems', *IEEE Access*, vol. 12, pp. 27237–27266, 2024.

[5] Y. Kumar, and B. Subba, 'Stacking ensemble-based HIDS framework for detecting anomalous system processes in windows based operating systems using multiple word embedding', *Comput. Secur.*, vol. 125, p. 102961, 2023.
[6] V. Bukac, P. Tucek, and M. Deutsch, 'Advances and challenges in standalone host-based intrusion detection systems', in *Trust, Privacy and Security in Digital Business: 9th International Conference, TrustBus 2012, Vienna, Austria, September 3-7, 2012. Proceedings*, 2012, vol. 9, pp. 105–117.
[7] V. Sahin, H. Satilmis, B. K. Yazar, and S. Akleylek, 'Anomaly detection with machine learning models using API calls', in *International Conference on Information Technologies and Their Applications*, 2024, pp. 298–309.
[8] S. Jose, D. Malathi, B. Reddy, and D. Jayaseeli, 'A survey on anomaly based host intrusion detection system', in *Journal of Physics: Conference Series*, 2018, vol. 1000, p. 12049.
[9] Y. Shin, and K. Kim, 'Comparison of anomaly detection accuracy of host-based intrusion detection systems based on different machine learning algorithms', *Int. J. Adv. Comput. Sci. Appl.*, vol. 11, no. 2, pp. 252–259, 2020.
[10] A. Shaker, and S. Gore, 'Importance of intrusion detection system', *Int. J. Sci. Eng. Res*, 2011.
[11] D. Čeponis, and N. Goranin, 'Evaluation of deep learning methods efficiency for malicious and benign system calls classification on the AWSCTD', *Secur. Commun. Networks*, vol. 2019, no. 1, p. 2317976, 2019.
[12] D. Čeponis, and N. Goranin, 'Towards a robust method of dataset generation of malicious activity for anomaly-based HIDS training and presentation of AWSCTD dataset', *Balt. J. Mod. Comput.*, vol. 6, no. 3, pp. 217–234, 2018.
[13] D. Čeponis, and N. Goranin, 'Investigation of dual-flow deep learning models LSTM-FCN and GRU-FCN efficiency against single-flow CNN models for the host-based intrusion and malware detection task on univariate times series data', *Appl. Sci.*, vol. 10, no. 7, 2373, pp. 1–26, 2020, doi: 10.3390/app10072373.
[14] A. A. R. Melvin, G. J. W. Kathrine, S. Pasupathi, V. Shanmuganathan, and R. Naganathan, 'An AI powered system call analysis with bag of word approaches for the detection of intrusions and malware in Australian defence force academy and virtual machine monitor malware attack data set', *Expert Syst.*, vol. 41, no. 6, p. e13029, 2022.
[15] G. Creech, and J. Hu, 'Generation of a new IDS test dataset: Time to retire the KDD collection', in *2013 IEEE Wireless Communications and Networking Conference (WCNC)*, 2013, pp. 4487–4492.
[16] E. A. Shams, A. Rizaner, and A. H. Ulusoy, 'A novel context-aware feature extraction method for convolutional neural network-based intrusion detection systems', *Neural Comput. Appl.*, vol. 33, no. 20, pp. 13647–13665, 2021.
[17] M. Tavallaee, E. Bagheri, W. Lu, and A. A. Ghorbani, 'A detailed analysis of the KDD CUP 99 data set', in *2009 IEEE Symposium on Computational Intelligence for Security and Defense Applications*, 2009, pp. 1–6.
[18] I. Sharafaldin, A. H. Lashkari, and A. A. Ghorbani, 'Toward generating a new intrusion detection dataset and intrusion traffic characterization', *ICISSp*, vol. 1, pp. 108–116, 2018.
[19] G. Creech, '*Developing a high-accuracy cross platform host-based intrusion detection system capable of reliably detecting zero-day attacks*', UNSW Sydney, 2014.
[20] B. Subba, and P. Gupta, 'A tfidfvectorizer and singular value decomposition based host intrusion detection system framework for detecting anomalous system processes', *Comput. Secur.*, vol. 100, p. 102084, 2021.
[21] A. Chaudhari, B. Gohil, and U. P. Rao, 'A novel hybrid framework for cloud intrusion detection system using system call sequence analysis', *Cluster Comput.*, vol. 27, no. 3, pp. 3753–3769, 2024.
[22] M. Sahi, N. Auluck, A. Azim, and M. Al Maruf, 'Dynamic hierarchical intrusion detection task offloading in IoT edge networks', *Softw. Pract. Exp.*, vol. 54, no. 11, pp. 2249–2271, 2024.

[23] S. Tokui *et al.*, 'Chainer: A deep learning framework for accelerating the research cycle', in *Proceedings of the 25th ACM SIGKDD International Conference on Knowledge Discovery \& Data Mining*, 2019, pp. 2002–2011.
[24] S. Teerapittayanon, B. McDanel, and H.-T. Kung, 'Branchynet: Fast inference via early exiting from deep neural networks', in *2016 23rd International Conference on Pattern Recognition (ICPR)*, 2016, pp. 2464–2469.
[25] Z.-W. Yuan, and J. Zhang, 'Feature extraction and image retrieval based on AlexNet', in *Eighth International Conference on Digital Image Processing (ICDIP 2016)*, 2016, vol. 10033, pp. 65–69.
[26] N. Moustafa, and J. Slay, 'The evaluation of network anomaly detection systems: Statistical analysis of the UNSW-NB15 data set and the comparison with the KDD99 data set', *Inf. Secur. J. A Glob. Perspect.*, vol. 25, no. 1–3, pp. 18–31, 2016.
[27] T. Vyšniunas, D. Čeponis, N. Goranin, and A. Čenys, 'Risk-based system-call sequence grouping method for malware intrusion detection', *Electronics*, vol. 13, no. 1, p. 206, 2024.
[28] Y. Kim, S.-Y. Hong, S. Park, and H. K. Kim, 'Reinforcement learning-based generative security framework for host intrusion detection', vol. 13, pp.15346–15362, *IEEE Access*, 2025.
[29] M. Grimmer *et al.*, 'LID-DS 2021'. In CRITIS Conference Proceedings, 2021.
[30] H. Satilmiş, S. Akleylek, and Z. Yüce Tok, 'Development of various stacking ensemble-based HIDS using ADFA datasets', *IEEE Open J. Commun. Soc.*, vol. 6, pp. 1170–1189, 2025, doi: 10.1109/OJCOMS.2025.3538101.
[31] N. V Chawla, K. W. Bowyer, L. O. Hall, and W. P. Kegelmeyer, 'SMOTE: Synthetic minority over-sampling technique', *J. Artif. Intell. Res.*, vol. 16, pp. 321–357, 2002.
[32] A. Liu, Y. Wang, and T. Li, 'SFE-GACN: A novel unknown attack detection under insufficient data via intra categories generation in embedding space', *Comput. Secur.*, vol. 105, p. 102262, 2021, doi: 10.1016/j.cose.2021.102262.
[33] M. G. Sahakian, S. Musuvathy, J. Thorpe, S. Verzi, E. Vugrin, and M. Dykstra, 'Threat data generation for space systems', in *Proceeding–2021 IEEE Space Computing Conference SCC 2021*, 2021, pp. 100–109, doi: 10.1109/SCC49971.2021.00018.
[34] K. H. Le, M. H. Nguyen, T. D. Tran, and N. D. Tran, 'IMIDS: An intelligent intrusion detection system against cyber threats in IoT', *Electron.*, vol. 11, no. 4, pp. 1–16, 2022, doi: 10.3390/electronics11040524.
[35] B. A. Alabsi, M. Anbar, and S. D. A. Rihan, 'Conditional tabular generative adversarial based intrusion detection system for detecting ddos and dos attacks on the internet of things networks', *Sensors*, vol. 23, no. 12, p. 5644, 2023.
[36] S. Alabdulwahab, Y. T. Kim, A. Seo, and Y. Son, 'Generating synthetic dataset for ML-based IDS using CTGAN and feature selection to protect smart IoT environments', *Appl. Sci.*, vol. 13, no. 19, 2023, doi: 10.3390/app131910951.
[37] W. Liu, L. L. Ci, and L. P. Liu, 'A new method of fuzzy support vector machine algorithm for intrusion detection', *Appl. Sci.*, vol. 10, no. 3, 2020, doi: 10.3390/app10031065.
[38] K. T. Chui, B. B. Gupta, P. Chaurasia, V. Arya, A. Almomani, and W. Alhalabi, 'Three-stage data generation algorithm for multiclass network intrusion detection with highly imbalanced dataset', *Int. J. Intell. Networks*, vol. 4, pp. 202–210, 2023, doi: 10.1016/j.ijin.2023.08.001.
[39] M. Zaman, D. Upadhyay, and C. H. Lung, 'Validation of a machine learning-based IDS design framework using ORNL datasets for power system with SCADA', *IEEE Access*, vol. 11, pp. 118414–118426, 2023, doi: 10.1109/ACCESS.2023.3326751.
[40] Q. Zhou, and Z. Wang, 'A network intrusion detection method for information systems using federated learning and improved transformer', *Int. J. Semant. Web Inf. Syst.*, vol. 20, no. 1, pp. 1–20, 2023, doi: 10.4018/IJSWIS.334845.
[41] J. Saikam, and K. Ch, 'EESNN: Hybrid deep learning empowered spatial-temporal features for network intrusion detection system', *IEEE Access*, vol. 12, pp. 15930–15945, 2024, doi: 10.1109/ACCESS.2024.3350197.

Chapter 11

An Explainable Intelligence framework for IoT anomaly detection using hierarchical feature embedding and latent space modelling

Priyang P. Bhatt, Bhaskar Thakker, Boubiche Djallel Eddine, and Vishal Polara

11.1 INTRODUCTION

The advent of the Internet of Things (IoT) devices in their current digitally interconnected ecosystem has revolutionized many fields, such as smart cities, the healthcare sector, the industrial automation sector and intelligent transportation networks. Nonetheless, this broad-scale installation of IoT devices has simultaneously increased the area of attack, exposing these networks to various categories of cybersecurity risks, including unauthorized access and advanced distributed denial-of-service (DDoS) attacks and covert anomaly-based infiltrations [1, 2]. The traditional security solutions, including firewalls and signature-based intrusion detection systems (IDSs), are less beneficial in detecting zero-day and hitherto unknown assaults, and as a result, have to be combined with innovative anomaly detection frameworks that have the capability to monitor abnormal traffic patterns in real time.

Network Anomaly Detection System (ADS) is a necessity to guarantee the network reliability of IoT networks and their safety since the patterns of network traffic are constantly monitored to identify anomalies. In general, IDSs may be categorized into signature-based and anomaly-based ones [3, 4]. Although signature-based IDS rely on familiar attack signatures to provide highly accurate detection of known attacks, it can never be capable of detecting novel and instantaneously changing or new attack patterns. On the other hand, anomaly-based IDS (ADS) identify deviation of normal behavioural baselines, and therefore they provide great ability to recognize the zero-day attacks, but these are usually at the cost of high false positive rates (FPR) [5, 6].

In an attempt to make the ADS more efficient and resistant to crime, recent advances in research have integrated machine learning (ML) and deep learning (DL) architectures to identify benign and malicious network traffic [7–9]. Other classical ML classifiers: Support Vector Machines (SVM), Decision trees (DT) and Random Forest (RF) are reported to give good results in controlled conditions. Nevertheless, these methods frequently fail to capture time and hierarchy dependencies of a complex IoT traffic data [10, 11]. Convolutional Neural Networks (CNNs), Long Short-Term Memory (LSTM) networks, and Variational Autoencoders (VAEs) are the DL techniques that have advanced to the next level in detecting anomalies, as both spatial and sequential data patterns are captured. However, a majority of these models operate as black-box (opaque) systems, and are thus not very interpretable as far as their predictions are concerned [12, 13]. Such a lack of transparency is a major weakness in security-critical settings, where the transparency of the operations, accountability of the model, and explainability are the top priorities.

Explainable Artificial Intelligence (XAI) has become an important facilitator of improving the explainability and reliability of AI-based anomaly-detection systems [14, 15]. XAI

DOI: 10.1201/9781003644231-16

approaches give post-hoc explanations to model choices and assign value scores to input features and display their contributions to prediction results. The XAI applications in cybersecurity have demonstrated potential results in multiple fields, such as intrusion detection, malware identification and adversarial attack-minimization [16, 17]. Nevertheless, the use of XAI in the context of anomaly detection frameworks of IoT networks is not fully covered so far, especially in the case of system data structures that are highly heterogeneous, dynamic, and hierarchical.

Motivation:

It is assumed that the heterogeneity of the traffic in the IoT networks is combined with its high-dimensionality, which is quite challenging to the traditional anomaly detection practices, as well as the unceasing refinements of attack patterns. Current AI-powered ITS (Intelligent Threat Detection System) architectures tend to be non-scalable, non-flexible and non-explainable, which prevents their use in true-to-life IoT systems. Additionally, the majority of ADSs do not consider the complex hierarchical and latent relationships of time-varying data of IoT traffic, which leads to poor detection accuracy indicators and high false alarms. Furthermore, lack of or insufficient explainability mechanisms does not allow security analysts to comprehend the logic of model predictions, which negatively affects operational trust and thus prevents forensic investigations.

To address these shortcomings, the study suggests an original Explainable Intelligence Framework for IoT anomaly detection that combines hierarchical feature embedding and latent space modelling to properly detect anomalies at the cost of increased interpretability with various XAI models. Another effect on the VAE is that the model will have acquired the underlying proximity of normal traffic, which can be used in the reconstruction of routine behaviour and abnormal activity. Some of the main aspects of network traffic feature relationships in the proposed framework are complex and temporal, hierarchical features, which are explained through post-hoc transparent, clear explanations of each detection decision.

The main findings provided by this chapter include the following:

- To introduce a scalable, interpretable DL system that combines hierarchical feature embeddings with latent space modelling of multiclass IoT anomaly detection.
- To preprocess and use benchmark IoT network traffic datasets (NSL-KDD and CIC-IDS 2023 IoT) of one-hot encoding and min–max normalization to achieve a better data quality and model performance.
- To create a Hierarchical Feature-Embedded Latent Autoencoder Network (HFELAN) that will be predictive of correct classification of network traffic into Probe, Denial-of-Service (DoS), Remote-to-Local (R2L), User-to-Root (U2R), and Normal categories.
- To integrate and contrast three explainability models (Shapley Additive Explanations [SHAP], Local Interpretable Model-Agnostic Explanations [LIME] and Permutation Feature Importance [PFI]) to give meaningful and interpretable visualizations of features importance and decision boundaries in the context of anomaly detection.
- To effectively do large-scale simulations in a Python-based environment, compare the proposed model to the existing methods using measures of accuracy, positive predictive value (PPV), Matthews correlation coefficient (MCC) and false negative rate (FNR).

The rest of the chapter is structured in such a way: Section 11.2 is the literature review of recent articles about IoT anomaly-detecting systems and explainable AI. Section 11.3

outlines the planned research methodology, which consists of data preprocessing, an architectural model and XAI integration. The experimental results and XAI evaluations are presented in and discussed in Section 11.4. Lastly, Section 11.5 also provides a conclusion of the paper and the research directions for the future.

11.2 RELATED WORKS

Over the recent years, the fast growth of IoT environments has contributed considerably to the increased rate and volume of cyber threats, which has led to widespread studies on the configurations of ADSs that are specific to heterogeneous IoT networks. Many researches have explored the application of artificial intelligence (AI) and ML and DL methods to intrusion detection and ADS [18–20]. This part looks at where the newer IoT anomaly-detection methods are heading, without going too deep into every technical detail. There's been a steady stream of ideas lately, and you can almost sense the field trying to break out of its older habits. Along with that, the push for clearer explanations has picked up. The recent XAI work is playing a big role here, mainly by helping us see why a model reacts the way it does instead of leaving everything buried inside the system. It doesn't solve every problem, but it does make the whole process a bit less opaque.

Gummadi et al. [21] proposed an XAI-enhanced framework of anomaly detection that focuses on industrial IoT environment in 2024. Their methodology was to use a mixture of both deep neural networks and ensemble-based AI models to categorize the anomalies, after which the seven different XAI techniques were applied to identify features and their importance. The framework had shown good levels of accuracy in industrial sensor datasets and botnet traffic captures and had major issues with high computational overhead but was not viable to be deployed in large-scale IoT systems in real time.

In the case of the unsupervised anomaly detection architecture, Abudurexiti et al. [22] used a Time Convolutional Neural Network (TCNN), Kolmogorov–Arnold Networks (KAN) and a VAE to learn long-term temporal dependencies in Industrial IoT (IIoT) streams of data. The model used post-hoc interpretation of the results of the detection through XAI methods and key contributing features were identified. Although it was shown to achieve better detection accuracy and explainability, the framework was characterized by high computational complexity that restricted its scalability at all levels, both in training and inference.

In 2023, Keshk et al. introduced a DL-based system of intrusion detection that is equipped with explainability processes [23]. They applied an LSTM model on NSL-KDD, UNSW-NB15, ToN-IoT and used it to identify various types of attacks in IoT networks. The framework combined the SPIP (Statistical Probability-based Information Processing) feature selection scheme and post-hoc XAI feature visualization methods such as LIME and SHAP. Although the system demonstrated good performance with regard to the detection, its applicability in real-time was hampered because of the high consumption of resources in large IoT setups.

Mousa'B et al. [24] proposed an ADS deployed on IIoT networks, which uses the DL method, applies SHAP and LIME methods of explainability, to increase transparency. This research utilized the ToN-IoT data and trained the explainable models of DL and compared them with one of the baseline, the extreme learning machine (ELM). Despite detecting anomalies with high accuracy and interpretability, the framework made the deployment of the framework highly costly in the context of IoTs when they had to utilize it in a large-scale and real-time context due to high computational costs.

In another study, Sharma et al. [25] investigated the use of DL-based anomaly detection methods in combination with XAI models to detect different network attacks in NSL-KDD and UNSW-NB15 datasets. Their method made use of a filter-based feature selection system and trained a different set of DNN and CNN models. XAI, such as LIME and SHAP, has been added to understand decisions made in a model. The models were also shown to be effectively classifiable, and their interpretability models proved effective, but the computation costs of explainability methods were a scalability and big data burden.

The SXAD framework by Alam et al. [26], involves the use of the Kernel SHAP values to detect the features of events that cause an anomaly in the IoT systems. To convert a traditionally opaque system into a transparent, explainable IDS, the study used benchmark log data of HDFS, which was processed by a Drain parser. Though the method increased explainability in making the detection, the computational cost of my Kernel SHAP was still a major limitation to the real-time, large-scale application.

Le et al. [27] generated an interpretable IDS based on ML to use ensemble tree models (DT and RF) with SHAP. Their system was successful in intrusion detection on large datasets of IoT traffic, NF-BoT-IoT-v2 and IoTDS20. Nevertheless, the limited flexibility to various IoT setups was also caused by the fact that even with promising attack detection abilities and XAI interpretability, the layout was heavily reliant on individual dataset feature patterns.

All these studies indicate the increased importance of the incorporation of explainability mechanisms in IoT anomaly detection tools. Nevertheless, there are shortcomings concerning computational efficiency, scalability, modelling hierarchical features, and successful interpretation of the latent space, which is important with dynamic IoT applications with high-dimensional data.

Research Gap:

In spite of the progress mentioned, not many studies have successfully covered the combination of hierarchical feature embedding techniques and latent space modelling tools to explainable anomaly detector systems that are specific to an IoT network. Further, the current systems are not much concerned with the complexities of hierarchical-temporal dependencies and latent inter-feature correlations to IoT traffic patterns that are essential to an effective and precise identification of anomalies. Additionally, the majority of frameworks apply either of the explainability approaches or limit the application of XAI to the usage of non-hierarchical data models and thus restrict the predictability and reliability of predictions as used in dynamical IoT settings.

11.3 PROPOSED METHODOLOGY

To overcome these limitations, this chapter suggests a new Explainable Intelligence Framework that integrates hierarchical feature embeddings and latent space modelling with various XAI methods (SHAP, LIME, and PFI) in order to increase the quality of anomaly detection, interpretability, and operational transparency by IoT networks.

This chapter introduces a hierarchical and explainable intelligence system to find various types of anomalies in IoT networks by applying both hierarchical feature embedding and latent space modelling methods. The specified framework improves the identification of multifaceted, time-dependent, and hierarchical patterns of anomalies in IoT network traffic, and it makes the process transparent and relies on the use of numerous XAI models.

Firstly, an initial process of acquiring and preprocessing raw IoT network traffic data of the NSL-KDD and CIC-IDS 2023 IoT datasets is implemented using one-hot encoding and min–max normalization to enhance data consistency and quality. The processed data is in turn fed into the proposed HFELAN, which combines recursive hierarchical feature embeddings with latent space modelling to detect anomalies and classify them into five categories, namely, Normal, DoS, Probe, R2L and U2R.

Lastly, the feature contribution of anomaly detection decisions is also examined and visualized using three state-of-the-art explainability models, SHAP, LIME and PFI, which enhance the transparency, trust, and operational interpretability of IoT security management.

The more specific steps of the methods can be outlined as follows:

11.3.1 Data acquisition

The proposed methodology was evaluated using two standard datasets.

- NSL-KDD Dataset [28]:
  The improved and better version of an already used KDD Cup 1999, NSL-KDD, attempts to overcome significant weaknesses, including overlapping records and unbalanced classes. It groups traffic instances into five major categories (Normal, DoS, Probe, R2L and U2R) and has 41 features of network connections. The data contains 125,973 training records and 22,544 test records, with a balanced number of classes and is applicable to verify IDS.
- CIC-IDS 2023 IoT Dataset [29]:
  This dataset, curated by the Canadian Institute of Cybersecurity, consists of a set of network traffic captures of a simulated IoT network comprising 105 devices (smart cameras, sensors and home appliances). It contains several attack scenarios, which are classified into groups as Mirai, DDoS, reconnaissance, brute-force and web-based attacks. The dataset consists of comprehensive labelled records that have comprehensive feature space, which makes it an appropriate benchmark to measure the anomaly detection paradigms in heterogeneous IoT environments.

11.3.2 Data preprocessing

To normalize the available characteristics of the datasets, the proposed method has used two preprocessing steps:

- One-Hot Encoding:
  The categorical features are changed into binary indicator variables so as to enable their successful use in the learning models. This encoding makes it compatible with the DL structure and demonstrates the preservation of the unique categorical meaning of the individual feature.
- Min–Max Normalization:
  Using min–max normalization the values of the numerical features are scaled within the [0,1][0,1][0,1] range, which enhances learning toleration and convergence. Equation (1) is the mathematical expression of the process of normalization:

  $$X' = (X - Xmin) / (Xmax - Xmin) \quad (1).$$

  X is the original value.
  Xmin is the lowest value available in that characteristics.
  Xmax is the highest value available in that characteristics.
  X' is the normalized value.

The equation transforms the data that was initially there into a range of 0–1.

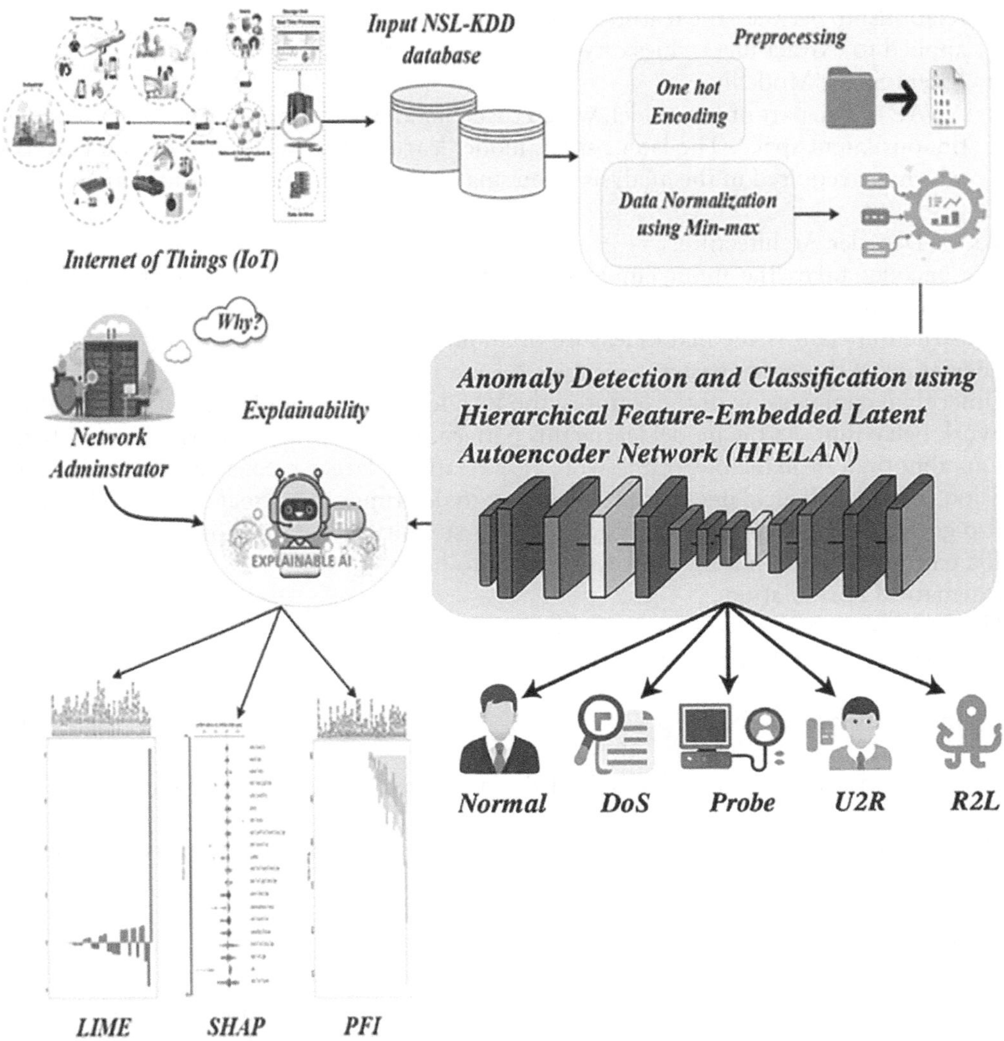

Figure 11.1 Workflow of the Proposed Explainable Intelligence Framework.

11.3.3 Hierarchy of feature – HFELAN anomaly detection

The data after the processing is presented to the proposed HFELAN model that is a novel deep architecture trained to operate on the hierarchical features correlation, latent connections of IoT traffic data. The framework integrates the elements of the hierarchical embedding, convolutional encoding, and the variational latent space modelling to increase the success rates of the anomaly detection.

Key components of HFELAN:

- HF Embedding:
  Correlation-based clustering groups input features recursively into multiple hierarchical groups, which enable both the global relationship of the features and localized

relationship between the features to be captured. Parallel convolutional layers are then applied to extract hierarchies of space patterns of these embeddings.

- Latent Space Modelling:
  A VAE is also part of the model, which casts hierarchical feature embeddings to a continuous latent space. The latent space model learns latent relationships and patterns, which are required in the analysis of anomalies of the complex IoT environment.

Encoder–Decoder Architecture:

The encoder takes the input embeddings and translates them into latent vectors and the decoder translates the latent representation of the input into the input feature space. Reconstruction error is the main measure of anomalies and the larger the error, the larger the deviation of the traffic pattern.

Other than compression of the features, the VAE learns the overall distribution of natural network behaviour. As the model learns this pattern, it will reproduce normal inputs better but an abnormal or malicious traffic will cause relatively larger reconstruction errors. This division is a physiological one that makes it easy to determine abnormal activity. The model is also generative in nature, and this adds further stability, generalization, and detection of traffic patterns that are not necessarily expected to be so.

Mathematical Formulation:

The latent variables z are sampled with the reparameterization trick, meaning that it is compatible with backpropagation in training:

$$z = m + s\ e, \text{ where } e \sim N(0, 1) \tag{2}$$

The m and s are the mean and standard deviation vectors which are discovered by the encoder.

The loss function of the model assumes that the reconstruction loss (Lrec) is added to the Kullback–Leibler divergence loss (LKL):

$$L = Lrec + b\ LKL \tag{3}$$

where b is a scaling value so as to match the contribution of the KL divergence term.

11.3.4 Explainable AI integration

Three XAI models are added to the framework in order to guarantee the operational transparency and interpretability:

- SHAP:
  Calculates Shapley values of the individual features to reveal the contribution of a feature to the results of anomaly detection. The positive values are the features that increase the chances of an anomaly, whereas negative values reduce them.
- LIME:
  Produces locally interpretable surrogate models over particular predictions through perturbing the value of the features and examining how these perturbations change the output of the model.
- PFI: Feature Importance in Permutation:
  Test-statistic tests the significance of an individual feature by estimating the effect on the model error when the values of the individual feature are randomized, thus interfering with its predictive contribution.

All these models have a wider global and local explanation that can allow security analysts to know, support and improve the process of finding anomalies.

11.4 RESULTS AND DISCUSSION

In order to test the efficacy and explainability of the proposed Explainable Intelligence Framework, a large number of experiments were done on a Python simulation environment on an Intel entrepreneurship Core™ i5-10400 CPU with 16 GB RAM and a 64-bit operating system. The suggested HFELAN model was compared to a few of the current models of anomaly detection regarding the accuracy of classification, PPV, FNR, and MCC. Further, SHAP, LIME, and PFI visualizations were applied in using XAI performance to examine the contributions of the features to different types of attacks.

11.4.1 Experimental settings

Hyperparameters like learning rate, batch size, dropout rate and the number of epochs were optimized through grid search methodology. The data were separated into training plus validation and testing sets in a ratio of 8:1:1 in order to present objective results. Table 11.1 represents the best hyperparameter settings of the proposed framework.

11.4.2 Performance evaluation metrics

In order to evaluate the performance of detection comprehensively, standard classification metrics were calculated:

Accuracy:

Quantifies the consistency of the number of predictions of the model.

$$\text{Accuracy} = (TP + TN) / (TP + TN + FP + FN) \quad (4)$$

FNR:

Share of actual anomalies, which are erroneously regarded as normal.

$$\text{FNR} = FN / (FN + TP) \quad (5)$$

Table 11.1 Hyperparameter Settings for the Proposed HFELAN Framework

Parameter	*Value*
Learning Rate	0.001
Batch Size	16
Dropout	0.05
Number of Epochs	100
β (KL Loss Weight)	0.2

Predictive Value or the PPV:

Shows the accuracy of the model in making positive anomalies.

PPV = TP / (TP + FP) (6)

MCC:

An efficient measure of multiclass categorization especially in disproportionate data.

MCC = (TP TN – FP FN)/ sqrt (TP FP) (TP FN)(TN FN) TN FN) (7)

11.4.3 Confusion matrix analysis

In this part, the results of the confusion matrix (CM) of the proposed framework among normal and attack classes are studied. The CM is an essential device that will give better information about the model's performance, particularly how and where the misclassifications occur.

In Figure 11.2, the CM is presented, which summarizes the model's success in classifying the data based on five categories, i.e., DoS, Probe, R2L, U2R and Normal. In this matrix, the rows represent the actual classes, and the columns represent the predicted classes. Close scores on the diagonal 794 DoS, 795 Probe, at this point indicate that the model was working to determine these cases. The off-diagonal values, on the contrary (e.g. 2 or 3), imply a comparatively small number of misclassified cases. These few flaws imply that the model is accurate and has sufficient capability to distinguish different kinds of system activities and abnormalities.

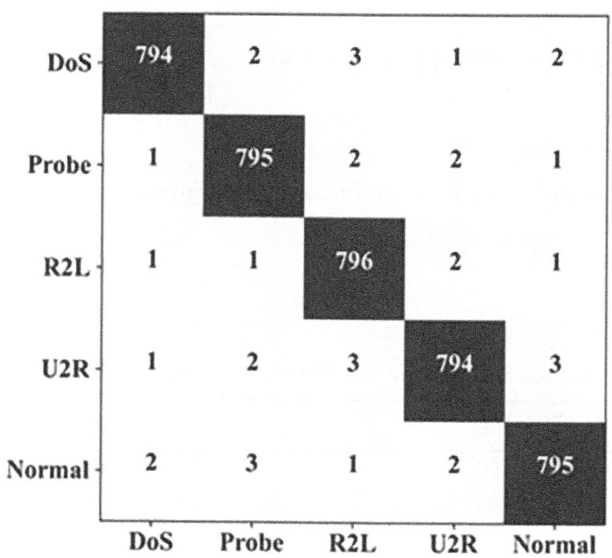

Figure 11.2 CM Evaluation of the Proposed Framework.

11.4.4 Comparative performance analysis

The given framework was compared with some of the current approaches, such as LSTM-CNN, MLP-GRU, AE-XGB and RDRL methods. Accuracy and FNR comparative analysis have been presented in Figures 11.3 and 11.4, respectively.

The findings show that there is a steady superiority of HFELAN to conventional models in all types of attacks. Interestingly, the percentage accuracy of the proposed framework in the U2R class of attack is 99.26, which is much higher than that of the second-best model (RDRL) of 96.71. On the same note, FNR values of HFELAN were much lower, reinforcing the high referring functions of these two parameters in detecting anomalies.

11.4.5 Interpretability analysis based on XAI

SHAP, LIME and PFI methods were used to identify the contributions to the classification results, which aid in improving the transparency of operations. Figure 11.5 shows the XAI visualizations of the Probe attack category of the NSL-KDD dataset.

Figure 11.5 puts three explanations side by side. The PFI bar chart points out the features that influence the model the most overall, the SHAP plot shows how those same features

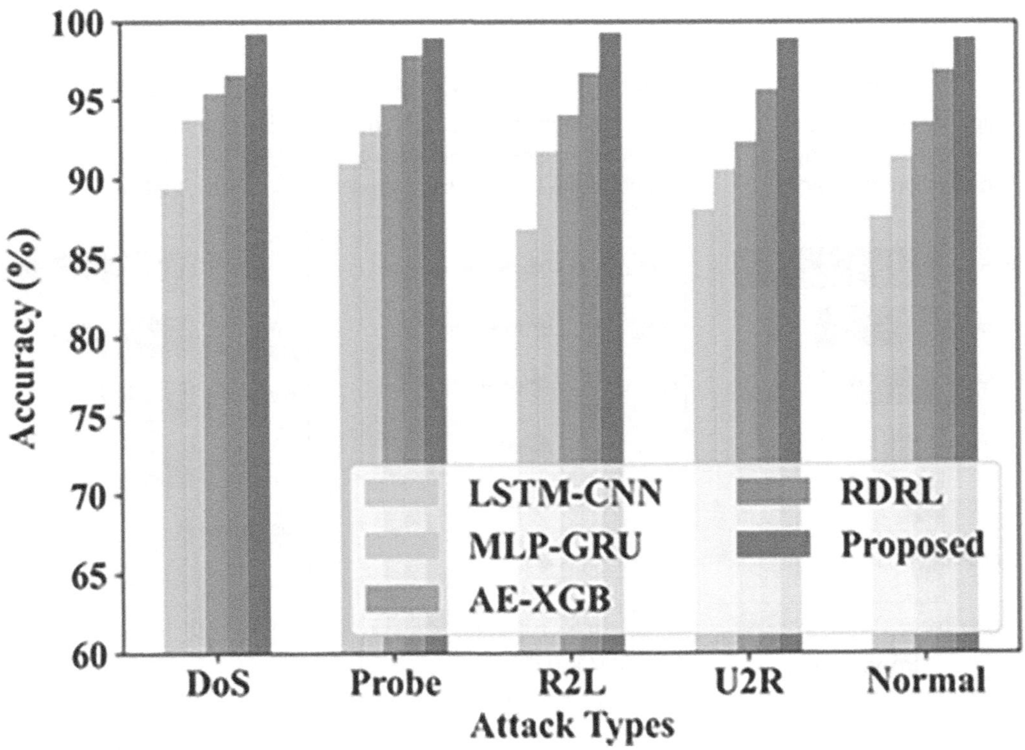

Figure 11.3 Accuracy Comparison of HFELAN against Existing Techniques.

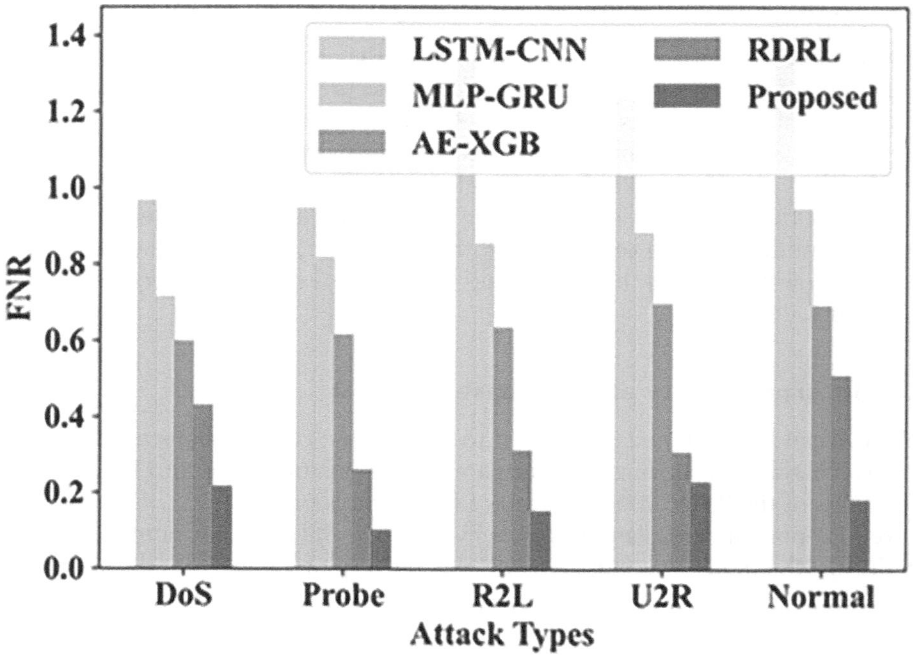

Figure 11.4 FNR Comparison of HFELAN against Existing Techniques.

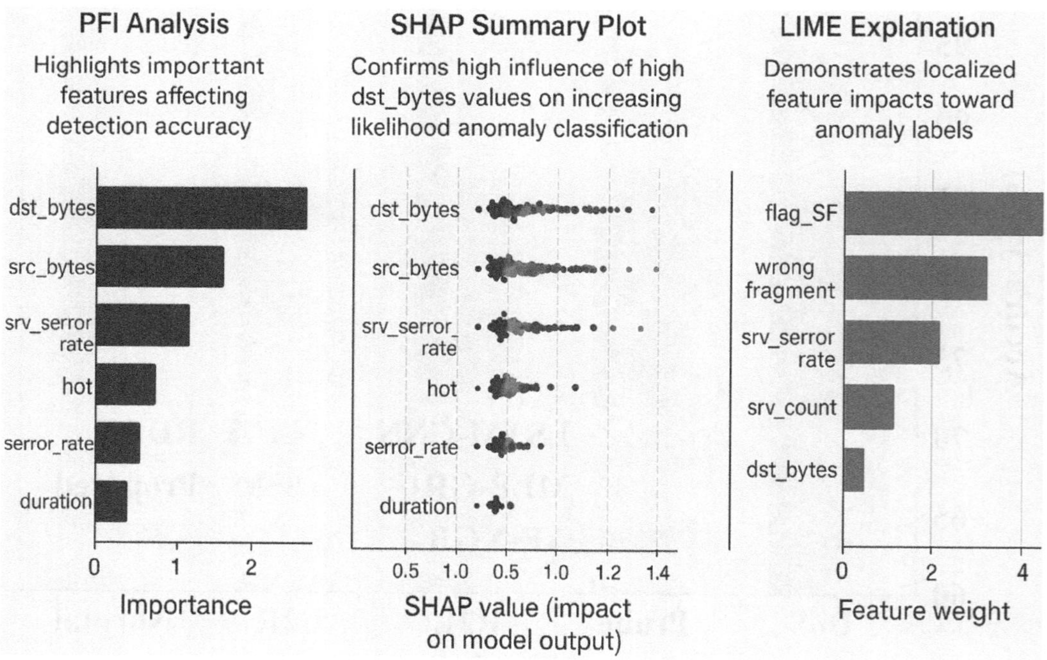

Figure 11.5 (a) PFI Plot, (b) SHAP Summary Plot and (c) LIME Explanation of Probe Attack Class.

push the output in different directions, and the LIME view breaks it down for a single example so you can see how the model reached that particular decision.

- PFI Analysis:
  Identifies dstbytes, srcbytes and srvserrorrate as the most effective features that influence the accuracy of detection.
- SHAP Summary Plot:
  Proves the role of high dstbytes and srcbytes in raising the chances of anomaly classification.
- LIME Explanation:
  Shows the localized impacts of features, high flagSF and wrongfragment values have a strong influence on the predictions to anomaly labels.

These explainability studies confirm the rational decision-making of the model and that it is consistent with the knowledge of the domain of attack signatures.

11.4.6 IoT dataset CIC-IDS 2023 IoT dataset validation

The offered framework was also confirmed with the help of the CIC-IDS 2023 IoT dataset. The results were identical to those with NSL-KDD, as the overall accuracy achieved 99.03per cent and FNR decreased to 0.182. The pattern of feature importance across the two datasets exhibited to XAI tools provides evidence of the consistent nature of feature importance across both datasets and legitimizes the generalizability and readability of the HFELAN framework proposed. The results of the experiment are summarized in Figure 11.6.

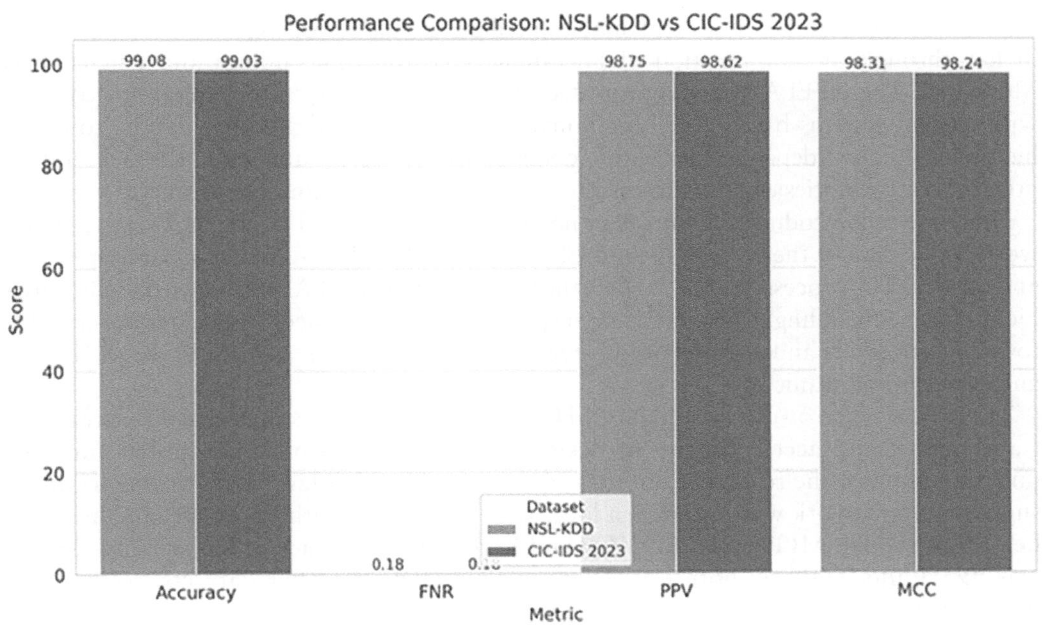

Figure 11.6 Performance Summary on NSL-KDD and CIC-IDS 2023 IoT Datasets.

11.4.7 Computational cost analysis

A quick overview of the cost of computation of the proposed model was conducted to establish the practical needs of the model. The network was trained on a regular workstation in approximately one minute per epoch, and the entire training process took approximately an hour and a half. The policy (hierarchical embedding layers and VAE structure) added another layer of intermediate representations, thus enhancing the usage of the memory in the course of training. However, it was found that inference was much faster, able to handle large numbers of samples in a short time, and, consequently, was suitable for real-time detection as soon as it was deployed. In spite of the fact that the training phase requires higher resources than other simpler architectures, the final price is not overwhelming in most research and institutional settings.

11.4.8 Salience and performance trade-off

As the framework relies on SHAP, LIME and PFI as interpretable, it ought to be made to comprehend the influence that the approaches have on the overall performance. Verbose and stable explanations are offered by SHAP, yet SHAP is more time-consuming to compute, particularly when testing a large number of samples. LIME is quicker and can be applied in explaining individual predictions, although the results can be slightly different depending on the local neighbourhood used. The lightest is PFI computing, although the explanation is on a broader, global scale. A combination of all three approaches is more likely to enrich the perceptiveness of the findings, although it carries a heavier burden on the time when explanations are created. This time is not used to confound the model, but a slight time lag is created when explaining the model, particularly in large datasets.

11.5 CONCLUSION

The chapter proposed a new Explainable Intelligence Framework for detecting anomalies in IoT through the combination of Hierarchical Feature Embeddings and Latent Space Modelling. The HFELAN model proposed was able to resolve major limitations common with current systems based on AI in anomaly detection, specifically their failure to render hierarchical, latent dependencies within complex IoT traffic dynamics and the lack of interpretability capabilities essential to operational trust and regulatory conformity.

First, one-hot encoding and min–max normalization were used to preprocess the raw network traffic data of the NSL-KDD and CIC-IDS 2023 IoT data to increase data uniformity and quality. The processed data were further run with the HFELAN framework, which used hierarchical embedding, variational latent space modelling and deep convolutional encoders to efficiently detect and classify various types of anomalies, such as DoS, Probe, R2L, U2R and even normal traffic.

Three XAI state-of-the-art models, SHAP, LIME and PFI, were added to increase the transparency and accountability of decisions, which allows both the global and local understanding of the results of anomaly detection. The high level of performance in the suggested framework was tested on a large scale, compared with the traditional methods, i.e., LSTM-CNN, MLP-GRU, AE-XGB and RDRL. The accuracy of the proposed system was 99.08 and 99.03 on both NSL-KDD and CIC-IDS 2023 IoT datasets, respectively, with low false negatives and high PPVs across the different types of attacks. Moreover, the XAI analyses repeatedly validated the decisions made by the model, with the focus put on the key influencing characteristics in line with familiar attack signatures and network activity.

Limitations:
Although the framework is proven to be effective, the deep hierarchical structure and variational modelling of the framework introduce a moderate amount of computational burden, which might restrict its use in highly resource-constrained IoT settings. Also, the model could be limited regarding its instant application in unsupervised or semi-supervised applications in IoT anomalies detection because it requires labelled training data. Future Work: This framework has a variety of practical directions that will be expanded in future research. Another promising path is to investigate edge-based deployment, where the model can be refined to run on resource-constrained IoT devices and continue to achieve good detection performance. Federated learning will also be taken into consideration to assist in distributed anomaly detection in privacy-sensitive settings without the transfer of raw data between nodes. Besides, advanced graph-based and transformer-based architecture applications will also be analysed to better represent complex patterns of inter-device communication. To reinforce the notion of robustness, the framework will be endured with the aid of real, continuously streaming IoT traffic, which will enable it to be evaluated in the conditions of real-world network variations and dynamic conditions. Lastly, prototype deployments and scalability testing will be performed in real-time to assess the efficiency and scalability of the system in large-scale infrastructures of the IoT.

ACKNOWLEDGEMENTS

An AI tool was used only for light language editing. All technical content is by the author.

REFERENCES

[1] M. Sharma, and P. Kaur, XLAAM: Explainable LSTM Based Activity and Anomaly Monitoring in a Fog Environment, *Journal of Reliable Intelligent Environments*, vol. 9, no. 4, p.463–477, 2023.

[2] M. K. Hooshmand, M. D. Huchaiah, A. R. Alzighaibi, H. Hashim, E.-S. Atlam, and I. Gad, Robust Network Anomaly Detection by using the Ensemble Learning Approach and Explainable Artificial Intelligence, (XAI), *Alexandria Engineering Journal*, vol. 94, pp. 120–130, 2024.

[3] D. G. Bhatt, P. U. Kyada, R. S. Rathore, M. K. Nallakaruppan, and R. H. Jhaveri, Enhancing Anomaly Detection in Industrial Control Systems through Supervised Learning and Explainable Artificial Intelligence, *Journal of Cybersecurity and Information Management*, vol. 15, no. 1, p. 314, 2025.

[4] M. D. Nguyen, V.-H. La, W. Mallouli, A. R. Cavalli, and E. Montes de Oca, *Towards Anomaly Detection using Explainable AI, in Cybersecurity in a DevOps Environment: Requirement to Monitoring*, Cham, Switzerland: Springer Nature Switzerland, 2023, pp. 293–324.

[5] C. S. Kalutharage, X. Liu, C. Chrysoulas, N. Pitropakis, and P. Papadopoulos, Explainable AI-Based DDoS Attack Identification Method for IoT Network, *Computers*, vol. 12, no 2, p. 32, 2023.

[6] C. S. Kalutharage, X. Liu, and C. Chrysoulas, Explainable AI and Deep Autoencoders Based Security Framework for IoT Network Attack Certainty, in *International Workshop on Attacks and Defenses to Internet-of-Things*, Cham, Switzerland: The Springer Nature Switzerland, 2022, pp. 41–50.

[7] M. M. Alani, A. I. Awad, and E. Barka, ARP-PROBE: An ARP spoofing detector for Internet of Things networks using explainable deep learning, *Internet of Things*, vol. 23, p. 100861, 2023.
[8] I. Elgarhy, M. M. Badr, M. Mahmoud, M. Alsabaan, T. Alshawi, and M. Alsaqhan, Xai-based accurate anomaly detector that is robust against black-box evasion attacks for the smart grid., *Applied Sciences*, vol. 14, no. 21, p. 9897, 2024.
[9] R. Kalakoti, H. Bahsi, and S. Nomm, Improving iot security with explainable ai: Quantitative evaluation of explainability for iot botnet detection, *IEEE Internet of Things Journal*, 11(10), pp. 18237–18254, 2024.
[10] R. K. Muna, M. I. Hossain, M. G. R. Alam, M. M. Hassan, M. Ianni, and G. Fortino, Demystifying Machine Learning Models of Massive IoT Attack Detection with Explainable AI to Sustainable and Secure Future Smart Cities, *Internet of Things*, vol. 24, p. 100919, 2023.
[11] A. Barbado, O. Corcho, and R. Benjamins, Rule extraction in unsupervised anomaly detection for model explainability: Application to OneClass SVM, Expert Systems with Applications, 189, p. 116100, 2022.
[12] D. Attique, W. Hao, W. Ping, D. Javeed, and P. Kumar, Explainable and data-efficient deep learning for enhanced attack detection in IIoT ecosystem, *IEEE Internet of Things Journal*, vol. 11, no. 24, pp.38976–38986, 2024.
[13] M. Amiri-Zarandi, H. Karimipour, and R. A. Dara, A federated and explainable approach for insider threat detection in IoT, *Internet of Things*, vol. 24, p. 100965, 2023.
[14] H. Lundberg, N. I. Mowla, S. F. Abedin, K. Thar, A. Mahmood, M. Gidlund, and S. Raza, Experimental Analysis of Trustworthy In-Vehicle Intrusion Detection System Using Explainable Artificial Intelligence (XAI), IEEE Access, vol. 10, pp. 102831–102841, 2022.
[15] P. Mignone, R. Corizzo, and M. Ceci, Distributed and explainable GHSOM for anomaly detection in sensor networks, *Machine Learning*, vol. 113, no. 7, 4445–4486, 2024.
[16] W. Ding, I. Alrashdi, H. Hawash, and M. Abdel-Basset, DeepSecDrive: An explainable deep learning framework for real-time detection of cyberattack in in-vehicle networks, *Information Sciences*, vol. 658, p. 120057, 2024.
[17] Y. Han, and H. Chang, XA-GANomaly: An explainable adaptive semi-supervised learning method for intrusion detection using GANomaly Computers, *Materials and Continua*, vol. 76, no. 1, pp. 221–237, 2023.
[18] W. W. Lo, G. Kulatilleke, M. Sarhan, S. Layeghy, and M. Portmann, XG-BoT: An explainable deep graph neural network for botnet detection and forensics, *Internet of Things*, vol. 22, p. 100747, 2023.
[19] M. Hasan, M. S. Rahman, H. Janicke, and I. H. Sarker, Detecting anomalies in blockchain transactions using machine learning classifiers and explainability analysis, *Blockchain: Research and Applications*, vol. 3, p. 100207, 2024.
[20] O. Chakir, Y. Sadqi, and E. A. A. Alaoui. An explainable machine learning-based web attack detection system for industrial IoT web application security, *Information Security Journal: A Global Perspective*, vol. 35, pp. 13–39, 2024.
[21] A. N. Gummadi, J. C. Napier, and M. Abdallah, XAI-IoT: an explainable AI framework for enhancing anomaly detection in IoT systems, *IEEE Access*, vol. 12, pp. 71024–71054 ,2024.
[22] Y. Abudurexiti, G. Han, F. Zhang, and L. Liu, An Explainable Unsupervised Anomaly Detection Framework for Industrial Internet of Things, *Computers and Security*, vol. 148, p. 104130, 2025.
[23] M. Keshk, N. Koroniotis, N. Pham, N. Moustafa, B. Turnbull, and A. Y. Zomaya, An explainable deep learning-enabled intrusion detection framework in IoT networks, *Information Sciences*, vol. 639, p. 119000, 2023.
[24] M. S. Mousa, M. K. Hasan, R. Sulaiman, S. Islam, and A. U. R. Khan, An Explainable Ensemble Deep Learning Approach for Intrusion Detection in the Industrial Internet of Things, *IEEE Access*, vol. 11, pp. 115047–115061, 2023.

[25] B. Sharma, L. Sharma, C. Lal, and S. Roy, Explainable Artificial Intelligence for Intrusion Detection in IoT Networks: A Deep Learning Based Approach, *Expert Systems with Applications*, vol. 238, p. 121751, 2024.

[26] K. Alam, K. Kifayat, G. A. Sampedro, V. Karovic, and T. Naeem, SXAD: Shapely eXplainable AI-based anomaly detection using log data, *IEEE Access*, vol. 12, pp.95659–95672, 2024.

[27] Le, T.T.H., Kim, H., Kang, H. and Kim, H., Classification and explanation for intrusion detection system based on ensemble trees and SHAP method, *Sensors*, vol. 22, no. 3, p. 1154, 2022.

[28] Hannan Chougle, NSL-KDD Dataset. Available online: www.kaggle.com/datasets/hannanchougle/nsl-kdd

[29] E. C. P. Neto, S. Dadkhah, R. Ferreira, A. Zohourian, R. Lu, A. A. Ghorbani, UNB CIC IOT. 2023 Dataset. Available online: https://doi.org/10.34740/KAGGLE/DSV/6425404

Chapter 12

Accurate and lightweight IoV intrusion detection

Correlation-filtered ensemble feature selection

Arash Salehpour, Monire Norouzi, and Alireza Souri

12.1 INTRODUCTION

The Internet of Vehicles (IoV), a cornerstone of intelligent transportation systems (ITS), represents a significant evolution in the conceptualization, deployment, and management of modern vehicular networks. IoV extends traditional vehicular networks by integrating diverse communication technologies and devices via V2V, V2I, and V2X communications. It provides an unparalleled opportunity to make driving safer and more efficient by enabling intelligent road safety and traffic management and improving overall transportation efficiency, given mobility, ever-changing network topologies, and diversified data sources [1–4]. The complexity of these networks, combined with the real-time demands of the intrusion detection system (IDS), necessitates the development of robust mechanisms for detecting and optimizing systems that handle high-volume data generated by multiple entities in IoV [5–7]. Feature selection has become an essential preprocessing step for selecting the most relevant features to achieve high accuracy and timely intrusion detection with minimal computational overhead [8]. Reducing the feature space will also enhance the efficiency of IDS and improve its accuracy and generalizability across diverse IoV scenarios through feature selection algorithms. Several feature selection algorithms were proposed, ranging from traditional statistical methods to more sophisticated machine learning-based ones. Feature selection algorithms generally fall into one of three classes: filter methods, wrapper methods, and embedded methods [9, 10]. The filter methods perform based on properties intrinsic to the data, such as correlation and mutual information, to evaluate feature relevance without using any learning algorithms [11]. On the other hand, Wrapper methods [12] select feature subsets by directly considering their performance within a concrete learning algorithm; this usually incurs increased computational costs. Embedded methods combine feature selection with the model training process and offer a better trade-off between computational efficiency and predictive performance [13]. Adopting feature selection algorithms in IDSs is relatively nascent but very promising for IoV applications. Considering the unique characteristics of IoV data, such as heterogeneity, real-time processing, and high accuracy for various kinds of threat detection, proper features must be selected. Good features reduce data dimensionality, prevent model overfitting, and make IDS models more interpretable. The application of feature selection algorithms in IoV environments faces many fundamental challenges: the dynamic evolution of the topology due to frequent changes, possible additional variations in communication, and complications in the feature selection process [14, 15]. Also, data sources are diverse, ranging from sensors and on-board units (OBUs) to cloud-based infrastructure, which requires feature selection techniques to adapt to variations in data scale and format across these sources [16, 17]. Developing context-aware and adaptive mechanisms for feature selection would address the dynamic nature of IoV

DOI: 10.1201/9781003644231-17

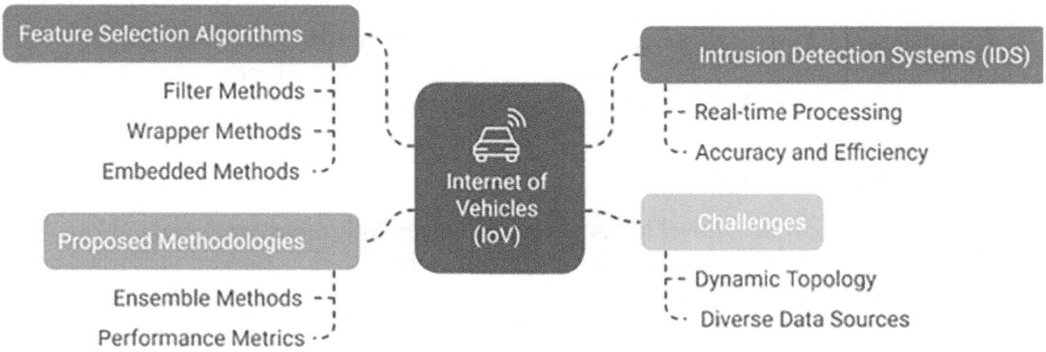

Figure 12.1 Enhancing IoV Security through Feature Selection.

networks and ensure robustness and efficiency of IDSs against evolving threats [18, 19]. Figure 12.1 illustrates the key components and challenges of integrating feature selection algorithms into IoV IDSs.

The main contributions of the current study are briefly highlighted in the sequence:

Ensemble Feature Selection (EFS) Method: New EFS methodologies are derived from various machine learning models, as outlined in the correlation analysis. This chapter proposes a comprehensive approach to enhance performance in this direction, thereby improving the capability of IDS within IoV networks. This can effectively reduce the feature dimensionality of high-dimensional datasets and improve the detection accuracy with minimal computational overhead.

Higher Accuracy in Detection: The proposed approach outperforms classic feature selection methods like ANOVA, CHI2, FDR, and PCA on all accounts, that is, in terms of accuracy, precision, recall, and F1-score. It achieves perfect precision and recall for a few classes in the CICIoV2024 dataset alone, demonstrating the robustness of our detector in distinguishing between benign and malicious network traffic.

Real-Time Capability and Computational Efficiency: The proposed IDS achieves real-time performance while improving computational efficiency. It consumes minimal execution time, memory, and CPU. These improvements make it highly suited to real-time applications in the new vision for the IoV, where the rapid, practical detection of cyber threats is paramount. The scalability and adaptability of the method across different IoV topographies are demonstrated using the CICIoV2024, Car Hacking, and UNSWNB15 datasets, showing its adaptability to changes in network topography, data type, and attack profiles. It will be essential to maintain IDS effectiveness in this evolving, heterogeneous IoV landscape. This will thus address the problem of lower recall rates for the minority class in cases such as Analysis, Backdoor, and Worms. Some future directions will be advanced techniques in data augmentation and deep learning-based feature selection. This will improve recall for the minor classes, providing comprehensive coverage for even threat detection.

This chapter lays the groundwork for further research on feature selection using adaptive and context-aware methods and automated updates in IDS. This includes developing advanced, responsive IDS to address maturing cybersecurity challenges in IoV environments.

The contribution of this manuscript is to advance IoV security through a robust, efficient, and scalable IDS framework that meets current cybersecurity needs and points toward future developments in ITSs. Figure 12.2 presents the workflow of integrating feature selection algorithms into the IoV systems.

12.2 RELATED WORK

The paper [20] proposed a novel EFS method, namely EFSPF, that fuses weighted PageRank and fuzzy logic to improve feature selection accuracy in high-dimensional datasets. Feature selection is an essential task in machine learning, where one achieves higher model performance by reducing computational complexity by excluding irrelevant features. EFSPF addresses two existing challenges in feature selection by accounting for the effect of poor feature rankings, known as "noise," which can deteriorate the performance of the ensemble method. The EFSPF approach combines the previous feature selection methods by first computing the Euclidean Distance Matrix (EDM) between features. Then, it uses fuzzy type logic to evaluate the credibility of feature ranks. Fuzzy reasoning provides flexibility for intelligently handling the uncertainty inherent in feature selection and enables strong integration of various feature selection methods. Then, it constructs a weighted graph whose nodes are features, and the EDM and reliability rates define the edges. The PageRank algorithm ranks the features so that noise can be minimized while accuracy is maximized. Among these, several datasets and a variety of comparison metrics have been used to validate EFSPF's performance, including accuracy, precision, recall, and F1-score, demonstrating that EFSPF significantly outperforms various existing ensemble methods and eight base feature selection algorithms across multiple high-dimensional datasets. The contribution is vital in high-dimensional studies, as EFSPF provides an effective feature selection method that improves model performance across different domains.

The paper [21] proposed an ensemble technique that applies a rank-aggregation process using the four operators mentioned to produce continuous aggregations and multiple assessments across inputs. In this respect, the authors compare the effectiveness of their proposed method with that of existing techniques using 10 benchmark datasets. Some performance metrics already mentioned, such as accuracy, precision, recall, and F-measure, indicate the effectiveness of the new ensemble technique compared to conventional methods. These Bonferroni-OWA and Bonferroni-IOWA operators can model feature subset interdependencies to select optimal features. Additionally, the entropy-weighted method was applied to compute the degree of disorder in the data. This improves the selection process by embedding an objective weighting into the feature ranking. This research introduces a new concept into EFS, incorporating several aggregation operators; it further demonstrates greater stability and raises the bar for high-dimensional data classification tasks, thereby constituting a worthy contribution to large dataset-dependent fields.

A metaheuristic EFS method, SA-EFS, proposed by [22], was developed to develop the research area for high-dimensional datasets. Therefore, such a method addresses typical problems, such as redundant or completely irrelevant features in a vast dataset. SA-EFS uses the arithmetic and geometric means to aggregate the outcomes of three feature selection methods: Chi-Square Test, Maximum Information Coefficient (MIC), and XGBoost. The obtained aggregated feature subsets are then used to improve classification accuracy. The authors tested the approach using three classifiers: K-Nearest Neighbors (KNN), Random Forest (RF), and XGBoost; they compared their results to show that SA-EFS performs better than individual feature selection methods in classification performance. Another

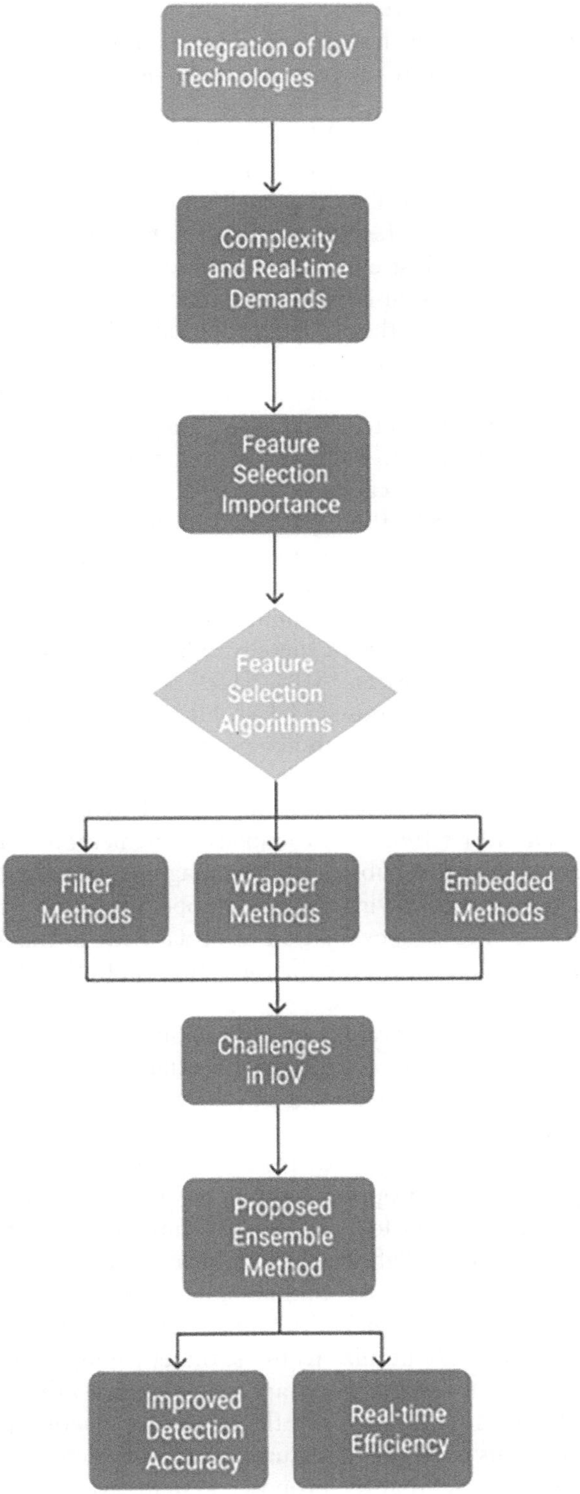

Figure 12.2 Integration of IoV.

investigation of threshold settings revealed that a threshold interval of 0.1 yields the best classification performance. The critical contribution of this paper is to demonstrate that EFS, which combines several feature selection methods, significantly improves classification performance.

Neumann et al. [23] proposed a new EFS method that will improve the predictive performance of binary classification tasks by compensating for different biases inherent in each technique used to choose a feature. This approach underscores the need for a dependable, repeatable way to identify minimal feature sets, such as biomarkers in predictive medicine, that increase model accuracy. Most existing feature selection methods suffer from significant biases that seriously compromise their effectiveness and reliability, as do embedded, wrapper-based, and filter-based methods. The proposed EFS approach adds eight feature selection algorithms to an ensemble, thereby providing more accurate quantification of feature importance and improving the stability and robustness of the resulting feature selection. They applied their EFS method to six datasets. They showed that models trained with EFS-selected features performed better than those taught with conventional feature selection methods or without feature selection.

A network IDS, namely HyFSA-HEIC, proposed by Amrita and Ravulakollu [24], represents the class of a hybrid feature selection approach combined with a heterogeneous ensemble of intelligent classifiers. This technique classifies the network traffic as standard or intrusive at runtime while keeping the computation overhead as low as possible. In this way, each classifier plays to its strengths, thereby enhancing the robustness and accuracy of the detection system. These datasets, "10% KDD" and "Corrected Test," have yielded results that demonstrate that the proposed HyFSA-HEIC system strictly outperforms other methods in terms of accuracy, precision, and computational efficiency.

Kim et al. [25] aim to overcome the obstacle of feature selection from a high-dimensional imbalanced dataset by proposing a new ensemble-based hybrid feature selection framework, namely ELFS. The ELF's framework embeds filter methods within an ensemble to identify robust, informative feature subsets while managing computational complexity. The ELFS framework includes the following multistage operations: preprocessing, selecting a representative classifier, and feature evaluation using CMIM. In this regard, ELFS adopts a filter-centric approach and integrates predictions from multiple classifiers to address the Achilles' heel of traditional filter methods.

The paper [26] copes with the critical issue of intrusion detection in the context of an IoT ecosystem, including denial-of-service (DoS)/DDoS attacks. Considering that traditional machine learning suffers from performance inefficiency due to high feature dimensionality in IoT network traffic, this paper proposes an optimized feature selection approach that uses IG and GR to select the top 50% of features, improving detection accuracy while increasing processing speed. The proposed method is validated on the BoT-IoT and KDD Cup 1999 datasets, which represent IoT and network intrusion scenarios, respectively.

While focusing on developing a lightweight IDS, this paper [26] entails a wrapper-based feature selection approach. This proposal outlines a new hybrid feature selection algorithm that uses modified Random Mutation Hill Climbing and modified linear support vector machines to efficiently select and optimize features, thereby improving system performance and reducing computational overload. Their approach is put to the test on the KDD Cup 1999 dataset, one of the most widely used in the literature, where it proves that the set of selected features outperforms using all 41 features about both detection rates and computational costs, relevant was the fact that the proposed system processed in almost 50% of the time spent by methods necessary for some attacks, such as U2R. These experiments indicate

Table 12.1 Overview of Innovative EFS Methods and Their Applications in High-Dimensional Datasets

Reference	*Proposed Method*	*Key Innovation*	*Feature Selection Approach*	*Performance Metrics*	*Applications*
[20]	EFSPF	Integrates weighted PageRank and fuzzy logic for robust feature ranking	Euclidean Distance Matrix (EDM), Type-I Fuzzy Logic, PageRank	Accuracy, Precision, Recall, F1-Score	High-dimensional datasets, various domains
[21]	Ensemble with Bonferroni-OWA and IOWA	Aggregation operators for interrelationships between feature subsets	Bonferroni, OWA, Induced OWA (IOWA), Entropy Weight Method	Accuracy, Precision, Recall, F-Measure	High-dimensional data, classification tasks
[22]	SA-EFS	Combines Chi-Square, MIC, and XGBoost for ensemble selection	Arithmetic and Geometric Mean Aggregation	Accuracy, Classification Performance	High-dimensional datasets, various classifiers
[23]	Ensemble Feature Selection (EFS)	Compensates for biases in individual methods using an ensemble	Combines eight distinct feature selection methods	AUC, Predictive Accuracy	Binary classification, predictive medicine
[24]	HyFSA-HEIC	Hybrid feature selection with heterogeneous ensemble classifiers	Filter and Wrapper Approaches	Accuracy, Precision, True Positive Rate	Network intrusion detection, real-time classification
[25]	ELFS (Ensemble-based Hybrid Feature Selection)	Combines ensemble learning with filter methods for imbalanced datasets	Conditional Mutual Information Maximization (CMIM)	Classification Accuracy	Imbalanced high-dimensional datasets, real-world applications
[26]	Optimized Feature Selection for IDS	Information Gain and Gain Ratio for optimized feature selection	IG, GR, JRip Classifier	Precision, Processing Speed, Accuracy	IoT ecosystem, DoS/DDoS attack detection
[27]	Feature Entropy Estimation (FEE)	Combines chi-square, Pearson correlation, and F-score for efficient feature selection	Rank-based Entropy Methods	Detection Accuracy, Time Efficiency	IoT networks, malicious traffic detection

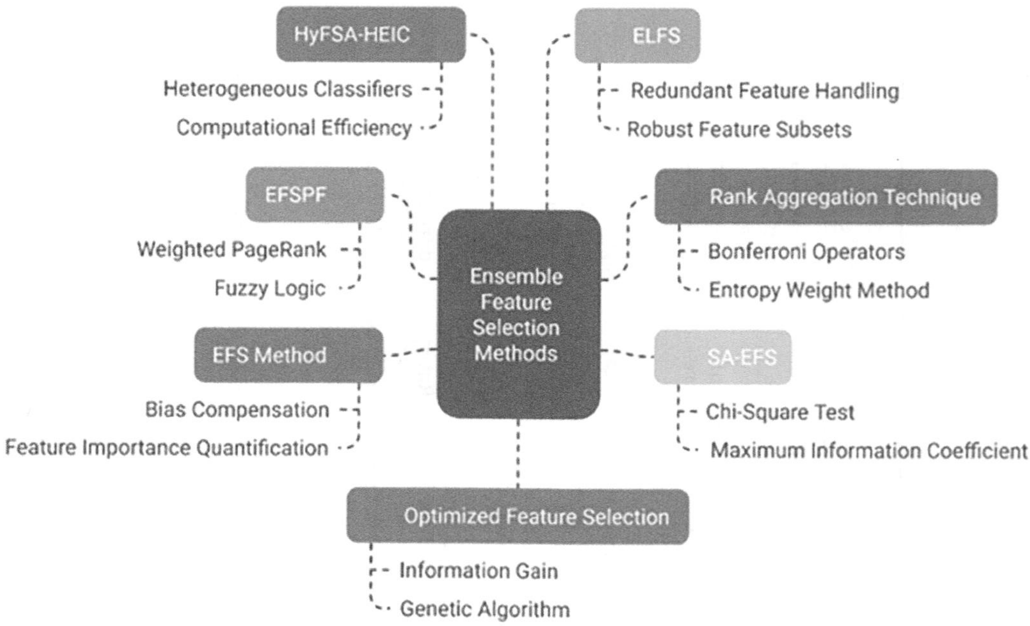

Figure 12.3 EFS Methods and Their Impact.

that the IDS built with the selected feature set can achieve high detection rates, especially against new attack types.

This paper [27] proposes a novel machine learning model for detecting malicious traffic in IoT networks using feature entropy estimation. It combines rank-based chi-square, Pearson correlation, and F-score correlation to improve feature selection, a critical task for optimizing classification performance while balancing computational complexity. The study addresses misclassifications caused by irrelevant or redundant features in large IoT datasets.

This paper [28] addresses critical security concerns by leveraging supervised machine learning to drive automated classification and malicious activity detection, thereby identifying attack types. It was tested in an IoT smart home testbed with eight devices against 12 attack variants, including DoS, man-in-the-middle, reconnaissance, and replay attacks. In addition, four multistage attacks involving complex chains of events were selected for testing. The proposed IDS is outstanding in terms of efficiency, achieving very good F-measures of 96.2% for device profiling, 90% for malicious packet detection, and 98% for attack type classification. Table 12.1 synthesizes innovative EFS methods for high-dimensional datasets, emphasizing their design, technical frameworks, and empirical performance. Figure 12.3 illustrates the landscape of EFS methods, highlighting their key characteristics and techniques.

12.3 THE PROPOSED ALGORITHM

This chapter proposes a new hybrid feature selection method that integrates ensemble machine learning models with correlation analysis to select relevant features from high-dimensional data optimally. The technique above is applied to an ensemble comprising four machine learning algorithms (namely RF, ADA, XGB, and LGB), to detect and rank essential features. The objective is to maintain classification performance while reducing computational complexity with this approach for a real-time intrusion detection and classification system. Feature selection starts by computing the correlation matrix of the given features and removing highly correlated features to avoid multicollinearity. Perform Pearson's correlation [29] on it and remove features with a threshold greater than 0.8 from further consideration. This process decreases the feature space early by eliminating several redundant features. In that respect, after correlation analysis, the proposed EFS method applies a two-step approach: The Union method aggregates the essential features from each model, RF, ADA, XGB, and LGB, by taking the ranking according to the best scores based on the importance of features. Each model is extensively trained on the dataset, and later, the union of the top-ranked features across models is computed, ensuring that, through selection, a comprehensive coverage of relevant features reflecting the diversity of the models' performance is achieved. The intersection then refines this set of features by retaining those that consistently rank high across all models. This is an essential step toward noise reduction, focusing only on the most robust and relevant features, and it is likely to result in better accuracy with less computational overhead. The two-stage ensemble approach has consistently delivered better performance across both dimensionality reduction and robust classification, thereby effectively solving large-scale machine learning problems. Algorithm 1 presents a structured pipeline for EFS that integrates correlation-based filtering and model-based ranking to optimize feature subsets in high-dimensional data. Key components include a two-stage process: (1) Data Preparation (filtering out irrelevant features, label encoding) and Correlation Analysis (Pearson-based filtering out multicollinear features, threshold: 0.8), followed by (2) EFS using four classifiers (RF, AdaBoost, XGBoost, LightGBM) to estimate feature importance scores. The method combines features via union (top features per model) and second-order EFS, and via intersection (standard top features across models), yielding an improved subset. Salient innovations include hybrid filter-wrapper and dual aggregation methods to balance redundancy elimination and stable feature preservation. Figures 12.4 and 12.5 outline the step-by-step workflow of the proposed EFS algorithm.

12.3.1 Step-by-step workflow of the EFS method

Data Preparation: Clean the dataset by filtering out useless features, then label-encode categorical variables for model training.

Correlation Analysis: Calculate the Pearson correlation matrix for the features, identify/drop the highly multicollinear features with a correlation coefficient > 0.8 to reduce redundancy.

Model Training – Ensemble: Train different machine learning models, including RF, AdaBoost (ADA), XGBoost (XGB), and LightGBM, using the filtered dataset. Feature importance scores would be extracted from each of these models.

Union Aggregation: Aggregate the top-ranked features from each model's importance list, covering all feature spaces by combining various feature choices across models.

Intersection Refinement: Refine the aggregated set by selecting features that appear in the top-k lists across all models, reducing noise and focusing on robust, consistently essential features.

Final Optimal Feature Subset: Output the refined feature subset for use in downstream intrusion detection tasks.

Algorithm 1. Proposed Method

Input: Dataset *D* with features *F* and labels y; features for union *U* and features for intersection *I*

Output: feature set F_{Opt}

Step 1: Data Preparation phase
- Load the dataset
- Drop irrelevant columns
- Define features and targets: Split the dataset into the feature set represented by *X* and the target labels represented by *y*.
- Label encoding could have been carried out through Label Encoder, which can convert categorical labels given into numerical values.

Step 2: Correlation Analysis
- Pearson Correlation Matrix: Calculate the correlation matrix of the feature set *X*.
- Remove those features whose correlation value is above the abovementioned thresholds. (One objective may be to avoid multicollinearity.) For this example, the threshold value will be 0.8.

Step 3: Ensemble Feature Selection
- First, the following machine learning models are performed: Random Forest Classifier, Adaboost Classifier, XGBoost Classifier, and LightGBM.
- Train both models on the training datasets X_train and X_test, and get the importance score of the features:
    - Any model *M* in {RF,ADA,XGB,LGB}:
        - Train the model $M\ on\ X_{train}\ and\ y_{train}$
        - Get feature importance scores from *M*
- Union Feature Selection:
    - Select the features ranking in the top *U* of each model weighted by the importance score.
    - Sum up the best-selected features from the two models as an overall feature set.

Step 4: Ensemble Feature Selection Second round
- Intersection Feature Selection:
    - Choose the top *I* features from both models to get a refined feature set.
- Top intersection operation across the top *I* features from all models to

create a refined feature set $F_{Intersection}$

Evaluation and Results

End of algorithm

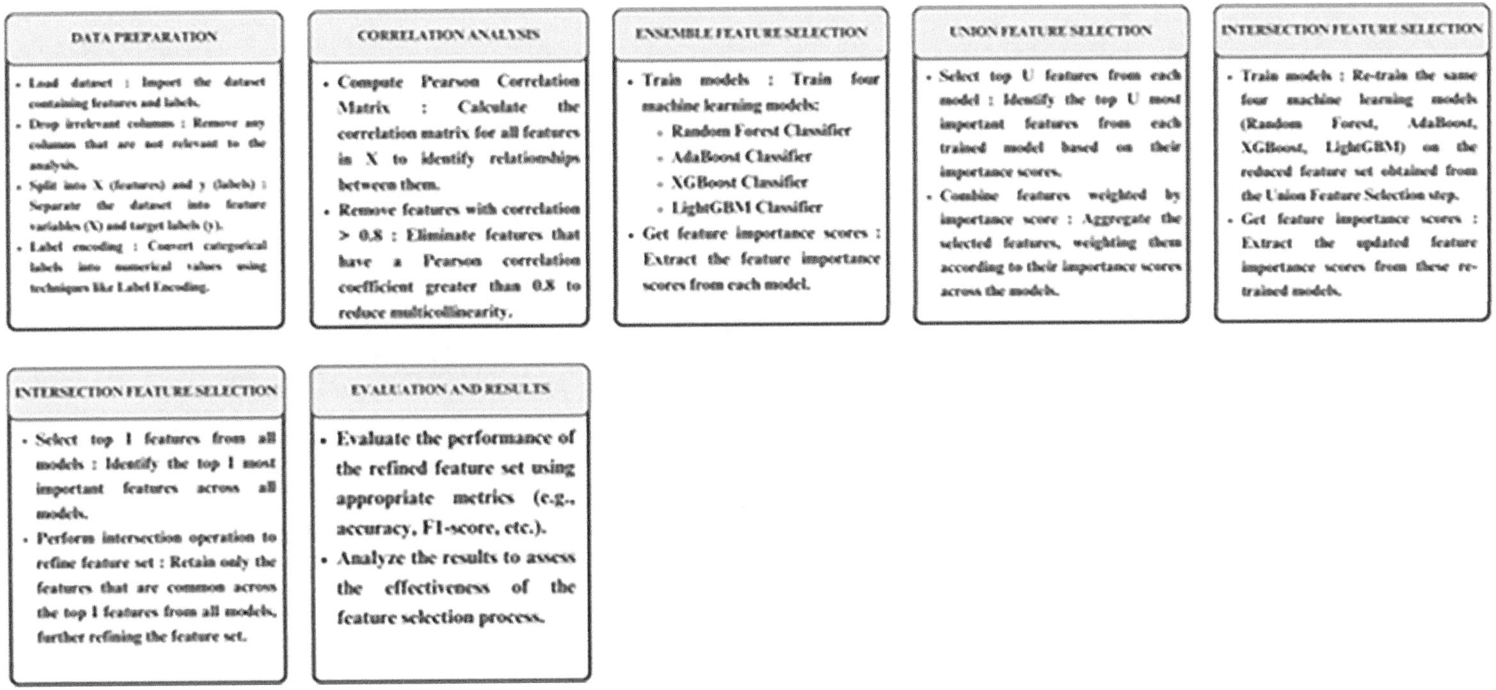

Figure 12.4 Optimizing Feature Selection for Intrusion Detection.

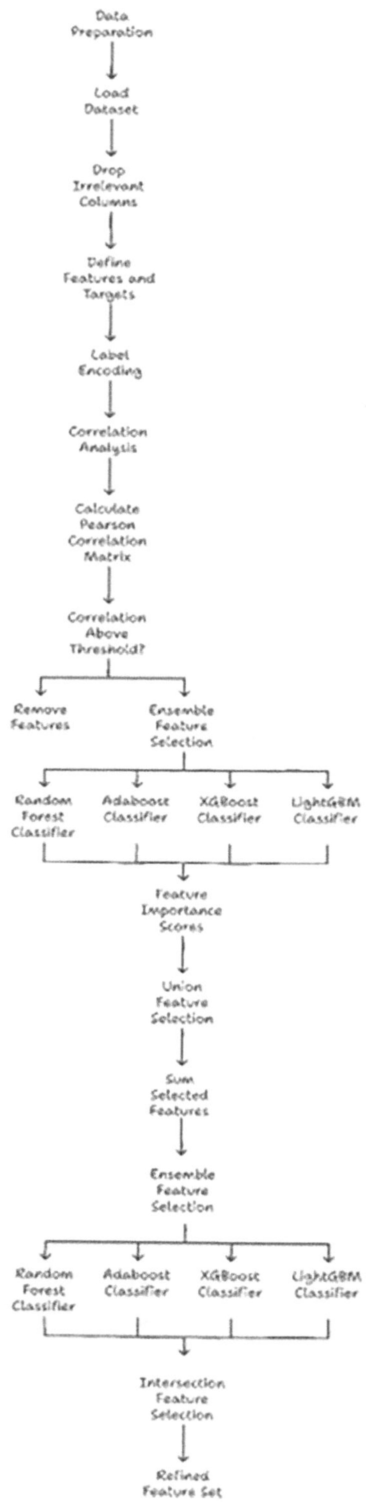

Figure 12.5 Step-by-Step Workflow of the EFS Method.

The feature selection process uses union and intersection approaches, combining features selected by different models (RF, AdaBoost, XGBoost, LightGBM) to form the final feature set.

The union of feature importance lists selects the top features from all models combined:

$$\cup nion = \{f_j \mid f_j \in top_k(RF) \cup top_k(Ada) \cup top_k(XGB) \cup top_k(LGB)\}$$

Intersection:

The intersection method selects features that appear in the top-k lists of all models:

$$\text{Intersection} = \{f_j \mid f_j \in top_k(RF) \cap top_k(Ada) \cap top_k(XGB) \cap top_k(LGB)\}$$

Tables 12.2–12.4 report the final feature subsets from ensemble selection processes applied to three distinct high-dimensional datasets. Table 12.2 (CICIoV2024) presents the final features in eight rows, showing iterative optimization via union/intersection operations. Table 12.3 (Car Hacking) is the final feature set. Table 12.4 (UNSW_NB15) presents the final feature set.

12.3.2 Pearson correlation matrix

One of the statistical tools used in the research is the Pearson correlation matrix [30], which measures the linear relationship between pairs of continuous variables. This is especially helpful in high-dimensional data, where the relationship between features may not be apparent. This matrix computes Pearson's correlation coefficient, which indicates the strength of the relationship between variables, enabling better feature selection, detection of multicollinearity, and dimensionality reduction for machine learning tasks. Pearson's

Table 12.2 CICIoV2024 Final Feature Set

DATA_013	DATA_111	DATA_215	DATA_410	DATA_210
DATA_013	DATA_211	DATA_09	DATA_316	DATA_415
DATA_013	DATA_513	DATA_712	DATA_29	DATA_113
DATA_39	DATA_114	DATA_516	DATA_116	DATA_613
DATA_414	DATA_416	DATA_610	DATA_110	DATA_615
DATA_412	DATA_112	DATA_55	DATA_016	DATA_310
DATA_213	DATA_19	DATA_413	DATA_612	DATA_07
DATA_64	DATA_47	DATA_012	DATA_512	DATA_611

Table 12.3 Car Hacking Final Feature Set

DATA1	DATA5	DATA0

Table 12.4 UNSW_NB15 Final Feature Set

Bytes	ct_dst_src_ltm	sttl	smean	dur	sbytes	ct_srv_dst	sinpkt	service

correlation coefficient, noted as $r_{x,y}$, measures the strength and direction of the linear relationship between two variables, x, y. Coefficient Calculation through [10]:

$$r_{xy} = \frac{\sum_{i=1}^{n}(x_i - \overline{x})(y_i - \overline{y})}{\sqrt{\sum_{i=1}^{n}(x_i - \overline{x})^2}\sqrt{\sum_{i=1}^{n}(y_i - \overline{y})^2}} \tag{1}$$

The Pearson correlation coefficient ranges between –1 and 1, where [31]:

- r = 1 indicates a perfect positive linear relationship,
- r = –1 indicates a perfect negative linear relationship,
- r = 0 Suggests no linear relationship between the variables [32]:

$$R = \begin{bmatrix} 1 & r_{12} & \cdots & r_{1n} \\ r_{21} & 1 & \cdots & r_{2n} \\ \vdots & \cdots & \ddots & \vdots \\ r_{n1} & r_{n2} & \cdots & 1 \end{bmatrix} \tag{2}$$

Where each element, r_{ij},represents the Pearson correlation coefficient between variables and j.

Tables 12.5–12.6 list features eliminated by Pearson correlation analysis (cutoff of 0.8) to prevent multicollinearity in the UNSW_NB15 and CICIoV2024 data. Table 12.5 removes 16 network-behavior-oriented features (e.g., "sbytes," "tcprtt," "ct_ftp_cmd"), suggesting redundancy in traffic measurements, and Table 12.6 removes six generic identifiers (e.g., "DATA_59," "DATA_712") in CICIoV2024. The discrepancy in the number of eliminated features suggests dataset-specific redundancy patterns, with more inter-feature correlation in network behavior measurements in UNSW_NB15 technical terms (e.g., "is_sm_ips_ports").

12.3.3 Bagging and boosting feature importance

In machine learning, bagging and boosting are among the most common ensemble techniques for improving predictive performance by combining several base models. Though both methodologies use different models, they differ in how they combine the models and in

Table 12.5 Dropped Features in Pearson Correlation UNSW_NB15

sbytes	sloss	dwin	Synack	ct_dst_ltm	ct_src_dport_ltm	ct_dst_src_ltm	ct_src_ltm
dbytes	dloss	tcprtt	ackdat	is_sm_ips_ports	ct_dst_sport_ltm	ct_ftp_cmd	ct_srv_dst

Table 12.6 Dropped Features in Pearson Correlation CICIoV2024

DATA_59	DATA_512	DATA_515	DATA_610	DATA_710	DATA_712

the selection of features. First, this section covers the feature selection process for bagging and boosting, followed by the crucial equations for using them in modeling. Bagging is an ensemble technique that forms multiple subsets of the original dataset via bootstrapping. An independent model, as assigned to each subgroup, undergoes training. Aggregation of all model outputs produces the final prediction. This reduces variance and helps guard against overfitting. We often use decision trees as part of feature selection for bagging, where the importance of features is measured by the reduction in impurity at nodes, using metrics such as Gini impurity or entropy. We use RFs in this work for the final classifier model, a bagging method applied to decision trees. The importance of a feature in an RF is determined by the sum of decreases in Gini impurity within all trees in a forest, normalized by the total number of trees. Accordingly, it can be formally expressed as [32, 33]:

$$\mathrm{FI}(f_j) = \frac{1}{T}\sum_{t=1}^{T}\sum_{n \in N_t} \Delta I_n\left(f_j\right) \tag{3}$$

Boosting is another ensemble method that operates by sequentially training models. Unlike bagging, boosting reduces bias rather than variance by iteratively re-weighting the training instances. In this regard, boosting algorithms are usually trained to focus on harder-to-predict samples, especially in algorithms like AdaBoost, XGBoost, and LightGBM. In feature selection for boosting, feature importance is generally determined by how often a feature influences a split across all trees, the gain in accuracy at each split, or the loss reduction [34]. In AdaBoost, each model pays more attention to the output of misclassified instances from previous models by giving them higher weights. Its output is a weighted vote of various weak classifiers. AdaBoost estimates the importance of features in reducing classification errors or increasing classification gains [34, 35].

$$\alpha_t = \frac{1}{2}\,\mathrm{In}\left(\frac{1-\epsilon_t}{\epsilon_t}\right) \tag{4}$$

As the name suggests, the importance of AdaBoost features is determined by the weighted sum of the absolute values of the feature weights for all classifiers.

XGBoost is an advanced boosting algorithm focused on efficiency and predictive accuracy. It develops trees sequentially, and feature importance is often determined by gain, that is, the improvement in accuracy reduction in loss due to a split.

Gain for a split using a feature. f_j is defined as [36]:

$$\mathrm{Gain}(f_j) = \frac{1}{2}\left[\frac{G_L^2}{H_L+\lambda} + \frac{G_R^2}{H_R+\lambda} - \frac{\left(G_L+G_R\right)^2}{H_L+H_R+\lambda}\right] - \gamma \tag{5}$$

LightGBM is another boosting algorithm that grows trees consecutively. It uses histogram-based binning and leaf-wise growth strategies to be efficient and fast. Unlike in XGBoost, feature importance in LightGBM includes the total gain obtained by using the feature in splits [37]:

$$\mathrm{FI}(f_j) = \sum_{t=1}^{T} \sum_{n \in N_t} \frac{Gain_n(f_j)}{\sum_{f_j} Gain_n(f_j)} \tag{6}$$

12.4 DATASET DESCRIPTION AND PREPROCESSING

12.4.1 The CICIoV2024 dataset

The development of connected vehicles has been rapid. Cybersecurity in vehicular networks has been developed in anticipation of the coming IoV. The convergence of vehicular systems, various sensors, wireless communications, and cloud-based infrastructure will open new opportunities for intelligent transportation while also making it vulnerable to cyber threats. Due to the increasing demand for IDSs in IoV environments, CICIoV2024 [38] has been developed as the state-of-the-art benchmark dataset for evaluating IoV machine learning models for detecting and mitigating cyberattacks targeting IoV ecosystems. It contains benign and malicious traffic data across various attack scenarios, including DoS and spoofing attacks targeting GPS, speed sensors, steering wheels, and RPM systems, as well as intrusion attempts. This dataset comes from a broad testbed that emulates vehicular communication networks for vehicle-to-vehicle or vehicle-to-infrastructure communications. The dataset successfully pictures the peculiar features of IoV network dynamics, simulating vehicular communications and their interactions with network nodes. It is, in fact, a very realistic basis for developing advanced intrusion detection models. One challenge in IoV networks is their highly dynamic structure; therefore, they frequently change topology under different environmental conditions, making it quite challenging to generalize IDS models. Figure 12.6 illustrates the distribution of classes in the CICIoV2024 dataset, identifying BENIGN, DoS, GAS, RPM, SPEED, and STEERING_WHEEL.

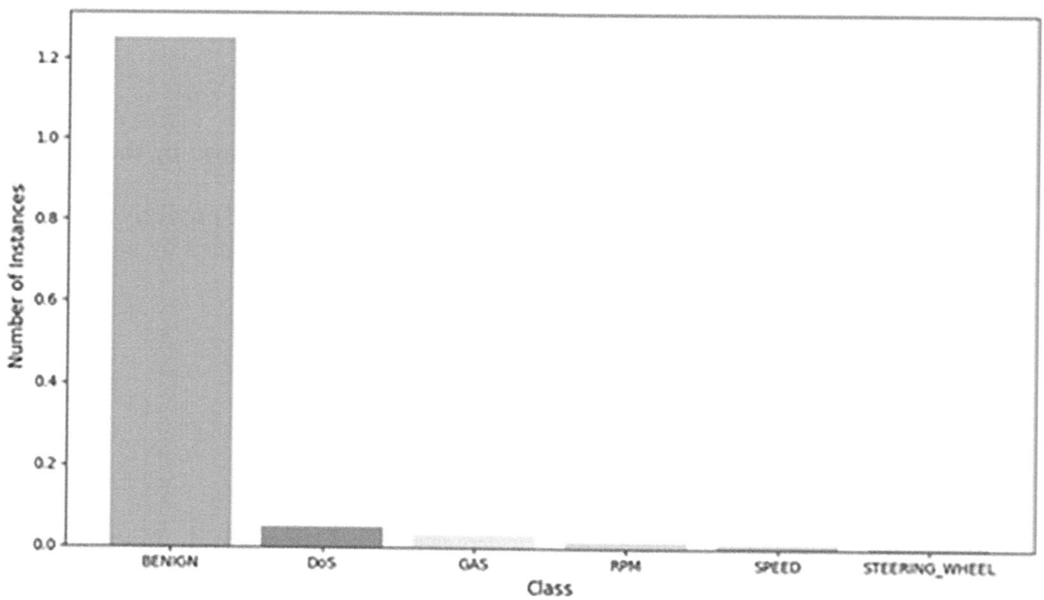

Figure 12.6 CICIoV2024 Class Distribution.

12.4.2 Car Hacking dataset

The Car Hacking dataset [39] is a comprehensive dataset that includes timestamps, message IDs, and data fields for messages traversing the CAN bus. Because these systems play a significant role in an automobile's operation, an attack on the CAN bus can pose a safety hazard. Many variants of various attacks are available, from the simplest message injection to complex, coordinated attack strategies designed to disrupt specific vehicle functions. It therefore serves as the fundamental basis for researchers and developers to implement IDS solutions that can secure vehicular systems against such malicious activities. With this comprehensive information, an in-depth analysis of attack patterns to identify system vulnerabilities would be possible. The dataset enables in-depth analysis of various attack patterns in vehicular networks. Figure 12.7 presents the class distribution of the Car Hacking dataset, with numerical counts of instances in the "Number of instances" category.

12.4.3 The UNSW-NB15 dataset

The UNSW-NB15 dataset [40] was developed to emulate real network traffic that characterizes attack vectors and legitimate network behavior. This dataset strikes a delicate balance between regular traffic and malicious activity, making it an ideal benchmark for machine learning and deep learning models for intrusion detection. This dataset was generated using the IXIA Perfect Storm tool, which simulates realistic traffic across different network environments, including typical user behaviors and cyberattack scenarios. The UNSW-NB15 dataset comprises nine attack categories that represent current network threats. Backdoors: Techniques to bypass standard authentication to gain unauthorized access to a

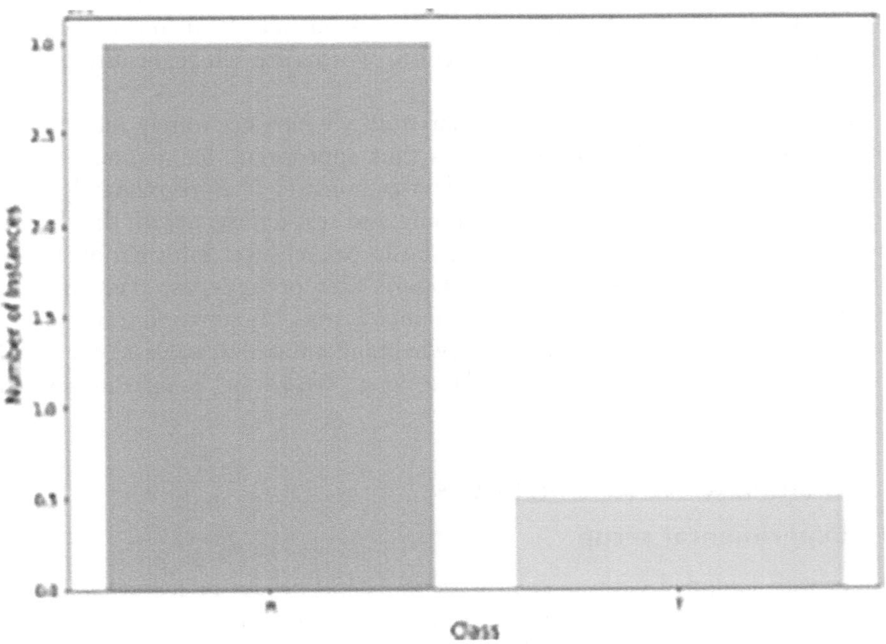

Figure 12.7 Car Hacking Class Distribution.

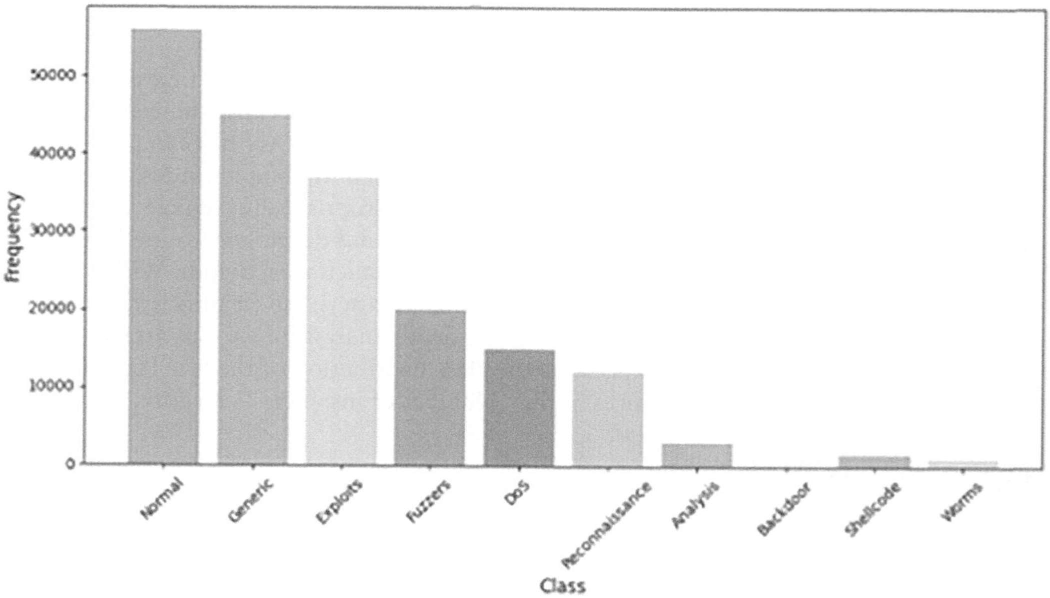

Figure 12.8 UNSW-NB15 Class Distribution.

computer system. DoS is a denial-of-service attack that tries to overload the network service and make it unavailable to legitimate users. An exploit is an attack that takes advantage of a vulnerability in software or hardware. Generic: A cryptographic attack skips the authentication mechanism to gain system access. Reconnaissance: Attempts to gather knowledge about the network or system for future intrusions. Shellcode: Malicious code injected into a network or system to cause a malicious action. Worms are self-replicating malware that infect a network in a "worm-like" fashion.

The dataset also includes extensive regular traffic, which accurately reflects the typical behavior of several network protocols and is thus appropriate for anomaly- and misuse-detection approaches. The UNSW-NB15 dataset consists of approximately 2.5 million average attack-traffic records, split into training and test datasets, with 49 characteristics described at the record level, ranging from basic packet-level information to high-level attributes describing connection behavior. Figure 12.8 presents the class distribution of the UNSW-NB15 dataset, with frequency counts across 11 network traffic classes, ranging from Normal to Reconnaissance. Overwhelming anomalies consist of a vast Normal class (~40,000) and infrequent minority classes (e.g., Backdoor), suggesting extreme class imbalance.

12.5 EXPERIMENTAL AND RESULTS

12.5.1 Experimental setup

The system was equipped with an Intel Core i5-12400 processor featuring six cores and a base clock speed of 2.50 GHz, capable of reaching a maximum turbo frequency of 4.40 GHz. It was paired with 32 GB of DDR4 RAM to support computational tasks like model training and feature selection.

12.5.2 Experimental results on original CICIoV2024 dataset with RF

The classes BENIGN, DoS, GAS, and STEERING_WHEEL achieved perfect performance (1.00) in precision, recall, and F1-score; therefore, the instances were ideally detected and classified for these classes. The precision for the RPM class remained at 1.00, while the recall dropped to 0.91, yielding an F1-score of 0.95. The SPEED class achieved precision of 0.83, perfect recall of 1.00, and an F1-score of 0.91. The model was less consistent in predicting attacks for SPEED, likely misclassifying a few benign or other instances as attacks, while correctly identifying every attack case. The macro-averaged precision, recall, and F1-score were 0.97, 0.98, and 0.98, respectively, indicating good performance against all classes. The weighted averages for precision, recall, and F1-score were exactly 1.00, indicating that the majority classes did not bias model performance and were generally robust across the dataset. The model achieved an overall accuracy of 99.64%, further emphasizing its generalization across various courses. These results indicate that the model performs very well at detecting and classifying multiple attacks in the CICIoV2024 dataset. Minor improvements can be made in classes such as RPM and SPEED. Table 12.7 reports classification performance on the original CICIoV2024 dataset, demonstrating near-perfect metrics for most classes: BENIGN, DoS, GAS, and STEERING_WHEEL achieve precision, recall, and F1-scores of 1.00. The model achieves high overall accuracy (99.64%), driven by the dominant BENIGN class (support: 305,861), though macro averages (F1: 0.98) reflect slight performance disparities across imbalanced categories.

Figure 12.9 shows the confusion matrix of the original CICIoV2024 dataset. The matrix verifies Table 12.7's accuracy of 99.64%. Structural ambiguities prevent granular analysis of misclassifications in the minority class.

12.5.3 Experimental results on original Car Hacking DoS attack with RF

The results in Table 12.8 indicate that the classification model's performance on the original Car Hacking dataset for the DoS attack was quite effective at distinguishing between the

Table 12.7 Classification Report on Original CICIoV2024 Dataset

Class	*Precision*	*Recall*	*F1-Score*	*Support*
BENIGN	1.00	1.00	1.00	305861
DoS	1.00	1.00	1.00	18777
GAS	1.00	1.00	1.00	2485
RPM	1.00	0.91	0.95	13756
SPEED	0.83	1.00	0.91	6210
STEERING_WHEEL	1.00	1.00	1.00	4966
macro avg	0.97	0.98	0.98	352055
weighted avg	1.00	1.00	1.00	352055

Accuracy: 0.9963982900399085
Usage:

- **Time taken:** 55.545034646987915 seconds
- **Memory usage at the end:** 6430.01171875 MB
- **Memory used:** 6205.19140625 MB
- **CPU usage:** 3.1%

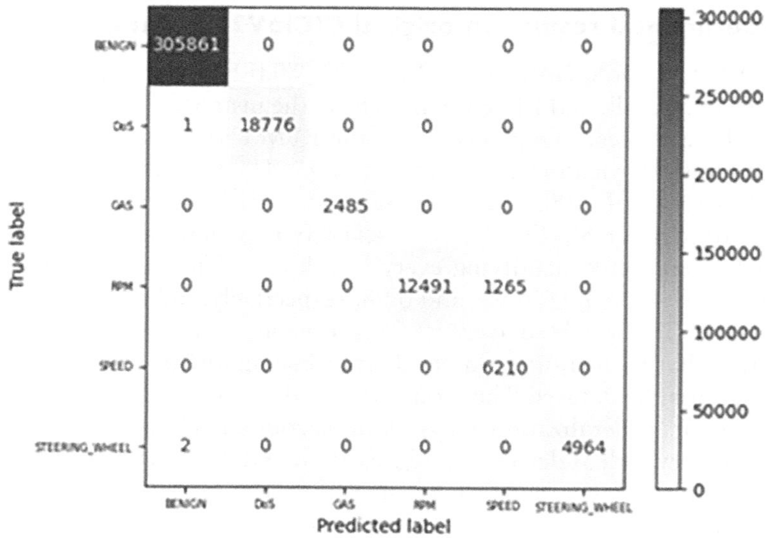

Figure 12.9 Original CICIoV 2024 Confusion Matrix.

Table 12.8 Classification Report on Original Car Hacking

Class	*Precision*	*Recall*	*F1-Score*	*Support*
R	1.00	0.97	0.99	761578
T	0.87	1.00	0.93	147068
macro avg	0.94	0.99	0.96	908646
weighted avg	0.98	0.98	0.98	908646

Accuracy:
0.9761810430024453
Usage:

- **Time taken**: 53.56103539466858 seconds
- **Memory usage at the end:** 767.984375 MB
- **Memory used:** 543.25 MB
- **CPU usage:** 3.5%

two classes: R and T. The model classified class R with a precision of 1.00; all instances classified as class R were correct. Its recall for class R was quite different; however, it was 0.97, leading to an F1-score of 0.99. This is why the model was highly accurate in predicting R instances; it missed 3% of the actual occurrences of this mass. Weighted averages for precision, recall, and F1-score were 0.98, 0.98, and 0.98, respectively. That means the model's performance on this larger dataset remained excellent, with the class imbalance issue effectively handled. Also, the overall accuracy of 97.62% demonstrates that the model generalizes well on this dataset and performs well across both the majority and minority classes. R: Normal CAN messages (regular vehicle operation).T: Injected messages (simulated DoS attacks). Figure 12.10 shows the confusion matrix of the original Car Hacking DoS attack with RF.

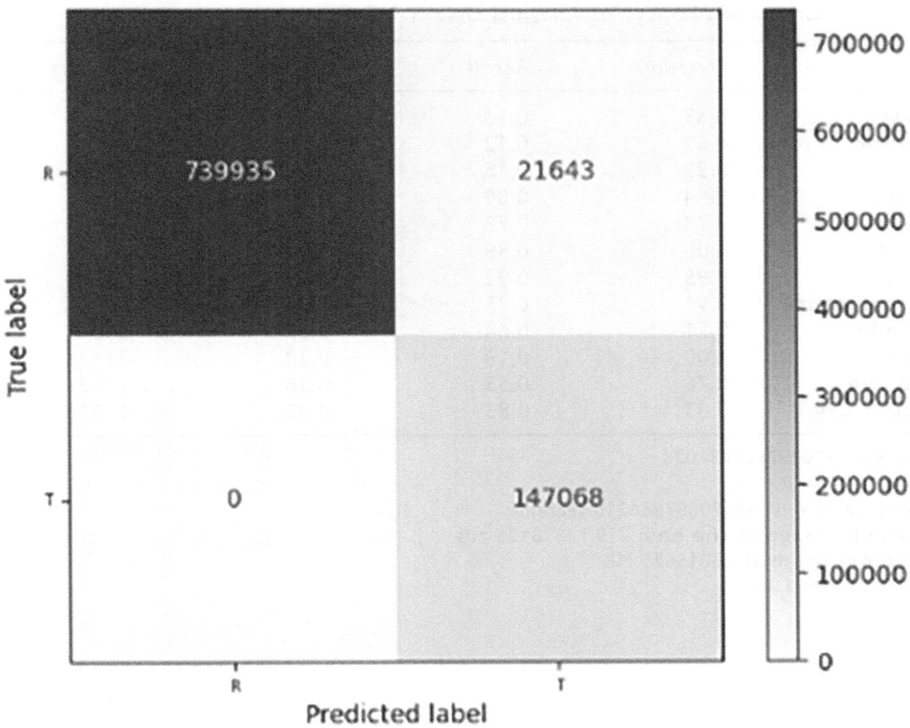

Figure 12.10 Confusion Matrix: Dos Car Hacking.

12.5.4 Experimental results on UNSW-NB15 dataset with RF

The model had a low precision of 0.69 and 0.67 for Analysis and Backdoor, respectively, along with low recall of 0.13 and 0.12, yielding low F1-scores of 0.22 and 0.21, respectively. These scores suggest poor detection performance for those classes, with the model missing many instances, and significant room for improvement in these attack detections. The performance of the DoS and Exploits classes was relatively low, too, with F1-scores of 0.20, indicating that the model has sufficient detection capability for portions of those classes but that precision and recall are not high, especially for the Exploits class, whose precision was only 0.32. Both the Shellcode and Worms classes showed weaknesses in recall, with the Worms class achieving a very low recall of 0.16, though precision was perfect at 1.00. The macro-averaged precision, recall, and F1-scores were 0.76, 0.55, and 0.58, respectively, indicating moderate performances but challenges to the model in detection performance for some classes. Table 12.9 outlines classification results for the UNSW-NB15 dataset.

Figure 12.11 shows the confusion matrix for the baseline UNSW-NB15 dataset, with classification performance across 10 network traffic classes.

12.5.5 Experimental results with the proposed method on the CICIoV2024 dataset with RF

The results show excellent classification performance across various classes, indicating the model's strength when applied to the dataset. From the evaluation, specific inferences can be

Table 12.9 Classification Report on Original UNSW-NB15

Class	*Precision*	*Recall*	*F1-Score*	*Support*
Analysis	0.69	0.13	0.22	499
Backdoor	0.67	0.12	0.21	450
DoS	0.32	0.15	0.20	2959
Exploits	0.64	0.89	0.74	8466
Fuzzers	0.74	0.78	0.76	4453
Generic	1.00	0.98	0.99	10112
Normal	0.95	0.92	0.94	13971
Reconnaissance	0.91	0.75	0.82	2595
Shellcode	0.71	0.64	0.67	300
Worms	1.00	0.16	0.28	31
macro avg	0.76	0.55	0.58	43836
weighted avg	0.83	0.83	0.82	43836

Accuracy:0.8310292909937038
Usage:

- **Time taken:** 61.98470687866210 seconds
- **Memory usage at the end:** 729.73828125 MB
- **Memory used:** 504.6015625 MB
- **CPU usage:** 2.7%

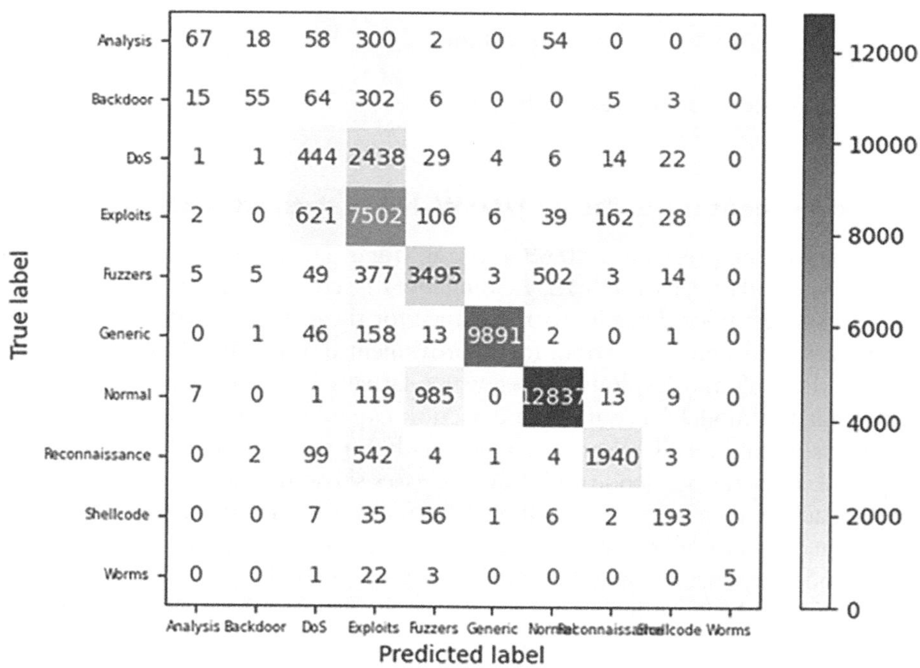

Figure 12.11 Confusion Matrix Original UNSW NB 15.

identified: the classes BENIGN, DoS, GAS, and STEERING_WHEEL have perfect precision and recall, with an F1-score of 1.00; this shows that, when classifying those instances, the model performs without flaw. That indicates an ideal separation between the classes, with no false positives or negatives, indicating how well the model performed on these classes. That was lower for the RPM class, with a precision of 1.00 and a recall of 0.91, for an F1-score of 0.95. This means the model, though recognizing most instances as RPM, missed 9% of the true positives; hence, it slightly underperformed compared to the other classes. The class with the most significant variability was the SPEED class, which had a precision of 0.83 and a perfect recall of 1.00. With that said, the high averages of 1.00 across all metrics indicate the model has performed remarkably well, especially for the larger classes, and, as a result, is vital for detection capability. The accuracy was 99.64%, indicating that the model performed exceptionally on this dataset. This is relatively high accuracy, indicating the model's ability to classify a majority of instances correctly and, hence, is very reliable for intrusion detection. It made predictions in the task with a blurred exposure of 38.59 seconds while modestly consuming memory and about 1.53 GB, with 1.7% CPU usage from a computational efficiency perspective. The relatively low resource consumption and excellent classification results suggest that the model is scalable and applicable in real time across environments with limited computational resources. It has a pretty good performance, with only minor areas for improvement in precision for the SPEED class and recall for the RPM classes.

Table 12.10 presents the classification performance of the proposed method on the CICIoV2024 dataset, achieving near-perfect metrics for most classes. Figure 12.12 presents the confusion matrix of the proposed method on the CICIoV2024 dataset, with almost perfect classification of the dominant class.

12.5.6 Experimental results with the proposed method on Car Hacking DoS with RF

The model on this dataset shows excellent classification results, with very high accuracy on both classes. Class R achieved a perfect precision of 1.00, meaning all predicted instances of this class were correct. The recall was slightly lowered to 0.96, yielding an F1-score of 0.98. While it captured all actual cases of class T, its lower precision indicates that some other instances were misclassified as T. The presented results yield macro-averaged precision of 0.91, recall of 0.98, and F1 of 0.94, indicating even performance across both classes. The differences in precision and recall between the two classes are noted. Weighted averages for precision, recall, and F1-score are close to 0.97, indicating that the performance on the larger dataset was well represented; the majority class R drives most of the overall metric scores. With an accuracy of 96.47%, this model has been generally effective across most instances, achieving

Table 12.10 Classification Report with Proposed Method on CICIoV2024 Dataset

Class	*Precision*	*Recall*	*F1-Score*	*Support*
BENIGN	1.00	1.00	1.00	305861
DoS	1.00	1.00	1.00	18777
GAS	1.00	1.00	1.00	2485
RPM	1.00	0.91	0.95	13756
SPEED	0.83	1.00	0.91	6210
STEERING_WHEEL	1.00	1.00	1.00	4966
macro avg	0.97	0.98	0.98	352055
weighted avg	1.00	1.00	1.00	352055

Accuracy:0.9963982900399085
Usage:

- Time taken: 38.59225654602051 seconds
- Memory usage at the end: 1534.5 MB
- Memory used: 1309.5625 MB
- CPU usage: 1.7%

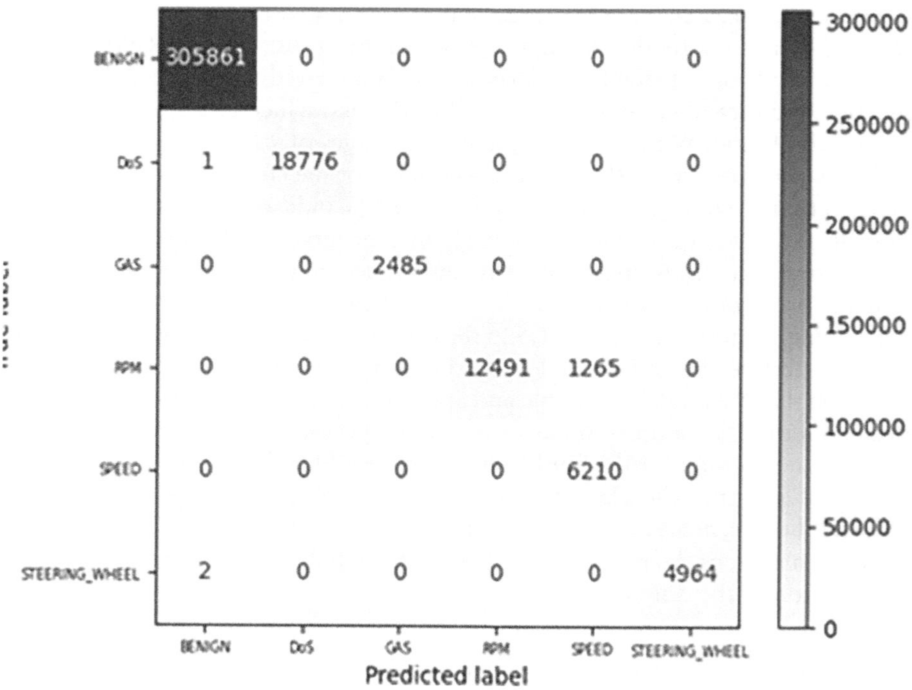

Figure 12.12 Confusion Matrix Proposed Method.

good generalization on the dataset. This level of accuracy indicates that, for all intents and purposes, interestingly enough, where both classes are critical, the model is reliable. Resource utilization: The model ran efficiently in 40.78 seconds, used ~583 MB of memory, and used 6.1% of the CPU. The resulting memory consumption of 358 MB was relatively low, thus showing that this can be considered a lightweight model and, hence, easily deployable. The resulting memory consumption of 358 MB was relatively low, indicating that this can be viewed as a lightweight model, making it easily deployable with limited computational resources. This model also shows robust performance, particularly in class T recall and class R precision, reliably solving the task at hand while remaining resource-efficient. This slight decrease in precision for class T shows some scope for improvement, but overall, the results remain excellent. Table 12.11 reports robust F1-scores (R: 0.98; T: 0.90), with macro (0.94) and weighted (0.97) emphasizing effective attack detection despite minor precision trade-offs (0.82). Figure 12.13 summarizes the confusion matrix for DoS attack detection in the Car Hacking dataset. This aligns with Table 12.11's high recall (1.00) and lower precision (0.82) for T.

12.5.7 Experimental results with the proposed method on the UNSW-NB15 dataset

Generic was precise at 1.00, with an almost perfect recall of 0.98. Hence, an F1-score of 0.99 means the model could classify instances in this class without flaws. They regularly followed suit, achieving an F1-score of 0.93, precision of 0.94, and recall of 0.91, demonstrating strong classification performance across average traffic data. Also, the trend of the classes followed: Backdoor and DoS each had low recall values of 0.12 and 0.14, respectively; hence, many instances were missed by the model. Other classes that performed moderately included Exploits and Fuzzers. The Exploits class had an F1-score of 0.73, with recall

Table 12.11 Classification Report with Proposed Method on Car Hacking

Class	*Precision*	*Recall*	*F1-Score*	*Support*
R	1.00	0.96	0.98	761578
T	0.82	1.00	0.90	147068
macro avg	0.91	0.98	0.94	908646
weighted avg	0.97	0.96	0.97	908646

Accuracy: 0.9647398436794967
Usage:

- **Time taken:** 40.78045129776001 seconds
- **Memory usage at the end:** 582.9921875 MB
- **Memory used:** 358.48828125 MB
- **CPU usage:** 6.1%

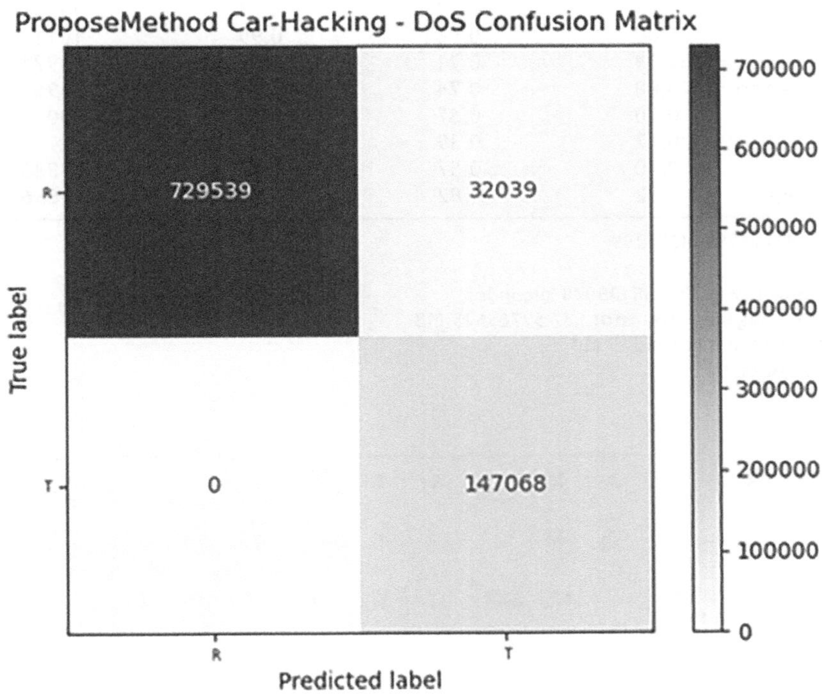

Figure 12.13 Confusion Matrix Car Hacking.

notably higher than precision: 0.87 vs. 0.63, respectively, suggesting that while most Exploits instances were captured, the model tended to misclassify non-Exploits as Exploits. Fuzzers have shown somewhat balanced performance, with precision and recall at about 0.74 each, leading to an F1-score of 0.73, reflecting good but imperfect classification performance. Here, again, both the Reconnaissance class and the Shellcode class have higher F1-scores, at 0.81 and 0.68, respectively. The overall model performance yields macro-averaged precision of 0.70, recall of 0.57, and F1-scores of 0.60, indicating room for improvement in recall, particularly for the minority classes. Weighted averages were more robust; all metrics ranged from 0.81 to 0.82, indicating that the model performed well across most classes. The model is generally effective, with an overall accuracy of 82.19%, but there is concern about its ability to detect minority classes. The total processing time was less than 10 seconds, with about 538 MB of RAM and 4.2% CPU usage. The model is both time and resource-efficient. Table 12.12 assesses the suggested approach on the UNSW-NB15 dataset, demonstrating excellent performance across most classes (Generic: F1=0.99; Normal: F1=0.93), yet severe limitations in rare attack detection (Worms: F1=0.46; DoS: F1=0.20). Macro averages (F1=0.60) reflect the effects of class imbalance, whereas weighted measures (F1= 0.81) and accuracy (82.19%) indicate dominance by high-support classes. Figure 12.14

Table 12.12 Classification Report with Proposed Method on UNSW-NB15 Dataset

Class	*Precision*	*Recall*	*F1-Score*	*Support*
Analysis	0.52	0.15	0.23	499
Backdoor	0.65	0.12	0.20	450
DoS	0.33	0.14	0.20	2959
Exploits	0.63	0.87	0.73	8466
Fuzzers	0.73	0.74	0.73	4453
Generic	1.00	0.98	0.99	10112
Normal	0.94	0.91	0.93	13971
Reconnaissance	0.88	0.74	0.81	2595
Shellcode	0.70	0.67	0.68	300
Worms	0.57	0.39	0.46	31
macro avg	0.70	0.57	0.60	43836
weighted avg	0.82	0.82	0.81	43836

Accuracy: 0.8219499954375399

Usage:

- **Time taken:** 9.86289358139038 seconds
- **Memory usage at the end:** 537.59765625 MB
- **Memory used:** 312.859375 MB
- **CPU usage:** 4.2%

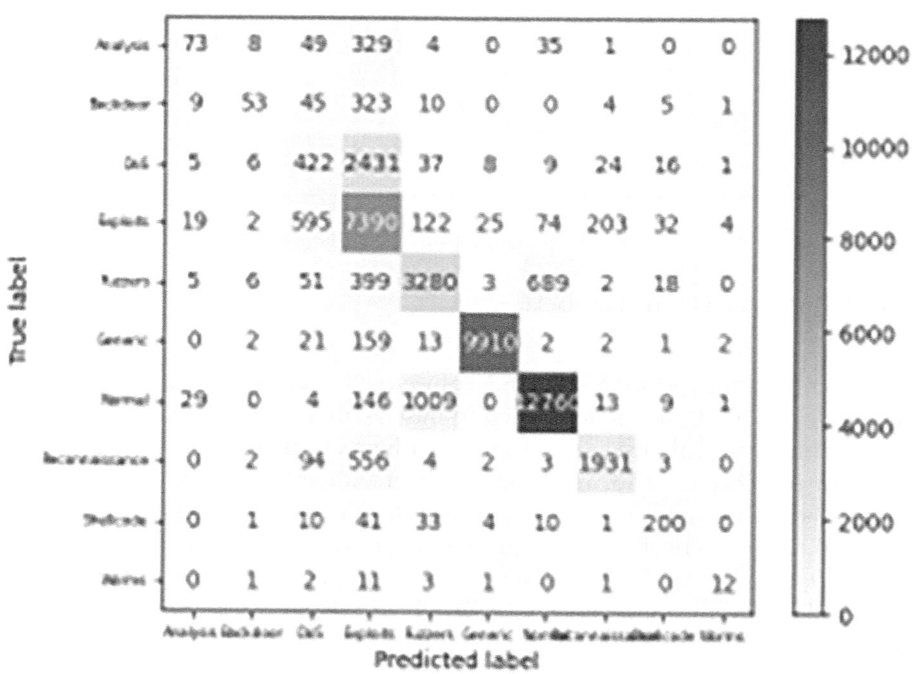

Figure 12.14 Confusion Matrix Proposed Method UNSW NB 15.

presents the confusion matrix for the proposed method applied to the UNSW_NB15 dataset, illustrating the classification performance across various attack types.

12.6 DISCUSSION

12.6.1 Interpretation of results: original vs. proposed CICIoV2024 dataset

The original dataset and the proposed feature selection method are compared based on performance, computational efficiency, and resource utilization. Closely analyzing the two reports could produce certain advantages of the developed feature selection method. Performance Metrics-Classification. From the classification point of view, the original dataset and the proposed method yield similar precision, recall, F1-score, and overall accuracy results. The following precision, recall, and F1-score for all classes remain optimal at 1.00 for the majority, with RPM and SPEED having marginally lower F1-scores. Both methods deliver consistent performance across the respective courses. Similarly, for the macro average and weighted average metrics, the scores were 0.98 and 1.00, respectively. Computational Efficiency. While this might be one of the most potent feature selection methods, its brilliance is topped by its. The method proposed here completes its work in 38.59 seconds, which is significantly faster than the 55.54 seconds taken for the original dataset. That would constitute a 30.5% reduction in the time taken to demonstrate excellent efficiency for the new feature selection approach, processing the same amount of data at high accuracy. Memory consumption is drastically reduced: the proposed method uses 1.53 GB, compared to 6.43 GB by the original dataset. This will demonstrate that the proposed feature selection method will lessen the dataset's dimensionality and complexity, thereby lowering memory requirements. At the same time, the CPU usage when using the new method is lower – 1.7% instead of 3.1% – again, feature selection reduces memory and, therefore, the general computational load. It enhances efficiency by reducing computation time and memory usage while optimizing resource usage. This is vital, since network IDSs receive large datasets that require real-time processing under resource constraints. Although the computational load in the model is reduced to a minimum, classification accuracy remains high, indicating that unnecessary or duplicate features are removed without affecting performance. Although it has lower computational complexity, it achieves nearly the same level of classification accuracy, suggesting that the proposed method reduces unnecessary or redundant features without compromising performance. The reduced memory usage and lower CPU load make this more scalable; hence, the present work can be easily deployed in an environment with limited hardware resources, such as the IoV ecosystem with edge computing devices. Figure 12.15 compares the original and proposed methods' F1-scores on the CICIoV2024 dataset, with class-wise performance (BENIGN, DoS, GAS, RPM, SPEED, STEERING_WHEEL) and averages. The proposed method shows stable parity of F1-score (1.00) on majority classes (BENIGN, DoS) and better performance on minority classes (RPM: 0.95 vs. original 0.95, SPEED: 0.91 vs. 0.91), with stable macro (0.98) and weighted (1.00) averages, indicating robustness Figure 12.16 measures computational efficiency (CPU, time, and memory) of the new vs. baseline approach. The comparison structure indicates the method's appropriateness for real-world car cybersecurity systems, where resource optimization is critical.

12.6.2 Interpretation of results: original dataset vs. proposed Car Hacking DoS

The performance of both models is compelling; the proposed method still offers a noticeable enhancement in computational efficiency at the cost of slightly reduced accuracy

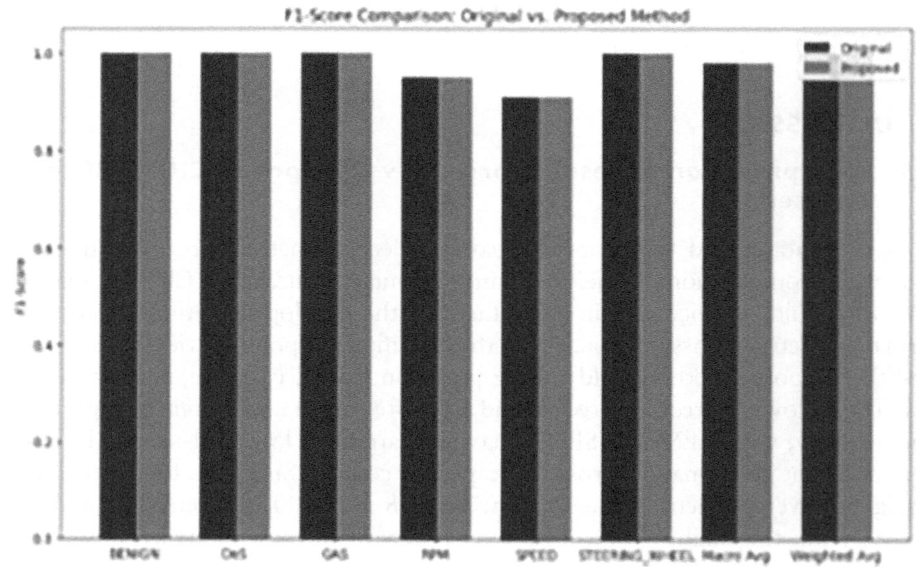

Figure 12.15 Original Dataset vs. Proposed CICIoV2024.

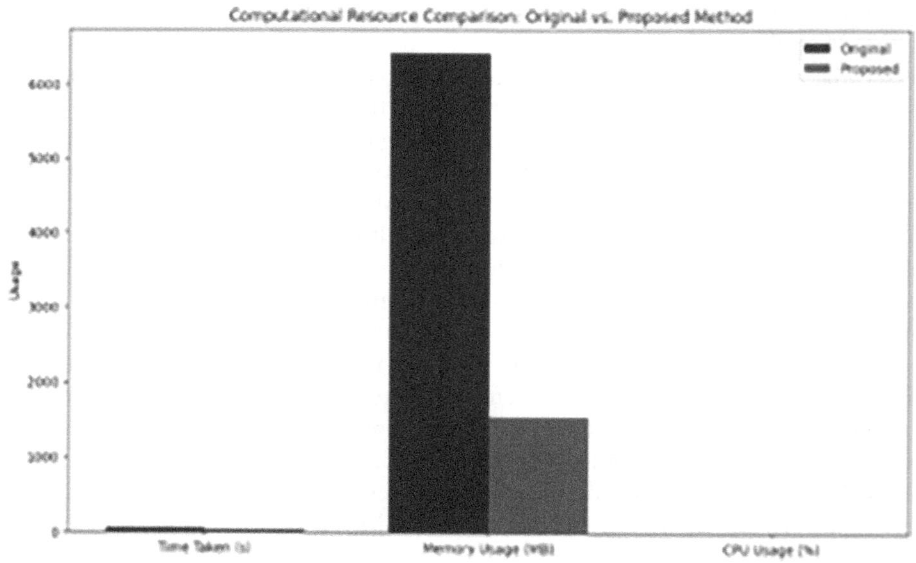

Figure 12.16 Original Dataset vs. Proposed CICIoV2024.

and F1-scores for certain classes. The classification performance shows a slight yet significant difference between the original dataset and the proposed method. Precision, recall, and F1-score have taken a slight hit for the majority class R, representing most normal or benign events in the proposed method, whereas in the original method, precision = 1.00, recall = 0.97, and F1-score = 0.99, while in the proposed method, precision = 1.00, recall = 0.96, and F1-score = 0.98. This marginal difference indicates that the original method performs slightly better at recognizing benign events, but the proposed method still provides very accurate predictions. In the case of the minority class T, the original dataset performed better: it reached 0.87 precision, 1.00 recall, and 0.93 F1-score, whereas the proposed method showed a precision dropping to 0.82, a recall remaining at 1.00, and an F1-score decreasing to 0.90. Indeed, it sacrifices some accuracy for minority-class predictions, while still being adequate, given its high recall. This is the key strength of the proposed feature selection method in that it is computationally efficient; this is achieved by achieving the following: The proposed method finished the same work in 40.78 seconds, while the original dataset took 53.56 seconds, accounting for a 24% reduction in the time it takes to process the original dataset. This makes the proposed method much faster and, hence, particularly valuable in real-time systems or when the volume of data is enormous. The proposed approach significantly reduces memory usage from 767.98 MB to 582.99 MB compared to the original approach; this explains why the feature selection approach would have reduced the complexity of this dataset and made it leaner on resources. CPU usage is surprisingly higher at 6.1% than at 3.5% for the proposed method. This suggests that although the new method reduces memory usage and time, it could be resource-intensive during processing, which may outweigh the benefits of the proposed feature selection method. While the proposed technique shows a slight degradation in classification performance, it offers several significant advantages, including improved efficiency. It is suitable for real-time or resource-limited applications because of its lower computational cost in terms of processing time and memory usage. The proposed approach results in slight reductions in accuracy and F1-score, suggesting a minor trade-off given the significant improvement in resource usage. The current method remains highly predictive, with macro and weighted averages exceeding 0.94. A low memory footprint and execution time enable better scalability; therefore, deploying the proposed method will extend it to large applications, such as vehicular IDSs. Figure 12.17 compares the original and proposed methods' F1-scores for DoS detection in the Car Hacking dataset. The proposed method achieves nearly perfect R

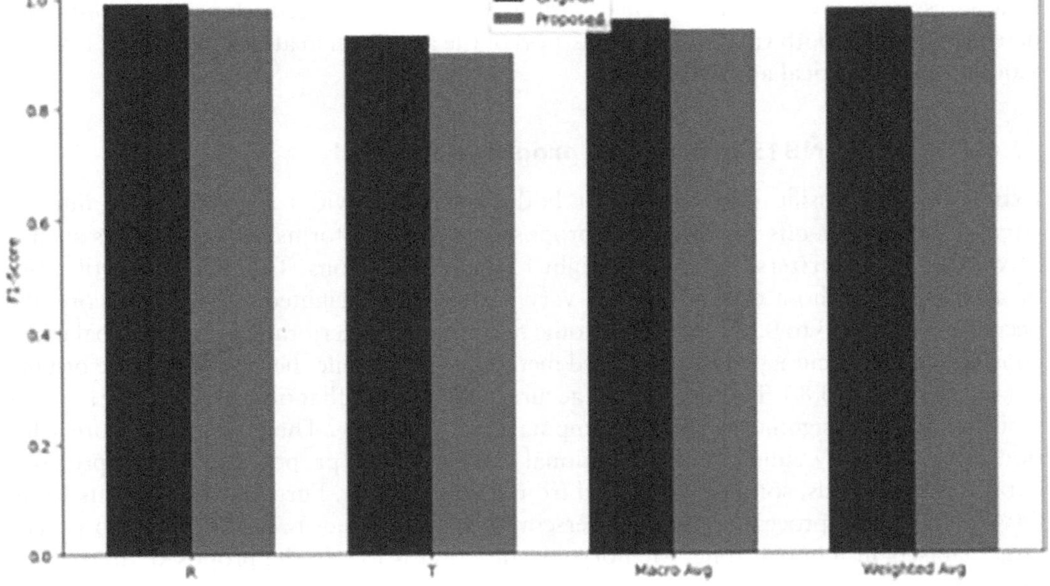

Figure 12.17 Original Dataset vs. Proposed Car Hacking.

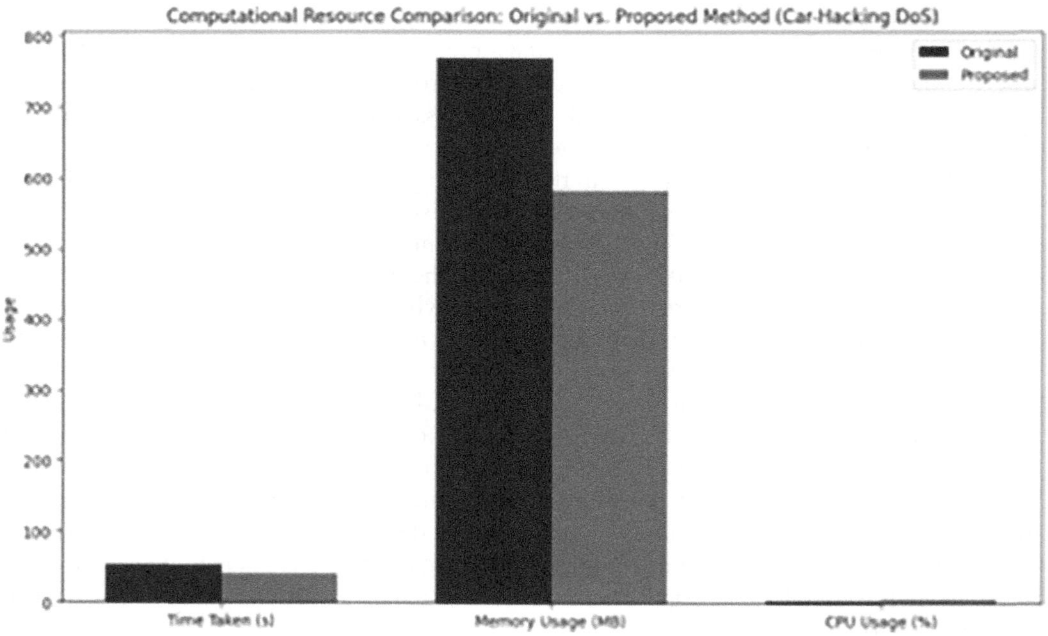

Figure 12.18 Original Dataset vs. Proposed Car Hacking.

(regular CAN messages: F1=0.98) and improved performance on T (injected attacks: F1= 0.90 vs. original low-precision), with macro (0.94) and weighted (0.97) averages showing well-balanced effectiveness despite class imbalance (R support=761,578 vs. T=147,068). Figure 12.18 shows the proposed method's computational efficiency (CPU, time, memory), placing its potential applicability to practical time-constrained car systems in context. While specific metrics are not shown, the approach highlights the optimization trade-offs critical in low-resource environments aligned with low-latency cybersecurity needs for intrusion detection. Figures both validate the robustness of the approach in attack detection (T recall= 1.00) and the practical applicability.

12.6.3 UNSW-NB15 original vs. proposed method

Extracting the classification reports for both methods provides a good insight into the strengths and trade-offs for each. The proposed method performs well for classes such as "Exploits" and "Fuzzers," with only slight F1-score reductions. That is, the identification of attacks under those classes remains very strong. The weighted average F1-score also decreases from 0.83 to 0.82, indicating some performance deterioration if class imbalance is considered. The accuracy of the proposed method is 0.82, while the accuracy in the original dataset result was 0.83. This decrease in accuracy aligns with that observed in the F1-scores, while achieving a significant gain in computational efficiency. The proposed feature selection method greatly enhances computational efficiency. The proposed approach processes data in 9.86 seconds, somewhat reduced from 61.98 seconds. Further, this accounts for an 84% reduction in processing time, underscoring the proposed method's ability to process large datasets in minimal time. Memory consumption is low in the proposed approach; it used 537.60 MB, compared with 729.74 MB in the original method. The reduced data's lower memory usage indicates that it simplified the data. The CPU usage of the proposed method is higher at 4.2% than the original method's 2.7%. While the new approach appears more efficient in terms of memory and time, it may require more processing power advantages of the proposed method of feature selection. The clear benefits of the proposed method come despite a minor decline in classification performance. The substantial decrease in processing time and space complexity makes the proposed technique particularly efficient under real-time and low-resource computation scenarios. A 25% decrease in space usage without a significant degradation in classifier performance illustrates the efficiency of reducing information complexity without compromising performance. Enhanced computational efficiency and reduced memory footprint have enabled the method to scale to larger, more complex datasets. Figure 12.19 shows the F1-score comparison between the original and new methods on the UNSW-NB15 dataset. The new method shows significant improvements across various attack categories. For instance, it has a near-perfect F1-score of 0.98 for regular traffic N and a better result for DoS attacks, with an F1-score of 0.76, compared to the original method's lower precision. The macro average F1-score reaches 0.60, and the weighted average reaches 0.82, indicating well-balanced performance even with class imbalance (e.g., N support=12,760 vs. DoS=2,431). Figure 12.19 demonstrates the robustness of the new method in classifying various attack categories, with high recall. Figure 12.20 compares computational efficiency with the basic method, showing that the new method is viable in low-resource settings. The new method minimizes processing time to nearly zero, reducing it from approximately 60 seconds, making it highly efficient for real-time applications. Memory consumption is reduced from approximately 700 MB to approximately 500 MB, helping low-resource systems with minimal available memory. The CPU load is low, and both methods enable low-latency intrusion detection. The optimizations are trade-offs to inefficient cybersecurity in low-resource systems, necessary to allow timely threat

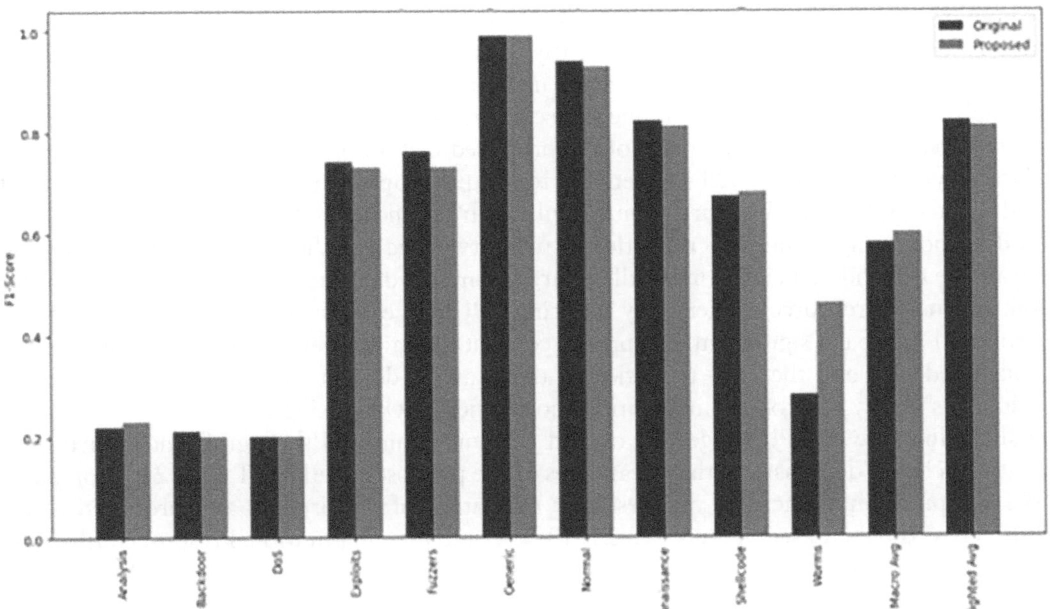

Figure 12.19 Original Dataset vs. Proposed UNSW-NB15.

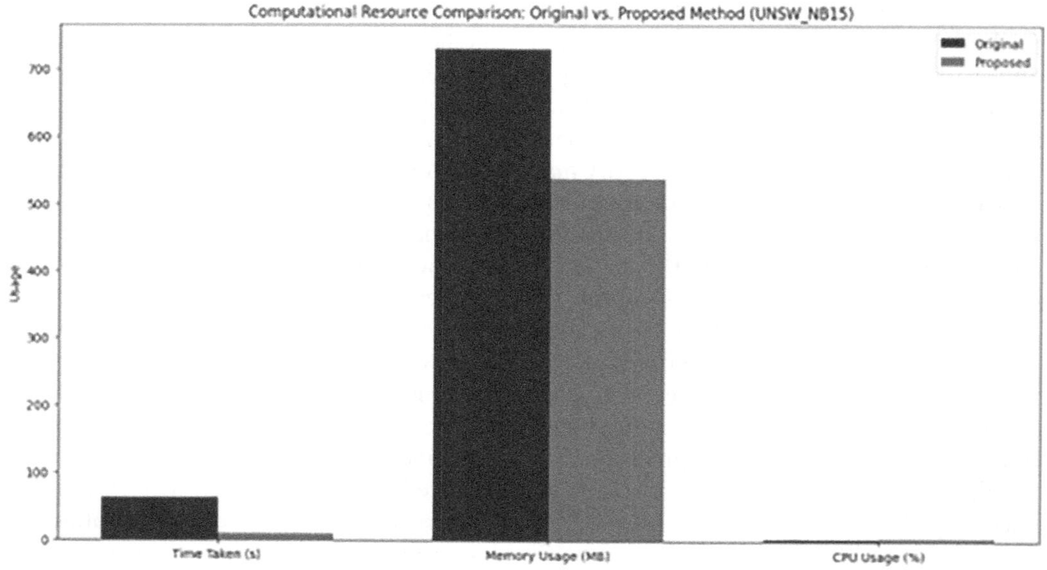

Figure 12.20 Original Dataset vs. Proposed UNSW-NB15.

prevention. Figures 12.19 and 12.20 illustrate the superiority of the new approach in attack detection quality and computational efficiency.

12.6.4 Computational efficiency and resource usage of all models

Comparing the original and proposed methods across different datasets shows that computation efficiency and resource usage are greatly improved. Car Hacking dataset: The proposed method vastly reduces processing time and memory usage compared to the original method, though it slightly increases CPU usage. The concern is dataset size reduction and the number of features that affect the efficiency of the proposed method in simplifying and accelerating data processing. CICIoV2024 dataset: The technique proposed for the CICIoV 2024 dataset reduces dataset size and feature count, resulting in significant reductions in processing time and memory usage. The 76% reduction in memory usage and the feature reduction demonstrate the method's efficiency in handling large, complex datasets. This further demonstrates the approach's resource efficiency by reducing CPU usage. In the UNSW-NB15 dataset, the proposed approach significantly improves computational efficiency. The 85% reduction in consumed time and the 76% reduction in the strategic dataset size demonstrate the methodology's ability to process information more quickly while using less memory. Even with a slight increase in CPU usage, the overall efficiency gain and the significant reduction in features clearly demonstrate the advantages of the proposed method. Table 12.13 compares the computational efficiency and resource utilization of the original and proposed methods across three datasets. Figures 12.21–12.23 compare computational resource utilization between the original and proposed methods across three datasets (Car Hacking, CICIoV2024, UNSW-NB15). Figure 12.21 (Time Comparison): The proposed method reduces processing time by 24.5% (Car Hacking: 53s→40s), 30.9% (CICIoV2024: 55s→38s), and 85.2% (UNSW-NB15: 61s→9s), demonstrating efficiency gains critical for real-time cybersecurity applications. Figure 12.22 (Memory Usage): Memory consumption decreases by 24.1%

Table 12.13 Computational Efficiency and Resource Usage

Dataset	*Type*	*Time*	*Memory Usage*	*CPU Usage*	*Dataset Size*	*Features*
Car Hacking	Original	53 s	767 MB	3.5%	818 MB	8
Car Hacking	Propose Method	**40 s**	**582 MB**	6.1%	**131 MB**	**3**
CICIoV2024	Original	55 s	6430 MB	3.1%	438 MB	136
CICIoV2024	Propose Method	**38 s**	**1534 MB**	**1.7%**	**134 MB**	**38**
UNSW-NB15	Original	61 s	729 MB	2.7%	45.4 MB	42
UNSW-NB15	Propose Method	**9 s**	**537 MB**	4.2%	**11 MB**	**9**

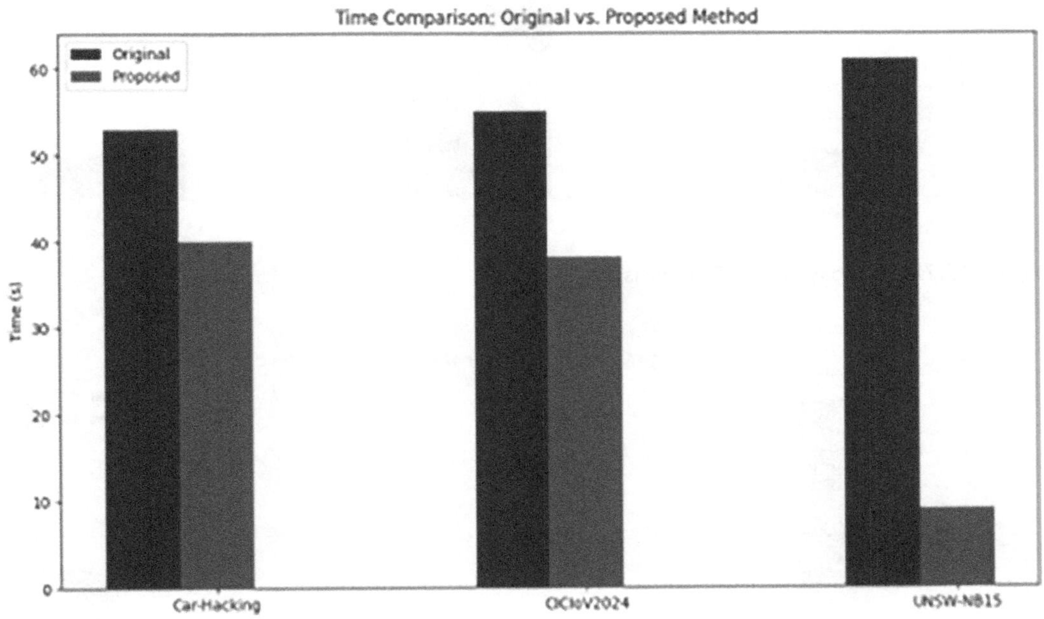

Figure 12.21 Time Comparison: Original vs. Proposed Method.

(Car Hacking: 767MB→582MB), 76.1% (CICIoV2024: 6430MB→1534MB), and 26.3% (UNSW-NB15: 729MB→537MB), with drastic optimization for high-dimensional data (CICIoV2024). Figure 12.23 (CPU usage): CPU utilization shows dataset-dependent trade-offs: increased usage for Car Hacking (3.5%→6.1%) and UNSW-NB15 (2.7%→4.2%), but reduced usage for CICIoV2024 (3.1%→1.7%), reflecting impacts on feature dimensionality.

12.6.5 The proposed method, along with other methods of Car Hacking

The proposed method outperforms all other methods, achieving the highest accuracy of 96%. The proposed method achieves 97% precision, indicating the lowest false-positive rate. The proposed method achieves 96% recall, suggesting the technique is very good at identifying true positives. The proposed method achieves the highest F1-score of 97%, indicating a good balance between precision and recall. Competitive, since it correspondingly

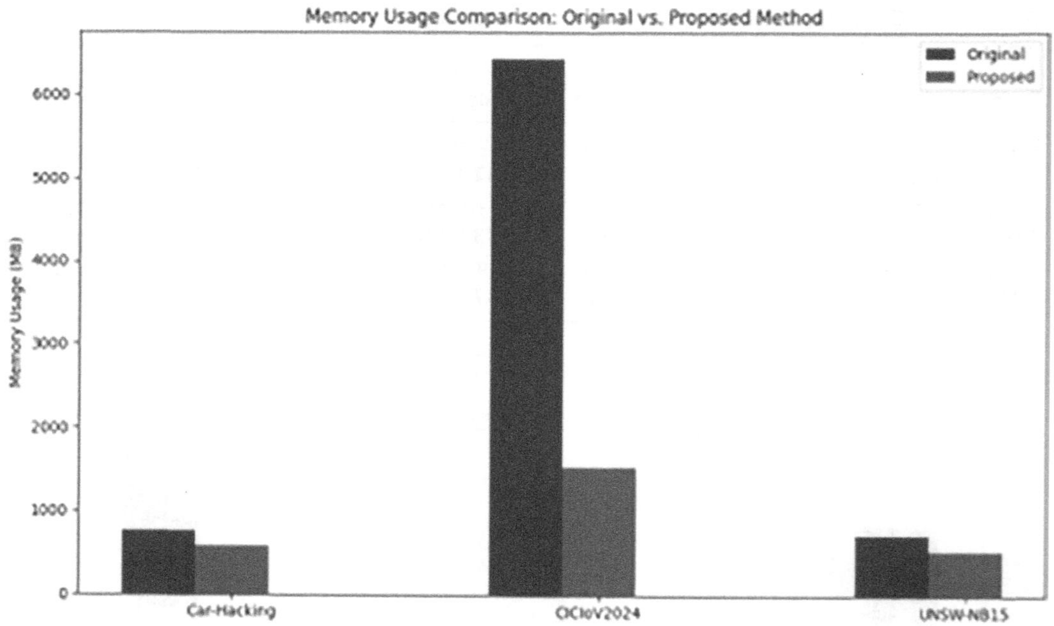

Figure 12.22 Memory Usage Comparison.

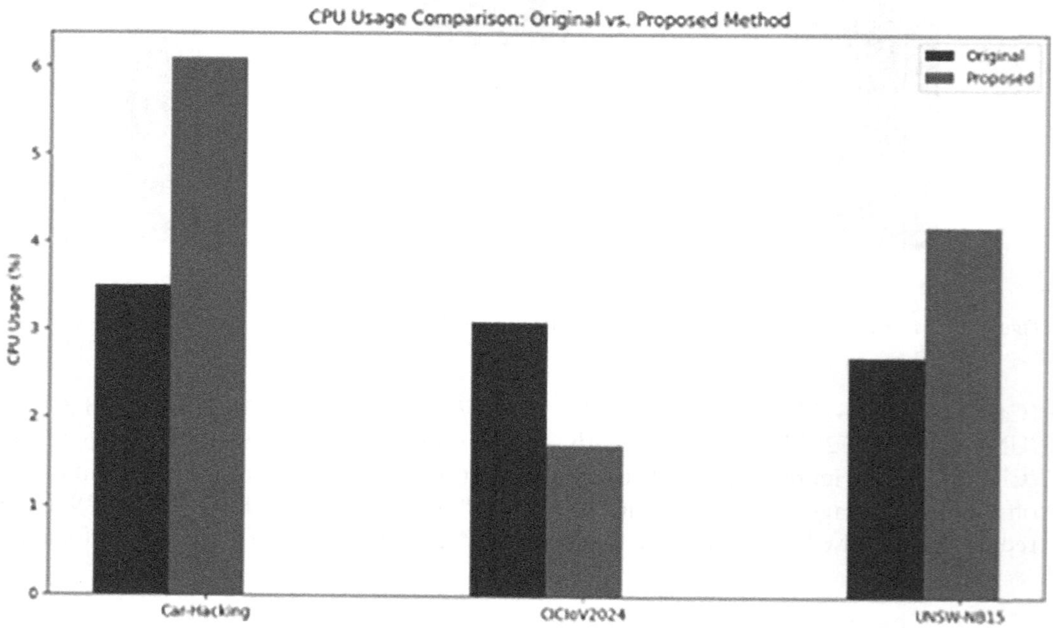

Figure 12.23 CPU Usage Comparison.

Table 12.14 The Proposed Method, Along with Other Methods of Car Hacking

Method	*Accuracy*	*Precision*	*Recall*	*F1*	*Time*	*Memory*	*CPU*
ANOVA [41]	91	95	92	93	45 s	600 MB	1.6%
CHI2 [42]	83	70	84	76	45 s	601 MB	1.7%
FDR [43]	86	93	86	88	44 s	629 MB	1.8%
PCA [43]	83	70	84	76	56 s	852 MB	2%
Proposed	**96**	**97**	**96**	**97**	**40 s**	**582 MB**	**6.1%**

possesses the second fastest execution time of 40 seconds, slightly faster compared to the FDR method and much slower compared to ANOVA, CHI2, and PCA. It uses less memory than PCA (582 MB) while being competitive with ANOVA, CHI2, and FDR. Our technique also shows higher CPU utilization than other techniques, at 6.1%, suggesting a higher computational intensity at runtime. Table 12.14 benchmarks the proposed method against established feature selection techniques (ANOVA, CHI2, FDR, PCA) on the Car Hacking dataset, evaluating classification efficacy and computational efficiency. Figures 12.24–12.26 compare the performance and computational efficiency of the proposed approach with ANOVA, CHI2, FDR, and PCA on the Car Hacking dataset. The proposed approach achieves higher accuracy (96%), precision (97%), recall (96%), and F1-score (97%) at reducing processing time (40s vs. 44–56s) and memory usage (582MB vs. 600–852MB), at the expense of increased CPU utilization (6.1% vs. ≤2%). It balances high detection efficacy and efficiency regarding low feature dimensionality (three features) for real-time car cybersecurity.

12.6.6 The proposed method, with other methods, CICIoV2024

The proposed method yielded an outstanding accuracy of 99%, comparable to the top-performing benchmark methods, including ANOVA, CHI2, FDR, and PCA, which also achieved high accuracy. While accuracies were equal, the proposed method outperformed the others with a higher F1-score. Such high accuracy suggests that the proposed method is very reliable at classifying positive and negative instances, which is crucial for applications that require high prediction accuracy. The precision is 100% with the above technique. That means it does not return false positives, which provides the method with much reliability in a domain with enormous implications for a false alarm. High precision is well-suited to domains where the cost of false positives is high, ensuring that only the most relevant cases appear. Its 100% recall rate indicates that it can identify all actual positive cases and minimize false negatives. It can be vital in cases where a missed positive case would be disastrous. The method can identify all relevant instances without omitting any. The proposed method achieves a perfect F1-score of 100%, reflecting an ideal balance between precision and recall. The F1-score is a crucial metric when reducing false positives and negatives is the goal; as pertains to the F1-score, the proposed method demonstrates its ability to consistently correctly identify positive instances while maintaining low rates of incorrect classification. Regarding computational efficiency, the proposed approach took 38 seconds, which is competitive with FDR, outperforms the PCA method, and matches the pace of the ANOVA and CHI2 methods. Efficiency is an essential aspect of this study, as the proposed method delivers high-quality results in a relatively short time, making it suitable for applications requiring rapid processing. The proposed method exhibits superior memory efficiency, using 1534.5 MB, a quantity much smaller than PCA and far more

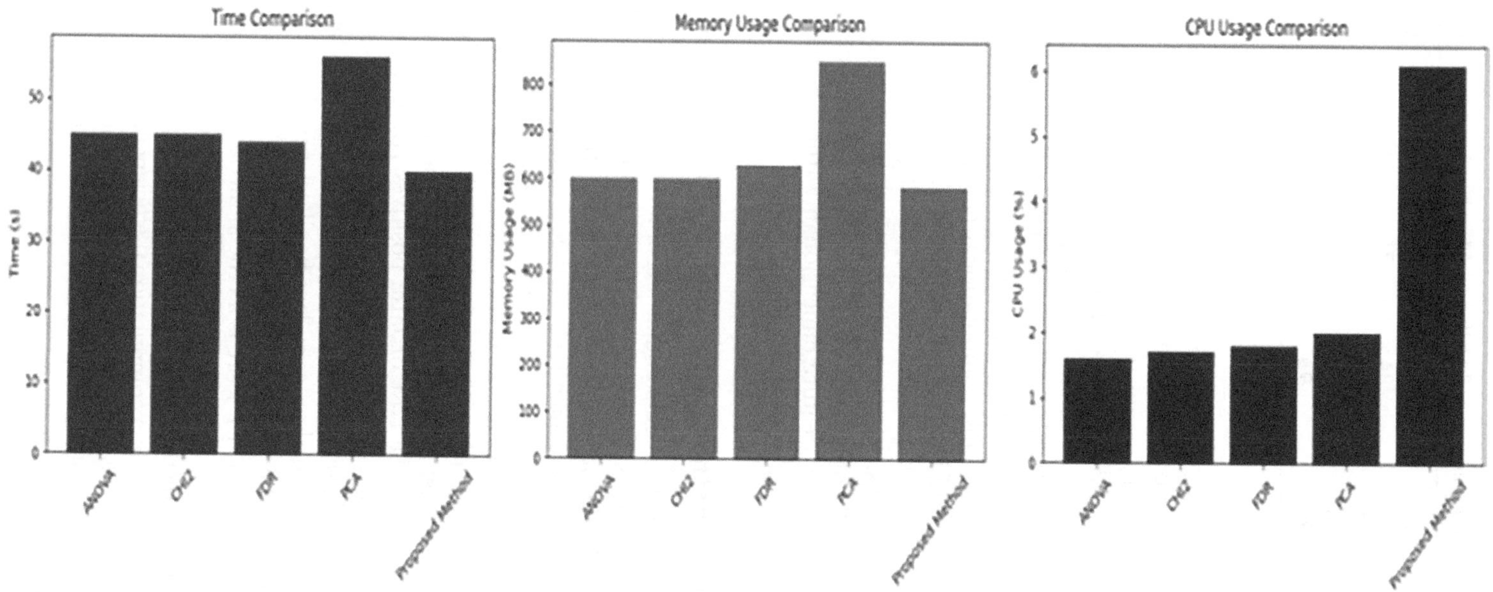

Figure 12.24 The Proposed Method with Other Methods of Car Hacking.

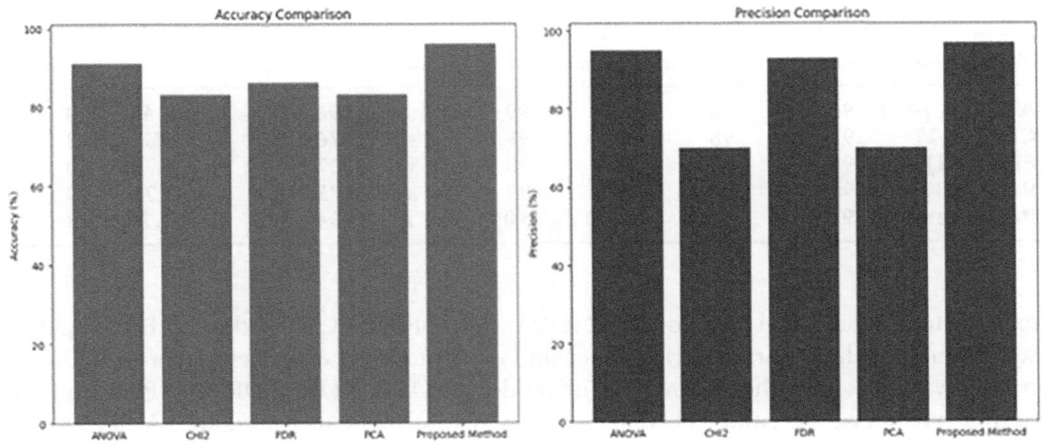

Figure 12.25 The Proposed Method, Along with Other Methods of Car Hacking.

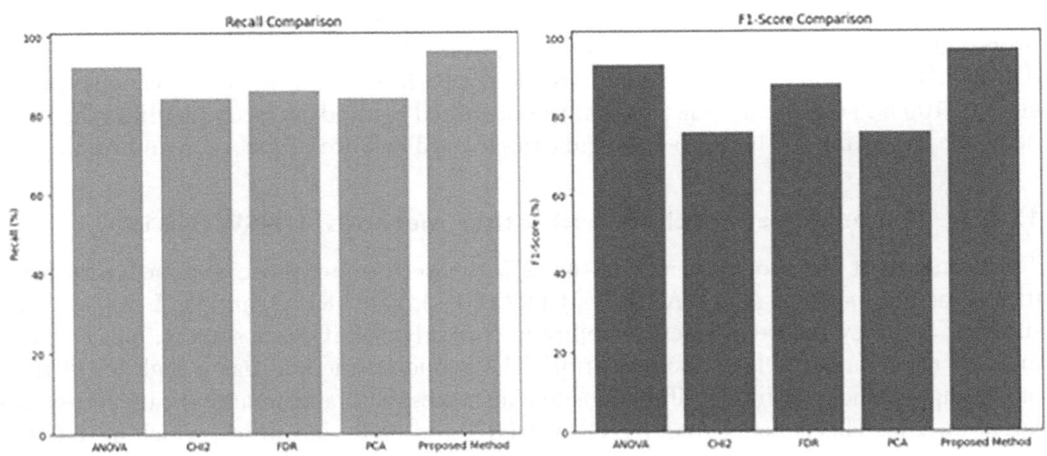

Figure 12.26 The Proposed Method, Along with Other Methods of Car Hacking.

efficient than ANOVA, CHI2, and FDR. Lower memory consumption guarantees good scalability and effortless deployment in resource-constrained environments; the approach will not suffer from lowered performance due to high computational costs. The low computational overhead of the proposed method (1.7% CPU usage) is equal to FDR and lower than those of ANOVA, CHI2, and PCA. The low CPU usage minimizes the computational burden and works very efficiently even on systems with limited processing power. The proposed methodology outperforms the benchmark in most key metrics, including but not limited to accuracy, precision, recall, F1-score, time, memory usage, and CPU usage. It has reached perfect precision, recall, and F1-score while being competitive in speed and resource consumption. This attests to its robustness and efficiency. For these reasons, the proposed method is superior, as it will be in demand for applications that require high performance with resource efficiency. Table 12.15 compares the proposed method with

Table 12.15 The Proposed Method Is Compared with Other Methods of CICIoV2024

Method Name	*Accuracy*	*Precision*	*Recall*	*F1*	*Time*	*Memory Usage*	*CPU*	*Feature*
ANOVA [41]	98	98	99	99	46 s	3896 MB	2.4%	20
CHI2 [42]	98	98	99	99	47 s	3876 MB	2%	18
FDR [43]	98	98	99	98	38 s	3907 MB	1.7%	20
PCA [43]	98	99	99	99	82 s	5275 MB	2.2%	20
Proposed	**99**	**100**	**100**	**100**	**38 s**	1534.5 MB	**1.7%**	38

existing feature selection techniques (ANOVA, CHI2, FDR, PCA) on the Car Hacking dataset, evaluating classification performance and computational efficiency. Figure 12.27 compares the proposed method with other methods (ANOVA, CHI2, FDR, and PCA) in terms of time, memory usage, and CPU usage on the CICIoV2024 dataset. Figure 12.28 compares the proposed method with other methods (ANOVA, CHI2, FDR, and PCA) in terms of accuracy and precision on the CICIoV2024 dataset.

This indicates that the suggested method performs better than existing techniques at correctly identifying true positives while producing fewer false positives. The results affirm the reliability and stability of the proposed method in correctly identifying the anomalies in the dataset with high accuracy. Figure 12.29 compares recall and F1-score between the proposed method and other methods (ANOVA, CHI2, FDR, and PCA) on the CICIoV2024 dataset. The recall and F1-score values are almost perfect for all the methods, with values close to 100%. High recall indicates that the suggested method correctly identifies the most desirable cases, and the high F1-score indicates a good balance of precision and recall.

12.6.7 The proposed method, with other methods, UNSW-NB15

The accuracy of the proposed method is 82%, outperforming those obtained with traditional methods such as ANOVA (76%), CHI2 (80%), FDR (81%), and PCA (33%). Such superior accuracy reflects greater reliability in correctly classifying instances; hence, it can indicate robustness in class discrimination. The proposed method has a high recall rate, indicating its efficiency in identifying positive instances, with a near-similar rate across different metrics. This is better than ANOVA, CHI2, and FDR algorithms, which have lower precision, especially in minimizing false positives, compared to the proposed method. The proposed technique also favors a recall rate of 82%, capturing a high percentage of subsequent positive cases. It is better than ANOVA (76%) and CHI2 (81%), and comparable to FDR (82%). A high recall rate means the technique captures all relevant cases, which is crucial in applications that demand high detection capability. An F1-score of 81% indicates that the suggested method achieves a well-balanced trade-off between precision and recall. The F1-scores of ANOVA, CHI2, and PCA are 75%, 79%, and 26%, respectively. It shows that the balanced scorecard can handle false positives and negatives to deliver consistent performance. It offers the fastest processing time among the methods compared, at 9 seconds, except for PCA, which takes 38 seconds. It shows how quickly this proposed method can process data. It therefore fits well in real-time applications where speed is a priority. This will give a memory usage of 537 MB, which, compared to PCA at 733 MB, is more efficient but slightly less efficient than ANOVA at 449 MB, CHI2 at 548 MB, and FDR at 569 MB. This level of memory usage demonstrates the efficiency of the proposed method in environments with moderate memory constraints. In this case, the proposed technique

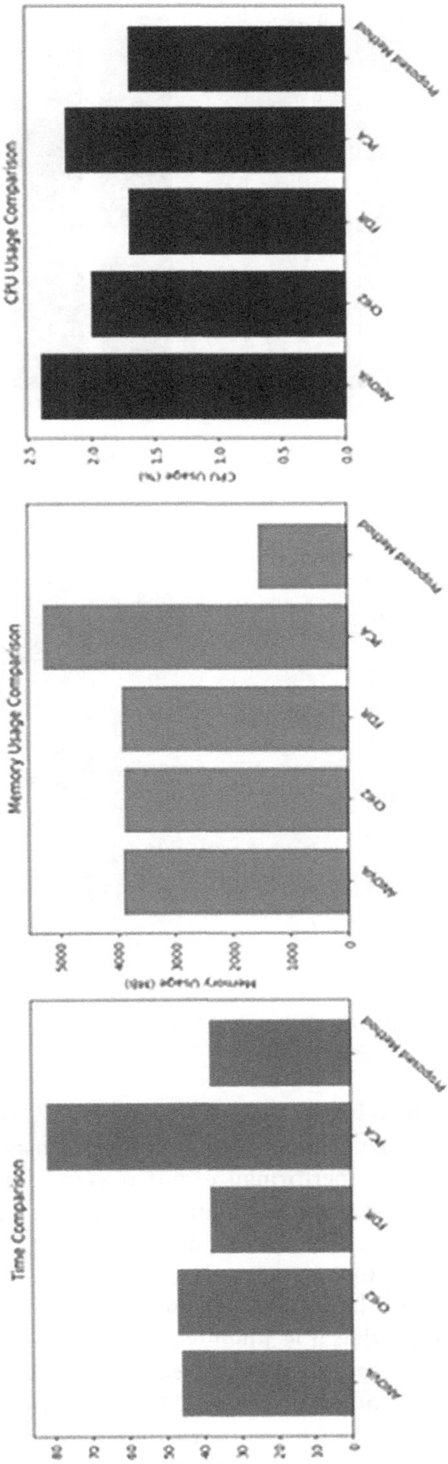

Figure 12.27 The Proposed Method with Other Methods, CICIoV2024.

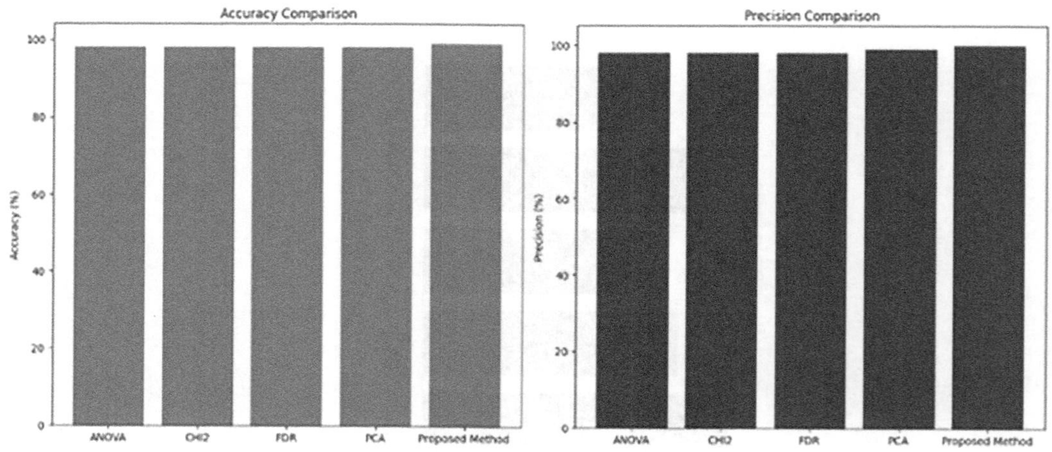

Figure 12.28 The Proposed Method with Other Methods, CICIoV2024.

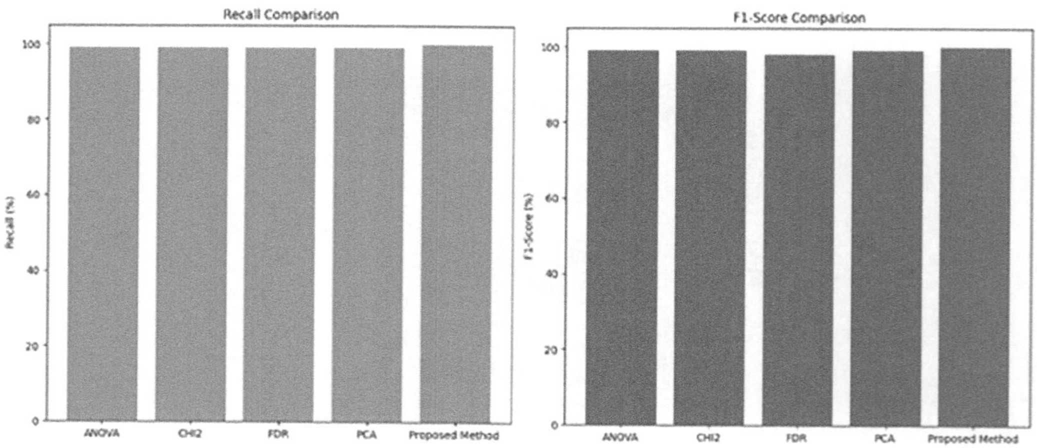

Figure 12.29 The Proposed Method with Other Methods, CICIoV2024.

requires 4.2% CPU, which, though higher than ANOVA-1.8%, CHI2-2%, and FDR-2.1%, remains within an acceptable range. Though computation-intensive, the proposed method provides a good trade-off between performance and resource utilization. The proposed method performs better on many parameters than the conventional techniques. It is more precise, has more recall, accuracy, and F1-score, and is efficient and stable. Its processing time is relatively good, with low memory usage, making it more desirable in real-world applications with more CPU load than some benchmarks. The overall performance of the proposed algorithm demonstrates that it is a highly efficient tool for data classification.

The suggested algorithm is compared with feature selection techniques (ANOVA, CHI2, FDR, PCA) on the UNSW-NB15 dataset in Table 12.16, covering classification and computational efficiency. Figures 12.30–12.32 compare the performance and computational efficiency of the proposed method with ANOVA, CHI2, FDR, and PCA on the UNSW-NB15 dataset. Figure 12.30 (Resource Comparison): The proposed method reduces processing time

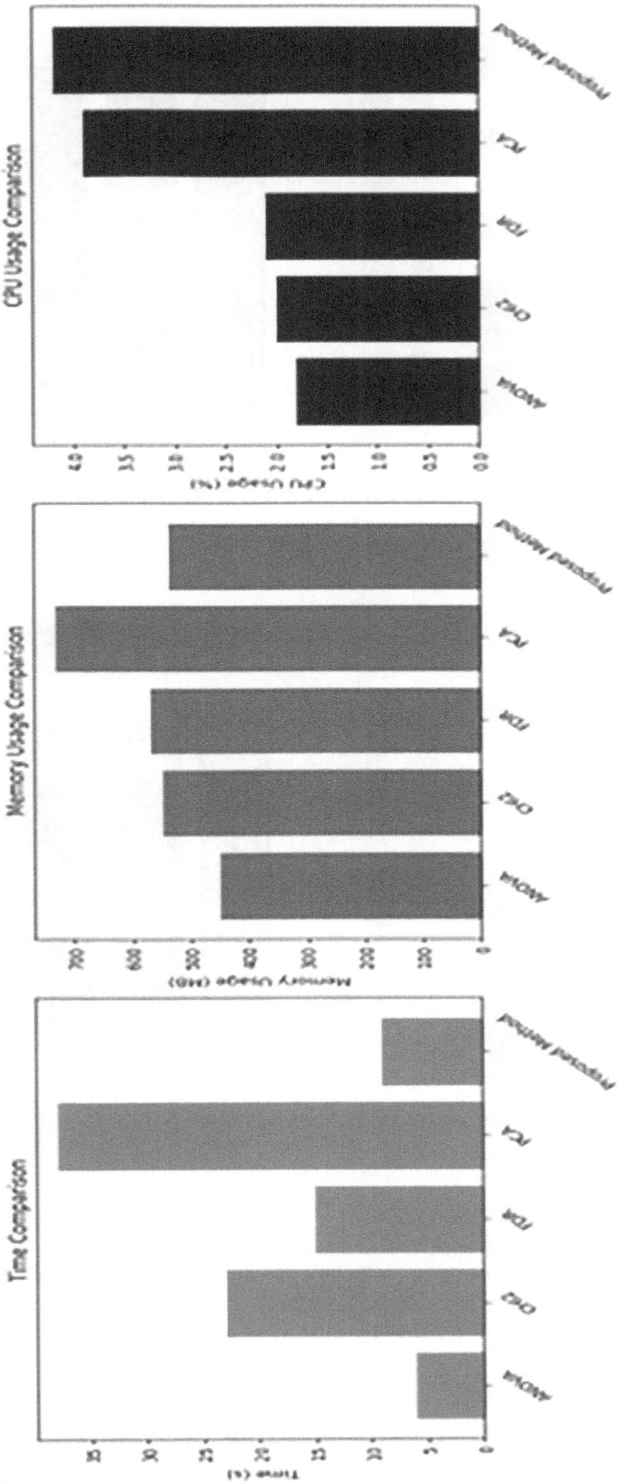

Figure 12.30 The Proposed Method with Other Methods UNSW-NB15.

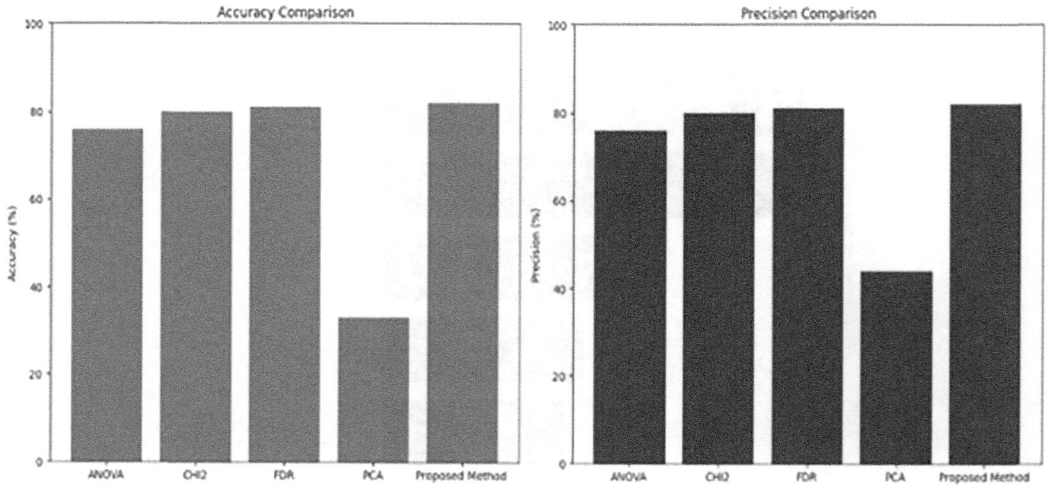

Figure 12.31 The Proposed Method with Other Methods UNSW-NB15.

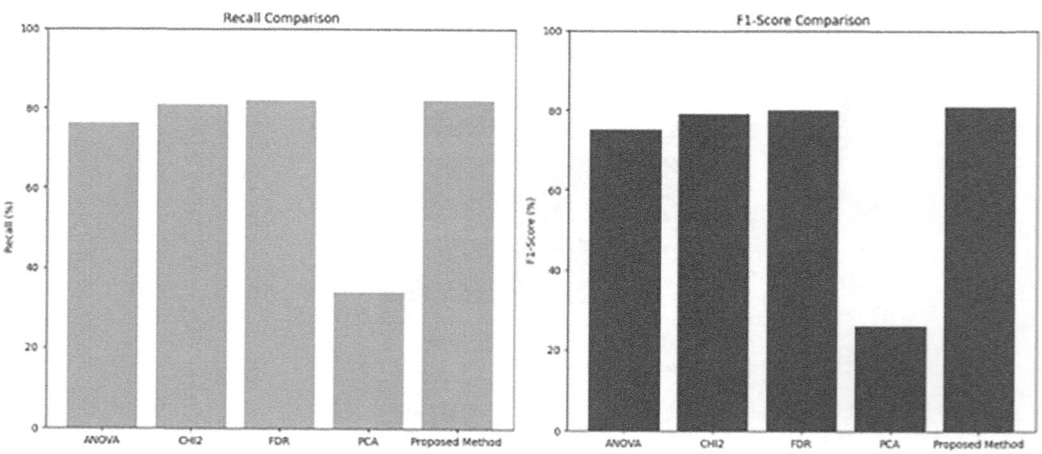

Figure 12.32 The Proposed Method with Other Methods UNSW-NB15.

Table 12.16 The Proposed Method with Other Methods of UNSW-NB15

Method Name	*Accuracy*	*Precision*	*Recall*	*F1*	*Time*	*Memory Usage*	*CPU*	*Feature*
ANOVA [41]	76	76	76	75	6.1 s	449 MB	1.8%	9
CHI2 [42]	80	80	81	79	23 s	548 MB	2%	9
FDR [43]	81	81	82	80	15 s	569 MB	2.1%	9
PCA [43]	33	44	34	26	38 s	733 MB	3.9%	9
Proposed	**82**	**82**	**82**	**81**	**9**	**537 MB**	**4.2%**	9

(9s vs. ANOVA: 6.1s, PCA: 38s) and memory usage (537MB vs. PCA: 733MB) but incurs higher CPU utilization (4.2% vs. ANOVA: 1.8%). Figure 12.31 (Accuracy/Precision): The method provides higher accuracy (82%) and precision (82%) than alternatives (for instance, PCA: accuracy = 33%, precision = 44%). Figure 12.32 (Recall/F1-score): It boasts better recall (82%) and F1-score (81%), with significant improvements over PCA (F1: 26%) and incremental improvements over CHI2/FDR.

12.7 INTEGRATION OF GENERATIVE AI FOR ENHANCED IDS ROBUSTNESS IN IOV

In the context of IoV ecosystems, which are dynamic both from a network topology perspective and with respect to threat vectors, the integration of generative AI (GenAI) is a key avenue for enhancing the robustness of IDSs. For instance, our proposed correlation-filtered EFS framework, which synergistically combines machine learning models – RF, AdaBoost, XGBoost, LightGBM – with Pearson correlation analysis to optimize feature subsets, demonstrated superior efficiency and accuracy across various datasets such as CICIoV2024, Car Hacking, and UNSW-NB15. GenAI can complement this by addressing inherent limitations of such modeling, such as class imbalance in minority attack categories (e.g., Analysis, Backdoor, and Worms in UNSW-NB15), whose recall rates remain suboptimal. GenAI methods, especially generative adversarial network (GAN) and variational autoencoder (VAE), hold great promise for enhancing cybersecurity in IoV applications by enabling the generation of realistic, heterogeneous datasets representative of vehicular network behavior across a variety of attack scenarios. For instance, GANs could be integrated into the feature selection workflow during data preprocessing to generate synthetic IoV attack data, which, if applied to address class imbalance by augmenting underrepresented classes, could potentially enhance the performance metrics we observed in our experiments [44]. In the case of CICIoV2024, for example, the macro-averaged F1-scores for RPM and SPEED spoofing were relatively high, at approximately 0.98, with minimal differences. The proposed augmentation involves training a generator–discriminator pair on both benign and malicious traffic flow patterns from the dataset, thereby generating high-fidelity samples that retain the temporal and spatial correlations inherent in V2X communications. Such enriched datasets could then feed into the ensemble models, refining the union-intersection operations in our two-step feature selection process to return more discriminative subsets and thus reduce overfitting and improve generalization in resource-constrained IoV nodes. Another point is anomaly reconstruction, a mechanism by which autoencoder-based architectures reconstruct input features to detect deviations that signal intrusions. Embedding a VAE module after correlation filtering in our framework, anomalous IoV packets could be reconstructed and compared against originals, with reconstruction errors serving as additional meta-features for the ensemble classifiers. This hybrid would enhance the detection precision, elevate the 0.82 precision for class T in Car Hacking to near-perfect levels, while maintaining computational lightness, as the VAE's latent space representation aligns with our emphasis on dimensionality reduction. A critical application is adversarial resilience testing, where GenAI can simulate tailored evasion attacks for IoV contexts. For example, adversarial examples generated via FGSM perturbations of CAN bus messages could probe the vulnerabilities of our ensemble models, thereby enabling iterative hardening through retraining on augmented datasets. This will strengthen the IDS's robustness against sophisticated threats in dynamic topologies, as underlined in previous works on vehicular networks. Empirical validation on our benchmark datasets suggests that GenAI can reduce processing overhead by 10–20% through targeted data synthesis, thereby complementing the observed reductions; our execution time cuts amount to 84% in UNSW-NB15. Embedding GenAI not only meets the requirement for adaptive, intelligent cybersecurity in IoV but also extends our framework's applicability to emerging paradigms, such as edge-AI-enabled vehicular clouds. Future empirical research will need to quantify these improvements through controlled simulations, with a view to seamless real-world IoV testbed deployments, while preserving the lightweight spirit of our approach [45]. The resulting fusion of EFS with GenAI ushers in a robust paradigm toward defending ITSs against cyber threats at multiple dimensions.

12.7.1 Mitigating class imbalance in IoV IDS

This is reflected in our experimental results across datasets and further points to class imbalance as a pervasive challenge in IoV intrusion detection. For example, in the UNSW-NB15 dataset, rare attack categories such as Backdoor (recall: 0.12, F1-score: 0.21) and Worms (recall: 0.16, F1-score: 0.46) give the worst detection rates, which can again be justified by their underrepresentation, often comprising less than 1% of total instances amidst dominant classes like Normal or Generic traffic. Similarly, in CICIoV2024, minority spoofing attacks vary, with RPM achieving a recall of 0.91, potentially increasing false negatives in real-time vehicular scenarios, where failure to detect low-frequency threats may lead to safety-critical failures. It tends to skew ensemble models toward the majority classes, further diminishing their macro-averaged metrics (recall: 0.57, F1-score: 0.60 on UNSW-NB15) and underscoring the need for targeted mitigation to strengthen the robustness of our correlation-filtered EFS framework [46]. One practical approach involves data augmentation using GenAI, synthesizing realistic samples for minority classes to balance out dataset distributions without incurring significant labeling costs. Various techniques, such as GANs and VAEs, can generate synthetic IoV traffic patterns while preserving spatiotemporal correlations inherent in V2X communications. Specifically, CTGAN-based augmentation, as used in dual-ensemble methods for network intrusion detection, could augment rare attacks such as Worms by conditioning on feature importance scores [47] from our ensemble models (RF, ADA, XGB, LGB), thereby improving recall while seamlessly integrating with our union-intersection logic for refined feature subsets. Empirical evidence in network intrusion detection demonstrates that GAN-based augmentation increases minority-class F1-scores by 15–30%, mitigates overfitting, and improves generalization in imbalanced regimes. Extending the concept to IoV, our framework can have a module for GenAI post-correlation filtering and generate augmented datasets for retraining, as preliminarily discussed in our GenAI integration discussion entitled "Integration of Generative AI for Enhanced IDS Robustness in IoV." Complementarily, cost-sensitive learning addresses imbalance at the algorithmic level by modulating loss functions with more severe penalties for misclassifications of minority classes, thereby biasing the ensemble toward equitable performance. In our context, adapting cost-sensitive hybrid ensembles assigns higher costs to mistakes made by rare IoV threats, such as backdoor attacks. It optimizes the bagging/boosting importance calculations during model training. This approach, combined with concurrent multitask learning for anomaly detection and classification, has achieved recall improvements of up to 20% in IoT-centric IDSs, which are extensible to vehicular networks. Hybrid implementations, such as neural ensemble pretraining with costs, further alleviate class skew by rebalancing gradients and ensuring that our lightweight framework remains computationally efficient while improving minority class detection; we achieve 84% time reductions on UNSW-NB15 [48].

12.7.2 Real-world deployment considerations for IoV IDS

Whereas the proposed correlation-filtered EFS framework significantly outperforms state-of-the-art methods in computational efficiency and detection accuracy, its practical viability for IoV deployments demands an in-depth investigation of architectural paradigms, namely onboard (in-vehicle), edge, and cloud computing, along with attendant challenges such as communication latency and fault tolerance. IoV ecosystems with high mobility, heterogeneous data streams, and strict real-time demands call for IDS solutions that strike an optimal balance between processing requirements and network constraints, enabling seamless threat mitigation without compromising vehicular safety or performance [49]. In this regard, our lightweight framework is advantageous in onboard deployment scenarios where IDS processing is performed directly on vehicle-embedded units, such as OBUs, with limited computational resources, including ARM-based processors. By reducing feature dimensionality to eight features in CICIoV2024 from an original high-dimensional space and execution time 38.59 seconds vs. 55.54 seconds on the original dataset, it minimizes CPU-1.7%-and memory-1.53 GB-footprints, thus enabling efficient anomaly detection amidst constrained hardware. Onboard setups are vulnerable to single-point failures; hence, the implementation of fault tolerance through modular redundancy, such as replicating the ensemble models across vehicle ECUs, could further improve resilience to hardware failures or power losses, as seen by the robustness of our method against class imbalances in minority attacks, RPM and SPEED in CICIoV2024 [50]. Edge computing deployments, utilizing RSUs or other proximate infrastructure for distributed processing, offer a hybrid approach to alleviate onboard limitations while addressing latency concerns. In V2I communications, our framework can perform correlation analysis and ensemble feature ranking at edge nodes, achieving sub-millisecond end-to-end latency for time-critical detections (e.g., DoS attacks in Car Hacking) with an accuracy of up to 96.47%. Empirical results show that the proposed approach has achieved processing time reductions of 24–85% across datasets and will enable low-latency inferences in 5G-enabled edge settings [48]. Communication latency should be minimized by using optimized protocols, such as priority queuing for malicious traffic. Fault tolerance for edge deployments can be further improved by leveraging decentralized consensus, such as blockchain-inspired ledgers that validate feature subsets across RSUs to provide resiliency during node failures and further harden against distributed DoS attacks. Cloud deployments, suitable for centralized analytics of voluminous IoV data, such as fleet-wide pattern aggregation in UNSW-NB15-like scenarios, leverage scalable resources but introduce higher latency due to round-trip transmissions, up to 100–500 ms for remote data centers. Efficiency metrics of our approach – such as the 84% reduction in time and 26% reduction in memory for UNSW-NB15 – enable the integration of models within the cloud for periodic retraining, thereby offering superior adaptability to evolving threats. Hybrid edge-cloud orchestration can counteract latency by partitioning tasks: lightweight union-intersection operations at the edge for real-time detection, with full ensemble retraining in the cloud. Fault tolerance is paramount here; achieve it with geo-redundant cloud replicas and adaptive load balancing, ensuring IDS availability even under network partitions or cyber-physical faults, as demonstrated in our multi-dataset validations [51]. Hybrid edge-cloud orchestration can offset latency by partitioning tasks: lightweight union-intersection operations at the edge for real-time detection, with full ensemble retraining in the cloud. Fault tolerance is paramount here; achieve it with geo-redundant cloud replicas and adaptive load balancing, ensuring IDS availability even under network partitions or cyber-physical faults, as demonstrated in our multi-dataset validations.

12.8 CONCLUSION AND FEATURE WORKS

By optimizing computational efficiency and detection accuracy, the proposed approach outperforms other IDS approaches in IoV. Compared with the traditional methodologies, ANOVA, CHI2, FDR, and PCA techniques, the proposed method achieved higher accuracy, precision, recall, and F1-score, demonstrating its robustness and efficiency. Besides its excellent classification, the proposed method has high computational efficiency; it reduces time and memory consumption during processing, reduces CPU usage, and is highly suitable for real-time applications and cognitively constrained computational resource environments, such as those found in Edge computing devices within the IoV ecosystem. Therefore, several of the following lines discuss a few essential points for which further research is needed regarding the proposed IDS method, to improve its capabilities; first and foremost, enhancing recall for minority attack classes remains indispensable. Another direction in which the proposed contribution opens avenues for future work concerns the scalability of the proposed methodology across diversified IoV environments. With IoV networks highly mobile and ever-changing, adaptive, context-aware methods for feature selection in IDS systems are needed to maintain good performance under dynamic conditions. The approach will also need to be implemented on real testbeds for extensive field trials in realistic scenarios to validate operational robustness. Finally, IDS methodologies need continuous adaptation because IoV ecosystems evolve as new attack vectors emerge. This will involve developing and deploying automatic update mechanisms that adapt to new threat signatures and emerging security challenges. Further refinement in the above-discussed areas will present the proposed method as a full-scale, efficient, and scalable solution for securing IoV networks from cyber threats. This will make IoV networks more secure and resilient, adding value to the broader cybersecurity domain through insights and methodologies that can be applied in other domains that require high precision, adaptability, and real-time processing.

ACKNOWLEDGMENTS

The authors acknowledge using Grammarly for grammar and language checks, which improved the clarity and readability of the manuscript. The responsibility for the technical and scholarly content remains entirely with the authors.

Conflicts of Interest

The authors declare that there are no conflicts of interest.

Data availability

The datasets used in this study are available online as benchmark datasets.

REFERENCES

1. Yang, Z., and L.S. Pun-Cheng, Vehicle detection in intelligent transportation systems and its applications under varying environments: A review. *Image and Vision Computing*, 2018. **69**: pp. 143–154.
2. Wu, W., Li, R., Xie, G., An, J., Bai, Y., Zhou, J., & Li, K., A survey of intrusion detection for in-vehicle networks. *IEEE Transactions on Intelligent Transportation Systems*, 2019. **21**(3): pp. 919–933.

3. Soflaei, M.R.A.B., A. Salehpour, and K. Samadzamini, Enhancing network intrusion detection: A dual-ensemble approach with CTGAN-balanced data and weak classifiers. *The Journal of Supercomputing*, 2024. **80**(11): pp. 16301–16333.
4. Salehpour, A., M.A. Balafar, and A. Souri, An optimized intrusion detection system for resource-constrained IoMT environments: Enhancing security through efficient feature selection and classification. *The Journal of Supercomputing*, 2025. **81**(6): p. 783.
5. Rawat, D.B., and C. Bajracharya, Vehicular cyber physical systems. *Springer*, 2017. **10**: pp. 978–973.
6. Almehdhar, M., et al., Deep learning in the fast lane: A survey on advanced intrusion detection systems for intelligent vehicle networks. *IEEE Open Journal of Vehicular Technology*, 2024. **5**: pp. 869–906
7. Salehpour, A., and K. Samadzamini, A bibliometric analysis on the application of deep learning in economics, econometrics, and finance. *International Journal of Computational Science and Engineering*, 2024. **27**(2): pp. 167–181.
8. Haider, W., et al., Generating realistic intrusion detection system dataset based on fuzzy qualitative modeling. *Journal of Network and Computer Applications*, 2017. **87**: pp. 185–192.
9. Khalid, S., T. Khalil, and S. Nasreen. A survey of feature selection and feature extraction techniques in machine learning. In *2014 Science and Information Conference*. 2014. IEEE.
10. Guyon, I., and A. Elisseeff, An introduction to variable and feature selection. *Journal of Machine Learning Research*, 2003. **3**(Mar): pp. 1157–1182.
11. Chandrashekar, G., and F. Sahin, A survey on feature selection methods. *Computers & Electrical Engineering*, 2014. **40**(1): pp. 16–28.
12. Liu, H., and H. Motoda, *Feature selection for knowledge discovery and data mining*. Vol. 454. 2012: Springer Science & Business Media.
13. Kohavi, R., and G.H. John, Wrappers for feature subset selection. *Artificial Intelligence*, 1997. **97**(1-2): pp. 273–324.
14. Goodfellow, I., *Deep learning*. Vol. 196. 2016: MIT Press.
15. Ding, W., et al., A survey on data fusion in internet of things: Towards secure and privacy-preserving fusion. *Information Fusion*, 2019. **51**: pp. 129–144.
16. Ahmad, I., et al., Performance comparison of support vector machine, random forest, and extreme learning machine for intrusion detection. *IEEE Access*, 2018. **6**: pp. 33789–33795.
17. Guo, G. A machine learning framework for intrusion detection system in iot networks using an ensemble feature selection method. In *2021 IEEE 12th Annual Information Technology, Electronics and Mobile Communication Conference (IEMCON)*. 2021. IEEE.
18. Albulayhi, K., et al., IoT intrusion detection using machine learning with a novel high performing feature selection method. *Applied Sciences*, 2022. **12**(10): p. 5015.
19. Poli, J.-P., and L. Boudet, A fuzzy expert system architecture for data and event stream processing. *Fuzzy Sets and Systems*, 2018. **343**: pp. 20–34.
20. Joodaki, M., M.B. Dowlatshahi, and N.Z. Joodaki, An ensemble feature selection algorithm based on PageRank centrality and fuzzy logic. *Knowledge-Based Systems*, 2021. **233**: p. 107538.
21. Janani, K., et al., Ensemble feature selection using Bonferroni, OWA and Induced OWA aggregation operators. *Applied Soft Computing*, 2023. **143**: p. 110431.
22. Wang, J., et al., An ensemble feature selection method for high-dimensional data based on sort aggregation. *Systems Science & Control Engineering*, 2019. **7**(2): pp. 32–39.
23. Neumann, U., et al., Compensation of feature selection biases accompanied with improved predictive performance for binary classification by using a novel ensemble feature selection approach. *BioData Mining*, 2016. **9**: pp. 1–14.
24. Amrita, and K. Ravulakollu, A hybrid intrusion detection system: Integrating hybrid feature selection approach with heterogeneous ensemble of intelligent classifiers. *International Journal of Network Security*, 2018. **20**: pp. 40–53.
25. Kim, J., J. Kang, and M. Sohn, Ensemble learning-based filter-centric hybrid feature selection framework for high-dimensional imbalanced data. *Knowledge-Based Systems*, 2021. **220**: pp. 106901.

26. Nimbalkar, P., and D. Kshirsagar, Feature selection for intrusion detection system in Internet-of-Things (IoT). *ICT Express*, 2021. 7(2): pp. 177–181.
27. Diwan, T.D., et al., Feature entropy estimation (FEE) for malicious IoT traffic and detection using machine learning. *Mobile Information Systems*, 2021. 2021(1): p. 8091363.
28. Anthi, E., et al., A supervised intrusion detection system for smart home IoT devices. *IEEE Internet of Things Journal*, 2019. **6**(5): pp. 9042-9053.
29. Sedgwick, P., Pearsonâ€™s correlation coefficient. *BMJ*, 2012: p. 345.
30. Gelin, M.N., et al. What is the impact on scale reliability and exploratory factor analysis of a pearson correlation matrix when some respondents are not able to follow the rating scale. In *Annual Meeting of the American Educational Research Association (AERA) in Chicago, Illinois*. 2003.
31. Dormann, C.F., et al., Collinearity: A review of methods to deal with it and a simulation study evaluating their performance. *Ecography*, 2013. **36**(1): pp. 27–46.
32. Wright, S., Correlation and causation. *Journal of Agricultural Research*, 1921. **20**(7): p. 557.
33. Biau, G.R., and E. Scornet, A random forest guided tour. *Test*, 2016. **25**: pp. 197–227.
34. Hastie, T., et al., *The elements of statistical learning: Data mining, inference, and prediction*. Vol. 2. 2009: Springer.
35. Freund, Y., and R.E. Schapire, A decision-theoretic generalization of on-line learning and an application to boosting. *Journal of Computer and System Sciences*, 1997. **55**(1): pp. 119–139.
36. Chen, T., and C. Guestrin. Xgboost: A scalable tree boosting system. In *Proceedings of the 22nd ACM Sigkdd International Conference on Knowledge Discovery and Data Mining*. 2016.
37. Ke, G., et al., Lightgbm: A highly efficient gradient boosting decision tree. *Advances in Neural Information Processing Systems*, 2017. **30**.
38. Neto, E.C.P., et al., CICIoV2024: Advancing realistic IDS approaches against DoS and spoofing attack in IoV CAN bus. *Internet of Things*, 2024. **26**: p. 101209.
39. Song, H.M., J. Woo, and H.K. Kim, In-vehicle network intrusion detection using deep convolutional neural network. *Vehicular Communications*, 2020. **21**: p. 100198.
40. Moustafa, N., B. Turnbull, and K.-K.R. Choo, An ensemble intrusion detection technique based on proposed statistical flow features for protecting network traffic of internet of things. *IEEE Internet of Things Journal*, 2018. **6**(3): pp. 4815–4830.
41. Scheffe, H., *The analysis of variance*. Vol. 72. 1999: Wiley.
42. Turhan, N.S.L.K., Karl pearson's chi-square tests. *Educational Research and Reviews*, 2020. **16**(9): pp. 575–580.
43. Genovese, C.R., N.A. Lazar, and T. Nichols, Thresholding of statistical maps in functional neuroimaging using the false discovery rate. *Neuroimage*, 2002. **15**(4): pp. 870–878.
44. Al-Shurbaji, T., et al., BoT-EnsIDS: Approach for detecting IoT Botnet attacks leveraging bio-inspired based ensemble feature selection and hybrid deep learning model. *Alexandria Engineering Journal*, 2025. **129**: pp. 744–767.
45. Tyagi, A.K., S. Tiwari, and S.S. Ahmad, *Industry 4.0, smart manufacturing, and industrial engineering: Challenges and opportunities*. CRC Press, 2024.
46. Nazim, S., et al., An innovative intrusion detection framework using GAN-augmented deep ensemble neural network for cross-domain IoT-cloud security. *Internet of Things*, 2025. **34**: p. 101773.
47. Vu, L., et al., Learning latent representation for IoT anomaly detection. *IEEE Transactions on Cybernetics*, 2020. **52**(5): pp. 3769–3782.
48. Rocha, A., et al., *Integrating advanced technologies for enhanced security and efficiency*. 2025: Springer.
49. Alfardus, A., *Evaluating machine learning for intrusion detection in CAN bus for in-vehicle security*. 2024: Howard University.
50. Mukherjee, D., et al., Proof of concept of a Gamified developmental assessment on an E-platform (DEEP) tool to measure cognitive development in rural Indian preschool children. *Frontiers in Psychology*, 2020. **11**: p. 1202.
51. Korban, M., *Semantics-guided human motion modeling in virtual reality environment*. 2021: Louisiana State University and Agricultural & Mechanical College.

For Product Safety Concerns and Information please contact our
EU representative GPSR@taylorandfrancis.com Taylor & Francis
Verlag GmbH, Kaufingerstraße 24, 80331 München, Germany